W9-ASC-211

LEARNING THEORY
AND
PERSONALITY DYNAMICS

Selected Papers

By

O. HOBART MOWRER, Ph.D.

RESEARCH PROFESSOR OF PSYCHOLOGY
UNIVERSITY OF ILLINOIS

THE RONALD PRESS COMPANY · NEW YORK

2

Library of Congress Catalog Card Number: 50-11151

PRINTED IN THE UNITED STATES OF AMERICA

To MOLLY

PREFACE

In both the title and the organization of this volume a distinction between "learning theory" and "personality dynamics" is implied, yet the artificiality of such a distinction will be immediately apparent. Ultimately, these two expressions refer to essentially the same set of realities; they refer to the processes and principles according to which the human personality or "mind" develops and functions.

It is nevertheless useful, at least for the present, to preserve this distinction, for it serves to remind us of some of the exciting and important facts about contemporary psychological science. It reminds us that our knowledge in this area has been derived from two distinct scientific approaches, two roads to the same destination: that of the laboratory and that of the clinic. A few decades ago these two approaches seemed to have little in common and to be aiming in different directions. But today, with a growing number of younger psychologists who have respectable training in the concepts and techniques of both experimental and clinical psychology, the trend toward integration and unification is widespread and vigorous. Today it is by no means uncommon to find psychologists who are equally versed and interested in laboratory research and in psychotherapy or other clinical work and who move freely, both in their thinking and in their activities, from one to the other.

The present volume, though not primarily historical in its aim, reflects certain phases of a developmental trend which has led us from an era in which the accent in psychology was upon "schools" to the more felicitous contemporary state of relative unity. More importantly, the volume is designed to give the reader, in addition to some historical perspective, a picture of current problems and issues in this rapidly moving discipline.

Most of the studies included here have already been published in various scientific periodicals or in monographic form; but there are eight papers, of rather varied nature, which are previously unpublished. In the normal course of events these would have appeared in the periodical literature within the next year or two. In the interest of making the volume as current and as complete as possible, they have instead been included here.

As already intimated, separation of the studies comprising this volume into two categories has involved a number of rather arbitrary decisions. From the beginning of the work represented here, the author has been mindful of "personality" problems when he wrote on the subject of "learning," and the reverse has been equally true. Yet a roughly accurate division seemed possible and probably desirable.

Several of the earlier studies appearing in this volume are mainly concerned with the psychology of fear and related states. This approach to the broader field of learning theory, though unconventional, has certain advantages. Of all the secondary drives, fear lends itself most readily to experimentation, and yet it had been comparatively little studied. Moreover, through the investigation of this seemingly narrow field one is quite naturally led to a concern with learning theory in its fully inclusive sense, as will be apparent from the later studies appearing in Part I. And there is the additionally fortunate circumstance that the study of fear provides a particularly meaningful bridge from experimental psychology to clinical psychology. As Freud has aptly remarked, anxiety is "the fundamental phenomenon and the central problem of neurosis."

The primary objective of Chapters 1–8 is to show (*a*) that the so-called secondary ("psychogenic") drives are *learned* and (*b*) that, once learned, they serve to motivate and, when terminated, to *reinforce* behavior, just as the primary ("viscerogenic") drives do. These studies were predicated on the assumption that there is but one basic learning process. In Chapter 9 a new and more secure position is taken, namely that there are *two basic learning processes:* one *problem solving,* which occurs when a drive (primary or secondary) is reduced; and the other *conditioning,* which occurs on the basis of sheer contiguity or double stimulation and which accounts for the acquisition of the secondary drives. In Chapter 10 further evidence is adduced in support of this two-process conception of learning. And Chapters 11 and 12 indicate how a two-factor theory of learning articulates with "insight" and related phenomena.

Although the topics covered in Part II are varied, there are certain common underlying themes. Throughout there is a concern with the relationship between learning theory and psychoanalytic thought; and the impact of culture theory and social-structure theory will also be apparent. The conviction thus evidenced that a comprehensive science of human personality must have a broad, interdisciplinary base had its inception during the six years that the author was on the staff of the Institute of Human

Relations at Yale University and was later reinforced by stimulating associations at Harvard University with members of the Department of Social Relations.

In Part II the reader will note a growing skepticism regarding certain psychoanalytic doctrines and principles. Freud, it appears, created not one all-inclusive, internally consistent system, but several partial and contradictory systems. On the basis of mounting clinical experience and experimental evidence, the author has come to reject a number of the Freudian formulations and has elaborated or revised others. The emerging systematic position is most fully developed in Chapters 18–22. The two concluding chapters deal with aspects of the psychology of language.

Three types of use can be visualized for this volume: (*a*) as a reference work; (*b*) as a textbook or text-supplement in graduate courses on learning theory, language, personality, or psychotherapy; and (*c*) as a possible guide to persons in neighboring sciences who are interested in interdisciplinary research. In general, the arrangement of the studies constituting each of the two parts of the volume is chronological. While Part I is logically prior to Part II, each part can be read independently, as can most of the individual chapters.

In order to integrate the studies with one another and to orient and correct the whole with respect to the expanding field of psychology and social science generally, prefatory remarks are inserted at the beginning of each chapter. Bracketed inserts and footnotes are occasionally used for similar purposes. Cross-references to the studies appearing in this volume are indicated by arabic chapter numbers enclosed in parentheses; reference to the work of other investigators is made by author's name and year of publication, as listed in the bibliography.

To those students and former colleagues who have collaborated on studies which appear in this volume, the author is indebted not only for their permission to reproduce these studies but also for the memory of many pleasant personal associations. The specific nature of the collaboration in each of these studies is indicated in the respective chapter prefaces. For assistance in the preparation of the typescript, illustrations, bibliography, and indexes, the author acknowledges the skillful services of Miss Norma Lowry and Mrs. William A. Ruyter.

O. H. M.

Urbana, Illinois
October, 1950

ACKNOWLEDGMENTS

The author wishes to thank the following authors, publishers, and others for their permission to reprint selections from copyrighted works in this volume:

American Journal of Orthopsychiatry, for republication of the articles appearing in this volume as Chapters 14 and 18.

Appleton-Century-Crofts, Inc., for excerpts from *Theories of Learning* by E. R. Hilgard, copyright 1948 by Appleton-Century-Crofts, Inc., in Chapter 11.

Harvard Educational Review, for republication of the articles appearing in this volume as Chapters 9, 16, and 23.

Harvard University Press, for republication of Chapter 35 from *Contemporary Psychopathology,* edited by S. S. Tomkins, copyright 1943 by Harvard University Press, appearing in this volume as Chapter 13.

Journal of Abnormal & Social Psychology, for republication of the articles appearing in this volume as Chapters 13 and 17.

Journal of Comparative and Physiological Psychology and the authors, for excerpts from "Studies in Motivation and Retention" by L. I. O'Kelly and A. W. Heyer, Jr. (*J. comp. physiol. Psychol.,* **41,** 466–78), in Chapter 12; also this *Journal,* for republication of the article appearing in this volume as Chapter 5.

Journal of Experimental Psychology, for republication of the articles appearing in this volume as Chapters 3, 6, and 7.

The Journal Press and the authors, for excerpts from "The Postulation of Two Different but Functionally Related Mechanisms in Adaptive Behavior" (*J. gen. Psychol.,* **41,** 111–23) by G. K. Yacorzynski and from "Variant Meanings of the Terms 'Conditioning' and 'Conditioned Response' " (*J. soc. Psychol.,* **28,** 248–55) by Donald O. Cowgill, in Chapters 11 and 10 respectively.

Joseph Wood Krutch, for excerpts from his *Edgar Allan Poe,* copyright 1926 by Alfred A. Knopf, Inc., in Chapter 22.

Liveright Publishing Corporation, for excerpts from *A General Introduction to Psychoanalysis* by Sigmund Freud, copyright 1920, 1935 by Liveright Publishing Corporation, in Chapter 19.

N. R. F. Maier, for excerpts from his *Frustration: The Study of Behavior Without a Goal,* copyright 1949 by McGraw-Hill Book Company, Inc., in Chapter 12.

Philosophical Library, Inc., for excerpts from "Recent Developments in Conditioning," by J. D. Harris, which appears as Chapter 10 in *Twentieth*

Century Psychology, edited by P. L. Harriman, copyright 1946 by Philosophical Library, Inc.

Progressive Education, for republication of the article appearing in this volume as Chapter 20.

Psychological Monographs and the American Psychological Association, for republication of the monographs appearing in this book as Chapters 2 and 4.

Psychological Review, the American Psychological Association, Inc., and the author, for excerpts from "The Formation of Learning Sets" by Harry Harlow (*Psychol. Rev.,* 1949, 51–65), in Chapter 11; also the Association and the *Review,* for republication of the articles appearing in this volume as Chapters 1 and 15.

The Ronald Press Company, for excerpts from *The Meaning of Anxiety* by Rollo May, copyright 1950 by The Ronald Press Company, in Chapter 20.

Rutgers University Press, for excerpts from *Sex, Symbolism, and Psychology in Literature* by R. P. Basler, copyright 1948 by Rutgers University Press, in Chapter 22.

The Viking Press, Inc., for excerpts from *Edgar Allan Poe,* edited by Philip Van Doren Stern, copyright 1945 by The Viking Press, Inc., in Chapter 22.

Certain other permissions are acknowledged in footnotes in the text, as required by individual contractual arrangements.

CONTENTS

Part II

PERSONALITY DYNAMICS

ILLUSTRATIONS

TABLES

LEARNING THEORY
AND
PERSONALITY DYNAMICS

INTRODUCTION [1]

Ideally, the psychology of learning and an adequate conception of human personality should be roughly coexistential. Here we are attempting to come nearer that ideal state of affairs by considering some of the implications which learning theory has for the better understanding and more efficient practical management of the many problems involved in psychotherapy.

More specifically we are concerned with the implications of that particular version of learning theory which has been associated with the name of Clark L. Hull. But since the areas of agreement between Hull's work and that of other systematists are constantly growing, we will necessarily be considering not only Hull's formulations but those of other investigators as well.

What I shall have to say falls into four parts, the first having to do with the phenomenon of secondary reinforcement, the second with the question as to whether there are two types or only one basic type of learning, the third with the relation between gradients of reinforcement and neurosis, and the fourth with a further analysis of neurosis and the conditions necessary for its effective treatment.

I. Secondary Reinforcement

Psychotherapy and learning research have very different backgrounds. It is not surprising that they long stood apart and have only recently begun to merge. Psychotherapy has been pre-eminently a human enterprise and has been carried on mainly under religious and medical auspices. Learning research, on the other

[1] [This paper, initially entitled "Systematic Implications of Hull's Learning Theory for Psychotherapy," was presented at a symposium held in connection with the Boston meeting of the American Psychological Association, in 1948. It is used here as an introduction to the other studies comprising this volume for the reason that it is relatively comprehensive in scope and serves to delineate the field with which the volume, as a whole, is concerned. However, it is far from self-sufficient as it stands and must rely heavily, both for logical and empirical substantiation, upon the studies which follow. As indicated in the Preface, reference to other studies appearing in this volume will be made by means of Arabic numerals, enclosed in parentheses. Reference to the works of others and to studies by the author which do not appear in this volume is made by name of author and year of publication. Material which has been added to studies as originally written is enclosed in brackets, as is this footnote.]

hand, has made extensive use of animal subjects and has taken place mainly in the experimental laboratory.

Much of this research has been focused upon the question of how living organisms learn in problem situations where the problem is a *primary drive,* such as hunger, thirst, cold, or pain. By contrast, the problems with which a neurotic human being struggles, and which he often brings to the psychotherapist, are very different. The neurotic's principal complaints are about anxiety and so-called symptoms, which we now know are defenses that the individual uses, consciously or unconsciously, to protect himself against anxiety and, perhaps secondarily, to gain partial satisfaction of desires whose direct gratification is blocked. Anxiety and the other drives underlying neurotic behavior are *highly complex* and are far removed from the elemental motives which the laboratory worker has traditionally used in the study of problem solving in lower animals.

In recent years, however, learning researchers have gone well beyond their former, limited preoccupations and have broadened their purview to include fear and to some extent anger and the appetites as motives, or problems, around which learning may center. At the same time clinicians have been learning to think more precisely about the nature of neurotic symptoms. Many now look upon symptoms simply as habits which serve to reduce anxiety and related tensions, much as eating reduces hunger, drinking reduces thirst, and resting reduces fatigue. Neurotic symptoms, in other words, are problem-solving, just as behavior in general is.

These developments, on the part of both clinicians and learning researchers, have gone a long way toward establishing a common language and an integrated set of concepts. At our recent professional meetings and in our journals there has been a steady crescendo of interest along these lines, which is certainly indicative of growth in a desirable direction. But many baffling problems remain unsolved. We do not know, for example, whether secondary reinforcement occurs only when a secondary drive is reduced or whether it may also occur when an appetite is aroused, a tension reduction merely anticipated (8, 10, 12). Nor do we have any very confident understanding of the ultimate nature of anxiety (19).

II. Two Basic Learning Processes or One?

While the work on secondary reinforcement—to which Hull, Spence, Miller, Tolman, and their students have all importantly contributed—while this work has opened up many new and exciting possibilities of rapprochement between learning theory and clinical theory, there is a more fundamental problem which has been less widely recognized. Common sense makes implicit reference to three forms of learning, the outcomes of which are often characterized as *habits, attitudes,* and *understandings.* And psychologists employ a similar classification when they speak of trial and error or problem solving, conditioning or emotion learning, and insight.

Hull has attempted to reduce all these phenomena to a basic, primitive reinforcement process: the process that occurs when a drive is lessened, a tension relieved, a pleasure experienced. Hull's theory works well enough for the learning that occurs in connection with simple problem solving. Regardless of whether the problem is a primary drive such as hunger or a secondary drive such as fear, we know that behavior which is instrumental in eliminating it is reinforced and tends to occur when the problem recurs.

But when it comes to accounting for conditioning, Hull's formulation is extremely awkward. For more than ten years I tried to make a monistic conception of learning work, but was forced to abandon it. There are clinical, experimental, logical, and common-sense considerations which all suggest that there are two fundamentally different learning processes, which may be most simply referred to as *solution learning* and *sign learning.* In the one case the subject acquires a tendency to action, an action which is the *solution* to some problem, be that problem either a primary drive or a secondary one. In the other case the organism acquires what may be most inclusively referred to as an *expectation, predisposition, belief,* or *set.* It is through the latter kind of learning that secondary drives, or emotions, become connected with new objects, thus *creating* "problems" where formerly there were none. In other words, solution learning is problem solving, drive reducing, pleasure giving, whereas sign learning, or conditioning, is often—perhaps always—problem making. In terms of the effector systems and the neural tracts involved and the conditions under which they occur, these two forms of learning appear to be basically different (9, 10).

The adoption of a twofold conception of learning, as opposed to Hull's monistic hypothesis, has many important implications, only two of which can be mentioned here.

By 1911 Freud had identified "two principles of mental functioning," as he called them. These, he believed, play roles which, in normality, are harmonious, but which, in neurosis, are antagonistic. These two principles are the pleasure principle and the reality principle. Although Freud was not always consistent or explicit in the definition and application of these two principles, it is clear that they meant for him something very similar to what we have here designated as the two basic learning processes. Solution learning, problem solving, effect learning, or trial and error, as it has been variously called, is clearly related to what Freud termed the pleasure principle. And in sign learning, or conditioning, it is equally evident that we are dealing with the process whereby we learn, not what is pleasurable and relieving, but what is actual, true, real. Many of the things that Freud had to say in terms of the pleasure and reality principles about repression, resistance, transference, and related clinical phenomena can now be meaningfully translated into the language of learning theory, provided that that theory posits the two basic learning processes just described (9, 15, 18).

A monistic conception of the learning process, by its very nature, fails to provide the possibility of dynamic opposition which is apparently necessary for the understanding of neurosis. On this score Hull's system is no exception. In his *Principles of Behavior,* Hull (1943) speaks of "maladaptive" behavior simply as habits which fail to extinguish as rapidly as environmental change demands. Some clinicians have a conception of neurosis which is almost equally simple; but an adequate understanding of neurosis and of the conditions of treatment involves far more complex considerations, to which we shall return presently (see also 18, 19).

Here I want to point out a second consequence which follows from the adoption of a dual conception of learning. Earlier in this paper I made reference to what many believe is a third form of learning, namely insight or so-called cognitive learning. These latter terms have often been used to signify different things. Some of the phenomena they have been used to denote can probably be accounted for in terms of sign learning. But a more complex explanation is necessary in other instances. I am not sure that we can explain all the remaining cases of so-called insight in this way, but many of them can be accounted for by distinguishing clearly between those psychological processes which are *inductive* and those which are *deductive.* Solution learning and sign learning, it would appear, are both forms of induction; they are the processes whereby living organisms build up what logicians call "propositions," or what Kresh has termed "hypotheses."

But then, after two or more of these propositions have been established, they can be used to arrive, swiftly and often very accurately, at new propositions. This latter procedure is the familiar one of deduction, which recent investigations have shown to be by no means restricted to verbalizing organisms; and further inquiry seems likely to show that much of what has passed as insight learning is not learning at all, in the strict sense of that term, but a kind of higher activity—or complex habit—that utilizes the results of learning but is not learning itself (11, 12).

I mention this approach to the problem of insight for two reasons: (*a*) it gives promise of reconciling some of the differences between Hull and such writers as Tolman and Lewin; and (*b*) it provides a means of further integrating the psychology of learning with clinical theory and practice. It must be kept in mind that clinical psychology makes extended use of the concept of insight, and if learning theory is to provide a competent conceptual underpinning, it must fully acknowledge and clearly account for this phenomenon.

III. Gradients of Reinforcement and Persistent Nonintegrative Behavior

While it would thus appear that Hull's monistic account of the learning process is at variance with the requirements of sound clinical theory, his emphasis upon gradients of reinforcement is extremely useful. As one of the first steps in developing a systematic theory of neurosis, we must have a clear understanding of what has sometimes been called persistent nonadjustive behavior or, as I prefer, persistent nonintegrative behavior. Here gradients of reinforcement are of critical importance.

In 1945 A. D. Ullman and I published a paper in which we attempted to resolve "the paradox of persistent nonintegrative behavior," i.e., behavior which persists despite the fact that it is more punishing than rewarding or behavior which is abandoned despite the fact that it is more rewarding than punishing. This analysis made extensive use of reinforcement gradients. It was then already well established, largely as a result of the work of Hull and his students, that "if a response is immediately followed by a rewarding state of affairs (drive reduction), the tendency for the response to occur in the same problem situation in the future is reinforced more than if there is a delay between the occurrence of the response and the reward" (15, page 426). And it was equally well known that "if a response is immediately followed by a punishing state of affairs (drive increase), the kinesthetic and other stimuli resulting from the making of this response become more strongly conditioned to the emotional response of [fear] than if there is a delay between the occurrence of the response and the punishment" (page 426). Said otherwise, solution learning is a function of the temporal interval between *response* and *reward,* and sign learning is a function of the interval between *the sign* and *the thing or event signified.*

On the basis of these facts it is readily demonstrable, both theoretically and experimentally, that if a given response is followed by *two* consequences, one rewarding and one punishing, persistent nonintegrative behavior may result. If the rewarding consequence is smaller than the punishing one but occurs considerably *earlier in time,* behavior may be perpetuated despite its being more punishing than rewarding. And likewise, if the rewarding consequence of a response is larger than the punishing consequence but occurs considerably *later in time,* behavior may be inhibited despite its being more rewarding than punishing.

In the paper cited (15) it was suggested that there is probably an important relationship between the phenomenon of persistent nonintegrative behavior and neurosis, but it was not maintained that nonintegration was the whole story. In the experimental demonstration of persistent nonintegrative behavior which we reported, we were dealing with subjects (laboratory rats) with rather severe native limitations on their integrative ability, and the tasks we set them simply fell beyond their ability to master. But in neurotic human beings the problem is hardly one of ability at all, certainly not of ability in the sense of innate intelligence. Although neurosis may bring a kind of stupidity in its wake, there seems to be no very important correlation between intelligence, in its native sense, and predisposition to neurosis.

In other words, neurosis is not to be explained solely in terms of the complexity of environmental stresses, or solely in terms of the subject's innate ability, or, indeed, even by a combination of these two variables. The *X*-factor which is needed to complete the equation is one which, as process, is appropriately termed *socialization* and which, as end product, is known as *character.* Here the interplay between the two basic forms of learning—between reward learning and conditioning, between love and discipline, between self-indulgence and self-restraint—seems to be critical; but we are only now beginning to see how to formulate significant experimental problems in this area (16, 18, 19, 20, 22).

IV. Socialization, Character, and Psychotherapy

On an earlier page I have referred to the fact that Hull has commonly characterized as "maladaptive" habits which fail to extinguish as rapidly as environmental change would ideally seem to demand. Although Hull's system is derived more directly from the work of Pavlov than from Freud, it is interesting to note that in this particular Hull is closer to Freud than to Pavlov. For Pavlov, maladaptive, or "neurotic," behavior was the result of actual damage to the brain cells, produced either functionally (i.e., by conflict) or by trauma of one kind or another. Although extinction was one of Pavlov's own concepts, he did not use extinction failure in any important sense to account for the behavior disturbances which he termed neurotic.

Freud, on the other hand, made extensive use of this type of explanation. He did not, to be sure, employ the term "extinction," but he spoke of fixation, the timelessness of the unconscious, the excessive severity of the superego, and the repetition compulsion—all of which imply that something has been learned which is then retained longer than it should have been for the most efficient and realistic functioning of the individual. In this respect he and Hull have more in common than do Hull and Pavlov.

Pavlov's interpretation of neurosis rests upon the purely somatic thinking which was common in medical circles half a century ago and which gave us the term "neurosis"—an "osis" of the nerves. Hull's and Freud's approaches are strictly functional, and in this respect are superior to that of Pavlov, but there is a question as to whether either Hull or Freud has touched the heart of the neurotic problem.

Much current psychotherapy is predicated on the assumption that neurosis is simply a result of mislearning and overlearning, and much time is accordingly spent in trying to get the patient to "reality test," i.e., to perform acts which he has long thought of as dangerous but which realistically are not, and to "discriminate" between "then and now," i.e., to see that conditions have changed, that attitudes, beliefs, and practices which, though perhaps justified at an earlier stage in the patient's life history, are no longer necessary or useful.

It is generally conceded that the results of contemporary psychotherapy are not as good as they ought to be. Nor have our therapeutic endeavors pointed the way to an effective mental hygiene program. Full comprehension of the dynamics of a disease in the field of medicine leads not only to efficient treatment but also to a drop in the incidence of the disease. Psychotherapy, if sound, ought then to generate a philosophy of life which, by permeating the home and society generally, would function as a preventive as well as a corrective. That the indices of neurosis and personal disorganization in our time show no signs of declining would seem to justify a searching re-examination of our most fundamental and most cherished premises in this area (18, 20, 22).

In view of the recent advances which have been made in our knowledge in a number of related fields, it seems possible that we may now be able to see neurosis and its treatment and prevention in a new light. We now know, thanks to the work of anthropologists and other social scientists, that human personality is only to a very small degree the product of independent learning; it is mainly the outcome of the imposition of the enormous accumulation of vicarious learning which we call *culture.* And we know that culture has two major subdivisions. Some items of culture help us solve immediate problems; they provide welcome answers to difficulties which we all encounter. But at the same time culture also contains elements which, at least in the early stages of life, are odious to the human animal. These are the moral injunctions which are essential to the continued functioning of the group but which the infant looks upon as foreign and functionless, arbitrary and needless barriers in the path to pleasure.

Here we are obviously dealing with phenomena which are related to the pleasure principle and the reality principle, to solution learning and sign learning. Moreover, culture stands for a long-term strategy; it stands for restraint, renunciation, and sacrifice. It stresses the future, whereas the untutored human animal, like animals in general, is much more disposed to live in the present. Here, then, we are dealing with the problem of time binding, of integrating the future and the present, of learning how to surmount the natural limitations imposed by the natively given gradients of reinforcement.

Without further elaboration it is apparent that personal maturity presupposes an enormously complicated and protracted type of learning, a type of learning which is *so* complicated and *so* protracted that it can occur only under the peculiarly favorable auspices of the *good family.* No other induction in the entire field of social science is better established than the proposition that personal disorganization and inadequacy are functions of family disorganization and inadequacy. Yet it has become a widespread clinical belief that neurosis occurs because the family has done its work all too well, made the "superego too severe," the conscience too demanding and inflexible. According to this perception of the situation, the task of psychotherapy is to help the patient move in the direction opposite to that in which the parents tried—and supposedly succeeded only too well—to take him.

Clinical experience does not support this view. The persons whom one sees clinically present, with monotonous regularity, a history, not of overlearning, but of underlearning. Personality immaturity is almost synonymous with neurosis, and the only way to maturity and personal normality is in the direction in which the family and other socializing institutions are designed to carry the child. If neurosis were simply a question of overlearning or mislearning, the condition ought to be self-correcting; for all that we know of habits and attitudes which cease to be reinforced indicates that they sooner or later extinguish (6). Neurosis, on the other hand, may last a lifetime, and the reason is that a neurotic is a person who has reached adulthood without having learned the things that he needs to know for happy, integrated existence; and once an individual is "on his own," the possibility for the continuation or resumption of this learning is exceedingly limited. The familiar slogan, "Even your best friends won't tell you," is peculiarly apposite here. Once we reach physical maturity, no one is likely to play the parental role with us, with the result that we may continue for the rest of our lives as half-formed human beings, able neither to abandon nor to complete the enterprise that was started but which, for whatever reason, was left unfinished.

Traditionally, religion has afforded human beings an opportunity to continue, as adults, to enjoy and profit from an extension of the child-parent relationship. Through prayer the adult was enjoined to keep in touch with his "heavenly father"; and, to make communication easier and more tangible, worldly emissaries of God were provided in the person of priests, ministers, and others whose duty it was to admonish and confess their "children." For many modern men and women, religion, because of its reliance upon supernaturalism, has lost its appeal and efficacy; and it is for such persons that psychotherapy may be uniquely indicated. In it the neurotic and the immature find an opportunity to resume and, in the fortunate case, complete the unfinished business of growing up. But because therapists frequently appear to misconceive the nature of this task, the outcome is often disappointing.

The gist of what I have tried to say in this paper is that clinical theory will profit by interaction with learning theory, but that it is a mistake to suppose that the profit will be in only one direction. Learning theory is still far too simple to encompass all the complexities of socialization and character formation. Neurosis is not a question of overlearning; and it does not represent just a failure of extinction. It is rather a question of underlearning, a failure of learning which is so involved that it can occur only in the home *or* in the approximation of the child-parent relationship which has traditionally been available in religion and is now being developed in the guise of modern psychotherapy.

PART I
LEARNING THEORY

CHAPTER 1

A STIMULUS-RESPONSE ANALYSIS OF ANXIETY AND ITS ROLE AS A REINFORCING AGENT

[During the period of time which has elapsed since original publication of the first of the papers comprising this volume, the greatest single advance in American psychology has probably been the increased emphasis on *secondary motivation.* This has done much to bridge the gap between the earlier work on animal motivation—which was concerned almost exclusively with primary drives—and the observations which had been reported concerning human motives.

As a result of the work of the last ten or twelve years, it is now clear (*a*) that secondary drives are *learned* (see Footnote 3 below) and (*b*) that, once learned, they serve as a basis for *further learning.* These two findings do much toward providing a systematic framework which is logically adequate for encompassing the intricate elaboration of drives and behavior known as *personality.* These findings serve particularly to call attention to the dual nature of learning, which will be subsequently discussed under the headings of *conditioning* and *problem solving;* and they also contribute to a more satisfactory understanding of *language functions.*

The present paper, originally published in *The Psychological Review* (1939), considers "anxiety" as an instance of secondary motivation and shows its double status as both a product and a producer of learning. The paper involves a combination of fact and theory drawn from both academic psychology and psychoanalysis, and establishes the conceptual setting for a number of the other papers included in this volume.

A word of explanation is necessary concerning the use of the term *anxiety* in this paper. Because much of what is here said applies equally to *fear,* the two terms are to be considered as synonymous. However, there are good grounds for defining them differently. One commonly made distinction is alluded to in Footnote 1. Other considerations will be discussed in Part II (see especially 19).]

Within recent decades an important change has taken place in the scientific view of anxiety (fear),[1] its genesis, and its psycho-

[1] Psychoanalytic writers sometimes differentiate between anxiety and fear on the grounds that fear has a consciously perceived object and anxiety does

logical significance. Writing in 1890, William James stoutly supported the then current supposition that anxiety was an *instinctive* ("idiopathic") reaction to certain objects or situations, which might or might not represent real danger. To the extent that the instinctively given, predetermined objects of anxiety were indeed dangerous, anxiety reactions had biological utility and could be accounted for as an evolutionary product of the struggle for existence. On the other hand, there were, James assumed, also anxiety reactions that were altogether senseless and which, conjecturally, came about through Nature's imperfect wisdom. But in all cases, an anxiety reaction was regarded as phylogenetically fixed and unlearned. The fact that children may show no fear of a given type of object, e.g., live frogs, during the first year of life, but may later manifest such a reaction, James attributed to the "ripening" of the fear-of-live-frogs instinct; and the fact that such fears, once they have "ripened," may also disappear he explained on the assumption that all instincts, after putting in an appearance and, as it were, placing themselves at the individual's disposal, tend to undergo a kind of oblivescence, or decay, unless taken advantage of and made "habitual."

Some years later John B. Watson (1928) demonstrated experimentally that, contrary to the Jamesian view, most human fears are specifically relatable to and dependent upon individual experience. Starting with the reaction of infants to loud sounds or loss of physical support, which he refused to call "instinctive" but did not hesitate to regard as "unlearned" or "reflexive," Watson was able to show, by means of Pavlov's conditioning technique, that an indefinitely wide range of other stimuli, if associated with this reaction, could be made to acquire the capacity to elicit unmistakably fearful behavior. This was an important discovery, but it appears to have involved a basic fallacy. Watson overlooked the fact that "loud sounds" are intrinsically *painful,* and he also overlooked the fact that "loss of physical support," although not painful in its own right, is almost certain to be followed by some form of stimulation (incident to the stopping of the body's fall) that is painful. The so-called fearful reaction to loss of support—if not confused with an actual pain reaction—is, therefore, in all probability itself a learned (conditioned) reaction, which means that, according to Watson's observations, human infants show no innate *fear* responses whatever, merely innate *pain* responses.

---

not. Although this distinction may be useful for some purposes, these two terms will be used in the present paper as strictly synonymous.

Freud seems to have seen the problem in this light from the outset and accordingly posited that *all* anxiety (fear) reactions are probably learned;[2] his hypothesis, when recast in stimulus-response terminology, runs as follows. A so-called "traumatic" ("painful") stimulus (arising either from external injury, of whatever kind, or from severe organic need) impinges upon the organism and produces a more or less violent defense (striving) reaction. Furthermore, such a stimulus-response sequence is usually preceded or accompanied by originally "indifferent" stimuli which, however, after one or more temporally contiguous associations with the traumatic stimulus, begin to be perceived as "danger signals," i.e., acquire the capacity to elicit an "anxiety" reaction. This latter reaction, which may or may not be grossly observable, has two outstanding characteristics: (*a*) it creates or, perhaps more accurately, consists of a state of heightened tension (or "attention") and a more or less specific readiness for (expectation of) the impending traumatic stimulus; and (*b*), by virtue of the fact that such a state of tension is itself a form of discomfort, it adaptively motivates the organism to escape from the danger situation, thereby lessening the intensity of the tension (anxiety) and also probably decreasing the chances of encountering the traumatic stimulus. In short, *anxiety (fear) is the conditioned form of the pain reaction,* which has the highly useful function of motivating and reinforcing behavior that tends to avoid or prevent the recurrence of the pain-producing (unconditioned) stimulus.[3]

In the mentalistic terminology that he characteristically employs, Freud (1936) has formulated this view of anxiety formation and its adaptational significance as follows:

---

[2] Freud (1936) has explicitly acknowledged the possibility of anxiety occurring, especially in birds and other wild animals, as an instinctive reaction; but he takes the position that in human beings, instinctive anxiety (not to be confused with "instinctual" anxiety, i.e., fear of the intensity of one's own organic impulses) is probably nonexistent or is at least inconsequential.

[3] [It is today an open question whether fear ("anxiety") is more properly conceived of as "the conditioned form of the pain reaction" or whether there are two forms of fear, one conditioned and the other unconditioned, the latter occurring as a parallel reaction to noxious stimulation, along with pain. One contemporary expert in this field (Miller, 1950) inclines to the latter view, as indicated by his classification of fear as an *acquirable* drive. Conditioned fear reactions certainly function as the anticipatory equivalents of pain and thus, by motivating the organism at the *secondary* level, aid it in avoiding the actual experiencing of pain as a *primary* drive. But it may indeed be true that fear is not the conditioned form of the pain reaction as such. Learned fears may be acquired on the basis of an associative shifting of a more primal reaction which occurs, along with pain, as a part of the organism's total response to noxious stimulation. In this case, we would certainly be justified of speaking of both conditioned and unconditioned fears. This is a problem which calls for more extended analysis, but it is not of critical importance for present purposes.]

Now it is an important advance in self-protection when this traumatic situation of helplessness [discomfort] is not merely awaited but is foreseen, anticipated. Let us call the situation in which resides the cause of this anticipation the danger situation; it is in this latter that *the signal of anxiety*[4] is given. What this means is: I anticipate that a situation of helplessness [discomfort] will come about, or the present situation reminds me of one of the traumatic experiences which I have previously undergone. Hence I will anticipate this trauma; I will act as if it were already present as long as there is still time to avert it. Anxiety, therefore, is the *expectation of the trauma* on the one hand, and on the other, an *attenuated repetition of it* (pp. 149–50).

Affective [anxiety] states are incorporated into the life of the psyche as precipitates of primal traumatic experiences, and are evoked in similar situations like memory symbols (p. 23).

Anxiety is undeniably related to expectation; one feels anxiety *lest* something occur (pp. 146–47).[5]

According to views expressed elsewhere by Freud, expectation and anxiety lie along a continuum, with the former merging into the latter at the point at which it becomes uncomfortably intense, i.e., begins to take on motivational properties in its own right [see the following paper]. The preparatory, expectant character of anxiety is likely, however, to be obscured by the fact that danger situations sometimes arise and pass so quickly that they are over before the anxiety reaction—involving, as it does, not only an augmentation of neuromuscular readiness and tension but also a general mobilization of the physical energies needed to sustain strenuous action—has had an opportunity to occur. The result is that in situations in which danger is so highly transitory, as, for example, in near-accidents in motor traffic, anxiety is commonly experienced, somewhat paradoxically, *after* the danger is past and therefore gives the appearance of being indeed a useless, wasted reaction (*cf.*

---

[4] [Freud's use of the word "signal" in this context is likely to be confusing. Ordinarily we think of fear, not as being in itself a signal, but as being a *reaction to a signal.* By speaking of "the signal of anxiety," Freud was here referring, not to the objects or events which serve to arouse fear, but to the premonitory, or warning, function of fear itself. He meant that fear is a "signal" of impending pain. Fear, in other words, is the subjective equivalent or counterpart of an external or objective warning signal.]

[5] [Although Freud was a pioneer in establishing the distinction between "fear" and "anxiety," he was not always consistent in his use of these terms. Sometimes he spoke, for example, of "normal anxiety," "moral anxiety," and "neurotic anxiety" (1933), by which he meant, respectively, *objective fear, moral, or social, fear,* and *irrational fear.* In keeping with the terminology which he elsewhere employed, it is only the last of these that qualifies as "anxiety." According to this usage, "neurotic anxiety" is redundant, for there is no other kind. See papers dealing with anxiety (19, 20, 22) in Part II.]

James, 1890).[6] It must not be overlooked, however, that situations of this kind are more or less anomalous. The fact that in a given situation the element of danger disappears before flight, for which the anxiety preparedness is most appropriate, has had time to occur, does not, of course, mean that anxiety preparedness in the face of danger is not in general a very adaptive reaction.[7]

As early as 1903, Pavlov (1928) expressed a point of view that bears a striking resemblance to the position taken by Freud in this connection. He said: "The importance of the remote signs (signals) of objects can be easily recognized in the movement reaction of the animal. By means of distant and even accidental characteristics of objects the animal seeks his food, avoids enemies, etc." (p. 52). Again, a quarter of a century later, Pavlov (1938) wrote as follows:

> It is pretty evident that under natural conditions the normal animal must respond not only to stimuli which themselves bring immediate benefit or harm, but also to other physical or chemical agencies—waves of sound, light, and the like—which in themselves only *signal* the approach of these stimuli; though it is not the sight and sound of the beast of prey which is in itself harmful to the smaller animal, but its teeth and claws (p. 14).

Although both Pavlov and Freud thus clearly recognize the biological utility of anticipatory reactions to danger signals, there is an important difference in their viewpoints. Pavlov emphasizes the mechanism of simple stimulus substitution (conditioning). According to his hypothesis, a danger signal (the conditioned stimulus) comes to elicit essentially the *same* "movement reaction" that has previously been produced by actual trauma (the unconditioned

[6] [Writing in 1921, Max F. Meyer remarked: "In connection with 'instincts' it has become the custom among psychologists to speak of 'emotions.' From the social point of view emotions are most curious phenomena. But if we analyse them psychologically, we find that they are nothing but 'wasted' reflexes and habits" (p. 212). Thus, "'Fear,' running away, is a habit based on negative localization" (p. 212). And later Meyer remarks, "Any wasted reflex or habit may be called an illusion (just as it may be called an emotion)" (p. 226). Yet we find this same author, in unguarded moments, speaking as if emotions were of very considerable importance, as, for example, when he says, "The cooling by conduction of heat through the tissues covering the body is little to be feared as long as the warm blood etc." (p. 214). These quotations illustrate the *tour de force* by which the Behaviorists tried to found a science of behavior which would have no need or place in it for the concept of emotion or secondary drive. In a sense, the whole of the present volume may be said to be dedicated to the "rediscovery" of emotion. But the behavioristic phase was a useful one in that it purged psychology of a lot of verbiage and cleared the way for significant new developments, both conceptually and methodologically. For a revival of interest in the question as to whether emotion is "wasted" ("disorganizing") or useful ("organizing"), see Leeper (1948) and Young (1949).]

[7] Cf. the discussion of the "startle pattern" by Landis and Hunt (1939).

stimulus). It is true that the blink of the eyelids to a threatening visual stimulus is not greatly unlike the reaction made to direct corneal irritation. A dog may learn to flex its leg in response to a formerly neutral stimulus so as to simulate the flexion produced by an electric shock administered to its paw. And a small child may for a time make very much the same type of withdrawal reactions to the sight of a flame that it makes to actual contact with it. However, any attempt to establish this pattern of stimulus substitution as the prototype of all learning places severe restrictions on the limits of adaptive behavior: it implies that the only reactions that can become attached to formerly unrelated stimuli (i.e., can be learned) are those which already occur more or less reflexly to some other type of stimulation.

According to the conception of anxiety proposed by Freud, on the other hand, a danger signal may come to produce any of an infinite variety of reactions that are wholly unlike the reaction that occurs to the actual trauma of which the signal is premonitory. Freud assumes that the first and most immediate response to a danger signal is not a complete, overt reaction, as Pavlov implies, but an implicit state of tension and augmented preparedness for action,[8] which he calls "anxiety." This state of affairs, being itself a source of discomfort, may then motivate innumerable random acts, from which will be selected and fixated (by the law of effect) the behavior that most effectively reduces the anxiety. Anxiety is thus to be regarded as a motivating and reinforcing (fixating) agent, similar to hunger, thirst, sex, temperature deviations, and the many other forms of discomfort that harass living organisms, which is, however, presumably distinctive in that it is derived from (based upon anticipation of) these other, more basic forms of discomfort.[9]

By and large, behavior that reduces anxiety also operates to lessen the danger that it presages. An antelope that scents a panther

---

[8] Cf. the revised theory of conditioning proposed by Culler (1938).

[9] Freud has never explicitly formulated this view in precisely these words, but it is clearly implied in various of his writings. [The above sentences rather clearly intimate that there are *two* forms of learning, two types of "reinforcement" —conditioning and problem solving or law-of-effect learning. Through the former, fear motives are acquired, and through the latter fear-reducing responses are found and fixated. This point of view becomes explicit in later studies (9, 10). In an earlier paper (Mowrer, 1938c), an attempt was made to provide a formula for reducing all learning to a single process, and a similarly monistic position has been taken in certain of the other papers here included (4, 5, 8). In the course of the decade represented by the studies included in this volume, there has thus been a shift from a monistic to a dualistic position; but, as the present article indicates (see also Mowrer, 1941c), a dualism has been at least incipient from the beginning.]

is likely not only to feel less uneasy (anxious) if it moves out of range of the odor of the panther but is also likely to be in fact somewhat safer. A primitive village that is threatened by marauding men or beasts sleeps better after it has surrounded itself with a deep moat or a sturdy stockade. And a modern mother is made emotionally more comfortable after her child has been properly vaccinated against a dreaded disease. This capacity to be made uncomfortable by the mere prospect of traumatic experiences, in advance of their actual occurrence (or recurrence), and to be motivated thereby to take realistic precautions against them is unquestionably a tremendously important and useful psychological mechanism, and the fact that the forward-looking, anxiety-arousing propensity of the human mind is more highly developed than it is in lower animals probably accounts for many of man's unique accomplishments. But it also accounts for some of his most conspicuous failures.

The ostrich has become a proverbial object of contempt and a symbol of stupidity because of its alleged tendency, when frightened, to put its head in the sand, thereby calming its emotional agitation but not altering the danger situation in its objective aspects. Such relevant scientific inquiry as has been carried out indicates, however, that infrahuman organisms are ordinarily more realistic in this respect than are human beings. For example, if a dog learns to avoid an electric shock by lifting its foreleg in response to a tone, it will give up this response entirely when it discovers that the tone is no longer followed by shock if the response is not made. Human beings, on the other hand, are notoriously prone to engage in all manner of magical, superstitious, and propitiatory acts, which undoubtedly relieve dread and uncertainty (at least temporarily) but which have a questionable value in controlling real events.[10] The remarkable persistence of such practices may be due, at least in part, to the fact that they are followed relatively promptly by anxiety-reduction, whereas their experienced futility at the reality level may come many hours or days or even months later.[11] The persistence of certain forms of "unrealistic" anxiety-reinforced behavior may also be due to the fact that in most societies there seem always to be some individuals who are able and ready to derive an easy living by fostering beliefs on the part of

---

[10] Under some circumstances, e.g., when warriors are preparing for battle, malevolent incantations or similar anxiety-reducing magical procedures may, of course, be objectively efficacious, not, to be sure, in the supposed magical way, but in that they alter human conduct in crucial situations (i.e., make the warriors bolder and better fighters).

[11] Cf. Hull's concept of the "goal gradient" (Hull, 1932). [See also 15.]

others in "unrealistic" dangers. For the common man protection against such "dangers" consists of whatever type of behavior the bogey-makers choose to say is "safe" (and which furthers their own interests).

Yet other forms of "unrealistic" anxiety-reinforced behavior are to be observed in the symptomatic acts of the psychoneuroses. According to Freud, anxiety is in fact "the fundamental phenomenon and the central problem of neurosis" (1936). He further says:

> Since we have reduced the development of anxiety to a response to situations of danger, we shall prefer to say that the symptoms are created in order to remove or rescue the ego from the situation of danger. . . . We can also say, in supplement to this, that the development of anxiety induces symptom formation—nay more, it is a *sine qua non* thereof, for if the ego did not forcibly arouse the pleasure-pain mechanism through the development of anxiety, it would not acquire the power to put a stop to the danger-threatening process elaborated in the id (1936, pp. 112–13).

Willoughby (1935), in a scholarly, well-documented paper, has previously stressed the similarity of magical rites (including religion) and neurotic symptoms and has shown that both types of behavior spring from the common propensity of human beings to deal with their anxieties unrealistically, i.e., by means which diminish emotional discomfort but do not adaptively alter external realities. This excellent study has, in the present writer's opinion, only one important weakness: it takes as its point of departure what Freud has called his "first theory" of anxiety formation (1894), which he subsequently abandoned for the one outlined above. In brief, Freud's earlier supposition was that anxiety arose whenever a strong organic drive or impulse was prevented from discharging through its accustomed motor outlets. According to this view, inhibition was the primary state, anxiety the resultant. In all his more recent writings, on the other hand, Freud takes the position, here also adopted, that anxiety (as a reaction to a "danger signal") is primal and that inhibition of anxiety-arousing, danger-producing impulses [12] is a consequence (1936).[13] Reaction mech-

[12] One of Freud's most fundamental discoveries, basic to the understanding of reaction formation, repression, projection, and other neurotic mechanisms, is that organic impulses, even though they are not consciously experienced and identified, may function as "danger signals" and thereby evoke anxiety. This relatively simple yet frequently misapprehended finding (Freud has himself contributed to the confusion by sometimes speaking as if anxiety *is* the "danger signal," instead of a *reaction* to it) can be readily translated into Pavlovian terminology by saying that an organic need or drive, which has in the past led to overt behavior that was severely punished, will tend upon its recurrence, even at low intensities, to elicit a conditioned pain (anxiety) reaction. Yet, as

anisms (magic, symptoms, etc.) that contribute to this end tend, for reasons already given, to be reinforced and perpetuated. Willoughby's analysis is not of necessity predicated upon Freud's original view of anxiety formation and would seem to gain rather than lose cogency if based instead upon his more recent formulations.

Magical and neurotic practices constitute a very perplexing and challenging problem from the point of view of traditional psychological theory; but, as Allport (1937) has recently pointed out, so also do many other types of human activity that are commonly regarded as both rational and normal. Allport rightly stresses the inadequacies of the conditioned-reflex concept as a comprehensive explanation of learning and personality development in general. He also justly criticizes the view that all human conduct is to be accounted for in terms of trial-and-error striving to eliminate immediately felt organic needs. The fact is that much of modern man's most energetic behavior occurs when his organic needs are ostensibly well satisfied. In an attempt to account for this state of affairs, without, on the other hand, falling back on a forthright mentalistic type of approach, Allport elaborates the view, previously advanced by Woodworth, that habits themselves have an ongoing character, independent of the motivation that originally brought them into being, and that this type of habit momentum constitutes a form of self-sustained motivation. Allport calls this the principle of "functional autonomy" and relies heavily upon it in developing his "psychology of personality."

In the estimation of the present writer, "functional autonomy" is on a par with "perpetual motion." Its author clearly perceives an important psychological problem, but it seems unlikely that his

---

will be shown in a later paper on the so-called "experimental neurosis" (18), Pavlov and his followers have largely ignored this possibility of internal, as well as external, stimuli acquiring "signal" value, i.e., becoming "conditioned," and have consequently made apparent mysteries of some laboratory observations which, when viewed more broadly, seem completely intelligible.

[13] [Here is an example of the undesirability of equating fear and anxiety. If anxiety, strictly speaking, is fear that has lost its object through repression, then it is clearly inappropriate to regard "anxiety" as causal with respect to repression. The practice consistently followed in the later studies appearing in this volume is to assume that, prior to repression, the individual experiences fears and guilts which have fully conscious objects and that it is only *after* repression that *anxiety* can be experienced. (See, however, the later discussion on "normal anxiety"). It should also be noted here that in these early papers the author accepted Freud's view that when there is a conscious conflict between social fear (superego) and some impulse such as lust or hostility (id), it is the latter which tends to fall under repression. As will be evident later (18, 19, 20), the author's present position is that repression far more commonly goes in the opposite direction and that anxiety thus represents a threatened "return," not of repressed lust or hostility, but of repressed, repudiated guilt feelings. This change in viewpoint has widely ramified implications which will be considered later.]

is a scientifically tenable solution to it. The position here taken is that human beings (and also other living organisms to varying degrees) can be motivated either by organic pressures (needs) that are currently present and felt *or* by the mere anticipation of such pressures and that those habits tend to be acquired and perpetuated (reinforced) which effect a reduction in *either* of these two types of motivation. This view rests upon and is but an extended application of the well-founded law of effect and involves no assumptions that are not empirically verifiable. It has the further advantage that it is consistent with common-sense impressions and practices and at the same time serves as a useful integrational device at the scientific level.[14]

The present analysis of anxiety (anticipation, expectancy) and its role in shaping both "adaptive" and "maladaptive" behavior in human beings is also consistent with the growing tendency to eliminate the distinction between learning through "punishment" and learning through "reward." The earlier view was that so-called punishment "stamped out" habits and that reward "stamped" them "in." This distinction now appears to have been spurious and to have depended upon a selectivity of emphasis or interest (1938c). If an individual is motivated by an internal discomfort or need (produced by his own metabolic processes), and if another individual provides the means of eliminating it, and if, in the process, the first individual acquires new behavior, this is called learning through "reward." But if a second individual supplies the need (by inflicting or threatening to inflict some form of discomfort) and if the affected individual supplies the means of eliminating this discomfort (by flight, inactivity, propitiation, compliance, or the like) and if, in the process, this individual acquires new behavior, then this is called learning through "punishment." The truth of the matter seems to be that all [problem-solving] learning presupposes (*a*) an increase of motivation (striving) and (*b*) a decrease of motivation (success) and that the essential features of the process are much the same, regardless of the specific source of motivation or of the particular circumstances of its elimination.[15]

---

[14] [For further discussion of these and related problems, see 2, 3, 4, 5.]

[15] According to this point of view, old habits are eliminated, not by being "stamped out" or extracted "by the roots," but by the functional superimposition of new, more powerful antagonistic habits (1938c). Anxiety may thus be said to exercise an "inhibitory" effect (see foregoing discussion of Freud's "first theory" of anxiety) upon established behavior trends mainly through its motivation and reinforcement of opposing behavior trends. In this way emphasis falls primarily upon the positive, habit-forming consequences of anxiety and only secondarily and indirectly upon its negative, inhibitory functions.

There is, however, one practical consideration to be taken into account. Although learning through "punishment" does not seem to differ basically from learning through "reward," interpersonal relationships are likely to be affected very differently in the two cases. If the method of "reward" is employed, interpersonal relationships are likely to be made more positive (i.e., approach tendencies will be strengthened); whereas, if the method of "punishment" is employed, interpersonal relationships are likely to be made more "negative" (i.e., avoidance tendencies will be strengthened).[16] From a purely social point of view, it is therefore preferable to employ the method of "reward," whenever this is possible; but "punishment" may have to be resorted to if no *organic* needs are present to be "rewarded" or if means of rewarding them are not available. Punishment (or the threat of punishment, i.e., anxiety) is particularly convenient in that it can be produced instantly; but this advantage is accompanied by disadvantages which cannot be safely disregarded.

Even the practical basis just suggested for distinguishing between learning through reward and learning through punishment becomes tenuous when one considers the type of situation in which one person withholds from another an expected reward. This, in one sense, is a form of "punishment," and yet its effectiveness is

[16] [If one explicitly adopts a two-factor theory of learning, the import of the above statements becomes much clearer. It is indeed true that living organisms tend to behave in fundamentally the same way with respect to primary drives, regardless of whether they result from the organism's own metabolism or from some external agency, i.e., the organism tends to find and fixate upon whatever responses are drive-reducing. Thus problem-solving learning involves *both* "punishment" and "reward," in the sense that it can occur only when there is, to begin with, a *problem* and, sooner or later, a *solution*. It is therefore only when one turns to conditioning—or "concomitant learning," as Kilpatrick has called it (1925)—that these terms become really meaningful. If an incidental stimulus is concomitant with the *onset* of a drive, it becomes connected with a very different reaction from what it becomes connected with if it is concomitant, or contiguous, with the *termination* of the drive. In the first case, the incidental stimulus soon acquires the capacity to arouse *fear*, whereas in the second case it acquires the capacity to arouse *hope* or some form of *appetite*. Thus, if one shows a dog a bone and then subjects the dog to electric shock, the bone will become a danger signal; but if one shows the dog the bone and lets him eat it, the bone, subsequently, will elicit tail-wagging and salivation. Although our experimental evidence is still incomplete on this score, it appears that it is drive onset and drive termination that are important here, rather than the specific nature of the drive itself. Unfortunately there seems at present to be no way of making dogs or other laboratory subjects suddenly and powerfully hungry. Thus we lack the opportunity to test the assumption that stimuli associated with such an event would be fear-producing. But an exploratory study by Coppock (1949) indicates at least this, that human beings do not develop fear (as indicated by the galvanic skin response) if a signal is associated with shock termination, whereas they do if it is associated with shock onset; and it would probably be a safe assumption that, in the former case, they developed a real "appetite" in response to the signal, although this was apparently not specifically ascertained (see 9 and 10).]

based upon the principle of "reward." This complicated state of affairs seems especially likely to arise in the parent-child relationship and has implications that have been but slightly explored in stimulus-response terms.

Summary

In contrast to the older view, which held that anxiety (fear) was an instinctive reaction to phylogenetically predetermined objects or situations, the position here taken is that anxiety is a learned response, occurring to "signals" (conditioned stimuli) that are premonitory of (i.e., have in the past been followed by) situations of injury or pain (unconditioned stimuli). Anxiety is thus basically anticipatory in nature and has great biological utility in that it adaptively motivates living organisms to deal with (prepare for or flee from) traumatic events in advance of their actual occurrence, thereby diminishing their harmful effects. However, experienced anxiety does not always vary in direct proportion to the objective danger in a given situation, with the result that living organisms, and human beings in particular, show tendencies to behave "irrationally," i.e., to have anxiety in situations that are not dangerous or to have no anxiety in situations that are dangerous. Such a "disproportionality of affect" may come about for a variety of reasons, and the analysis of these reasons throws light upon such diverse phenomena as magic, superstition, social exploitation, and the psychoneuroses.[17]

Moreover, by positing anxiety as a kind of connecting link between complete well-being and active organic discomfort or injury, it is possible to reconcile the fact that much, perhaps most, of the day-to-day behavior of civilized human beings is not prompted by simultaneously active organic drives and the fact that the law of effect (learning through motivation reduction) is apparently one of the best established of psychological principles. This is accomplished by assuming (*a*) that anxiety, i.e., mere anticipation of actual organic need or injury, may effectively motivate human beings and (*b*) that reduction of anxiety may serve powerfully to reinforce behavior that brings about such a state of "relief" or "security." Anxiety, although derived from more basic forms of motivation, is thus regarded as functioning in an essentially parallel manner as far as its role as an activating and reinforcing agent is

---

[17] [For a somewhat different approach to this problem, see 18, 19, 22.]

concerned. This analysis is consistent with the common-sense view in such matters and does not conflict with any known empirical fact. Finally, it has the advantage of being open to objective investigation and of giving rise to a host of problems that have scarcely been touched experimentally (2).

CHAPTER 2

PREPARATORY SET (EXPECTANCY)—SOME METHODS OF MEASUREMENT

[In some ways the use of the terms "preparatory set" and "expectancy" in the title of this paper was unfortunate, for they fail to call attention to the extent to which the paper is concerned with the problem of secondary motivation. However, this concern is repeatedly expressed in the text. Thus: "As previously posited, expectancy or preparatory set is itself a form of discomfort. . . . [By] regarding both expectancy of 'reward' and expectancy of 'punishment' as forms of discomfort (rather than as one being 'pleasant' and the other 'unpleasant'), it is possible to account for the motivational value of each on the basis of a single, unitary principle. This is in keeping with an attempt which has been made elsewhere to show that so-called 'learning through reward' is not basically different from 'learning through punishment.' [See 1, footnote 16.] By eliminating this traditional distinction, a real advance can be made toward a simpler, more coherent and comprehensive theory of behavior" (pages 60–61).

As indicated in the preceding paper, all emotions have an "expectant" or anticipatory quality and are "sets" for one form of activity or another. The present paper is therefore in series with the first and addresses itself particularly to the task of finding objective, operational ways of identifying some of the derived drive states; hence, the emphasis on *measurement.*

Earlier writers had commonly subsumed under the term *attention* many of the phenomena here discussed. Behaviorists, eschewing such mentalistic concepts, tended to speak instead of *posture, sense-organ orientation,* and other *motor equivalents.* The present paper demonstrates the unreliability of purely muscular indices of secondary-drive sets and suggests instead the concept of *tension.* The tension concept is clearly related to that of secondary motivation and emotion.

This study was originally published as a *Psychological Monograph* (1940) and represents the culmination of a line of thought developed in three other studies (Mowrer, 1938c; Mowrer, Rayman, and Bliss, 1940; and Mowrer, 1941b), which are not here included.]

Introduction

Although affording a possible basis for more significant future inquiry, animal studies of motivation have not to date materially increased our understanding of human motivation. This seems to be largely due to the fact that experiments in this field have been concerned almost exclusively with organically specific sources of motivation such as thirst, hunger, temperature variations, sex, electric shock, and so forth. Civilized human adults also respond (though often less obviously than do animals) [1] to these primary drives or needs, but the greater part of their daily activities, often of a most strenuous nature, occurs when these basic needs are apparently well satisfied. How can this important fact be accounted for in a way that is consistent with what is known concerning the operation of the principles governing primary motivation?

With the passing of nativistic conceptions of human nature on the one hand and rationalistic conceptions on the other, psychologists and other behavioral scientists have been hard put to give a convincing account of the springs of human action. Gradually, however, there is emerging from a variety of sources what appears to be a realistic, workable solution to the problem. Such key concepts as "attitudes" (sociology), "need for security" (social work), "tension" (psychiatry), and "anxiety" (psychoanalysis) all involve the assumption that human beings are capable of being motivated, not only by organic needs (discomforts) that are immediately present and felt, but also by the mere *anticipation of such needs.* Most men obviously do not wait until they are actually hungry or unsheltered or attacked by their enemies before they begin making appropriate responses. If "work" has one outstanding characteristic, it is surely that it aims (i.e., on the average tends) not only to remove organic pressures that are already present but also to lessen the prospects of re-experiencing them in the future. Human beings have a strong impulsion to put as much "distance" between themselves and the brink of real privation as possible; and it is this "need for security"—not actual, immediate want—that keeps most men at their jobs and largely shapes their political, economic, and social ideologies.[2]

Academic psychologists have been aware of the forward-look-

---

[1] Cf. Brogden (1939b).

[2] There is nothing mysterious or teleological about the assumption that anticipation of organic needs can function as a source of motivation. All the basic needs are types of discomfort and are in the broad sense "painful." Anticipation

ing functions of the human mind, but the successful scientific investigation of a phenomenon involves more than mere recognition of its reality. Lindner (1938) has recently reviewed the attempts of the early introspectionalists to analyze the anticipatory processes and concludes that the work of these writers "nets us very little" (p. 225). On one point, however, these writers were in fair agreement, namely, that anticipation or expectancy [3] is commonly accompanied by a feeling of "strain," which they sought to localize in the skeletal musculature. Lange (1888), carrying this type of

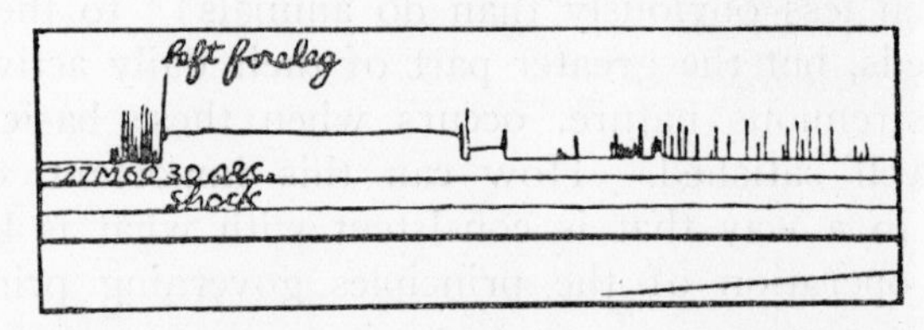

FIG. 1.—Record of foreleg flexions of a sheep with "experimental neurosis." The above record, reproduced from Anderson and Liddell (1935), shows (top line) the left foreleg flexions of a "neurotic" sheep before and after one of a series of paired presentations of the sound of a metronome and an electric shock (at point indicated). Note the numerous anticipatory flexions prior to stimulation, which, according to these writers, always had the effect of quieting the animal, "no matter how nervous it might have been before this stimulation. The period of quiet usually lasted about a minute and then the nervous movements began again. The shock appeared to relieve the tension which had been rising since the last test" (p. 358).

analysis a step further, reached the conclusion that, as James (1890) has rephrased it, "ideational preparation itself is a consequence of muscular adjustment, so that the latter may be called the essence of the attentive process throughout" (p. 444). If, as this view held, anticipation of an impending event were not only accompanied by, but actually dependent upon, characteristic changes in the subject's motor apparatus, all that would be needed to make this phenomenon objectively identifiable and measurable (and thus lay the foundation for its scientific study) would be the development of refined meth-

---

of a need is also "painful" and carries with it motivational potentialities which may be great or small but which are functionally similar to the need that it presages. Anticipation, or expectancy, thus serves as an immediate, current motive for adaptive behavior and provides the necessary connecting link between basic needs that are not present but will tend to recur in the future and the related activity of the present. A more extended analysis of this problem has appeared elsewhere (Mowrer, 1938c).

[3] Warren's *Dictionary of Psychology* (1934) defines "expectancy" as "the prospective chance of an occurrence based on experience" and differentiates it from "expectation" which it defines as "a mental attitude characterized by tension and characteristic of attention." Boring (1933), Cowles and Nissen (1937), Grether (1938), Humphreys (1939b), Woodworth (1938), and other recent writers have, however, used "expectancy" in the sense of the second of these definitions; in the present study the two terms will be employed interchangeably.

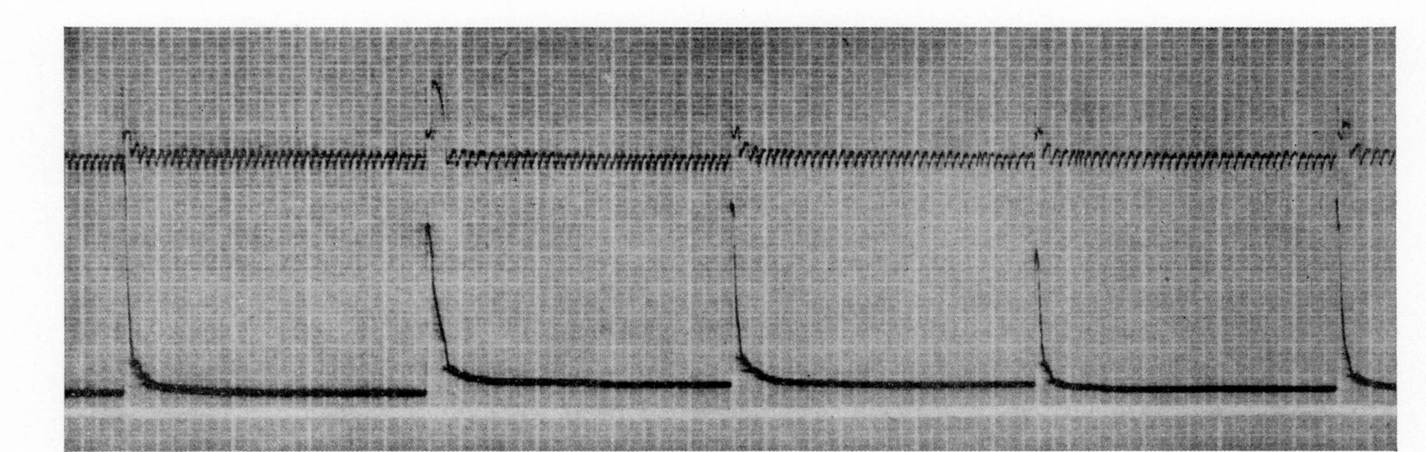

Fig. 2.—Record of foreleg flexions and breathing of a rat in response to shock. The lower black line shows the right foreleg flexions produced in a rat by a momentary shock administered to this member every 20 seconds. The upper line represents the concomitant breathing behavior of the animal. Neither type of response gives any reliable indication of expectation of shock on the part of the rat (see text).

ods of detecting minute muscular changes. Within the past two decades such technical progress has been made in this connection that virtually any type of muscular activity, however subtle, can be detected and recorded. But application of these improved methods has not confirmed the assumption of a necessary connection between anticipation and muscular activity. Woodworth (1938) has reviewed some of the major attempts that have been made to demonstrate a muscular basis for quickness of simple reaction time (which is known to be a function of anticipation) and shows that the results have been distinctly unsatisfactory. The negative findings of Hathaway (1935), who used action-current recording, are especially noteworthy in this connection.

In extreme cases, where anticipation is so highly developed that it reaches the anxiety level and, to speak loosely, "spills over" into motor channels, it can often be detected in gross behavior. The so-called "nervous" movements of human beings are taken, as a matter of course, to indicate apprehension and "worry" on the part of the person showing them. Agitated behavior of a comparable kind has also been reported by various animal experimenters. For example, Anderson and Liddell (1935) have published a record of the foreleg flexions of a sheep suffering from an "experimental neurosis," in which anticipation of a recurrent electric shock to this member was clearly revealed by anticipatory reactions of the leg before each occurrence of the shock (at intervals of one to four minutes), after which the leg remained quiet for a time. This record, described as typifying the behavior of this and other "neurotic" sheep, is so dramatic that it is here reproduced as Figure 1.

On the other hand, there are many instances in which expectation of an impending event is by no means so immediately evident. The lower black line in Figure 2 shows the right foreleg flexions produced in an albino rat by an electric shock administered to this member every 20 seconds. Here, it will be noted, there are no anticipatory reactions whatever, despite the fact that the shock had been administered more than 50 times at the standard interval before this particular record was taken. Other rats showed essentially the same behavior under these conditions, the only outward signs of apprehension being occasional outbursts of generalized struggling.[4] Yet, as results that will be discussed below (page 42) plainly indicate, the absence of gross, overt reactions of an anticipa-

[4] These animals were immobilized by a method similar to that described by Schlosberg (1934). This investigator also reports that the only gross indication of anticipation of shock manifested by rats under the conditions of his experiment took the form of generalized struggling.

tory character does not prove that these animals had no appreciation of the imminence of the successive shocks.

Variation in pulse, blood volume, respiration, metabolism, galvanic skin resistance, and other "physiological changes" have, of course, commonly been employed as indices of apprehension, and for some purposes they have turned out to be very useful. However, much the same criticism applies to them that has just been made of tonicity changes and overt agitation as measures of this psychologically significant phenomenon, namely, that they give positive results only when anticipation becomes sufficiently intense to "overflow," in this case, into the autonomic nervous system. The

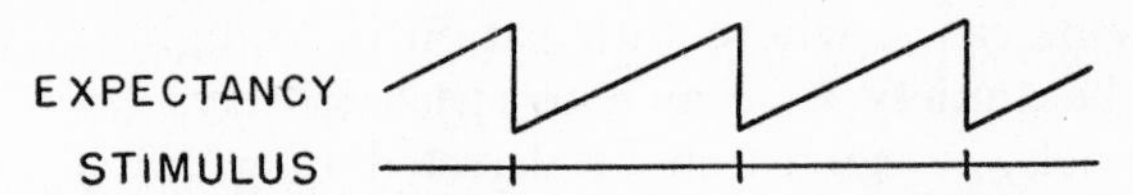

Fig. 3.—Hypothetical course of expectancy of a stimulus. This diagram, reproduced from an earlier study by the writer (Mowrer, 1938c), represents the hypothetical course of expectancy between successive presentations of a psychologically significant stimulus. While admittedly schematic, the general shape of the upper line was suggested by the comments of subjects who had served in a study of the galvanic skin response to electric shock.

upper black line in Figure 2 represents the breathing of the rat whose leg flexions are recorded immediately below. It will be observed that this "physiological" measure gives no reliable indication of expectation of the shock prior to its occurrence.

In an analysis of the learning process as exemplified in conditioning, which has appeared elsewhere (Mowrer, 1938c), the writer has posited (on the basis of the spontaneous comments of subjects used in an investigation of the galvanic skin reaction to electric shock) that if a stimulus is presented recurrently, at regular temporal intervals, expectation of that stimulus rises and falls in the manner indicated in the schematic diagram reproduced in Figure 3. The assumption that was made at the time of the original publication of this diagram, but not incorporated in it, was that if a stimulus does not occur at the expected point, expectancy may remain constant for a time, or perhaps even mount a little higher than usual, and will then undergo a relatively gradual decay.

As early as 1929, Schilder published a somewhat similar curve, also based on introspective data, purporting to show the rise and fall of expectation (as manifested by feelings of "tension") when a flash of light occurred and was regularly followed, five seconds later, by an electric shock. Here, again, the actual occurrence of the expected event, although painful, is represented as bringing about "relief," in the sense of lowering tension (cf. Figure 1).[5] Schilder's original diagram is reproduced in Figure 4.

Apparently unfamiliar with either of the diagrams just referred

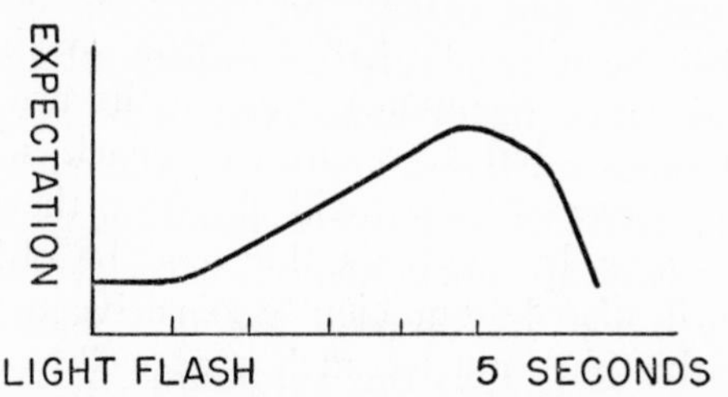

FIG. 4.—Schilder's curve of rise and fall of expectancy. Schilder (1929) has presented the above curve purporting to show the rise and fall of expectancy when a light is flashed and is then followed, 5 seconds later, by an electric shock. The curve is based on the introspective reports of human subjects.

to, Woodworth (1938) published three hypothetical curves showing possible ways in which "readiness" might be assumed to develop during a twenty-four-second "foreperiod" between a warning signal and the stimulus to which a simple, overt reaction is to be

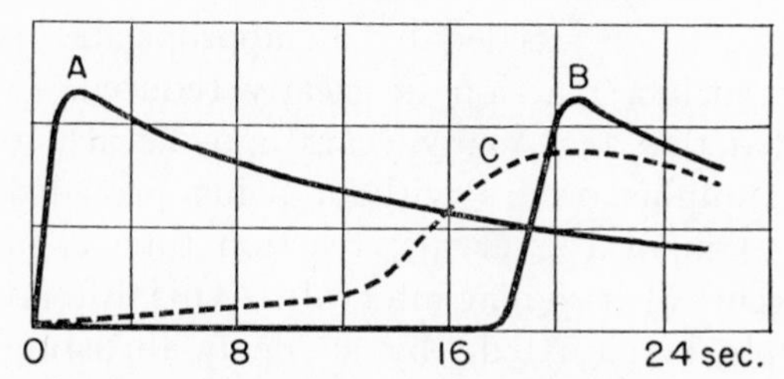

FIG. 5.—Woodworth's "possible curves of readiness." "Possible curves of readiness in a long foreperiod. The fore-signal comes at 0. If curve *A* is correct, readiness is immediately pushed to maximum. If *B* is correct, readiness is pushed to a maximum at the moment when the stimulus is expected. If *C* is correct, there is no sharp peak of readiness in a long foreperiod" (Woodworth, 1938, p. 317).

made. These curves are reproduced in Figure 5. Curve *C,* it will be noted, follows somewhat the same course as the curves reproduced in Figures 3 and 4.

---

[5] [This is probably the dynamics of "masochism." "Dabrowsky (1937) has recently reported an interesting study on self-torture and comes to the conclusion that self-inflicted physical pain usually serves to alleviate a more excruciating form of inner, mental anguish. Freud (1920a) has repeatedly commented upon the tendency for hysterical and other neurotic symptoms to disappear whenever a form of physical suffering intervenes. Thus, masochistic behavior in general can be regarded as relieving, through the infliction of one form of pain or tension increase, another and less tolerable form of suffering" (Mowrer, 1938c, p. 87).]

The dilemma is thus apparent. The phenomenon of expectancy, or anticipation, can be detected with a considerable degree of delicacy by the method of introspection, but it cannot be precisely quantified by this method. On the other hand, the same disadvantage does not inhere in the use of overt agitation (including muscle-thickening and tremor techniques) [6] nor in the use of the so-called physiological measures, but these methods lack sensitivity. Continued scientific progress in this field requires, therefore, the application of other methods, methods that will be objectively quantitative but that will also be sufficiently sensitive to permit effective investigation of this phenomenon at low as well as at high levels of intensity. The present study is directed to this end.

Method I. Reaction Time

The difference in the latency of a simple reaction, such as releasing a key in response to a light or tone, that is observed with human subjects when the reaction stimulus is presented with and without "warning" clearly shows the role of expectancy, or preparatory set ("attention"), in determining the time required for such a reaction to occur. Preceded by an appropriate "ready" signal, the latency of such a reaction is greatly reduced. When Wundt (1880) reported this fact many years ago, he also remarked that if a reaction stimulus occurs without being preceded by a signal, but at *regular* temporal intervals, reaction time is briefer than if the stimulus occurs at irregular intervals. This difference, he found, could be sharply accentuated "by suddenly thrusting into a long series of equidistant [homogeneous] stimuli a much shorter interval which the observer [subject] does not expect. . . . The time of reaction may then easily be lengthened to one quarter of a second with strong signals, or with weak ones to a half second" (pp. 242–43).

The close positive relation between quickness of reaction and expectancy, or readiness, seems to offer one relatively simple yet sensitive method of objectively investigating the latter phenomenon. It is always an advantage whenever a phenomenon that defies direct quantification can be made a function of time. For present purposes it is assumed that the relation between expectancy and quickness of reaction is linear; but if subsequent inquiry should

[6] That expectancy can vary widely without concomitant changes in the skeletal musculature is clearly indicated by the results of an independent investigation (Mowrer, Rayman, and Bliss, 1940).

reveal a curvilinear relation instead, the implications of the following experiment would not be materially altered.

In order thus to obtain an *objective* record of the course of expectancy during the interval between successive presentations of a stimulus at a standard temporal interval, 100 male college students were submitted to the following procedure.[7] They were seated comfortably in a soundproof room and instructed to hold down a telegraph key, conveniently placed on an arm of the chair, with a gentle but continuous pressure until they heard a tone (42 d.b. above threshold, with pitch of 800 d.v.) in a pair of telephone receivers located at a distance of 3 feet. Upon hearing the tone, the subjects were to release the telegraph key as quickly as possible and thereby terminate the tone. They were given a special incentive to do their best by being told that when the session (which lasted about 14 minutes) was over they would be informed as to how fast their reactions had been and how they compared with other subjects in this respect. Upon withdrawing from the soundproof room, the experimenter extinguished the light (with appropriate explanation to the subject) in order to eliminate visual distraction.

Each subject first received 20 tones at an unvarying interval of 12 seconds, during the presentation of which the average latency of reaction for all subjects dropped from 369.78 milliseconds, on the first trial, to 231.70 ms., on the eighth trial, and then remained approximately constant for the next 12 trials. Following these 20 preliminary, or "training," trials, each subject received, without any break in continuity, 49 additional tones (making 69 in all), which also came at 12-second intervals, except on the twenty-first, twenty-seventh, thirty-fifth, forty-first, forty-eighth, fifty-fifth, sixty-first, and sixty-eighth trials. On these "test" trials, the tones came after intervals of 3, 6, 9, 12, 15, 18, 21, and 24 seconds, in balanced random order. The average reaction times of all subjects on these 8 test trials were, respectively, as follows: 293.57, 254.44, 243.39, 229.02, 234.78, 239.35, 238.41, and 243.47 ms. These values are represented graphically in Figure 6. As had been anticipated (see Figures 3 and 4), reaction time was found to be longest (expectancy lowest) when the tone came at the 3-second interval. As the test interval approached the standard interval, the reaction time became progressively shorter (with rising expectancy) until, at the 12-second test interval—which was, of course, the same as the standard interval—the obtained reaction time was "normal," viz., 229.02

---

[7] The writer is indebted to N. Nelson Rayman and Eugene L. Bliss for assistance in carrying out the investigation here reported.

ms., as compared with the average of 231.70 ms. that was achieved by the eighth trial in the preliminary series and was maintained with relatively little variation on the standard-interval trials that were interposed (5 to 7 in succession) between the 8 test trials. As the test intervals varied beyond 12 seconds, up to 24 seconds, the average reaction time again increased but not to the same heights it had reached on the shorter test trials, which was also in keeping with the prediction.

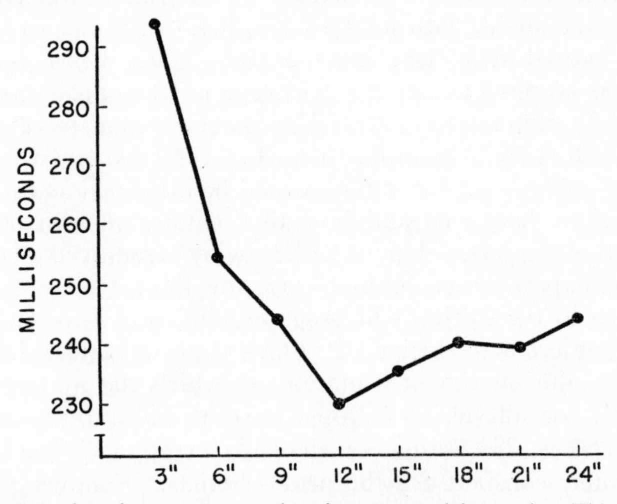

FIG. 6.—Reaction times at expected and unexpected intervals. This curve represents the average reaction time (in milliseconds) of 100 male college students as a function of the interval between successive presentations of the reaction stimulus (tone). The standard interstimulus interval was 12 seconds, but occasionally the stimulus occurred at one of the "test" intervals indicated along the abscissa.

The reliability of the difference between the average reaction time on the 3-second test trial and 12-second test trial is indicated by a critical ratio of 8.67. The critical ratio of the difference between the average reaction time on the 6-second and 12-second trials is 4.32; between the 9-second and 12-second trials is 2.50; and between the 24-second and 12-second trials, 2.31. The critical ratios of the other differences were not computed, but the consistency of the trend toward longer reaction times from the 12-second to the 24-second test trials indicates their probable reliability.

It has been assumed that many subjects would resort to counting as a means of trying to judge more accurately the time of occurrence of the successive tones. Casual questioning indicated, however, that relatively few of our subjects made any attempt to do this and that those who did soon abandoned it as more confusing than helpful. They found, in general, that they could make what seemed to them to be the quickest reactions if they simply waited between presentations of the tone, passive but alert. Somewhat surprisingly, it was found that the presentation of the tone at test intervals shorter than 12 seconds did not significantly affect the average reaction time on the next, immediately succeeding standard 12-second trial, although the longer test intervals (18, 21, and 24 seconds) tended to have a slight effect in the direction of lengthening the next reaction. However, this effect disappeared completely by the time of the second succeeding standard-interval trial.

Some apprehension was also experienced on the grounds that the subjects might discover the approximate frequency with which the test trials were interposed between the more numerous standard-interval trials, with a resulting disturbance of the usual course of expectancy at these points. Fortunately this does not seem to have been the case. In the first place, many subjects apparently did not consciously differentiate the 9- and the 15-second test intervals from the standard 12-second intervals. Furthermore, one test trial, namely, that involving the 12-second interval, was actually identical with the standard-interval trials, which made it additionally difficult to determine when test trials, discernible to the subject only on the basis of irregularity of interval, were to occur. The fact that subjects did not establish any periodic expectation of test (irregular) intervals is indicated by the close similarity between the average reaction time of 229.02 ms. that was obtained at the 12-second test interval and the average reaction times of 228.69 ms., 227.81 ms., and 231.18 ms. obtained on the 3 immediately preceding standard-interval trials and by the average reaction time of 221.81 ms. obtained on the immediately succeeding standard-interval trial.

Another way of graphically presenting the data obtained in this experiment is to plot each of the reaction-time averages for the group as a whole on the 8 test trials in terms of what *percentage* it is of the average of the reaction-time averages obtained on the 3 (or any other arbitrary number of) standard-interval trials immediately preceding the test trial. This procedure is followed in the broken-line graph that appears in Figure 7. The first point on this graph, for instance, was determined by dividing 293.57 ms. (average reaction time for all subjects on the 3-second test trial) by 227.28 ms. (average of 227.20 ms., 231.88 ms., and 222.76 ms., which were the reaction-time averages for all subjects on the 3 preceding standard-interval trials). The remaining 7 points on this curve were determined in a similar manner. It will be noted that the shape of this curve is almost identical with that of the curve obtained by simply plotting the absolute reaction-time averages, in terms of milliseconds, for the 8 test trials (Figure 6). The similarity of these curves indicates, again, that the "base line," composed of the average reaction times on the standard-interval trials, remained relatively constant throughout.[8] There is, moreover, this

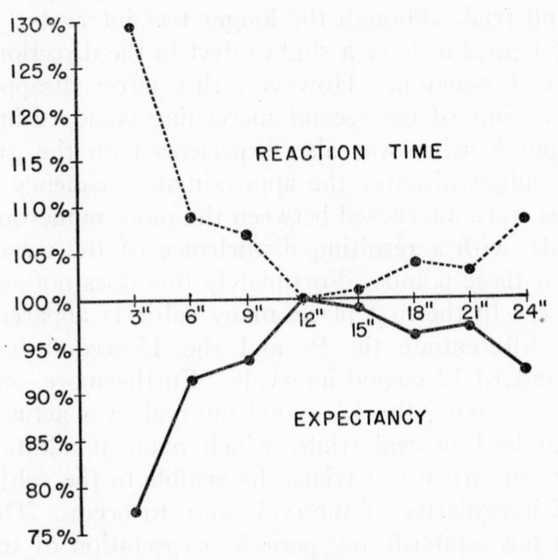

FIG. 7.—Method of translating reaction times into an expectancy curve. The dotted-line curve shows the extent (in terms of percentages) by which the average reaction time of 100 male college students on "test" presentations of the reaction stimulus (tone) at the intervals indicated along the abscissa exceeded the average reaction time of the same subjects on the three standard-interval presentations of the stimulus that immediately preceded each "test" presentation. The solid-line curve is the reciprocal of the dotted-line curve and is assumed to represent the course of "expectancy."

additional advantage in reproducing the data in this way, that by plotting the reciprocal of the broken-line curve representing reaction time in Figure 7, it is possible to obtain a second curve, which, by hypothesis, represents the course of expectancy between successive stimulus events at the standard interval of 12 seconds and which is necessarily also expressed in terms of percentages rather than in absolute units (such as milliseconds) that are not appropriate. This "curve of expectancy" is represented by the solid line in Figure 7.

[8] It may be well to remind the reader at this point that the eight test trials were interspersed among the last 49 standard-interval trials in a prearranged but perfectly balanced, random order for the group as a whole. Any trend shown by the curves presented in Figures 6 and 7 cannot, therefore, be due to the order in which the test trials were presented.

The shape of the curve thus derived, from strictly empirical data, confirms the suppositions previously advanced. It shows, first of all, that when a stimulus event occurs after a standard, recurrent temporal interval and produces an appropriate response, readiness to repeat that response (expectation of the stimulus) immediately drops markedly, then mounts to a maximum at the point in time coinciding with the end of the next standard interval. If the expected stimulus and prepared-for response do not occur at this point, there is, at least under the conditions of this experiment, a relatively gradual decline thereafter in readiness to make such a response, which presumably implies a corresponding decline in expectation of the stimulus. It was previously conjectured that if the stimulus did not occur at the end of the standard interval, the curve of expectancy (readiness) might continue to rise for a little while, before starting to decline. No such tendency is noted in the curve in Figure 7. It may well be, however, that such a "hump" would be obtained under other experimental conditions, particularly if the expected stimulus event were somewhat more "traumatic" than a tone of moderate intensity can be said to be.[9]

It may be asked whether the sudden lowering of expectancy immediately after the occurrence of an expected stimulus-response sequence may not represent a simple refractory-phase phenomenon of some kind. Under such circumstances the subject is, to be sure, "refractory" in the sense that he shows a reduced readiness to make the response in question (as indicated by increased response latency), but this effect is demonstrably not due to any kind of "physiological limit," which is what the term "refractory phase" properly implies. Numerous studies[10] have shown that the most favorable interval between the warning stimulus and the reaction stimulus in simple reaction-time experiments is relatively brief.

---

[9] This supposition is supported, albeit somewhat obliquely, by the fact that a number of investigators (cited by Hovland, 1936) have found that after a series of paired presentations of a conditioned and an unconditioned stimulus (the latter usually of a noxious character), the responses obtained on the second and third presentations of the conditioned stimulus alone, unaccompanied by the unconditioned stimulus, are likely to be somewhat larger than the response obtained on the first so-called nonreinforced presentation of the conditioned sitmulus. After this initial rise in response magnitude, the size of the reactions to the successive nonreinforcement conditioned stimuli gradually undergoes a decrement, leading to ultimate extinction. Hovland (1936) has undertaken an analysis of the conditions under which this effect occurs and has come to the conclusion that it is a function of the accumulation or nonaccumulation of "inhibition of reinforcement" during the successive paired presentations of the conditioned and unconditioned stimuli. Humphreys (1939a, 1939b, 1940a) has reported more recent findings which he interprets on the basis of an expectancy hypothesis that accords well with the theoretical position taken in the present paper.

[10] See, for example, those reviewed by Breitwieser (1911).

Woodrow (1914), using foreperiods ranging from 1 to 24 seconds, has studied this problem systematically and found, with earlier investigators, that the fastest reactions occur with a preparatory interval of about 2 seconds. In the light of this fact it is clear that the longer reaction times obtained in the present study on the 3-second test trial than on the standard-interval trials cannot have been due to any kind of physical limitation of the reacting organism. However, in order to verify this conclusion under the conditions of the present investigation, a few subjects, after they had served in the main experiment and had had a brief rest period, were asked to return to the soundproof room, where they were again seated and given the same instructions as before. But now, instead of being presented with a series of tones at 12-second intervals, they received tones every 3 seconds. After the first two or three responses, these subjects began to make reactions that were decidedly faster than their reactions had been under the first conditions. If, then, after this new rhythm of expectation was well established (i.e., after reaction times became fairly constant) a 12-second interval was interposed, the latency of the ensuing reaction was always dramatically increased. Such an effect is obviously not explainable in terms of "refractory phase," yet it is strictly comparable to the phenomenon manifested in the main experiment.

In a later report evidence will be presented which shows that under some conditions expectancy apparently occurs as an unlearned phenomenon, but there can be scarcely any question that the particular curve shown in Figure 7 is a learned phenomenon. Variation in the length of the standard interval between successive presentations of the reaction-evoking stimulus, in the nature and intensity of this stimulus, and in the amount of "practice" permitted before the introduction of test trials would undoubtedly have noticeable effects in this connection. Nevertheless, the curve here presented is probably representative, in a general way, of the type of curve obtainable under a variety of circumstances. It is believed that the general shape of this curve, involving a relatively rapid rise to the maximal point and then a more gradual decline, can be derived from the concept of "stimulus traces" and from the principle of "generalization of conditioning," but this, too, will have to be postponed until a later study.

Finally, it may be asked whether there is any difference between the phenomenon of "expectancy" and what has been traditionally connoted by the older term "attention." Since the latter has usually been defined in diffuse, mentalistic terms, on which no two writers could agree, it is difficult to determine whether the "faculty" that "attention" was supposed to represent is or is not the same as such a specific, operationally definable concept as expectancy. For some few writers, it is clear that "attention" prominently involved the notion of preparation for impending action. James (1890), for example, in discussing the "intimate nature of the attentive process," concluded that there are "two physiological processes [which] immediately suggest themselves as possibly forming in combination a complete reply," to wit: "(1) The accommodation or adjustment of the sensory organs; and (2) the anticipatory preparation from within of the ideational centres concerned with the object to which the attention is paid" (p. 434). His use on a subsequent page (439) of such expressions as "anticipatory thinking," "preparation to react," "premonitory imagination," and "expectant attention" leaves little doubt of the similarity of his conception of the so-called "attentive process" and what is here designated as expectancy, or preparatory set.[11] Used in this sense, there can be no objection to regarding "attention" as simply a synonymous term for the phenomenon that is here the primary object of quantitative study. However, an examination of the earlier works that purported to "measure attention" leaves no doubt as to the need for a new attack upon this problem, for new terms, and for a new perspective.[12]

Method II. Reaction Magnitude

From a number of incidental observations that have previously been reported,[13] it is evident that under appropriate circumstances the size of the reaction elicited by a standard stimulus affords an index of the extent to which that stimulus is expected and prepared for by the reacting organism. One of the most explicit instances of this type of observation is reported by Pavlov (1927), who says:

> The experiment just described [on temporal conditioning in dogs] may be performed with the following modification. The animal can be given food regularly every thirtieth minute, but with the addition, say, of the sound of a metronome a few seconds before the food. The animal is thus stimulated at regular intervals of thirty minutes by a combination of two stimuli, one of which is the time factor and the other the beats of the metronome. In this manner a conditioned reflex is established to a

---

[11] The writer feels no hesitancy in employing these two latter terms interchangeably. They are assumed to be merely two aspects of the same basic phenomenon.

[12] For an excellent review of this literature, see Philip (1928); also Whipple (1924).

[13] See, for example, Darrow (1938), Freeman (1939), Hilgard and Biel (1937), Landis and Hunt (1939), and Tuttle (1924).

compound stimulus consisting of the sound plus the condition of the hemispheres at the thirtieth minute, when both are reinforced by food. Further, if the sound is now applied not at the thirtieth minute after the preceding feeding, but, say, at the fifth or eighth minute, it entirely fails to produce any alimentary conditioned reflex. If it is applied slightly later it produces some effect; applied at the twentieth minute the effect is greater; at the twenty-fifth minute greater still. At the thirtieth minute the reaction is of course complete (p. 41).

If the results of this experiment had been presented in precise quantitative terms, i.e., number of drops of saliva elicited by the metronome at the various temporal intervals, so that these values could have been plotted graphically, it is clear that the resulting curve would have started at zero and gradually ascended to a maximum at the standard 30-minute interval. Unfortunately, Pavlov gives no account of any attempt having been made in his laboratory to determine how the size of the salivary response would have been affected had the sounding of the metronome been delayed beyond the point at which expectation of feeding was maximal.

Despite the suggestiveness of the findings reported by Pavlov and of those obtained by other experimenters under widely diverse conditions, it appears that the only systematic and quantitatively exact attempt to investigate response magnitude in relation to a standard interval between successive stimulus presentations was recently made by Brown (1939) in the same laboratory from which the present study comes. This writer first presented individual rats with 35 instantaneous shocks, which were delivered at regular 12-second intervals from a small, "free-floating" grill on which the animal stood. Following this training series, each animal continued to receive shocks at 12-second intervals, except for occasional test shocks that were administered after intervals of 3, 6, 9, 12, 15, 18, 21, and 24 seconds. These test trials were given in a random, balanced order, and the size of the jump made to each presentation of the shock was linearly recorded by photographic means.

In keeping with the results of the reaction-time experiment reported in the preceding section, Brown found the smallest average magnitude of response at the 3-second test interval, with progressively larger responses up to the 12-second test trial. However, on the 15-second test trial, there was a sharp, statistically reliable drop in the average size of reaction, followed by a rise on the 18-second test, a still further rise on the 21-second test, and finally a drop on the 24-second test. It will be recalled that the reaction-time curve for human subjects (Figure 6) showed no such fluctuations at the longer test intervals, manifesting instead a gradual increase in latency on the successive test intervals longer than the standard interval. If subsequent research confirms this difference between the shape of the "expectancy curve"[14] obtained from human beings and from rats, it may be found explainable on the grounds that the symbolic processes (speech) cause a kind of perseveration of readiness in human beings that is not possible in rats. It is noteworthy that the drop obtained by Brown in the magnitude of response on the 15-second test trial comes at a point at which expectancy would have been lowest if stimulation had occurred at the standard interval, i.e., 3 seconds beyond the 12-second interval. If this drop obtained by Brown on the 15-second test interval is confirmed, it will have extensive theoretical implications which cannot, however, pertinently be gone into at this time.

The findings that are now to be described were obtained in an as yet unpublished investigation which was carried out by Professor Clark L. Hull, with an objective in view different from the present one, namely, the conditioning of the galvanic skin reaction of human beings to a "patterned" stimulus. At the suggestion of Dr. Douglas G. Ellson and with the permission of Professor Hull, the writer has analyzed the results of this study in terms of the magnitude of response as a function of the amount of time elapsing between successive stimulus presentations. Since the responses were sometimes elicited as conditioned reactions, i.e., by the conditioned stimulus alone, and sometimes as unconditioned reactions, i.e., by the conditioned and unconditioned stimulus (shock) in combination, it is desirable to present the data obtained under the two conditions in separate graphs. The solid-line curve in Figure 8 shows the average magnitude of the *conditioned* responses obtained at the step interval shown along the abscissa, which represent the time in seconds since the preceding stimulus presentation. The broken-line curve, on the other hand, shows the frequency with which presentation of the conditioned stimulus occurred at the various step intervals. Although the correspondence is not perfect, it will be noted that in general the largest magnitude of response was obtained when the conditioned stimulus was presented at the most commonly used intervals, i.e., between 30 and 50 seconds after the last stimulus presentation. When a stimulus was presented at an

[14] Mention should be made of the fact that Brown interpreted his data as showing the operation of a "temporal gradient of reinforcement" rather than an "expectancy curve." However, since the present writer assumes that expectancy is developed on the basis of the former principle, there is no basic incompatibility between the findings or the implications of the two studies.

uncommon temporal interval (shorter than 30 seconds or longer than 50 seconds), the size of the reaction was appropriately diminished, thus indicating, according to the writer's interpretation, that the magnitude of the conditioned G. S. R. (galvanic skin response) obtained under these circumstances was positively correlated with the degree to which stimulation was expected by the subjects.

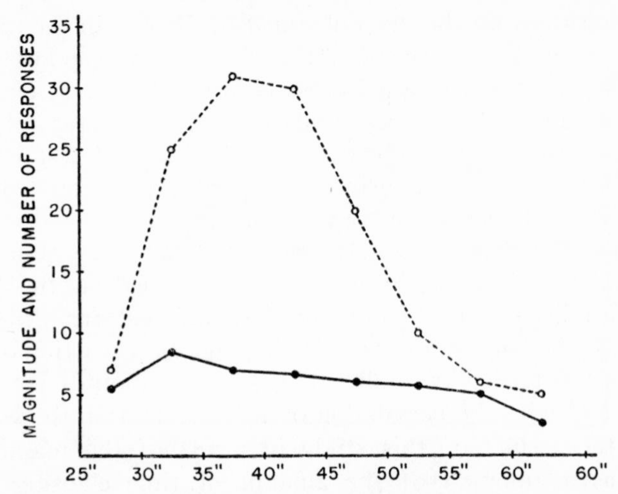

FIG. 8.—Magnitude and frequency of galvanic skin response to a conditioned stimulus. The solid-line curve represents the average magnitude of galvanic skin response elicited by a conditioned stimulus, presented at the various temporal intervals indicated (along the abscissa) after the preceding stimulus-response sequence. The dotted-line curve represents the frequency with which the conditioned stimulus occurred at these intervals. The data (obtained through the courtesy of Professor Clark L. Hull) on which these curves are based represent the responses of eight human subjects during a single experimental session.

Casual inspection of the data constituting the solid-line graph in Figure 8 indicates that the differences between successive points on the curve are probably in no case reliable, as measured by usual statistical devices. However, the smoothness of the curve warrants placing considerable confidence in its significance.

The size of the *unconditioned* G. S. R., as a function of the temporal interval elapsing since the preceding stimulus presentation, is represented by the solid-line curve in Figure 9. The dotted-line curve shows the frequency with which the unconditioned stimulus was presented at the various step intervals. As in the case of the conditioned G. S. R., the magnitude of the unconditioned G. S. R. also shows a positive correlation with the point in time at which the subjects had empirical grounds for most strongly expecting stimulation. Here again there is probably not a reliable difference between any two successive points on the solid-line curve as measured by usual statistical methods, but the tendency for this curve to follow the distribution curve is extremely suggestive.

By using a procedure similar to that employed by the present writer in connection with the study of reaction time reported in the preceding section or by Brown in the study of response magnitude already described in this section, it seems virtually certain that the magnitude of the G. S. R., produced by a standard stimulus,

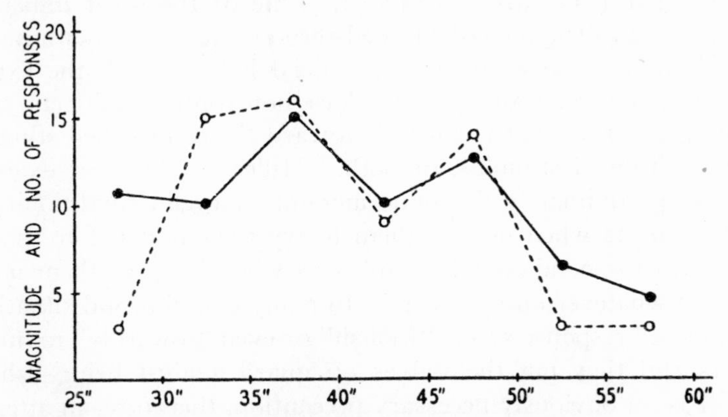

FIG. 9.—Magnitude and frequency of galvanic skin response to an unconditioned stimulus (shock). The solid-line curve represents the average magnitude of the G. S. R. elicited by an unconditioned stimulus (shock) when presented at the various temporal intervals indicated after the preceding stimulus-response sequence. The dotted-line curve represents the frequency with which the unconditioned stimulus occurred at these intervals. The data on which these curves are based were obtained under the conditions stated in the legend to Figure 8.

could be used as a highly reliable and refined measure of expectancy of that stimulus. It will be noted, however, that this statement is not inconsistent with the remark made in the introductory section to the effect that the G. S. R., along with the other "physiological changes," is not a very adequate *direct* measure of expectancy. The method that is elaborated here consists, not in relying upon the galvanic skin resistance (or potential) to change concomitantly with expectancy, but rather in using the size of the reaction produced by *a standard stimulus* as a measure of this phenomenon. Evidence published elsewhere (Mowrer, 1938c) indicates that expectancy can change within broad limits without this being at all evident in the G. S. R. "base line." It is only, in other words, when expectancy or, to use another term proposed by Darrow (1938), the "excitation background" is sampled, or "tapped," in the manner here indicated that the G. S. R. takes on a high degree of refinement as a measure of this phenomenon.

The use of the magnitude of the response made to a standard stimulus as a measure of expectation of that stimulus would thus appear to open up new research possibilities of some importance. However, one complication can already be anticipated, namely, that a positive correlation between response magnitude and expectancy will be found only in those cases in which there is a "positive attitude" on the part of the subjects, i.e., a set to perform the response in question when the expected stimulus occurs rather than a set not to perform it ("negative attitude"). One of the great difficulties in attempting to use the conditioned-response technique with human beings is that, because of complex social habits which the experimenter often cannot or at least does not control, subjects spontaneously adopt a negative attitude toward the conditioned stimulus, the unconditioned stimulus, or both. Miller (1935), for example, obtained approximately the same amount of eyelid conditioning in human subjects when he told them to try their best not to make a response to the conditioned stimulus as when he gave them no instructions whatever on this score. In many experimental situations, a conditioned response seems "foolish" or even "cowardly" to human subjects and they put themselves on guard against being "shown up." It is an obviously necessary precaution, therefore, in attempting to use response magnitude as a measure of expectancy to bear in mind that the correlation between the size of the response and the degree to which the stimulus that elicits the response is expected may be either positive or negative, depending upon the character of the prevailing "attitude" or "set" of the subject.[15]

A further indication of the role of negative attitude on the part of human subjects in certain types of conditioning experiments is the finding, reported by Calvin (1939), that better eyelid conditioning is obtained with an irregular interval between successive paired presentations of the conditioned and unconditioned stimulus than with a regular interval. On the basis of the principle of "temporal

[15] It might appear that there is here a basis for questioning the parallelism between expectancy and preparatory set that is implied in the title of this study and is explicitly posited at various points in the text. If preparatory set can be either "positive" or "negative," with expectancy in both cases "positive," then the two must be independent phenomena, not simply different aspects of the same phenomenon. This difficulty disappears, however, when it is recalled that a so-called "negative" attitude or set is quite as *active* a state, when viewed psychophysiologically, as is a "positive" set, and that the terms "positive" and "negative" are meaningful in this context only with reference to one particular, selected type of performance. With reference to some other (usually antagonistic) type of performance, a so-called "negative" set is, necessarily, "positive." Viewed in this light, expectancy is always positively correlated and varies concomitantly with preparatory set, providing the behavior for which the latter is appropriate is properly defined.

conditioning," better conditioning would have been predicted in the latter case. As the present writer views the matter, the reverse finding can only mean that the subjects in this study had a strongly negative attitude toward blinking in response to the conditioned stimulus and that this attitude was able to manifest itself most effectively when the occurrence of the conditioned stimulus was anticipated with a relatively high degree of accuracy (thus giving inferior "conditioning" at the regular intervals). On the other hand, when the paired presentations came at irregular intervals, with resulting inability on the part of the subjects to know exactly when to expect stimulation, they were often caught "off guard" and blinked "in spite of themselves" (thus giving superior "conditioning").[16] On the assumption that animals lower than man would not have the same incentives as human beings for manifesting a negative attitude in a conditioning experiment of this kind, it would be very instructive to repeat Calvin's experiment with animal subjects. This should provide a reasonably crucial test of the validity of the interpretation that has just been proposed of the findings reported by this investigator.

It is not, however, to be supposed, because infrahuman organisms are less disposed to show negative attitudes toward what would seem to be natural reaction tendencies (i.e., are less "inhibited") than are human beings, that this type of phenomenon is altogether absent in them. By means of appropriate "conflict" situations, a wide variety of such attitudes could presumably be created at will. Ellson (1939) has, in fact, already called attention to what would appear to be an excellent instance of this kind, all the more dramatic because of its subtlety. In an experiment conducted by Ivanov-Smolensky, which is reported by Pavlov (1927), the salivary reaction was independently conditioned to two tones of different pitch. The conditioned reaction to one of these tones was then repeatedly extinguished and the size of the reaction to the other tone tested at varying intervals after the last of a series of nonreinforced presentations of the first tone. Pavlov says that "all

---

[16] Support for such an interpretation is found in a recent study by Yacorzynski and Guthrie (1937). They say: "There is evidence that the conditioned voluntary response [which was here investigated] appears oftener when the interval is unusually long or short. The subject is then caught off his guard because the inhibitory set [spontaneously established by the subjects] is also conditioned with its time interval. Furthermore the conditioned voluntary response according to our records starts strong, diminishes after an 'error' [i.e., a 'conditioned response'] and then builds up increased certainty until another 'error' occurs with a consequent decrease in certainty of response. . . . Many subjects reported that, after being once taken by surprise in this 'error,' their whole attention was given to keep from being 'caught' again" (pp. 251–53).

the reflexes [to the second tone] were found to undergo inhibition, but in a varying degree" (p. 165). Ellson has taken some of the results obtained in this experiment, which Pavlov presents tabularly, and has arranged them graphically in the form of two curves. With

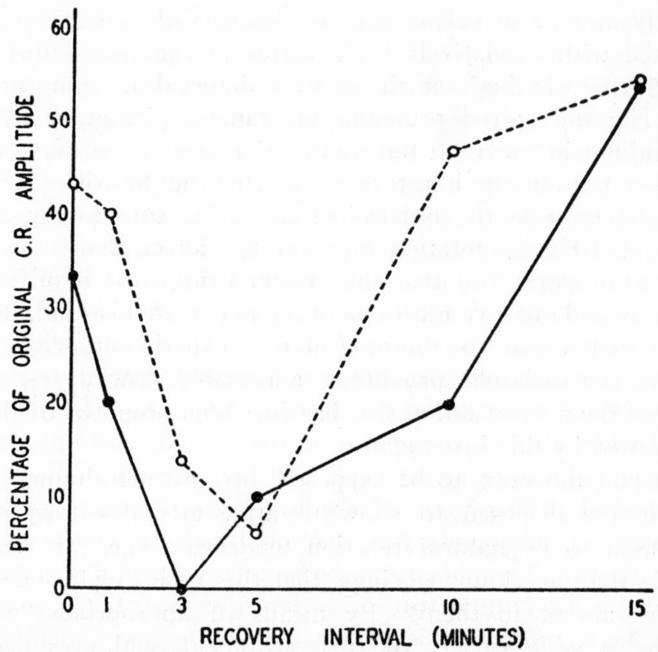

FIG. 10.—Inhibition of a conditioned reaction by previous extinction of a similar reaction. Both curves in the above figure (based on data obtained from Pavlov, 1927) show the varying extent to which the extinction of a conditioned salivary response to a tone of one pitch inhibits the conditioned reaction to a tone of another pitch when the latter tone is presented at various temporal intervals after the extinction of the response to the first tone. According to the interpretation suggested in the text, the maximal depression of the conditioned reaction to the second, nonextinguished tone occurs at the 3- and 5-minute intervals after extinction of the response to the first tone for the reason that the successive nonreinforced presentations of the first tone probably also occurred at approximately these intervals (Ellson, 1939). It was therefore at these intervals that the animal's expectation of food was lowest and its "negative attitude" toward all conditioned stimuli (signals of food) strongest.

Ellson's permission, these two curves are reproduced in Figure 10. From these it will be seen that when the second (nonextinguished) tone was presented 0 minutes and 1 minute after the last nonreinforced presentation of the extinguished tone, a significant reaction was obtained, whereas at the end of 3 minutes and again at 5 minutes there was relatively little response. At the end of 10 minutes the nonextinguished tone again produced a sizable reaction, and a still larger reaction at the end of 15 minutes. Pavlov interpreted the smallness of response produced by the nonextinguished tone at the 3-minute and at the 5-minute intervals after extinction of the other tone as meaning that this was the amount of time required for the "inhibitory process" supposedly generated by the extinction of the conditioned reaction to the first tone to "irradiate" from its point of initiation at one cortical locus out over the rest of the "acoustic analyzer." The greater magnitude of response obtained after the longer intervals of delay Pavlov explained as due to the "inhibitory process" having presumably irradiated maximally and then having "receded" before the occurrence of the second tone.

Ellson pertinently notes that the interval between successive paired presentations of conditioned and unconditioned stimuli used in Pavlov's laboratory frequently ranged between 3 and 5 minutes. On the assumption (*a*) that this was the rate used in establishing the conditioned salivary reactions in the experiment under discussion and (*b*) that it was also the rate at which the conditioned reaction to the one tone was systematically extinguished, it is easy to see why the conditioned reaction to the second, nonextinguished tone was minimal when elicited at the end of the 3- and 5-minute intervals. It was precisely at these intervals that, as a result of the repeated nonreinforced presentation of the first tone, expectation of food was lowest. Consequently the magnitude of the salivary reaction made to all stimuli would tend to be especially small at just this time. At other points, both before and after this one, there would presumably be a somewhat less accentuated "negative attitude" and other stimuli would have a proportionately greater effect. In other words, the curves reproduced from Ellson in Figure 10 may be said to portray the curve of expectancy during a period when expectancy drops to a minimum instead of rising to a maximum, as it did, for example, in the Pavlovian experiment described at the outset of this section.

This interpretation may seem somewhat hypothetical, and it will certainly need to be buttressed by further research before complete dependence can be placed on it. It shows, however, the ramified implications of the expectancy concept and demonstrates its possible usefulness as a means of eliminating the dubious "brain physiology" of Pavlov as an explanatory basis for many important empirical observations.

Method III. Implicit Conditioning

In an earlier study (Mowrer, 1938c) a distinction was drawn between new stimulus-response sequences that appear because of (*a*) genuine learning and (*b*) the development of preparatory sets, or states of readiness, to such a point that they can be "tripped" and transformed into overt action by stimuli which, without such a background of preparedness, would not ordinarily produce a response of this kind.[17] At that time the supposition was also advanced that the phenomenon of conditioning, as it is somewhat loosely conceived, is sometimes dependent for its occurrence upon one of these mechanisms, sometimes upon the other. To the extent that conditioning in any particular experimental situation is dependent upon the second of these mechanisms it is, in effect, an index of the underlying state of the organism that is here termed expectancy or set. There has already been occasion in the preceding section to refer to experimental situations in which the magnitude of conditioned responses does indeed afford a reasonably satisfactory measure of this phenomenon. In many types of situations, however, conditioned reactions of an overt, easily observed character are relatively slow to manifest themselves and are decidedly unstable. This can scarcely mean that in these instances—sometimes involving hundreds of successive presentations of paired stimuli—the first of the pair, the so-called secondary or conditioned stimulus, has acquired no meaning, no signal value, no significance to the organism. It is, in other words, extremely unlikely in such cases that the subject does not "know" that the one stimulus, of an intrinsically innocuous nature, is to be followed by another, less innocuous stimulus. In situations in which the occurrence of a conditioned reaction has no "defense" value, i.e., does not enable the organism to avoid or at least diminish the intensity of the noxious, unconditioned stimulus, the failure of conditioning is not very mystifying.[18] However, the writer has observed a number of cases in which rats and other laboratory animals (sometimes even human subjects) fail to develop conditioned reactions under the seemingly optimally favorable condition in which such a re-

[17] Cf. Hull's distinction between what he has termed Alpha conditioning and Beta conditioning (1934a).

[18] [This problem is more fully analyzed in later studies (6, 7, 9). An element of obscurity exists in the above discussion because of the ambiguous meaning of the term "conditioned response." It was here being used in the traditional sense of any response that is elicited by a signal, or so-called conditioned stimulus. Many of the difficulties inherent in the above discussion disappear when "conditioning" is more precisely defined as the process whereby emotional reactions, and these alone, are acquired. Behavioral adjustments which are then made to the resulting emotional tensions are not "conditioned responses" but are "problem solutions," just as are the responses that become standardized in a problem box or a maze. Thus, the absence of a specified overt action in a given situation may or may not indicate a "failure of conditioning." Conditioning occurs whenever there is emotional learning, regardless of whether such learning is reflected by adjustments involving the skeletal musculature; see (9).]

action provides the possibility of avoiding the unconditioned stimulus completely.

Such a failure of conditioning seems to be a regular occurrence under the following circumstances: If a rat is placed on a grill that can momentarily be energized with electricity and if on each occasion that the resulting shock is presented a tone of moderate intensity is sounded for one second in advance, never will the rat, even after innumerable presentations of tone and shock in combination, make a quick, decisive jump in response to the tone of the kind that it makes to the shock.

This is not an appropriate time to try to determine what precisely is the reason for the failure of conditioning under the circumstances just described, but it is certainly not attributable to sheer stupidity on the part of the rat. After as few as two or three paired presentations of the conditioned and the unconditioned stimuli, one can observe reactions, such as flattening of the ears and disturbed breathing, that clearly indicate that the tone has become a signal of impending shock. That the tone produces a definite expectancy of (readiness for) shock can, moreover, be further demonstrated by the following procedure.

If, after a number of paired presentations of tone and shock at a standard rate, the shock is presented at the usual time but is not preceded by the tone, the size of the reaction produced thereby is likely to be materially smaller than the reactions made to the joint presentations of tone and shock that precede and follow. The upper record in Figure 11 shows a series of jumping responses made by a rat to tone and shock in combination, with an occasional interpolated shock without tone. It will be noted that when the shock thus comes without warning, the size of the resulting jump is greatly reduced.[19] The lower record in Figure 11 shows the complete ineffectualness, on the other hand, of the tone alone as far as the production of a jump, as a conditioned response, is concerned.[20] This augmentation of the reaction to the *unconditioned* stimulus, by virtue of its being preceded by a warning, or conditioned, stimulus (which does not, however, produce a gross, overt response in its own right), is here termed "implicit conditioning."

Data affording an opportunity for exact, quantitative comparison

---

[19] A comparable effect can, of course, readily be demonstrated in human subjects with respect to the latency of a simple reaction by occasionally presenting the reaction stimulus without the warning stimulus that has ordinarily preceded it on prior presentations.

[20] The mechanical details of the method by which these records were obtained have been given in another paper (13).

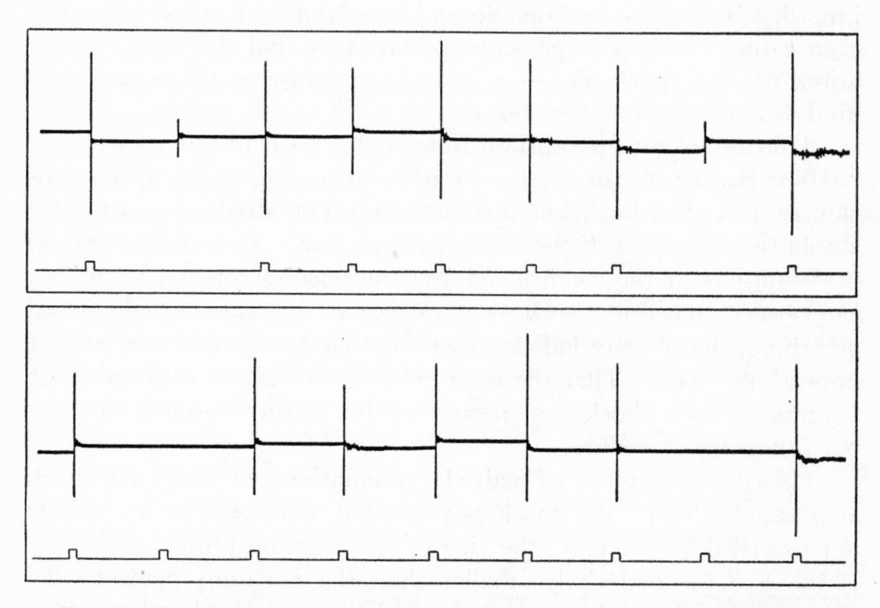

FIG. 11.—Jumping responses of a rat to: shock and tone combined, shock presented without tone, and tone presented without shock. The vertical lines in the upper record show the magnitude of 9 successive jumps produced in a rat by a momentary electric shock of standard intensity applied regularly every 20 seconds through the grill on which the animal was standing. All presentations of shock, except the second and eighth, were immediately preceded by a tone of 1 second's duration (see line at bottom of record). It will be noted that the magnitude of jump to shock when preceded by tone was much greater than when not preceded by tone, thus indicating "implicit conditioning." The lower record shows the failure of the tone alone to produce a detectable overt reaction.

of the magnitude of response obtained with and without the warning signal—from which the expectancy-producing efficacy of the signal could be determined—were not obtained for the reason that comparable responses could be produced only so long as the rat remained in approximately the same position on the grill. If the animal turned, for example, from a position in which the long axis of its body was at right angles to the small individual steel rods constituting the grill to a position in which the long axis of its body was parallel to the bars, a somewhat different intensity of shock was almost certain to be experienced, with a resulting change in the magnitude of response thereby produced. The two records that are reproduced in Figure 11 were obtained from animals that remained in virtually the same location with reference to the grill during the succession of stimulations indicated. The relatively great amount of variability arising from alterations in the rat's location on the grill would have so obscured the differential effect of shock with and without the warning signal that the results obtained would probably have been statistically unreliable, if all reactions had been included. If all reactions had not been included, the application of statistical method would, of course, have been a travesty. Since the effect of the warning signal was, however, so striking when an animal did not change its position (as the upper record in Figure 11 shows), it seemed better to make no attempt at exact quantification until other techniques have been worked out for investigating this phenomenon which do not involve such a large element of uncontrolled error. Such techniques can undoubtedly be devised.

Method IV. Electroencephalography

The methods of objectively investigating expectancy that have been discussed in the preceding sections, while relatively satisfactory in some respects, have one common defect: they do not provide a means whereby the course of this phenomenon can be continuously followed in a single, individual subject. For some purposes the possibility of obtaining such a record would be highly desirable; fortunately, this possibility seems at last to be at hand, in the form of the electroencephalogram or so-called "brain waves" of Berger. Experimental attempts have repeatedly been made to correlate the presence or absence of these rhythmical electrical pulsations from the cerebral cortex with the presence or absence of various kinds of sensory stimulation or muscular activity, such as clenching the fists, talking, and so forth. The somewhat disconcerting finding has been, however, that no such correlation of a one-to-one, unvarying character exists, with the result that many have come to regard the Berger rhythms and their coming and going as an interesting but as yet rather meaningless curiosity. On the other hand, those investigators who have worked most intensively in this field have maintained that, despite the superficially capricious nature of these electrical effects, they correspond to psychologically significant states of the nervous system. This point of view is well represented in the following quotation from Jasper (1937):

> The idea of levels of cortical excitatory state or of cortical activation is admittedly a rather vague concept, but it has proven of value as a working hypothesis for the purposes of describing certain systematic changes in cortical potential patterns associated with conditions of the organism usually described by the terms "excited," "aroused," "emotionally tense," "very alert," "intense concentration" (of attention), etc., as opposed to conditions of relaxation, drowsiness, and sleep. . . . It was first pointed out by Berger and later confirmed by many investigators that, in general, the maximal regularity and amplitude of the alpha rhythm in man is observed under optimal conditions of relaxation. Intense worry, emotional excitement, or severe apprehension often results in apparent suppression of the alpha rhythm except for rare groups of waves in a long record (pp. 456–57).

It does not appear to be an unreasonable assumption that the "cortical excitatory state" which this writer here proposes as the negative correlate of Berger rhythms is the same phenomenon that has been referred to throughout the present study as expectancy or preparatory set. Perhaps the best evidence in support of this supposition is the fact that the temporarily depressing effect that certain forms of stimulation have upon the principal, or "alpha," type of brain waves can be readily "conditioned" to stimuli that initially have no such effect. In an investigation by Cruikshank (1937) it was necessary to give a "preparatory signal" consisting of the command, "Eyes open," before presentation of a visual stimulus, the inhibiting effects of the latter on the alpha waves being the main object of experimental interest. The use of such a signal was found highly unsatisfactory from the point of view of the main purpose of the experiment for the reason that "after two or three presentations of the preparatory signal at a constant interval before the light the brain potentials would become conditioned to react to the preparatory signal before the light flash. The auditory signal itself would have no appreciable effect on the brain potentials before this conditioning. . . . The preparatory signal was necessary in order to make the position of the eyes and the general attitude of the subject more constant from one stimulus to the next" (Jasper, 1937, p. 627).

Incidental observations of a similar character have also been reported by Loomis, Harvey, and Hobart (1936) and by Howard (1935). Travis and Egan (1938) have recently investigated this phenomenon more systematically than had previous investigators, but with essentially the same findings. They say: "The statistically significant increase in effectiveness of tone during the conditioning series as compared to that of tone alone, preconditioning, is the essential finding of this study" (p. 526). In an unpublished exploratory study by the writer, it has been found that a tone likewise quickly acquires the capacity to depress the alpha rhythm if it is paired with an electric shock, rather than with a visual stimulus. So-called "verbal conditioning" was even found to be obtainable by simply *telling* a subject, after a series of tones without shock, that on the next presentation of tone, shock would shortly follow.

Of significance is the finding, reported by various writers (Adrian and Mathews, 1934; Bagchi, 1937; Durup and Fessard, 1936; Howard, 1935), that visual stimulation per se, which has sometimes been regarded as the necessary cause of alpha-rhythm depression, will have such an effect only when it is "meaningful." As Russell (1927) has pointed out, a stimulus event is said to be "meaningful" when it has symbolic implications, i.e., is a signal or sign of something else. Employing the basic conditioned-response formula of Pavlov, this writer says: "Originally, stimulus *A* produced reaction *C;* now stimulus *B* produces it, as a result of association. Thus *B* has become a 'sign' of *A,* in the sense that it causes the behavior appropriate to *A.* All sorts of things may be signs of other things, but with human beings words are the supreme example of signs" (p. 82). In other words, therefore, a "meaningful" stimulus, visual or otherwise, is one that arouses an expectation of consequences ("unconditioned stimuli") that are important to the organism in their own right, i.e., are possessed of *intrinsic* response-producing potentialities. The fact that visual stimulation produces a depression of the alpha rhythm in human beings more frequently than do other forms of stimulation can only indicate, according to this interpretation, that visual stimuli, in general, are more meaningful. Jasper (1937), in discussing this problem, has reached the following conclusion:

> The prepotency of visual stimuli in this regard for man may be related to the behavioral significance of vision at the higher levels of encephalization of function rather than there being a specific relation of the alpha

rhythm to the visual mechanism as such. . . . It is interesting to note that a sound imitating the rat's squeal was found most effective in blocking the slow cortical potentials in the rat, accordings to Travis and Milisen, and that tactual and auditory stimuli were more effective than visual stimuli in blocking the slow rhythms in the cat, according to Rheinberger and Jasper (p. 466).[21]

Rheinberger and Jasper (1937) have reported an observation that seems to afford an especially neat illustration of the point that stimuli which depress brain potentials do so by virtue of their arousal of a state of expectancy. They found, quite by chance, that a cat will usually stop showing the alpha rhythm if, during an experimental session, it develops a need for elimination. One has only to recall the type of treatment to which most cats are subjected at one time or another for indiscreet elimination in order to see why such a form of internal stimulation might be highly "symbolic" for the cat, arousing a lively anticipation of punishment.

Only one fact thus far reported in the literature seems to oppose the hypothesis that large, regular alpha waves signify mental relaxation and that small, depressed waves signify alertness and expectation. This is the finding, reported by Bagchi (1937), Jasper, Cruikshank, and Howard (1935), and others, that a stimulus which occurs "unexpectedly," with a "startle" effect, is more likely to depress the alpha rhythm than is the same stimulus if the subject is thoroughly adapted to it. Does not such a finding show, contrary to the foregoing hypothesis, that the more a stimulus is expected the *less* effect it is likely to have on the alpha rhythm? This apparent dilemma breaks down when it is recalled that the statement that a person is adapted to the occurrence of a given stimulus event is not the same as saying that he *expects* it. As the term *expectancy* is employed in the present paper, it implies a state of active preparedness for a given type of stimulus-response sequence. Adaptation is the antithesis of this. It implies that a particular stimulus or stimulus situation has lost its "meaningfulness," that the reaction formerly made to it has, in conditioned-response terminology, become "extinguished." Thus the statement that an "unexpected" stimulus is especially likely to be followed by a depression of the brain potentials really means that such a stimulus is especially likely to be "meaningful" to the subject, i.e., especially likely to arouse a

---

[21] The visual-mindedness of man is indicated by such expressions as "insight," "foresight," "far-sighted," and "to see," meaning "to understand." For a further discussion of this subject and a comparison of man and the lower animals on this score, see Collins (1922) and Smith (1928).

state of expectancy, in a way that an "adapted" (extinguished") stimulus would not.

In spite of the large number of other factors that have been systematically explored in respect to their possible role in facilitating or depressing the electrical potentials of the cortex, it appears from the foregoing discussion that the variable that is probably most significant in this connection has as yet been studied only incidentally, in a sense, largely inadvertently.[22] The reasons for this are understandable. Before a phenomenon can become a satisfactory object of scientific inquiry, it must be capable of being (*a*) controlled and (*b*) measured. The present paper is intended as a step in the direction of making the phenomenon of preparatory set or expectancy scientifically amenable in these respects. To the extent that the techniques previously discussed and illustrated in this paper offer an opportunity for the control and measurement of this phenomenon, the way should be open for crucial verification of the major hypothesis that has been under consideration in the present section, namely, that expectancy varies inversely with the size and regularity of the type of brain wave designated as the alpha rhythm. Since the course of expectancy between successive stimulus events that occur at regular intervals has now been empirically, if somewhat laboriously, determined by the reaction-time technique (and confirmed by the other methods already considered), it would be a simple but highly useful task to determine the course of the alpha rhythm under the same conditions. Confirmation by such a method of the hypothesis stated above would not only bring new order into the field of electroencephalography, but it would also open up new possibilities for the more intimate study of a variety of problems that emerge from the theory of expectancy as a motivating and reinforcing agent that has been proposed by the writer (1938c).

Other Methods

Although less directly applicable to the empirical measurement of expectancy than the techniques discussed in the four preceding sections, there are a number of other possibilities in this connection that may be briefly outlined.

Sensory Hallucinations. It has repeatedly been noted in research on absolute sensory thresholds in human beings that if at

[22] The nearest to a systematic attempt that has apparently been made to date to investigate the effect of expectancy or set upon brain waves is the study recently reported by Knott (1939). See also Bakes (1939).

a point in time at which the presentation of a stimulus is expected by the subject no stimulation is given, an hallucinatory perception of stimulation is very likely to be reported. Attention has also frequently been called to the fact that simple sensory hallucinations can often be produced in human beings by the use of suggestion, i.e., by the establishment of a strong expectation of stimulation of a given kind by verbal means. This relationship between expectancy and sensory experience has been considered at greater length in an earlier paper (Mowrer, 1938c) and need not be further discussed here, except to say that it apparently affords an opportunity for the detection of expectancy that has not been as yet systematically explored. How useful such an index might prove to be for quantitative purposes is at present conjectural.

THE TIME ERROR. One of the commonest sources of annoyance in the field of psychophysical comparisons is the fact that of two stimuli presented in succession, the latter is likely to be consistently overestimated by a slight amount. In seeking to explain this so-called negative time error it has been necessary to raise the basic question as to how the intensity of two stimuli, presented serially, can be compared at all. The first stimulus has disappeared before the second occurs. How, therefore, can a sensation that no longer exists be compared with one that is current? The hypothesis most widely accepted in this connection is derived from the work of Muller and Schumann (1889) on weight-lifting. Their supposition was that the lifting of a weight of given mass establishes a set (*Einstellung*) appropriate to the lifting of a second weight of the same mass. The next weight actually lifted is, therefore, judged as lighter or heavier than the first in terms of whether the set is more than adequate or less than adequate for the lifting of the second weight. In order to explain the time error, Woodworth (1938) has assumed that a certain amount of effort is required to maintain a given set and that with the passage of time such a set tends to "sag," i.e., to become progressively less adequate for the lifting of a weight of the same mass as the weight first lifted. The result would be that of two weights of identical mass lifted in succession, the second would, on the average, be judged as heavier and that a constant error in the same direction would be introduced in the judgment of successively lifted weights of different mass. This explanation of the time error is supported by the fact that it tends to become greater as the comparison interval is increased and by other facts too complex to be discussed in the present connection. It is only necessary to note here that if this hypothesis is correct, the time error should provide a basis for the study of expectancy inasmuch as it is regarded as a necessary correlate of preparatory set.

"ASSOCIATION" AND "PROJECTION" TECHNIQUES. Psychological conflict has been defined (Luria, 1932), at its simplest level, as readiness to react to the same stimulus in contradictory ways, with one of these reaction tendencies dominant and the other subordinate. Even the most smoothly coordinated of human behavior probably involves an undercurrent of conflict, but so long as the discrepancy in the strength of rival reaction tendencies is relatively great, little importance or interest attaches to this state of affairs. When, however, opposing impulses are more nearly matched, the submerged one is likely to exert its influence either by diminishing the smoothness and efficiency of the main stream of integrated behavior or by extruding itself in the superficially meaningless acts known as "symptoms." Under the latter circumstances the affected individual is often unable to account for his own eccentricities and, disturbed by this, seeks the aid of persons who are specialists in the use of various techniques that have been developed during recent decades for the purpose of "unmasking" troublesome impulses. The well-known "association test" was one of the earliest devices developed in this connection. More recently the so-called "projection" techniques have emerged. Psychoanalysis is yet another method of achieving the same end. But regardless of the particular technique employed, the finding is essentially the same: inhibitions always involve expectations (conscious or unconscious) of inimical consequences if the inhibited impulse were allowed forthright expression. Thus, the investigation of submerged, conflicting behavior trends is necessarily a study of expectancy, of the source and objects of anxiety.

"HYPOTHESIS" FORMATION. If, on a series of occasions, experimentally controllable event *X* has uniformly been followed in the experience of a given individual by experimentally controllable event *Y*, and if that individual has been asked to indicate on each occurrence of event *X* whether he does or does not expect it to be followed by event *Y*, he will soon be expressing uniformly positive expectations. If event *X* now ceases to be followed by event *Y*, the subject will express a few "false" positive expectations and will then abruptly begin to express uniformly negative expectations. This change from what may be termed a strongly positive "hypothesis" to a strongly negative one presumably occurs by degrees, but the all-or-none method of responding that is imposed upon the subject by the conditions of the experiment conceals all indication of the gradualness of this transition. If, however, the results obtained from a *large number* of persons under the same conditions are analyzed, i.e., if the number of "yes" and "no" votes is tabulated on each successive occurrence of event *X,* it will be found that the change from the positive to the negative "hypothesis" is not abrupt for the group as a whole. Humphreys (1939a) and Humphreys, Miller, and Ellson (1940) have recently conducted experiments of this kind (cf. 7) and have presented curves portraying group changes in "hypothesis" or "attitude," which probably parallel the changes in the *degree of certainty* felt by each individual subject in expressing his expectations during the transitional period. This is a new and interesting possibility as far as the objective measurement of expectancy is concerned. How valid it is remains to be determined. If, for example, the Gestalt contention that changes in "hypothesis" (expectancy) always occur suddenly, through "insight," is correct, then the apparent gradualness of the transition from one hypothesis to another that is suggested by the experiments cited is purely an artifact (cf. 11). The other experimental findings presented in this paper suggest, however, that this is probably not the case.

"Incentive" as a Measure of Expectancy. In a number of studies it has been demonstrated that the tenacity with which an animal will "work" in an experimental situation is a function not only of the intensity of the organic need that is being employed as the so-called "drive" but also of the size of the "reward" (i.e., the extent of drive reduction) that the animal expects to receive for its efforts. Fletcher (1939), for example, has shown that, with hunger held constant, chimpanzees will work reliably harder to pull in a weighted food box if they see the experimenter put a large piece of food into it than if they see him put in a small piece. In the former case, the animal's "incentive" is said to be stronger, which can only mean, since the strength of drive is constant and since the lure is seen only momentarily, that the difference in vigor of response in the two cases is occasioned solely by a corresponding difference in expectancy. As previously posited (1), expectancy or preparatory set is itself a form of discomfort, and if the sight of a large piece of food can be assumed to produce (as a conditioned reaction) a stronger expectancy, i.e., a greater readiness to eat, than the sight of a smaller piece of food, it is then understandable why "incentives" of varying size have differential motivational efficacy.

It may be noted in passing that by thus regarding both expectancy of "reward" (decreased drive) and expectancy of "punishment" (increased drive) as forms of discomfort (rather than as one being "pleasant" and the other "unpleasant"), it is possible to account for the motivational value of each on the basis of a single, unitary principle. This is in keeping with an attempt that has been made elsewhere (Mowrer, 1938c) to show that so-called "learning through reward" is not basically different from "learning through punishment." By eliminating this traditional distinction, a real advance can be made toward a simpler, more coherent, and more comprehensive theory of behavior.

Implications

By and large, psychological writers can be divided into three groups on the basis of their views concerning the learning process: (*a*) those who believe that all learning follows the principle of association through temporal contiguity (simple conditioning), (*b*) those who believe that all learning occurs according to the law of effect, and (*c*) those who believe that learning can come about through the operation of both principles. As originally formulated the law of effect had two subprinciples: (*a*) that stimulus-response connections are strengthened or "stamped in" by satisfying ("pleasant") consequences and (*b*) that stimulus-response connections are weakened or "stamped out" by painful ("annoying") consequences. Recently there has been a tendency to abandon this dichotomous formulation and to assume instead that the law of effect operates only in a positive direction, that established habits disappear only as a result of their being overlaid by the acquisition of new habits. As pointed out previously (Mowrer, 1938c), (1), this revision of the law of effect has considerably increased its force and attractiveness. There has been, however, one major source of objection to it as a comprehensive theory of learning. Students of human learning have repeatedly asked what "drive" is "satisfied" when, for example, a subject memorizes a series of nonsense syllables. And animal experimenters have asked where the element of "pleasure" or "gratification" is in the conditioning of a simple withdrawal response, where the conditioned stimulus, for example, is a tone and the unconditioned stimulus a momentary electric shock that cannot be avoided.

These have not been idle questions. For some time it has been clear that if the law of effect is to be seriously considered as the universal mechanism underlying all learning, the concept of "gratification" or "pleasure" must be extended beyond the notion of fulfillment of basic organic needs. As stressed in the introductory section of this paper, learning can obviously occur, particularly in human beings, when all such needs are apparently well taken care of. Eschewing such vague, unanalyzed concepts as "need for new experience," "wish for superiority," "desire for social approval," and so forth, the present writer believes that the extension of the source and scope of motivation required in this connection can be accomplished by simply adding, to the organically specifiable needs, the notion of expectancy, i.e., a state of tension or discomfort involving anticipation of the recurrence of one or more of these needs. The evidence mobilized in the preceding sections of this paper gives empirical support for the assumption, scarcely debatable on common-sense grounds, that such a state of tension is high before the occurrence of a repeated noxious stimulus event (such as the momentary shock commonly employed in conditioning a simple defense reaction) and low immediately thereafter (see Figure 3), thus providing appropriate conditions for the operation of the law of effect. It follows from this analysis that, other things being equal, the greater the extent of the drop in expectancy-tension after the occurrence of a stimulus-response sequence, the greater the "reinforcing," or learning-inducing, value of this drop. Direct experimental confirmation of this inference has already been obtained and will be published shortly, thereby lending further strength to the underlying assumptions.[23]

Contending against the English "empiricists," who held that the human "mind" is composed of "associations" that are acquired,

---

[23] Brown (1937) has recently reported the interesting finding that in memorizing nonsense syllables, human subjects show maximal galvanic skin responses to those syllables that are learned first, i.e., those that occur at the beginning and at the end of a series. In view of the relationship between expectancy and the G. S. R. as noted above, this is an extremely suggestive observation. The discovery of Muenzinger (1934c) and others that "shock for right responses" in a discrimination experiment with rats may facilitate learning also appears relevant in this connection. [The above discussion resolves the paradox of why it is that "punishing" events may also be "rewarding": if an event such as a brief electric shock is preceded by a lively expectation, i.e., fear, of that event, then the occurrence of the shock reduces the fear and thus provides a reinforcement (though a somewhat ambiguous one) for whatever acts immediately precede it. (See the experiment of Whiteis, reported in 9; see also 12.) But this analysis leaves unanswered the question as to how the *fear itself* is learned. Hull's system of postulates (1943, 1949) requires that the fear be learned on the basis of primary-drive reduction, such as that provided by the termination of an electric shock. We now have evidence that fear is learned on a different basis, namely that provided by the principle of contiguity, and that it is not shock termination that is crucial in this respect but shock *onset* (9, 10).]

more or less passively, as a consequence of the impingement of stimuli from the external world, James (1890) long ago took the position that learning is essentially an active process, for the occurrence of which "attention" is an indispensable prerequisite. In this stand James would certainly be heartily supported by most present-day educators. As one writer (Philip, 1928) says:

To the extent that an individual is able to give attention is he able to bring more or less into play his powers of acquiring knowledge. . . . There is no doubt that the lack of the requisite amount of attention greatly decreases the efficiency of one's mind. The estimation of the composite thing known as intelligence is quite important; of importance too is the determination of the extent to which mental forces may be concentrated on the task at hand (p. vii).

May (1939) has recently commented upon the extent to which anxiety (anticipation of "punishment") is conventionally employed to motivate classroom learning. This mechanism probably operates in a number of ways not ordinarily recognized. When, for example, a teacher says (in however pleasant a voice), "Attention, boys and girls," there tends to be aroused on the part of the pupil an expectation that something is going to be demanded of him, that all will be well if he can meet this demand, but that if he cannot "something will happen." He may be somewhat vague as to what this "something" will be, but he knows that it will be a "loss" to him, loss of some accustomed privilege or of his own physical and emotional comfort (at least temporarily). Freud (1936) has shown that anticipation of such a loss is the essence of anxiety; it is also the essence of what is here termed expectancy, of which anxiety is but a special, more accentuated form (1).

From principles now at hand, a deduction of highly practical character can be made, namely, that in order for classroom learning to proceed efficiently, the arousal of anxiety must be followed as promptly as possible by its dissipation, after a "correct" reaction is made. A good teacher, in other words, knows how to turn the "heat" off as well as turn it on. But even such a teacher is likely to be relatively ineffectual (*a*) in the case of children whose performances fail (for whatever reason) to approximate the class standard and who, sensing this, remain ill at ease and apprehensive and (*b*) in the case of children whose level of anxiety is chronically so high, due to "neurotic" mechanisms, that it is virtually impossible to produce a significant reduction in it at appropriate points in the educational program. A more or less successful attempt has been made in some schools to deal with the first of these problems by the creation of "opportunity" classes (in which poor students can do "average" work) and to meet the second by referring children to appropriate agencies for psychotherapy.

These considerations apply with equal force to the training that children receive in the home which is commonly referred to as the socialization process. Most parents would impulsively deny that they train their children primarily by means of fear, insisting instead that they sway them through "love." Careful analysis shows, however, that the latter type of influence is no less dependent upon the arousal of apprehension than is control by the threat of corporal punishment. Among other writers, Anna Freud (1931) has stressed this point of view. She says:

> In the earliest years, the child is under the domination of two powers, an inner one, due to the pressure of its own instincts, and an external one, due to the commands and prohibitions of parents. . . . Thus the power of the parents is the source of a twofold anxiety, which makes the child amenable to upbringing. Further, there is the fear of being injured by the parents if their wishes are opposed. . . . Secondly, there is the fear of the loss of love of parents [with resulting deprivations]. Psychoanalytic pedagogy regards the threat of castration [physical punishment] and the threat of the loss of love, both of which are used to a greater or less extent by all parents, as the two chief factors which make possible the upbringing of the child (p. 565).

Without an adequate appreciation on the part of parents of the nature of the forces they are employing in their role as educators, it is not surprising that the personality development of their children often proceeds along lines contrary to their avowed wishes and to dictates of the culture. Nor is it surprising that in the so-called maladjusted adult the source of his difficulties is commonly traceable to anxieties that stem from childhood.

In order, therefore, to approach the problem of education, with its broad and vital social implications, in the soundest, safest manner, it is clearly essential that the conditions and consequence of the use of expectancy or anxiety as a motive for learning be more thoroughly understood than they have been in the past. The present paper represents an attempt, at an elementary level, to further this sort of understanding.

CHAPTER 3

ANXIETY REDUCTION AND LEARNING

[The emotion of fear ("anxiety") is commonly thought of as an outcome of punishment; and since punishment tends to *inhibit* the behavior to which it is applied, fear itself is often conceived of as having primarily an inhibitory function. In the present study and the immediately following ones, experimental evidence is advanced to show that fear is pre-eminently a *drive,* a goad to *action,* and that ensuing drive reduction provides emphatic reinforcement of such action. These are the basic facts about fear, and its inhibitory role is derived therefrom: fear can be used to block established habits because, through its agency, new habits of an antagonistic nature can be quickly established. Since fear is itself learned, through conditioning, and since it then calls for new learning, in the nature of problem solving, it lends itself admirably to the laboratory study of secondary motivation and reinforcement. Its study also illustrates the advantages of a two-factor conception of learning.

The paper here reproduced was originally published in *The Journal of Experimental Psychology* (1940).]

I. The Problem

That a reduction in the intensity of the psychosomatic state known as dread, apprehension, nervousness, tension, fear, or anxiety can function as a "satisfying state of affairs" (as defined by Thorndike's law of effect) and thereby bring about the learning of new stimulus-response sequences ("connections") is indicated by various clinical as well as common-sense observations (A. Freud, 1937; S. Freud, 1936; Mowrer, 1). So far as the writer is aware, however, no previous attempt has been made to submit this proposition to experimental verification.[1] More specifically, the hypothesis un-

[1] Interest has occasionally been expressed in the relation between various indices of "emotion" and learning in particular situations. For example, Brown (1937) has reported a correlation of .80 between the size of psychogalvanic response made by human subjects to serially presented nonsense syllables and the readiness with which these syllables were memorized. This finding, like many others that might be cited, is highly suggestive but has only an indirect bearing upon the problem at hand. For a discussion of the relation of emotion to "education," see Lund (1939).

der examination here is that just as a reduction in hunger, reduction in thirst, reduction in sex drive, reduction in fatigue, reduction in oxygen lack, or reduction in any other organic "need" or "discomfort" tends to "reinforce" the behavior which brings about (or is at least temporally contiguous with) such a reduction or state of "relief," so likewise is a reduction in the particular form of discomfort called anxiety effective in fixating behavior that is associated therewith.

Instead of first stating the systematic assumptions underlying the present study and then describing the experimental procedure and results, it seems preferable in this instance to follow the opposite course. Since some of the problems here involved are relatively complex and as yet not completely solved, it is desirable to keep the theoretical part of this paper as concrete and unambiguous as possible. This end seems most likely to be attainable by going directly to an account of methodology and empirical findings, which can then serve as a fixed reference point for the subsequent theoretical analysis.

II. Apparatus and Subjects

The apparatus employed in the present study (see Figure 12) is a modified version of the device first described by Culler, Finch, and Girden (1934) for use with cats and later adapted by Hunter (1935b) for use with rats. It consists of a circular grill which is divided into eight individually electrifiable sections, enclosed by inner and outer walls of transparent celluloid (20 inches high). The grill itself is composed of small, radially placed, stainless steel rods and is 5 inches wide, with an internal diameter of 18 inches.

When a naïve animal (rat or guinea pig) is first placed in this type of apparatus and current is applied to the particular section of the grill on which it happens to be located, it may churn its feet rapidly up and down, leap into the air, or engage in other equally futile agitated behavior. Very shortly, however, it is certain to try running (which sometimes occurs immediately); and since this behavior carries the animal off the charged section of the grill and thereby affords escape from shock, only two or three applications of the shock are required to make this reaction prompt and specific. Although running is not, therefore, a wholly "unconditioned" response to shock under these circumstances, it can be so regarded for present purposes.

As a conditioned stimulus, a relatively pure tone (800 d.v. in pitch, 60 d.b. above human threshold) was presented through headphones which were located 3 feet directly above the grill. All

Fig. 12.—Apparatus for the conditioning of a simple locomotor response.

experimentation was carried out in a sound-proofed room, with visual and auditory cues from the experimenter excluded. The unconditioned stimulus (shock) was derived from a 60-cycle, 500-volt source of alternating current, with a standard limiting resistance in series with the subject (3,000,000 ohms for rats, 500,000 ohms for guinea pigs). A small rotary selector switch permitted prompt application of current to any of the 8 sections comprising the grill.

Various conditioning setups of other types were tested before the one here described was adopted. It has an advantage over any arrangement demanding immobilization of subjects in that it saves time and avoids artifacts due to struggling. The modified activity cage described by Brogden and Culler (1936) seems to be quite as satisfactory for use with guinea pigs as the circular grill arrangement, but it does not serve so adequately with rats for the reason that they have a tendency to keep running more or less continuously in it, which they do not do in the circular grill. The circular grill is likewise superior to the two-compartment device first described by Dunlap, Gentry, and Zeigler (1931) and later modified by Warner (1932b), Hunter and Pennington (1939), and others.[2] In this latter type of apparatus strong conflict tends to be generated by the fact that the subject is forced to shuttle back and forth between only two positions, movement to either of which means going back to a place where punishment may just have been received. In the circular grill, on the other hand, an animal can always move on to a relatively "new" position, one that is less strongly associated with punishment than the place it has just left and is therefore more acceptable. The only complication that arose in connection with the use of the circular grill in the present investigation was that occasionally a rat tried to perch on one of the low crosspieces separating adjacent sections of the grill (see Figure 12) and thereby avoid shock completely. When this happened, which was relatively infrequently, the rat was immediately dislodged by the experimenter.[3]

The 18 albino rats (12 males and 6 females) used in this investigation were obtained from the Wistar Institute (Experimental Colony Strain) and were approximately six months old. They had had no prior experimental use.

---

[2] [An apparatus of this kind was shortly developed (Mowrer and Miller, 1942) which proved satisfactory. It has been employed in a number of the studies which appear later in this series. See especially (4), page 94.]

[3] Following the completion of the study here reported, this defect was remedied by removing these separators and making the whole surface of the grill perfectly flat.

The 20 guinea pigs (10 males and 10 females) which were also employed were obtained from a local breeder. Little was known concerning them except that they were healthy young adults, with no prior laboratory experience.

III. Procedure

Three distinct conditioning procedures were employed in this investigation and were carried out first with 3 groups of rats and then with 3 groups of guinea pigs.

The Group I procedure was as follows. At the beginning of each experimental session, each animal was placed in the apparatus and allowed 1 minute of habituation. The conditioned stimulus, i.e., tone, was then presented for 5 seconds, at the end of which time, if the rat had not moved out of the section in which it was sitting at the onset of the tone, shock was administered. On moving to another section of the grill, the rat escaped the shock and the tone was turned off by the experimenter. If, on the other hand, when the tone was presented, the rat made the required movement within the 5-second interval following its onset, the tone was immediately terminated and no shock was applied.[4] Successive tones, or tone-shock combinations, were presented regularly every 60 seconds. Training lasted for 10 days, each animal receiving 24 conditioning trials (tones or tone-shock combinations) each day.

The Group II procedure was exactly the same as the Group I procedure except for the fact that instead of successive tones, or tone-shock combinations, occurring at regular 60-second intervals, they were presented at 3 different intervals—15, 60, and 105 seconds—in a revolving random order. During the course of each daily session of 24 trials, each of these intervals was used 8 times, with the result that the *average* interval was exactly 60 seconds. The average rate of presentation of stimuli was thus the same for

---

[4] The practice of omitting shock when a conditioned response occurs, instead of having it invariably follow the conditioned stimulus, has been adopted because of the better conditioning obtained in this way by Culler, Finch, Girden, and Brogden (1935), Hunter (1935b), and others. However, the termination of the conditioned stimulus upon the occurrence of a conditioned response, instead of permitting it to continue for a fixed interval, seems not to have been previously described. Exploratory work indicates that this method may be superior to the conventional one; a more definitive study of this problem is now in progress (see 4). [Note that in this study the author was still following the common practice of referring to the overt behavior elicited in a threat situation as a "conditioned response." The more precise terminology subsequently adopted (9) would require that in an experiment of this kind, fear alone be spoken of as the "conditioned" reaction and that the behavioral adjustment made to the fear be looked upon as a "habit," essentially similar to the habits which are acquired as solutions to the motivational problems or tasks which other drives present.]

Group I subjects and Group II subjects; but in the first case the rate of presentation was constant, whereas in the second case it was irregular.

The Group III procedure was again exactly like the Group I procedure save for one difference. In the Group I procedure nothing happened to the subjects during the 60-second intervals between successive tones or tone-shock combinations. In the Group III procedure, however, these intervals were punctuated by the interpolation of shocks every 15 seconds (i.e., at 15, 30, and 45 seconds during each 60-second interval). These interpolated shocks were of the same intensity and were escapable in exactly the same way (i.e., by flight to other sections of the grill) as were those which were paired with the tone. They could not, however, be avoided.

In short, the Group II procedure differed from the Group I procedure only in the matter of temporal regularity-irregularity of tone (or tone-shock) presentations, whereas the Group III procedure differed from the Group I procedure only in the matter of the filled-unfilled character of the intervals between successive presentations of tone (or tone and shock).

IV. Results

The results, in terms of rate and amount of conditioning, obtained for the three groups of rats used in this investigation are represented graphically in Figure 13. The ten successive points comprising each of the three curves show the average number of conditioned responses made by the 6 animals (4 males and 2 females) in each group during each of the 10 successive daily training sessions. It will be noted that the number of conditioned responses made by Group I is consistently superior to the number of conditioned responses manifested by either Group II or Group III. The critical ratio of the difference between the amount of conditioning obtained in Groups I and III is 3.36.[5] This means, according to Fisher's (1938) "Table of *t*," that the chances are more than 99 in 100 that this difference is real (i.e., caused by the conditions of the experiment). The critical ratio of the difference between the amount of conditioning obtained in Groups I and II is 1.63, which, in terms of *t*, means that there are about 85 chances in 100 that it is

[5] This value was obtained by taking the *total* number of conditioned responses made by each animal during all 10 training sessions as the basis for computing the standard deviation of the distribution (σ). This practice of treating an animal's whole performance as a single 'test score' is followed throughout, except as otherwise indicated.

real. The critical ratio of the difference between Groups II and III is 1.88, which, again in terms of *t,* means that the chances are 90 in 100 that the difference is real. The average number of conditioned responses made by the Group I animals during the entire 10-day training period was 200.0, by the Group II animals 178.7, and by the Group III animals 138.5.

The results obtained from the three groups of guinea pigs under the same conditions as employed with the three groups of rats are

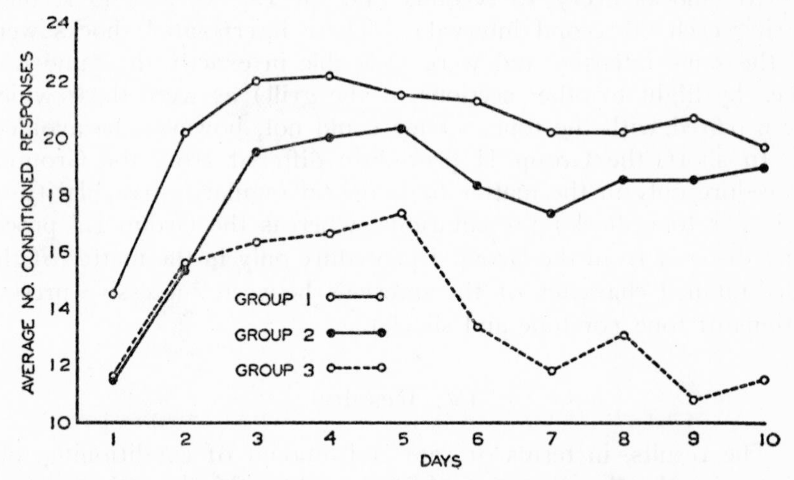

FIG. 13.—Amount of locomotor conditioning obtained in three groups of rats in which reinforcement (anxiety-reduction) was systematically varied.

presented in Figure 14. In general pattern, the findings are very similar. In both types of subjects, the Group I procedure gave the best conditioning and the Group III procedure the worst, with the Group II procedure intermediate. Although the rate of conditioning was much faster in the rats than in the guinea pigs, the rats and guinea pigs alike showed a tendency for the conditioning in Groups I and II eventually to become equalized and for the conditioning in Group III to show an initial rise and then a marked deterioration. Statistical analysis indicates that in the case of the guinea pigs the chances are about 94 in 100 (C. R. = 2.21) that the difference between Groups I and III is real and about 92 in 100 (C. R. = 2.02) that the difference between Groups II and III is real. The difference between Groups I and II is, by the same criterion, much less reliable (C. R. = .67), due to the virtual equalization of performance during the latter half of the training period. However, if one takes the performance of these two groups on the second, third, and fourth days of training, one finds that the chances are about 97 in 100 (C. R. = 2.61) that the difference during this selected part of the procedure is real. The fact that this difference disappears as training is prolonged does not mean that it is not real in the beginning. The average number of conditioned responses made by the Group I animals during the entire training period was 137.1, by the Group II animals 116.5, and by the Group III animals 64.2.[6]

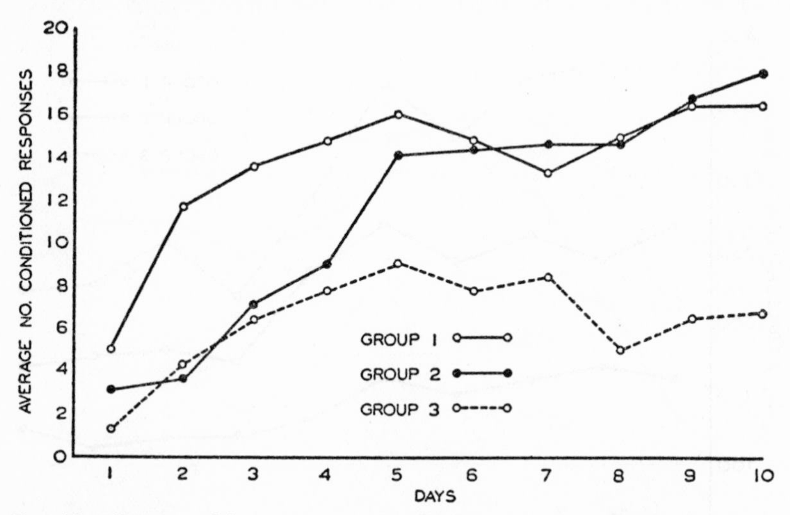

FIG. 14.—Amount of locomotor conditioning obtained in three groups of guinea pigs in which reinforcement (anxiety reduction) was systematically varied (as in Figure 13).

The relatively high *t* values and the marked similarity in the pattern of the differences obtained between the Group I, Group II, and Group III procedures with both rats and guinea pigs as subjects seem unequivocally to support the conclusion that these differences are significant.

The activity that subjects manifest during the intervals between successive paired presentations of conditioned and unconditioned stimuli has been regarded by most investigators as a nuisance, something to be either ignored or designedly minimized by whatever means available. In the present study this activity has been taken into account and carefully recorded, on the assumption that it is related to and may throw light upon the dynamics of the condition-

[6] It will be noted that these figures are considerably lower than those obtained from the corresponding groups of rats. The superiority of the performance of the latter type of subjects is further indicated by their lower variability. The rats had coefficients of variability of 6.1 (Group I), 14.9 (Group II), and 21.8 (Group III), as against 44.3 (Group I), 36.4 (Group II), and 73.3 (Group III) for the guinea pigs.

ing process as a whole. Figures 15 and 16 show for rats and guinea pigs, respectively, the average number of sections of the circular grill traversed per daily training session by the animals in Groups I, II, and III.[7] Although differing considerably in absolute value, the findings for the two types of subjects are here again very much alike. In both cases, the Group III animals consistently show the greatest amount of activity, the Group I animals show the next

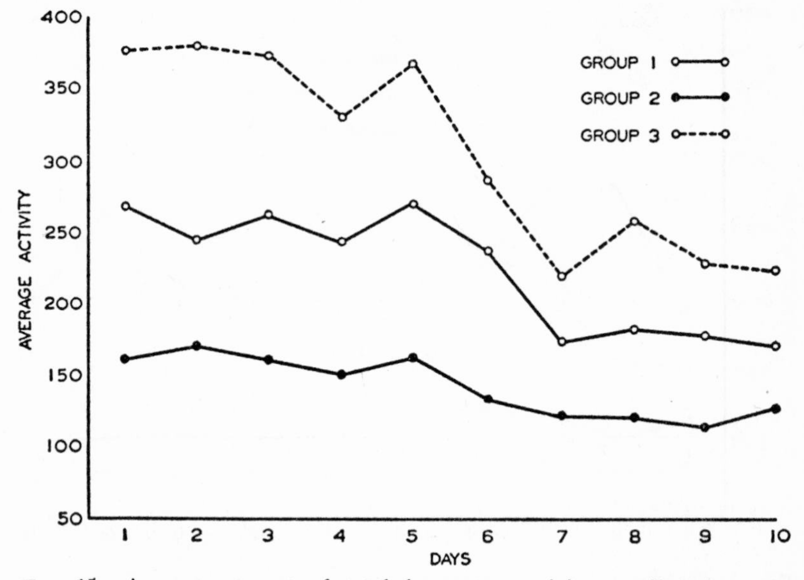

Fig. 15.—Average amount of total locomotor activity manifested per daily training session by rats during the development of a conditioned locomotor response (compare Figure 13).

greatest amount, and the Group II animals show the least. The critical ratios of the differences between these groups are 3.37 (I–II), 4.41 (II–III), and 1.78 (I–III) for the rats and 3.38 (I–II), 9.30 (II–III), and 6.88 (I–III) for the guinea pigs. There can thus be little question of the reliability of these differences.

With the hope of securing an additional basis on which to compare the amount of conditioning obtained in both rats and guinea pigs by the three procedures here employed, all subjects were submitted, on the day following the completion of the 10-day training period, to a standard 24-trial extinction series. Each ani-

[7] These averages are based upon all the activity manifested by each animal during the experimental session, including not only the "spontaneous" locomotion that occurred between trials but also the responses resulting directly from application of the conditioned and unconditioned stimuli.

mal was put into the apparatus, habituated as usual, and then presented with 24 tones at regular 1-minute intervals. If, within 5 seconds after the onset of tone, an animal moved to another section of the grill, the tone was promptly turned off and a conditioned response recorded; if the animal did not move, the tone was left on for the full 5-second period and then turned off, with no shock in either case. Figure 17 shows the extinction curves for the 3

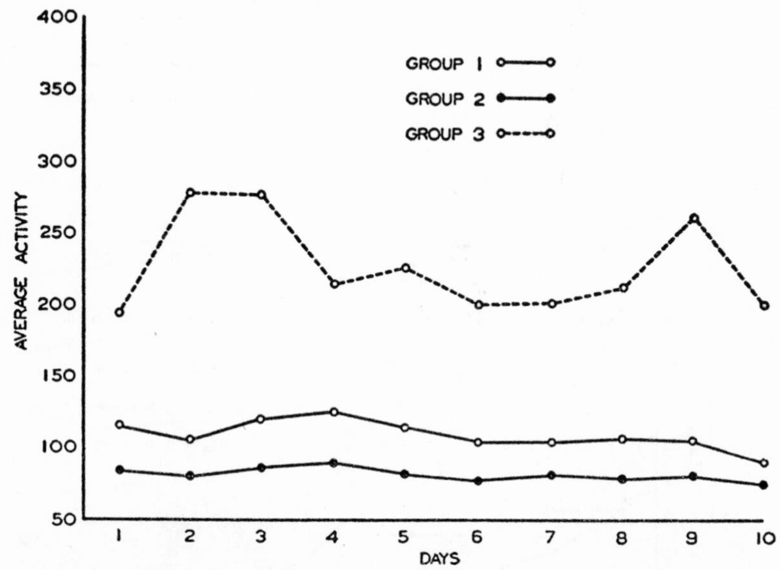

FIG. 16.—Average amount of total locomotor activity manifested per daily training session by guinea pigs during the development of a conditioned locomotor response (compare Figure 14).

groups of rats, and Figure 18 shows the corresponding curves for the 3 groups of guinea pigs. In general, they tell much the same story as do the acquisition curves (Figures 13 and 14). Resistance to extinction is markedly greater in both the Group I and Group II animals than in the Group III animals. In the case of the rats, the resistance of the Group I animals seems to be slightly greater than that of the Group II animals; but in the case of the guinea pigs this relationship is reversed. No attempt has been made to determine the statistical reliability of these differences.

The total locomotor activity manifested during the extinction trials by both rats and guinea pigs is shown, respectively, in Figures 19 and 20. Here some marked dissimilarities are evident. Although the Group II animals hold the intermediate position in both cases, the Group I and Group III curves are exactly reversed. The

Group III rats continue to show the greatest activity during extinction, as they did during acquisition; but the Group III guinea pigs show the least activity during extinction, instead of most as they

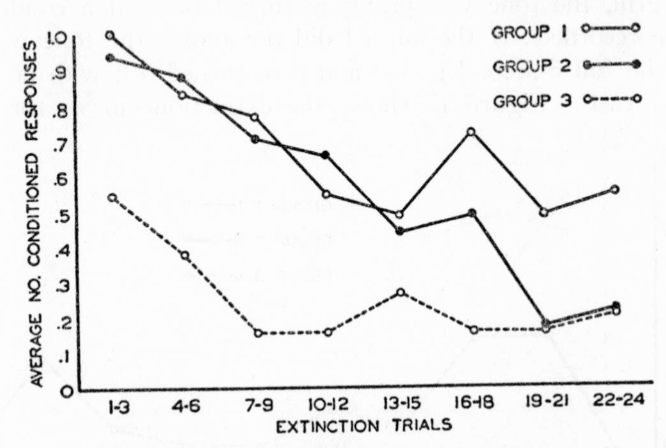

Fig. 17.—Extinction of a conditioned locomotor response in rats.

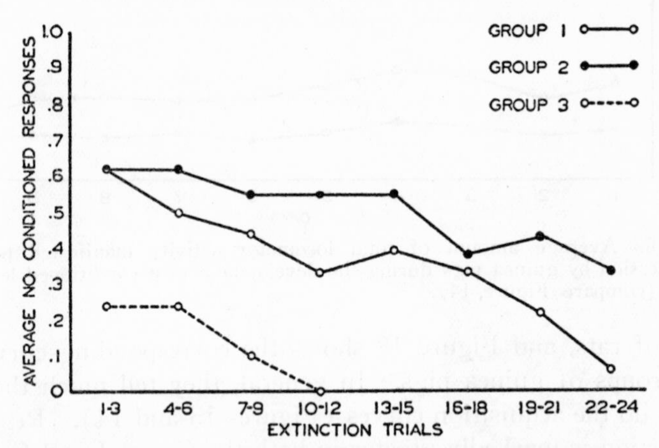

Fig. 18.—Extinction of a conditioned locomotor response in guinea pigs.

did during acquisition. Still other differences are to be noted, which will be discussed later.

V. Discussion

Evidence which has been presented elsewhere (2, see especially Figure 3) indicates that when a stimulus is recurrently presented to an organism at regular temporal intervals, expectation of (preparedness for) this stimulus mounts as the time approaches for its presentation, suddenly drops when the expected stimulus occurs (and is reacted to), then begins to mount again, and so on. When this phenomenon of expectancy, or preparatory set, is sufficiently

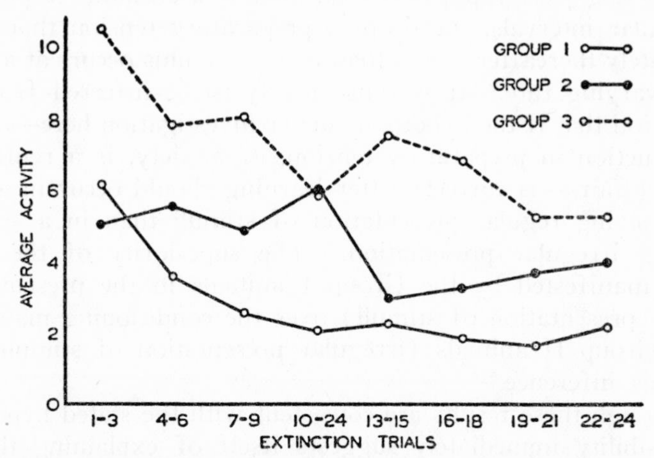

FIG. 19.—Average amount of total locomotor activity manifested per trial during extinction of a conditioned locomotor response in rats (compare Figure 18).

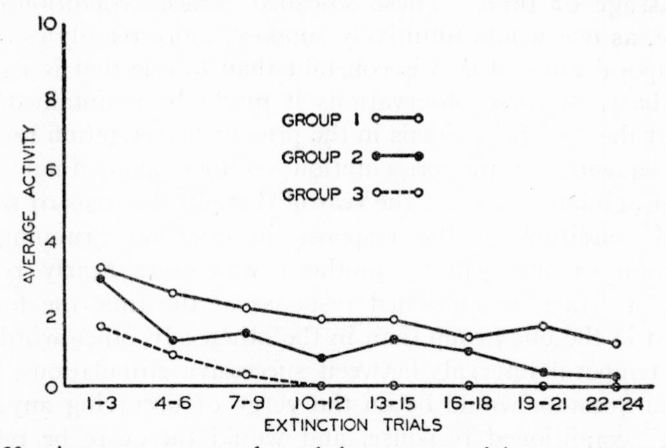

FIG. 20.—Average amount of total locomotor activity manifested per trial during extinction of a conditioned locomotor response in guinea pigs (compare Figure 19).

highly developed to be "uncomfortable," i.e., takes on motivational properties in its own right, its reduction should, on the basis of the hypothesis stated at the outset of this paper, provide a "satisfying state of affairs" and thereby "reinforce" accompanying behavior. As a corollary of this proposition, it is to be supposed that, within limits, the greater the extent of such a drop in preparatory tension (dread, anxiety) at any given point in time, the greater its reinforcing, or learning-producing, potentialities.

Again on the basis of evidence reported in the study cited in the preceding paragraph, it is clear that if a stimulus is presented at irregular intervals, the drop in preparatory tension that occurs immediately thereafter is less than if the stimulus occurs at a standard, unvarying rate. It is consequently to be inferred from this observation that if the hypothesis under investigation here—namely, that reduction in preparatory tension, or anxiety, is a reinforcing state of affairs—is correct, better learning should occur in a situation involving regular presentation of stimuli than in a situation involving irregular presentation. The superiority of the conditioning manifested by the Group I animals in the present study (regular presentation of stimuli) over the conditioning manifested by the Group II animals (irregular presentation of stimuli) confirms this inference.[8]

Although these results are consistent with the stated hypothesis, the possibility immediately suggests itself of explaining them in another way. Pavlov (1927) and other investigators have shown that conditioned responses can be established on the basis of the mere passage of time. These so-called "trace" conditioned reactions are, as one would intuitively suppose, more readily established to a temporal interval that is constant than to one that is irregular. On the basis of these observations it might be maintained, therefore, that the Group I animals in the present investigation responded more frequently to the presentation of tone alone than did the Group II animals solely for the reason that, on the basis of so-called temporal conditioning, the response in question (running from one section of the grill to another) was more nearly ready to occur as a "trace" conditioned response at the time the tone was presented in the one group than in the other. In other words, with regular temporal intervals between successive stimulations, the response in question would be on the verge of occurring anyway, as a "trace" conditioned response, and would therefore be relatively easy to "trip" by the tone; whereas, with irregular intervals between successive stimulations, the response would be less highly prepared at any particular point in time at which the tone hap-

[8] Preliminary experimentation has indicated that this difference appears only if the absolute duration of both the regular and the irregular intervals is relatively brief. If, for example, an interval of 120 seconds (instead of 60 seconds) were permitted between trials in the regular order of presentation and if intervals of 75, 120, and 165 seconds (instead of 15, 60, and 105) were permitted between trials in the irregular procedure, any difference in results would probably be much reduced if not obliterated entirely.

pened to occur, with the result that the tone would be less effective in eliciting the response. If this simple view of the matter were correct, there would be no need to posit differential anxiety-reduction to account for the differing amounts of conditioning obtained in the Group I and Group II animals.

The procedure employed with the Group III animals was specifically designed to test the soundness of the foregoing explanation. It will be recalled that in the case of the Group III subjects, tone (or the tone-shock combination) occurred, as in the Group I procedure, at regular 60-second intervals but that shocks were interpolated every 15 seconds. The Group III animals were thus forced to make a response, i.e., move to another section of the grill, regularly every 15 seconds, one fourth of the time in response to tone (or tone and shock) and three fourths of the time in response to shock alone. In view of both the brevity and the regularity of this 15-second interval, temporal conditioning should, theoretically, have occurred especially quickly; and if the development of conditioned reactions to tone were primarily dependent upon this underlying temporal conditioning, then the Group III animals should have shown superior learning. However, this was not the case: the conditioning obtained in the Group III animals was decidedly inferior.[9]

[9] After this paper was in press, Mr. William D. Orbison called the writer's attention to a possible alternative explanation of this finding. Since the interpolated shocks could not be circumvented by anything the subjects could do, whatever they did just preceding the shocks was necessarily "punished." However, as Brogden, Lipman, and Culler (1938) have pointed out, a shock administered to a small animal such as the rat or guinea pig from a grill is probably less "punishing" if the animal assumes a preparatory crouch than if the animal is running at the moment of shock onset. Thus, a recurrent shock which is inescapable tends to be met by immobility; whereas, a shock which can be averted by anticipatory running tends to perpetuate this type of behavior. In the procedure employed with the Group III animals in the present study, conflict may, therefore, have been generated as follows: whereas the interpolated (inescapable) shocks tended to immobilize the animals, the shock which followed the tone only if the animal did not make a conditioned response tended to produce anticipatory running. A glance at the Group III curves in Figures 13 and 14 suggests that during the early part of the 10-day experimental period the subjects were trying to make an adjustment to the situation by means of the latter type of behavior; but since this did not prove satisfactory, they soon resorted to the other mode of adaptation, namely, anticipatory crouching, with a resulting deterioration in their "conditioned-response" scores. The fact that the activity record of the Group III rats broke sharply (see Figure 15) on the same day that their conditioned-response score dropped most markedly, namely, on the sixth day, would tend to support this interpretation, although the activity record of the Group III guinea pigs showed no such slump (see Figure 16). Although this "conflict" explanation of the inferior conditioning obtained with the Group III animals is somewhat different from the one proposed in the text, it is similar in that it, too, involves a law-of-effect view of the conditioning process instead of the traditional associationistic theory. Furthermore, there appears to be such an intimate connection between anxiety and conflict that the two alternative hypotheses here proposed may ultimately reduce to essentially the same thing. [In speaking of "a law-of-effect view of the conditioning process" as opposed to "the

These results do not, of course, deny the reality of temporal conditioning, but they do indicate that it alone cannot provide a comprehensive explanation of the results obtained in the present study. On the other hand, the anxiety-reduction hypothesis does provide such an explanation. Speaking loosely, it may be said that the poorness of the learning obtained in the Group II and Group III animals was because they were given less opportunity to "let down" between trials than were the Group I animals. In other words, they were kept in a more or less chronic state of apprehension or suspense. In the Group II animals this was accomplished by "keeping them guessing" as to when each succeeding stimulation was to occur. In the Group III animals, this element of uncertainty was presumably absent, but the stimuli came in such rapid succession that one stimulus had no more than occurred when the next one began to be "expected."[10] In either case, conditioned reactions to the tone were relatively "unrewarding" in that little was gained in the way of anxiety reduction when they occurred; whereas, in the case of the Group I animals each response was followed by a relatively long, unvarying period of no stimulation, with correspondingly great anxiety reduction.

The fact that the Group II animals showed conditioning which, although inferior to that of the Group I animals, was markedly superior to that of the Group III animals indicates, presumably, that the Group II procedure was such as to permit a degree of anxiety reduction between trials that was less than that permitted by the Group I procedure but greater than that permitted by the Group III procedure. Direct measurement of the respective amounts of anxiety reduction permitted under the conditions of the three procedures would have been a decided advantage, but this did not seem possible. Superficially it might appear that the total amount of activity displayed by the various groups of animals (Figures 15 and 16) would provide an empirical index of the amount of tension they were under. It is true that the Group III animals, which were conjecturally kept most anxious, showed a uniformly

traditional associationistic theory," I was clearly preoccupied with the subject's *overt* behavior, which was motivated by fear and reinforced by fear reduction. I was not thinking of the process whereby *fear itself* was learned. Although I have considered the possibility that even fear is acquired on the basis of the law of effect (Mowrer, 1938c; see also 8), I have more recently come to the conclusion that we are here dealing with two fundamentally different forms of learning (see 9, 10).]

[10] That the Group III procedure kept apprehension chronically high is indicated by the fact that the Group III rats made repeated efforts to "leave the field" by trying to jump out of the apparatus. This behavior was not quantified but was very striking.

higher level of total activity than did the other two groups. However, it is impossible to say to what extent this greater activity was due to anxiety and to what extent it represented responses made directly to the numerous interpolated shocks. More meaningful perhaps is the fact that the Group I animals showed a consistently higher level of total activity than did the Group II animals. Two alternative interpretations of this difference are possible. It can be assumed, on the one hand, that greater activity represents greater anxiety and that the Group I animals were consequently more anxious; or it can be assumed that greater activity represents a relative absence of anxiety, in which event the Group I animals would be viewed as less anxious. Observations made on rats and guinea pigs in other experimentally produced danger situations suggest that the latter supposition may be the more valid one. However, additional experimentation, aimed specifically at this problem, will be necessary before a completely reliable decision can be reached on this score.

Another objection that may be raised to the interpretation of the findings of the present study in terms of differential anxiety reduction is that anxiety itself is a learned phenomenon and should not therefore be used as a basis for explaining further learning.[11] The writer (1) is in full agreement with the proposition that anxiety is a learned phenomenon, but it does not follow from this that anxiety cannot function as a motive, and its reduction as a reinforcing agent, for further learning. Numerous recent studies in the field of motivation have made it clear that in man and the lower animals alike there are both innate (primary) and derived (secondary) forms of motivation. The position here taken is that anxiety falls into the latter category. Just how the cyclic rise and fall of anxiety, or preparatory tension, posited above as a condition of recurrent noxious stimulation is acquired is an important problem, but its solution does not necessarily have to be completed before use can be made of the phenomenon itself as an explanation of other findings.

It is unfortunate that the hypothesis here advanced lacks the great simplicity of the associationistic theory of conditioning advocated by Pavlov and his followers. There is, however, no point in venerating a theory because of its simplicity if it is demonstrably inadequate to account for all the relevant facts. Some of the many

[11] [The implication of circularity is here completely avoided if one posits two principles of reinforcement, two types of learning. Thus, the principle of contiguity (of tone and shock) accounts for the acquisition of the fear reaction; and the law of effect explains the development of those overt responses which are fear-reducing.]

weaknesses of the view that mere paired presentation of stimuli provides the necessary conditions for conditioned-response learning have been previously enumerated (2) and need not be repeated here. It is, however, instructive to note that under the conditions of the present experiment, best conditioning occurred precisely in those animals which received *fewest* paired presentations of tone and shock. Since the results presented in Figures 13 and 14 are in terms of the average number of conditioned reactions shown by the various groups of animals during the course of each daily training session, and since a conditioned response is defined as one that occurs to a tone which is not followed by shock, it is axiomatic that the animals showing the best conditioning must have received the smallest number of paired presentations of tone and shock. In view of this fact it follows that the goodness of learning in a situation of this kind is not determined exclusively or even predominantly by the temporal pairing of stimuli but by some other factor. The assumption here made is that this other factor is the presence or absence of a reinforcing state of affairs as defined by the law of effect. The temporal contiguity of stimuli seems important only from the point of view of determining what stimuli will become functionally connected with what responses; it presumably does not determine whether such connections will or will not occur.[12]

Two other implications are to be briefly noted. It is well established that human beings memorize verbal material more efficiently with distributed practice than with massed practice. Without attempting to evaluate or compare the virtues of other theories which have been advanced to account for this phenomenon, it is worth observing that a possible explanation follows fairly directly from the foregoing discussion. In the learning of verbal material, motivation is ordinarily supplied, not by primary motives

[12] [A two-factor theory of learning greatly simplifies the analysis of this problem. It assumes that, in an experiment such as the present one, fear is acquired on the basis of sheer contiguity. But when the extent of fear acquisition (conditioning proper) is being measured by the occurrence or nonoccurrence of an overt response, such as running, this response will not be an entirely satisfactory index of fear acquisition, since it is affected, not only by the intensity of the fear which produces it, but also by the extent to which the overt response is reinforced, in keeping with the law of effect, through fear reduction. Thus, when an animal makes a so-called conditioned response, i.e., runs in response to the fear produced by the warning signal, the running response—as a solution to the problem of fear—is reinforced, but the fear itself—as a premonition of shock—tends to undergo extinction. Likewise, when the running response does not occur following tone, there is no reinforcement of it, but the tone-fear connection is strengthened by the association of tone and shock. There is thus, of necessity, a reciprocal relationship between these two types of learning in a situation of the kind here described. (For further consideration of this problem, see 10.)]

such as hunger or thirst, but by some form of tension or mild anxiety (anticipation of being ridiculed for poor performance, being called stupid, or the like). Reinforcement may be assumed to occur when the subject reproduces a correct item and is permitted to know that it is correct. Let this state of affairs be thought of as involving tension reduction. However, each successive task that is set the subject involves the possibility of failure, i.e., arouses new tension, and the more rapid the rate at which these tasks are presented, the less the tension will drop after each correct response. Parents soon learn the wisdom of spacing their demands upon small children for acquiring new responses. Each demand for learning produces an increased tension (renewed anticipation of failure, punishment, etc.), and if such demands come in too rapid succession, tension will remain chronically so high that the proper tension reduction ("success") cannot be experienced after a good performance to insure its fixation. Laboratory evidence in support of this theory as to why distributed practice is so much superior to massed practice in certain types of learning situations will be discussed in a later report.

The other implication of the present findings that seems noteworthy bears upon some experimental results reported by Calvin (1939). This investigator found that human subjects show better eyelid conditioning when an irregular temporal interval is allowed between successive paired presentations of the conditioned and unconditioned stimulus than when a regular interval is employed. In a previous publication (2), the present writer has suggested that this finding may be due to the fact that human beings tend to develop a "negative attitude" in many conditioning situations and that the more precisely they can judge when a conditioned stimulus is going to occur, the more effectively they can guard against the occurrence of a conditioned response. In the same study it was also conjectured that since the complex social factors that are presumably responsible for the development of negative attitudes on the part of human subjects in conditioning situations are not operative in animals, the latter should show better rather than poorer conditioning when the rate of stimulus presentation is regular. The results of the present investigation support this hypothesis.

Before concluding this paper it is perhaps worth calling attention to the fact that the curves for conditioning (Figures 13 and 14) and those for total activity follow divergent courses. Whereas the former present a general pattern of increment, the latter show more or less decrement. The conditioning process is thus to be seen as one of progressive differentiation and specification of response. In describing the development of a conditioned paw-retraction response in dogs, Culler, Finch, Girden, and Brogden (1934) say:

> During the early periods of training, the shock often evokes vigorous and varied activity (yelping, jerking, twisting, evacuation, to mention only the more evident manifestations of fright, escape or defense). . . . In these earliest stages we find no trace of a localized reaction (foot-withdrawal); the animal's activity all belongs to the general pattern of escape-defense. Now and then it misses the shock, but only by accident; the right forepaw moves in accord with general somatic activity and not in any adaptive manner. . . . Later, on the contrary, when the animal has achieved an adaptive response (foot-withdrawal prior to shock) there is but little resemblance. The localized, individuated response of a well-trained dog is as unlike his original excited, diffuse behavior as two acts can well be (p. 224).

Although it is evident that the process of individuation was to some extent involved in the conditioning of the locomotor response investigated in the present study, it was much less pronounced than in the situation just described. This fact probably accounts in large measure for the relatively greater ease of conditioning of a gross locomotor response than of a more limited and specific reaction such as paw retraction. Schlosberg (1934) experienced great difficulty in obtaining a stable conditioned leg-withdrawal response in rats, and the present writer has found in unpublished work that it is correspondingly hard to condition a type of pedal-pressing response which has been described elsewhere (18). If a generalization is here warranted it would seem to be that the more a conditioned response is permitted to resemble the response initially made to the unconditioned stimulus, the more rapidly conditioning proceeds.[13] There seems also to be a rather nice correlation between the phylogenetic position of an organism and the extent to which conditioned responses can be made to differ from their unconditioned prototypes. Man undoubtedly stands at the top of this scale. Whereas the conditioned responses which lower animals learn to make to signals of danger are, for example, usually not very different from those which they would make if the signified trauma were actually present, man, on the other hand, is readily capable of acquiring responses to danger signals that differ drastically from the behavior which would be manifested in

[13] [Empirical confirmation of this inference is supplied by the two following studies, 4 and 5.]

the face of the danger itself. This difference in ability is, however, apparently one of degree and is in no sense absolute.

Summary

The primary purpose of the present study was to test the hypothesis that anxiety reduction acts as a reinforcing state of affairs (as defined by the law of effect). To this end three experimental procedures, designed to provide three different degrees of anxiety reduction, were carried out, with both rats and guinea pigs as subjects. The results indicate that anxiety reduction is positively correlated with learning, thereby supporting the supposition that it is a reinforcing agent.

Various implications of this finding are discussed and contrasted with alternative interpretations suggested by the conditioned-reflex (associationistic) conception of the learning process. The latter is found deficient because of its emphasis upon the importance of mere temporal contiguity (paired presentation) of stimuli and its neglect of the factors of motivation and motivation reduction.

CHAPTER 4

AVOIDANCE CONDITIONING AND SIGNAL DURATION—A STUDY OF SECONDARY MOTIVATION AND REWARD

["The position is taken in this study that no comprehensive theory of avoidance conditioning is possible without taking the concomitant phenomenon of anxiety and its role as a reinforcing agent into systematic account" (page 124). In other words, it is here maintained that a simple associationistic account of the way in which living organisms acquire defense reactions is manifestly inadequate, and that the acquisition and perpetuation of such reactions prominently involve the law of effect. The experimental findings here reported support this position, but the accompanying theoretical analysis is now seen as unsatisfactory in one important respect: whereas the position taken in this study is that both fear and the defense reactions which it instigates and reinforces are acquired on the basis of a single learning process, present indications are that there are *two* forms of learning —problem solving *and* conditioning—and that all overt, skeletal adjustments (including what are here called "avoidance conditioned reactions") are acquired on the basis of the former and all emotional reactions (including fear) are acquired on the basis of the latter. If the reader keeps this dualistic conception of learning in mind and translates into these terms the results here reported, he will find that passages which seem somewhat involved are considerably clarified.

The reader is likely to have special difficulty with the concept of "parasitic reinforcement," which was introduced, under this name, for the first time in this study, although the underlying logic had been anticipated in earlier studies (Mowrer, 1938c; 2). The concept was rendered necessary by the attempt which the writer was still making, when the present study was published, to support a monistic theory of learning. With the development of a two-factor theory, "parasitic reinforcement" became unnecessary, although such a theory does not necessarily preclude its existence. Two-factor theory merely makes the phenomenon, if it exists, relatively unimportant (cf. 5, page 145).

This study was first published as a *Psychological Monograph* (1942), jointly with Ross R. Lamoreaux.]

Introduction

For the past quarter of a century much of the theorizing as well as research that has been carried out by American psychologists in the field of learning has been based on the supposition that the conditioned reflex is, as John B. Watson termed it, the "fundamental unit of habit." Since the phenomenon of conditioning has been traditionally linked, from Pavlov on, with the conception of learning through association, or paired presentation of stimuli, this has meant that associationism has been the predominant, if not exclusive, learning doctrine for a large group of workers in this field.

Within recent years, however, it has become increasingly clear that conditioning, on the one hand, is neither basic nor simple, and that associationism, on the other hand, is grossly inadequate as a theoretical interpretation. A decade ago Dunlap (1932) commented that conditioning, far from being the prototype of all other learning, is actually "among the most complicated of learning processes" (p. 85). Thorndike (1931) has likewise said that "the conditioned reflex is the one type of learning that manages, even more completely than maze learning, to conceal the true nature of the learning process in a mass of special conditions" (p. 113). And experiments by Hunter (1935a), Brogden, Lipman, and Culler (1938), and others on the relative efficacy of the "classical" vs. "instrumental" conditioning procedures (cf. Hilgard and Marquis, 1940) have not only further stressed the complexity of conditioning but have also seriously undercut the logic of association theory.

In a series of earlier papers (1, 2, 3; Mowrer, 1938c, 1941a; Mowrer and Miller, 1941) evidence has been advanced for believing that learning, in both conditioning and trial-and-error situations, is dependent, not upon the mere association, or temporal contiguity, of stimuli (or responses), but rather upon the occurrence of a state of affairs which has been variously designated as goal attainment, problem solution, pleasure, success, satisfaction, gratification, adjustment, re-establishment of equilibrium, motivation reduction, consummation, reward.[1] The Law of Effect, as recently reformulated by Thorndike (1931) and others (Hull, 1937; Mowrer, 1941a; Muenzinger and Fletcher, 1936), thus becomes the basic determinant of all learning. The present study represents an application of this point of view in the realm of

[1] For an analysis of other factors in conditioning, see Girden (1938), Grether (1938), Harris (1941), Hull (1934c), and Mowrer (1938c; 3).

avoidance conditioning and attempts to resolve certain paradoxes which well-established facts in this field constitute for associationism.[2]

I. Analysis of a Paradox

The experiment by Brogden, Lipman, and Culler which has already been cited serves especially well as a point of departure for showing the fatal defects in associationism. These writers have shown that conditioning is markedly superior in guinea pigs if the conditioned stimulus (a 1,000-cycle tone) is followed by the unconditioned stimulus (electric shock) only when the conditioned response (a short run in a modified activity cage) fails to occur within a stipulated period of time (2 seconds). In other words, these writers report better conditioning, i.e., a higher incidence of anticipatory responses to the "danger signal," in the group of animals in which shock was avoidable than in the group in which it was not.

From a common-sense point of view, this finding is not very surprising. But if considered in the light of traditional conditioning theory, it constitutes a paradox. As Hilgard and Marquis (1940) point out, the "classical" conditioning procedure has involved invariable pairing of the conditioned and unconditioned stimulus, on the assumption (derived from association theory) that this would provide maximal facilitation of the conditioning process. Yet the findings of Brogden, Lipman, and Culler show that, at least under the experimental conditions which they employed, an "instrumental" procedure, in which a conditioned response *prevents* pairing, gives decidedly better results than does the "classical" procedure. This breakdown of association theory raises the question as to whether "effect" theory can provide a more satisfactory explanation of the observed facts.

An important consideration which traditional conditioning theory has not ordinarily taken into account is the fact that the so-called unconditioned response is always, in well-designed experiments, more or less heavily rewarded. Thus, in the experiment just cited, the guinea pigs quickly learned to run in response to the

[2] Some writers have equated associationism, in the sense of Pavlovian stimulus substitutionism, with the stimulus-response "connectionism" of Thorndike. Instead of lumping both Pavlov and Thorndike together as associationists and contrasting them with the Gestalt, or "field theoretical," writers, the line should be drawn with Pavlov on one side and with Thorndike and the field theorists on the other. In so far as Gestalt psychology has a theory of learning and a concept of reinforcement, the resemblance to the law of effect is certainly greater than to the Pavlovian position. The "pleasure principle" of Freudian psychoanalysis is also far more closely related to the law of effect than to stimulus substitutionism.

electric shock (i.e., to make the so-called unconditioned response) because this action (by revolving the cage the required amount) automatically terminated the shock. And as long as the experimental conditions remained unchanged, running in response to shock would continue to be highly rewarding. This is obviously an instance of simple trial-and-error learning which is readily explicable in terms of "effect" theory.[3]

Fortunately no new principle is needed to account for the development of conditioning in this situation. Since the tone and the shock occur in close temporal proximity, they constitute together the stimulus compound which produces the running response. Since this response is rewarded (by shock reduction) on each occurrence, it becomes more and more strongly connected, not only to the shock, but also to the tone. Since the onset of the tone occurs somewhat in advance of the onset of the shock, there is an opportunity for the response to the tone alone, when this connection becomes sufficiently strong, to occur in advance of the shock. When the running response thus "moves forward" and occurs to the tone alone, it is said to have become "anticipatory" or "conditioned." But the same basic mechanism of reinforcement is responsible for the strengthening of both the connection between the shock and the response (trial-and-error learning) and the connection between the tone and the response (conditioning proper).[4]

---

[3] Failure to appreciate the importance of the rewarding, or adjustive, function of the unconditioned response has led to much confusion. The bothersome phenomenon of "adaptation" to the unconditioned stimulus, which tends to occur when this stimulus is of *fixed* duration, is a case in point. Culler and his associates (1935) have rightly stressed the methodological advantage of making the unconditioned stimulus subject to termination by the unconditioned response, although they have not offered a systematic explanation of this advantage.

(It nows appears that we have partially misunderstood the writings of Professor Culler on this score. In correspondence recently received from him, he states that it has been the practice in his laboratories to use an unconditioned stimulus (shock) of "fixed duration, except as it is *terminated by the animal's response.*" In other words, the shock lasts for a brief, fixed period (0.1 second or 0.2 second) unless the subject makes the appropriate escape response *within this period.* One of the reasons which Professor Culler gives for using a shock of limited duration is that subjects sometimes adjust to a prolonged shock by "freezing" to the grill instead of running, jumping, etc. As pointed out elsewhere (Mowrer, 1942), this immobilization to shock will not occur if the shock circuit is suitably designed. Other experimentation now in progress (10) is aimed at empirically testing the relative desirability of using a shock of fixed vs. variable duration in conditioning work. Our results to date support the position adopted above, namely, that, other things being equal, better conditioning results if the shock is always terminated on the basis of what the subject does rather than after any arbitrarily fixed interval.)

[4] [In the light of later studies this statement now appears to be inadequate. Effect learning is certainly responsible for the connection between the shock and the response which eliminates the shock, and for the connection between fear of the shock and the response that eliminates this fear. However, for reasons

Although it is possible, as just indicated, to bring conditioning within the framework of "effect" learning theory,[5] the paradox created by the superiority of the "instrumental" conditioning procedure over the "classical" procedure remains. On the basis of the analysis suggested above, the strengthening of the connection between the tone and the running response is dependent, no less than in association theory, upon the paired presentation of the tone and the shock. Since it is *escape from shock* which reinforces both the response to the tone and the response to the shock, there can obviously be no reinforcement, from this source at least, if the shock does not occur in conjunction with the tone. But, as the findings of Brogden, Lipman, and Culler indicate, a procedure which permits *avoidance of shock* results in better conditioning than does a procedure permitting only escape from shock.[6, 7] Association theory provides no satisfactory way of accounting for this finding, but by extending the analysis already undertaken in terms of the Law of Effect an explanation is soon forthcoming.

A reinspection of the results reported by Brogden, Lipman, and Culler reveals that there are really two paradoxes to be accounted for instead of one. Not only must an explanation be found for the fact that the instrumental conditioning procedure showed an over-all superiority to the classical procedure; some way must also be found of accounting for the fact that the animals which were subjected to the classical procedure made as many conditioned responses as did the other group in the beginning; but later, instead of making more and more conditioned responses, they made fewer and fewer. In other words, after an initial period in which the learning curves for both groups rose in a virtually identical manner, the curve for the classical-procedure group continued to rise for a time but more slowly, and then progressively deteriorated, whereas the curve for the instrumental-procedure group mounted steadily to a 100 per cent criterion. See Figure 21.

---

which will be reviewed later, it now seems likely that the fear itself is acquired through a different learning process, that of *conditioning*.]

[5] Cf. Hull (1937).

[6] The expressions *escape from* and *avoidance of* a noxious stimulus have sometimes been used in conditioning literature as more or less synonymous. In the present paper they are intended to have very distinct connotations. *Escape from shock* will here mean that the shock has impinged upon the subject but is then by some means terminated. *Avoidance of shock,* on the other hand, will mean that, in a situation in which shock might have occurred, it does not.

[7] When Brogden (1939a), using dogs as subjects, subsequently compared the classical and the instrumental conditioning procedures, he obtained about the same amount of conditioning in both cases. This finding appears to have been due to the circumstance that what was intended to be the classical procedure was actually also instrumental.

On the basis of these facts it would seem that with the initial appearance of a conditioned response (through the process of "parasitic" reinforcement [8]), new factors enter into the situation. It is as if there were one mechanism for bringing the conditioned response into existence, another mechanism for perpetuating it if it is "successful," and yet another mechanism for suppressing it if it as a failure.[9] If the conditioned response serves any "purpose,"

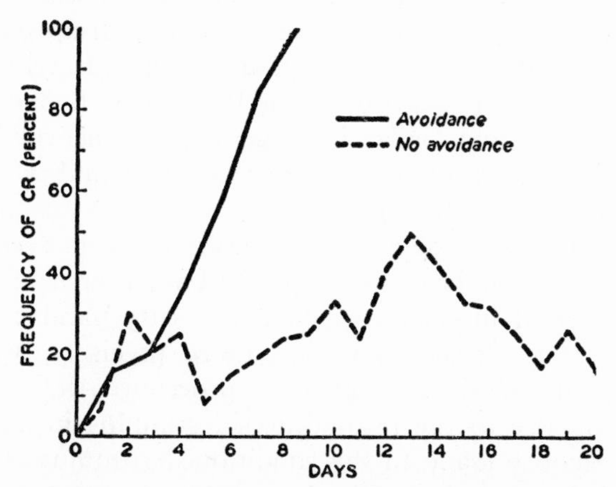

FIG. 21.—Comparison of amounts of conditioning obtained in two groups of guinea pigs. Based on the use of the "classical" (no avoidance) and the "instrumental" (avoidance) training procedures. This graph is a slightly modified version (reproduced from Hilgard and Marquis, 1940) of curves originally published by Brogden, Lipman, and Culler (1938).

i.e., if its occurrence averts (or substantially lessens) the impact of the noxious stimulus, it is perpetuated; but if the response has no such efficacy, it is in some way actively depressed. The problem is to determine precisely how this species of "reality testing" is so nicely accomplished.[10]

---

[8] "Parasitic" reinforcement is here used to designate the strengthening of the tone-running (conditioned) sequence through the action of the basic rewarding situation provided by the shock termination. The strengthening of the shock-running (trial-and-error) sequence may, in contradistinction, be termed "intrinsic" reinforcement.

[9] In order to avoid possible confusion, attention should be called to the fact that in both instrumental and classical conditioning, the procedure is exactly the same (uniform paired presentation of the conditioned and unconditioned stimulus) up to the point that the first conditioned response occurs. The mechanism through which the conditioned response makes its appearance is, therefore, necessarily the same in both cases. Only with the advent of a conditioned response do the procedures and the underlying mechanisms become differentiated.

[10] The expression "reality testing," as employed clinically, usually refers to situations which are analogous to the omission (extinction) of a conditioned avoidance reaction, "to see if the danger is still there" (cf. French, 1937). The type of "reality testing" here referred to is of a different kind, serving to determine whether the conditioned response will "do any good."

Let us first search for a possible mechanism whereby a conditioned response which proves "useless"—as conditioned responses nearly always do in classical conditioning—may be eliminated. Present evidence indicates that any response, if not in some manner rewarding, will cease to occur if repeatedly elicited.[11] But this fact is of little assistance in the present instance, since the task here is to explain how it is that a conditioned response that is being constantly reinforced "parasitically" may nevertheless disappear.[12] It is not, therefore, a question of accounting for the disappearance of a response in the absence of reinforcement (simple extinction) but rather of discovering some negative factor which operates in the direction of inhibiting or at least depressing the conditioned response, despite continued reinforcement of the kind which brought it into existence.

From a common-sense standpoint it would seem reasonable that if an animal gets "punished" regardless of whether it makes a given response or not, it might as well "take it easy" and not make the response. Or, to speak somewhat more precisely, we may say that since, in the classical conditioning procedure, the subject has to make one response to the unconditioned stimulus in any event, an additional response made to the conditioned stimulus is a waste of effort. In other words, a shock and two responses represent a more "punishing" combination than do the shock and a single response. Therefore, not making a response to the conditioned stimulus is from this point of view more economical and efficient than is making one: hence the tendency, when the classical conditioning procedure is followed, for the conditioned response, after making its appearance and proving ineffective, to disappear. As Brogden, Lipman, and Culler point out in connection with their experiment on guinea pigs, "Nothing was to be gained by turning the cage, since the shock came anyway; so when the tone began, they literally 'sat tight,' held the breath, and tensely awaited the shock" (p. 111).[13]

---

[11] One should perhaps say, "any *learned* response," although even reflexes can often be markedly diminished if repeatedly elicited in circumstances which deprive them of their normal functional utility (Mowrer, 1934).

[12] This phenomenon, which Wenger (unpublished manuscript) and Hovland (1936) have termed "inhibition of reinforcement," is not confined to the realm of avoidance conditioning. Pavlov (1927) discusses it at length in connection with classical salivary conditioning experiments. The problem in its broader ramifications will be considered in detail later.

[13] A little later these writers remark: "One group [of animals] finds a solution by turning the cage [in response to the tone]; the other, faced with an unavoidable shock, so places and tenses the trunk and limbs as to minimize its effects" (p. 111). This intimation that the classical-procedure group actually reduced the noxiousness of the shock by not responding to the tone seems un-

Although perhaps possessing some validity, this explanation is not very rigorous or compelling. A more satisfactory hypothesis is the following.[14] All striped-muscle reactions produce proprioceptive, or "backlash," stimulation. If, therefore, a given reaction, such as running, occurs to a noxious (unconditioned) stimulus, the resulting response-produced stimulation *follows* the noxious stimulus and will have no special significance. But if, on the other hand, the same response occurs to the conditioned stimulus in a classical conditioning procedure, then the response-produced stimulation will *precede* the noxious stimulus and will itself become (along with the conditioned stimulus proper) a "danger signal." The occurrence of running as a conditioned response thus becomes "punishing," i.e., arouses anxiety, and the subject is more or less powerfully motivated *not* to engage in this kind of behavior, since not doing so is rewarded through anxiety reduction (3). Thus a "secondary" (emotional) source of reinforcement tends to inhibit the conditioned running response (by rewarding inaction) even though the mechanism of "parasitic" reinforcement continues to strengthen it.[15] This inference is consistent with the observation that animals in a classical conditioning experiment are in obvious conflict between a tendency to make the conditioned response and a tendency not to make it

justified. The cage had, in any event, to be turned a certain amount before the shock would go off. This could hardly be done either more promptly or less painfully by refusing to move until the shock actually occurred (cf. footnote 2).

[14] This hypothesis was suggested to the senior author by some informal remarks made by Mrs. Barbara Lyndon. Miller and Dollard (1941) have independently evolved a similar theory. The basic idea involved in both cases is inherent in Freud's conception of inhibition as "a restriction which the ego imposes on itself in order not to arouse anxiety" (1936, p. 37).

[15] [In terms of two-factor theory, the analysis of this problem would go as follows. In the beginning of an experiment employing the so-called classical conditioning procedure, wherein the conditioned stimulus is, let us say, a tone and the unconditioned stimulus an electric shock of fixed duration, the first learning consists of the formation of a connection between tone and fear. Fear then motivates an overt response of some sort, but the shock follows all the same. Thus, the second thing learned is that action is followed by shock, and this fact tends, for reasons given above, to inhibit the action. In this way we deduce the fact that, as shown by the experiment of Brogden, Lipman, and Culler, the incidence of overt responses in a so-called classical conditioning experiment first rises (reflecting the association tone-is-followed-by-shock) and then falls (reflecting the association response-is-followed-by-shock). The first association tends to produce action, the second one inaction. Since it is the same shock that follows both the tone and the organism's response thereto, the fear aroused in both cases is presumably about equal. That inaction eventually predominates may be accounted for by the fact that action, or "work," is itself somewhat punishing (6); and, where the forces producing it and those otherwise tending to inhibit it are equal, what might be called the "effort syndrome" casts the deciding vote, in favor of inaction. We thus have a situation analogous to that existing in physical machines: where forces tending to produce motion are evenly opposed by forces tending to inhibit it, the result is no motion, since all physical systems have more or less resistance in the form of friction and tend to come to rest when not effectively propelled.]

(Brogden, 1939a). If, as in the experiment reported by Brogden *et al.*, the tendency not to make the conditioned response eventually dominates, this can only mean that the anxiety reduction resulting from not making the response is more powerful than is the parasitic reinforcement.

Viewed in this light, the slowness which subjects (both human and infrahuman) have sometimes shown in developing conditioned responses in experimental situations becomes less a reflection upon their intelligence and the efficacy of conditioning as a method than upon the understanding employed in devising the experimental procedure. The analysis just proposed to account for the conflict necessarily engendered in the classical conditioning procedure has various implications which cannot here be relevantly discussed. The immediate aim has been merely to account for the fact that a conditioned response, after first normally developing, tends, in a classical conditioning procedure, to become erratic and to deteriorate.

The task which now confronts us and the one with the most direct bearing upon the experiment shortly to be reported is to determine what sort of new mechanism, if any, comes into play when circumstances are such that a conditioned response serves to prevent the occurrence of the unconditioned (noxious) stimulus. Under these circumstances the connection between the conditioned stimulus and the response in question can be parasitically (associatively) reinforced only when the response fails to occur to the conditioned stimulus alone and is elicited by the added influence of the unconditioned stimulus. The question is whether there is any other source of reinforcement whereby a conditioned avoidance response may be perpetuated, independently of parasitic reinforcement.

In discussing what he has called the "dilemma of the conditioned defense reaction," Hull (1929) has formulated this problem as follows:

> For a conditioned defense reaction to be wholly successful, it should take place so early that the organism will completely escape [avoid] injury, i.e., the impact of the nocuous [unconditioned] stimulus. But in case the unconditioned stimulus fails to impinge upon the organism, there will be no [?] reinforcement of the conditioned tendency which means (one would expect) that experimental extinction will set in at once. This will rapidly render the conditioned reflex impotent, which, in turn, will expose the organism to the original injury. This will initiate a second cycle substantially like the first which will be followed by another and another indefinitely, a series of successful escapes [avoidances] alternating with a series of injuries. From a biological point of view, the picture is de-

cidedly not an attractive one. . . . The problem presents a fascinating field for experimental investigation (pp. 510–11).

Viewing the problem again from a common-sense standpoint, one might say that it is rewarding *not* to receive the noxious stimulus which the conditioned stimulus presages and the conditioned response averts. But such a statement is obviously vague and incomplete. In the final analysis reward appears always to involve the elimination (or reduction) of actual stimulation, i.e., a state of discomfort, or motivation. Therefore, *not getting something* can hardly, in and of itself, qualify as rewarding. Not getting "punished," or "injured," is rewarding *only if punishment is expected,* i.e., only if the subject is anxious or fearful, and if this expectation in some way gets *reduced.* In other words, if a conditioned avoidance reaction occurs when the subject is anxious and if the subject then ceases to be anxious (or becomes less so), such a response would be reinforced and might be perpetuated as long as the danger situation served to arouse a state of anxiety in the subject.

We know, of course, that fear, as an "emotional" reaction, is aroused by precisely the same sort of stimuli that produce conditioned avoidance responses, namely, by "danger signals." We have, therefore, good reason for positing that fear is likely to accompany avoidance reactions. We also know that, other things being equal, fear is likely to diminish with the termination of the danger signal. We thus arrive at the deduction that *conditioned avoidance reactions which terminate the conditioned stimulus (danger signal) will be reinforced by the resulting diminution of anxiety and will tend to be perpetuated, independently of the mechanism of parasitic reinforcement.* Just as the unconditioned reaction serves to reduce or eliminate the unconditioned stimulus (primary motive) and thereby perpetuates itself, the conditioned reaction, if it reduces or eliminates the conditioned stimulus (and thereby the secondary motive of fear), will likewise tend to perpetuate itself.[16, 17]

---

[16] Sheffield (1941) has proposed a different analysis of this problem which, in the writers' opinion, fails to take all the facts into account. [In a more recent study (1948), Sheffield reports a repetition (with minor modifications) of the Brogden-Lipman-Culler experiment, and tries to show that "contiguity" theory is alone sufficient to account for the results obtained. I now concede that "effect" theory alone is not adequate to account for the results here reported, but I am equally convinced that neither is contiguity theory. I now believe that *both* effect and contiguity are necessary to explain the results obtained in a wide variety of experiments, including the ones here discussed. For an analysis of the Brogden-Lipman-Culler experiment, in terms of Tolman's theory of learning, see Osgood (1950). These recent studies, by Sheffield and by Osgood, will be considered more fully later (10).]

[17] [It now seems likely that fear becomes connected with a danger signal

In a state of nature any overt response which serves to reduce the danger of one organism being attacked by another will ordinarily also eliminate or at least substantially reduce the cues which elicit this response. However, in the conditioned-response laboratory the seemingly universal practice has been to employ conditioned stimuli of arbitrarily fixed duration.[18] If the hypothesis which has just been proposed is correct, one would expect variations in the duration of the conditioned stimulus in relation to the time of the occurrence of the conditioned response to influence the extent to which the conditioned response can survive, without parasitic reinforcement. It is well established that the optimal condition for learning of a trial-and-error nature is one in which the factor of reward, or "success," comes immediately after the occurrence of the "correct" response. If the reward either precedes or follows this response by an appreciable length of time, other responses will be more strongly reinforced, with consequent impairment of the learning of the "correct" one. Since this is true,[19] it follows that if the anxiety which is aroused by a danger signal terminates either significantly before or after the occurrence of the conditioned avoidance reaction, this reaction will be reinforced less than if the anxiety were to terminate with the occurrence of the avoidance reaction. And since anxiety tends to be coterminous with the danger signal, it further follows that the conditioned avoidance response should be more quickly acquired and better retained if the conditioned stimulus ceases *with* the response than if it ceases either *before* or *after* the response.[20] This inference has been tested in the experiment which will now be reported.

---

through pure contiguity, without any reference to the reinforcing state of affairs provided by the termination of the associated trauma. And since overt avoidance behavior seems to develop as a reaction to fear, rather than as a *direct* reaction to the danger signal, the concept of "parasitic reinforcement" becomes superfluous. Whether this type of reinforcement is nevertheless a reality remains an open question see (9).]

[18] [Cf. preceding chapter.]

[19] Cf. Hull's discussion of the "temporal gradient of reinforcement" (1942).

[20] A conditioned response is thus seen to be *avoidant* as far as the unconditioned stimulus, or primary motive, is concerned; but in respect to the secondary motive of fear it is an *escape* reaction. Thus, continued successful avoidance of the primary noxious motive is made possible through the reinforcement provided by escape from the secondary motive. In other words, a response which develops on the basis of parasitic reinforcement may be perpetuated by a new form of intrinsic reinforcement which is made possible by the phenomenon of secondary motivation (cf. 5).

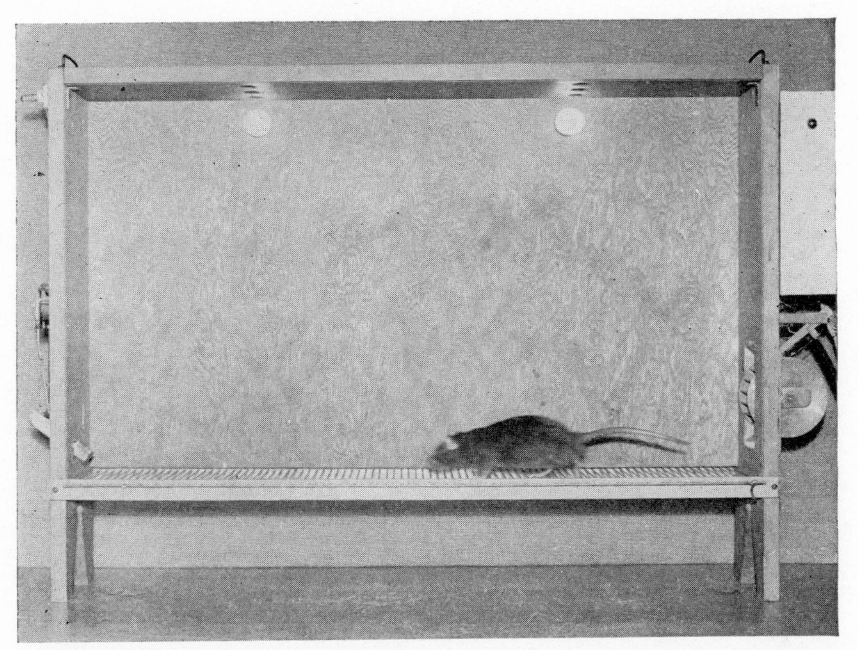

FIG. 22.—Apparatus for conditioning a simple locomotor response in the rat. All experimentation was carried out in a sound-proofed room with the apparatus internally illuminated and with a one-way screen between the rat and the experimenter. The experimenter presented the conditioned and unconditioned stimuli by means of a remote-control box.

II. Subjects, Apparatus, and Procedure

Laboratory avoidance conditioning in human beings is so likely to be complicated by uncontrolled factors [2, 3] that it seemed desirable to employ animal subjects in the present investigation. Twenty-four rats (Lashley strain), ranging from four to six months of age, were divided into 3 groups (1 male and 7 females to the group).

In Group I the procedure was as follows: After a rat had been placed in the apparatus shown in Figure 22,[21] it was allowed to remain unmolested for 2 minutes. At the end of this time a *buzzer* (ordinary annunciator type), which was mounted on the back of the apparatus, was sounded for 1 second. Following the onset of the buzzer, the rat had 5 seconds in which to make the response of moving from one half of the grill to the other (the dividing line being indicated by the white stripe on the interior wall of the apparatus). If the rat did not make the required response during this 5-second period, an electric charge was applied to and maintained on the rat's half of the grill until the response occurred. (The flow of current was approximately 1.1 milliamperes at 180 volts, with a 350,000-ohm fixed resistance in series with the subject, whose own resistance was usually about 1,000,000 ohms.) The number of "spontaneous" crossings from one half of the grill to the other was recorded, as were the latencies of both the conditioned and the unconditioned responses. The interval between successive trials was always 2 minutes.[22] All animals received 10 trials a day for 10 days, making 100 trials in all.

The procedure employed with the animals in Group II was exactly the same as the Group I procedure save for the fact that the

---

[21] This apparatus has been described in detail elsewhere (Mowrer and Miller, 1942).

[22] This interval may have been unnecessarily long; equally good results might have been obtained with an interval as brief as one minute. Earlier studies (3; Mowrer and Orbison, "Signal Intensity and Rate of Presentation as Factors Influencing Conditioning," Unpublished; Schlosberg, 1936) indicate, however, that intertrial intervals of substantially less than one minute result in inferior conditioning. Evidence has likewise shown that the use of a fixed interval between successive trials actually gives less "temporal" conditioning, i.e., fewer "spontaneous" responses between stimulus presentations, than does the use of a variable intertrial interval. If, for example, in trying to avoid temporal conditioning, the policy be adopted of withholding stimulation until the animal has been *quiet* for a certain period, then inactivity is the state which always precedes stimulation and thus becomes "dangerous." If, on the other hand, the stimulation comes on a fixed schedule, regardless of whether the animal has just been quiet or active, then quietness is not specifically penalized and activity is not unduly encouraged. As the results which are reported later clearly show, the amount of "spontaneous" or "interval" activity which occurred in this experiment was remarkably small.

buzzer was of variable rather than of fixed duration. In Group II the buzzer came on and stayed on in all cases until the rat made the required response, regardless of whether this response occurred within the initial 5-second period, to the buzzer alone, or had to be forced by means of the shock. In both instances the buzzer ceased the moment that the response occurred.

The animals in Group III were also exactly treated as were those in Groups I and II except as regards buzzer duration. In their case the buzzer always lasted for 5 seconds after the crossing response occurred, regardless of whether this was on a conditioned or unconditioned basis.

There were thus provided for Groups I, II, and III conditions in which the conditioned stimulus terminated, respectively, *before, with,* and *after* the crossing response, irrespective of whether it occurred as a conditioned or as an unconditioned response. (If in the case of the Group I animals a conditioned response occurred less than 1 second after the onset of the buzzer, the buzzer did not, of course, terminate *before* the conditioned response occurred; but since the conditioned response usually had a latency of over 1 second, this was not a serious consideration.)

It will be noted that in all 3 groups the so-called instrumental conditioning procedure was employed, i.e., the unconditioned stimulus (shock) was in all cases avoided if the crossing response occurred within the prescribed 5-second period after the onset of the conditioned stimulus (buzzer); and if the unconditioned stimulus was not thus avoided, it lasted only until the rat made the appropriate escape reaction.

In order to avoid possible ambiguity concerning the three procedures just described, they are schematically represented in Figure 23. Here the response, when elicited by shock, is represented as always occurring after an interval of 2 seconds (i.e., 7 seconds after buzzer onset). It will be understood, of course, that this interval was actually subject to considerable variation, being frequently either longer or shorter than the arbitrarily selected 2 seconds. The latency of the response when elicited by the buzzer alone is also arbitrarily represented as being 2 seconds. Here there was likewise much variability. But these oversimplifications, if kept in mind, will not impair the usefulness of Figure 23 as a kind of blueprint of the experiment as a whole.

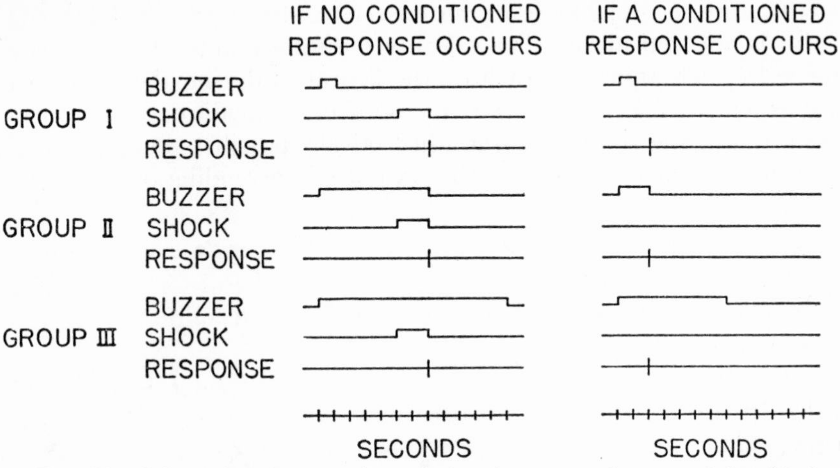

IF NO CONDITIONED RESPONSE OCCURS
IF A CONDITIONED RESPONSE OCCURS
GROUP I BUZZER SHOCK RESPONSE
GROUP II BUZZER SHOCK RESPONSE
GROUP III BUZZER SHOCK RESPONSE
SECONDS SECONDS

FIG. 23.—Schematic representation of the three procedures used in this investigation.

III. Results

The data obtained in this study fall into three main categories: number of conditioned responses, number of "spontaneous" responses, and latency of both conditioned and unconditioned responses. These items will be presented and statistically analyzed in this order, followed by a brief description of miscellaneous findings.

NUMBER OF CONDITIONED RESPONSES. The three curves shown in Figure 24 indicate that, whereas the incidence of conditioned responses in Group I was slightly superior to that of Group III, the incidence of such responses in Group II was decidedly superior to that of both Groups I and III. In order to obtain an estimate of the reliability of these differences, the following procedure was carried out. From Figure 24 two sources of variability in the incidence of conditioned responses are immediately evident: variability between groups and variability between days. Inspection of the original data reveals, moreover, a third source of variability, namely, variability between animals. But since the traditional "critical-ratio" technique of determining the reliability of a difference between two means takes only two sources of variability into account—in this case, variability between animals and between groups—it becomes essential, if this technique is to be employed efficiently, that the variability between days be in some manner eliminated from consideration.[23]

[23] If this were not done, spuriously large standard deviations would be obtained, with the result that the reliability of the differences between groups would be spuriously low.

This can be done by ignoring the day-to-day scores of individual animals and considering instead only the total number of responses made by each animal in each of the 3 groups during the course of the experiment, as a whole, i.e., the number of conditioned responses made out of the 100 which were theoretically possible (but unlikely). For the 8 animals in Group I these values, in ascending order, were:

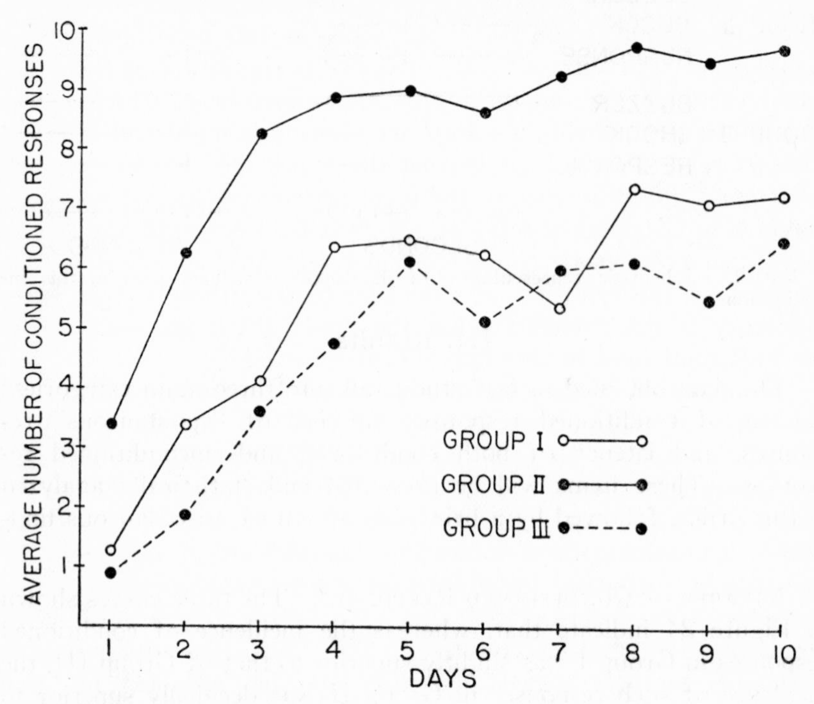

FIG. 24.—Average number of conditioned responses made by three groups of rats on each of 10 successive days.

31, 39, 49, 51, 57, 61, 74, 78. For the animals in Group II, they were: 64, 74, 79, 80, 86, 91, 93, 94. And for the animals in Group III, they were: 22, 23, 28, 53, 58, 60, 63, 65. (The number of unconditioned responses made by any particular animal during the whole experiment is, of course, 100 minus his conditioned-response score.)

When these data are subjected to treatment according to the critical-ratio method,[24] it is found that the C. R. of the difference between Groups I and II is 4.076, between Groups I and III, 0.973, and between Groups II and III, 4.761. Since n-1 was used in computing the standard error of the group means, it is legitimate to

[24] See Garrett (1939), pp. 210–15.

translate the C. R.'s thus obtained into *t*-values. When this is done (see Fisher's "Table of *t*," 1938, p. 177), it is found that the differences between the incidence of conditioned responses in Groups I and II and Groups II and III are "significant at the 1 per cent level." According to the logic of the "null hypothesis," this statement means that if the Group II procedure were not really superior to the Group I and Group III procedures, differences of the obtained magnitude would occur only once in 100 repetitions of the experiment. (In fact, a C. R. of 3.499 is significant at the 1 per cent level under the conditions of this experiment, which means that the C. R.'s actually obtained are even more highly reliable, but Fisher's table does not go beyond the 1 per cent level.) On the other hand, the difference in the incidence of conditioned responses obtained in Groups I and III (C. R. = 0.973) is significant only at the 35 per cent level. Since the 5 per cent level is conventionally accepted as the criterion of scientific trustworthiness, this latter difference is not "reliable"; but the other differences—which are the important ones in this experiment—are highly so.

Examination of the conditioning scores listed above shows that the range of these scores is only 30 (64–94) for the Group II animals, as against 47 (31–78) and 43 (22–65) for the Group I and Group III animals, respectively. The standard deviation for the scores of Group I is 16.10, of Group II, 10.42, and of Group III, 18.77. Converting these values into "coefficients of variability,"[25] and thereby correcting for differences due to the absolute values of the three group means, one obtains a *V* of 29.27 for Group I, 12.62 for Group II, and 40.37 for Group III. Such large differences in variability as these suggest that they may be "reliable," i.e., that the three groups may have actually differed not only in the average incidence of conditioned responses but also in the magnitude of "individual differences," or "variance within groups."

Determination of the reliability of the difference between two *V*'s is at best a cumbersome procedure and, when small numbers of subjects are involved, is subject to considerable error. However, a convenient and more accurate method of achieving the same end is described by Lindquist (1940, pp. 60–66) and is based on Fisher's *z*-test (not to be confused with his *z*-test in relation to correlation, or *r*). Employing this method one finds an *F* of 2.387 for the difference in variability between Groups I and II, an *F* of 1.359 for the difference between Groups I and III, and an *F* of 3.245 for the difference between Groups II and III. An *F*, based on groups con-

[25] See Finner (1935, p. 164).

taining 8 subjects (thus having 7 degrees of freedom), is significant at the 5 per cent level if it equals or exceeds 3.79. Although the obtained F-values for Groups I and II and for Groups I and III fall considerably below this figure, the F for Groups II and III (namely, 3.245) approaches this figure and therefore approximates significance at the conventional level of 5 per cent. This finding supports the suspicion that the 3 groups of animals employed in this experiment differ significantly in the variability (as well as in the means) of their conditioning scores.

This finding might be interpreted as meaning that the animals constituting Groups I, II, and III were not assigned to these groups on the basis of a truly random selection. Since there is, however, no empirical reason for believing that this was the case, the more plausible alternative is the assumption that the three different experimental procedures which were employed resulted, not only in differences in average incidence of conditioning, but also in differences in "individual differences." This latter supposition is further supported by Figure 25. Here it will be noted that the trial-to-trial variability manifested by Group II is conspicuously lower than that manifested by the other two groups. It is true that this kind of variability is not the same as individual-difference variability; but since Group II ranks lowest in both respects, a presumption is established that the experimental conditions under which the three groups of animals were tested actually influence not only the average amount of conditioning but also the factor of variability, as reflected by both indices.

No attempt has been made to establish the statistical reliability of the differences in the trial-to-trial variability of the three groups, since the use of the critical-ratio technique (otherwise indicated here) presupposes that the variations from trial to trial are normally distributed. From inspection this appears not to be the case; but since the differences in variability are so striking inspectionally, there is no urgent need for a statistical estimate of their reliabilities.

Although the group differences in the variability of conditioning obtained in this investigation were not predicted, they can be explained in a manner consistent with the general theoretical position outlined in the introduction, as will be shown later.

From Figure 25, it is evident that not only was there a day-to-day increment in the number of conditioned responses made by the various groups (see Figure 24) but that there was also a trial-to-trial increment. In order to make this latter phenomenon more obvious, the average number of conditioned responses made by all animals in each of the three groups on each of the 10 trials given on each day are presented in Figure 26. As might have been expected, this arrangement of the data again shows the Group

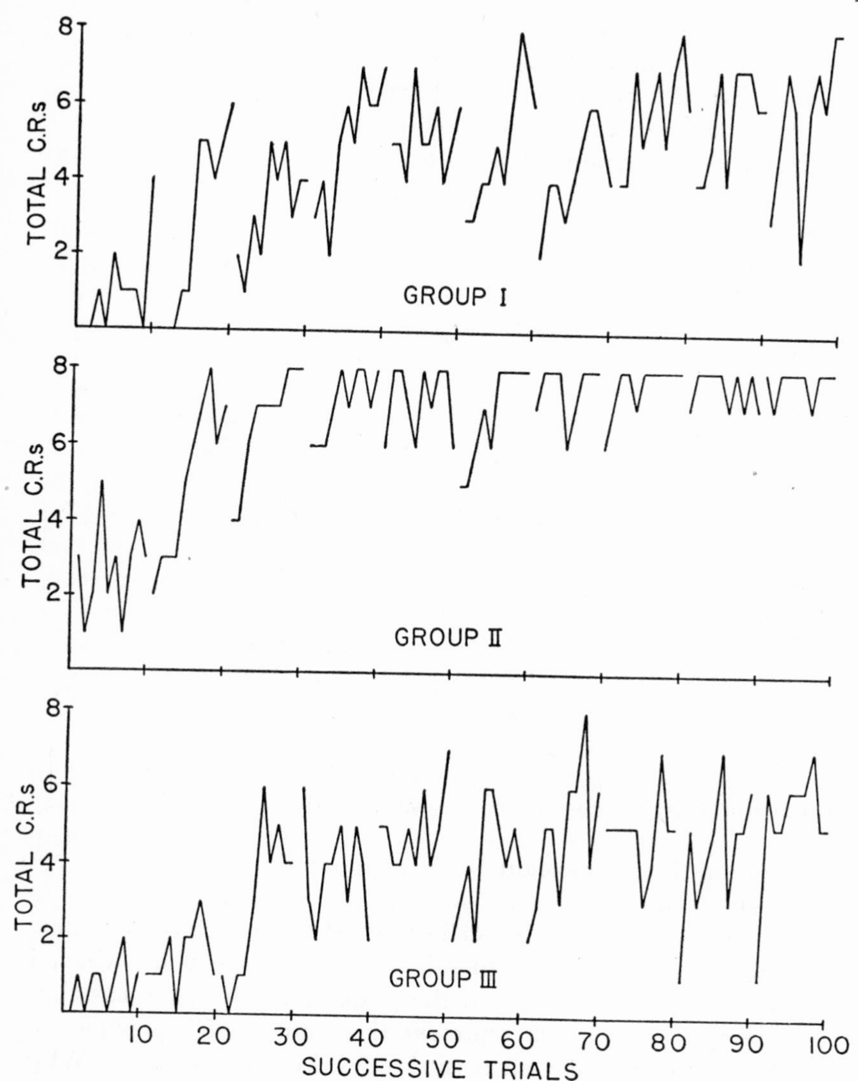

FIG. 25.—Total number of conditioned responses made by all subjects in Groups I, II, and III throughout the experiment. These curves are designed to show the group differences in variability from trial to trial. The discontinuities in the curves separate each day's trials from those of the preceding and following days.

II animals to be markedly superior to the Group I and Group III animals, with the former slightly better than the latter. Since these curves are based on the same data as are the curves presented in

Figure 24, the reliabilities of the differences between them are the same as those between the curves in Figure 24.

Number of "Spontaneous" Responses. The three curves shown in Figure 27 represent the averages of all responses, including conditioned, unconditioned, and "spontaneous," made on the 10 successive days of experimentation by the animals in Groups I, II, III. Since each animal necessarily made a combined total of

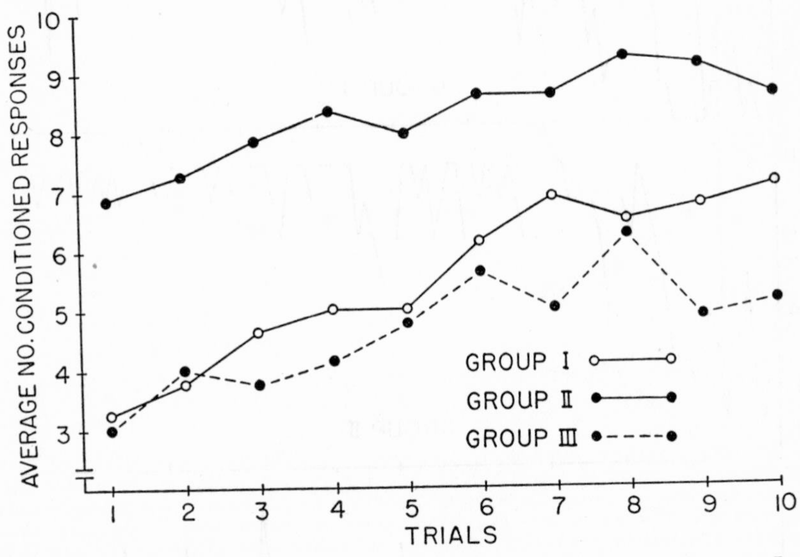

Fig. 26.—Average number of conditioned responses made by Groups I, II, and III on trials 1–10 on all 10 days of the experiment.

10 conditioned and unconditioned responses during each daily session of 10 trials, the average number of "spontaneous" responses can be readily ascertained by deducting 10 from each of the values represented in Figure 27. In other words, if the point which is labeled "10" on the ordinate of the graph is taken as the base line, the respective curves then represent the number of "spontaneous" responses made on the successive days by each group. When computed by the method described in the preceding section, the critical ratio of the difference in spontaneous responses made by Groups I and II is found to be 1.960, by Groups I and III 2.848, and by Groups II and III 1.188. According to Fisher's "Table of *t*," these critical ratios are significant at the 10 per cent, 2 per cent, and 30 per cent levels respectively. The values ("spontaneous" responses only) from which these critical ratios were derived are:

for Group I, 14, 16, 107, 107, 157, 191, 226, 239; for Group II, 18, 26, 28, 50, 76, 91, 96, 158; and for Group III, 4, 20, 41, 52, 52, 54, 64, 87. Although the range of scores in the three groups differs considerably,[26] the coefficients of variability are relatively constant, being 66.44 for Group I, 69.41 for Group II, and 54.00 for Group III. Since these values are so nearly the same, it seemed scarcely worth while applying a z-test to them; for all practical

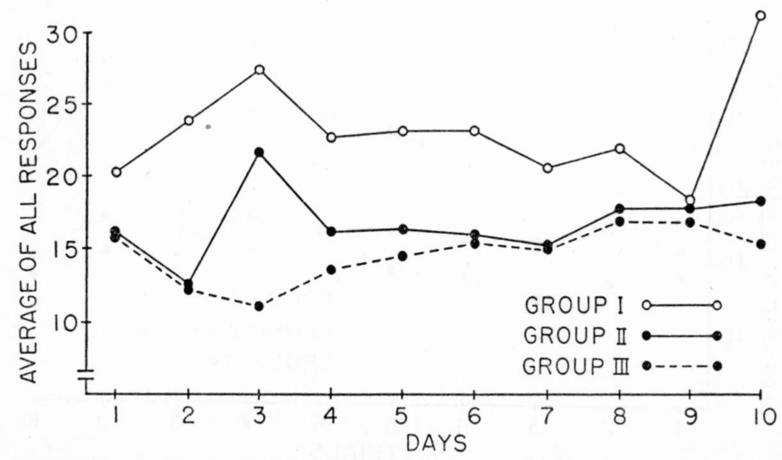

FIG. 27.—Average number of responses (conditioned, unconditioned, and "spontaneous") made by Groups I, II, and III on each of the 10 successive days of the experiment. Since the average number of conditioned plus unconditioned responses was always 10 per day, the number of "spontaneous" responses alone can be determined by regarding 10 on the ordinate of the graph as the base line. The sudden rise in the Group I curve on the 10th day was caused by a single animal and does not, therefore, represent a general trend.

purposes the differences between them can be assumed to be nonsignificant.

Noteworthy is the fact that the number of "spontaneous" responses made by the three groups of subjects does not correspond in any direct manner to the incidence of conditioned responses in the three groups. Whereas Group II, for example, is highest in conditioned responses, it is intermediate in spontaneous responses. This finding shows that the higher incidence of conditioning in Group II was not due to a higher level of general activity. In fact, when the rank-order correlation between conditioned responses and spontaneous responses is computed for all animals used in the whole experiment, an r of $-.13$ is obtained, which is nonsignificant. When,

[26] It is also striking how large the range is in all groups in relation to the mean. In other words, the individual differences in respect to number of "spontaneous" responses is, for some reason, unusually great.

however, the correlations between conditioned and "spontaneous" responses within each of the three groups are computed, an *r* of +.59 is obtained for Group I, +.47 for Group II, and +.78 for Group III. Since the number of subjects in each group is comparatively small, these values are not very reliable, but they probably indicate a real trend for conditioned and "spontaneous" responses to be positively correlated *within* groups. Reasons why they are not correlated *between* groups will be considered in a later section,

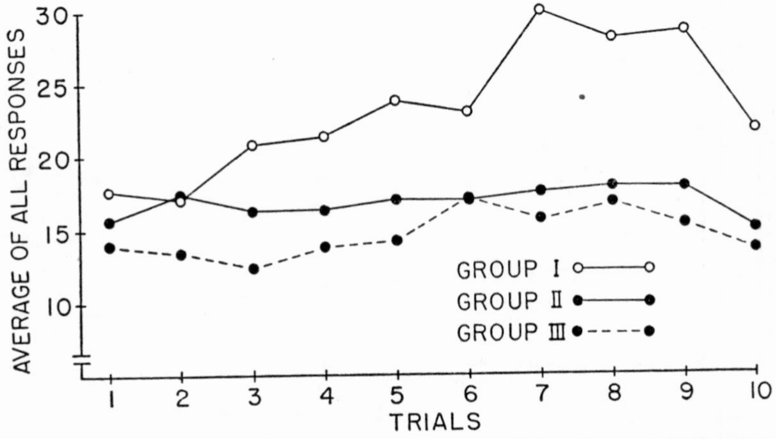

FIG. 28.—Average number of responses (conditioned, unconditioned, and "spontaneous") made by Groups I, II, and III on trials 1–10 on all 10 days of the experiment.

as will the meaning of the word "spontaneous" as used in the present context.

In Figure 27 there is no very clear-cut trend in the amount of "spontaneous" activity observed from day to day. When these responses are analyzed, as they are in Figure 28, on the basis of their average incidence on each trial within the 10 different daily sessions, Groups II and III again show no particular trend, although Group I shows a marked upward trend. An explanation of this latter phenomenon will be suggested later. Since the same basic data were employed, the reliabilities of the differences between the three curves in Figure 28 are the same as in Figure 27.

RESPONSE LATENCIES. Although no record was kept of the points at which "spontaneous" responses occurred during the two-minute intervals between trials, the latencies of all conditioned and all unconditioned responses, with respect to the onset of the conditioned stimulus, were timed to within 0.1 second. The daily averages of these values for Groups I, II, and III are represented in the three curves shown in Figure 29. As might have been expected, the Group II animals showed consistently shorter latencies than did either the Group I or the Group III animals. Not only do the latency curves reflect the same over-all superiority of the Group II procedure as do the conditioned-response curves: they inversely parallel them almost exactly. If Figure 24 is inverted and held in front of a mirror, the resemblance to Figure 29 is striking indeed,

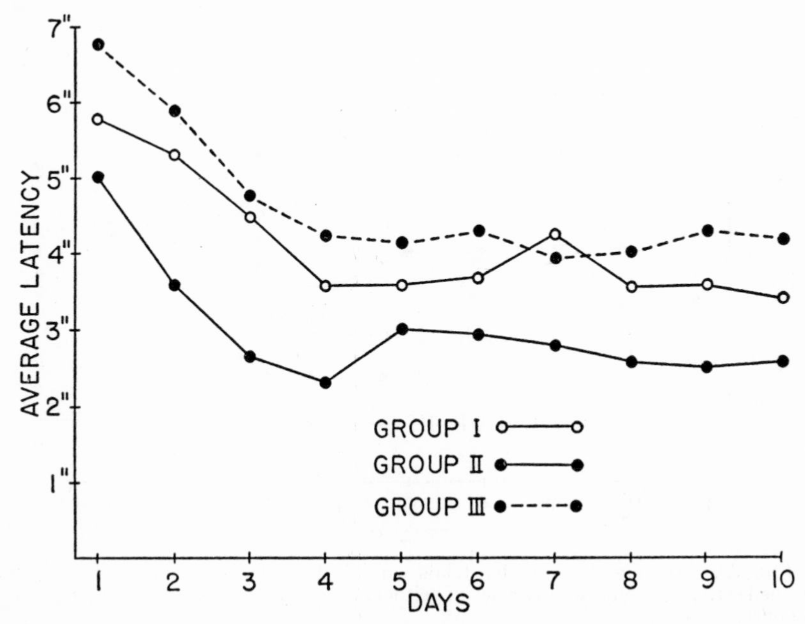

FIG. 29.—Average latency, by days, between onset of the conditioned stimulus and occurrence of either a conditioned or an unconditioned response.

extending even to the coincidence of the points at which the curves for Groups I and III cross each other. Response latency and incidence of conditioned responses may be said, therefore, to be more or less equivalent measures of the same phenomenon, at least as far as the present type of experimental situation is concerned. This is not, however, surprising when it is remembered that the criterion of a conditioned response is a temporal one.

When the latency data are arranged by trials, the curves presented in Figure 30 are obtained. Here again there is a marked resemblance to the conditioned-response curves shown in Figure 25, although the correspondence is not quite so close as between the curves in Figures 24 and 29. Although all 3 curves in Figure 30 show a substantial over-all decrement from trial 1 to trial 10, it must be realized that this is a composite picture of what happened throughout the experiment. On the first 3 or 4 days, when learning was most rapid (see Figure 29), there was also the greatest trial-to-trial latency decrement. During the latter part of the experiment, there was comparatively little change as regards both day-to-day and trial-to-trial performances. If the experiment had been continued for another ten days, it is conceivable that a point would have been reached at which the latencies of the earlier re-

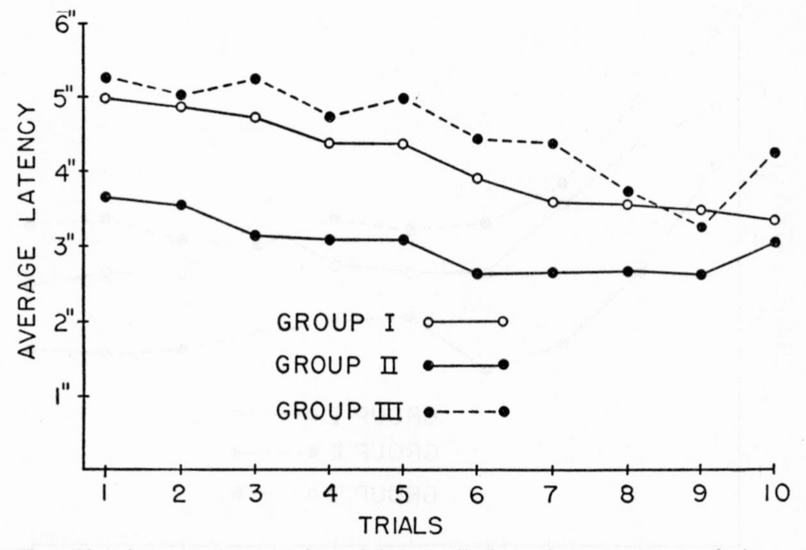

Fig. 30.—Average latency, by trials on all days, between onset of the conditioned stimulus and occurrence of either a conditioned or an unconditioned response.

sponses on a given day might have become actually shorter than those of the later responses on that day, due to the absence of further learning and the operation of opposing forces such as fatigue, loss of emotional tension, or the like.

Although it would have been readily possible to compute critical ratios of the differences between the averages of the latency data presented in Figures 29 and 30, this did not seem called for inasmuch as the earlier analysis of the conditioned-response data had already shown a satisfactory differentiation between Group II and Groups I and III.

Of especial value in providing an overview of the results of the experiment as a whole are the three histograms represented in Figure 31. These show the number of responses which occurred in Groups I, II, and III at various step intervals (0.0–0.3 second, 0.4–0.7 second, 0.8–1.1 seconds, 1.2–1.5 seconds, etc.) after the onset of the conditioned stimulus. By virtue of the practice, common to all group procedures, of allowing an interval of 5 seconds between the onset of the conditioned stimulus and the unconditioned stimulus, all responses which occurred within this interval are con-

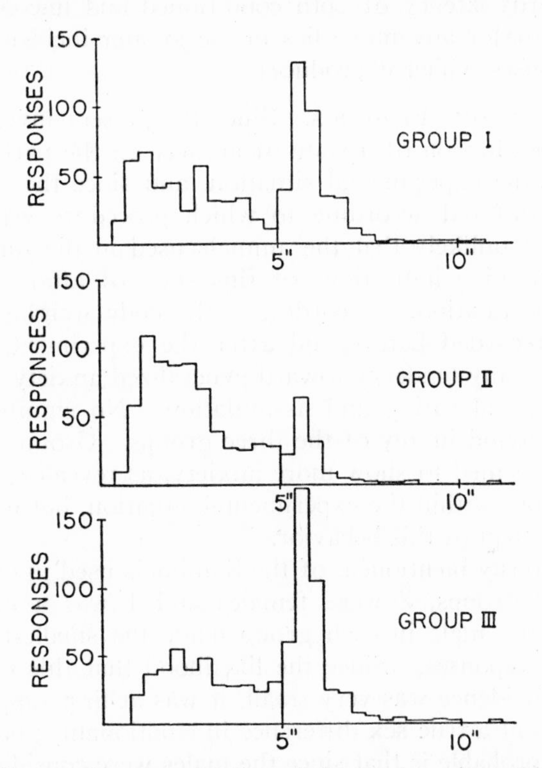

FIG. 31.—Histographic representation of the number of conditioned responses (within 5 seconds) and the number of unconditioned responses (after 5 seconds) occurring at various step intervals after onset of the conditioned stimulus. In Group I there were three unconditioned responses with latencies too long to be represented here (16.0 seconds, 17.8 seconds, 18.0 seconds). In Group III there were five such responses (16.0 seconds, 19.8 seconds, 14.6 seconds, 35.6 seconds, 13.2 seconds).

ditioned responses and all those which occurred afterwards are unconditioned responses. These histograms show not only the greater incidence of conditioned responses in Group II but also reveal the group differences in response latencies just described. Due to the greater incidence of conditioned responses in Group II, the average latency of all conditioned and all unconditioned responses (800 in all) made by this group was only 2.99 seconds, as against 4.11 seconds for Group I and 4.6 seconds for Group III. The latencies of the conditioned responses alone were 2.40 seconds, 2.40 seconds, and 2.83 seconds for Groups I, II, and III respectively. The average latencies for the unconditioned responses made by the three groups were, in order, 6.28 seconds, 6.00 seconds, and 6.29 seconds. Although the Group II procedure thus seems to be somewhat superior as regards latency of both conditioned and unconditioned responses, its major advantage lies in the greater incidence of conditioned responses which it produces.

MISCELLANEOUS FINDINGS. Since the present investigation involved the production of a state of anxiety on the part of the subjects within the experimental situation, and since the adjustmental possibilities differed according to which procedure was employed, it seemed not unlikely that the animals used in the three different groups might give indications of this state of affairs outside the experimental situation. Accordingly, the body weights of all subjects were recorded before and after the experiment, on the assumption that any tendency toward generalized anxiety might interfere with normal eating and assimilation. No significant weight change was found in any of the three groups. Group I and Group III animals seemed to show more anxiety, as revealed by urination and defecation, within the experimental situation, but no systematic records were kept of this behavior.

As previously mentioned, of the 8 animals used in each of the 3 experimental groups, 7 were females and 1 was a male. As it turned out, the male in each group made the smallest number of conditioned responses. Since the likelihood that this outcome was merely a coincidence was very small, it was at first supposed that it might represent a true sex difference in emotionality; but what now seems more probable is that since the males were considerably larger than the females, the shock which they received was less painful (due to smaller current density) and that they accordingly showed less conditioning, because of weaker motivation. This explanation is, however, conjectural. The problem deserves to be investigated systematically.

One other incidental finding is worth noting. The average latency of the response made by all animals in all groups on the first trial of the experiment (trial 1, day 1) was 6.15 seconds. On the second trial, the average latency was 6.39 seconds, and on the third trial, 6.45 seconds. On succeeding trials, this average declines. But the question is: Why did it rise on the second and third trials? If the buzzer-shock combination is first presented when a rat is on the right half of the grill, for example, escape from the shock involves his crossing to the left half. Since the animal has never previously been shocked on the left half of the grill, moving toward it and away from the charged right half will presumably involve little or no conflict. But when, on the second trial, the left half of the grill is electrified, the adjustive response consists of returning to the right half, where the rat has been shocked only a little while before. The conflict arising on this second trial presumably accounts for the increase in average latency from 6.15 seconds on the first trial to 6.39 seconds on the second. This type of conflict seems to disappear rapidly as training proceeds and interferes surprisingly little with the efficiency of the general conditioning procedure. It should be remembered, however, that a 2-minute interval was always allowed between trials; a briefer trial-to-trial interval would almost certainly cause this conflict to be more pronounced.

IV. Discussion

INTERPRETATION IN TERMS OF ANXIETY REDUCTION. The results of this study confirm the prediction that better avoidance conditioning will take place if the conditioned stimulus or "danger signal" terminates with, rather than either before or after, the conditioned response.[27] Such a confirmation strengthens the hypothesis from which the prediction was derived, namely, that *once a conditioned response has developed on the basis of "parasitic" reinforcement, it tends to be independently reinforced and perpetuated, providing that it terminates the danger signal and thereby reduces the subject's attendant anxiety.* In other words, a response which results in the *avoidance* of a primary (unconditioned) noxious stimulus may continue to occur to the appropriate danger signal for a long time, without further "parasitic" reinforcement, because *its occurrence provides escape from a secondary form of noxious stimulation, namely, fear.* Since fear, however painful it may be, will not kill an organism,[28] whereas the thing feared may

[27] Since the above was written, personal correspondence received from Professor Elmer Culler reveals that in unpublished experimentation he, too, has found that a variable conditioned stimulus gives better results than does one of fixed duration. He says: "My own observation confirms what you say, that the animal conditions more quickly and seems in general more alert and responsive if the sound is turned off at the instant of response; in other words, if the animal gets rid of the sound by reacting to it. I have made use of this method a good many times in conditioning animals myself; I thus agree that the animal works best when he is given opportunity to learn both that his response terminates the shock, and also that his response terminates the sound which signals or symbolizes the oncoming shock." Cf. also Parmenter (1940) on the use of a variable conditioned stimulus in producing extinction.

[28] In making this statement it is realized, of course, that if fear becomes too intense and can be reduced in no other way, suicide may be resorted to. Chronic anxiety states may also result indirectly in death by creating gastrointestinal,

do so, it is as if nature has provided this surrogate motive and source of reinforcement as a means of perpetuating responses which serve to keep the organism from re-experiencing the original, potentially fatal motive.

This interpretation squares with a number of observations which are not easily explained by the traditional associationistic theory of conditioning. A number of years ago Lashley (personal communication; see Hilgard and Marquis, 1940, p. 12) found in experiments on conditioned finger withdrawal in which respiration and heart rate were concurrently recorded that the withdrawal responses continued only so long as the visceral indices of fear continued to be elicited by the conditioned stimulus. When the conditioned stimulus ceased to produce emotional upset, the overt finger response quickly disappeared. This finding substantiates the hypothesis that the conditioned avoidance response is fear-motivated and will continue to resist extinction, in the absence of parasitic reinforcement, only so long as it continues to receive reinforcement through fear reduction.[29] Naturally such a response may have some "momentum" or "reserve" derived from past reinforcements, but this can be counted on to perpetuate the response for only a few elicitations if the secondary reinforcement here described does not occur.

That fear is intimately related to the perpetuation of conditioned avoidance response is likewise indicated by the observation, described by Hamel (1919) and confirmed by others, that such a response is more readily established and maintained if a strong rather than a weak unconditioned stimulus is used. On the basis of classical association theory, conditioning should result merely from the paired presentation of two stimuli, providing only that the second stimulus is barely strong enough to elicit the desired response. Intensity of the unconditioned stimulus beyond this point should have no significance, yet it patently does. On the basis of the hypothesis here proposed, there are two reasons why avoidance conditioning is positively related to the intensity of the unconditioned stimulus. The more intense this stimulus is, the greater will be both the intrinsic and the parasitic reinforcement produced by its termination. And since the fear response (itself a product

---

cardiac, and other "functional" disturbances which eventually produce genuine organic pathology. But these facts are not inconsistent with the thesis that fear is, in general, less harmful biologically than the thing feared.

[29] Another interesting fact, reported by various investigators (Hamel, 1919; Upton, 1929; Weaver, 1930) is that visceral disturbances always seem to be conditioned first, before overt avoidance responses develop.

of parasitic reinforcement)[30] is proportional to the intensity of the trauma which the danger signal presages, then the second-order reinforcement provided by fear reduction will be positively related to the intensity of the unconditioned stimulus.

Considerable discussion has taken place in recent years as to why it is that the conditioned response nearly always differs in detail from the so-called unconditioned response and may even be quite radically different. An example of the latter type is the difference between the behavior of a man whose house is actually on fire and the behavior of the same man if he is merely apprehensive lest his house should catch afire. On the basis of classical associationism, i.e., simple stimulus substitutionism, one would expect all conditioned responses to be more or less exact replicas of unconditioned responses. The present hypothesis, on the contrary, provides for a different possibility. Just as any response which reduces a primary motive will become more and more strongly connected with that motive, so will any response which reduces a secondary motive likewise become more and more strongly connected with that motive. In the present investigation, it so happened that the same response that reduced shock also reduced the secondary motive of fear by terminating the conditioned stimulus; but other responses not infrequently occurred while the buzzer was sounding, and if any one of these had been systematically followed by buzzer termination, it would very probably have been learned.[31] It is true that, by the mechanism of parasitic reinforcement, the same response which reduced the unconditioned stimulus tends to become specifically connected with the conditioned stimulus; but, as already shown, parasitic reinforcement is not the only mechanism which is operative in avoidance conditioning.

That fear is the common denominator in all avoidance conditioning situations is indicated, first of all, by the observation reported by Liddell, James, and Anderson (1935), and by others, that extinguished avoidance response can usually be revived by one or two presentations of the unconditioned stimulus alone. This reinstates apprehension and fear, and as a result the avoidance response returns without further paired presentation. The point is similarly made by the finding of Finch and Culler (1935) and of Brogden (1940a) that once an avoidance response is established, it can be kept going under threat of shock administered at ana-

[30] [For experimental evidence for believing that fears are learned on the basis of contiguity rather than as a result of "parasitic reinforcement," see 10.]

[31] [Subsequent experimentation by the writers has confirmed this inference (see 5).]

tomical loci remote from the point of application of the shock employed in the original conditioning. It also seems probable, if it has not indeed already been demonstrated, that a conditioned avoidance response, if it reduces the danger signal, could likewise be perpetuated indefinitely if the *nature,* as well as the locus, of the noxious stimulus were changed. That is to say, if a conditioned response were established with electric shock as the unconditioned stimulus, this response could probably be kept permanently alive under threat of the subject's being beaten, burned, or pained in any of various other ways.[32]

Especially pointed in this connection are the comparative data reported by Brogden (1940b) on the resistance to extinction of the same response, which was acquired in the case of one group of dogs as a means of securing food and in another group as a means of escaping (and avoiding) shock. This writer summarizes his results by saying that "conditioned flexion [of a dog's left fore-limb] originally reinforced with shock [reduction] will persist without reinforcement after a lapse of 6 months, over thrice as long as will conditioned flexion originally reinforced with food [hunger reduction]" (p. 287). Although Brogden inclines to the view that the passage of time is responsible for the differential resistance to extinction in the two cases, the hypothesis here proposed would explain this discrepancy as due to the fact that extinction of a hunger-motivated response starts as soon as the response ceases to result in hunger reduction, whereas a fear-motivated response may continue to be reinforced through fear reduction long after the situation has changed so that the conditioned stimulus will no longer be followed by the unconditioned stimulus if the conditioned response does not occur, i.e., after the danger signal ceases to signify real, objective danger. It is instructive that all instances of so-called "failure of extinction" reviewed by Hilgard and Marquis (1940) involve responses of the avoidant type. That all instances of "repetition compulsions" and of "functional autonomy" involve subtle sources of anxiety reduction also seems likely but cannot be fully demonstrated on the basis of available data.

The preceding discussion involves an assumption which has not been made explicit up to this point, namely, that fear, as a form of motivation which is itself due to a conditioned visceral reaction (Hilgard and Marquis, 1940; Mowrer, 1938; Wenger, unpublished manuscript), is easier to establish and harder to extinguish than

---

[32] See also studies by Miller (1941) and by Mowrer (3) demonstrating the reinforcing value of anxiety reduction, as distinct from reinforcement derived from the paired presentation of conditioned and unconditioned stimuli.

are conditioned skeletal responses. Clinical as well as experimental observations support this assumption but do not explain the underlying mechanics of the difference. That the fear response may be biologically very useful as a means of converting a weak but highly significant stimulus (danger signal) into a powerful motive, capable of eliciting and sustaining the most vigorous and varied behavior, is evident; but why it is that this "amplification" system is so exceptionally sensitive and efficient, in comparison with other conditioned responses, requires independent investigation.

Other Hypotheses Examined. As pointed out at the beginning of this section, the experimental findings of the present study confirm the prediction that if a conditioned avoidance response terminates the danger signal, it will persist longer, without parasitic reinforcement, than if the danger signal is of arbitrarily fixed duration.[33] Although empirical confirmation of a prediction strengthens the hypothesis from which it is derived, the same prediction can often be made on the basis of other hypotheses. In the present instance there are at least three such hypotheses, which will be examined and evaluated in turn.

1. Pavlov (1927) and his students have shown that if a conditioned stimulus terminates well before food is presented to a hungry dog, a less vigorous conditioned salivary response is established than if the conditioned stimulus lasts until the food appears. The former procedure has been termed "trace conditioning" and is superficially parallel to the Group I procedure employed in the present investigation. On the basis of the demonstrated inferiority of trace conditioning of the Pavlovian type, the Group I animals in the present study might have been expected to make a comparatively poor showing. There are, however, two salient differences between the Pavlovian situation and the one here employed. In the first place, Pavlov was using a training procedure in which the emotional reaction to the conditioned stimulus was appetite rather than anxiety; termination of the conditioned stimulus would there-

[33] [This statement should now be modified to read: "If a conditioned avoidance response, so-called, terminates the danger signal, it will persist longer, without further pairing of the signal and the punishing stimulus, than if the danger signal is of arbitrarily fixed duration." In other words, if the secondary drive of fear is held constant, an overt response which causes the fear-producing signal to go off immediately will be reinforced more than if the stimulus goes off before or after the response occurs. Obviously, if the intensity of the fear drive is varied, in whatever manner, the incidence of overt fear-motivated behavior will also tend to change; and if this occurs when an attempt is being made to compare the effects of different points of signal termination, the causal factors in the situation will tend to be confounded.]

fore be expected to have different functions in the two cases. Furthermore, Pavlov used the classical conditioning procedure, whereas the present writers employed the instrumental procedure. Even if the instrumental procedure were used in both types of situations, an important difference would remain in that in the one instance the so-called unconditioned stimulus (food) would be omitted if the conditioned response did not occur, while in the other instance the unconditioned stimulus (shock) would be omitted if the conditioned response did occur.[34] These considerations make it hazardous to interpret the findings of the present investigation in terms of Pavlov's observations and theories.

It could likewise be maintained on the basis of Pavlovian researches that the inferior conditioning obtained in the Group III animals was due to extinction, adaptation, or the like, which was occasioned by the fact that the conditioned stimulus always lasted for 5 seconds after the conditioned (or unconditioned) response occurred. So far as the writers are aware, no experiment has ever been carried out in which the conditioned stimulus has been continued for a fixed interval after the presentation of food in the Pavlovian type of situation; but they predict that the results of such a procedure would not be very different from the results secured by the usual procedure of terminating the conditioned stimulus when food is presented. Instead of trying to interpret the findings of the present investigation in terms of Pavlovian theory, it might be more profitable to examine Pavlovian findings in the light of present theory. This will not be attempted at this time, but the prediction is made that a salivary conditioning procedure, patterned after the Group II procedure here described, in which food would be presented as soon as the conditioned response occurs and withheld if the conditioned response does not occur within a standard period of time, will give better results than usually obtained by the Pavlovian procedure, and that the troublesome phenomenon of "inhibition of reinforcement" would be entirely averted.

2. Another alternative interpretation of our results is that the buzzer which served as the conditioned stimulus was so loud that

---

[34] To describe both food and shock as unconditioned stimuli is to illustrate the looseness and ambiguity with which the concept of the unconditioned stimulus has been used. If one is to be consistent about the matter, the unconditioned stimulus in the Pavlovian situation must be defined as sight of food *plus hunger*. Since food alone will not make a satiated animal eat and since hunger alone, in the absence of food, likewise does not elicit eating reactions, the response to food plus hunger is clearly a *patterned*, or discriminative, reaction which has itself been learned. In the case of avoidance conditioning, on the other hand, the response to the so-called unconditioned stimulus is not in this sense also patterned.

its termination was intrinsically rewarding, quite aside from any anxiety reduction that might have been involved. If this were the case, it would follow that a procedure in which the buzzer terminated at the instant that the conditioned response occurred would perpetuate a conditioned response better than a procedure in which the conditioned stimulus ended either significantly before or after the conditioned response. It has been shown elsewhere (Mowrer and Orbison, unpublished study) that if conditioned stimuli of varying intensities are employed with the Group II type of procedure, an intense conditioned stimulus produces better conditioning than does a weaker one. It may be, therefore, that part of the differentiation between the Group II results and those for Groups I and III was a function of the intrinsic reward value of buzzer termination. There are, however, other facts which make it unlikely that this is the sole, if even a partial, explanation of this differentiation.

In unpublished experimentation by the senior author it was found very difficult, if not impossible, to teach rats to perform any specific response as a means of terminating a sound which was far more intense than the one used in the present investigation as the conditioned stimulus. Moreover, if the intrinsic rewarding function of buzzer termination were marked, extinction in the Group II procedure would never occur, which has been shown in an independent study by the writers not to be the case. Finally, if buzzer termination had an intrinsically powerful rewarding, or reinforcing effect, the buzzer would be expected to have proportionately great potency as a motive. Although it must not be supposed that the buzzer had no motivational properties in its own right, these seem to have been comparatively trivial since, as Figures 27 and 28 show, Group I, for which buzzer duration was briefest, displayed the greatest number of "spontaneous" responses, whereas Group III, for which buzzer duration was greatest, showed the fewest "spontaneous" responses. Group II, for which buzzer duration was intermediate, showed an intermediate number of such responses. There is thus an inverse relation between "spontaneous" response and buzzer duration, which is opposite to what would be expected if the buzzer were a powerful motive in its own right.

3. It is also conceivable that the Group II procedure proved superior because of the so-called "law of emphasis," or "vividness." It is true that in Group II the "emphasis" conjecturally created by buzzer termination coincided with the occurrence of the conditioned responses, while in Groups I and III it did not. The results may,

therefore, be said to be consistent with the "emphasis" hypothesis. Whether it is actually the "emphasis" factor or anxiety reduction which accounts for the superiority of the Group II procedure could presumably be determined by substituting for buzzer termination, as the hypothetical "emphasizer," a flash of light or some similar distinctive stimulus which would not have, however, any particular value as a "safety" signal. The writers predict that such a stimulus would not materially affect the incidence of conditioning.[35]

Some Incidental Considerations. Turning to the incidental findings of this investigation, it is noteworthy, first of all, that there was a relatively large positive correlation between the incidence of conditioned responses and the number of spontaneous responses made between trials in each group, considered separately, although there was no such correlation when all groups were considered together. How can this outcome be explained? The solution seems to hinge upon the fact that in the present investigation there were two distinct sources of so-called spontaneous responses. Every student of conditioning knows that if a noxious stimulus is repeatedly presented at regular intervals, with or without an accompanying signal, subjects almost invariably show "temporal conditioning," i.e., they remain relatively inactive for a time immediately after each stimulation but then begin, as the time for the next stimulation approaches, to make, with increasing frequency, the response which is under investigation (along with other unrecorded responses) (2). The greater this tendency to make spontaneous, or anticipatory, responses on the basis of temporal conditioning, the greater the likelihood that the conditioned stimulus proper will elicit a response.[36] This observation probably explains why it is that, with conditioning procedure held constant, the subjects in the present investigation showed positive correlations between conditioning and spontaneous activity.

When, however, the conditioning procedure was varied, as it was in the three different groups, a new factor entered into the picture. It will be recalled that in the Group I procedure, the buzzer

[35] Professor D. P. Boder of Illinois Institute of Technology has expressed to the writers an intention of carrying out an experiment of this kind. [See 11.]

[36] Pavlov (1927), Hull (1942), and others have pointed out that temporal conditioning must be based upon some intraorganismic process, or neural reverberation, set going by preceding stimulation. This "stimulus trace," when it reaches the appropriate point (determined by the rate of previous stimulations), tends, in a way not yet understood, to elicit the response in question. Seemingly correct in principle but incomplete, this interpretation overlooks the fact that the first conditioning in a situation of this kind involves visceral reactions (Upton, 1929; Weaver, 1930) which are concomitants of anxiety. Once anxiety occurs, it may be that so-called spontaneous responses are produced by it rather than by the stimulus trace alone.

was sounded for only 1 second, with 4 seconds of grace intervening before the shock occurred. This meant that in those instances in which a conditioned response did not occur and the shock was presented, there were, in a manner of speaking, two stimuli which preceded the shock—buzzer and silence. Both, therefore, became dangerous and tended to elicit running (as well as other) responses.[37] Since a running response was counted as conditioned only if it occurred within five seconds after the onset of the buzzer and since silence persisted indefinitely, one can see why the animals in this group, being more or less "left up in the air," made many responses which would necessarily be counted as "spontaneous." The Group II and Group III animals, on the other hand, were never shocked after the buzzer had quit sounding; for them, therefore, silence was safe instead of dangerous. They would consequently be expected to show comparatively few spontaneous responses, in keeping with the observed facts. Since the Group I animals made the greatest number of spontaneous responses and made relatively few conditioned responses, one sees why the overall correlation between these two types of reaction was nil, even though it was relatively high in all three groups, considered separately.[38]

In the preceding discussion the assumption has repeatedly been

---

[37] The technically more exact characterization of the situation would be to say that both the buzzer and its "trace" preceded the shock and therefore became danger signals.

[38] These observations raise an incidental problem of very considerable interest. If, as in the Group I procedure, a danger signal terminates before the affected organism has had time to make the appropriate reaction, how is the organism to "know" when it is safe? The fact that the Group I animals made the greatest number of "spontaneous" responses suggests that they were indeed somewhat "insecure" or "nervous," i.e., were uncertain as to when they were in danger and when they were not. The animals were not, however, entirely without cues in this situation. Since the shock, if it occurred, always came 4 seconds after the buzzer (which lasted one second) had ceased, this point on the stimulus trace of the buzzer represented the region of "maximum danger," and later points on the trace became progressively less ominous. But even if the shock had occurred (in the event of no conditioned response) at highly irregular intervals after the buzzer had ended, there would still have been a means of determining when the shock had been averted and when it had not. Since the stimulus trace of the buzzer and the stimulus trace of the avoidant response would *never precede* the shock, then this combination would mean *safety,* as opposed to the *danger* implied by the buzzer trace alone. In short, as soon as the animal learned to *discriminate* between buzzer trace alone and buzzer trace *plus* response trace, it would "know" when it was safe and when it was not. Thus, even though conditions were such that there was no change in the *external* stimulus situation when the right response had been made, an animal could eventually learn, on the basis of *internal* cues, to feel rewarded (freed from anxiety) when it had behaved "properly." This analysis would appear to take us near an explanation (cf. the psychoanalytic conception) of certain forms of "compulsive" behavior seen in human beings and is suggestive of a way in which the notion of "conscience" as "internalized authority" can be made more concrete and objective.

made that, given appropriate conditions, anxiety results in agitated, restless behavior. The symptoms of common "nervousness" obviously support this supposition; but it is a no less familiar observation that anxiety may also inhibit or paralyze action. Why fear, or anxiety, has sometimes the one effect and at other times exactly the opposite one is a problem that has occasioned much speculation but now appears readily solvable. Whether fear results in agitation and flight or in frozen inaction seems to be primarily, if not exclusively, a function of the locus of the danger signal. If the danger signal is an *external* one, such as the buzzer employed in the present investigation, the resulting anxiety is almost certain to produce activity, since such behavior, if it carries the organism away from the danger situation or eliminates the danger signal in some other way, is more or less powerfully reinforced by anxiety reduction. On the other hand, if the danger signal is *internal,* consisting of proprioceptive stimuli produced by a previously "punished" response, then the resulting anxiety is equally likely to inhibit activity, since this is the most direct means of eliminating the danger signal and thereby reducing anxiety. The hypothesis that anxiety reduction reinforces whatever type of behavior accomplishes this end thus proves a unifying principle, explaining why it is that anxiety produced by "prodding," on the one hand, and by "punishment," on the other hand, have such unlike effects.[39]

CONDITIONING AS PROBLEM SOLVING. Comparatively few writers on the subject have explicitly regarded conditioning as a type of "problem solving." One obvious reason for this is that so long as a classical conditioning procedure is employed, no real solution to the problem thereby created is in fact possible.[40] There are, however, numerous advantages in taking a functional—some might miscall it a teleological—view of conditioning. Some of these advantages have already been indicated. Two others remain to be discussed.

In the investigation here reported, all subjects actually faced, as is always true in conditioning situations involving a noxious

[39] From this it follows that if an organism is being "prodded" but at the same time "punished" for every attempted adjustment to the first source of discomfort, persistent anxiety will result. Such a state seems to be a prelude to all neuroses.

[40] Cf. experiment by Brogden, Lipman, and Culler which was described in the introductory section. See also Girden (1938), Hunter (1935a) and Woodworth (1938). In personal correspondence, Professor H. S. Liddell has likewise expressed the conviction that classical conditioning procedure is "biologically senseless."

unconditioned stimulus, two problems rather than only one. The first of these was the problem created by the occurrence of the electric shock. The solution to this problem consisted of the animal's running to the opposite end of the apparatus. Some learning was involved in perfecting this simple adjustment; but since running in response to noxious stimulation of the feet has almost inevitably received some previous reinforcement, this response is likely to be relatively high in the initial hierarchy of responses made by rats to shock. Such learning as is involved at this level of adjustment is therefore likely to occur very rapidly.

The other problem which the subjects in this study had to face was that created by the anxiety caused by the danger signal. Anxiety, like shock, is also a noxious stimulus, or drive, and similarly demands adjustive action. The solution to this second-order type of problem was very easy of attainment in the Group II procedure, consisting of the same response as that required to shock, namely, merely running to the opposite end of the apparatus. This response immediately eliminated the danger signal and was reinforced, presumably, by marked anxiety reduction. In the Group I and Group III procedures, on the other hand, no such ideal solution was available. It is true that if, in either case, an animal responded to the danger signal within 5 seconds after its onset, the animal avoided shock; but as already pointed out, such a response was not accompanied by buzzer termination and anxiety reduction. In other words, in both the Group I and Group III procedures the best possible solution to the problem created by the buzzer-induced anxiety was distinctly inferior to the solution that was possible in the Group II procedure. It is almost axiomatic, therefore, that the incidence of conditioned responses in these two relatively unfavorable procedures should have been significantly lower than in the optimal Group II procedure.

This line of analysis leads to an explanation of the finding that the Group I and Group III animals showed not only less conditioning but also greater variability than did the Group II animals, both as regards "individual differences" for the experiment as a whole and trial-to-trial group performances (see Figure 25). When one views the problem created by the buzzer in the 3 groups in terms of the goodness of adjustment (to anxiety) which was possible, it becomes understandable that the procedure which provided the best possibility of adjustment (Group II) should have produced least variability. If an organism has found a good solution to a problem, it is much less likely to continue "searching" for a better one than is an organism that has found a less good solution or none at all. In other words, since exploratory behavior plays so large a role in the adjustmental process, the continuation of response variation in the latter type of situation is clearly an advantage biologically. As Dodge (1931) has pointed out and Boring (1941) has re-emphasized, we have been too long content to regard behavior variability as a statistical rather than as a psychological problem. The connection between this phenomenon and what may be called goodness of adjustment is patent but needs to be investigated in detail.

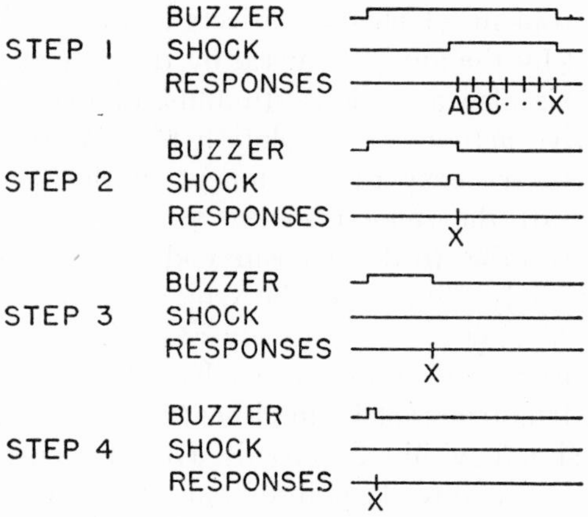

FIG. 32.—Schematic representation of the relation between trial-and-error learning and conditioning.

Of particular interest from a systematic point of view is the fact that by regarding conditioning as a kind of second-order problem-solving behavior, it can be brought into an orderly relationship to so-called trial-and-error learning, or "simple" problem solving. This relationship is schematically represented in Figure 32. Originally (step 1) the buzzer does not "mean" danger to the rat and elicits no response of any interest (to the experimenter). When the shock occurs, it produces various responses, *A, B, C, . . . X* happens to be the "correct" (shock-reducing) response, consisting in this instance of running to the opposite end of the apparatus. After a few repetitions, *X moves forward*—or *upward,* if one wishes to preserve the hierarchical conceptualization—and occurs without delay or intervention of other responses, when the shock is presented (step 2). This "coming forward" is, of course, the phenomenon ordinarily designated as trial-and-error learning and is based upon the mechanism of "intrinsic" (shock-reduction) reinforcement mentioned above. But while this first-order type of learning has been going on, something else has been happening, i.e., a connection has been developing, not only between the shock and *X*, but also (by "parasitic" reinforcement) between the buzzer and *X*. Under the ideal conditions provided by the Group II procedure, it is usually only a matter of a few more trials after the shock-*X* connection has become prompt and specific until the buzzer-*X* connection becomes strong enough for the buzzer alone to elicit *X* (step 3). When this happens, a conditioned response is said to have occurred. In other words, the response, *X*, has continued its forward march and has become anticipatory, or avoidant, with respect to the shock. If, as in the Group II procedure, the conditioned response immediately terminates the buzzer, it has a tendency to move forward still further and to occur the instant that the buzzer is sounded (step 4). Trial-and-error learning and conditioning thus become merely different aspects of, or stages in, a single, continuous adjustive process.[41]

This continuity between trial-and-error learning and conditioning has been generally overlooked, or ignored, in the past, largely for the reason that most investigators have concerned themselves more or less exclusively with only one of these phenomena. Both must be studied, preferably simultaneously, if their complementary, interrelated character is to be observed and understood.

The distinction which Pavlov (1927) and his followers have made between unconditioned and conditioned responses was adumbrated in 1906 by Sherrington, who proposed a functional division of behavior into *consummatory* responses and *anticipatory* responses. Although useful as a first approximation, this dichotomy

---

[41] The schematization shown in Figure 32 is deliberately incomplete (for sake of simplicity) in that it shows *X* as the only response occurring to the buzzer. As indicated earlier, a conditioned stimulus almost always elicits many responses other than the one which the experimenter is specifically prepared to observe and record. In a situation of the kind under discussion, the conditioned stimulus always produces more or less anxiety, which may then produce a wide variety of reactions in its own right. [An analysis of this same problem in terms of a two-factor theory of learning would go something like this. Through trial-and-error learning, the overt response which is effective in terminating the shock moves forward, as shown in steps 1 and 2. But at the same time, a second form of learning is occurring: through conditioning, the fear reaction, which was originally elicited by the shock, becomes shifted to the buzzer signal. As this happens, a *derived* form of trial-and-error learning begins: the overt response which is effective in terminating *the fear* moves forward, as shown in steps 3 and 4. There is thus trial-and-error learning (a) at the primary-drive level and (b) at the derived-drive level; but in both instances it is essentially the same form of learning that is involved. However, the "leap" from the lower of these levels to the higher one is evidently made possible by a different form of learning, namely conditioning. If this type of analysis is correct, then one should apply the term "conditioned reaction" not to the overt response that serves to terminate the danger signal and the attendant fear, but rather to the connection between the signal and the fear. See 9 and 10.]

is not entirely satisfactory for the reason that a response which is anticipatory with respect to one type of problem (drive) may be consummatory with respect to another. Thus, in the present study a conditioned response made under the Group II procedure is indeed anticipatory, or avoidant, with respect to the shock; but it is consummatory with respect to the anxiety created by the buzzer.[42] This fact provides a partial explanation of how it is that so much behavior gives the illusion of being either teleological (caused by events that have not yet occurred) or "functionally autonomous" (persisting without motivation and reward). In the Group II procedure, which seems fairly to typify those situations in which avoidance conditioning most commonly and efficiently occurs in nature, shock avoidance is reinforced and perpetuated by anxiety reduction. The shock, without occurring, does indeed seem to influence the animal's behavior; but this relationship is only apparent. As already shown, the animal's behavior can be entirely accounted for in terms of the danger signal, ensuing anxiety, and anxiety reduction, without any reference to the shock, except to the extent that its *past* occurrence in conjunction with the danger signal is responsible for the development of the anxiety reaction and for the parasitic reinforcement which initially brings the avoidance response into existence.

Although no empirical data are reported in this study concerning extinction, the hypothesis supported by the results which are here described generates certain definite expectations concerning extinction. On the basis of this hypothesis, one would predict that if three groups of subjects were all conditioned by the same procedure, i.e., by either the Group I, Group II, or Group III procedure, and were then submitted, respectively, to extinction involving each of these three procedures, marked differences in resistance to extinction would be found, corresponding to the effectiveness which the three procedures have in producing conditioning. This prediction can be easily tested and, if confirmed, would provide further substantiation of the general point of view here advanced.

There is a growing body of evidence that extinction depends upon the existence of an unfavorable balance between the fatigue (stimulation increase) generated by an act and the amount of reward (stimulation decrease) thereby attained. (See 6.) This hypothesis provides an explanation of why it is that massing of trials accelerates extinction and retards acquisition (3). Car-

[42] Another difficulty arises in trying to determine, in a series of instrumental acts such as those involved in running a maze, which responses are anticipatory and which consummatory.

ried a step further, this analysis leads to another prediction. In any situation in which anxiety is the chief motive, anxiety reduction (reward) is a function, among other things, of the rate at which the danger signal is presented. From this it follows that massing of trials would be even more effective in producing extinction and in retarding acquisition in the case of avoidance conditioning than in other forms of conditioning. Further investigation will be required to determine whether this is actually true.

So-called "spinal conditioning" is one of the few phenomena which do not readily fit into the theory of avoidance conditioning here advanced.[43] Since the autonomic nervous system is presumably disconnected in a spinal-conditioning preparation from the caudal segment of the central nervous system in which conditioning occurs, it is unlikely that anxiety can play any role in learning of this kind. This (plus the sparsity of association centers outside the brain) may account for the fact that spinal and other forms of subcortical conditioning are, as Pavlov has shown (1927), ordinarily so difficult to be obtained. That spinal conditioning can occur at all may conceivably be due entirely to the parasitic reinforcement produced by termination of the unconditioned stimulus.

Summary

Earlier experimentation has shown that the "instrumental" conditioning procedure gives results which are dramatically superior to those obtained by the "classical" conditioning procedure in situations in which the unconditioned stimulus is an electrical shock or similar noxious event. Analysis of the reasons for this difference leads to the deduction that the "instrumental" procedure should give better results still if modified so that the conditioned stimulus, or "danger signal," terminates at the moment that the conditioned response occurs, instead of lasting for an arbitrarily fixed period of time.

This deduction is tested with three groups of rats in which the conditioned stimulus regularly terminates before (Group I), with (Group II), and after (Group III) the conditioned response. The fact that the second of these procedures gives conspicuously better conditioning than either of the other two is taken as confirmation of the hypothesis from which the deduction was derived. This hypothesis, in brief, is that *a conditioned avoidance response de-*

[43] [A study recently reported by Kellogg (1949) has reopened the question as to whether "spinal conditioning" really occurs.]

velops on the basis of "parasitic" reinforcement but is independently perpetuated, under favorable conditions, by the reinforcement resulting from the anxiety reduction which accompanies termination of the conditioned stimulus. Possible alternative interpretatons of the obtained results are evaluated and differential predictions made.

The Group II procedure was found to give not only better conditioning but also less variability. If conditioning, like trial-and-error learning, is seen as an adjustive process, this finding becomes intelligible, since variability would be expected to be inversely correlated with the goodness of the adjustment which any particular conditioning procedure makes possible.

Although there are pronounced group differences in the number of "spontaneous" responses made between trials, there is no over-all correlation between such responses and conditioning. This finding negates the otherwise possible inference that the greater number of conditioned responses made by the Group II animals was due merely to a greater tendency toward agitated behavior. The fact that there is, however, a sizable positive correlation between these two phenomena within each of the three groups is discussed and an explanation proposed.

The latencies of both the conditioned and the unconditioned responses made by the animals in all three groups were recorded and analyzed. These data again show the Group II procedure to be markedly superior to the other two and lead to a further discussion of the continuity between trial-and-error learning and conditioning.

The position is taken that no comprehensive theory of avoidance conditioning is possible without taking the concomitant phenomenon of anxiety and its role as a reinforcing agent into systematic account. When this is done, numerous problems, which have been perpetual paradoxes from the point of view of associationism, become readily solvable. Some of the questions considered in this connection are:

a) Why do conditioned skeletal responses of an avoidant nature soon disappear when the conditioned stimulus ceases to produce visceral disturbances?

b) Why is avoidance conditioning proportional to the intensity of the unconditioned noxious stimulus?

c) Why are avoidance responses often very different from the responses made to the so-called unconditioned stimulus?

d) Why can an avoidance response be perpetuated by dangers very different from the one involved in the original conditioning situation?

e) Why are avoidance responses more resistant to extinction than are other conditioned responses?

f) Why does behavior sometimes seem to be "teleological" or "functionally autonomous"?

g) Why does "classical" conditioning result in "inhibition of reinforcement"?

h) Is the "massing of practice" more influential in determining avoidance conditioning and extinction than in determining other kinds of learning?

i) Why does anxiety sometimes produce activity and at other times inhibit activity?

CHAPTER 5

FEAR AS AN INTERVENING VARIABLE IN AVOIDANCE CONDITIONING

[This study follows as a direct sequel to the preceding one and, in one sense, completes the cycle of inquiry which was initiated by the paper here reproduced as Chapter 1. It confirms, more directly and more decisively than do the other studies, the hypothesis put forward in that paper, namely that fear is fundamentally a drive, a producer of *action;* that fear reduction is a powerful reinforcer of such action; and that the *inhibitory* effect of fear is an indirect rather than a direct one.

The results of this study confirm certain well-known clinical views concerning the nature of neurotic symptoms (as "habits" which reduce anxiety), but they raise important difficulties for traditional learning theory. They show that some of the responses which have commonly been termed "conditioned responses" are heavily dependent upon motivation and "effect." This outcome at first seemed to cast doubt upon the reality of conditioning, as that form of learning which purportedly occurs through the mere paired presentation, or contiguity, of stimuli, without any reference to "effect." What later became evident was that the concept of conditioning has been brought into jeopardy through *misuse* and *overextension.* As a restricted process, whereby *emotional* reactions are acquired, conditioning still appears to be a genuine phenomenon; but it should not be extended to include the process whereby "habits," i.e., responses involving the skeletal musculature, are acquired (see 9, 10).

Although the present study takes the useful step of positing fear as an *intervening variable* between the danger signal and the *so-called* conditioned response (rather than viewing both as immediately produced by the conditioned stimulus, or danger signal), it does not take the next requisite step of regarding fear itself as a truly conditioned reaction, which is acquired in a manner qualitatively distinct from the process of reinforcement whereby problem-solving behavior is acquired. (This step is anticipated when the authors say: "Whether an anticipatory response which reduces fear but is radically different from the response which reduces the traumatic stimulus of which the fear is premonitory should be called a 'conditioned response' is perhaps debatable; but it is certainly legitimate to say that it is produced by the conditioned stimulus, provided we do not lose sight of the fact that the occurrence of the fear is an essential intermediate step." (See page

131.) Bracketed footnotes are again used as an aid to the reader in giving the experimental findings here reported the fully elaborated interpretation which now seems appropriate.

This paper was initially published, jointly with Ross R. Lamoreaux, in *The Journal of Comparative Psychology* (1946).]

Conditioning has commonly been assumed to exemplify associative learning in purest form. But the acceptance of such a view has led to so many difficulties that most contemporary students of learning have either abandoned it altogether or introduced extensive qualifications.

The basic defect in a purely associative interpretation of conditioning is that it denies or at least neglects the phenomenon of motivation. For Pavlov and many of his earlier followers, the mere *paired presentation* (in *temporal contiguity,* as traditional associationists would say) of two stimuli was all that was necessary for conditioning to occur, provided the second of these stimuli, the so-called unconditioned one, was capable from the outset of producing some uniform response. Thus, the ticking of a metronome followed by the presentation of food was regarded as sufficient to cause the salivary response, which initially occurred only to the food, to come forward in time, and to occur, as a so-called conditioned response, to the metronome alone. One discovers only incidentally in reading Pavlov that, in order for this type of learning to take place, it was necessary for his experimental animals to be *hungry;* and nowhere does Pavlov seriously consider the possibility that perhaps the most significant thing about the food, or so-called unconditioned stimulus, in experiments of this kind is, not that it produces salivation, but that it *reduces hunger.* We now know that to talk about the metronome and the food as if they were the only relevant variables in the experimental situation is to obscure important psychological realities and to torture one's conception of the learning process into a mold that is not only vastly oversimplified but probably also wrong in principle.[1]

Actually Pavlov's famous reference experiment with the salivary response is a peculiarly bad one for understanding the condi-

[1] For Pavlov the strengthening, or reinforcement, of new stimulus-response connections was exclusively a function of paired presentation of stimuli. Our assumption is that reward, in the sense of drive reduction, is the critical element in reinforcement (cf. Hull, 1943; Mowrer and Lamoreaux, 3). [The author's current view is that there are *two* learning processes, two forms of reinforcement: problem solving, which is based on drive reduction; and conditioning, which apparently involves pure contiguity (9, 10).]

tioning process. Bekhterev's technique for studying avoidance conditioning (Pavlov's work was largely restricted to appetitive conditioning) makes it possible to see—or, should we say, impossible not to see—the really essential variables. As a result of observing animal subjects in experiments in which the unconditioned stimulus was an electric shock, Finch and Culler (1935) came to the conclusion that "the primary [unconditioned] stimulus plays a dual role in conditioning. (*a*) It determines the character or *pattern* of the response. . . . (*b*) It provides the *incentive* or drive needed to actuate this response pattern" (p. 660). And Cole (1939), Grant (1939), Razran (1936), and others have also stressed the motivational implications of the conditioning procedure. But perhaps the most crucial demonstration of the inadequacy of a strictly associationistic interpretation of conditioning was reported by Brogden, Lipman, and Culler (1938). These investigators found that if they omitted the unconditioned stimulus (shock) whenever their subjects responded to the conditioned stimulus (tone) alone, they obtained conditioning that was decidedly superior to that produced by the procedure, dictated by Pavlovian theory, of having the conditioned stimulus invariably followed by the unconditioned stimulus. The present writers have elsewhere discussed (4) what seem to them to be the salient theoretical implications of this finding and have reported original data which indicate that the *instrumental* conditioning technique [2] employed by Brogden, Lipman, and Culler can be made to give even better results if, in addition to omitting the unconditioned stimulus when a conditioned response occurs, one also immediately terminates the conditioned stimulus (instead of having it continue for an arbitrarily fixed period of time).

These and other observations now make it evident that no *simpliste* interpretation of conditioning, as pure associationism, is tenable.[3] No longer can we close our eyes to the role of motivation and reward in conditioning, any more than we can in trial-and-error learning. But unlike trial-and-error learning, which can

---

[2] Hilgard and Marquis (1940) are responsible for introducing the useful expressions *instrumental conditioning* and *classical conditioning* to designate, respectively, conditioning procedures of the type just described and the unvarying paired presentation of stimuli as employed by Pavlov. [As names for two different laboratory procedures, these terms are still useful; but the term "instrumental conditioning" is misleading if it is applied to the process whereby "instrumental," i.e., problem-solving, responses are acquired. There is, strictly speaking, *only one* form of conditioning, and that is the "classical" form, i.e., the form which is dependent solely upon contiguity.]

[3] [This statement should now read: "These and other observations now make it evident that many so-called 'conditioned responses' are misnamed; more correctly designated, they are problem-solving responses which are based upon secondary drives—the *true* conditioned responses."]

be validly exemplified with hunger, thirst, pain, and other *primary* drives, an adequate conceptualization of conditioning seems to require the introduction of *secondary* drives, or emotions.

In an earlier paper (3) one of us has already reviewed the evidence for believing that the emotion of fear is itself a conditioned response. Thus, if a painful or traumatic stimulus which (to use Cannon's expression) produces a "physiological emergency reaction" is preceded by some initially neutral stimulus, this neutral stimulus will tend to acquire the capacity to elicit the "emergency reaction" in advance of the occurrence of the original trauma. When this occurs we say that the originally neutral stimulus has become a "danger signal" for the subject and produces a *fear reaction.* Traditionally we have tended, in experiments involving a noxious unconditioned stimulus, to glue our eyes and our recording instruments so exclusively on some overt response that we have overlooked the concomitant emotional learning that invariably occurs.[4] There have, to be sure, been numerous studies of "emotional conditioning." But the almost universal practice has been to center attention either upon some overt, behavioral reaction or upon some physiological process. Our proposal is that the physiological, or emotional, conditioning is basic and that no proper understanding of overt, or behavioral, conditioning is possible save in the context of the accompanying emotional events. We take this position not only because of the experimental findings which have already been reviewed but because of still another paradox which we believe can only in this way be satisfactorily resolved.

I. Noncorrespondence Between Conditioned and Unconditioned Responses

If conditioning were the simple process of stimulus substitution, or associative learning, it is sometimes said to be, a conditioned response should be an exact replica of the reaction made to the so-called unconditioned stimulus. Sometimes, during the early stages of conditioning, this is indeed the case; but more commonly the *CR* differs from the *UnCR* both quantitatively and qualitatively. Hilgard and Marquis (1940), after surveying the literature on this problem, conclude that the reaction to a conditioned stimulus can take any of four forms: (*a*) it may be a more

[4] Kilpatrick (1925) has been particularly vocal in calling attention to the dangers of this fallacy in education. Cf. other educational and clinical writers who emphasize the importance of always considering the "whole child" (Burton, 1944; Hopkins, 1941).

or less perfect reproduction, or "redintegration," of the unconditioned response; (*b*) it may be a "fractional component" of the unconditioned response; (*c*) it may serve as a preparation, or "set," for the unconditioned stimulus; or (*d*) it may be a response which is due, not to conditioning proper, but to the "sensitization" produced by the unconditioned stimulus alone (hence the term "pseudo-conditioning"). Much of the mystery concerning the noncorrespondence which is thus evidenced between conditioned responses and their putative unconditioned prototypes can, we believe, be removed by introducing the concept of fear as an intervening variable in all conditioning experiments in which the unconditioned stimulus is a noxious one.[5]

In the study already cited (4), the present writers have shown that an avoidance *CR* is acquired much more quickly in rats if the *CS*, or "danger signal," terminates the instant the *CR* occurs, instead of a few seconds before or a few seconds afterwards. From this and related findings (1, 3), it appears that, once the *CS* has become capable of arousing fear, termination of the *CS* and the attendant reduction in fear constitute a rewarding state of affairs which powerfully reinforces the connection between the fear and whatever behavior immediately precedes (i.e., ordinarily "causes") the fear reduction.

In a situation involving a traumatic (unconditioned) stimulus and a warning (conditioned) stimulus, there are thus *two* types of problems to be solved. Once the traumatic stimulus impinges upon the organism, the organism will engage in whatever type of behavior is best calculated to eliminate that stimulus; but when the warning signal occurs alone, the organism will be motivated only by fear and will engage in whatever type of behavior is best calculated to eliminate this painful emotion.[6]

---

[5] Tolman (1932) has most pertinently elaborated the general notion of intervening variables in the behavior of living organisms. In the present study no attempt is made to determine whether the intervening variable with which we are here concerned, namely, "fear," has the status of a mere construct or is a drive whose reality can be independently demonstrated. Lacking a precise empirical index of fear in our subjects, we assume that it has, technically, the status of a construct; but its reality and drive quality could almost certainly be independently confirmed.

[6] This analysis is, of course, strictly behavioral and "noncognitive." In human beings, with their verbal prolixity, there is a tendency to interpret behavior teleologically, to say, for example, that one seeks shelter *in order* to avoid being rained on rather than saying that one seeks shelter *because* one is afraid of being rained on. The degree of fear consciously experienced in such a situation may be hardly perceptible, but it seems far safer to assume that it must invariably be present, in some degree, as the cause of the observed behavior than to assume that the behavior is purely "rational," i.e., determined by "ends" rather than by causes, or "drives." (This, incidentally, serves as an example of an anticipatory

If the same response that eliminates the traumatic stimulus will also, when made anticipatorily, eliminate the premonitory warning and the attendant fear, then the so-called conditioned and unconditioned responses will be more or less identical. Or, in other words, if the same action provides the solution to the problem occasioned by the secondary drive as well as to the one occasioned by the primary one, then one and the same response will become habitual to both types of drive. But if the situation is such that the response required to eliminate the warning signal and the attendant fear is *different* from the response which must be made when the trauma itself occurs, then the so-called conditioned response and the unconditioned response can be expected to differ accordingly. Obviously such responses may differ slightly or quite radically, but this noncorrespondence, whatever its magnitude, need occasion no perplexity if the two responses are seen as the solutions to two different problem situations.

Whether an anticipatory response which reduces fear but is radically different from the response which reduces the traumatic stimulus of which the fear is premonitory should be called a "conditioned response" is perhaps debatable; but it is certainly legitimate to say that it is produced by the conditioned stimulus, provided we do not lose sight of the fact that the occurrence of fear is an essential intermediate step. Strictly speaking, the *CS* produces the fear which then elicits the fear-reducing response—a response which, as we have seen, may be either the same as or markedly different from the response which has been found most appropriate to the unconditioned stimulus.[7]

---

response which is much the same as the response made to the unconditioned stimulus proper, namely, rain. But if one is about to start on a walk at a time when "it looks like rain," instead of running back into the house, one may pick up an umbrella or a raincoat and proceed with the walk. Here the anticipatory, or "conditioned," response is very unlike the "unconditioned" response.)

[7] This analysis may not be valid for those conditioning experiments involving the blink, the knee jerk, and other reflexive or highly automatic responses in which the optimal interval between the conditioned and the unconditioned stimulus has been found to be from 0.2 second to 0.4 second (a time which is probably too brief to allow for the succession of events posited above). We still do not know very much about what actually happens in these experiments, and it is probably not very important that we should. That such experiments involve highly special and artificial conditions is indicated by the fact that in ordinary life the delay between the appearance of a danger signal—as, for example, the signs occurring in a state of nature that an enemy is near or spoken warnings as used by human beings—and the impingement of the "unconditioned stimulus" is usually much longer than a fraction of a second. It can hardly be a disadvantage, therefore, if our theoretical analysis of the conditioning process is such as to account more satisfactorily for the type of learning that occurs under ordinary circumstances than for the segmental response modifications that are produced under extraordinary conditions in the laboratory.

In the following pages we describe an experiment which we believe exemplifies and confirms the foregoing analysis.

II. Synopsis of Procedure

The main object of this paper is to report an experiment in which rats learned to make a conditioned, or anticipatory, response which was radically unlike the response made to the original, so-called unconditioned stimulus. Such learning, it is believed, constitutes an enigma for association theory but can be satisfactorily accounted for by effect theory.[8] However, in order to demonstrate this type of learning unambiguously, it was necessary to introduce a number of controls which, if not clearly differentiated, may obscure the central purpose of the experiment.

In the main experimental group, the conditioned and the unconditioned responses acquired by the subjects were radically different. But for theoretical reasons which will be considered later, it was desirable to have a control group in which the conditioned and the unconditioned responses were the same. It was likewise desirable to have yet another group in which a conditioned response was established but without the existence of any uniform or standardized response to the unconditioned stimulus.

The second type of control had to do with the nature of the conditioned stimulus, i.e., it was necessary to make sure that the *CS* was not of such a nature that its termination might be assumed to be inherently rewarding, independently of its capacity to produce a reward through fear reduction.

And the third type of control relates to the nature of the conditioned and unconditioned responses. Lest our subjects have some original predisposition to make one type of response to the conditioned stimulus and a different one to the unconditioned stimulus, it was necessary to divide our subjects in such a way that the response which was conditioned in one group would be the unconditioned response in another group, and vice versa.

This is the type of experiment which lends itself ideally to a

---

[8] [Although this study in many ways anticipates the development of a two-factor theory of learning, such a theory is not here made explicit. By properly redefining conditioning, we find that it is a real phenomenon and that it conforms to the expectation, generated by association theory, that the conditioned response should be the same as the unconditioned response, or at least the same as some segment thereof. Thus, if electric shock produces both pain and fear, a signal of shock will be expected to, and does, elicit fear. It is only when the term "conditioning" is misapplied to skeletal responses which are learned on the basis of problem solving that the enigma of noncorrespondence between "conditioned" and "unconditioned" responses arises.]

Fisher factorial design. In such a design, the variables which are introduced solely as controls unfortunately tend to assume a prominence equal to the major variable, thus somewhat obscuring the main purpose of the experiment and swamping the reader with secondary details. But the efficiency of such a design (in terms of number of subjects required) and the unique possibility it affords for testing for "interaction" between different variables more than offset the disadvantages.

In the light of these considerations, the present investigation was factorially designed, but an attempt will be made to describe the procedure employed in such a way as to presuppose only a minimal knowledge of Fisher's experimental and statistical methods.

III. Apparatus and Subjects

The apparatus used in this investigation is shown in Figure 22 (4). Fully described elsewhere (Mowrer and Miller, 1942), it calls for little additional comment here except a word about the nature of the conditioned stimulus. In order to avoid one of the possible sources of ambiguity mentioned in the preceding section, it was necessary to set up the experiment in such a way that the termination, or "off" effect, of the conditioned stimulus could not be inherently rewarding. The best way of doing this which occurred to us was to use as the conditioned stimulus, not a sound, light, or any other stimulus whose termination could be suspected of providing some intrinsic element of relief, but a *change in the pattern* of the illumination of the apparatus. It was accordingly decided that one pattern should consist of the illumination provided by the two small (10-watt) electric lamps located on the interior rear wall of the apparatus (see Figure 22, page 95) and that the other pattern should consist of the illumination provided by a single, similar lamp located on the table directly beneath and about equally distant from the two ends of the apparatus (but now shown in Figure 22). As a further precaution it was decided that with half of our subjects, the conditioned stimulus should consist of a shift in the pattern of illumination from the two lights to the one and that with the other half it should consist of a shift from the one light to the two. In this way it was possible to have a distinctive visual "danger signal" without, however, introducing any marked change in the total intensity of visual stimulation impinging upon the subject.

The alternating electric current, which provided the unconditioned stimulus (and was administered from the grill which constituted the floor of the apparatus), represented a flow of 1.1 milliamperes (assuming the average resistance of a rat on the kind of grill used in this apparatus to be approximately 1,000,000 ohms).

The subjects were 24 male Lashley-strain rats, four to six months of age.

IV. Experimental Design and Procedure

The 24 subjects employed in this investigation were randomly divided into 3 major groups of 8 animals each. In Group I the correct response to the conditioned stimulus, i.e., the response which terminated the *CS* and was rewarded by a diminution of fear, was very different from the correct response to the unconditioned (shock) stimulus. In Group II the correct responses to the conditioned and to the unconditioned stimulus were one and the same. In Group III, there was no correct, or standard, response which our subjects could make to the unconditioned stimulus, since the latter was of fixed (2 seconds) duration and could not be terminated by any particular response on the part of our subjects. However, in the latter group there was the same opportunity for the subjects to terminate the conditioned stimulus by making the appropriate response as existed in the other two groups. (See first column in Table 1.) [9]

In order to meet the problem of the conditioned stimulus, discussed previously, it was necessary to divide the 24 animals comprising Groups I, II, and III into 6 subgroups, such that for half the animals in each major group the conditioned stimulus consisted of the overhead lamps going *off* (and the alternative single

[9] [Difficulty has been reported, on the basis of the description given in this section, in fully understanding the procedure here employed. It is suggested that the remainder of the section be read and that, if the procedure is not then intelligible, the rest of this footnote be read: The central point of the experiment was simply this: to show that, by an appropriate procedure, it is possible to establish in rats shock-avoidance (i.e., so-called "conditioned") responses which are quite different from shock-escape (so-called "unconditioned") responses. Thus, the conditions were such that certain rats found that they could escape from shock-on-grill by running to the opposite end of the apparatus; but they also discovered that in order to *avoid* shock (escape from fear-of-shock), when the danger signal was given, they had to make a quite different response, i.e., they had to leap into the air. For reasons given in the text, other rats were subjected to conditions such that they could escape the shock by leaping into the air, but in order to *avoid* it they had to do something else, namely run to the opposite end of the apparatus. Both sets of these animals, together, comprised Group I, i.e., animals for which the *CR* and the *UnCR*, so-called, were *different*. These animals are compared with those in Group II, for which the *CR* and *UnCR* were the *same*. They are also compared with those in Group III, wherein there was no standard response which could be called an *"UnCR,"* since the shock was of fixed duration and could not be escaped from by means of any response (but see page 144).]

lamp coming on) and for the other half of the animals in each major group the conditioned stimulus consisted of the overhead lamps coming *on* (and the alternative single lamp going off). The possibility that such differences as were obtained in the conditioning of Groups I, II, and III were due to the inherent properties of the conditioned stimulus was in this way largely eliminated. For purposes of convenience, the 6 subgroups thus created may be designated as Group I-Off and Group I-On, Group II-Off and Group II-On, and Group III-Off and Group III-On. Each of these subgroups consisted of 4 animals. (See second column in Table 1.)

Although seemingly less urgent than the problem of controlling the conditioned stimulus, it was also thought desirable to counterbalance the two types of response used in this investigation, namely, leaping into the air and running to the opposite end of the apparatus, in such a manner as to avoid any ambiguity in the meaning of the results obtained in Groups I, II, and III. This problem seemed most likely to arise in the interpretation of the results for Group I, in which the conditioned and unconditioned responses were purposely different. If, for example, running had been exclusively used as the conditioned response and jumping as the unconditioned response, the question would have arisen whether the same results would have been obtained if the conditioned response had been jumping and the unconditioned response running. Again it was decided to meet this problem by the simple expedient of having the conditioned response for half the animals in Groups I, II, and III consist of running and for the other half of jumping.

It was, of course, necessary to avoid having the nature of the conditioned response (running vs. jumping) vary in such a way as to be "confounded" with the nature of the conditioned stimulus (overhead lights off vs. overhead lights on). This was done by symmetrically dividing the 6 subgroups already described into 12 sub-subgroups, each of which contained 2 animals. In keeping with the nomenclature already suggested, these sub-subgroups may be designated as: Group I-Off-Jump, Group I-Off-Run, Group I-On-Jump, Group I-On-Run; Group II-Off-Jump, etc. (See third column in Table 1.)

This experimental design is represented schematically in Table 1. Although based upon the old and familiar device of counterbalancing factors which are likely to produce "constant errors," such an arrangement makes possible the application of modern statistical methods which utilize *all* the obtained data instead of discarding all but those findings which are of the most immediate

TABLE 1

SCHEMATIC REPRESENTATION OF THE FACTORIAL DESIGN USED IN THIS EXPERIMENT

NOTE.—The first factor (Groups column) involves the general conditioning procedure; the second factor (Subgroups column) refers to the nature of the conditioned stimulus; and the third factor (Sub-subgroups column) refers to the nature of the conditioned response.

Groups ($N = 8$)	Subgroups ($N = 4$)	Sub-subgroups ($N = 2$)	Subjects
I—*CR* and *UnCR* different	*CS* = Lights off	*CR* = Jumping	1 1a
		CR = Running	2 2a
	CS = Lights on	*CR* = Jumping	3 3a
		CR = Running	4 4a
II—*CR* and *UnCR* the same	*CS* = Lights off	*CR* = Jumping	5 5a
		CR = Running	6 6a
	CS = Lights on	*CR* = Jumping	7 7a
		CR = Running	8 8a
III—No standard *UnCR* —(*UnCS* of fixed duration)	*CS* = Lights off	*CR* = Jumping	9 9a
		CR = Running	10 10a
	CS = Lights on	*CR* = Jumping	11 11a
		CR = Running	12 12a

TABLE 2

DETAILED RESULTS OBTAINED IN THIS STUDY

NOTE.—For an indication of the conditions under which each of the 24 subjects was trained, see Table 1.

Subjects	Number of Conditioned Responses Made per Day												Total *CR*'s
1	1	8	6	8	9	10	10	9	10	10	10	10	101
1a	0	2	6	6	5	1	0	2	0	0	1	0	23
2	0	3	4	6	10	7	10	9	10	10	10	10	89
2a	2	7	9	9	10	9	10	10	10	10	10	10	106
3	0	0	0	0	0	0	0	0	0	0	0	0	0
3a	0	0	0	0	0	0	0	0	0	0	0	1	1
4	1	0	3	6	4	7	10	8	10	10	10	10	79
4a	3	8	10	10	9	10	10	10	10	10	10	10	110
5	1	2	6	4	8	8	8	8	8	9	9	8	79
5a	0	7	9	9	9	9	9	10	9	10	10	9	100
6	1	6	10	9	9	9	10	10	10	10	10	10	104
6a	3	9	10	9	10	10	10	9	10	10	10	10	110
7	0	5	6	7	10	9	9	9	10	9	9	9	92
7a	1	4	7	7	7	7	7	10	9	10	9	10	88
8	2	6	7	10	8	10	10	9	10	10	10	10	102
8a	3	8	8	10	9	10	10	10	10	10	10	9	107
9	0	6	8	8	9	9	9	10	9	10	10	9	97
9a	3	6	6	8	10	7	9	10	6	10	10	10	95
10	0	0	4	4	8	6	3	7	7	8	7	9	63
10a	7	9	8	10	10	10	9	10	10	10	10	10	113
11	0	0	8	9	10	9	9	10	10	10	10	10	95
11a	1	7	8	6	6	6	8	10	9	10	9	9	89
12	2	3	8	10	10	9	10	9	10	10	10	10	101
12a	2	3	4	6	6	6	6	7	6	9	10	10	75

interest. These methods will be referred to again in the next section.

After the 24 animals which were used in this study had been randomly assigned to the 12 sub-subgroups, or "cells," just described, they were each submitted to 10 conditioning trials per day for a period of 12 days. Each animal was put into the apparatus and allowed 1 minute for habituation.[10] The conditioned stimulus was then applied. If a conditioned response occurred, the *CS* was

[10] There was one exception to this rule. When put into the apparatus on the first day, each animal was required to remain in either the right or the left half of the apparatus for a minimum of 1 minute before experimentation was started. This precaution was taken as a means of allowing exploratory behavior largely to disappear before the *CS* was applied and thereby avoiding the occurrence of "false" *CR*'s on the first trial. After one or two paired presentations of the *CS* and *UnCS*, the animals became sufficiently frightened so that there was little random behavior between trials.

immediately terminated and the *UnCS* was not applied. But if, within 5 seconds after the onset of the *CS*, a conditioned response did not occur, the *UnCS* was applied until the appropriate *UnCR* had occurred (as in Groups I and II) or for a fixed period of time (as in Group III). In all cases in which a *CR* did not occur, the *CS* remained on while the *UnCS* was applied, i.e., the *CS* and the *UnCS* overlapped and terminated together. One minute was allowed between successive trials.[11]

All experimentation was carried out in a soundproofed room with a one-way screen between the experimenter and the apparatus. Mention should also be made of the fact that subjects 1, 2, 3, 4, 5, 6, 7, 8, 9, 10, 11, and 12 (see Table 1) were first used in this investigation, with subjects 1a, 2a, 3a, 4a, 5a, 6a, 7a, 8a, 9a, 10a, 11a, and 12a being run about one month later.

V. Results

Table 2 shows the over-all results obtained in this experiment. This table can be thought of as a continuation (from left to right) of Table 1, with the "Subjects" column overlapping.

When the average number of conditioned responses made per day by the 8 animals in Group I (subjects 1–4a in first column of Table 2), by the 8 animals in Group II (subjects 5–8a), and by the 8 animals in Group III (subjects 9–12a) are plotted graphically, the three curves shown in Figure 33 are obtained. If all 24 subjects are divided according to whether they were trained with the *CS* consisting of the overhead lights being turned "off" or "on" (i.e., 1–2a, 5–6a, and 9–10a as compared with 3–4a, 7–8a, and 11–12a), the two curves shown in Figure 34 are obtained. Likewise, if all 24 subjects are divided into two groups according to whether the *CR* consisted of jumping (as it did in 1–1a, 3–3a, 5–5a, 7–7a, 9–9a, and 11–11a) or running (as it did in 2–2a, 4–4a, 6–6a, 8–8a, 10–10a, 12–12a), the two curves shown in Figure 35 result.

Since this experiment was factorially designed, the question of the reliability of the differences between the various groups can best be approached through an analysis of variance (Fisher, 1937; Lindquist, 1940). As will be seen from inspection of Table 3, the *F*-test shows that the variance introduced by the differences in

---

[11] With the particular instrumental conditioning procedure used with all subjects in this study, i.e., with the *CS* terminated as soon as the *CR* was made and with the *UnCS* omitted, there were so few "spontaneous," or "temporal," *CR*'s between trials that the usual expedient of using irregular intervals between trials was unnecessary.

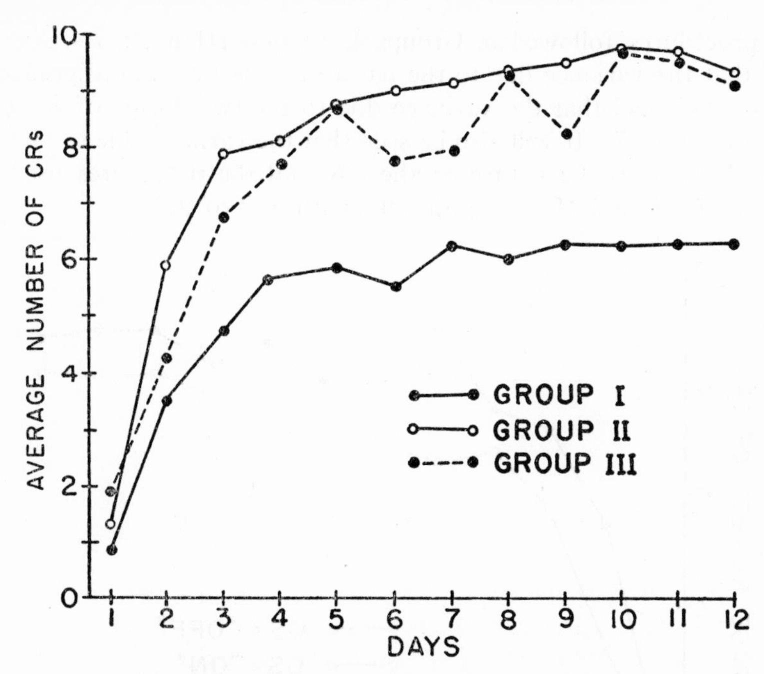

FIG. 33.—Curves showing average number of conditioned responses made by Groups I, II, and III. The experiment lasted 12 days, and each animal received 10 conditioning trials per day. There were 8 animals in each group.

TABLE 3

ANALYSIS OF VARIANCE OF TOTAL NUMBER OF CONDITIONED RESPONSES

Source of Variance	Degrees of Freedom	Sum of Squares	Mean Square	*F*-Value
Total	23	23,542.625		
Between groups	2	5,225.250	2,612.6	5.66 (P = .02)
Type of *CS*	1	828.375	828.4	1.80 (P = .23)
Type of *CR*	1	3,725.042	3,725.0	8.08 (P = .015)
Interaction: Groups-*CS*	2	1,261.750	630.9	
Interaction: Groups-*CR*	2	5,244.083	2,622.0	5.69 (P = .02)
Interaction: *CS-CR*	1	590.042	590.0	
Interaction: Groups-*CS-CR*	2	1,133.583	566.8	
Between paired rats receiving same experimental treatment (estimate of error)	12	5,534.500	461.2	

the procedures followed in Groups I, II, and III has a *P*-value of .02, that the variance due to the nature of the *CS* is nonsignificant ($P = .23$), and that the variance due to the two forms of the *CR* has a *P* of .015. It will also be seen that the variance due to "interaction" between the nature of the *CR* and the procedures used in Groups I, II, and III is significant (with a *P* of .02).

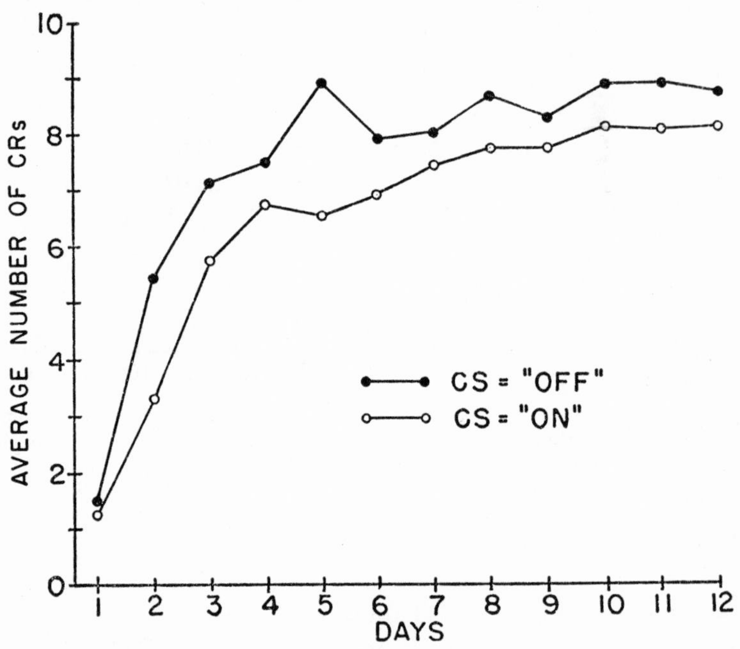

Fig. 34.—Average number of conditioned responses made by the 24 animals used in this experiment, divided according to the nature of the conditioned stimulus.

This analysis of variance gives us all the statistical information we need, except for an estimate of the reliability of the differences between Groups I and II, I and III, and II and III. Applying the appropriate *t*-test (Helson, 1942; Lindquist, 1940), we find that the differences between Groups I and II and Groups I and III are significant at the .01 level, whereas the difference between Groups II and III is nonsignificant ($P = .54$).

VI. Discussion

The main object of this experiment was to determine whether a conditioned response of an avoidant nature can be established which is completely unlike the response elicited by the so-called unconditioned stimulus.[12] Such a finding, it was reasoned, would further discredit the traditional interpretation of avoidance conditioning as simple stimulus substitution and would strengthen the position that in order to give a really adequate account of this type of learning, fear must be posited as an intervening variable. If a rat's running

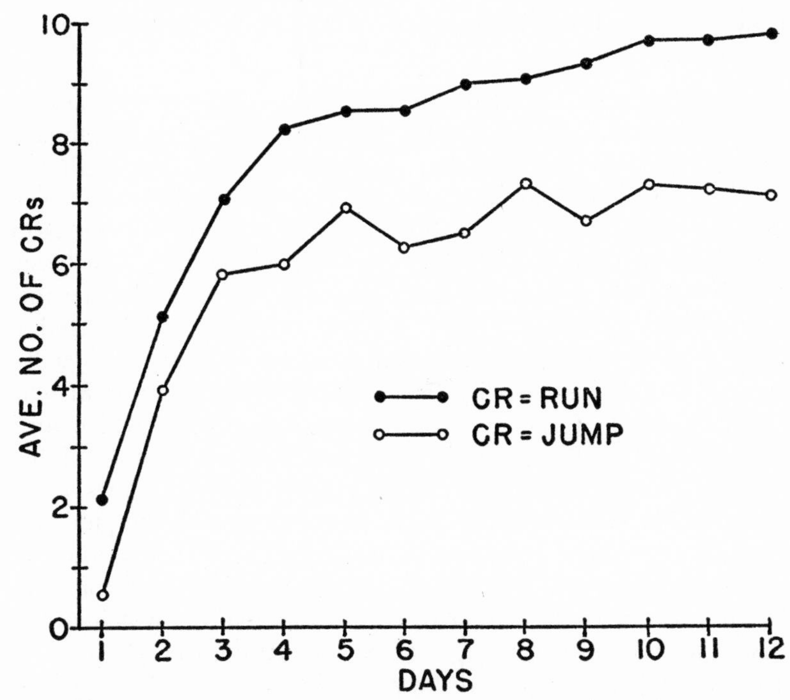

FIG. 35.—Average number of conditioned responses made by the 24 animals used in this experiment, divided according to the nature of the conditioned response.

on all four legs be accepted as "completely different" from its leaping from its hind legs vertically into the air, then the main purpose of this study may be said to have been satisfied.[13] Our results indicate that rats can learn to react to a *CS* with either of these responses when the correct response to the *UnCS* is the opposite one. In fact, during the last 4 days of the experiment, 5 of the 8 animals

---

[12] We use the expression "so-called unconditioned stimulus" for the reason that in this study the responses to it were largely learned (on a trial-and-error basis), being therefore only slightly if at all reflexive or "unconditioned."

[13] Any of a number of other responses might have been employed in this study—biting at the bars which constituted the floor grill of the apparatus, sitting up on the hind legs, churning the feet rapidly up and down in one spot, etc. Running and leaping vertically into the air were selected as the two responses which seemed the most unequivocally "different."

with which this hypothesis was tested gave absolutely perfect, 100 per cent conditioning (see Table 2).

As a means of comparing the speed of learning under these conditions and under the two more conventional conditioning procedures, and of controlling two possible sources of artifact, the total investigation (involving 24 animals) was factorially designed in the manner already described. Our main finding must now be considered against the background of the results provided by the entire study.

Difference in CS Not Significant. The counterbalancing of an illumination change in one direction against an illumination change in the opposite direction was a safeguard against the possibility that the termination of the *CS* might be inherently rewarding to our subjects and would thus vitiate our efforts to demonstrate the role of fear as a secondary reinforcing agent. Our results indicate that this precaution was probably unnecessary inasmuch as the curves shown in Figure 34 are so nearly similar and the reliability of the difference between them is so slight. As will be seen, such difference as exists is in favor of the animals in which the *CS* consisted of the overhead lights going "off," which meant that at the end of the *CS* they came "on." This finding might at first seem to oppose Keller's (1941) finding that in rats a drop in illumination is intrinsically rewarding and an increase punishing; but it will be remembered that in speaking of the *CS* as the overhead lights going "off" or "on," we are only using a convenient shorthand for a change in pattern of illumination which did not greatly alter the amount of light actually reaching the subject's eyes. Thus, although the difference between the two curves appearing in Figure 34 is uniformly in favor of the 12 animals for which the *CS* consisted of the overhead light being turned "off," this difference is so small and statistically so nonsignificant that it can safely be dismissed from further consideration.

Effects of the Two Types of *CR* Considered. On the other hand, the results obtained from the use of two types of *CR* turn out to be important in a variety of ways. That the curve reproduced in Figure 35 for the 12 animals for which the *CR* consisted of running should be consistently and significantly superior to the curve for the 12 animals for which the *CR* consisted of leaping into the air is not surprising. One of the present writers, in unpublished research, has confirmed James' (1941) finding that the amount of work involved in performing a response is negatively correlated with the ease of conditioning; and Mowrer and Jones (6) have shown that the work factor is positively correlated with the tendency for a response to become extinguished. That the jumping response was more effortful than running can hardly be doubted, but the influence of this factor manifested itself in a curious way. When we divide up the results for the 24 animals used in this experiment, not only according to the general conditioning procedures, but also according to the nature of the conditioned response, we obtain Table 4.

TABLE 4

NUMBER OF CONDITIONED RESPONSES MADE BY EACH OF 24 ANIMALS, BROKEN DOWN IN TERMS OF CONDITIONING PROCEDURE AND TYPE OF CONDITIONED RESPONSE

I—Jump		II—Jump		III—Jump	
1	101	5	79	9	97
1a	23	5a	100	9a	95
3	0	7	92	11	95
3a	1	7a	88	11a	89
Average	31.25		89.75		94.00
					71.66
I—Run		**II—Run**		**III—Run**	
2	89	6	104	10	63
2a	106	6a	110	10a	113
4	79	8	102	12	101
4a	110	8a	107	12a	75
Average	96.00		105.75		88.00
					96.58
All Group I Animals		**All Group II Animals**		**All Group III Animals**	
Average	63.63		97.75		91.00

Here we note, first of all, that in Group III there is a reversal of the trend for the running response to condition more readily than the jumping response. In fact, if we apply a technique suggested by Dr. Daniel Horn for "correcting for interaction," we obtain an "adjusted mean" for the III-Jump animals of 99.6 and for the III-Run animals of 69.7. There is thus a mean difference of 29.9 in favor of the III-Jump animals. This difference is almost reliable at the 0.5 level of significance.

The explanation of this reversal of the general tendency for the running response to condition more easily than the more effortful jumping response is probably as follows. It will be remembered that in the Group III procedure, the *UnCS* was of arbitrarily fixed duration. We had initially assumed that this would mean that there would be no differential reinforcement of any particular response to the *UnCS*. However, it is now clear, in retrospect, that the response of leaping into the air provided at least momentary relief and almost certainly received more reinforcement than any other response which occurred to the *UnCS*.[14] This fact probably predisposed the animals in both III-Run and III-Jump not only to make jumping responses to the *UnCS* but also (for reasons which will be considered shortly) to the *CS*. This unanticipated and uncontrolled source of reinforcement of the connection between the conditioned stimulus and the jumping response appears to have operated in all the Group III animals in such a way as to more than counteract the over-all tendency for the less effortful running response to condition more readily.

In Table 4 we also note that although the superiority of conditioning of the running response is clearly manifested in the Group II animals, this difference is peculiarly striking in the Group I animals. We have already seen that the interaction between type of *CR* and general conditioning procedure is highly significant statistically, and it is now evident that most of this interaction is contributed by the animals in I-Jump. However, the meaning of this find will be clear only after we have considered the relative merits of the Group I, Group II, and Group III procedures.

Two Sources of Reinforcement of the *CR*. While the results for the 8 animals which were subjected to the Group I procedure show that it is possible to establish conditioned responses which are radically unlike the response made to the unconditioned stimulus, it is also evident that it is *more difficult* to obtain conditioning with this procedure than it is with either the Group II or the Group III procedure. Why should this be the case?

The fact that conditioning can be obtained with the Group I procedure cannot, we believe, be explained on the basis of so-called associative learning. In order to account for this type of conditioning, we must apparently make three assumptions not found in association theory: (*a*) that the *CS* acquires the capacity to elicit

[14] In this respect jumping was an unfortunate choice for a response to be contrasted with running. One of the other responses mentioned in footnote 13 might have been preferable from this standpoint.

the secondary motive of fear, (*b*) that under appropriate conditions (see below) this motive produces a variety of more or less "random" response, and (*c*) that the termination of the *CS* and the resultant reduction in fear reinforces the connection between the fear and whichever one of these random responses happens to bring about the fear reduction, regardless of whether this response is the same as or different from the response which solves the problem presented by the *UnCS* or primary drive. But the fact that the Group II and Group III procedures give reliably better conditioning than the Group I procedure suggests that the secondary reinforcement provided by fear reduction is not the only factor which determines what response will become the one characteristically made to the *CS*. Having demonstrated the reality of independent secondary reinforcement in avoidance conditioning, let us look for the other source of reinforcement.

Common observation indicates that when an electric current is applied to an experimental animal, the current produces not only pain ("shock") but also fear (cf. 1, Footnote 3). Therefore, whatever response is found effective in eliminating the pain also serves to reduce the accompanying secondary drive of fear. This means that there is not only a strengthening of the connection between pain-plus-fear and this response but also between fear alone and this response. This type of learning is properly designated as "associative" or "redintegrative" learning.[15]

This analysis enables us to see why the Group I procedure produced reliably less rapid conditioning than did the Group II procedure, with the Group III procedure falling somewhere between. In the Group II procedure, we have two types of reinforcement cooperating to strengthen the connection between fear and the same response as was made to the fear and shock in combination. However, in the Group I procedure, we have a conflict. Here there is a tendency for the fear to elicit—through associative reinforcement—the same response as has been made to the fear and shock

---

15 [This statement calls for revision. According to the author's present views, the expression "'associative' or 'redintegrative' learning" should be regarded as synonymous with "conditioning." There is certainly a resemblance between conditioning and the type of learning referred to above in that in both instances part of a total stimulus compound which initially elicited a given response later does so alone. But it now looks as if the particular type of learning here under discussion is simply a special case of problem solving, i.e., it involves a situation in which *two drives* are simultaneously active and simultaneously reinforce a common response. The fact that one of these drives alone proves capable, subsequently, of eliciting this response is not surprising and needs no principle to explain it other than that of problem solving. Perhaps nothing more is here involved than is implied by Freud's concept of "multiple causation," or "overdetermination," of behavior. Cf. discussion of "parasitic reinforcement," in (4).]

together. But there is also a tendency for the fear to elicit—through what we have called independent secondary reinforcement—a response which is very different from the response made to the fear and shock together. And it is presumably only when the independent secondary reinforcement can be made stronger than the associative reinforcement that one gets conditioning of the kind exemplified in Group I.[16]

Letting these two types of reinforcement, independent secondary and associative, be represented, respectively, by the letters X and Y, we may say that in the Group II procedure the reinforcement of the conditioned response is $X + Y$, whereas in the Group I procedure it is $X - Y$. This interpretation squares with the results actually obtained. And since, in the Group III procedure, there was only (or at least mainly) one source of reinforcement, namely X, we expect, and find, the goodness of conditioning to be represented by a value less than $X + Y$ but greater than $X - Y$.

With this notation in mind, let us look again at Table 4. Taking the amount of conditioning obtained in each of our three groups as an index of the net strength of reinforcement, we may set up three equations:

$$
\begin{aligned}
&(1) \quad X - Y = 63.63 \quad \text{(Group I conditioning)}\\
&(2) \quad X + Y = 97.75 \quad \text{(Group II conditioning)}\\
&(3) \quad X = 91.00 \quad \text{(Group III conditioning)}
\end{aligned}
$$

If our experiment were perfectly controlled, we should expect the value for X, derived from Equations (1) and (2), to be the same as the value for X given in Equation (3). Solving Equations (1) and (2), we find $X = 80.60$ ($Y = 17.06$). But Equation (3) gives $X = 91.00$. This discrepancy suggests that our experiment was *not* perfectly controlled; and the most obvious interpretation of this discrepancy is that in Group III, some Y (associative reinforcement) was present, in addition to X (independent secondary reinforcement).

This type of analysis also enables us to see why, in Group I, half of the animals showed so much better conditioning than the other half. In the case of the I—Run animals the X-reinforcement of the running response was soon able to overcome the opposing Y-reinforcement of the *more effortful* jumping response and thus

[16] [This statement should now be modified to read: "And it is presumably only when the independent secondary reinforcement (fear reduction), which occurs when the danger signal terminates, can be made stronger than the reinforcement which occurs when the shock terminates (and the accompanying pain and 'unconditioned' fear lessen) that one gets learning of the kind exemplified in Group I."]

produce a stable *CR* of running; but in the I—Jump animals the *X*-reinforcement of the jumping response was unable (save in one of our four animals) to overcome the *Y*-reinforcement of the *less effortful* running response. These two factors—differential reinforcement and differential effortfulness of the two responses—thus "interacted" to depress the conditioning in the I—Jump animal and to facilitate it in the I—Run animals.

Associative Reinforcement Re-examined. In conditioning, where the *CR* and the *UnCR* are strikingly dissimilar, association theory breaks down completely. In order to have a satisfactory alternative explanation, we must resort to what has just been termed "independent secondary reinforcement," i.e., to the notion of a rewarding state of affairs provided by a reduction in the secondary drive of fear. But we have also just seen that even where conditions are such as to result eventually in a *CR* which differs markedly from the *UnCR,* there is nevertheless a strong tendency, especially in the early stages of training, for the *CR* and *UnCR* to be alike. This, by definition, is associative learning; but in accounting for it we have discarded association theory and again resorted to the concept of fear as a secondary motive. Is this really necessary? Would it not be simpler and perhaps also more nearly correct to omit any reference to fear in this type of conditioning and interpret it entirely in terms of associationism? This theory, being essentially "peripheral" in character, holds that learning results directly from the paired presentation of two external stimuli, the *CS* and the *UnCS*. Can it be shown that, even when the *CR* and the *UnCR* are virtually identical, it is still necessary to posit fear as an intervening variable?

Whether the paired presentation of a *CS* and a noxious *UnCS* automatically results in the development of an avoidant *CR,* without the concomitant occurrence of fear, could be interestingly tested in animals which have been sympathectomized. Here one would have living organisms in which the central nervous system (including the so-called associative centers) and the afferent and efferent pathways are entirely intact but in which the auxiliary autonomic mechanism which mediates the secondary drive of fear had been eliminated. Here the opportunity for purely "associative learning," as traditionally conceived (and also "cognitive reorganization"), would presumably be unimpaired; but our prediction is that actual avoidance conditioning would be strikingly depressed, if not altogether absent.[17]

[17] [Such an experiment has recently been carried out by Solomon (1950).]

The experiment just described would, we believe, give very illuminating results, but it is technically very difficult. Let us therefore suggest another experiment which is more feasible. Suppose that rats were individually put into an apparatus similar to the one used in the present investigation and a buzzer were sounded for 5 seconds, at the end of which time an electric shock of fixed duration were presented. Since the buzzer and shock would thus be turned off after an arbitrarily fixed period of time, without any reference to what the animal was doing at the end of this time, no particular random response would be differentially reinforced.[18] Suppose, then, that subsequently these animals were put back into the apparatus and were taught to shuttle from one half of the apparatus to the other across a barrier (not present in the first stage of training) whenever shock were presented on that half of the grill on which they happened to be standing. In this second stage of training the buzzer would not be presented at all. Later, when the buzzer was sounded alone, what would these animals do?

According to the traditional associationism, with its emphasis on the purely external, or "objective," factors in the situation, one would expect these animals to engage in the same random and confused behavior in response to the buzzer alone which they had previously manifested in response to buzzer and shock together. On the other hand, if one looked at the situation from the standpoint of the theoretical position taken by the present writers, one would predict that the animals, when presented with buzzer alone, would make the same response which they had just learned to make to the shock alone, i.e., that they would tend to shuttle to the other end of the apparatus. Results obtained in a very similar experiment recently carried out by May *et al.* (1948) suggest that this is actually what would happen.[19]

How can such results be explained? In the face of such findings classical conditioning theory is helpless. But if we introduce the notion of fear, the explanation is simple. In the first stage of training, the animals, while failing to learn to make any specific overt response to the buzzer and shock, do learn to *be afraid* when the buzzer is sounded. In the second stage of training, the rats learn to shuttle in response to *shock-plus-fear*. Later, when fear alone, aroused not by shock but by the buzzer, is operative, the animals

[18] Leaping into the air would, for reasons given above, probably be an exception to this statement; but for purposes of the experiment here outlined, this fact would presumably be of no importance.

[19] [Cf. experiments recently reviewed by Miller (1950). See also 12, wherein fear is discussed as a "mediating response"; cf. Osgood (1951).]

make the same response to this secondary drive which they had previously learned to make to the primary drive of shock and fear in combination.[20]

With the traditional associationism so clearly inapplicable, some writers will seize upon May's results as illustrating "insight," "latent learning," "change in the psychological situation," or some similarly "cognitive" process. Going to an extreme of anthropomorphism, it might even be said that here is proof of "reasoning," in which the rat says to himself something like this: "Crossing the barrier and getting into the opposite end of the apparatus is the way to *escape* from electric shock. The buzzer is a *warning* that shock may recur. Therefore, the way to *avoid* the shock is to get over into the opposite end of the apparatus whenever the buzzer occurs."

But if Lloyd Morgan's canon is cogent, it would surely favor the hypothesis that the rat, having learned to be afraid when the buzzer sounds and to shuttle in response to fear and shock acting conjointly, will make the same response to fear acting independently. Our position is that this is also what happens in avoidant conditioning of the conventional type, where the *CR* is a more or less exact and obvious replica of the *UnCR*. Since, by positing fear as an intervening variable, we can account not only for conventional but also very eccentric forms of conditioning, we conclude that this hypothesis is superior to an interpretation whose range of application is so much more limited.

OTHER IMPLICATIONS. It may be argued that since our intervening variable, namely fear, is itself a product of learning, it cannot be legitimately used to account for further learning. Or, to put the same thing differently, it may be said that one cannot explain one type of learning in terms of prior learning. Actually, willingness to do just this seems to be an absolutely necessary step if we are to articulate the scientific study of learning with human or even animal behavior as we observe it in everyday life. Dewey (1938) has differentiated between good and bad pedagogical methods in terms of the way they influence the student's attitude toward further learning. Attitudinal psychology in general (including the work

[20] At first glance it may appear that this is merely another instance of pseudo-conditioning, where an animal, "set" to make a particular response to a noxious stimulus, makes this response to any other stimulus which is able to "trip" this "set" and throw the animal falsely into overt action. May and his associates have shown, however, that their subjects will *not* shuttle in response to buzzer alone, after having been taught to do so to shock alone, if the initial stage of training (paired presentation of buzzer and shock, which converts the buzzer into a danger signal) is omitted. There is thus apparently no question of their results being due to so-called pseudo-conditioning.

of Tolman and others on the concept of "expectancy") presupposes that learned behavior influences further learning. Miller and Dollard (1941) have shown how essential is the concept of "social learning." And Chein (1944) has recently suggested that "a structured set of interrelated motives" probably forms the core of the empirically experienced "self," or "ego."[21]

That there can be no adequate psychology of the abnormal which does not give emotions and attitudes a prominent systematic position is today a foregone conclusion. Pavlov's (1927) attempt to extend the same narrow formulae into which he forced his experimental results with animals over into the field of psychiatry is eloquent testimony of their inadequacy. One of the keys to Freud's success is that from the outset he saw fear, lust, and anger—or, more accurately, fear *of* lust and anger, i.e., "anxiety"—as the central problem in the psychoneuroses.[22]

Finally in acknowledging the secondary motive of fear as a significant variable which commonly intervenes between external stimulation and overt behavior, we resolve a systematic difficulty which has long harassed the law of effect and kept it from developing into a comprehensive theory of learning. If behavior is always motivated and must be rewarded in order to persist, how is it that *anticipatory* responses, especially of an avoidant nature, are often among the most energetic and persistent which living organisms display? Difficulty in answering this question has made proponents of effect theory equally easy marks for the associationists, with their pat mechanical conception of conditioning, and for those writers who like to stress the role of purely "rational," or "cognitive," factors in behavior. We now see that behavior which is avoidant with respect to a primary drive (or "unconditioned stimulus") is likely to be rewarded by a reduction in the secondary drive (fear) which instigates it. In this way so-called anticipatory, or "foresightful," behavior can be made to conform very acceptably to the requirements of the law of effect, and seemingly "purposive," or "teleological," responses are accounted for well within the framework of ordinary scientific causation.[23]

---

[21] It is suggestive that in common language we identify our "selves" with our emotions in a way that we do not with external stimulation. Thus one says, "I *am* afraid," but only *sees* lights, *hears* sounds, etc. Alcohol, tobacco, and certain other drugs which change the experience of self are known to have their chief physiological effects on those mechanisms which mediate the emotions. Sleep, as an interlude in self-awareness, cannot occur if one is emotionally too excited or anxious.

[22] [For a revision of the Freudian theory of anxiety, see (19).]

[23] [The missing link in this logic is any reference to the question as to how fear itself is acquired and perpetuated. This problem has been touched upon in some of the preceding papers and is given detailed attention later (9).]

Summary

In the foregoing pages we have described an experiment in which a deliberate attempt was made to establish conditioned responses which were radically different from the type of response which our subjects (rats) made to an unconditioned stimulus. This attempt was successful. Since traditional associationism cannot easily account for our results, we offer an alternative hypothesis.

The electric shock which constituted the unconditioned stimulus in this study was a primary (unlearned) drive. The conditioned stimulus (change in the pattern of illumination) aroused the secondary (learned) drive of fear. If, under circumstances of this kind, the response which is effective in eliminating the primary drive serves also to eliminate the secondary drive, then the "conditioned" (anticipatory) response and the "unconditioned" response will be substantially the same; but if conditions are such that one type of response is necessary to eliminate the primary drive and a different response to eliminate the secondary drive, then the so-called *CR* and the *UnCR* will tend to differ appropriately.

However, our results show that even where the primary and the secondary drives call for quite different responses, there is a tendency for the response made to the primary drive also to occur to the secondary drive. The reason for this is that a noxious primary drive, such as electric shock, tends to be accompanied by the secondary drive of fear; and any response which occurs to and eliminates the shock and fear in combination will tend to occur to fear alone when elicited by a warning, or danger, signal.

Thus two distinct sources of reinforcement are detected in avoidance conditioning, the one tending to strengthen the connection between fear and whatever response reduces the fear (independent secondary reinforcement) and the other tending to strengthen the connection between fear and whatever response eliminates the situation (shock and fear combined) of which the fear is premonitory (associative, or reintegrative, reinforcement).

Since fear is itself a product of learning, it may be contended that it cannot legitimately be used as a basis for explaining further learning. Our position is that only by making precisely this assumption can we hope even to begin to bridge the gap between the objective study of behavior and "ego psychology."

CHAPTER 6

EXTINCTION AND BEHAVIOR VARIABILITY AS FUNCTIONS OF EFFORTFULNESS OF TASK

[Any careful investigation of the psychology of fear leads to a consideration of the inhibition of behavior which is produced by means of so-called "punishment." Other writers have suggested that this effect comes about by virtue of "punishment" having the capacity to neutralize or reverse the effects of previously experienced "reward." It now seems that inhibition occurs rather as a result of *conflict,* which consists of the incompatibility of the punished response and the response(s) which the punishment itself and the associated fear call forth (1, 2, 3, 4, 5). (What is said here is intended to apply only to the inhibition of overt *behavior.* How emotional reactions are negatively modified is an independent and, as present, not well understood problem.)

In this paper the same logic is extended to account for the inhibition of habits, not by punishment in the ordinary sense, but by what is often referred to as "extinction." In extinction the only apparent source of conflict is that provided by the *fatigue* resulting from the recurrent, unrewarded preformance of a habit. The experiment here reported was designed to test the deduction that, with other things equal, effortful responses, i.e., responses whose performance generates relatively great fatigue, will extinguish (inhibit) more quickly than less effortful ones. This inference was confirmed at a high level of confidence.

The same type of reasoning was also used to make certain predictions concerning the relation between effortfulness of task and *behavior variability,* as manifested under conditions both of reward and nonreward. Although the results indicate that there is a significant relationship here, it is in the *reverse* direction to that anticipated. An analysis of this paradoxical outcome leads to the topic of "cognition," which is considered in the two following, and later, papers.

This paper, which originally appeared in *The Journal of Experimental Psychology* (1943), was jointly prepared with Helen M. Jones.]

This study deals with two distinct but related problems. The first is that of the relationship between the energy or effort involved in performing a habit and the rate at which this habit extinguishes (through nonrewarded repetition). The second problem is that of the relationship between the effortfulness of a habit and the tendency shown by living organisms to vary the behavior involved in the execution thereof.

Growing evidence indicates that extinction is a motivated adjustment in which fatigue plays an important role (Mowrer, 1941a). If this is true, it follows that the extinction of an effortful habit will proceed more rapidly than will the extinction of a relatively effortless but otherwise comparable habit. Is this expectation empirically confirmed, and if so, what, precisely, is the relationship between the factor of effortfulness and the rate at which extinction occurs?

It has repeatedly been noted that in situations in which there are two or more equivalent ways of reaching the same goal, living organisms do not readily fixate on one of these ways to the exclusion of the others, but instead continue, often for a very long time, to vacillate between the available alternatives. Since this form of behavior variability is something of a paradox from the point of view of any simple conception of habit formation, we raise a second question: Is this form of behavior variability, or oscillation, in any way related to the absolute level of effort which the affected organism must exert in reaching the goal?

Although there is some disadvantage from an expository standpoint in considering these two problems in the same study, there is the compensating advantage that, by using an appropriate experimental design, both problems can be investigated at the same time with only slightly more labor than either would occasion if attacked alone; and there is, moreover, a theoretical connection between them which will be more evident if the two problems are considered together rather than separately.

The problem of the effortfulness of task in relation to extinction will be considered first, then that of effortfulness in relation to behavior variability, and finally their interrelationship.

I. Extinction and Effort

Following the lead of Thorndike (1933), the traditional assumption has been that reward strengthens and punishment weakens a habit. But of these two "laws of effect," only the principle of reward has been found to be fundamental, for through it the phenomena subsumed under the principle of punishment can be derived. It is, for example, a familiar fact that a hungry animal, which has learned to obtain food by pushing a bar, can be made to abandon this habit if a sufficiently strong electric charge is put on the bar. Superficially, it does indeed appear that the "punishment" received when the bar is touched specifically weakens the original bar-pressing habit; but closer analysis shows that what actually happens is that the new motive, namely shock, merely calls forth a response which is incompatible with the original adjustment to the hunger motive, namely, the response of withdrawing from the bar, instead of pushing it. A *conflict situation* is thus produced in which the adjustment to the new, more urgent motive becomes dominant, without, however, necessarily weakening the original habit, *except in the sense of overlaying or superseding it.* Both of these responses are acquired, presumably, on the basis of the law of reward (reduction of hunger, reduction of shock), and the inhibitory effect is due to the fact that the responses are mutually incompatible, and unequally instigated.[1]

For some years it has been known that "punishment" is not, however, the only means by which habits can be inhibited: they can also be inhibited by their own nonrewarded repetition. Various hypotheses have been advanced as to the explanation of this effect; but in the present paper the assumption is made that the inhibition of a habit through nonrewarded repetition, i.e., by "extinction," works in fundamentally the same way as does inhibition through "punishment." In extinction the competing motivation is, we assume, the *fatigue* which is created by the organism's own activity; whereas in so-called punishment, the competing motivation is externally imposed.[2] The adjustment demanded by punishment may take the form of withdrawal or avoidance behavior which is necessarily incompatible with the action which occasioned the punishment. On

---

[1] [This account of the psychology of punishment is, of course, highly abbreviated. It omits all reference to the *conditioning* that would occur in a situation such as that described. Shock-on-bar serves not only to make the rat take his paws *off* the bar; it also makes him *afraid* of the bar. That is to say, since sight-of-bar has been followed by pain-to-paws, the former becomes capable of arousing fear; and the tendency for the rat to reduce this fear is to move away from, i.e., to *avoid* the bar. Thus the complete sequence would be: (1) under hunger instigation, the rat approaches and touches the bar; (2) the pain resulting from the shock produces a new instigation, which outcompetes the bar-pressing habit and forces the rat to release the bar, thus reinforcing the response, or habit, of letting-go-of-charged-bar; (3) at the same time, by conditioning, the sight of the bar is becoming a danger signal; and (4) through problem solving, this time at the level of secondary motivation, the animal learns to reduce the fear by staying away from the bar.]

[2] [To the statement, "the competing motivation is externally imposed," should be added, "and then becomes *internalized in the form of fear.*" This commonplace conversion of physical pain into psychic pain (i.e., fear) can probably be regarded as a very elemental form of what psychoanalysts have called *introjection.* For a discussion of the form of introjection known as identification, see 21 and 24.]

the other hand, the adjustive behavior to the discomfort (fatigue) produced by the organism's own activity is simply that of resting, or inactivity; but this behavior is also incompatible with the continued performance of the original response. In both cases new responses are thus instigated and reinforced which interfere with and, if sufficiently strong, inhibit the initial behavior. The modification of behavior, produced by the fatigue motive, is, we assume, basically the same as that produced by any other competing ("punishing") motive.[3] Both extinction and punishment, therefore, involve conflict between two or more responses which are differentially instigated.

The theory that extinction is a result of the interference of one habit with another has been previously suggested by Guthrie (1935) and by Wendt (1936), who explain the inhibition as rivalry between different reaction systems. These writers did not, however, recognize fatigue as the specific cause of the rivalry. Pavlov (1927) has considered fatigue as a possible explanation of extinction but discarded it for what seem to us to be quite insufficient reasons. Brogden, Lipman, and Culler (1938), finding that three times as many trials were required to extinguish a conditioned response in dogs as to establish it (with electric shock as the unconditioned stimulus), have conjectured that "the only incentive for extinction is inertia. The dog might keep on reacting forever were it not easier now and then to stand still" (p. 112). Though fatigue is not stressed by these three writers as the explicit cause of extinction, it is nevertheless clearly implied. The interference, or conflict, theory of extinction which is subscribed to in this paper (cf. Mowrer, 1941a, Miller and Dollard, 1941, and Hull, 1943) has the advantage of making possible a single, comprehensive explanation of the inhibition produced both by so-called punishment and by extinction, and leaves no need for positing a separate theory of "adaptation" as proposed by Hilgard and Marquis (1940) or the "central inhibitory process" of Pavlov (1927).

---

[3] For present purposes, "fatigue" or "effort" may be defined as the internal stimulation which results from the contraction of skeletal muscles. This stimulation may be either specific or general; and it may be weak or strong. Specifically, "fatigue" refers to the stimulation of the particular muscles, tendons, and joints which are involved in the execution of any given reaction; in its more general aspect, it refers to the diffuse effects produced by the spread (through the blood stream) of the waste products of the local action. Both types of stimulation are stronger (*a*) if the reaction is performed against much rather than little resistance, (*b*) if the reaction is performed repetitively rather than singly or sporadically, and (*c*) if the organism is undernourished, aged, arthritic, or diseased. The specific, localized stimulus effects of action, if weak, serve mainly as cues for guiding action (kinesthesis); only when this and the more generalized form of action-produced stimulation become relatively intense do they take on motivational power, i.e., function as "fatigue."

PROBLEM. If fatigue is the motive for extinction, it follows that the rate of extinction should be positively correlated with the effortfulness of the task, that is, the rate at which the fatigue is generated. The verification of this inference is the principal objective of the first part of this study.

APPARATUS. A front view of the apparatus employed in this experiment may be seen in Figure 36*a*. This apparatus is made of wood with a glass front and wire flooring. The inside measurements are approximately 12 × 12 × 6 in. The food trough is located in the center of the back panel midway between 2 brass bars (¼ in. in diameter) which extend horizontally into the box a distance of 4½ in. Guards were installed over the bars to prevent the animals from climbing over and standing on them, thus ensuring a more uniform type of operation. Each bar required a minimum downward pull of 5 gm. and an excursion of approximately ½ in. to activate the electrical food-delivery mechanism which is located on the back of the apparatus (Figure 36*b*). A description of this delivery mechanism will be found in an article by Mowrer and Miller (1942). The food used in this experiment consisted of 2 parts Purina Dog Chow and 1 part macaroni flour, molded into cylindrical pellets approximately ¼ in. long and ⅛ in. in diameter. In order to secure the varying degrees of effort required to depress the bars, at different stages in the experiment, lead weights were added in appropriate number to the yokes attached at the opposite ends of the bars (see Figure 36*b*).

SUBJECTS AND TRAINING PROCEDURE. Thirty Lashley-strain female rats (four to six months old) were reduced and held for the duration of this investigation to 15 per cent below normal body weight. The animals were given 8 days of habituation to the apparatus, to the type of food used as reinforcement, and to being handled. During this time they also learned to push each of the 2 bars as a means of obtaining food. The detailed procedure was as follows. In order to accustom the animals to finding food in the trough, they received 20 pellets a day for 2 days with both bars absent. On the third and fourth days this procedure was repeated but with the experimenter clicking the electrical delivery mechanism so that the animals would learn to associate the sound of the click with the delivery of the food (Skinner, 1938). On the fifth day one bar was inserted and each animal was required to depress it in order to receive a pellet of food. To preclude any tendency for position or recency to act differentially on the establishment of preference, half of the animals were given access to the right bar

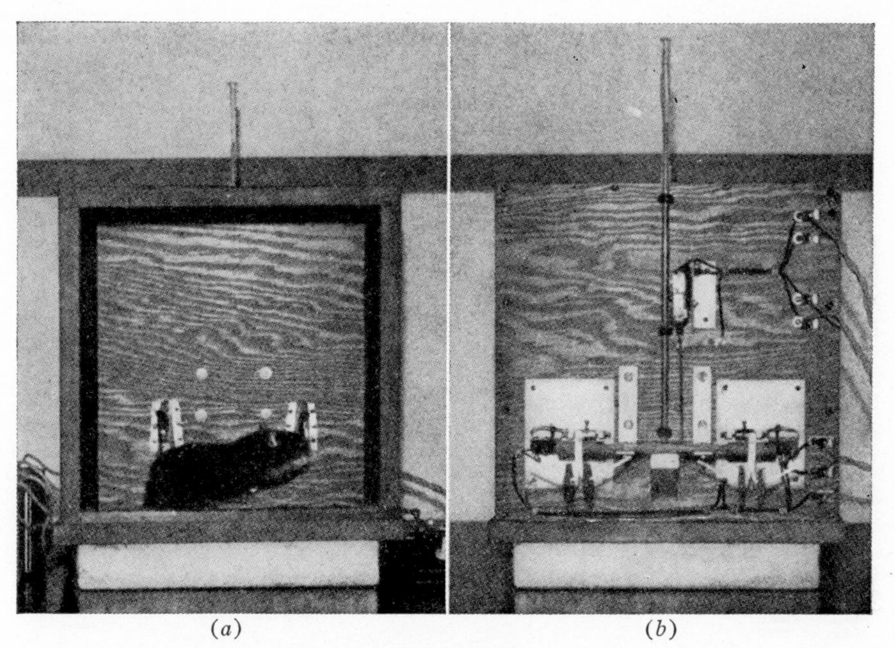

(*a*) (*b*)

Fig. 36.—Front and rear views of apparatus used in this study.

on this day and half to the left. The bars were alternated during the sixth, seventh, and eighth days, at the end of which time each animal had thus made a total of 80 rewarded responses, 40 on the right bar and 40 on the left. Beginning on the ninth day, both bars were left in the apparatus, a response on either producing a pellet of food.[4]

The remainder of the training procedure is graphically represented in Figure 37. The amount of effort required to push the

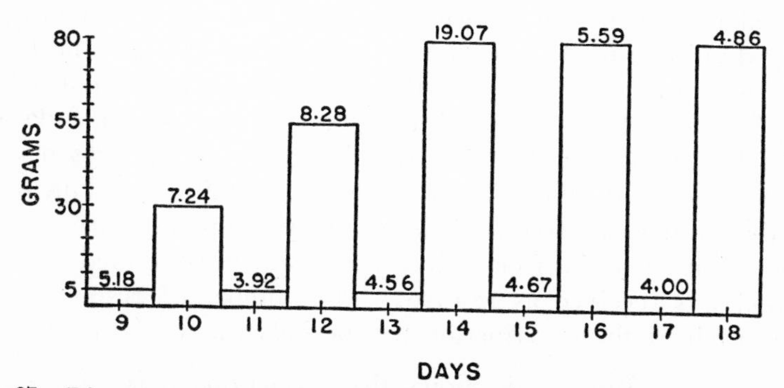

FIG. 37.—Diagrammatic representation of procedure used to teach subjects to press bars requiring varying amounts of effort. The values given at the top of each column represent the average times (in minutes) required by all subjects to make the 20 responses constituting each day's training performance.

bars on the ninth day was the same as on the previous days, namely, 5 gm. On the tenth day, however, the difficulty of the task was increased to 30 gm. This was reduced to 5 gm. on the eleventh day and increased to 55 gm. on the twelfth. Again there was a return to 5 gm. on the thirteenth day, and this weight was alternated with 80 gm. for the remaining 5 days of the training period.[5]

The alternation between the 5- and 80-gm. levels of difficulty was continued until the animals took very little longer to perform

[4] For purposes of the part of this study which has to do with extinction and effort, one bar would have served as well as two. The double bar arrangement was made necessary by the second part of the experiment having to do with behavior variability.

[5] This peculiarly complicated procedure seemed necessary for the following reasons. If all subjects had been trained to press the bar with only one level of effort involved, there was the danger that they might have been differently affected by the three levels of difficulty used in extinction (quite aside from the direct effects of the effort factor), because a particular level of difficulty during extinction happened to be similar to or different from the one used during acquisition. On the other hand, if all animals had been trained with the bar response requiring the same level of effort during acquisition as was to be required during extinction, there would presumably have been variations in the resistance to extinction shown by the three groups, even if tested under precisely the same extinction conditions. The procedure actually adopted avoids both of these difficulties.

20 responses under the one condition than under the other. Indicated on the top of each column of the diagram shown in Figure 37 are the average times required each day by all animals to make the 20 responses. These times are shown in minutes and hundredths of minutes. As training progressed, we see that the time involved in making the 20 80-gm. responses declines until, in the end, it is only slightly greater than the time required to make 20 5-gm. responses.[6]

Extinction. Up to this point all the animals had received identical treatment. They were now, on the nineteenth day, randomly divided into 3 groups. For one group the bars henceforth required 5 gm. of effort, for the second an intermediate amount of 42.5 gm., and for the third, 80 gm. On each of the 3 days immediately following acquisition training, each animal was placed in the apparatus and allowed to remain for 20 minutes. During this time the animal was free to make as many bar-pressing responses as it chose, but since the food-delivery mechanism contained no pellets, no food was received as reward. The number of responses made during each of these extinction test periods was carefully recorded.

Results. Figure 38 shows the extinction curves for each of the three groups of animals on the three extinction days. That effortfulness of the task is inversely related to the number of extinction responses is indicated by the finding that Group I, for which the task was easiest (5 gm.), clearly made the greatest number of responses; Group III, for which the task was most difficult (80 gm.) made the smallest number of responses; and Group II, with a task of intermediate difficulty (42.5 gm.), made an intermediate number of responses. Even in the first minute of nonrewarded repetition the effect of the effortfulness of the task was noticeable, since the 5-gm. group made an average of 17 responses in the first minute, the 42.5-gm. group an average of 15.9 responses, and the 80-gm. group an average of 12 responses. On the last day of extinction the curves naturally draw together and show some overlapping as complete extinction is approached by all three groups.

---

[6] The increment in the time required to make 20 5-gm. responses on the thirteenth and fifteenth days over that required on the eleventh day may be accounted for as follows. On the twelfth and fourteenth days, the effort demanded was 55 and 80 gm. respectively. It was noticed that on a day following one on which the task had been unusually difficult, the animals were at first reluctant to start work. They would look at both bars, explore a bit, and finally push with much more energy than the task demanded. Consonant with the law of least effort, however, this excessive exertion was gradually reduced to correspond to the demands of the task. By the seventeenth day learning was so far advanced that there was no hesitation in responding immediately, regardless of the level of difficulty, and the time required to make the 20 responses on this day was again practically the same as it had been on the eleventh.

Another way of presenting the results obtained in this study may be seen in Figure 39, which shows the average number of responses made by each group during all three extinction days. The 5-gm. group made an average of 350.3 responses during this entire period, the 42.5-gm. group an average of 248.4 responses, and the 80-gm. group an average of 110.7 responses. That these results are statistically significant is indicated by the finding that for the

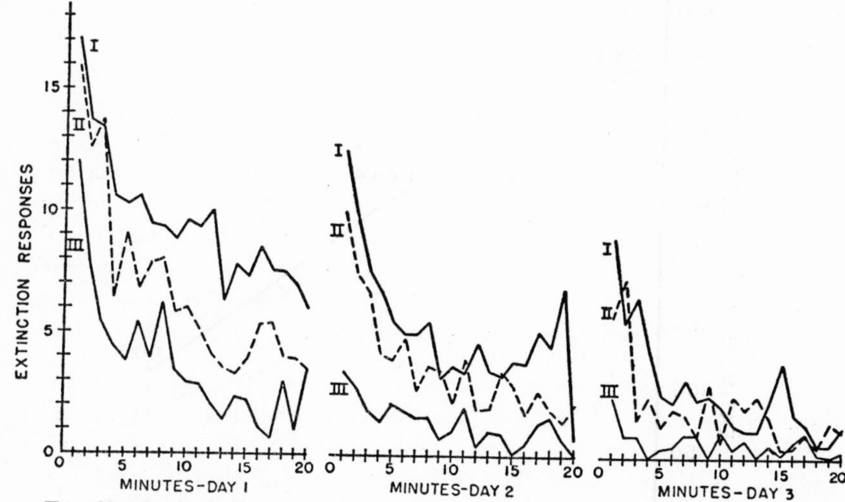

FIG. 38.—Curves showing the course of extinction of a habit when that habit is easy (I), hard (III), and intermediate (II) with respect to the effort required to execute it.

5-gm. and 42.5-gm. groups the critical ratio is 1.93, for the 42.5- and 80-gm. groups it is 2.69, and for the 5-gm. and 80-gm. groups it is 8.00. All these values are significant at the .05 level or better. From these results the hypothesis is clearly confirmed that extinction is related to the effortfulness of the task.

One striking, but not unexpected, incidental result of this experiment was that during extinction individual differences among the animals were found to be a function of the degree of effort involved. The behavior of the 5-gm. extinction group was surprisingly uniform, but in the 42.5- and 80-gm. groups some animals showed signs of frustration and aggression, consisting of excessively vigorous pressing of the bar, gnawing at the guards and other parts of the apparatus, jumping, and other agitated behavior. Using the coefficient of variation, $V = \frac{100\sigma}{M}$, it was found that for the 5-gm. group, $V = 1.95$, for the 42.5-gm. group, $V = 5.73$, and for the 80-gm. group, $V = 5.16$. Calculating the coefficient of variation without a Group II aberrant animal which made more responses than did any animal in Group I, the *V* for the 42.5-gm. group is then 4.1, thus showing a progressive increase in variability as the effort of the task was increased. This is consistent with the results of previous investigations by Mowrer and Lamoreaux (4) and Whiting and Mowrer (14) which disclosed individual differ-

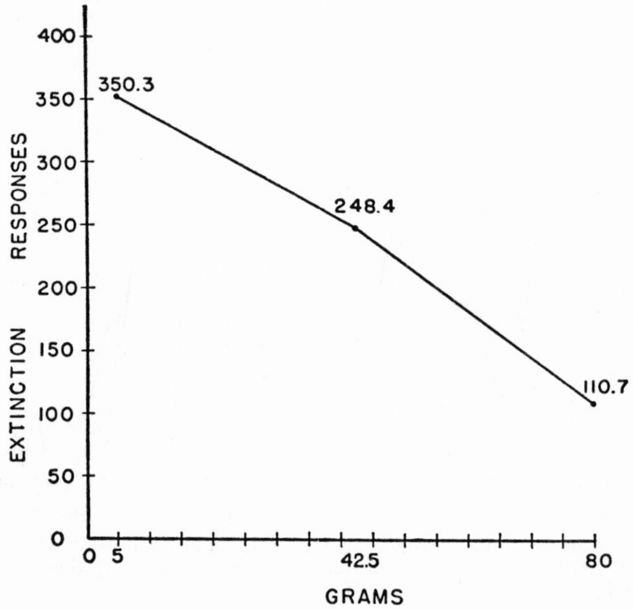

FIG. 39.—Curve showing the average number of responses made during three standard extinction periods as a function of the effortfulness of the task.

ences to be greater when a learning task is difficult than when it is easy.

DISCUSSION. Figure 38 suggests a problem which the fatigue theory of extinction has to face. If it is the response of resting which interferes with the original response of pushing the bar, and if it is admitted that fatigue disappears with rest, then why do not the three curves start at the same point on the three days of extinction? Why, on the second day, does the bar-pressing start at a lower level for all three groups than on the first, and on the third day at a still lower level than on the second?

This phenomenon may be accounted for in the following manner. During acquisition the response of pressing the bar has been followed by a reduction in hunger and so has been reinforced. At the same time it has also been connected with the cues of the total situation, such as the click of the food-delivery mechanism, the lights and shadows in the box, the odors of the apparatus, and so on. The whole pattern of stimuli provided by the apparatus has thus acquired some capacity for producing the bar-pressing response through the principle of associative reinforcement (Mowrer, 1941a). During extinction, however, the response of pushing the bar does not result in hunger reduction, whereas the response that does get reinforced is resting. The situational stimuli which had previously become connected with the bar-pressing response now become connected with the resting response. In other words, the sign-function, or "meaning," of the experimental situation changes from place-where-rat-reduces-hunger-by-pressing-bar to place-where-rat-gets-tired-and-has-to-rest. It is, then, this shift due to associative learning that causes the animals to respond differently on successive extinction days even though the hunger motive is held constant and the opposing fatigue motive is also approximately the same at the beginning of each daily experimental session. Extinction is thus seen to be a true, though somewhat complicated, learning function (cf. Hull, 1943, and Miller and Dollard, 1941).[7]

It is interesting to note that if the curve shown in Figure 39 were extrapolated to the right, it would cross the base line at about 110 gm., thus suggesting that with the bar response requiring this amount of effort, extinction would be immediate and complete, i.e., that the task would be so arduous that the animals could not perform it at all. If, on the other hand, the curve were extrapolated to the left—to the point where the bar-pressing required, hypothetically, no effort at all—extinction would occur at about 373 responses. If our hypothesis—that the fatigue, or effort, generated by the nonrewarded repetitions of a habit is the cause of extinction—is valid, then one would be forced to predict that a habit requiring zero effort should occur an infinite number of times. Why, then, does the curve shown in Figure 39 suggest a finite number of responses at zero effort?

Obviously the 5 gm., 42.5 gm., and 80 gm. required to press the bar during extinction do not represent all the work done during the extinction period. Also effortful are raising the forelegs to the bar to depress it, going to and from the food trough, etc. The amount of effort involved in these actions is not directly measurable; but fortunately the extent of this effort can be at least roughly esti-

[7] [This analysis is strictly in accord with the account of inhibition-through-punishment which is given in Footnote 1. In the one case the bar "shocks you" —in the other it "tires you." But in both cases there is presumably conditioning of fear, which tends to produce bar-avoidance, though the emotion generated in the one case is considerably less intense than in the other.]

mated. Since 5 is one sixteenth of 80, one would be led to expect the 5-gm. group to make sixteen times as many responses as did the 80-gm. group, if bar-pressing were the only source of fatigue or effort. But from the number of extinction responses made by these two groups, it would appear that the work performed by the 80-gm. group was only about 3 times, rather than 16 times, as great as that performed by the 5-gm. group, since the latter made 3 times as many responses. Evidently a constant factor should be added to the 5 and 80 which makes the total amount of effort involved for the 80-gm. group only 3 times that of the 5-gm. group. If 32.5 is added to 5, the result is 37.5. This amount multiplied by 3 is 112.5. If 32.5 is added to 80 the result is likewise 112.5. The effort exerted by the 80-gm. group per trial would thus be 3 times that exerted per trial by the 5-gm. group. It may be assumed, therefore, that the effort involved in getting in position to push the bar, going to look for food, etc., is about 32.5 gm., irrespective of the effort directly involved in pushing the bar. If, therefore, the graph shown in Figure 39 were shifted to the right 32.5 units, there would then be the requisite amount of space on the left for the curve to be deflected upward toward infinity in accordance with the expectations of this theory.

II. Variability and Effort

The results which have just been described are in complete accord with findings previously reported by Crutchfield (1939), Fitts (1940), James (1941), and Brogden, Lipman, and Culler (1938) and with the general conception of the law of least effort as formulated by Wheeler (1940) and with Hull's law of less work (1943).[8] More novel are our results concerning the relation between effortfulness of task and behavior variability.

---

[8] [Solomon (1948a) has recently published an extended review of the literature in this area. He has also published (1948b) an empirical confirmation of the findings reported in the first part of this article. Rohrer (1947), in reviewing the literature on the effect of massed vs. distributed extinction trials upon the rate of extinction, finds the results somewhat inconsistent: some studies show massed trials more conducive to extinction, while others show no difference. Rohrer's own results "favor the massed condition when the response being extinguished [is] one with high habit strength" (p. 492). This outcome is certainly consistent with a fatigue theory of extinction. That depressant drugs facilitate extinction and excitant drugs retard it (Hilgard and Marquis, 1940) is likewise in keeping with the expectations generated by such a theory. (In reading Rohrer's study one needs to note the rather special way in which he uses the terms "internal inhibition theories" and "interference theories." The fatigue theory as outlined above and by Miller and Dollard (1941) and by Hull (1943) is certainly a kind of "interference" theory, yet Rohrer does not so classify it. He concludes that it is "a compromise between the internal inhibition theory of Pavlov and the interference type of theory" (p. 490).]

In a situation in which there are two or more ways of attaining the same goal, living organisms often behave in such a manner as to create a learning-theory paradox. On the first trial, the goal will be reached by one particular means or route. This fact indicates an initial preference for this in contrast to the alternatives. And since the route which is initially selected leads to reward, this preference should be further enhanced, with the result that the organism's performance would be promptly and permanently fixated. But this, as even the most casual observation will indicate, is rarely what occurs: instead of the initial response, or response-series, being immediately stereotyped,[9] the organism usually continues to show a considerable, though eventually diminishing, amount of exploration and response variations. How is this interesting, and biologically significant, phenomenon to be explained?

It was formerly the practice to refer to the varied responses which an organism displays in a trial-and-error learning situation as *random,* i.e., as due to uncontrollable and unpredictable circumstances. But as Miller and Dollard (1941) and other recent writers (Mowrer, 1941a; Shaffer, 1936) have shown, the successive responses which are made in such a situation occur according to a predetermined order, or hierarchy, and each unsuccessful ("erroneous") response ("hypothesis") gives way in turn to the next because of the inhibition (conflict) produced by its own nonrewarded repetition. That variation should occur among *unsuccessful* responses is thus well accounted for, but the question remains as to why living organisms should vacillate between two or more *successful* responses.[10] In situations in which the alternative adjustments involve unequal amounts of effort or reward, one can see an evolutionary, or survival, value in an organism's being able to manifest at least enough variation to insure discovery of the best solution. Such a statement does not, however, offer an *explanation* of the phenomenon in question for the reason that it does not designate the relevant variables, or determinants. Presumably the same determinants as cause this "adaptive" variation in behavior are also responsible for the ostensibly "nonadaptive" variability that occurs between alternative adjustments of equal merit. At least this is the

---

[9] See Guthrie and Horton (1937) and Cutsforth (1930) for studies reporting unusually prompt stereotyping. See also Whiting and Mowrer (1943) for a discussion of the role of anxiety in producing "curiosity" behavior.

[10] Also implied is the question as to why living organisms show variations in the particular movements, or actones (cf. Murray, 1938), involved in performing what, from a molar standpoint, is the *same* act or habit. This kind of variability is obviously related to the ability to eliminate awkward unessential movements and to develop "skill."

hypothesis which prompted the experimentation shortly to be described.

In commenting upon the objectively useless variability which occurs in the behavior of organisms in situations where there are two or more precisely equivalent routes to the same goal, various writers have suggested that this phenomenon may be due to an inherent tendency on the part of nervous tissue to vary or fluctuate in its functioning in such a way as to produce the instability noted in overt behavior. Thorndike, for example, says:

> There are subtle differences in the brain and nerves and muscles of the individual from minute to minute which cause a multiplicity or variety of responses to the same external situation (1931, p. 10).

A similar conception is implied by Maier and Schneirla, who say:

> The order in which these reactions appear may depend upon the excitatory threshold of each manner of response, or it is possible that the responses are an expression of a tendency to vary behavior (1942, p. 119).[11]

Most explicit and complete is Hull's recent discussion. This writer, positing a "spontaneous oscillation in irritability of the neural conduction elements which mediate behavior" and a "random and spontaneous firing of the individual neurons throughout the nervous system" (1943, p. 310), has formulated the following formal postulate:

> Associated with every reaction potential ($_{s}E_{r}$) there exists an inhibitory potentiality ($_{s}O_{r}$) which oscillates in amount from instant to instant according to the normal "law" of chance, and whose range, maximum, and minimum, are constant (p. 319).

It is indeed unlikely that any nervous system would be capable of preserving exactly the same level of excitability, or reactivity, from day to day or even from moment to moment. But recourse to this imperfection of nervous functioning as an explanation of the type of behavior variation which is here under consideration seems somewhat premature. The older assumption that the response variation which occurs in trial-and-error behavior was due to "chance" served only to obscure a problem and delay its solution. To the present writers, the use of such terms as "chance," "random," and "spontaneous" in attempting to explain behavior oscillation in situations involving various routes to the same goal can only

[11] Cf. Krechevsky (1937), Adams (1931), Gengerelli (1930).

arouse the suspicion that here again we may be employing language which provides nothing more than a pseudo-solution.[12] Since the concept of inhibition through the nonrewarded repetition of responses has provided an apparently valid explanation of response variability in *trial-and-error* situations, a thoroughgoing attempt should be made to account for the variability which occurs in *trial-and-no-error* situations on the same basis before resorting to any hypothetical neurological explanation which, as Hull warns, generates a certain fatalism as to the possibility of ever achieving "precise prediction of the specific behavior of any organism at any given moment" (1943, p. 318).

The justification for invoking a dubious neurological hypothesis to explain behavior oscillation decreases still further when we note that no less than seven methods have previously been described whereby this phenomenon can be experimentally manipulated. Elliott (1934) has shown that rats vacillate between 5 alternate routes to food significantly less when very hungry than when only slightly or moderately hungry (cf. Hamilton (1916)). Hamilton and Krechevsky (1933) and Everall (1935) report that the administration of an electric shock before the point of choice in a T-maze creates a marked tendency toward "perseveration," i.e., loss of normal variability ("plasticity"); and Everall (1935) finds that temporal delay produces a similar effect. Hamilton and Ellis (1933) describe a loss of variability following experimentally induced brain lesions. Pavlov (1927), Hamilton (1916), Witkin (1937) and others have advanced evidence that "distraction" also increases response variation. Krechevsky and Honzik (1932) and Hall (1936) find that response vacillation is a function of level of learning, being, in general, greatest in the early stages and least in the later stages. Heathers (1940) reports that vacillation between two alternative routes to equivalent goals (in a T-maze) is greater when trials are massed than when distributed and suggests an explanation in terms of Dodge's conception of "refractory phase" (cf. Dennis (1939)). If response vacillation is thus subject to modification by such a variety of means, appeal to a neurologi-

[12] This statement is intended to apply no less to situations in which the alternative routes or ways of reaching the goal are unequal than to those situations in which the alternatives are equal. The so-called law of least effort, as variously formulated by Wheeler (1940), Gengerelli (1930), Tsai (1932), Waters (1937), and others, undoubtedly provides a descriptively correct statement of the tendency of living organisms to select, other things being equal, the least effortful means of solving the problem. (See also Adams, 1931.) But more fundamental is the question which we pose: How to explain the response variation which must occur before a "selection" may be said to have been made.

cal explanation (which really does not explain but merely replaces one mystery by another) appears to be quite unnecessary.[13]

PROBLEM. As previously noted, the mechanism which is responsible for extinction seems to operate as a "self-correcting" device whereby living organisms are forced (without external interference, or "punishment") to abandon useless (unrewarding, wrong) behavior and to try out other, possibly more efficacious (rewarding, right) responses. It would seem reasonable to suppose that the same mechanism is probably also responsible for the variations in behavior which occur when there are two or more (either equally or unequally good) routes to the same goal. Since "wrong" responses which are effortful extinguish more quickly than do relatively effortless responses (see part I above) and since effort is required in making "right" responses no less than in making "wrong" ones, it would seem to follow that, other things being equal, the more effortful the alternate routes to a goal, the greater should be the tendency for living organisms to become extinguished ("refractory") with respect to one of the routes and therefore likely to resort to the other, thus showing a pattern of successive alternations, or oscillation. As the results reported below indicate, this, however, is too simple a view of the matter.

RESULTS AND DISCUSSION. It will be recalled that in order to determine the effects of effort on rate of extinction, we trained our subjects according to the special procedure described in the first part of this study (see Figure 37). This procedure provided for a 10-day training period during which the level of effort required to execute the rewarded task was varied on successive days as follows: 5, 30, 5, 55, 5, 80, 5, 80, 5, 80 gm. Since two strictly equivalent bars were available throughout this period, the procdeure used in connection with our first problem provided an excellent opportunity for also testing the hypothesis just advanced that, when equivalent responses are equally effortful, living organisms vacillate between them more, i.e., show less stereotyping, than when the responses are relatively effortless. A careful record was accordingly kept during this 10-day period of the order in which all animals

[13] If one attempts to explain the apparent capriciousness of living organisms in choosing alternate routes to the same goal in terms of "spontaneous" neural oscillations, it would be equally logical to try to account in the same way for the "vicarious trial-and-error behavior" (*VTE*) which occurs at choice points in mazes and in discrimination learning. Far from being a kind of *paralysis agitans,* this behavior has been shown by various researches (Muenzinger, Bernstone, Richards, L., 1938; Muenzinger and Gentry, 1931; Tolman, 1938) to be a definite aid to economical learning, which is probably itself a product of earlier learning.

chose the two bars which were thus available to them in making the 20 responses which were permitted each day. In Figure 40 will be seen the results, first of all, in terms of the amount of vacillation (percentage of trials on which there was a shift from one bar to the other) which occurred each day. Contrary to our expectations, it was found that this phenomenon was related in no detectable

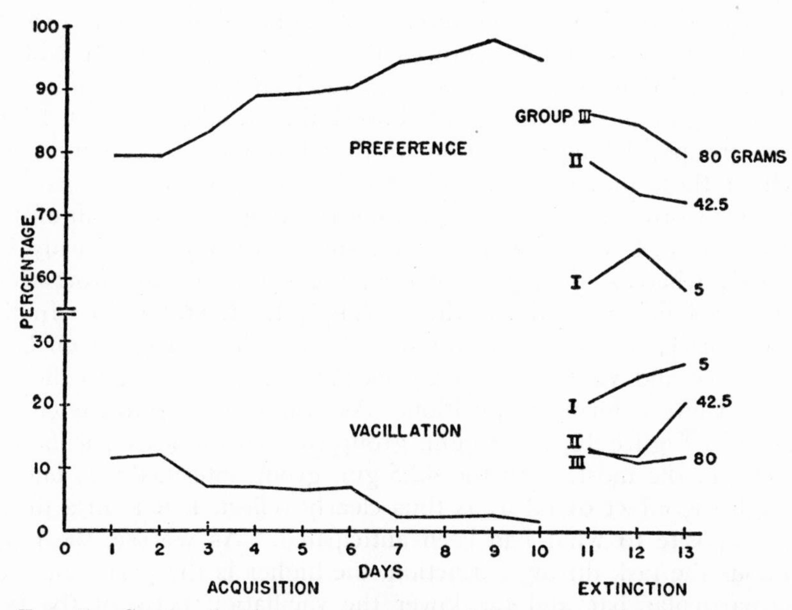

FIG. 40.—Curves showing two measures of response variability (vacillation and preference) as functions of level of effort involved. During the 10 days of acquisition, the effort factor was varied as follows: 5, 30, 5, 55, 5, 80, 5, 80, 5, 80 grams without, however, affecting either measure of response variability. During extinction, on the other hand, when the effort factor was varied by groups but not from day to day, there is a clear indication of causal relationship.

manner to the level of effort required to execute the bar-pressing task. The only consistent trend was a gradual decrease in the amount of vacillation from the beginning to the end of this period.

As might have been expected, it turned out that preference for a given bar (measured in terms of the percentage of trials on which each animal selected its favored bar) was inversely related to the vacillation measure just described (see upper curve in Figure 40), but this measure likewise failed to show any perceptible effect of the day-to-day variations in the level of effort required to perform the bar-pressing task. In keeping with the inverse relationship between these two measures of variability, there was, however, a gradual increase in the stability of preference during the 10-day period.

Since the procedure employed in the first part of this study readily permitted it, the tendency to vacillate between the two equivalent bars was recorded not only during acquisition but also during extinction, with highly interesting results. By referring to Figure 40 it will be seen, in the first place, that during extinction both the vacillation and preference measures show trends exactly the reverse of what they showed during acquisition. (It will be remembered that all the animals had received the same training up to the beginning of extinction but were then randomly divided into three groups; during extinction we therefore have three curves for each of these measures instead of only one as during acquisition. In other words, during the acquisition training, variations in effortfulness of task were introduced on successive days as already indicated; whereas, during extinction, the variations in effort were introduced in terms of the three groups, I, II, and III.) In the second place, the weight factor does have a decided effect on both preference and vacillation during extinction, in contrast to the absence of effect during acquisition. As can be seen from the curves shown in Figure 40, the 80-gm. group showed the least vacillation, the 5-gm. the most, with the 42.5-gm. group intermediate; but although the effect of effort is thus clearly reflected, it is in a direction opposite to what had been anticipated. As we see, the more arduous the task during extinction, the higher is the preference for one particular bar and the lower the vacillation between the two bars, whereas we had originally assumed that the greater the effortfulness of the task the lower would be the preference and the greater the amount of vacillation.

In an unpublished experiment carried out some years ago by the senior author and William D. Orbison, it was likewise found that when rats were allowed to run to a common goal via either of two equivalent maze routes, they showed reliably less vacillation when these two routes were both relatively long than when they were both short. But since the factor of effort cannot be varied in a maze situation without also varying the time factor, these results were not taken as necessarily disproving the hypothesis that, with other factors held constant, effortfulness and variability should be positively correlated. However, since the results of the present experiment, in which the time factor was held virtually constant (see Figure 37), also fail to show the expected positive correlation, the hypothesis can be regarded as definitely disproved.

An explanation of the finding that under at least certain conditions behavior variability is negatively, rather than positively, correlated with effortfulness of task has not yet been fully worked out; but one possibility is that the inhibitory effects generated by the repeated performance of a task generalize more strongly to a similar or equivalent task when these tasks involve a high degree of effort than when they involve a low degree of effort. Most of the work which has been done on generalization has had to do with *stimulus* equivalence; further research on the laws governing the generalization of equivalent *responses* may or may not confirm the foregoing conjecture. However, in showing that under at least some circumstances the effort factor is capable of influencing response variability we have added another variable to the seven previously listed by means of which response variability can be experimentally controlled and to this extent have further discredited the type of neurological hypothesis previously advanced by various other writers.

Summary

This study takes as its point of departure the hypothesis that the elimination of a response, or habit, through its own nonrewarded repetition involves a conflict in which the fatigue thus generated instigates a response (resting) which is incompatible with and therefore tends to inhibit the original response. Such an hypothesis is confirmed by the finding that the rate at which a nonrewarded response extinguishes is highly correlated with the effortfulness of that response. It is also confirmed by the well-known tendency for an extinguished response to reappear after a lapse of time, since the motive which produces the inhibitory response of resting, namely, fatigue, is thereby eliminated. The fact that the amount of recovery following successive extinctions becomes progressively smaller and may eventually reach zero is due to a change in the "meaning" of both situational and organic cues, which follows familiar learning principles.[14]

---

[14] [Using the empirical findings reported in this article as a point of departure, Hull (1943) has coined the term "reactive inhibition" (I_R) and "conditioned inhibition" ($_sI_R$) to refer, respectively, to the two phenomena described in the above paragraph. Kimble (1949) has recently defined the first of these terms as follows: "Reactive inhibition is essentially a negative [why "negative"?] drive state closely allied to pain avoidance [why not simply "pain"?]. It is a *response-produced* inhibition which results from or accompanies all effortful behavior whether reinforced or not and dissipates during periods of rest. In this respect I_R resembles [is?] fatigue" (p. 15). With the minor changes indicated in this statement, I would certainly subscribe to it. However, there is a subtle but important difference in the way in which Hull defines "conditioned inhibition" and the way in which I regard it. Again paraphrasing Hull, Kimble says: "Since pauses [in an effortful performance], however slight, serve as reinforce-

If extinction is thus conceived as a "self-correcting" mechanism (in principle no different from "punishment"), by means of which behavior which has previously been but is no longer rewarding is eliminated, then the role of extinction in producing the response variation which is so essential in trial-and-error learning becomes obvious. But living organisms not only manifest and then abandon "erroneous" responses; they also often show considerable variability in situations in which there are two or more equally "correct" responses. If only one motive were involved in situations of this kind, the observed response vacillation would be quite incomprehensible; but since we know that fatigue is generated no less by the performance of responses which lead to reward than by those which do not (assuming that they occur equally often), one is justified in supposing that the resulting conflict, or "ambivalence," is in some way responsible for the capriciousness just mentioned. Since the effortfulness of a response is known to be positively correlated with the rapidity with which that response extinguishes if reward is withdrawn, it was conjectured that the more effortful two alternative routes to the same goal are, the greater would be the "ambivalence" toward each route and the greater the tendency to vacillate between them. The experimental results here reported do not, however, confirm this expectation. Alternative hypotheses are considered, which will be tested by later research.

---

ments [i.e., are fatigue reducing], it follows that the response of resting will become conditioned to whatever stimuli are present in the learning situation. This conditioned resting response tendency is conditioned inhibition ($_sI_R$), the secondary inhibition component represented in the total inhibitory potential" (p. 15). I believe it is a misleading oversimplification to speak of a "conditioned resting response tendency." As I have indicated in Footnote 7, what is conditioned is *mild fear,* representing anticipation of the *mild punishment of fatigue.* And since the proprioceptive and other stimuli associated with a given performance become signals of the fatigue which the performance engenders, they, then, become capable of eliciting the mild fear state. *This* is conditioning. What the organism *does* about such a derived drive is a matter of *problem solving.* Since inaction serves to eliminate the fear-producing stimuli and thus the fear, then inactivity, or "resting," becomes reinforced in precisely the same way that any other problem-solving response does. I believe that omission of *emotion* as an intervening variable in cases of this kind is a serious imperfection in Hull's theoretical system. (The issue raised here is actually that of the nature of *secondary reinforcement.* Hull assumes, as the foregoing passages indicate, that incidental stimuli which accompany a primary reinforcing state of affairs acquire, through conditioning, secondary reinforcement potential. I tend rather to the view that secondary reinforcement can occur only when a secondary drive state is already existent and a stimulus- or situation-change releases secondary-drive reduction. Thus, secondary reinforcement is less a matter of the appearance of a signal of primary drive reduction than it is of the disappearance of a signal of primary drive increase (or drive continuation). This issue, which calls for much further analysis, both logical and empirical, than it has thus far received, has been alluded to in the Introduction and will be discussed again in a later study (17).]

A Supplementary Experiment

[After the foregoing study had been published, it occurred to the authors that there is another possibility of accounting for the spontaneous alternation of equivalent responses which has not previously been explored. A series of experiments by Lumley (1931, 1932) and by Spragg (1933, 1934, 1936) has shown the tendency for responses (e.g., turns in a maze) which occur near the goal to come forward, as "anticipatory intrusions," and produce "errors"

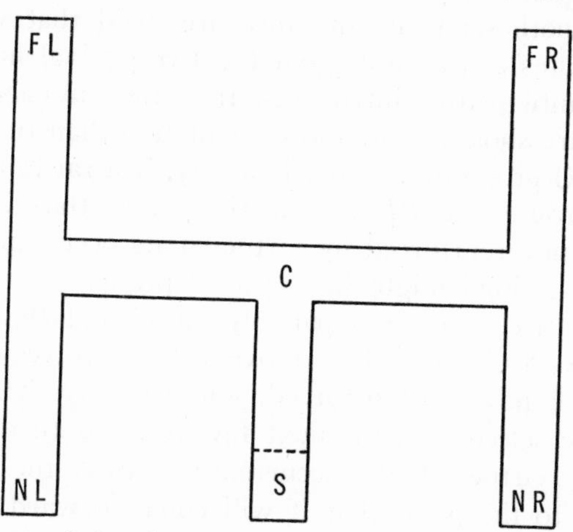

FIG. 41.—A maze designed to test the hypothesis that behavior variability is caused by "anticipatory intrusions."

earlier in the performance (cf. also Hull, 1934). The same phenomenon is, of course, also well known in serial learning involving nonsense syllables. It seemed likely, therefore, that at least in some situations behavior at a choice point, where the subject has to select one of two (or more) alternative routes to the same goal, might be influenced by anticipations of this kind. Thus, as a result of a subject's repeatedly reaching a goal by means of a given series of movements, it might be supposed that the anticipatory intrusion, or "coming forward," of one of the later movements in the series would throw the subject into quite a different series of movements, which would result in its reaching the goal by an alternative route.

A maze of the kind shown in Figure 41 seemed to offer a good means of testing this line of thought. Let us suppose that rats are used as subjects and that two groups are subjected to the two following procedures. With one group, after an animal is released at *S* (start), food will always be available both at *FL* (far left) and *FR* (far right). With the other group, the maze is baited, instead, at *NL* (near left) and *NR* (near right). Let us call the first procedure the **S**-procedure and the second procedure the inverted-**U**-procedure, since these two letters roughly describe the nature of the paths which are involved in the two cases. In the first case, regardless of whether the subject goes to the right or the left at choice point *C*, the last correct turn made before reaching the goal is the *opposite* of the turn made at *C*. In the second case, regardless of the direction of choice at *C*, the last correct turn made before reaching the goal is in the *same* direction as the turn made at *C*.

If the hypothesis is in any measure valid that vacillation between two routes to the same goal (or two equivalent goals) is influenced by anticipatory intrusions, then the animals subjected to the **S**-procedure should show more vacillation than the animals subjected to the **U**-procedure. That is to say, if a rat in the first group follows the route *S-C-FL* a few times and thus has the right-turning tendency reinforced by virtue of its occurrence nearest the goal, such an animal might be expected presently to make this response prematurely, or anticipatorily, at *C* and thus be launched on the route *S-C-FR*. The movements involved in following this route will now be reinforced, and we may therefore assume that it will be selected on the next few trials, until the left-turning tendency, by virtue of its occurrence nearest the goal, will be strengthened to the point that it will come forward and cause the animal to turn left at *C*, thus putting it back on path *S-C-FL*. This sequence of events might be expected to continue indefinitely, resulting in frequent reversals in the nature of the choice-turn at *C*.

On the other hand, if a rat in the second group follows the route *S-C-NL* a few times and thus has the left-turning tendency strongly reinforced by virtue of its occurring near the goal, then such an animal might be expected to have an ever-growing tendency to turn left at *C*, since this is the direction of turn which is being most strongly reinforced as the animal nears its goal at *NL*. Likewise, if a rat in the second group takes the route *S-C-NR* and thus has the right-turning tendency reinforced by virtue of its occurring near the goal, then such an animal might be expected to have an ever-growing tendency to turn right at *C*, since this is the direction of turn which is being most strongly reinforced as the animal nears its goal at *NR*. Thus, once an animal has traversed either *S-C-NL* or *S-C-NR* a time or two, one might suppose that, other things being equal, the route originally chosen would be permanently fixated, or at least that there would be much less vacillation between routes than in the case of the **S**-procedure.[15]

Suffice it to say here that fairly extended preliminary tests did not reveal any consistent difference between **S**-procedure animals and **U**-procedure animals. We were at the time surprised by this outcome—and still do not understand it!]

---

[15] For simplicity of analysis, no reference is made in the foregoing paragraphs to the fact that the rats in both groups could make errors at the choice point midway between *FL* and *NL* and at the choice point midway between *FR* and *NR*. However, one might expect that directional factors, resulting from the presence of food at *FL* and *FR*, in the one case, and at *NL* and *NR* in the other, would reduce the extent of errors of this type. Empirical observations confirmed this supposition.

CHAPTER 7

HABIT STRENGTH AS A FUNCTION OF THE PATTERN OF REINFORCEMENT

[The present study, undertaken in defense of the law of effect as a universally adequate theory of learning, brings the authors, in the end, to a consideration of alternative views. One interpretation of the experimental results here reported—the "response-unit hypothesis"—is consistent with the view that all learning is effect learning. But another interpretation—the "discrimination hypothesis"—which is equally efficient in accounting for the empirical facts, goes beyond the law of effect. It posits that over and above the influence of effect, certain "cognitive" factors may be operative in this experiment—factors which, while not too precisely identified, suggest the possibility of a *second kind* of learning: namely, purely associative learning, or conditioning.

This study touches upon "ego psychology" and leads naturally to the paper which follows.

As in the case of the preceding one, this paper was coauthored by Helen M. Jones and appeared in the *Journal of Experimental Psychology* (1945).

Toward the end of this chapter there are two long bracketed inserts which connect this study as originally published with observations and theoretical considerations which have been more recently published. Since this volume went to press, an admirably comprehensive review of the problem of partial reinforcement has been published by Jenkins and Stanley (1950). The reader will find this review particularly valuable for its account of the early history of the problem and its discussion of methodological and statistical complications. See also Grant, Riopelle, and Hake (1950).]

It was long assumed that the basic truth concerning the psychology of learning was embodied in the law of exercise (repetition, use, frequency), which held that every performance of a habit necessarily strengthened that habit. But evidence gradually accumulated which suggested that "exercise," as such, has little, if anything, to do with the strength of a habit. It was rather the presence or absence of *reward* (law of effect) that seemed crucial, since only rewarded responses grow stronger with repetition and nonrewarded (or punished) responses are actually inhibited thereby. Even this proposition, that every rewarded repetition of a habit strengthens it, has, however, recently been questioned. It is our purpose to consider whether the doubt which has thus been thrown on this proposition is justified.

If it be assumed that reward is the essential factor in strengthening a habit and that nonrewarded repetitions have a weakening effect, it would seem to follow that habits which are rewarded every time they occur would be strengthened more than habits which are rewarded only intermittently. But recent experimentation has brought the validity of this inference under suspicion. When "resistance to extinction," i.e., the extent to which a previously rewarded habit will continue to occur after reward is eliminated, is used as a measure of habit strength, it is found that a habit which has been developed on the basis of intermittent reward is, by this criterion, "stronger" than a habit which has been continuously rewarded. The experiment here reported represents an attempt to explain this paradox and to show that the experimental facts are actually consistent with the law of effect.

I. Formulation of the Problem

Since the present investigation was prompted largely by Humphreys' research on intermittent vs. constant reinforcement, it is necessary to begin with a brief description of this work.

Humphreys performed three experiments with human subjects, in the first of which he used the conditioned eyelid response (1939b), in the second a verbal response (1939a), and in the third the conditioned psychogalvanic response (1940a). In all three experiments a conditioned stimulus was followed by the unconditioned stimulus 100 per cent of the time in one group, whereas in a second group, the conditioned stimulus was followed by the unconditioned stimulus only 50 per cent of the time, in a predetermined but unpredictable order (though never with more than two reinforced or two nonreinforced trials in succession).[1] In each

[1] For Pavlov and many of his followers, the establishment of conditioned responses was assumed to involve nothing more than the paired presentation of the conditioned and the unconditioned stimulus. But it is now clear that even in avoidance conditioning of the kind employed in Humphreys' three experiments, the learning that occurs is subject to the same principles as control trial-and-error learning, where drive and reward play such an unmistakable role (Mowrer, 1941a; 4; 5). Therefore, whenever we use the term "reinforcement" we assume it to imply reward (drive reduction), even though it be in describing experiments in which the experimenter thought of reinforcement in purely Pavlovian (associationistic) terms. [The term "reinforcement" as it applies to learning theory has

experiment Humphreys found that the 50 per cent reinforcement group showed reliably greater resistance to extinction than did the 100 per cent reinforcement group.

Discarding Hull's "excitatory potential" concept (1938), Skinner's "reflex reserve" theory (1938), and Hovland's hypothesis of "extinction of reinforcement" (1936) as inadequate to account for his findings, Humphreys has put forward the alternative suggestion that "conditioned responses are a consequence of anticipated reinforcement, extinction [a consequence] of anticipated nonreinforcement and that the role of frequency in the repetition of reinforcement and nonreinforcement is by way of its influence on the subject's expectation of the stimuli which are to appear" (1939b, p. 150). Elsewhere, Humphreys says that the fact that discontinuous reinforcement produces greater resistance to extinction than does continuous reinforcement is "apparently due to difficulty in forming an hypothesis of continuous nonreinforcement after discontinuous reinforcement in acquisition" (1940a, p. 74).

More recent investigations by Humphreys (1940b) and Finger (1942a, 1942b), with rats as subjects, have likewise shown greater resistance to extinction after discontinuous than after continuous reinforcement. But Brown [2] has questioned whether Humphreys' "expectation" hypothesis is scientifically meaningful at the infrahuman level and has proposed an alternative interpretation. Brown suggests that an understanding of the results obtained with intermittent reinforcement hinges on the definition of the word "response." Let us suppose that a hungry animal has been trained with intermittent reinforcement to press a bar as a means of obtaining food, i.e., has sometimes been rewarded after pressing the bar once, sometimes after pressing it twice, sometimes after pressing it three times. The "response" which is thus effective in securing food consists, therefore, sometimes of one, sometimes of two, sometimes of three individual bar depressions. During extinction, ani-

---

had a curious history. It first came into general usage as a result of Pavlov's (1927) employment of it to designate the strengthening of a conditioned response through the paired presentation of the conditioned stimulus and the unconditioned stimulus. As a result of Hull's (1943) attempted reduction of all learning to drive reduction and his use of "reinforcement" to designate this type of event, the term has recently come to mean, rather generally, the strengthening of a stimulus-response connection through "reward." Many writers now speak of "contiguity theory" and "reinforcement theory" as denoting, respectively, association and effect (Sheffield, 1948). Strictly speaking, "reinforcement" simply means "strengthening," and if there are two kinds of learning, as maintained in this volume (9, 10), then there are two kinds of "reinforcement." But this issue is of no great immediate relevance since the Humphreys effect apparently applies to both forms of learning.]

[2] Dr. Judson S. Brown—personal communication. [Cf. Hull, 1941.]

mals trained to depress the bar more than once as a means of getting food might, consequently, be expected to depress the bar more times *but not necessarily to make more "responses" as thus defined* than animals which, having been rewarded consistently rather than intermittently, have learned exclusively a "response" consisting of *only one* depression of the bar. In other words, Brown's suggestion is that we may have been deceiving ourselves in this type of situation by equating the term "response" to single bar depressions instead of interpreting it to mean the total sequence, or *pattern,* of behavior leading up to the reward.[3]

The foregoing considerations raise the following specific question: If one uses as the unit for measuring resistance to extinction the same pattern of behavior which served as the instrumental "response," or "act," during acquisition, will intermittent reinforcement still produce greater habit strength than does reinforcement that is continuous?

In order to answer this question it seemed desirable to carry out an experiment involving one group of rats in which reward would follow each bar depression, three groups whose response pattern, or unit, would always consist, respectively, of two, three, or four depressions of the bar, and a final group which would be rewarded not only discontinuously but also randomly, on the average after every two and one half bar depressions.

The reason for this particular combination of groups is that prior experiments on intermittency of reinforcement have been to some extent confounded: groups of subjects which have been rewarded continuously and, necessarily, regularly have been compared with groups which have been rewarded discontinuously *and irregularly.* This confounding leaves open the question whether the obtained results are due to one, the other, or both of these factors. In our experiment, Group I is rewarded regularly and continuously, Groups II, III, and IV are rewarded regularly but discontinuously, and Group V is rewarded discontinuously and irregularly. In this way we have a combination of groups which makes possible all the comparisons necessary to determine whether it is to discontinuity, irregularity, or both that the phenomenon in question is attributable.[4]

---

[3] Cf. Murray's (1938) similar emphasis upon the distinction between what he terms "actones" and "acts."

[4] We are indebted to John L. Wallin for useful suggestions concerning the logic and design of this experiment.

II. Apparatus

The apparatus used in this experiment has been fully described elsewhere (6). It consists, essentially, of a wooden box, approximately 1 foot square, with a glass front and a wire-mesh floor. Originally there were 2 quarter-inch brass rods which extended horizontally into the box on either side of the food trough, which was located in the center of the interior rear wall; but for the purposes of this experiment, only the bar on the right was used.

In order to avoid differential auditory cues following bar depressions which were and were not to produce food, the automatic delivery mechanism employed in earlier experiments was disconnected and the food (a small, cylindrical pellet of Purina Dog Chow) was manually released by experimenter from the rear of the apparatus into the chutelike trough. However, the criterion as to when the bar had been pushed down sufficiently far to count as a full depression was standardized by a system of electrical contacts and a relay which caused a small light to flash on in experimenter's (but not in the rat's) field of vision whenever the bar was depressed by a predetermined amount. This electrical setup was also arranged so that each flash of the light signified a full excursion of the bar, i.e., the bar could not be depressed until the light came on and then "jiggled" as a means of making multiple flashes of light. Once the light had come on it would stay on until the bar was released and allowed to return to its normal position; only by means of another complete depression of the bar could the light be made to come on again.

A cumulative work recorder, which has also been separately described (Mowrer, 1943), was connected to the apparatus so that each time the light flashed a small increment of change was registered. Records thus obtained will be reproduced on a later page.

The reasons for arranging the apparatus so that only complete, discrete bar depressions would cause the light to flash and the recorder to operate are obvious, but the precautions taken to eliminate differential cues require a word of explanation. It was felt that if bar depressions which produced food resulted in a sound (due to the automatic delivery mechanism) which was noticeably different from the sound accompanying depressions which did not produce food, the animals would simply learn to go to the bar and pump away until they got the auditory cue signifying the reward. Similarly, in extinction there would have been a tendency to keep pushing the bar until the telltale sound occurred. It therefore seemed desirable to circumvent the entire problem by simply eliminating all differential cues. By releasing the pellet manually, it was possible to make the accompanying sound almost imperceptible; and by withholding the pellet until the animal came and looked in the trough, we prevented even this slight noise from serving as a cue as to whether any given bar depression would or would not be followed by food. The only way an animal could "know" when he had pushed the bar enough, without actually going and looking in the trough, was on the basis of his own kinesthesis.[5]

III. Procedure

HABITUATION AND ACQUISITION. Thirty Lashley-strain male rats (four months old) were reduced and held for the duration of this investigation to 15 per cent below normal body weight. At the outset of the experiment, each animal was given 20 pellets of food in the apparatus for purposes of habituation. On the first training day, the bar (requiring a minimum pull of 5 gm. to depress it) was inserted into the apparatus, and the animals were required to push it in order to obtain the food. Each animal was given 20 trials. This same procedure was repeated on the second and third days. On the fourth day the animals made the first 5 responses with the bar requiring a downward pull of 5 gm. as usual, but for the next 5 responses the bar was weighted so as to require a pull of 15 gm., and on the final 10 responses the bar required a pull of 30 gm. During the remainder of the experiment, the bar was kept weighted so as to require this latter amount of downward pressure to operate it.[6]

On the fifth day, after the preliminary training just described, the animals were randomly divided into 5 groups. The animals in Group I were rewarded after every bar depression, those in Group II after every second bar depression, those in Group III after every third, those in Group IV after every fourth, and those in Group V in random order, after 1, 2, 3, or 4 bar depressions but,

[5] Earlier unpublished research indicates that rats can learn to discriminate between 1 and 2 bar depressions and between 2 and 3, but beyond this their discrimination becomes unreliable. In the present experiment, multiple bar depressions often occurred between inspections of the food trough, but the more usual procedure in all groups was to press, look; press, look; etc.

[6] The bar was made easy to depress during the early phase of training, and reward was provided after each response in order to get the bar-pressing habit established more quickly and more reliably than would have been possible if the various conditions employed in the later part of the experiment had existed from the beginning. Our reason for increasing the effort required to depress the bar on the fourth day of training was that we wanted this act to be the major element in the total sequence of behavior involved in going back and forth between the bar and the trough, eating the food, etc.

on the average, after 2½. These different procedures were followed from the fifth through the eleventh day, the animals in each group being given 20 reinforcements (pellets) daily, as on days 1 to 4. By the end of the eleventh day each animal had thus received 220 reinforcements, the first 80 of which had been received under the same (preliminary) conditions for all groups, and the last 140 under conditions which were distinctive for each group.

EXTINCTION. Extinction began on the twelfth day and continued through the thirteenth and fourteenth days. The animals were left in the apparatus for 20 minutes on each of these days, free to press the bar at will but given no food whatever. (Outside the experimental situation, they received enough food to keep them at the standard body weight mentioned previously.) The number of bar depressions made during this period was counted by the observer and recorded automatically.

IV. Results and Interpretations

Groups I, II, III, and IV will be discussed first, inasmuch as the problem investigated with the animals comprising these 4 groups is that of the effect of continuous reinforcement (Group I) vs. discontinuous, or intermittent, reinforcement (Groups II, III, and IV). Group V poses the separate question of the importance of irregularity, or randomness, as opposed to regularity of reinforcement (Groups I–IV).

V. Continuous vs. Discontinuous Reinforcement

Table 5 gives the average number of bar depressions made by Groups I, II, III, and IV during the 3 days of extinction. Figure 42 shows the actual extinction performances on day 1 and day 3 of typical animals in Groups I and IV. These records for individual animals give a graphic equivalent of the corresponding group averages of 77.4, 15.8, 155.1, and 42.2 in Table 5. From Table 5 it is evident (*a*) that all groups made progressively fewer bar depressions on the 3 days of extinction and (*b*) that the animals in Groups I to IV made progressively more bar depressions on each of the 3 days of extinction, as well as for the 3 extinction days considered as a whole (see Totals). From Figure 42 it is further evident (*c*) that, as has repeatedly been noted by other

TABLE 5

AVERAGE NUMBER OF BAR DEPRESSIONS MADE ON THREE SUCCESSIVE DAYS OF EXTINCTION BY GROUPS I, II, III, AND IV

NOTE.—The bottom line (Totals) gives the average number of bar depressions made by each group during all three extinction days.

Extinction Days	Groups			
	I	II	III	IV
1	77.4	105.5	113.8	155.1
2	34.8	60.5	74.3	75.0
3	15.8	22.0	27.4	42.2
Totals	128.0	188.0	215.5	272.3

investigators (Hilgard and Marquis, 1940; Hull, 1943), the rate of bar-pressing activity was greatest at the beginning of each extinction session and was thereafter negatively accelerated.

The three sets of curves appearing in Figure 43 present these same data in a somewhat different manner. They represent the average number of bar depressions made by each of the 4 groups, by 2-minute periods, during each of the 3 20-minute extinction sessions. The 3 trends mentioned in the preceding paragraph are again evident in Figure 43.

The relationship between resistance to extinction and the reinforcement ratio used during acquisition becomes especially clear in Figure 44. The broken line shows (cf. Totals in Table 5) the average number of bar depressions made during all 3 extinction days by the animals in Groups I, II, III, and IV. This number was 128.0 for Group I, 188.0 for Group II, 215.5 for Group III, and 272.3 for Group IV. An analysis of variance gives an F of 7.18 for the differences between these groups due to frequency of reinforcement, an F of only 4.43 being necessary for significance at the .01 level. The t-test shows significant differences at the .02 level or better between the mean of Group I and the means of all other groups and between the means of Groups II and IV.

From these results it would appear, in keeping with earlier findings, that not only is intermittent reinforcement reliably more effective than continuous reinforcement in establishing a tendency to depress the bar in the absence of reinforcement; it may also be said that, within the limits of this experiment, the functional relationship between these two variables is virtually linear. [See comments by Jenkins and Stanley (1950), Footnote 6, p. 218.]

Since the animals in Group I were rewarded during acquisi-

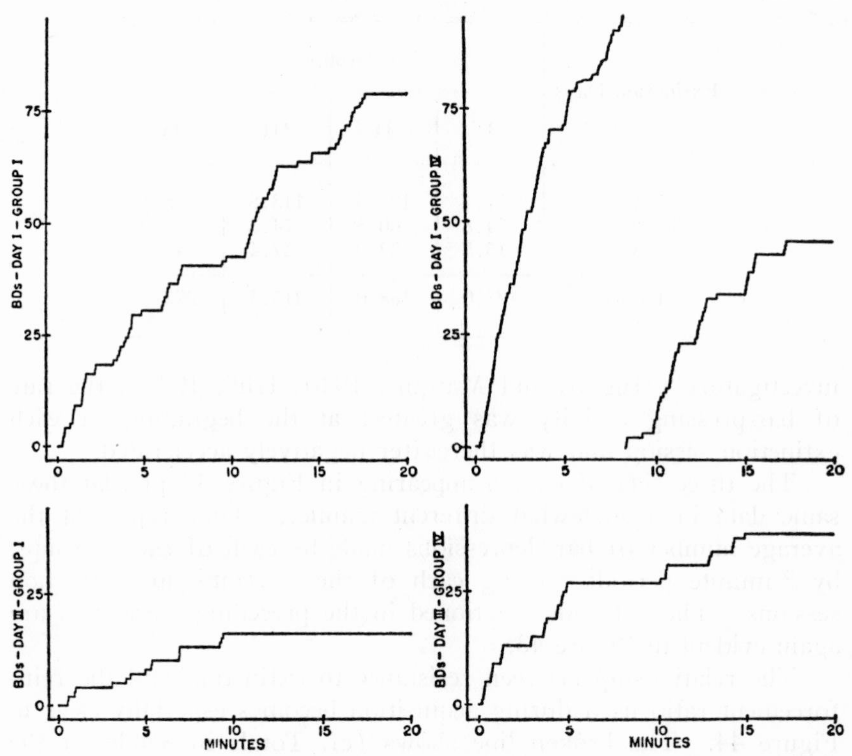

FIG. 42.—Graphic recordings of the performance of a typical animal in Group I and a typical animal in Group IV on Day 1 and Day 3 of extinction. These four individual recordings, representing 79, 16, 143, and 38 bar depressions (*BD*'s) respectively, correspond to the group averages of 77.4, 15.8, 155.1, and 42.2 in Table 5. The two curves in the upper right-hand recording should be thought of as continuous (cf. Mowrer, 1943).

tion every time they pressed the bar, whereas the animals in Groups II, III, and IV received reinforcement only one half, one third, and one fourth as often—and yet developed progressively greater apparent habit strength, as measured by resistance to extinction, it is easy to see how results of this kind might indeed seem incompatible with the assumption that every rewarded repetition of a habit strengthens it and nonrewarded repetitions weaken it. There are, however, at least two ways in which this paradox may be explained, well within the framework of effect-learning theory.

THE RESPONSE-UNIT HYPOTHESIS. The first of these explanations has already been suggested. Various studies (Hilgard and Marquis, 1940; Hull, 1943) have shown that the reinforcing effects of reward apply not only to the immediately preceding be-

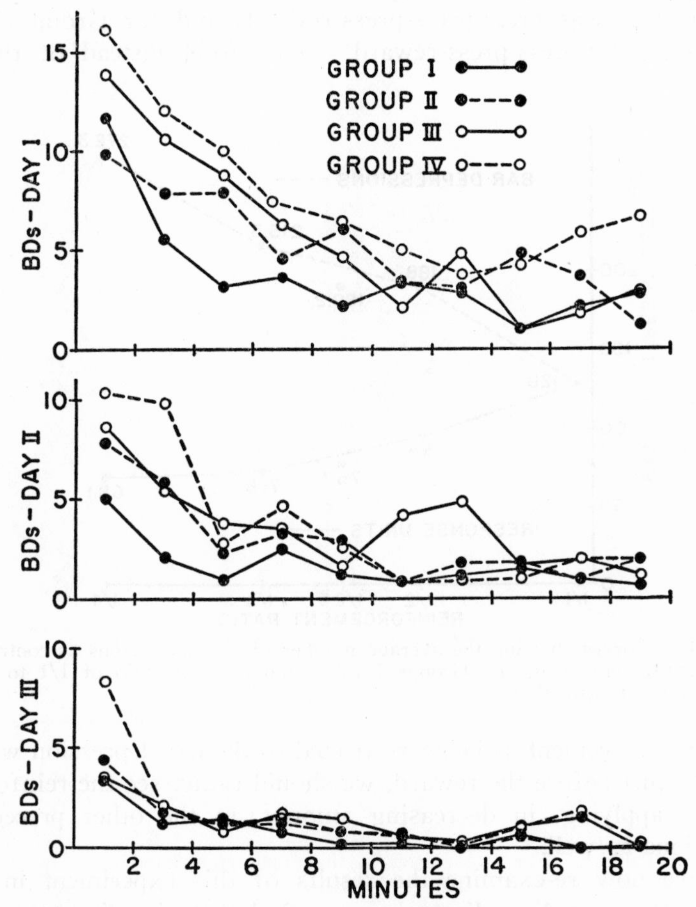

FIG. 43.—Curves showing the average number of bar depressions (*BD*'s) made by Groups I–IV on the 3 days of extinction. Each point on the curves represents the average number of bar depressions made in a 2-minute interval.

havior but also, to a diminishing extent, to the behavior which is temporally more remote from the advent of reward. According to this principle (the "gradient of reinforcement"), we know that under the conditions of the present experiment it was possible for an animal to be somewhat reinforced for pressing the bar even when this behavior did not immediately produce food. Thus, because an animal was, for example, rewarded only after pressing the bar twice, we should not think of this as press-failure, press-reward, but rather as press-press-reward. It will be recalled that in this part of the experiment the animals were all trained, after the fourth day, according to some one definite pattern. The pattern for Group I was press-reward; for Group II it was press-press-reward; for Group III it was press-press-press-reward; and for Group IV it was press-press-press-press-reward. Therefore, instead of think-

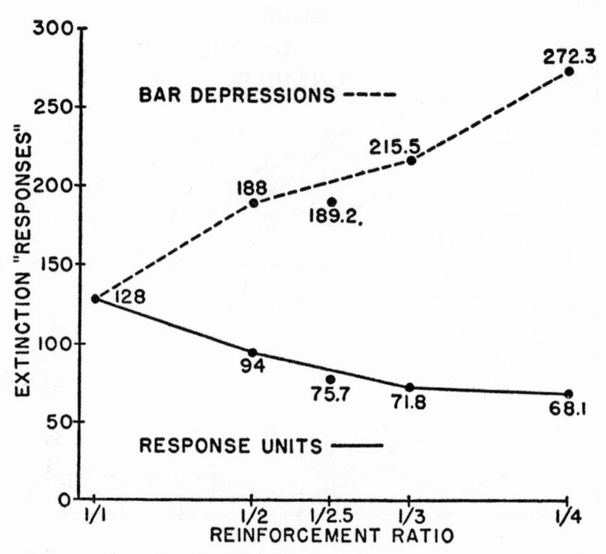

Fig. 44.—Curves showing the average number of bar depressions as contrasted with response units made by Groups I–IV (reinforcement ratio of 1/1 to 1/4) on all 3 days of extinction.

ing of reinforcement as being restricted to the bar depression which occurred just before the reward, we should rather see the reinforcement as applying, in decreasing amount, to the other preceding depressions as well.

If we now re-examine the results of this experiment in the light of the preceding discussion, we find that the discontinuous-reinforcement groups did *not* make more extinction "responses," defined in terms of the pattern, or unit, of bar depressions which was rewarded during acquisition, than did the continuous-reinforcement group. During extinction the animals in Group I repeated the response unit which had previously been rewarded 128.0 times (128.0 ÷ 1), the animals in Group II repeated their response unit 94.0 times (188.0 ÷ 2), those in Group III, 71.8 times (215.5 ÷ 3), and those in Group IV 68.1 times (272.3 ÷ 4). By thus using as a definition of "habit," or "response," the total unit of bar depressions which was rewarded in each of the four groups of animals during acquisition, we find that the apparent advantage of so-called intermittent reinforcement disappears (see solid line, Figure 43). The hypothesis that rewarded repetitions of a habit (so defined) strengthen it is, therefore, still tenable.[7]

A subsidiary problem remains, however. Since we are proceeding on the assumption that every rewarded repetition of a habit (defined as the total response unit, or instrumental act) strengthens it, and since each of the groups of subjects in the present experiment made the same number of rewarded response units during acquisition, each group might have been expected to make approximately the same number of response units during extinction. But as Figure 43 indicates, the average number of extinction response units becomes progressively smaller as we go from Group I to Group IV, being 128.0, 94.0, 71.8, and 68.0, respectively. The t-value for the differences between the mean thus obtained for Group I and the means of the other three groups and between the mean for Group II and that for Group IV all show significance at the .05 level or better, thereby indicating that the downward slope of the solid line in Figure 43 is statistically reliable and scientifically meaningful.

In a previous paper (6) we have shown that if a response requires more effort to perform, it will extinguish more quickly than if it requires less effort. Obviously, a response unit consisting of four bar depressions requires more effort than a response unit of only one depression. It is not surprising, therefore, that the former extinguishes more rapidly than the latter.

Equally plausible is an explanation based on the fact that even though all the bar depressions involved in a response unit of four depressions receive some reinforcement, they do not receive the same amount, since the one nearest the reward gets most, the one preceding somewhat less, the one preceding that one still less, and

---

[7] Sears (1943) has recently commented on the difficulty involved in precisely defining the term "instrumental act" and has to a considerable extent anticipated the above analysis by pointing out that "all activity preceding the goal response appears to come under this heading and to undergo reinforcement. If a given *movement* must be performed twice before the goal is reached, then the *pair* of movements becomes the instrumental act to the goal response. If later these acts are repeatedly performed without any reward occurring, it is to be expected that more *single* movements would occur during the extinction process if a *pair* of movements was the unit that had originally been reinforced than if a *single* movement had been the unit" (p. 84). Skinner (1938) has similarly remarked: "This is fundamentally a problem in the definition of a unit of behavior. As a rather general statement it may be said that when a reinforcement depends upon the completion of a number of similar acts, the whole group tends to acquire the status of a single response, and the contribution of the reserve tends to be in terms of groups" (p. 300).

the original one in the series least of all.[8] On the other hand, if the response unit consists of only one bar depression, it always receives the same, maximal amount of reinforcement (provided that the animal goes immediately to the trough and eats the food). Therefore, although the behavior involved in pressing the bar will be considerably more reinforced in Group IV than in Group I, it will not be reinforced *four times* as much. Consequently, when the behavior which occurs during extinction is analyzed in terms of response units, Group I will necessarily rank highest, with Groups II, III, and IV following in order.

Whether one or both of the two mechanisms just described—greater effortfulness of multiple than of single bar depressions, or the greater average but smaller total reinforcement received by single than by multiple depressions—were actually involved in producing the downward slope of the solid line in Figure 44 is a question which cannot be answered on the basis of our present data.

THE DISCRIMINATION HYPOTHESIS. The second way of explaining the results obtained with intermittent reinforcement depends upon the concept of discrimination, or sign-learning. Let us, for the moment, disregard the immediately preceding analysis in terms of response units. Viewing the continuous- and discontinuous-reinforcement procedures afresh, we see that the animals in Group IV, for example, had no means of differentiating so sharply between the acquisition situation and the extinction situation as did the animals in Group I. For the Group I animals, the act of pressing the bar had always "meant" that food would follow, i.e., during acquisition the kinesthetic and other stimuli which accompanied the performance of this movement became conditioned to the responses involved in turning from the bar to the trough and consuming the food.[9] On the other hand, in the case of the Group IV animals the kinesthetic and other stimuli accompanying bar depression were ambiguous, since they were sometimes followed by eating responses and sometimes by pressing the bar again, once

[8] Hull (1943) has recently reported evidence that in order for a response on the part of a rat to be reinforced by a subsequent reward it must occur within 30 seconds of that event. In the present investigation, all of the bar depressions comprising a response unit often occurred within a 30-second period (even in Group IV), but this was not always the case. (This statement is based on general observation; we have no systematic data.)

[9] [The terminology of this paragraph is obviously confused. At the outset a distinction is implied between solution-learning and "discrimination, or sign-learning." However, as the use of the term "conditioning" has just indicated above, the writers were still not clear about the proper distinction between problem-solving and conditioning. But awareness of the existence of two learning processes is unmistakably implied in Footnote 11.]

again, and still again. Therefore, with the onset of extinction, when food did not follow the first, second, or even third depression of the bar, the situation was not yet any different, psychologically, from what it had been during acquisition. Only after at least four bar depressions had occurred and not been followed by food did the "meaning" of the situation begin to change for the Group IV rats and then probably only very slowly. One would accordingly expect that the tendency to press the bar would wane much less quickly in the discontinuous- than in the continuous-reinforcement groups.

We suspect that this explanation is essentially what Humphreys had in mind in speaking of the greater difficulty which subjects trained with discontinuous reinforcement have in changing from an "expectation," or "hypothesis," of reinforcement to one of non-reinforcement than do subjects trained with continuous reinforcement. Our alternative statement merely attempts to make explicit some of the intermediate steps which were apparently implicit in Humphreys' reasoning. [Cf. also Virginia Sheffield, 1949.]

The plausibility of the foregoing interpretation is increased by the observation, reported by Pavlov (1927) and confirmed by others, that in learning experiments in which subjects are continuously reinforced, extinguished, retrained, re-extinguished, etc., extinction and relearning both take place with increasing speed. This finding suggests that the receiving of the reward has psychological implications over and beyond the automatic action of the law of effect. It suggests that the absence of reward, on the first trial of successive extinctions, may come to signify to the subject that further response is, at least for the time being, futile, i.e., the stimuli associated with the absence of reward become conditioned to resting instead of working, just as the presence of reward, on the first trial during successive relearning periods, may come to signify to the subject that the opposite situation now prevails.[10] Thus, in an experiment in which hunger is the principal drive, the subject learns to discriminate sharply between two total patterns: hunger-(and-fatigue)-plus-stimuli-associated-with-*getting-food* and hunger-(and-fatigue)-plus-stimuli-associated-with-*not*-getting-food. To the

[10] Cook and Harris (1937), Cole (1939), and Mowrer (1938c) have shown that it is possible to produce almost instantaneous "extinction" and "relearning" of involuntary conditioned responses in human subjects by means of signals or verbal instruction to the subjects indicating changes in experimental conditions. All these investigators used avoidance rather than appetitive conditioning, which probably means that they were simply manipulating the secondary motive of fear symbolically instead of requiring their subjects to build up their own inductive generalizations, or "hypotheses." Cf. Krechevsky (1932a) and Brunswik (1939) for a discussion of this problem as it relates to the behavior of rats.

first configuration the subject learns to make food-seeking responses; to the second configuration the subject learns to make resting responses.[11]

It is obvious that if reinforcement is discontinuous during acquisition, acquisition will be harder to discriminate from extinction (ergo, greater "resistance to extinction") than if reinforcement has been continuous. And not only would we expect to encounter this type of confusion on the first transition from acquisition to extinction; if, as in Pavlov's experiment, we passed a number of times from the one condition to the other, we should expect less rapid discriminative learning where acquisition involved discontinuous reinforcement than where it involved continuous reinforcement.

This type of analysis turns out to have an unsuspected advantage: it suggests why it is that in previous experiments on continuous vs. discontinuous reinforcement, there has been the confounding, already noted, of the continuity-discontinuity factor with the regularity-irregularity factor. The research in this field was started by Humphreys, using college students as subjects.[12] Knowing that

---

[11] In acknowledging the "sign-function" of success and failure, one does not need to repudiate the law of effect, as Tolman, Hall, and Brentnall (1932), for example, suggest. It would appear that we are dealing here with a mechanism which often supplements and on occasion even supersedes simple law-of-effect learning, but this is no proof that the latter is not a perfectly valid phenomenon. Our guess is that in those situations in which one nonrewarded repetition of a response (or a signal of some kind—see Footnote 10) causes a sudden cessation ("extinction") of response what happens is that a strong *emotion* (anticipation of many nonrewarded, futile performances of the response) is aroused which serves to counteract the habit strength, or response tendency, built up by the preceding rewarded repetitions of the response. Likewise, a single rewarded repetition of a response (or a signal from the experimenter—see Footnote 10) may likewise serve as a kind of all-clear sign which removes the depressing effect of many antecedent nonrewarded repetitions of a response (or of an earlier signal from the experimenter) and thus releases the tendency to make the response in question. Or it may be that a single success or some other sign that reward will now follow if responses are resumed may serve, not merely to banish "discouragement," but also to arouse an emotion of "hope" which suddenly energizes the response tendency. Thus a single success or failure (or a signal or word with the same implications) may cause an abrupt change in behavior of the kind that has often been accepted as proof of "insight," "change in hypothesis," or "alteration in cognitive structure" and as disproof of the law of effect. In our judgment this is not a real antithesis and should not cause the cleavage which exists today between those learning theorists who stress the role of effect and those who stress so-called cognition. What we are suggesting is that *emotion* is the key to the controversy and may enable us to build up a more unified structure of behavior theory, from the lower to the higher levels of complexity, than now exists. The present hypothesis would seem to have especially promising applications to discrimination learning and in resolving such paradoxes as Hull (1943) has recently pointed out in connection with "patterning." It may also be useful in more correctly interpreting "latent learning."

[12] Skinner's work (1938) on discontinuity of reinforcement with rats actually antedates that of Humphreys, but it was only with the publication of Humphreys' findings that general interest in this problem was stimulated. Brogden (1939a), Cole (1938), and Brunswik (1939) have also published data on the effects of intermittent reinforcement, showing that, in general, acquisition of a given habit

such human beings can *count,* he may have anticipated that the effects of discontinuity could be demonstrated only if he made the reinforcement procedure not only discontinuous, but also irregular, since by counting a human being can detect a change from an acquisition to an extinction situation quite as accurately if the reinforcement has been discontinuous as if it has been continuous, provided the reinforcement has been regular. In other words, for a human being who, during discontinuous but regular reinforcement, makes each unrewarded trial distinctive by performing the "pure stimulus act" (Hull, 1930) of saying "one," "two," "three," etc., failure of reward to follow, for example, a fourth trial after three nonrewarded ones can be just as significant as the occurrence of a single nonrewarded trial following continuous reinforcement.

As Riess (1943) has pointed out, the rudimentary function of counting is to make possible the same sharpness of discrimination between 10 and 11, or 100 and 101, otherwise identical, successive events (reactions) as between 0 and 1 or 1 and 2 such events. With such precision of discrimination possible by means of counting, it is questionable whether the Humphreys effect can be demonstrated in human subjects with discontinuous but regular reinforcement.

VI. The "Continuity-Noncontinuity" Issue

[Within recent years there has been a great deal of discussion between "cognition" and "reinforcement" theorists concerning the nature of discrimination learning. Because of the special relevance of this issue to the present analysis, it seems desirable to insert here a section which was not a part of the paper as originally published.

Prentice (1949), in a compact and carefully reasoned paper entitled "Continuity in Human Learning," has summarized the essential features of the continuity-noncontinuity issue and has reported the results of a well-designed experiment. He begins his paper by noting that:

> The "continuity" vs. "noncontinuity" issue has usually been confined to discrimination learning in the laboratory rat. The original observations of Lashley (1929), the ingenious experiment by McCulloch and Pratt (1934), the countering experiments by Krechevsky (1938), the series of investi-

occurs more slowly with intermittent than with continuous reinforcement (cf. also Finger, 1942a). Of these three writers Cole alone was interested in the possible effects of intermittent reinforcement on resistance to extinction and he only incidentally. Insofar as his results can be compared to those of Humphreys and Finger they are, however, confirmatory.

gations by Spence (1936, 1940, 1945), and all the controversial articles and notes and comments (Haire, 1939; Lashley and Wade, 1946; McCulloch, 1939a and 1939b; and Prentice, 1946) have concentrated their attention on what happens when an albino or hooded rat is confronted with a problem requiring sensory discrimination (p. 187).

Prentice defines the "continuity" principle as holding "that learning is essentially a matter of strengthening connections between specific stimuli and specific responses, and that the course of solution is determined rigorously by a summation of the rewards and punishments administered trial by trial" (p. 188). "The hypothesis that learning may be 'noncontinuous,' " he says, "is based on the assumption that factors of attention, perceptual organization, and the like will limit the efficacy of reward and punishment to something less than the entire stimulus situation. Associations will then be formed only between the responses and those aspects of the stimulus situation which are in some sense obtrusive or central or 'attended to' " (p. 188). Said otherwise, the "continuity" theory holds that on each successive trial, the reward or punishment received, respectively, for the correct or incorrect responses *gradually* strengthens the one and weakens the other until a perfect or near-perfect performance is attained. The "noncontinuity" theory, on the other hand, holds that the solution to a discrimination problem comes as a result of the subject's suddenly "seeing" a consistent difference between the positive and negative stimuli which he has not previously noticed; i.e., the solution comes through "insight."

By way of summarizing his experiment and the results obtained, Prentice says:

A conditional visual discrimination was taught to two groups of human subjects. One group learned the problem to criterion after having previously had 20 trials on the opposite problem. All subjects gave running verbal accounts of their reasoning. Even when all subjects who had showed any signs of attending to the relevant cues before reversal were dropped from consideration, this group learned significantly *slower* than the control group. These results seem to support a "continuity" notion. On the other hand, the decrement in rate of learning was almost exactly equal to the number of trials on the "reversed" problem. This means that there is, strictly speaking, no negative transfer; so that certain difficulties are raised for interpretations based on simple associative [reinforcement] concepts. . . . These results are interpreted as indicating the need for experimental and theoretical advances toward an understanding of the relation between theories which emphasize respectively the cognitive and the response aspects of learning (p. 194).

More specifically, the task of the subjects was this. They were seated before a fiberboard panel, in the center of which could be exposed, side by side, two visual figures. One of these figures was always a circle and one was always a square, but they differed in a number of other ways which were not identified for the subjects. On each trial the subject was required to "choose" the figure which he thought was "correct" by pressing one or the other of two telegraph keys located on the table, side by side, immediately in front of the fiberboard panel. On correct choices a green light, mounted toward the top of the panel, came on; on incorrect choices, a buzzer sounded. The subjects were told "to learn to get the light every time, never the buzzer" and "to *think aloud*" (thus enabling the experimenter to have some index as to when the subject got the right hypothesis about the principle governing the correctness of choice and also indicating whether the hypothesis was arrived at slowly or suddenly).

The control-group subjects were allowed to work on the problem with one set of principles governing the correctness of choice throughout; these subjects required, on the average, about 41 trials to learn the discrimination to criterion. In the case of the experimental subjects, for the first 20 trials the rules governing the correctness of choice were just the reverse of those employed with the control group. However, on the 21st trial, the rules were changed so that they were the same as those employed throughout with the control group. Under the experimental conditions, the subjects required about 62 trials to learn to criterion, as opposed to 41 for the control-group subjects.

Noncontinuity theory holds that presolution, or preinsight, trials are of no significance, either positively or negatively. If, therefore, as their verbalizations indicate, the subjects in this experiment did not usually get the right hypothesis before the 21st trial, what happened prior to that trial would be of little importance; and both groups might be expected to require the same total number of trials to reach a common criterion. As Prentice notes, "there is good reason to accept [the obtained] results as indicating that the experimental group was slowed down by the reversal treatment" (p. 190). The fact that the two groups required, respectively, 41 and 62 trials on the average rather than the same number of trials goes contrary to noncontinuity theory; but neither were the results precisely what one would expect on the basis of continuity theory.

Since it took the control group 41 trials to master the discrimination, and since it took the experimental group almost exactly the same number of trials (42) to master the discrimination after the rules governing the discrimination were reversed, the following difficulty arises. If, during the first 20 trials, the subjects in the experimental group were getting reinforced in a set of habits opposite to that which they eventually had to learn, then a good many unlearning trials might have been expected to be needed before these subjects would be on an even footing with the control subjects. In other words, continuity theory would predict a certain amount of "negative transfer" from the first to the second set of learning conditions. No such interference or transfer effect was observed. As Prentice remarks:

> To put it another way, we should find negative transfer in the sense that the experimental group should need significantly more trials *after reversal* than the control group needed all together. This result does not appear, and consequently the experiment must cause difficulty for the kind of associationism that has been fostered by (e.g.) Spence (p. 191).

That these findings constitute an enigma is well recognized by Prentice, as indicated by his remark that "the plain fact is that the relationship between cognition and action in complex learning situations still needs to be elucidated" (p. 193).

A measure of elucidation of these results can be achieved by thinking about them in the context of the present paper. Through the work of investigators already cited, we know that if a series of reinforced learning trials is followed by a series of nonreinforced trials and if this alternation of reinforcement and nonreinforcement occurs a number of times, the subject will shift more and more quickly from performance to nonperformance to performance, etc. In such a sequence, it appears that the first trial in a series of reinforced or nonreinforced trials comes to have a *sign function.* If the first nonreinforced trial has been repeatedly followed by other nonreinforced trials, it comes to mean: "Conditions are now such that work will produce no results; I might as well stop and rest." And if the first reinforced trial has been repeatedly followed by other reinforced trials, it comes to mean: "Conditions are now such that work will produce results; I should start responding again." (This is admittedly a loose way of speaking, but it seems to make for quicker communication than would a more precise formulation. For a relatively rigorous but protracted statement, see Footnote 11.)

In other words, it would seem that "reinforced trials" and "nonreinforced trials" may have a *double* function: they may provide either an increment or a decrement in reinforcement as conceived by reinforcement theorists, *and* they may take on a cognitive, or meaning, function, thereby producing changes which are quite disproportionate to the effects of reinforcement or nonreinforcement in the strict sense of these terms.

This inference is consistent with a two-factor theory of learning which differentiates between solution learning and sign learning. When a response is followed by a given reward (or solution), the connection between the underlying drive (or problem) and this response is strengthened, trial by trial; and when a response is not followed by the appropriate reward, this response is weakened (interfered with), trial by trial. When a first trial is reinforced and followed by other reinforced trials and when such a sequence is repeated a number of times, the first reinforced trial in each series of reinforced trials comes to "mean," through conditioning, that other reinforced trials will follow; and when a trial which is not reinforced is followed by other nonreinforced trials and when such a sequence is repeated a number of times, the first nonreinforced trial in a series comes to mean, in like manner, that other nonreinforced trials will follow.

This conception of learning as involving two distinct processes—problem solving and conditioning—satisfactorily accounts for the results obtained in series of reinforced and nonreinforced performances; and I believe it also can be made to account for the otherwise paradoxical results reported by Prentice. "Continuity" theory depends exclusively upon the notion of reinforcement in the problem-solving sense; "discontinuity" theory depends exclusively, or at least very largely, upon something which is much closer to conditioning, i.e., the kind of learning that brings "expectations," "meanings," and similar cognitive phenomena into being. On the basis of this admittedly sketchy analysis, it appears that Prentice's results can be satisfactorily accounted for by neither continuity nor noncontinuity theory for the reason that a fully adequate account of what happens in complex learning situations, such as the one under discussion, calls for an explanation involving *both* kinds of learning.

In relatively abstract terms, it appears that Prentice's results can be best explained in this way. If "reinforcement" learning were alone operative, the initial "mistraining" given to the experimental-group subjects should have produced negative transfer; if "cognitive" learning were alone operative, the "mistraining" should have had no effect whatever. Actually, the mistraining did have an effect in the sense of increasing the total number of trials required by the experimental-group subjects; but it did not produce any negative transfer. This intermediate result can be interpreted as meaning that both types of learning were operating and produced a compromise effect. With each subsequent reversal of the rules governing correctness of choice (if the experiment had been so extended), it could be predicted that the influence of sign learning would increase and that the influence of solution learning, in its primitive sense, would decline.]

VII. Regular vs. Irregular Reinforcement

The foregoing discussion provides a convenient setting for the description of the results obtained from our Group V animals, which, it will be recalled, received reinforcement both intermittently and randomly, but on the average after every 2½ depressions of the bar. These animals depressed the bar a mean number of 189.2 times during the 3 days of extinction. The point corresponding to this value has been indicated in Figure 44. Dividing 189.2 by 2.5 (the figure comparable to the response units of the other 4 groups), we find that the Group V animals made 75.5 repetitions of their hypothetical average response unit. The point corresponding to this value has likewise been indicated in Figure 44.

From these results it is evident that the greater resistance to extinction obtained in this experiment following discontinuous (Groups II, III, and IV) than continuous (Group I) reinforcement is probably in no way contingent upon the factor of irregularity of reinforcement. In fact, as a glance at Figure 44 will indicate, our Group V animals depressed the bar actually somewhat less frequently during extinction than would have been expected from interpolation on the curve representing the performances of the regular reinforcement groups (I, II, III, and IV).

Unfortunately, there is no way of determining whether the obtained downward deviation of the Group V results is due to the factor of irregularity or to factors which the experimenters did not attempt to control, i.e., "chance." If the Group V animals had been irregularly rewarded after pushing the bar either 2 or 3 times, on the average, instead of 2.5 times, their extinction scores would then have been directly comparable, statistically, to those for the Group II or the Group III animals.

That this procedure was not followed is now a patent defect in the design of the experiment. However, from a common-sense standpoint our results indicate clearly enough that, for rats at least, it is discontinuity of reinforcement, rather than irregularity, that accounts for the greater resistance to extinction resulting from a training procedure involving both discontinuity and irregularity of reinforcement. Therefore, the confounding of the discontinuity and irregularity factors which has been noted in previous studies is probably unimportant and was even necessary if this phenomenon was to be demonstrated in human subjects, due to the latter's tendency to count and thereby render discontinuous and continuous reinforcement much more nearly equivalent, psychologically, than they otherwise would be.

VIII. Other Implications

As we have seen, there are two about equally plausible ways in which the Humphreys effect can be accounted for: by the "response-unit hypothesis" and by the "discrimination hypothesis." Naturally the question arises as to which of these is the more valid, and experiments can probably be devised (though not easily) which would throw light on this problem.[13] However, in situations of this kind we fall perhaps too easily into the practice of taking an either-or attitude, of assuming that where two or more mechanisms may account for a given result one must ultimately prove significant and the other not. Actually we know that in all but the most simplified types of psychological situations the observed outcome is nearly always "overdetermined," i.e., is a product of multiple processes acting, and interacting, simultaneously. It may well be, therefore, that *both* of the explanations advanced above to account for the Humphreys effect are valid.

One other implication of research on continuous vs. discontinuous reinforcement in relation to "resistance to extinction" should be noted. In an experiment reported by Whiting and Mowrer (1943),

---

[13] The response unit and the discrimination hypothesis are designed to account for the greater resistance to extinction (in the sense of more "work" done) following discontinuous than continuous reinforcement. They make no assumption concerning the effect of regular vs. irregular reinforcement. That the findings of this investigation indicate that, in rats at least, the factor of regularity-irregularity is of little or no importance in this connection *may* have implications for the relative validity of these two hypotheses, but if so these implications are so subtle as to be obscure to the present writers. [Sheffield (1949) has recently reported an experiment which she believes provides a differential test of these two hypotheses. She thinks her results support the discrimination hypothesis and make "the idea of a response unit untenable" (p. 524). However, this author concedes that "from this [the response-unit] hypothesis it would probably be predicted that spacing of training trials would make it difficult for a sequence of behavior to be reinforced as a 'unit' and would therefore cause a breakdown in the usual advantage of partial reinforcement in extinction" (p. 524; cf. references in the present paper to the relationship between the response-unit hypothesis and reinforcement gradients). Since the "spacing of training trials" was the independent variable in Sheffield's experiment, it is therefore hard to see the basis for her assumption that the results support one rather than another of the hypotheses, when both would predict the obtained outcome.]

it has been discovered that when rats, previously punished for taking the shorter route to the goal on a D-shaped maze, found that the punishment (an electric shock) was no longer in force, they precipitously reverted to this route. This behavior was contrasted with the behavior of human beings, who often show lifelong tendencies to refrain from doing certain things they have been taught to regard as "wrong" even though the external sanctions originally used to set up such attitudes have long since disappeared.[14]

This difference between the behavior of rats and human beings raises the question as to what it is about the education, or "socialization," of the latter that creates conscience, character. The psychology of conscience is undoubtedly complicated, but one consideration seems obvious: in the experiment reported by Whiting and Mowrer (1943), the rats discovered that the punishment always occurred at a certain point along the shorter route to the goal. If they got past this point, they were safe and had no reason to feel "guilty." In learning to run the "social maze" which parents and others set for them, children, on the other hand, discover at an early age that punishments, even though indefinitely delayed, may still be forthcoming; and certainly parents are likely to foster the impression on the part of their offspring that their "sins" must ultimately be found out and that retribution will surely follow.

Thus it is that at least a part of that kind of conscience which is based on fear is probably set up. But if conscience is an institution whereby the individual punishes himself (i.e., his conscience "hurts" him) for acts, contemplated as well as actually performed, which are likely to bring external disapproval, so is there a comparable mechanism, based on hope and faith, which makes for perseverance in the face of adversity, in a word, "morale." Very small children display both the moral and the morale aspects of conscience in only incipient amounts, and much of their "character training" consists of attempts to bring about development along these lines. As part of such a

[14] Whether the original (usually parental) sanctions become "introjected" and form a permanent part of the personality ("superego") needing no further reinforcement from the external world or are subtly strengthened periodically by other (community) sanctions is one of the important and difficult psychological problems of our time. It is perhaps the central point of issue between Freudian psychoanalysis, with its emphasis upon the past (childhood), and the followers of Karen Horney and members of the Washington ("interpersonal relations") School of Psychiatry, for whom the current life situation of the individual is of greatest importance. This problem is also related to the question as to whether emotions (attitudes) are "autonomous" (Allport) or require at least occasional reinforcement, like any other learned response. Professor F. J. Shaw (personal correspondence) has remarked, "We still face the problem of the apparent resistance of the anxiety state itself to extinction. This strikes me as a rather difficult problem for reinforcement theory whereas Guthrie's theory might have less difficulty with this particular problem."

program they are commonly encouraged to keep plugging away if they do not immediately reach their (legitimate) goals and are admonished, when confronted by failure, to "try, try again."

Even in the course of ordinary events, children learn to carry out long sequences of action where the reward is so remote that in the beginning it can sustain endeavor for only a short time. Thus, a small child, though capable of endless activity at home, will quickly report being "tired" if taken for a walk. But it is almost certainly not so much fatigue as it is "extinction," or "loss of interest," that is responsible for his lagging steps. He puts one foot forward, then the other, then the one, then the other, etc., etc., and nothing happens. Only gradually, with encouragement from his elders and periodic indulgences—a look at the train here, an ice cream or candy there—does the child get so he can, at the age of five or six, set out on a long walk with only a single destination or objective in mind. His "resistance to extinction" has increased, in a manner probably not fundamentally different from that used in producing the Humphreys effect. By requiring rats to push a bar at first only a few times for a piece of food, then a larger and a larger number of times, Skinner (1938) was able to get one eventually to make 192 responses for a single piece of food, and there was no indication that this number necessarily represented the limit of which the rat was capable. Did these rats have "morale"? They certainly had "hope," "faith."

Somewhere between fear and faith—the pivotal concepts of most religions—lies the truth about conscience. Any improvement in our understanding of how they work is a contribution to the psychology of character, and character defects. Here, it would seem, is a most promising point of articulation between scientific learning theory and education, ethics, psychotherapy, and other practical problems of both a social and individual nature.

Summary

In this paper an attempt is made to show that the Humphreys paradox—that habitual responses which are rewarded only intermittently are apparently stronger than those which are rewarded after each occurrence—does not invalidate the law of effect. Experimental results are reported which confirm Humphreys' empirical findings but which can be explained either by the "response-unit hypothesis" or by the "discrimination hypothesis," both of which are consistent with the view that reward is the fundamental and crucial determinant of habit strength.

The response-unit hypothesis defines a "response" not as a single, isolated movement but as the totality of behavior which leads to a given goal. For example, the fact that a rat has to press a bar three times in order to get a pellet of food does not mean that three separate acts, or "responses," have been performed; the sequence of three bar depressions is here conceived as a unitary, integrated, instrumental performance. When "response" is thus redefined in terms of the whole pattern of behavior which proves effective in producing reward during acquisition, the Humphreys paradox disappears. When "response" is thus redefined, it is found that intermittent reinforcement, far from producing greater "habit strength," actually produces reliably less than does continuous reinforcement.

But there is another equally plausible approach to this problem. If, during acquisition, a response (conceived as a more or less isolated movement) occurs repeatedly but is rewarded only now and then, the transition from acquisition to extinction will not be discriminated as sharply as if acquisition has involved reward for each and every response. With "faith" thus established that failure will ultimately be followed by success, "discouragement" is slower to set in (ergo, greater "resistance to extinction") when there is a change in objective conditions from acquisition (occasional reward) to extinction (no reward whatever).

This second interpretation involves the introduction of *intervening variables* ("faith," "discouragement"), factors which disrupt the direct, one-to-one relationship observed in the simplest kinds of situations (and subjects) between reward and behavior. Here we are approaching the realm of "ego psychology," but it should not be supposed that there is any discontinuity between the fundamental laws of learning that can be so easily demonstrated at the lower levels of behavior and the generalizations that seem to hold best at the higher levels. The intervening variables which operate at the higher levels and which complicate the simple relationships observed at the lower levels between reward and the behavior-changes which we call learning are themselves products of former learning—i.e., "emotions," "secondary drives," "expectations," "attitudes," "sentiments," "conscience."[15]

---

[15] We do not overlook the fact that "thoughts" and "ideas" are also important intervening variables, but the intrapsychic use of symbols is so intimately tied up with emotions that in stressing the latter we are necessarily subsuming the former. It is a common form of human vanity to make thoughts a "higher" and emotions a "lower" mental process, but from a dynamic standpoint, the emotions are both genetically and energetically basic. Emotions supply the rudiments of "reason" and remain its driving force no matter how refined or elaborated it becomes (15).

Here we are dealing with a distinction similar to the one which Murray (1938) has made between *viscerogenetic needs* and *psychogenic needs.* And when there are psychogenic needs (secondary drives) operating within an organism, we do not expect the viscerogenetic needs (primary drives) to produce the same results as when psychogenetic needs are absent.[16] When these two types of "needs," or drives, come into opposition, there will necessarily be *conflict* (sometimes "character"); and we know that the outcome is rarely a matter of simple algebraic summation (15). The various "dynamisms" (Freud), or "self-systems" (Sullivan), go into action, with the endlessly complicated results which we see clinically (as well as in the "experimental neuroses" of animals) and even in ordinary, "normal" human behavior.

IX. The Role of Secondary Reinforcement

[Since the publication of this paper there has been comparatively little new work on the problem of continuous vs. discontinuous reinforcement. Humphreys (1948) and Calvin (1948) have published abstracts of studies which seem to bear upon this issue only peripherally; and Skinner (e.g., 1948) has continued to use intermittent reinforcement as a more or less standard learning condition in the investigation of related phenomena, but has not dealt specifically with the problem which is under examination in this paper. Postman (1947) and Hilgard (1948) have reviewed the relevant literature without making any special innovations in the matter of interpretation.

However, in a paper which appeared in 1946, Denny introduced the concept of secondary reinforcement in a way which had not been previously suggested. He points out that in so-called intermittent reinforcement the "nonreinforced trials" are nonreinforced only with respect to the reinforcing agent provided by the experimenter and that on such trials the subject may well receive secondary reinforcement—for example, from the goal box (though empty) or from other incidental features of the experimental situation which have been associated with the primary reinforcement provided by the experimenter.

---

[16] [Again it is apparent how close this paper verges upon a two-factor conception of learning. It distinguishes between habits which are motivated by primary drives (viscerogenic needs) and habits which are motivated by secondary drives (psychogenic needs), but it does not explicitly differentiate between the learning whereby such habits come into existence and the learning whereby the secondary drives (attitudes, emotions) are acquired. By making this distinction explicit, the central argument of the paper is further consolidated.]

After considering the explanation of certain results reported by Humphreys (1943) in terms of response-patterning (see above), Denny says:

> There is, however, still another factor that seems to have been overlooked by Humphreys in his interpretation of these experiments. This is the principle of secondary reinforcement. It is entirely possible that secondary reinforcement was operative in the partial reinforcement groups on those trials in which the unconditioned or reinforcing stimulus was omitted. For it has been shown by Bugelski (1939) and Skinner (1938) that the click accompanying the movement of the lever just preceding the food reward in the Skinner box can acquire subgoal or secondary reinforcing properties. Considering that Humphreys gave all his subjects 100 preliminary training trials in which a buzzer was followed immediately by food, it is not unreasonable to assume that the buzzer served as a secondary reinforcing agent, thus providing reinforcement on what were ostensibly nonreinforced trials.
>
> On the basis of this analysis it is presumed that the experimental finding of approximately equal amounts of learning with either partial or consistent reinforcement is due to the operation of secondary reinforcement. If experimental conditions could be arranged so that secondary reinforcement was not present on the nonreinforced (i.e., nonfood) trials, it would be possible to test this hypothesis: the inference is that under such conditions a difference would be obtained in the amount of learning under partial and full reinforcement (pp. 375–376).

Denny then describes an experiment which was designed to test the above inference.

> The results in terms of over-all learning scores (number of correct responses on test trials) and in terms of final level of performance (per cent correct responses) revealed no differences between the partial and continuous reinforcement groups in the control condition [in which no attempt was made to control secondary reinforcement], whereas significant differences were found in the experimental condition [arranged so as to minimize the effects of secondary reinforcement] (p. 388).

Denny's graphs show that when the factor of secondary reinforcement was present, a 50 per cent reinforcement group of subjects (rats) and a 100 per cent reinforcement group learned at about the same rate; however, when, in two otherwise comparable groups the factor of secondary reinforcement was absent, learning occurred at quite different rates (although the amounts of learning *per reinforcement* proved to be nearly identical).

There can be no doubt that Denny's point is well taken concerning the operation of secondary reinforcement in learning situations of the kind this investigator employed—a simple T-maze, with hunger-motivated rats. Indeed the authors of the present paper, aware of the results reported by Skinner and Bugelski concerning the reinforcing effect of the sound produced by a food-delivery mechanism even though it delivers no food, were careful in the experiment here reported to avoid this artifact (see last paragraph of section headed "Apparatus"). In their experiment the question may therefore be legitimately raised as to whether secondary reinforcement was not fairly well excluded. The only source of stimulation which was especially associated with food-getting were the proprioceptive and other stimuli which were concomitants of the bar-pressing responses; and since, in Group IV for example, even these stimuli were followed by food only one time in four, it is hard to see how they could have had much secondary-reinforcement potency.

Denny's experiment is rendered less significant than it would otherwise have been by the fact that the Humphreys extinction effect did not appear in either the two so-called control groups (secondary reinforcement present) or in the two experimental groups (secondary reinforcement absent), i.e., in neither pair of groups did partial reinforcement give any greater resistance to extinction than did continuous reinforcement. The prediction was that by controlling the factor of secondary reinforcement the *rate of acquisition* could be made to vary as between subjects that received continuous primary reinforcement and subjects which received only intermittent (50 per cent) primary reinforcement. This prediction was confirmed; but in order to create conditions which would give positive results on this score, something was apparently done which nullified the Humphreys extinction effect no less in those groups where secondary reinforcement was present than it was in those groups in which it was not. It would have been consistent with Denny's assumptions to find that exclusion of secondary reinforcement during acquisition would have eliminated the difference in resistance to extinction between partial and full reinforcement groups; but it did not follow from his assumptions that, under the conditions of his experiment, he would also find no difference in extinction rates in groups in which secondary reinforcement was operative during acquisition.

Denny's analysis leaves a number of questions unanswered. For example, in one of Humphreys' studies (1940) it was demonstrated that the difference in resistance to extinction could be produced with a conditioning procedure which involved the galvanic skin reaction to electric shock and threat of shock. Denny does not attempt to explain how the principle of secondary reinforcement, as he uses the term, could account for results of this kind.

Since in Denny's experiment the individual trials came at long intervals (20 to 30 minutes), and since, under these conditions, the Humphreys extinction effect was not forthcoming, it might be argued that the failure occurred because the response-patterning mechanism could not operate. This inference would tend to support the first of the two possible explanations advanced in the present study. On the other hand, it is to be noted that Humphreys, in the G. S. R. experiment just cited, obtained differential resistance to extinction under conditions wherein it would be hard for the response-patterning principle to operate. We are therefore still left without any clear-cut indication as to whether one or the other of these explanations, or perhaps a different one, is necessarily correct. It does appear, however, that the emphasis on the role of secondary reinforcement as an explanation is not very satisfactory.]

CHAPTER 8

THE LAW OF EFFECT AND EGO PSYCHOLOGY

[This paper was prepared for a symposium which was held at Harvard University in December, 1945. The two other persons who presented papers on this occasion were Gordon W. Allport and Phillip B. Rice. Their papers and subsequent discussion did much to change my position with respect to two issues: (*a*) One of the arguments advanced by Allport was influential in forcing me to abandon a strictly monistic conception of learning and to adopt a two-factor theory (see 9); and (*b*) certain of the problems here discussed contributed, at least indirectly, to the conception of anxiety which is developed toward the end of this volume (19). The reader will also note a special connection between what is said here and in the paper on "insight" (11).

The present paper was first published in the *Psychological Review* (1946), as were the companion papers by Rice and Allport.]

In his paper "The ego and the law of effect," Professor Rice (1946) has performed a singular service. With the detachment of a true philosopher and an incisively critical and discerning eye, he has surveyed some of the most controversial areas in the whole field of psychology and has produced a synthesis which we psychologists, with our intensely partisan and often narrow preoccupations, can read—and reread—with profit. As I have studied Dr. Rice's paper, it has been with a growing appreciation of its thoughtful subtleties as well as its systematic coherence and soundness.

Rice alludes to the challenging paper by G. W. Allport, "The ego in contemporary psychology" (1943), in which the author calls for a reconsideration of some of the phenomena which used to be subsumed under the terms "ego" and "self" but which, for several decades now, have been taken seriously only by the psychoanalysts and certain Gestalt theorists. Elsewhere (5, 7, 15) I have advanced parallel reasons for supposing that the time has come when "scientific," or "objective," psychology can profitably undertake the investigation of a number of long-neglected problems in this area, and that until this is done we shall have neither a comprehensive, a unified, nor a maximally useful science of human action and experience. I am therefore in complete accord with Rice's appraisal of the importance of Allport's paper, and it is the fact that Rice so successfully reconciles Allport's position with the systematic point of view with which I am most familiar and sympathetic that makes the former's paper, in my judgment, so valuable.

I shall first discuss some of the major problems which are suggested by Allport's paper and then speak about the particular resolutions of these problems which Rice has proposed.

I. Toward a More Precise Definition of "Ego"

Professor Allport has been a brilliant and unremitting critic of the law of effect. He has probed its soft spots and revealed its shortcomings perhaps more effectively than any other writer. But while acknowledging the timeliness and cogency of many of his strictures, one may variously interpret their implications. Allport himself has been inclined to replace the law of effect with such concepts as ego-involvement and functional autonomy—concepts which, if not contrary to the law of effect, are at least assumed to be independent of it. I prefer, with Professor Rice, to think that, although the law of effect has not always been aptly formulated, it nevertheless provides us with the firmest foundation on which to develop a truly adequate and comprehensive psychological theory.

Without attempting to be in any way thoroughgoing, let me cite a few of the reasons why I take this position.

1. The expression "the ego" itself raises problems. It suggests, for example, that "the ego" is a thing, a substance, a structure (Allport, 1943, p. 474). Neither post-mortem dissection nor vivisection has ever yielded such a structure. Obviously, "the ego" must refer to a process or processes. I should therefore prefer to see the term used only as an adjective, to denote, for example, ego processes and nonego processes.

2. Another implication of the term "the ego" seems to be that one either has an ego, a more or less full-blown one, or one does not have one at all. Allport explicitly states that small children do not have egos and that this part of the total person is an outcome of a particular type of development. But when, exactly, may a child be said to have acquired "an ego"? And what about animals? Do they have "egos"? If some do and some do not, what is the principle of differentiation? Again it seems to me desirable to speak of ego processes rather than egos. By so doing one is in a much better position to set up operational criteria for determining the

precise extent to which such processes may be said to be in operation in any given organism and at any given stage of development. My own understanding of what ego processes are suggests that they are gradually elaborated both as the human child develops and as one ascends the phylogenetic scale.

3. Allport seems to equate "ego" and "self." This, I think, is confusing. The self, or person, includes the total living organism. Thus, in common and accepted usage, if one cuts one's finger, one says, "I hurt myself." But one would hardly say, "I hurt my ego." This, along with the other difficulties mentioned above, is avoided if one thinks of ego, not as a *thing,* but as a process or processes.

4. The second term that strikes one in Allport's paper is "ego-involvement." Almost without exception, one can substitute the common term "interest" for "ego-involvement" in this paper without materially changing either the reader's impression or, I suspect, the author's intention. The term "interest" is a very common one in educational literature (Ulich, 1945), and its equivalent, "cathexis," appears frequently in psychoanalytic writings (Freud, 1935a). I question whether either of these terms means anything more than *emotional arousal,* either appetitive or affective. Appetitive emotions occur when one anticipates a satisfaction or consummation of some kind; the affects, notably fear and anger, appear when one anticipates a dissatisfaction of some kind. We know a good deal about both the genesis and nature of the emotions, and I see no advantage in separating ourselves from this knowledge by speaking of ego-involvement instead of emotional arousal.

5. The substitution of emotional arousal for ego-involvement has a number of clarifying consequences. Let me instance one. In his paper, Allport says: "Mental health and happiness, it seems, [do] not depend upon the satisfaction of *this* or *that* drive; [they depend] rather upon the *person* finding *some* area of success somewhere. The *ego* must be satisfied, not the hunger drive, nor the sex drive, nor the maternal drive, however temporarily insistent these segmental tensions may be" (Allport, 1943, p. 466). Note that the author does not include, for example, the *fear drive* in this connection. Can this be because of an implicit recognition that so-called ego satisfaction is actually emotional satisfaction? It is certainly true that a person can be hungry, thirsty, cold, tired, or sexually deprived and—if not *too* hungry, thirsty, cold, tired, or deprived sexually—may still be "mentally healthy and happy." But one can hardly be chronically fearful or hopeless and be mentally healthy and happy. The fulfilment of hopes and the reduction of fears are, I submit, the essence of ego satisfaction and are not, in principle,

different from the satisfaction of the so-called primary, or biologically given, drives.

6. In the foregoing paragraphs I have obviously been trying to show that we do not need a whole new set of terms and concepts to understand and explain the motivational and consummatory processes which occur in the case of "ego-involved behavior," as contrasted with ordinary behavior caused by the familiar drive mechanisms. Allport agrees that the law of effect works well enough in the latter case; it also works, I believe, in the former case.

But if we stopped here, I am sure no one would be satisfied, least of all myself. Allow me, therefore, to make my own principal criticism of the law of effect and see if this does not lead us more nearly to agreement.

The very expression "the law of effect" implies that actions have *only one* consequence, *only one* effect. It is recognized that this effect may be either rewarding or punishing, pleasurable or painful. But in any given instance the effect is singular. By contrast, I submit that if we are going to have a psychological theory that accords with common experience, we ought to speak of the "Law of Effects." In ordinary life, actions more commonly than not have *multiple* consequences, *multiple* effects, some rewarding, some punishing; some immediate and some remote. Psychoanalysis has explicitly recognized the admixture of pleasant and unpleasant consequences following any given action and has subsumed this fact under the term "ambivalence." Psychoanalysis has also recognized that consequences may be unevenly distributed in time, some being relatively immediate and others more or less remote, and it has subsumed this fact under the distinction between the *pleasure principle* and the *reality principle* (Freud, 1911).

7. The law of effect, as traditionally formulated, is an abstraction, or induction, from observations made in highly simplified laboratory situations in which the action of a living organism has a consequence or effect which is at one and the same time *unitary* and *immediate*. If a living organism performs an action which is solely and immediately satisfying, this action will (if the organism is "naïve") be repeated with increasing promptness when the same problem situation recurs. Similarly if a living organism performs an action which is solely and immediately punishing, this action will tend to be inhibited when the same problem situation to which it originally occurred recurs.

What the law of effect *does not* tell us is what living organisms will learn and do if they perform actions which are followed by consequences which are (*a*) both rewarding and punishing and/or (*b*) both immediate and remote. The investigation of these problems takes us into dynamic or, if you will, ego psychology. The processes by which consequences which are both rewarding and punishing are weighed and balanced and by which consequences which are both immediate and remote are integrated—these processes are, in my judgment, prominent among those which we may call the ego processes.

With this I believe Allport fundamentally agrees, for he explicitly states that the ego is the "conflict region" of the total personality and that it is "customarily occupied with the future" (Allport, 1943, p. 474). Those processes by which conflicts are resolved and by which the future is brought forward psychologically and integrated with the present can be called "ego processes" quite appropriately (15).

8. The *mechanisms* by which these processes are mediated are, of course, another story. These mechanisms importantly involve that type of behavior which we commonly refer to as symbolic, and I suggest that the study of so-called symbolic behavior, especially in small children and animals, on a very much intensified scale, is currently needed most urgently (15, 23). But I suspect that further research will show that symbolic behavior is itself learned and performed under substantially the same conditions as implied by the law of effect in connection with nonsymbolic behavior.

By admitting the phenomenon of *conflict* and the element of *time* into our systematic psychological theorizing, we are in a position to reconsider such concepts as reasoning, willing, and thinking, which, for the past thirty years, have been in general disfavor. However, if and as we now turn to reconsider them, it will be from a new and more secure standpoint (15).

I fully agree with Allport that the postwar period is likely to be one in which psychology makes momentous strides toward overcoming the narrowness and limitations which it imposed upon itself in its adolescent revolt against philosophy. It is an encouraging sign that a person such as Dr. Rice, a philosopher concerned with the problems of value, finds that psychology already has sufficient maturity to be of some assistance to him in his work; and I take it as an equally good omen that an increasing number of psychologists are becoming more concerned than they once were with problems of ethics, semantics, value, and other fields which formally fall within philosophy.

9. In attempting to build a systematic theory of behavior which will extend from the simplest to the most complex behavior of living organisms, one encounters a number of perplexities and complex-

ities, none of which, however, seems insurmountable. Let me mention but two.

If we agree that satisfaction is the cement that makes learning stick, whether this learning be mediated by symbolic or nonsymbolic processes, we are faced by the problem of defining "satisfaction." Most writers agree that satisfaction ought to be equivalent to pleasure and dissatisfaction equivalent to pain. But, then, what do we mean by "pleasure"? One view is that we can equate pleasure to drive reduction and pain to drive or drive increase. Some writers object that tension increase may, in some instances, be pleasant. Such instances are, I believe, deceptive and upon more thorough analysis turn out to be consistent with the thesis that satisfaction, pleasure, and drive reduction are strictly equivalent (15).

If, however, one wishes to temporize a bit, one may say that satisfaction is the subjective consequence of solving a problem. I see no objection to this statement.

10. The second problem which I wish to mention in this connection is that organisms in which the symbolic (or "ego") processes are poorly developed seem to exemplify clearly enough the "hedonism" implied by the law of effect but that organisms in which the symbolic processes are *well* developed often seem to transcend and even defy hedonism. Normal, personally mature human beings manifest sentiments of honor and obligation which seem to rise above all considerations of pleasure, satisfaction, or reward. We work, we save, we sacrifice. We try, as best we can, to be virtuous, and the common element in all virtue is renunciation. To put the problem in its most paradoxical form, it seems that human development requires that we learn *not* to learn under at least some circumstances or, one may say, we must come to feel rewarded because of not allowing ourselves to be rewarded. We must, in a word, become ethical beings, and this seems to imply a repudiation of hedonism and pleasure-seeking.

I have previously attempted to show the desirability of distinguishing between three frames of reference in behavior theory: the adaptational, or biological; the adjustive, or hedonistic; and the integrative, or ethical (Mowrer and Kluckhohn, 1943; 15). I cannot now review the various advantages which seem to me to result from distinguishing these three frames of reference. I need only say that, just as the hedonistic or adjustive processes are an outgrowth of adaptation as mediated by organic evolution, so is integration, or ethics, an outgrowth of the principles and processes of adjustment and hedonistic learning. In other words, although integrative behavior superficially seems to transcend the principles of adjustment, such behavior has been developed and is socially perpetuated precisely because it is, in the final analysis, *both* adjustive and adaptive.

II. Secondary Reinforcement and Higher Mental Processes

In a similarly synoptic manner, I shall briefly review Rice's paper, singling out for special comment those points which are particularly significant or which seem to me incompletely developed.

1. Writing in 1931, Thorndike referred to the law of effect as having been an "unpopular doctrine" (p. 33). The reasons for its unpopularity are complex and manifold, but prominent among them is the fact that from its inception it was coupled with the law of exercise. Between the two of them it is possible to "explain" everything in the field of learning but to predict nothing. These two "laws" are completely complementary in that whatever one cannot account for the other necessarily will (15). Convenient as such an *ad hoc* arrangement is, it is not the stuff from which science is made. Any theoretical system which can never be driven into a corner, which cannot be made to stand or fall on the basis of crucial experiments, has a spurious strength which in the end may be its undoing.

It was therefore a great advance when the advocates of the law of effect began to discard the false comfort provided by the law of exercise and set out to make the law of effect stand on its own merits, or not at all. This development, briefly alluded to by Rice, is constantly gaining experimental support and is of fundamental importance for any discussion of the current implications of the law of effect. It is regrettable that Thorndike himself, after having advanced some of the most coercive evidence against the law of exercise (1931, 1932), has shown a tendency in more recent writings to fall back upon his earlier faith in this dubious principle (1943).

2. Rice likewise comments upon the revision of the law of effect whereby its original bifurcated formulation has been replaced by a single, positive principle. Although it is perhaps too soon to conclude that learning is always and necessarily an irreversible, indelible process, there is considerable evidence that this may be the truth of the matter. After extensive experiments designed to compare the effects of "satisfiers" and "annoyers," Thorndike remarks, "Since in these experiments with these subjects, the wrong connections were simply displaced or nullified by the right ones, not intrinsically weakened, we may properly expect that something similar may hap-

pen in many sorts of learning, and we may increase our confidence in positive rather than negative learning and teaching" (1931, p. 46).

Important as it is, this finding may, however, be easily misinterpreted, a danger which is not lessened by the equivocal manner in which it has sometimes been presented. From incautious statements of this finding, one can get the impression that punishment has no effect whatever upon the behavior of living organisms. Such an inference is certainly at variance with the everyday evidence of one's senses. The fact which one needs to keep explicitly in mind in this connection is that, whereas satisfaction appears to have a directly reinforcing effect upon the stimulus-response sequences which precede or accompany satisfaction, the effect which punishment has upon behavior which precedes or accompanies it is a *secondary, indirect* one. That is to say, punishment does not weaken the "habit," or "connection," which it follows; it merely *inhibits,* or *interferes* with, it through the production of a conflict (Hilgard and Marquis, 1940; 6). In short, the punished habit is not "taken out by the roots" but is simply overlaid, suppressed, superseded by some new and more potent stimulus-response tendency.

When examined in detail, the effect of punishment seems to involve the principle of conditioning; i.e., the kinesthetic and other impulses which accompany a punished act become danger signals and set up a fear state which can be eliminated only by stopping the act which produces them. The process thus involved is pretty obviously both different from and more complex than the process involved in the straightforward strengthening of a stimulus-response sequence which results in satisfaction.

Although phrased differently, this interpretation is clearly implied in the following passage from Thorndike:

> Annoyers do not act on learning in general by weakening whatever connection they follow. If they do anything to learning they do it indirectly by informing the learner that such and such a response in such and such a situation brings distress, or by making the learner feel fear of a certain object, or by making him jump back from a certain place, or by some other definite and specific change which they produce in him. Satisfiers *seem* to act more directly and generally and uniformly and subtly . . . (1931, p. 46).

In summary, then, the law of effect, as currently formulated involves the single, unitary proposition that living organisms learn when and only when they solve a problem in the sense of reducing a tension, relieving a discomfort, deriving a satisfaction. It assumes that the effect of so-called punishment is simply to supply a second drive which leads to the learning of new habits which inhibit older ones and that conditioning, or associative learning, is a subsidiary and dependent form of behavior modification (4, 5). Such a conception of the learning process has the advantage of articulating easily and constructively with modern clinical theory and anthropological functionalism. It also provides, as will be shown later, a common denominator on which to base a reconciliation of learning theory and Gestalt psychology.

3. Rice is right in singling out the word "repetition" for special scrutiny both in connection with its implications for the law of effect and for Allport's criticisms of that law. It should be re-emphasized that, on the basis of the present formulations of the law of effect, repetition is important in the production of learning solely in the sense that repetitions—or, more accurately, occurrences—of a given stimulus-response sequence are productive of learning only if they are accompanied by satisfaction. It is not, in short, the repetition of a given act that leads to learning, but rather its *rewarded repetition.* Nonrewarding or punished repetitions of acts lead to their inhibition (6).

Rice suggests that small children, mental defectives, and compulsive neurotics sometimes repeat stereotyped, meaningless, unrewarding acts, but that normal adults do not. An alternative possibility is that the seemingly unrewarding repetitive activities sometimes seen in the former cases are unrewarding only in the sense that they do not lead to any externally discernible satisfaction but that they serve to *alleviate anxiety* and thus conform quite acceptably to the hypothesis that behavior is reinforced and perpetuated when and only when it is in some way satisfying (15).[1]

I would criticize Allport's example of the student who gets an A in a college course and yet does not repeat the course on grounds somewhat different from those which Rice employs. Note that the law of effect assumes that a response which has resulted in satisfaction on one or more occasions will be repeated subsequently only if the problem to which that response provides the solution *recurs.* This law does not assume that living organisms, after having solved a problem or satiated a drive, go on endlessly repeating—like a cracked phonograph record—the behavior which produced the satiation. As Rice says in another connection, one cannot get "satisfac-

[1] [It is still correct, on the basis of a two-factor theory of learning, to say that "behavior is reinforced and perpetuated when and only when it is in some way satisfying." The question that remains is how *emotions* are "reinforced and perpetuated." Two-factor theory holds that here it is contiguity that is important, rather than satisfaction.]

tion from problem solving unless there is a problem" (p. 311). The student does not repeat a course taken with a satisfactory mark for the reason that the situation or problem which caused him to take the course in the first place has been permanently eliminated. Only under the most unlikely circumstances can one think of the problem's possible recurrence.[2]

4. Rice usefully draws our attention to the fact that the performance of a satisfying action does two important things: (*a*) it reinforces the connection between the underlying drive and the action which brought the satisfaction about and (*b*) it leads to the development of what has been variously termed fixation on the goal-object, cathexis, expectation, appetitive conditioning, or interest. Educational writers (Ulich, 1945) have stressed the importance of the psychology of interest, and psychoanalysts (Freud, 1935a) have similarly emphasized the parallel concept of cathexis; but as far as laboratory experimentation is concerned, this phenomenon has been generally neglected. It is little wonder that we do not yet have a comprehensive and unified theory of learning!

A variety of incidental observations seems to make it nearly unavoidable that we assume (*a*) that "interests" are secondary drives and (*b*) that as such they can both motivate and reinforce behavior, in much the same fashion that primary drives do (MacDonald, 1946; 4). It has just been possible to show (5) that it is necessary to posit fear as an "intervening variable" (Tolman, 1932) in order to explain certain phenomena of avoidance conditioning; and the necessity seems hardly less great to suppose that appetitive drives, or "interests," can function similarly. This means that, even in infrahuman organisms, it is necessary to have a theory of learning, and of behavior generally, which explicitly acknowledges the importance not only of the primary but also of the secondary drives (Miller and Dollard, 1941). When this is done, the psychology of learning and ego psychology are brought tangibly nearer to each other; but as Rice suggests, there are no clearly established facts from the latter area which compel even a partial repudiation of the law of effect as the beginning and ultimate guiding principle of all learning. On the contrary, if properly interpreted, the facts impressively corroborate such a theory.

---

[2] Dr. Emanuel K. Bellar has suggested (in conversation) a different but not incompatible reinterpretation of Allport's example, namely, that getting an A in a college course may be thought of as comparable to a rat's successfully negotiating a single segment of a maze. Just as the rat is trying to get "through the maze," the student is trying to "get through college." There would, therefore, be no more reason to expect a repetition of a successful step toward the ultimate goal in the one case than in the other.

5. Once we posit that certain drives, which may function to produce new learning, are themselves the outcome of past learning, we are in a position to account for a number of previously bothersome phenomena. I can refer here to only a few of them.

Rice says:

> The only possibility of saving the law of effect, then, would seem to consist in finding *what* is reinforced by success or satisfaction, and therefore *what* it is that tends to be repeated. This implies that we should either replace "response" by some other concept, such as "interest," in the statement of the law, or else try to find some *aspect* or *feature* of the responses, rather than the response as a whole, which is reinforced by satisfaction; in the latter case, the feature selected must include for human activity, and possibly for some animal behavior, the core of what is intended by the vague term "interest" (1946, p. 310).

In the paragraphs which follow this quotation, Rice shows how productively the concept of interest can be used in accounting for very diverse behavior, and he shows equally convincingly that interest itself is a learned phenomenon which follows the law of effect. He then concludes:

> The upshot of all this is that the validity of the law depends on *what* is conceived to be satisfied or thwarted, and therefore reinforced or extinguished. Only because many proponents of the law, influenced by the cruder forms of reflexology, have focused on response mechanisms and goals rather than interests, and have ignored interests of high generality, has their proof of the law been so inadequate (p. 314).

The only ambiguity that seems to me to appear in Rice's analysis is his tendency to separate "responses" and "interests." Although the phenomena which he denotes by these two terms are importantly different, yet there is every reason to believe that they are *both responses,* the former being, in the main, overt skeletal responses and the latter being, in the main, covert, emotional responses. This terminology allows us to see "interests" as learned by past satisfaction in essentially the same way that other responses are learned; it shows how it is that interest-responses, or emotions, may serve to motivate and reinforce new learning; and it identifies the "goal-object," actual or symbolized (imagined), as the stimulus, or signal, which trips off, or arouses, "interest." [3]

---

[3] [This paragraph anticipates the line of thought which is presented in the next two papers. The principal difference lies in this, that here it is assumed that behavioral responses and emotional responses are "learned . . . in essentially the same way," whereas in later studies a dual process is posited.]

6. One of the most interesting ("emotion-arousing"?) and suggestive passages in Rice's whole paper is the following:

> These remarks fit in with Thorndike's own later statements about the law of effect [1931, 1932], though he has not given a precise reformulation of it. There he has tended to treat reinforcement in terms of "wants," "interests," and "attitudes," as well as in terms of stimulus-response connections; and where he does refer to responses he says that reinforcement can attach to any "part or feature" of them, that the response may consist of an idea, a mood, a liking, a craving, as well as a motor act, and that the reinforcement operates upon the "relevant" or "belonging" aspects of the response. And for human motivation, Thorndike stresses the "confirming reaction" or "O. K. reaction" as the kind of reward that is most potent. The confirming reaction is strongest when it is a gratification of the ego by way of self-esteem or a gratification of the superego by way of "conscience" (pp. 314–15).

These remarks have prompted me to review the literature on Thorndike's concept of "belonging," with the following questions in mind: (*a*) What were the experimental facts or circumstances which drove Thorndike to posit such a concept? (*b*) How is this concept related to or different from the Gestalt concept of "insight"?

The answer to the first of these questions may be very simply illustrated by reference to a single experiment, which is one among many which Thorndike has reported in this connection (1931, 1932). Thorndike asked a group of subjects to listen while he read the following sentences ten times:

> Alfred Dukes and his sister worked sadly.
> Edward Davis and his brother argued rarely.
> Francis Bragg and his cousin played hard.
> Etc., etc.

At the end of the tenth reading the subjects were asked to write answers to such questions as:

> What word came after "Francis"?
> What word came after "sadly"?
> Etc., etc.

From this experiment Thorndike discovered that his subjects could answer the first type of question much more readily than the second, and from this and related findings he concluded that mere repetition of a sequence of events or acts has little or nothing to do with learning, but that the presence or absence of something which he refers to rather inexplicitly as "belonging," or "belongingness," is of critical importance.[4]

Reviewing this work, Rock says:

> The principle of "belongingness" (which Saniford calls "that horrible word") represents one of the important new concepts which grew out of experimental work on other aspects of learning, and which was itself then subjected to experimental scrutiny. Belongingness is not strictly defined by Thorndike, but numerous illustrations indicate that if the things to be connected "belong" there is between them some sort of inherent bond, in the sense that the subject feels there is a certain fitness in connecting these things. This principle, which possesses something of both the nature and the vagueness of the Gestalt view, has been investigated or illustrated by some highly ingenious experiments. Certain of the aspects of belongingness are to be understood in terms of mind set, either habitual or temporary, while other aspects are related to meaning, though there appears to be more to the principle than either or both of these (1940, p. 756).

This capitulation on the part of Thorndike, as it seemed to some, was immediately seized upon and capitalized by the more zealous proponents of *Gestalttheorie*. In a pointedly titled article, "Thorndike's Theory of Learning as Gestalt Psychology," Brown and Feder announced that "in his latest writings Thorndike, himself long one of the staunchest supporters of psychological atomism, self-styled connectionist, has unwittingly gone over to the other side. Our specific aim in writing this paper is to show that Thorndike's theory of learning could be successfully rewritten in terms of Gestalt psychology without serious modification of the tenets of either" (1934, p. 426). Inescapably, "belongingness" was the central target of this attack, leading to the conclusion: " 'Belonging' or sense of relationship implies organization (i.e., *Struktur,* Gestalt), a property of wholes and only of wholes. . . . Thorndike and the Gestalt Psychologist are talking about the same sort of thing" (1934, pp. 428–29).

Anticipating reactions of this kind, Thorndike had already remarked in 1931:

> I hope that the sort of connection-system which I have described in these lectures is more acceptable than the kind against which configurationists like Köhler and Koffka and Ogden direct their criticisms—criticisms from which I have profited, and with which I often agree. . . . But I cannot see that such a connection-system requires aid from closure or

[4] Cf. Hartmann's four lists of words ranging in meaning from nonsense syllables to a complete sentence (1941, p. 292).

Prägnanz. The facts which they explain seem explainable nearly or quite as well by varied reaction guided by the satisfyingness of the results attained . . . (pp. 130–31).

Writing in 1935, we find Koffka sounding, in certain important respects, very much like Thorndike:

Since all problem solutions can be said to consist in finding the *fitting* part which will relieve the existing stress, a law of fittingness would be the most universal law to explain thinking, and with it the arousal of new processes. Such a law would be a generalization of the laws of good continuation and closure (1935, p. 638).

And in 1943 Thorndike, in turn, sounds much like Koffka, although in some respects still very different:

When one responds to the situation, "What is the square of 10?" by writing, saying, or thinking "100," the 100 clearly "belongs to" the "What is the square of 10?", is evoked by it, and presumably is physiologically linked to it as a latter part of some neural activity of which the earliest part represents the question. This belonging and physiological linkage may be present to some extent, however, when the response has no important fitness or relevance to the situation (1943, p. 25).

The question now is: How can the agreements between Thorndikians and Gestalt students of learning be consolidated and the remaining differences reconciled? One promising possibility will be discussed in the following section.

7. The whole of Rice's third section is devoted to the proposition that "the confirming reaction for humans, and to some small extent for higher animals, can attach directly to symbols" (1946, p. 316), which is to say, if I interpret the facts correctly, that living organisms which are capable of being emotionally aroused by appropriate signs may also be relieved, reassured, rewarded by other signs and that when the latter state of affairs occurs, there is satisfaction, just as there is when a primary drive is reduced or eliminated. Thorndike has called this emotional, or secondary, type of satisfaction the "confirming" or "O. K." reaction. It is, I suspect, also essentially what Gestalt writers have in mind when they use the term "insight" [cf. 11].

Let us take the familiar case of Köhler's ape, Sultan, contemplating the banana that lies out of reach beyond the bars of his cage. The experimenter has given him two bamboo sticks of about equal length, the ends of which will fit one into the other. After more than an hour of abortive attempts to reach and rake the banana toward him with the sticks, used individually, Sultan abandons the sticks and seems, at least temporarily, to give up his quest for the banana. The experimenter goes off and leaves Sultan under the observation of the keeper but still "in possession of his sticks."

Keeper's report: "Sultan first of all squats indifferently on the box, which has been left standing a little back from the railings; then he gets up, picks up the two sticks, sits down again on the box and plays carelessly with them. While doing this, it happens that he finds himself holding one rod in either hand in such a way that they lie in a straight line; he pushes the thinner one a little way into the opening of the thicker, jumps up and is already on the run toward the railings, to which he has up to now half turned his back, and begins to draw a banana towards him with the double stick" (1927, p. 127).

Let us abruptly stop this dramatic, rapidly moving picture at this point and review what has happened. The law of effect, as we traditionally know it, would certainly lead us to expect that if Sultan thus obtained the banana, on subsequent, similar occasions he would solve the problem in the same way, increasingly promptly and proficiently. But I think we can now predict that if, as Sultan suddenly started fitting the sticks together, the experimenter had taken the banana away, Sultan would have been scarcely less prompt in seizing and starting to fit the sticks together as soon as he saw the banana, on a later occasion, in its usual place. In other words, there is now no reason to suppose that learning can occur only when a primary satisfaction (such as hunger reduction) is experienced; current formulations of the law of effect include the possibility of learning resulting from secondary, or purely emotional, satisfaction.

Actually, if we read on, we find that adventitious circumstances developed in the experiment with Sultan which afforded a striking confirmation of the foregoing prediction. As it turned out, the smaller of the two sticks did not fit snugly into the larger one, with the result that, before the banana was obtained, the sticks fell apart "several times; each time Sultan rejoins the tubes immediately by holding the bigger one towards himself in the left and the thinner one in his right hand and a little backwards, and then sliding one into the other. *The proceeding seems to please him immensely*" (1927, p. 128, italics added).

Eventually Sultan makes the double stick work and obtains a banana, but there can hardly be any doubt that well in advance of this event the ape experienced considerable emotional satisfaction, which powerfully reinforced the stick-fitting-together response. The only question which remains is how and why this satisfaction came about.

Although we cannot answer this question in detail, we can answer it at least in principle. Whenever a living organism experiences a protracted primary drive, such as hunger, there develops an emotional state which can be characterized as *an anticipation of more hunger.*[5] Thus, to the primary drive is added a secondary drive of apprehension, discouragement, or the like. To take a familiar example, when one is ill one experiences not only the pain and inconvenience of the moment but also a foreboding lest the pain and inconvenience persist or even increase. When the doctor comes, examines us, and pronounces certain symbols, we immediately "feel a lot better," even though the physical basis of our condition has probably not altered in the slightest. In like manner, when Sultan was not only hungry but in prospect of continuing to be hungry indefinitely, he, too, "felt a lot better" when he hit upon a plan, or had an "insight," which he believed would bring his hunger to an end, or at least importantly reduce it.

How such "plans," "ideas," "insights" develop is still uncertain, but even here we are not entirely in the dark. First of all we know that plans are developed through either sensory or symbolic exploration of the situation and of the possible ways in which the problem presented thereby may be solved. As these possibilities are passed in review (cf. the variation of response in trial-and-error behavior), there is a constant appraising, a censoring or approving of them. At the human level, we consider and discard a succession of possibilities, until at length we hit upon one which elicits a "Ha, that's it. Now I have it!" The plan, or "insight," may, of course, be realistically wrong, impractical; but the self-administered satisfaction, the drop in emotional tension experienced at the moment is none the less real or effective in reinforcing the responses which have preceded it.

Although we know a good deal about the way signs, symbols, and situations may serve to arouse emotional states of various kinds, we know comparatively little about the way in which they may also serve to terminate such states. For example, there have been many laboratory studies of the behavior of living organisms in the presence of signs which have become "danger signals," but there have been few studies of "safety signals." However, the preliminary indications (Bugelski, 1938; Hilgard and Marquis, 1940; Hull, 1943; Miller and Dollard, 1941; 4) are that the latter are no less amenable to experimental analysis than the former, and that such analysis, particularly when carried on from the genetic stand-

[5] [For experimental confirmation of this hypothesis, see 17, cf. also Coppock and Mowrer, 1947.]

point, will do much to dispel the mystery implicit in such concepts as the Gestaltists' "goodness of figure" or Thorndike's "belonging."

Despite the unsolved problems which remain in this field, there is already much solid ground beneath our feet. No longer is there any reason for schools of thought to rise and flourish around the question as to whether learning occurs only when a primary drive is satisfied, as early formulations of the law of effect seemed to imply, or only when there is "insight," as many Gestalt writers have contended (cf. Hartmann's summary of the Gestalt standpoint, 1935). The more tenable and integrative position is that learning occurs when and only when a drive is reduced, a problem solved, a satisfaction derived, but that this satisfaction may stem from the reduction of *either* a primary or a secondary drive. This view is certainly implicit in the following passage by Thorndike:

Whatever else it may be, thought is a series of varied reactions. As the series occurs, one or another response is selected, emphasized, and allowed to determine the next thought, because it relieves some annoying irritation or lack or satisfies some craving in the thinker. Certain responses are disregarded or discarded as useless or harmful because they fail to satisfy or because they produce actual discomfort. These annoyances and satisfactions are no less real because they lack the sensuous or emotional qualities of electric shock, food, fear, or social approval. To be thwarted in solving a problem in arithmetic is as truly annoying as to be thwarted in getting out of a box to food or companions (1931, pp. 145–46).

As Gates says, ". . . the basal idea of the organism's own potency in influencing its own course of learning is the keystone of the Thorndike [newer] psychology of learning" (1942, p. 149).

In similar vein, Krechevsky, an investigator with strongly Gestaltist leanings, has maintained that behind the so-called random, or chance, trial-and-error behavior which one can observe in animal problem solving, there is nearly always a secondary, or symbolic, level of activity which results in "hypotheses" which are then tried out and if objectively unsuccessful are soon discarded for new ones.

Thus, "when we say that an individual has an 'hypothesis' we imply that the individual is contributing something to the situation. His behavior is not something forced upon him by the immediately presented stimuli. He has taken the problem-field and has brought to bear upon it all his past experiences. His 'hypothesis' originates to some degree *from within himself*. . . . An 'hypothesis' is the individual's interpretation of the data, it is not a phenomenon deriving from the presenting data alone" (1932b, pp. 531–32).

The question, as Krechevsky points out, is Where does the animal "get" these "hypotheses"? The Gestalt theory has one answer. Such behavior, or any behavior is an inevitable result of some stimulus configuration. The situation *forces* a specific response.[6] The relationship between stimulus field and response is as definite as it is mysterious (1932b, p. 531).

Although we do not know the historical facts, we may nevertheless assume, following Krechevsky, that in the case of Sultan, an "hypothesis" was formed before the animal actually began putting the sticks together and that this hypothesis generated a certain "faith" that the hunger problem could thus be solved, a "faith" which was in some way generalized, or transferred, from other problem-solving situations to this one and which would last for only a limited period of time if it met with consistent failure and frustration, i.e., would, like any other unrewarding reaction, eventually extinguish. Gestalt writers have undoubtedly rendered a real service in calling attention so insistently to learning that occurs without the involvement of *primary* satisfactions, thus forcing proponents of the law of effect to expand their concepts to include the possibility of learning through *secondary* drives and rewards; but certain of the Gestaltists' own speculative, or metapsychological, postulates seem increasingly wide of the mark, "irrelevant," lacking in "belonging" and "fittingness." Proponents of the law of effect have acknowledged their early errors and have made their concessions to *Gestalttheorie.* Are the advocates of the latter prepared to do as much?[7]

8. Because of his preoccupations as a professional philosopher, but equally by the very nature of the facts, Rice cannot fail to point out some of the ethical implications of the law of effect. For example, he asks:

> What can cause an individual to persist in a "style of life," or the pursuit of it? Observation suggests that he does so because he has found satisfaction, actual or imaginative, from that style of life, or because it promises to integrate the scattered elements of past satisfactions and lessen

---

[6] Cf. Rice's (1946) apt characterization of the a-historical bias of Gestalt psychology (pp. 318–19).

[7] [Although no explicit reference is made in the foregoing discussion to the problem of "latent learning," the problem is clearly implied. By positing secondary drives and their resolution as a source of reinforcement, we take one essential step toward making "reinforcement theory" more adequate on this score. However, in order to have an entirely satisfactory explanation of this phenomenon, it is apparently necessary also to posit a form of learning that is independent of reinforcement in the sense of drive reduction, namely contiguity learning. For recent studies on latent learning, representing differing points of view, see Karn and Porter (1946) and Seward (1949).]

past dissatisfactions, or because social rewards and punishments promote its adoption. But all these are operations of the law of effect (p. 313).

Elsewhere (15) I have developed at some length what seem to me to be the salient implications of learning theory for ethics, but it is sufficiently evident, without elaboration here, that as soon as we have a psychology of learning which can speak meaningfully about self-administered satisfactions, and dissatisfactions, we are in a position to begin dealing systematically and scientifically with problems of conduct, conscience, and morality. From the modern psychological clinic and consulting room, as from traditional religion and social precept, a good deal is already known in this area; but there are still many mysteries which urgently call for more precise investigation than has thus far been accorded them.

One may surmise that it was certain of these mysteries which prompted Allport to put forward his concept of "functional autonomy" (1937, 1940). It is true that a normally mature man or woman must have the capacity to persist in the face of punishment and to resist in the face of possible satisfactions in a way that implies a kind of immunity to and triumph over the law of effect; but as Rice points out, these facts constitute no paradox for the law of effect if one sees them in terms of "interests" of a sufficiently "high level of generality."

Scientific students of learning theory are thus coming to acknowledge the importance of "the moral problem." Will the professional moralists and theologians be equally amenable to scientific logic and concede that the ultimate *raison d'être* of morality lies in the psychology of learning?

9. This paper makes no claim to being either complete or entirely consistent. There are still many lacunae and paradoxes in our theory of learning. For example, take the problem, instanced by Allport (1943), Murray (1938), Lashley (1942), and many others, of *response equivalence*. Why living organisms do not immediately and permanently fixate upon whatever response or response sequence has been found to lead to satisfaction, but instead continue to show more or less behavior variability, is still an open question (Hull, 1943). Helen Jones and I (6) have made a number of attacks on this problem, but they have all been unsuccessful to date. This problem, along with many others, is of great systematic significance; but I concur fully in Rice's judgment that, despite the unresolved difficulties which remain, the law of effect is by all odds the most inclusive and predictively potent conception of learning which we have, and should be pushed to its limit.

CHAPTER 9

ON THE DUAL NATURE OF LEARNING—A REINTERPRETATION OF "CONDITIONING" AND "PROBLEM SOLVING"

["In the psychology of learning, there are three major traditions: hedonism, associationism, and rationalism. Many writers have attempted to base their understanding of learning exclusively upon one or another of these traditions; others have drawn unsystematically from all three. The position taken by the author of the present article is that there are *two basic learning processes*—'conditioning' (associationism) and 'problem solving' (hedonism)—and that rationality is a complex derivative of these other two. However, in order for such a synthesis to be possible, conditioning and problem solving must, the author believes, be defined in the rather special ways here proposed.

"If this type of formulation proves valid, it holds promise of not only resolving a number of theoretical paradoxes but of opening the way for new and important applications of the principles of learning in education, clinical work, human relations, and other related fields."

These paragraphs are quoted from the editor's introduction to this article as originally published in the *Harvard Educational Review* (1947).]

One of the distinguishing features of science is that it strives for maximal simplicity, parsimony, and consistency in its basic assumptions, whereas common sense is content with complexity, multiplicity, and inconsistency. Folk explanations often take the form of proverbs, which are notorious for their variety, unrelatedness, and mutual contradiction. Scientific explanations by contrast tend to be interrelated, rigorous, and systematic. Whereas common sense has an "explanation" for everything—once it has happened—but lacks general principles with high predictive power, the ways of science often bring its practitioners up short in the face of paradoxes and set problems which those who rely upon a ubiquitous eclecticism do not encounter.

The history of scientific learning theory, though brief, reflects some of the best traditions in scientific method. In America, William James was the first great writer in this field, and for him *repetition* was "the great law of habit." His student, E. L. Thorndike, found it impossible to make the law of repetition (or "use") account for all his experimental findings and posited the *law of effect* in addition. John B. Watson accepted the law of repetition (or "frequency") but rejected *effect* in favor of *recency*. At a somewhat later stage he came under the sway of Pavlovian thought and concluded that the *conditioned response* was the "fundamental unit of habit."

That these pioneer investigators have been in disagreement concerning their basic hypotheses has sometimes been allowed to overshadow the more important fact that they were all following the behest of science, that one's basic assumptions be explicit, simple, and, if possible, few in number. The wealth of experimental fact which has been accumulated during the past half-century as a result of the systematic formulations and logical deductions of these writers abundantly testifies to the value of this method.

During this period still other hypotheses concerning the learning process have been put forward, explicitly by Gestalt psychology, for example, and by psychoanalysis implicitly; but these hypotheses have not readily lent themselves either to precise experimentation or to rigorous logical analysis and may therefore be dismissed from further consideration at this time.[1]

Within the past two decades there have been no major innovations in basic learning theory, but many investigators have vigorously pursued the implications and possible relatedness of the various fundamental concepts which were formulated during the first and second decades of the century. The last and in many respects most ambitious attempt to base a psychology of learning exclusively upon the principle of conditioning was made by E. B. Holt (1931). While it is uniformly conceded that there is something real and important about the conditioning concept, it is now generally acknowledged that it does not provide a comprehensive learning theory. In the hands of E. R. Guthrie (1935), the principle of recency has received its most vigorous and able exploitation, but O'Connor (1946) has pointed out what would seem to be a fatal defect in this type of theory. The principle of repetition (use, exercise, frequency) has come in for a bombardment of criticism from many sides and is today perhaps the least important of the historically notable concepts in the field. By contrast, the law of effect, which

[1] The writer has recently discussed some of the implications of Gestalt psychology for scientific learning theory in an article entitled "The law of effect and ego psychology" (8). For a discussion of psychoanalysis in this connection, see "Time as a determinant in integrative learning" (15).

was for a long time "an unpopular doctrine" (Thorndike, 1931, p. 33), has stood up exceedingly well and is today probably more influential than any other single conception of the learning process.

For a number of years the present writer and a small group of colleagues and students have attempted to push the law of effect as hard and as far as possible in an effort to determine the full extent of its potentialities—and its limitations, if any. For a time it looked as if this law were indeed *the* basic law of learning, from which all seemingly divergent types of learning could be derived. This view was tentatively suggested by the writer in 1938 (1938c) and has been more confidently proposed in a series of later papers. McGeoch, in *The psychology of human learning* (1942), has taken a similar position; and numerous other writers have subscribed to this view in varying degree. But it remained for Hull in his *Principles of behavior* (1943), to make the first thoroughgoing attempt to make effect theory serve all purposes.[2]

The purpose of the present paper is to adduce evidence for believing that the law of effect is not valid as a *universal* principle of learning and that it has to be ranged alongside of a second, and independent, type of learning.

I. Association or Effect?

In 1934 Schlosberg published the first of a series of papers, by himself and others, which were designed to determine whether the type of learning which had become known as "conditioning" does or does not obey the law of effect. It had long been known, from the work of Thorndike and many others, that, at least under certain circumstances, responses which "solve problems," i.e., which get "rewarded," are reinforced and that those which "make problems," i.e., which get "punished," are inhibited. In other words, it is well established that in at least some situations responses are strengthened or inhibited according to their *effects*. The question, in simplest form, which Schlosberg and subsequent investigators set out to answer was, therefore, whether conditioned responses,

[2] It is debatable whether Thorndike can be said ever to have adopted this monistic conception of the learning process. In 1931, he wrote: "Repetition of a connection in the sense of the mere sequence of the two things in time has then very, very little power, perhaps none, as a cause of learning" (pp. 28–29). This might seem to constitute a repudiation of the law of exercise and an endorsement of the law of effect as the sole principle of learning. But in the next sentence he adds, "Belonging is necessary." Moreover, in later publications Thorndike (1943, 1946) has continued to speak as if exercise and effect were both valid principles (cf. later discussion of Thorndike on exercise and effect).

so-called, are likewise influenced by their effects or are governed by some other principle.

The nature and results of Schlosberg's first experimental approach to this problem are summarized by him as follows:

> In various [earlier] experiments utilizing shock as the unconditioned stimulus, two fundamentally different methods of administering the shock have been utilized. The first method involves the presentation of a shock of predetermined duration, regardless of the response made to the [immediately preceding] conditioned stimulus. In the second method the animal is arranged so that its response will either prevent or terminate the shock. Both methods have been used extensively [by others], apparently without any suggestion that they may be fundamentally different.
>
> [In the present experiment, one group of rats] were always stimulated [following the presentation of the signal] by a shock of 165-sigma [0.165 second] duration. [Another group of rats] were attached to the short-circuiting contacts described above, so that the first millimeter of tail withdrawal would terminate or prevent the shock, and keep it "shorted" until a movement in the reverse direction started. There is no significant difference between the results obtained from the animals that actually shortened the duration of [or avoided] the shock by every response made to it [or to the warning signal], and those that were always given a shock of predetermined duration. This result was very surprising to the writer (p. 322).

The results of this study seem quite unambiguous. They suggest that conditioning is a form of learning that is wholly dependent upon the paired presentation ("association") of two stimulus events, the conditioned stimulus and the unconditioned stimulus, and that it is wholly independent of and unrelated to that form of learning which is known to be dependent upon effect.

The following year, in 1935, Hunter (1935a) published a paper reporting experimental findings which seemed to have implications just the reverse of those of Schlosberg. Rats were again used as subjects, and the nature of the problem under investigation was much the same, but the experimental situation was different. Individually, the subjects were placed on a large circular grill (with appropriate sides and top) consisting of eight sections which could be independently energized by electric shock. At intervals of 1 minute a buzzer was sounded for 2 seconds. With one group of subjects, the presentation of the buzzer was invariably followed by an electric shock which was applied to whatever section of the grill the subject happened to be on at the moment. The shock was applied without regard to whether the subject had or had not moved on the grill in response to the conditioned stimulus. With the other group of subjects the buzzer was followed by shock only if the subject failed to respond to the buzzer by moving to another section of the grill, i.e., failed to make a "conditioned response." In other words, with the second group of subjects a conditioned response, so-called, was effective as a means of avoiding electric shock, whereas in the first group it was ineffective. Hunter comments upon his results as follows:

> Under the conditions of the present experiment, . . . there is a great superiority in the method of not giving the unconditioned stimulus if the conditioned response has been made (p. 144).
>
> Conditioning is quicker on the average if the unconditioned stimulus, shock, is not given after the conditioned response has been made. For ordinary purposes it is suggested that the conditioned and unconditioned stimuli should not always be paired; but that where the subject responds to the conditioned stimulus, the unconditioned stimulus should not be given because of its inhibitory effect upon previously occurring responses (p. 148).

The results thus obtained seem clearly to support the view that conditioning is dependent, not so much upon the paired presentation of the conditioned and unconditioned stimulus, as upon the *effect* produced by the conditioned response: if this response results in the avoidance of the noxious unconditioned stimulus, it will be more readily learned than if it has no such favorable, "problem-solving" consequence.

The year following the publication of Hunter's experiment, Schlosberg published a second paper (1936) in which the same problem was again attacked, with the same general procedure and with the same type of subject as used in his first study, but with the unconditioned stimulus now applied to the rat's leg rather than to the tail. Of his results the author says:

> In the experiments with the tail withdrawal it was found consistently that it made little or no difference in the rate of conditioning whether or not the rat could terminate or avoid the shock by withdrawing the tail. In the present experiments one rat of every experimental pair was trained with short-circuiting contacts arranged so that the first movement [of the leg] shorted the shock, while his experimental mate was trained without these contacts. An examination of the charts will show that the only pair of rats in which there was a clear difference in incidence of leg responses [to the conditioned stimulus] was the pair used in experiment I. In this experiment it was the *noSC* [no short circuit] rat that developed the leg withdrawal, despite the fact that the response did not terminate or prevent the shock. We thus find no more indication that anything comparable to the "law of effect" is working in the conditioned leg reaction than we did for the conditioned tail reaction. . . . In other words, success in avoiding

the shock led to extinction of response instead of "stamping it in." This would seem to be an example of what Hull has referred to as "the dilemma of the conditioned defense reaction" (p. 133).[3]

These findings confirm those reported by Schlosberg in 1934 and seemingly refute those reported by Hunter in 1935.

The next major contribution to this problem was reported by Brogden, Lipman, and Culler in 1938.

> Eight guinea pigs were prepared in the rotator, a modified activity-cage which has been found useful in conditioning small animals. Four of the animals (comprising Group *A*) were trained by the methods commonly employed in this laboratory; that is, the *US* (shock) occurs after *CS* (100-cycle tone) has continued just two seconds. The rotator is so devised that the animal, upon turning the cage an inch or more when the sound begins, escapes [avoids] the shock by breaking the high-voltage circuit through a pendulum. . . . Those [animals] of Group *B*, though exposed to the same situation (same sound, same shock, same test environment), were not allowed to escape [or avoid] the punishment by reacting; on the contrary, each stimulus presentation was reinforced with shock, whether the animal turned the cage or not (pp. 109–10).

In Group *A*, all subjects were soon making the prescribed response to the conditioned stimulus, and thus avoided the shock on 100 per cent of the trials, whereas the animals in Group *B* never made such a response on more than 50 per cent of the trials. Here, it seemed, was particularly dramatic proof that conditioned responses which are "rewarded," by shock-avoidance, are acquired much more readily than are conditioned responses which are "punished," i.e., followed by shock or some other form of noxious stimulation. On the basis of such evidence it would appear that so-called conditioned responses behave very much as do habitual responses in general, i.e., they obey the law of effect, and do not require any special principle for their explanation.

In the same year, the present writer (1938c) made and briefly reported an attempt to determine whether the galvanic skin response (of human beings) conditions any more readily when it is instrumental in avoiding the noxious stimulus of which the conditioned stimulus is premonitory than when the conditioned G. S. R. has no such effect. The results, as far as the experiment was carried, were inconclusive; but the indications were that the G. S. R. conditions no more rapidly when an instrumental procedure is followed than when the classical procedure is employed. This type of investigation should be repeated, but on the basis of the results

[3] This dilemma will be considered later in a different context.

obtained there is no basis for believing that the conditioning of the G. S. R. is in any way dependent upon its "effectiveness"; the acquisition of such a conditioned response seems to be wholly a function of the paired presentations of the conditioned and unconditioned stimuli.

But, beginning in 1939, the writer designed and, with the aid of collaborators, carried out a series of experiments, mainly with rats, which seemed to provide increasingly good evidence that so-called conditioned responses are acquired according to and obey precisely the same basic law of learning as do habits in general, namely, the law of effect.

This conclusion was supported by the results of the first experiment in this series in the following way. Using a circular grill very similar to the one previously employed by Hunter, the writer (3) subjected three groups of rats, and later three groups of guinea pigs, to three different experimental conditions. In one group of subjects, a conditioned stimulus (tone) was sounded for 5 seconds at regular minute intervals. If this *CS* elicited a response (a run to an adjacent section of the grill), the shock was omitted. In the second group, exactly the same procedure was followed, save that the trials came at irregular intervals, some of which were as brief as 15 seconds and some as long as 105 seconds, but which *averaged* 1 minute. In the third group, the same procedure was followed as with the first group except that at 15-second intervals during the minute-interval between trials the subject received a shock (without tone) and was forced to run to the adjacent section of the grill.

The findings were that the Group I animals conditioned very satisfactorily and that the Group II and Group III animals conditioned much less satisfactorily. These findings seemed to imply that when the interval between trials was of regular duration and free from disturbance, the satisfaction experienced by the subjects as a result of avoiding the shock which had previously been paired with the conditioned stimulus was greater than when the interval between trials was of irregular duration or when filled with disturbing events, i.e., recurrent electric shocks.[4]

It had previously been taken for granted by various writers that it is in some manner rewarding to an experimental subject to

---

[4] This interpretation is in keeping with Schlosberg's (1934) earlier finding that he could not obtain conditioning in rats when "double stimulation," i.e., conditioning trials, came at the rate of 1 every 9 seconds. When the rate of presentation was reduced to 1 trial every 72 seconds, conditioning was obtained.

avoid a noxious unconditioned stimulus. It is easily seen that it is rewarding to *escape* from such a noxious stimulus. But how can a shock which is *not experienced,* i.e., which is avoided, be said to provide either a source of motivation or of satisfaction?[5] Obviously the factor of fear has to be brought into such an analysis. *Fear* of electric shock, when aroused by a warning signal, can motivate living organisms, and reduction of such a state can powerfully reward them (5). Presumably the results just cited were obtained because, in the Group I procedure (free, regular intertrial intervals), the amount of fear reduction, or relief, which was experienced when a conditioned response was made was relatively great, whereas in Groups II and III (irregular, filled intertrial intervals), the amount of fear reduction experienced when a conditioned response was made was relatively slight.

It would thus appear that conditioned avoidance reactions are acquired readily or less readily, depending upon whether they are followed by a "satisfying state of affairs" or by an "annoying state of affairs." If earlier investigators have used primary drives, such as hunger and thirst, to the exclusion of the secondary drives, such as fear, in their study of the law of effect, this, it would seem, is an historical accident. Conditioned responses, so-called, are apparently merely those responses which are acquired as solutions to the problems presented by secondary drives, and as such are quite as much controlled by the law of effect as are other problem-solving responses.

This inference was confirmed by an experiment reported by Mowrer and Lamoreaux (4) in 1942. In this experiment it was found that if the conditioned stimulus (a buzzer) was terminated the instant that the subjects (rats) made a conditioned response (a brief run, to the opposite end of the apparatus, Mowrer and Miller, 1942), reliably better conditioning was obtained than if the conditioned stimulus was of arbitrarily fixed duration. The implication of this finding seemed clearly to be that the conditioned

[5] In a recent study by Whatmore, Morgan, and Kleitman (1945–46), this problem has been expressed as follows. Having found that dogs acquire a leg-flexion response more readily with an avoidance (instrumental) conditioning procedure than with a nonavoidance (classical) procedure, they say: "We find it difficult at the present time to explain why the avoidance conditioning procedure should work so well at lowering pathway resistances. Some type of reinforcing agent is necessary to maintain performance in the usual type of conditioning, but in avoidance conditioning we can find no such reinforcement. A possible explanation is that the dog is capable of some crude sort of thinking which enables it to realize that by lifting its paw its avoids an unpleasant sensation. It must be aware of the existence of something that it is not experiencing" (pp. 434–35). It is believed that the type of theoretical analysis developed in this paper resolves this paradox.

stimulus aroused fear and that when the so-called conditioned response occurred and the buzzer was immediately turned off, there was a corresponding reduction in fear which provided a "satisfying state of affairs" and thus reinforced the conditioned response more powerfully than did the termination of the *CS* (and the attendant reduction of fear) if it either preceded or followed the response by an appreciable length of time. From previous work on the "gradient of reinforcement," we know that a reward which precisely coincides with a given response reinforces that response more than does the same reward when there is an interval (either "forward" or "backward") between the reward and the response. The results obtained in the experiment just described indicate unmistakably that the termination of the buzzer provided a rewarding state of affairs and that this state of affairs was highly significant in determining the strength of the so-called conditioned response of running.

Additional evidence of the problem-solving nature of conditioned responses was forthcoming from a second experiment by Mowrer and Lamoreaux (5), published in 1946. If conditioning is merely a matter of associative learning in the sense that one stimulus becomes able to do the "work" of another one, i.e., elicit the same response, it might be expected that a so-called conditioned response would always be an exact replica of its unconditioned prototype. Yet the fact is that so-called conditioned responses often differ considerably from their prototypes.[6] If, on the other hand, a conditioned response is the solution to a secondary drive or "problem," such as fear, then it might be expected that that response will be "conditioned" which provides the best solution to this problem, regardless of whether it is the same as or different from the response made to the situation from which the secondary drive has been derived. Thus, it seemed possible that, for example, a rat which had learned to *escape* from an electric shock by running might learn to *avoid* the shock by jumping or doing something else radically different from running, provided only that this other response caused the danger signal to cease and the attendant fear to be reduced.[7]

Suffice it to say here that, in the experiment cited, this prediction was well confirmed. It was found possible to produce so-

---

[6] This problem will be considered again on a later page.

[7] In this way is resolved the question, raised on an earlier page, as to how the avoidance of shock can be rewarding. The fact seems to be that the *avoidance* of shock, or any other painful experience, is never, in and of itself, rewarding. The reward comes when the fear of such an experience is reduced or, still better, eliminated.

called conditioned responses, i.e., responses to a danger signal, which were as different as imaginable from the responses which the subjects regularly made to the pain-stimulus of which the danger signal forewarned. This finding cannot easily, if at all, be explained solely on the basis of associative theory.

In an unpublished study Lamoreaux and Mowrer (unpublished) have pushed the problem-solving conception of the so-called conditioning process one step further, identifying it with learning, or habit-formation, in general. In an earlier study (5) it had been pointed out that salivary conditioning as described by Pavlov can be interpreted simply as a matter of discrimination learning; and it now appeared that avoidance conditioning, which may at first seem to represent conditioning in purest form, might also be conceived in a similar fashion. It has been common practice to speak as if the conditioned stimulus in the Pavlovian type of experiment becomes the sole and sufficient cause of the salivary reaction which it elicits. Actually, it has long been known that the subject must also be *hungry* and must, as a rule, be in the *same situation* as the one in which food (the so-called unconditioned stimulus) has previously been received. Viewed in this light, the conditioning process may easily be interpreted as a process of discrimination, in which the subject learns to differentiate between hunger-situation-and-*CS* (to which it is appropriate to salivate) and hunger-situation-and-no-*CS* (to which it is not appropriate to salivate). In other words, the *CS,* in such experiments, seems to function more as a *cue* than as a *signal,* i.e., it tells the hungry animal *when* to expect food. If the animal were not hungry, the *CS* would not activate it, as, for example, a danger signal would.[8]

By contrast, in an avoidance conditioning experiment, the *CS* seems to be clearly a signal, and it is correspondingly difficult to see how the resulting learning can be thought of as discrimination. However even this difficulty vanishes when one takes into account a phenomenon which previous investigators have more or less systematically neglected. After a few paired presentations of the conditioned and unconditioned stimuli in an avoidance experiment, the response which is originally elicited exclusively by the unconditioned stimulus begins to occur, not only to the conditioned stimulus, or signal, but also between trials, "to the situation." These latter responses are commonly referred to as "spontaneous," or

[8] In keeping with this interpretation is the fact that in the early stages of such training a dog will salivate between the trials, showing that it has not yet clearly differentiated between situation-without-*CS* and situation-with-*CS*.

"interval," response, and are usually regarded as an uninteresting nuisance, to be minimized if possible and, if not, ignored.

Even the most superficial observation suggests that these interval responses occur because the subject is *afraid,* not only of the discrete stimulus, which has been associated with the *UnCS,* but also of the *whole experimental situation.* Therefore, the so-called conditioning which occurs in experiments of this kind, i.e., the process whereby the *CS* becomes increasingly efficient as an instigator of the responses in question, may well be thought of simply as a process whereby the subject learns that experimental-situation-without-*CS* is safe, whereas experimental-situation-with-*CS* is dangerous. As this kind of "cognitive restructuring" takes place, the interval responses, which are useless, disappear and the conditioned responses, which are useful, appear with mounting regularity.

In the study under discussion, the results were entirely consistent with this interpretation: when it was easy for the subjects to differentiate between the dangerous and the safe periods, "conditioning" proceeded rapidly: when it was difficult so to differentiate (due to special experimental conditions which cannot here be described), "conditioning" proceeded slowly.

Thus it came about, through the series of experiments just described, that even the avoidance response, which has often been assumed to typify conditioning in purest form, is reducible to an instance of simple problem-solving behavior, or habit formation.

Some years ago Thorndike (1931) remarked:

> I must admit that the reported phenomena of the conditioned reflex are a mystery to me in many respects. Just what their relation to ordinary learning is I do not know, but I am not convinced that they show its fundamental pattern and most general principles (p. 113).

More recently Morris (1946) in the concluding pages of his book, *Signs, language, and behavior,* has referred to "the great vagueness in the term 'conditioned response' " (p. 309).

Other investigators, on independent grounds, have thus arrived at the same conclusion as that toward which the foregoing series of experiments seems to point, namely, that "conditioning" is an ill-defined concept, that the phenomena subsumed under it are not fundamentally different from "habits" in general, and that the concept is more misleading than useful and may profitably be dropped.[9]

---

[9] It is interesting to examine Hilgard and Marquis' highly useful book, *Conditioning and learning* (1940), in this connection. Although the term "conditioning" is used in the title in such a way as to suggest that it is something different from "learning," the reader discovers that in the text itself these two terms are used as if they were more or less synonymous. Cf. later discussion of "instrumental" conditioning.

II. Association and Effect

Since science strives for parsimony in its basic assumptions, it is understandable that attempts should have been made to account for all learning solely in terms of the law of effect. While acknowledging the molar differences between "habits" and so-called conditioned responses, a number of writers have attempted to account for both as instances of the same fundamental learning process.

In 1938 the present writer (1938c) made such an attempt, as follows:

> Just as incidental . . . stimuli which are temporally contiguous with those responses which are made at the time of escape from hunger, for example, become integrated with the hunger stimulus into a total stimulus pattern which, with repetition, becomes more and more specifically connected with these responses, so would it appear that stimuli which are temporally contiguous with those responses which occur at the time of escape from an anticipatory tension [e.g., fear] likewise become integrated with the anticipatory tension into a total stimulus pattern which, with repetition, becomes likewise more and more specifically connected with these responses. Eventually such incidental stimuli may acquire sufficient excitatory value as to be capable alone of eliciting the responses with which they have been temporarily associated, without the accompanying presence of the original motivating stimuli (pp. 73–74).

In 1942 Mowrer and Lamoreaux (4) attempted to make this hypothesis more explicit by distinguishing between "parasitic" reinforcement and "intrinsic" reinforcement. "Parasitic" reinforcement is here used to designate the strengthening of the tone-running (conditioned) sequence through the action of the basic rewarding situation provided by the shock termination. The strengthening of the shock-running (trial-and-error) sequence may, in contradistinction, be termed "intrinsic reinforcement" (pp. 3–4). It was here again assumed that there was only one basic reinforcing process, namely, that which occurs when a drive is reduced, a problem solved.

The concept of "redintegration," which is very likely to be suggested to the reader by the foregoing quotations, is, of course, an old one. However, in these quotations the attempt is made to make redintegrative, or associative, learning dependent upon the law of effect, rather than to explain it in terms of a separate principle, as has been the common practice.

In Hull's 1943 book, *Principles of behavior,* there appears a section entitled "The conditioned reflex as a special case of ordinary learning reinforcement," in which the author develops the same monistic conception of learning.[10] He says:

> Because of the current differences of opinion concerning the relationship between selective learning and conditioned-reflex learning, an explicit and somewhat detailed comparison of them as types will be made. . . . [Illustrative examples] suggest that the differences between the two forms of learning are superficial in nature; i.e., that they do not involve differences in the conditions under which the principle operates. . . . On one critical point both cases are identical—the reinforcing state of affairs in each consists in the abolition of the shock-injury or need, together with the associated decrement in the drive and drive receptor impulse, at once after the temporal conjunction of the afferent receptor discharge and the reaction. This is, of course, all in exact conformity with the law of primary reinforcement formulated above. . . .
>
> Pavlov differs from the law of reinforcement by regarding as the critical element of the reinforcing state of affairs the occurrence of S_u, in this case the *onset* of the shock. On the other hand, the critical element in the reinforcing state of affairs by our own hypothesis is the reduction in the drive receptor impulse which accompanies the reduction of the need, i.e., reduction of the physiological injury of the feet, caused by the termination of the shock. . . .
>
> It is an easy matter to show the inadequacy of Pavlov's formulation as a general theory of learning. . . . It is not difficult to understand how Pavlov could have made such an error. His mistaken induction was presumably due in part to the exceedingly limited type of experiment which he employed (pp. 76–79).

Figure 45 presents these two theories of reinforcement diagrammatically. Each of these theories accounts well enough for those instances in which the response elicited by the *CS* is an exact replica of the response elicited by the *UnCS;* but a theory of conditioning must also be able to explain those instances in which the so-called conditioned response differs radically from the unconditioned response, as, for example, in the experiment by Mowrer and Lamoreaux (5), previously described. Such results can be made intelligible only if fear is posited as an intervening variable (cf. Tolman, 1932), and neither Pavlov's nor Hull's type of analysis has any place in it for such an intermediate factor. What clearly happens when a *CS* is paired with a noxious *UnCS* is that

---

[10] Cf. a series of papers by Youtz (1938a, 1938b, 1939) in which a number of seeming parallels between "Pavlovian" and "Thorndikian" learning are adduced. See also an earlier (1927) paper by Symonds.

the *CS* becomes a danger signal and arouses fear, and it is the fear which then serves to motivate the externally observed defensive behavior. The latter seems to be largely determined by effect learning and may be like or quite unlike the overt behavior aroused by the original noxious drive.

Having established this much, the question which now arises is: How is fear learned? Is it acquired on the basis of what happens at *O* or at *T* (Figure 45)? If Pavlov had ever interested himself in the phenomenon of fear, he would presumably have said that it

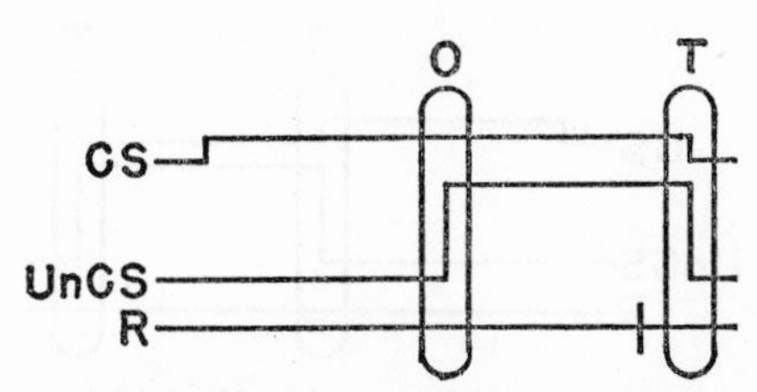

FIG. 45.—Diagram illustrating two theories of conditioning. According to Pavlov, reaction *R* becomes connected with the conditioned stimulus, *CS,* because of what happens at *O*. According to Hull, reaction *R* becomes connected with the *CS* because of what happens at *T*. For Pavlov it is the contiguity of the *CS* and the *onset* of the *UnCS* that is crucial, whereas for Hull it is the contiguity of the *CS* and the *termination* of the *UnCS* that is all-important. In this illustration, the *UnCS* may be thought of as any noxious stimulus, such as an electric shock, and the *CS* as any innocuous stimuli, such as a tone or a light.

becomes attached to the *CS* by virtue of the mere conjunction of the *CS* and the *UnCS*. Hull's theory, on the other hand, would lead us to expect that the fear would become attached to the *CS* because of the satisfying state of affairs experienced when the *UnCS* is terminated. The latter expectation is contrary to intuitive common sense and to biological considerations. Why, one asks, should living organisms be so constructed that they can learn to fear traumatic stimulation only when that stimulation is "all over"? Would it not seem preferable for them to be constructed in such a way that fear-learning is produced by the coincidence of a danger signal and the impact of the trauma?

In an experiment which will shortly be reported by Suter, Horton, and Traum (10), evidence has been obtained which shows that fear-learning is indeed dependent, not upon situation *T,* but upon situation *O* (Figure 45). The logic of this experiment is as follows. If the capacity of the *CS* to become a danger signal is dependent upon its coincidence with the termination of the *UnCS,* then the *CS* should become more ominous to the subject if it overlaps and terminates with the *UnCS* than if the *CS* does not overlap with the *UnCS,* as shown in Figure 46. It is not possible here to give all the details of this experiment; but the important fact for the present purposes is that the above prediction is not confirmed: there even appears to be a slight tendency for the *CS* to become more ominous to the subject if the *CS* and the *UnCS* do *not* overlap.

No one will gainsay the importance and legitimacy of the attempt to derive a single, monistic principle of learning. For the teacher of learning theory no less than for the investigator, it would be very convenient if learning were a simple, unitary process. But

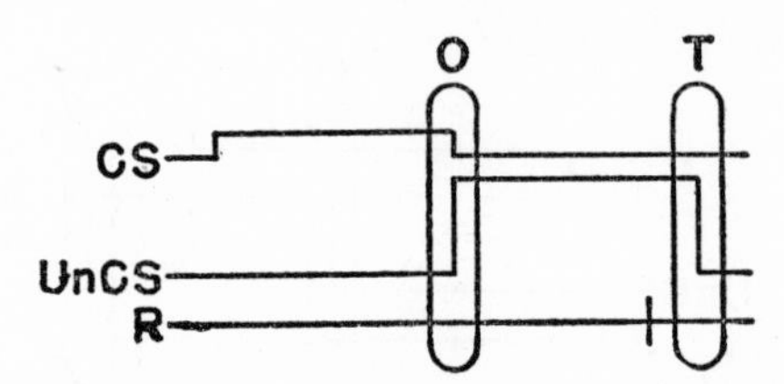

FIG. 46.—Diagram of experimental procedure in which the *CS* is turned off at *O* instead of being kept on until *T*, as in Figure 45. If the reinforcement of the connection between *CS* and *R* were dependent on what happens at *T*, this connection would be expected to develop less readily with this procedure than with the one depicted in Figure 45. The fact that the *CS-R* connection seems to develop just as readily when the *CS* terminates at *O* as when it extends to *T* suggests that for this kind of learning the reinforcement is provided by what happens at *O*, not at *T*. However, this analysis presupposes the division of labor posited in the text between reactions which are mediated by the autonomic nervous system and those mediated by the central nervous system. No attempt is made either in Figure 45 or in Figure 46 to indicate this relatively complex relationship.

the fact seems to be that learning is a more complicated procedure, and it is unrealistic to try to adduce a theory which does not appropriately acknowledge this complexity. We know that, in certain instances of learning, what happens when a drive is terminated and satisfaction is experienced is crucially important; but it now appears equally clear that certain other instances of learning depend upon the onset, rather than upon the termination, of a drive. Some other principle which is quite different from either the law of effect or the principle of association may ultimately make possible a unified theory of the reinforcement process; but for the present it seems necessary to assume that there are *two basic learning processes:* the process whereby the solutions to problems, i.e., ordinary "habits," are acquired; and the process whereby emotional learning, or "conditioning," takes place.[11]

[11] This conclusion has been forced upon the writer, not only by the experimental findings which are reviewed in this and the preceding section, but also by some particularly cogent and forceful criticisms which Professors P. B. Rice (1946) and G. W. Allport (1946) have recently directed against the author's earlier view that "living organisms learn when and only when they solve a prob-

This distinction, because it employs the term "conditioning," in a much more restricted and rigorous sense than has been common practice, immediately requires a word of explanation. As we have seen in the preceding section, the broader and more customary usage applies the term "conditioning" to the acquisition of any response which occurs to a signal, or *CS,* of any kind. This usage has broken down on both logical and pragmatic grounds and should be discontinued. As we have seen, many *so-called* conditioned responses are simply solutions to secondary-drive problems and are learned in the same way as are problem solutions in general, i.e., through trial-and-error and the law of effect.[12] But it is also apparent that the law of effect is not adequate to account for the process whereby these secondary drives are themselves acquired; and it is for this latter process, exclusively, that the term "conditioning" should be reserved.

Such a procedure has a number of advantages which will be reviewed in a later section; first, however, it will be useful to note certain other justifications for using the term "conditioning" in this, and only this, sense and for making the conditioning process separate and distinct from the learning process denoted by the law of effect.

---

lem in the sense of reducing a tension, relieving a discomfort, deriving a satisfaction" (8, p. 210). Although convinced of the validity and importance of the law of effect, Rice prefers "to leave it an open question whether the law of effect can be taken as the sole principle of learning, or whether a law of exercise is also needed, perhaps together with still other principles." "It is hard to see how mere exercise or repetition, without satisfaction or need-reduction, could fail to have some effect on the associative neural tracts, even though this effect may be slighter than the 'retroflex' action of reward" (p. 309). And Allport, while accepting effect as a secondary principle of learning, maintains that "effect cannot possibly be the *only* law of learning" (p. 338) and remarks that it is easy "to demonstrate that learning takes place when no drives have been reduced. Suppose while using a cleaning fluid I am careless with a match. . . . Suppose I mispronounce a word in a public speech . . . and suffer mounting shame and discomfort. Tension has been *created,* not reduced; *dissatisfaction* and not satisfaction has resulted; but in this sequence of events I shall surely learn" (p. 342). These criticisms are well taken, and it is hoped that the point of view presented in the present paper will meet them, but will, at the same time, avoid the manifest difficulties which multiple-principle learning theories have previously encountered (cf., for example, the later discussion of Thorndike's principles of effect and exercise).

[12] In earlier publications the author has stressed the usefulness of the distinction which Hilgard and Marquis (1940) have drawn between the "classical" conditioning procedure (invariable pairing of *CS* and *UnCS*) and the "instrumental" conditioning procedure (pairing of *CS* and *UnCS* only when the *CS* does not elicit the expected response). An "instrumental conditioned response" now appears to be a contradiction in terms. Only *skeletal* responses are instrumental in the sense of performing "work," producing "results," changing the external world; and if the term "conditioning" is to be restricted, as now seems desirable, to the process whereby responses of the smooth muscles and glands are acquired, it is clearly inappropriate to speak of a conditioned response as instrumental. This point will be returned to on a later page.

III. Collateral Support for a Two-Factor Theory of Learning

There are reasons other than that of conceptual convenience for supposing that there are two distinctive learning processes. In stressing the "unity of the individual," or the "organism as a whole," we are likely to gloss over the fact that in all mammals and in many other phyla the individual organism is divided into two great response systems, that of the *skeletal muscles* and that of the *smooth muscle* and *glands*. The responses mediated by the latter are appropriately termed *physiological,* whereas those mediated by the former are *behavioral* in the usual sense of that term. Just as an army must have both its "supply" units and its "action" units, so must the individual organism have organs of supply and organs of action.

The fundamental nature of this dichotomy is further emphasized by the fact that mammals and other complex living organisms have, not "*a* nervous system," but two distinct *nervous systems.* Responses of the skeletal muscles are mediated by the *central nervous system,* whereas responses of the visceral and vascular parts of the organism are mediated by the *autonomic nervous system.* In terms of structure and organization, as well as mode of functioning, these two nervous systems are radically different; and it is by no means unreasonable to suppose that the responses which they mediate are subject to very different learning processes.[13]

As a further parallel to this basic dichotomy we may note the familiar differentiation between *voluntary* and *involuntary* responses. Without exception, the visceral and vascular responses are beyond direct voluntary control, whereas all of the skeletal responses (with the unimportant exception of a few "reflexes") are or may be brought under voluntary control. Under ordinary circumstances, the visceral and vascular responses occur in a smoothly automatic fashion, and serve what Cannon (1932) has

[13] If one assumes that effect learning is basic and that conditioning is dependent upon it, then one might expect to find that, phylogenetically and ontogenetically, the central nervous system is laid down first and the autonomic later. Kempf (1918) believes that the autonomic is the primitive nervous system and far older than the central nervous system. Although the central nervous system is now "dominant" in higher organisms, this was presumably not the case at an early stage in organic evolution. And Hewer (1927) has shown that in the human embryo the unstriped musculature develops first, to be followed later by the striped musculature. There is thus converging evidence that the autonomic-physiological system is more primitive than the central-behavioral system. From this it may seem to follow that conditioning is the basic form of learning and effect learning a "secondary form" (as Allport has proposed, Footnote 11). Whether such an inference is justifiable, on the basis of present knowledge, is uncertain.

called the "homeostatic," or physiological, equilibrium-restoring function. These same responses may, however, be made to occur, not only in response to actual physiological needs, but also in response to conditioned stimuli, or signals, of various kinds. And when the visceral and vascular responses occur on the latter basis, as *anticipatory states,* they *produce,* rather than eliminate, physiological disequilibrium and are consciously experienced as *emotion.* As such, they play enormously important motivational roles, roles so important to the survival of the organism that it is easily understood why the learning of these responses should be automatic, involuntary, distinct from the type of learning whereby ordinary habits are acquired. Biologically, it is clearly necessary that living organisms be equipped with a nervous system which will cause to be fixated those skeletal responses which reduce drives and give pleasure. But it is equally evident that living organisms must also be equipped with another nervous system which will cause emotional responses to be learned, not because they solve problems or give pleasure in any immediate sense, but because without such responses the organism would have slight chance of survival. There are grounds for believing that all emotions (including fear, anger, and the appetites) are basically painful (i.e., all have drive quality); and it is hard to see how they could be acquired by the same mechanism which fixes those responses (of the skeletal musculature) which are problem solving, drive reducing, pleasure giving. The latter are learned when a problem is resolved, ended; whereas it is often necessary that emotional responses become conditioned to signals which are associated with the *onset,* not the termination, of a problem.[14]

Another way of making the same point is to note (as one of the author's students, Mr. C. G. Chmielenski, has recently done) that trial-and-error learning is parallel to what Freud (1911) has called the *pleasure principle,* whereas conditioning is more closely related to the *reality principle.* In other words, living organisms acquire conditioned responses, or emotions, not because it is pleasant to do so, but because it is *realistic.* It is certainly not pleasant to be afraid, for example, but it is often very helpful, from the standpoint

[14] This discussion raises a particularly important, but difficult question: How are appetites learned? Superficially they appear to represent an anticipation of drive reduction, or satisfaction. Thus, for example, salivation (as a physical concomitant of food appetite) may be said to represent an anticipation of hunger reduction. But whether an appetite is learned in the same way as are responses of the skeletal musculature which produce drive reduction, or by the mere pairing of a signal and food (as Pavlov apparently believed) is at present impossible to say. Even less is known about the conditions of anger learning.

of personal survival (cf. Mowrer and Kluckhohn, 1944, on the distinction between "adjustment" and "adaptation"). At the same time, it is biologically useful for living organisms to be able to learn those responses which reduce their drives, regardless of whether these drives be primary (as in the case of hunger) or secondary (as in the case of fear); but it is apparently quite necessary that the neural mechanism which mediates this kind of learning be different from the mechanism whereby emotional, or "attitudinal," learning comes about.

Nor does the usefulness of differentiating between conditioning and effect learning end here. Anthropologists are tending more and more to define "culture" as accumulated and transmitted problem solutions (Ford, 1939; Kluckhohn and Kelly, 1945; Linton, 1936). However, unless a distinction is immediately made, this definition leads to a serious dilemma; i.e., some items of culture, far from solving problems for the individual in any immediate sense, actually *make* problems for him. This dilemma is quickly resolved if we note that certain items of culture are problem solving primarily, or perhaps exclusively, in the sense of being *individually* useful; whereas certain other items of culture are problem solving primarily, or perhaps exclusively, in the sense of being *socially* necessary. By and large, the solutions to individual problems involve the central nervous system and the skeletal musculature, whereas the solutions to social problems involve the autonomic nervous system and the organs which mediate emotional responses. Intrinsically, it is hardly helpful to the individual to be told, "Thou shalt not do thus and so," but it may be socially very necessary, and, in the long run but not in any immediately discernible psychological sense, also advantageous to the individual.[15]

Similarly, in the field of education it is useful to differentiate between *teaching* and *training*. Teaching may be defined as the process whereby one individual helps another learn to solve a problem more quickly or effectively than would be likely on the basis of that individual's own unaided, trial-and-error efforts. Here we are dealing with "items of culture" which are individually helpful. Training, by contrast, may be thought of as involving learning whose primary objective is social rather than individual. In this connection one naturally thinks of "items of culture" which are associated with such words as "morality," "character," "social responsibility," etc. Such a distinction as the one here proposed

---

[15] Cf. Mowrer and Ullman (15) on the distinction between "adjustment" and "integration." See also the concluding paragraphs of the present paper on the "problem of conscience."

between teaching and training is helpful in deciding the oft-debated question as to whether "indoctrination" is a legitimate function of education. It is also relevant to some of the issues which have arisen between Progressive Education and more traditional educational philosophies.[16]

Although current laboratory practice is not completely differentiated in this connection, it may nevertheless be worth noting that the method of plotting "learning curves" tends to be different when trial-and-error learning is involved from what it is when

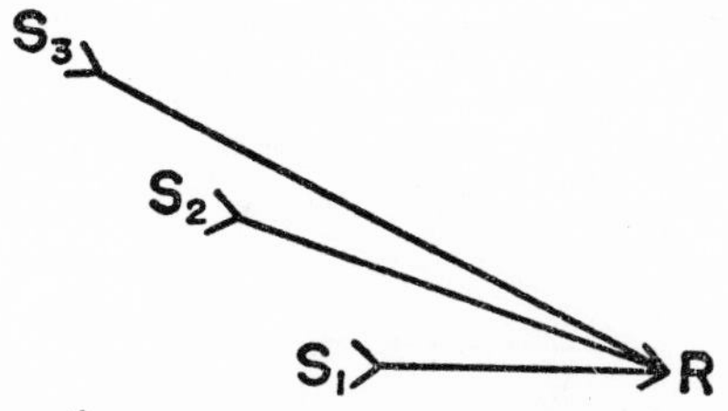

FIG. 47.—Diagrammatic representation of conditioning, or stimulus substitution. Originally only S_1 is capable of producing R; but as a result of the contiguous occurrence of S_2 and S_1, S_2 becomes able to elicit R. This change represents "first order" conditioning. And if R becomes attached to S_3 through the pairing of S_3 and S_2, this change is referred to as "second order" conditioning. In this type of learning, R is a response mediated by the autonomic nervous system.

conditioning is involved. What is probably the commonest procedure, in the former instance, is to note and graph the *time required* by the subject to make the "correct" response after the "problem" is presented. Learning is thus seen graphically as a descending curve. In the case of conditioning, on the other hand, the usual practice is to note whether a specified response does or does not occur (and possibly to what extent) in response to the so-called "conditioned stimulus." This type of learning is therefore represented graphically as an ascending curve.

An even more explicit difference arises from the fact that conditioning involves what may be termed stimulus substitution, whereas problem-solving learning involves response substitution. This contrast is presented diagrammatically in Figures 47 and 48.

In Figure 47, if S_1 is a stimulus which can be relied upon to elicit the emotional response R, and if S_2 is presented along with S_1, then S_2 quickly becomes a substitute for S_1. This is commonly known as "first-order" conditioning. But if, after S_2 has become

[16] Cf. also Kilpatrick's (1925) discussion of "concomitant" learnings, i.e., the unintentional emotional conditioning which often accompanies supposedly pure "teaching."

capable of producing the same response as S_1, S_3 is paired with S_2, then S_3 may become capable of eliciting the response in question. This is known as "second order" conditioning. Pavlov (1927) has shown that salivary conditioning in dogs can be carried to the "third order." How far "higher order" conditioning, involving different subjects and different responses, can be carried has not been fully determined. (To the reader who is not accustomed to think in terms of this type of learning, the analogy of the teaching of a foreign language by the "direct" and "indirect"

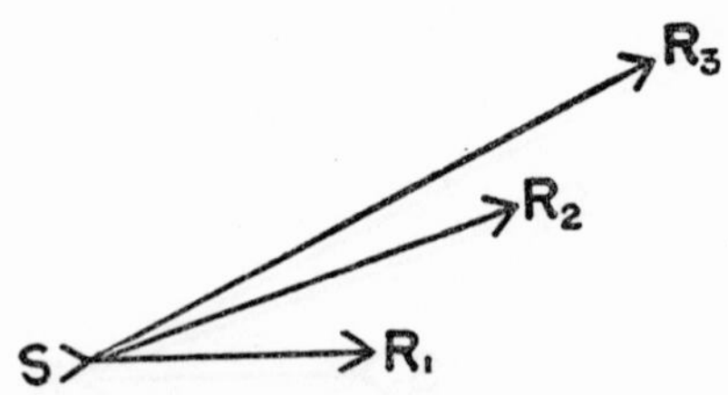

FIG. 48.—Diagrammatic representation of problem solving, or response substitution. Originally *S* produces R_1; but if R_1 does not lead to a satisfactory outcome, it is inhibited and R_2 occurs. If R_2 likewise fails to prove rewarding, R_3 occurs. If this latter response "solves the problem," i.e., eliminates *S*, the connection between *S* and R_3 is reinforced, and R_3 tends to replace both R_1 and R_3. In this type of learning R_1, R_2, and R_3 are mediated by the central nervous system.

methods may be useful. The first method corresponds roughly to first-order conditioning and the indirect method to second-order conditioning i.e., in the first case the "word" is associated directly with the "thing," whereas in the second case the "word" is expected to acquire the proper meaning by virtue of association with another "word," rather than with the "thing.")

The diagram shown in Figure 48 represents learning of the problem-solving, or response-substitution, type. If *S* is a drive, or a "problem situation," the subject's first response, R_1, may not be effective. It is followed by R_2, which may likewise not be effective. R_2 is followed in turn by R_3, which, let us suppose, is effective. On subsequent occasions, when *S* recurs, R_3 will tend to be the dominant response. It may be said to have become a substitute for R_1.

This distinction between conditioning and problem solving has recently been expressed by Scott (1947) somewhat differently but very explicitly, as follows:

> The behavior of an animal can be divided into two categories: modifiable and nonmodifiable behavior. In the first class falls most of the external behavior. If an animal's first reaction does not produce satisfactory adjustment to stimulation, he can alter it and produce a more satis-

factory one. In the second class is most of the internal behavior of an animal, including the secretion of glands and the contractions of smooth muscles. Such activities follow a standard pattern, and while they can be associated with certain stimuli, and thus be affected by learning, the nature of the reaction never varies except in its strength. In this same class of behavior also belong certain types of external behavior which have been usually termed reflexes. It is, of course, this nonmodifiable behavior which has the closest association with the term emotion (p. 279).[17]

That there is a fundamental difference between the two forms of learning which are here designated as conditioning and as problem solving is made clear in yet another way. There have been many experiments and discussions on "the gradient of reinforcement," but if there are two basically different types of reinforcement, one would expect to find *two* gradients of reinforcement. This expectation is well founded. In the gradient of reinforcement of the problem-solving type, the variable that is important is the interval of time between the occurrence of the correct response and the occurrence of the ensuing rewarding state of affairs. If this interval is short, the reinforcement is great; if the interval is long, then the reinforcement is slight. On the other hand, in the gradient of reinforcement of the conditioning type, the variable that is important is the interval of time between the occurrence of the *CS* and the occurrence of the *UnCS*. If the *CS* precedes the *UnCS* only slightly or actually coincides with it, then the reinforcement is great; but if the interval between the *CS* and the *UnCS* is longer, then the reinforcement is proportionately lessened. We thus arrive at what is one of the most clear-cut distinctions between the two types of learning which are here under discussion.

In summary, then, we see that there are many and highly diverse sources of evidence for the two-factor theory of learning which is here under consideration. Such a theory presupposes a delimitation of the term "conditioning" as it is usually employed and an extension of the traditional concept of "effect" learning. The term "conditioning" has commonly been used, erroneously as it now seems, to denote the process whereby a living organism comes to make any response, skeletal or visceral, immediate or delayed, to a stimulus which has "signal value." As we saw in the preceding

[17] This way of dichotomizing the responses of living organisms has the interesting incidental effect of resolving the question, Why do conditioned responses, so-called, sometimes differ from their unconditioned prototypes? The answer is that if the term "conditioned response" is restricted to visceral-vascular responses, the problem disappears, since such responses are always much the same, whether elicited by a *CS* or an *UnCS*. (This is not to say, however, that their subjective counterparts are necessarily the same. Cf. the earlier discussion of emotions as physiological preparations.)

section, this usage is too broad for precise scientific purposes. It now seems preferable to apply the term "conditioning" to that and only that type of learning whereby *emotional* (visceral and vascular) responses are acquired. By contrast, effect learning has been previously conceived as applying mainly in those situations in which the motive, or "problem," is an unlearned biological drive, such as hunger, thirst, pain, etc. It is now clear that effect learning must be expanded to include those situations in which the motive, or "problem," is a *learned* drive, i.e., an emotion such as fear or an appetite (1, 3, 4). Many responses involving the skeletal musculature, which have previously been termed "conditioned responses," are, in the present conceptual scheme, not conditioned responses at all. Only those responses which involve visceral and vascular tissue and which are experienced subjectively as emotion are assumed to be conditioned responses. If an emotion, or secondary drive, causes the skeletal musculature to be activated and if such activity results in secondary drive reduction, then the overt response thus acquired is here conceived as an instance of effect learning, not conditioning.

One other matter remains to be considered, although the limitations of both space and precise knowledge are such that it can be considered only in the most general terms. In the foregoing pages we have repeatedly spoken of *two* nervous systems, the central and the autonomic. We must now briefly examine their interrelationship and, in one important respect, the dependence of one upon the other.

Of the two, the central nervous system is the more complete, composed as it is of sensory nerves, internuncial nerves, and motor nerves, by means of which it is possible, at least in principle, for an impulse from any sense organ to be relayed to any part of the skeletal musculature. On the other hand, the autonomic nervous system, strictly speaking, is an exclusively motor, or efferent, system. As Fulton (1943) remarks, "The sympathetic chain and vagus obviously carry many afferent fibres, some sensory in nature, giving rise to visceral pain, and others involved in viscero-visceral and viscero-somatic reflexes that never reach consciousness. There is some question, however, whether such fibres should be classified as 'autonomic,' the term adopted by Langley for a purely efferent outflow, and it is perhaps better to use the standard morphological term 'visceral afferent' " (p. 194). It is obvious, therefore, that communication, if communication there be, between the so-called autonomic nervous system and the sensorium of the individual must be supplied by the sensory pathways of the central nervous system. And the fact that both external and internal stimuli of various kinds may activate the autonomic leaves no doubt that such communication does exist. The question is how and where it is that ordinary sensory impulses, traveling inward on the central nervous system, get shunted onto fibers communicating with the autonomic system.

For an answer we may again turn to Fulton. He says:

> Autonomic nerves . . . are in no way independent of somatic. The two are interdependent. . . . We find somatic and autonomic functions regulated from common levels in the cord, brain, stem, hypothalamus and cortex (p. 191). In the cortex there is extensive overlapping between autonomic and somatic motor representation, making possible unified correlation between the reactions of the two systems. In general, the topographical relation between the cortical areas influencing specific autonomic functions is close to the cortical area influencing the corresponding functions. Thus lacrimation is observed on stimulating the eye fields, salivation, on stimulation of the motor representation of the face and tongue (p. 444).

In other words, it is now established that there are numerous "representations" of the autonomic nerves in the most complex parts of the central nervous system, and that from the standpoint of neuroanatomy there is no difficulty in getting an impulse which enters the central nervous system from any sensory organ to discharge through the autonomic system. The structural basis is thus laid for the occurrence of that form of learning which is involved in conditioning; but how this is achieved, functionally, is still a mystery. What is important to note for present purposes is merely that, anatomically, there is just as much basis for assuming that conditioning occurs in the cerebral cortex as for supposing that problem-solving learning occurs there. There is, in other words, no neuroanatomical evidence which argues against the two-factor theory of learning, and there is some such evidence which is at least implicitly supportive of this theory.

IV. Adumbrations of This View

Writing in 1906, Sherrington proposed a twofold division of behavior into *anticipatory* responses and *consummatory* responses. Because the forwardmost, or "leading," part of an organism encounters new stimuli first, it is this part, i.e., the *head,* which has developed the "distance receptors": eyes, ears, nose, and, in some instances, "feelers." Responses which are elicited by stimuli impinging upon these receptors are, in one sense, necessarily *anticipatory,* since objects from which these stimuli emanate have themselves not yet come into direct contact with the organism. "Ability on the part of an organism to react to an object when still distant from it allows an interval for preparatory reactive steps which can go far to influence the success of attempts either to obtain actual contact or to avoid actual contact with the object. . . . The 'distance receptors' initiate anticipatory, i.e., precurrent, reactions" (p. 326).

By contrast there are the *consummatory* responses, responses of incorporation or of rejection, which occur when an object comes into direct contact with the organism. As its name implies, a consummatory response tends to be accompanied by a feeling of satisfaction, pleasure, gratification. And thus, reasoned Sherrington, "to consummatory reactions affective tone seems adjunct much more than to the anticipatory, especially the remotely anticipatory [responses to stimulation] of the projicient sense-organs" (p. 330).[18]

A number of subsequent investigators, including the present writer at one point (1941a), have accepted Sherrington's distinction between anticipatory and consummatory responses. They correspond in certain very obvious ways to the "conditioned" responses of Pavlov (who also referred to them as "anticipatory") and to the problem-solving responses which Thorndike and others have investigated. But a closer analysis shows that anticipatory responses, so-called, may also—in fact usually do—have a "consummatory" quality, no less than do the consummatory responses proper. As shown by the experiments of Mowrer and Lamoreaux which are cited above, there is now reason to suppose that living organisms experience satisfaction, not only when they *escape* from a noxious stimulus, such as an electric shock, which has actually impinged upon them, but also when they *avoid* such a stimulus and in so doing experience a reduction in the secondary drive of fear. That we should refer to the one of these responses, and not to the other, as "consummatory" seems highly arbitrary. Viewed in this larger setting—i.e., with the role of secondary as well as primary drives, and drive reductions, in mind—the distinction proposed by Sherrington between anticipatory and consummatory responses becomes

[18] Sherrington is here following an old and, as it now seems, fallacious conception of pleasure as an "emotion." Clarity seems best served if we think of "affective tone," or emotion, as attaching precisely to those stimuli which Sherrington says it is not attached to, namely, "distance stimuli," or signs. "Pleasure" is properly contrasted with "pain," or "drive," as a reduction in drive, whereas an emotion *is* drive, not drive reduction. A reduction in the intensity of an emotion, or secondary drive, provides pleasure, just as a reduction in a primary drive does, so it is hardly sensible to speak of a *reduction* in emotion as "emotion."

blurred and much less useful than it at first promises to be. What is important is the distinction between the skeletal responses and the visceral responses, between behavior and the accompanying interplay of emotion.

Sherrington was by no means unaware of the connection between the emotions and what he referred to as the anticipatory responses. Thus, he says in now quaintly archaic language, "The relative haste with which an animal when hungry approaches food offered to the visual field suggests that conation attaches to the visual reaction by association through memory with affective tone. By associative memory a tinge of the affective tone of the consummatory reaction may suffuse the anticipatory. The latter becomes indirectly a pleasure-pain reaction" (p. 331). But what Sherrington did not see was that the occurrence of feeling, or emotion, in response to stimulation of the distance receptors is often, perhaps always, a precondition for the occurrence of those overt skeletal responses of approach and avoidance which he called the "anticipatory" responses. In other words, it now appears that the only responses which are truly anticipatory are the emotional ones and that the skeletal responses which are activated by the emotions are just as "consummatory" as are those which are activated by the primary drives, such as hunger, thirst, pain, etc. The first reaction to a sign is, by this hypothesis, always an emotional one, and the resulting drive state is an *intervening variable* between the sign-stimulus and the "final common path," or overt behavior.[19]

[19] [This type of analysis dispels a number of apparent teleological paradoxes. It shows, first of all, that "anticipatory" skeletal responses are caused by forces which lie, not in the future, but in the present. In other words, these "anticipatory" responses are *caused, motivated by drives*—quite as much as are the skeletal responses of a so-called "consummatory" nature. But what of the emotional reactions? Is there not something telic, premonitory, futuristic about them? Certainly we cannot say that they are motivated, or caused, in the sense that skeletal responses are. Emotions are not "motivated"—they occur, not in response to drives, but in response to mere *signs* of drives. (For a minor qualification of this statement see 1, Footnote 3.) Signs may be stimuli which possess but infinitesimal intrinsic energy. How, then, is it that they can "produce" relatively profound "disturbances" in an organism? Just how the effect is achieved we do not know (whether by "avalanche conduction" or by some other means); but, at the descriptive level, we may liken the emotional apparatus to a "booster" system such as is used in long-distance telephone communication: it takes a small quantity of energy and "steps it up," "amplifies" it many times over, to the point that it can then *drive* the relatively resistant machinery of overt behavior. But the emotions are no more teleological than are skeletal responses. They serve to prepare the organism for impending events (which are more or less probable but may or may not happen) and are in this sense "anticipatory"; but it is *memory,* or *past learning,* that makes such reactions possible, not powers or processes that lie in the future as such. Similarly, in criticism of the law of effect, it has sometimes been claimed that teleology is here implied. Obviously a response which is followed by reward is not influenced, or affected, by that reward: the response is done and over with before

In one sense Sherrington may be said to have recognized the lack of a direct connection between signs and overt responses; for he remarks:

> The nerve fiber that starts from the receptor does not in many of the cases itself extend to, or send processes to, the mouths of the "final common paths." Instead of going so it ends often far short of them, and forms connection with other nerve fibers (internuncial paths), which in their turn reach distant "final common paths." This arrangement involves an intercalation of gray matter between the "private receptor" path and the "final common path" . . . (p. 328).

In these words Sherrington certainly provides a neurological "opening" for the occurrence of emotions as intervening variables. And, on a later page, after quoting Lloyd Morgan, he says:

> It is enough here that in regard to certain stimuli the new value—the meaning—which the projicient sensation [sign] has obtained has reinforced greatly the conative intensity of the reaction to the stimulus. It has given the stimulus increased force as a spring of precurrent actions aimed at a final consummatory one. It has been given this not by altering the external stimulus, nor the receptor-organ, but by, among other alterations, altering internal connections of the receptor arc. Thus it is that, be it by associative memory or other processes, the reactions of the "distance receptors" come in higher animals to reveal a conative driving force which is perhaps the end for which these psychoses exist (pp. 331–32).

Sherrington is neither entirely clear nor entirely consistent in his analysis on this score; but one here sees a great mind and an astute observer grappling with a very fundamental problem.

A decade later, by 1916, Pavlov's work on the conditioned response was becoming known in this country, particularly through the writings of Yerkes and Morgulis, Watson, and Lashley. In his presidential address to the American Psychological Association in that year, Watson (1916) remarked that "it is customary to make a distinction between (A) *conditioned secretion reflexes* and (B) *conditioned motor reflexes*" (p. 92). "The conditioned salivary reflex has at present no very wide sphere of usefulness or applicability" (p. 93). "Our own work has centered around the conditioned motor reflex of Bekhterev, since we find for his method an immediate and widespread usefulness" (p. 94).

---

the reward occurs. What *is* affected, altered by the reward, is *the organism,* which will show the "effect" of the reward in the form of a tendency to make more promptly, under similar conditions in the future, responses similar to the one which previously elicited the reward. This type of causality is surely as straightforward as one could ask.]

Watson recognized that so-called conditioned motor reflexes—such as retraction of the great toe in human subjects—"apparently can be set upon processes which are presided over by the autonomic system" (p. 98), yet his writings seem to have done a great deal to confirm the practice in this country of referring to various skeletal responses as "conditioned responses." At least it cannot be said that he did anything to restrict this term to visceral and vascular changes or to further the practice of thinking of skeletal responses, not as conditioned responses, but as problem-solving responses, acquired under the impact of effect learning.

In the same year Lashley (1916) spoke of the "relative independence of the salivary reflex from the complex conditions of reinforcement and inhibition which affect the activity of striped muscles" (p. 460); but he did not attempt on the basis of this distinction to establish a two-factor theory of learning.

One of the first and most explicit attempts along these lines came in 1935 when B. F. Skinner published a paper entitled "Two types of conditioned reflex and a pseudotype," in which he proposed a fundamental distinction between behavior which is acquired on the basis of what is ordinarily referred to as the law of effect and behavior which is acquired on the basis of the principle of conditioning, as elaborated by Pavlov (1927).

Two years later, Konorski and Miller (1937) expressed their essential agreement with the distinction drawn by Skinner, but raised certain questions concerning its validity.[20] They say:

> In our opinion, Skinner's main lines of analysis are correct. He rightly discriminates two types of conditioned reflex—his Type I against the classical Pavlovian types—and stresses the absence of the signalizing function in the former. Nevertheless, the very construction of his Type I is built up in a faulty manner and is not in agreement with the present state of experimental facts (p. 265).

In an attempt to support the latter statement, Kornorski and Miller cite some of their own earlier "physiological investigations of the phenomena which in psychology are known as habits" (p. 265) and call attention to certain dilemmas which they believe their findings raise for Skinner's differentiation. The precise nature of these findings is unimportant for present purposes. Suffice it to note that Skinner (1937) prepared a reply to Konorski and Miller in which he defended his original formulation; but this defense is involved and not particularly illuminating. It will, however, be

[20] For a review of related literature up to 1937, see Hilgard (1937). For a more detailed discussion of much of the same material, see Hilgard and Marquis (1940).

useful to quote, even though somewhat out of context, one passage from this paper of Skinner's as indicating an important line of thought which he was to develop later at greater length:

> Two separate points may be answered briefly. (1) It is essential in this kind of formulation that one reflex be considered at a time, since our learning data have the dimensions of changes in reflex strength. The development of an antagonistic response when a reinforcement in Type *R* is negative requires a separate paradigm, either of Type *R* or Type *S*. [The distinction between operant and respondent behavior and the special properties of the former will be dealt with at length in a work now in preparation. All conditioned reflexes of Type *R* are by definition operants and all of Type *S*, respondents; but the operant-respondent distinction is the more general since it extends to unconditioned behavior as well (p. 274).] (2) That responses of smooth muscle or glandular tissue may or may not enter into Type *R*, I am not prepared to assert. I used salivation as a convenient hypothetical instance of simultaneous fused responses of both types, but a skeletal response would have done as well. The child that has been conditioned to cry "real tears" because tears have been followed by positive reinforcement (e.g., candy) apparently makes a glandular conditioned response of Type *R*, but the matter needs to be checked because an intermediate step may be involved (p. 279).

Skinner ends this paragraph, and his article, by a brief reference to the experiments of Hudgins in which the smooth-muscle response involved in pupillary contraction is first conditioned and then brought under "voluntary" control, i.e., changed from a "respondent" to an "operant" type of behavior.

In the same year (1937), Schlosberg published a paper entitled "The relationship between success and the laws of conditioning." This paper is so carefully reasoned, so compact, and so freighted with important implications that it could be profitably quoted *in toto* in the present context. Since this is not possible, it must suffice instead to pick out for comment only a few of the paper's most salient features.

The paper opens as follows:

> The purpose of the present paper is to differentiate between two types of learning, namely, that involving simple conditioning and that involving the law of effect. . . . There are two somewhat different types of learning:
>
> (1) Simple conditioning, which applies particularly to diffuse, preparatory responses.
>
> (2) "Effect" learning, which applies particularly to precise, adaptive responses, and makes greater demands upon the nervous system than does simple conditioning (p. 379).

On a later page, Schlosberg says:

Skinner, in a recent paper, has clearly analyzed two types of simple stimulus-response situations and differentiated between them. His Type II conditioned response is clearly the conditioned response as defined above. Skinner also described a situation in which one response led to another stimulus-response sequence. He chose to call the behavior resulting from such situations conditioned response Type I. The present writer would prefer to call such situations by some other name, such as "problem-solving," to avoid confusion. But he is completely in agreement with Skinner in separating the two types of situations (p. 388).

The main purpose of Schlosberg's paper was to try to reconcile seemingly contradictory experimental facts (see previous section, Association or Effect? page 224); and he believed that this could be done if one made the type of distinction which is suggested in the foregoing quotations. It will not be necessary here to reconsider these issues; but it will be useful to quote, without attempting to supply the full context, a few particularly significant passages.

Let us turn now to a discussion of the conditioned reactions based upon shock. . . . The responses to shock may be grouped under two classes, namely, those responses, usually of skeletal muscle, that would remove the member from the locus of the shock and those reactions of muscle and gland that result from the shock but are not specific to the shocked area. The former are called "withdrawal" or "flexion" reflexes or responses and are sometimes classified as "defense" reactions. The less specific reactions have no convenient generic name. They include various changes in the breathing rhythm, pulse rhythm, electrical skin resistance, body volume, pitch of voice, and tonic change. Such responses may be referred to as emotional, attentional, anticipatory, or preparatory. They "condition" rather readily. But they probably do not materially modify the effectiveness of the unconditioned stimulus, even though they may occur as conditioned responses before the unconditioned stimulus (p. 385).

Schlosberg concludes:

It is thus possible to make a rough, and perhaps superficial distinction between diffuse preparatory responses, to which the laws of conditioning apply in a direct fashion, and precise adaptive responses, in which the law of effect seems relevant. The distinction, in common with most of those that are drawn in the biological sciences, is not to be construed too rigidly. Further, it is quite possible that the distinction is not an ultimate one, and that the facts referred to under the law of effect may eventually be reduced to terms of conditioning. But the distinction has some merit in ordering certain of the experimental results obtained in the field of learning (p. 390).

It is thus apparent how close Schlosberg came to the position taken in the present paper. The principal difference is that he did not quite clearly enough differentiate between the visceral and vascular responses and the skeletal responses and that he regarded both the "diffuse" and the "precise" responses to which he refers as essentially parallel and independent reactions to common stimuli. The position taken here is that conditioning of the visceral-vascular, or "diffuse," responses takes place first and that the accompanying emotional state provides the motivation, or problem, which produces the subsequently observed skeletal, or "precise, adaptive," reactions. In common with most psychologists of a decade ago, Schlosberg was here equating "problem" to "primary drive." It is now clear that we must extend our conception of "problem" to include the secondary drives and that we must think of the latter as themselves a product of learning, but of a particular form of learning, namely, conditioning.

It is unfortunate that Skinner insisted upon referring to both his Type I learning and Type II learning as forms of "conditioning." Nor has his alternative use of "Types *S*" and "Types *R*" and his introduction of the terms "operant" and "respondent" been in the interests of clarity and quickness of communication. Yet the fact remains that he has come nearer than any other writer to making precisely the distinction between the two basic forms of learning which is here being emphasized. In his book *The Behavior of organisms* (1938), he says:

> The distinction between Types *R* and *S* arising from their confinement to operant and respondent behavior respectively implies a rough topographical separation. Reflexes of Type *S*, as respondents, are confined to such behavior as is originally elicited by special stimuli. *The effectors controlled by the autonomic nervous system are the best examples,* one of which was used almost exclusively by Pavlov in his classical studies. . . . Most of the experiments upon skeletal behavior which have been offered as paralleling Pavlov's work are capable of interpretation as discriminated operants of Type *R*, . . . *It is quite possible on the existing evidence that a strict topographical separation of types following the skeletal-autonomic distinction may be made* (p. 112, italics added).

Although the foregoing passage was written and published some years before the present writer came to the point of view which is presented in this paper, it was only after this point of view was well stabilized that Skinner's formulation came to the writer's attention.[21] For the writer, it is therefore a source of special confidence in this point of view that Skinner arrived at it previously and quite independently.

That Skinner foresaw one of the most important implications that come from attempting to distinguish between *behavior,* as instrumental action, and *emotion,* as primarily a source of motivation, is indicated by the following quotation:

> There is little reason to expect conditioning of Type *R* in an autonomic response, since it does not as a rule naturally act upon the environment in any way that will produce a reinforcement, but it may be made to do so through instrumental means. In collaboration with Dr. B. B. Delabarre I have attempted to condition vasoconstriction of the arm in human subjects by making a positive reinforcement dependent upon constriction. These experiments have so far yielded no conclusive result, but there are many clinical observations that seem to indicate conditioning of this sort. The operant field corresponds closely with what has traditionally been called "voluntary" behavior, and the "voluntary" control of some autonomic activities is well established. The child that has learned to cry "real tears" and produces a reinforcing stimulus has apparently acquired a conditioned autonomic operant (pp. 112–13).

This is obviously the same problem on which the present writer [using the G. S. R.] reported preliminary evidence in his 1938 paper, which Skinner cites (p. 111) in the context of the foregoing quotation. [It is noteworthy that in both instances the results were "inconclusive."]

Some of the many other implications of this two-factor theory of learning will be considered in the two following sections.

By way of summarizing the present section, we may note that the basic distinction which is here being proposed corresponds roughly to that drawn by common sense between *habits* and *attitudes,* if by habits we mean learned responses of the skeletal musculature and if by attitudes we mean learned responses of glands, smooth muscle, and vasomotor tissue. But it is even more important to note that these two types of reactions are not strictly parallel or coordinate: habits function instrumentally, reduce drives, solve problems; attitudes, or emotions, although in one sense responses, are drives, or problems, which call forth skeletal responses and on the basis of which habits, as above defined, may then develop, just as they may on the basis of the primary drives.

It is difficult to see why so simple a conception as this one has

---

[21] As a result of conversation with Professor Skinner at the meeting of the American Psychological Association in Philadelphia, September, 1946.

been so rarely suggested and so little used to resolve the many dilemmas that haunt the theory of learning and of behavior generally.[22]

V. Clarifying Consequences

In the present section we shall review some of the paradoxes which are resolved by adopting the two-factor theory of learning presented in the preceding sections. In the final section, we shall consider, by contrast, some of the problems which remain unsolved or are specifically created by this theory.

Failures to Obtain "Conditioning." Nowhere is it more apparent how confused the concept of conditioning has been than in the numerous apparent failures to obtain this type of learning. Let us consider first an example of such a "failure" with animal subjects and then one involving human subjects.

In 1932 Warner published a paper entitled "An experimental search for the 'conditioned response,'" in which he reported a would-be conditioning experiment in which "no rat, even after 1,000 trials, responded to the sound or light by hopping [i.e., making a *CR*]. The secondary stimuli did come to affect the animals' behavior but not in this way. The most frequent responses given by them were change in respiratory rate and lowering of the head" (p. 112). Using a different experimental setup, Warner found it possible to produce successful avoidance reactions, but these reactions were very different from the so-called unconditioned responses of his subjects (cf. 5). "The four rats which quite consist-

[22] Since the above was written, an article entitled "Two kinds of learning," has been published by H. S. Tuttle (1946), in which the author adopts a point of view which is in many respects remarkably similar to the one here presented. He believes that "an extensive and ever increasing mass of data points cogently and uniformly to the conclusion that there are two distinct kinds of learning" (p. 267)—"affective learning," which he equates to Pavlovian conditioning, and "intellectual learning" which may be equated to what is referred to in the present paper as problem solving. It is significant that Tuttle, relying largely upon work in educational psychology (particularly that reported by Thorndike, in *The psychology of wants, interests, and attitudes,* 1935) should draw much the same inferences as seem to follow from the experimental and clinical data which are here reviewed. Tuttle concludes: "The discovery that affective learning is a second kind of learning is indeed momentous. During the next hundred years its effects upon social control and the guidance of learning will be nothing short of revolutionary" (p. 277). The present writer is less confident that the consequences of this point of view will be "revolutionary," but he agrees with many of the practical inferences which Tuttle draws, some of which rather neatly parallel the considerations which are suggested in the following section. See also Tuttle's comments on "morality . . . as a product of conditioning" (p. 275) and the concluding paragraphs of the present study, entitled "Learning and the problem of conscience." The reader's attention is also drawn to articles by Stevens (1942) and Maier and Schneirla (1942), in which somewhat different types of two-factor theories of learning are presented.

ently scrambled under the fence [which divided two compartments] in response to the shock did learn to get to the other side of the fence in response to the sound—*but by leaping over it*" (p. 113).

In conclusion, Warner says:

> Even though a rat be placed in a situation wherein all stimulation is relatively uniform with the exception of two potent stimuli, and even though these stimuli be often repeated in a close temporal juxtaposition, it does not necessarily follow that the response to one of these stimuli can ultimately be aroused by the presentation of the other (p. 113). . . .
>
> The conditioned response hypothesis has been just as susceptible to overapplication and misapplication as have, for example, the Freudian principles. One should not conclude that the hypothesis is faulty but rather that it should be employed far more critically, and that it should be made the subject of less speculation and more experimentation (pp. 113–14).

It will be neither possible nor necessary to go into all the probable reasons why Warner failed to get the kind of response-modification which he felt one should expect on the basis of traditional conditioning doctrine. Only two points are here essential. It will be noted, first of all, that by changing the definition of a "conditioned response" from a vague, conventional one to the more limited and precise one suggested above, an experiment which ostensibly failed to produce "conditioning" in the conventional sense changes to one in which "conditioning," in the restricted sense, was obviously obtained: "The secondary stimuli did come to affect the animals' behavior but not in this way. The most frequent responses given to them were change in the respiration rate. . . ." From this phrase it is apparent that the subjects did condition in the sense that they acquired an emotional response.

The other point to be noted is that at least part of Warner's failure to obtain avoidance reactions involving the skeletal musculature was due to a failure to appreciate the fact that such responses develop and persist only if they are *problem solving* with respect to the underlying emotion, in this case *fear*. As the various experiments reported in Section III indicate, it is possible to get rats to begin making such responses after 6 to 10 trials and, after 60 to 80 trials, to make these responses nearly 100 per cent of the time.

"Failures" to obtain conditioning have been reported particularly often when human beings have been used as subjects, but nowhere does one find a more illuminating example of this than in the article, already cited, which was published by Watson in 1916. Watson says:

> In the best cases we begin to get a conditioned reflex [flexion of the great toe] after fourteen to thirty combined stimulations. We have found several refractory subjects: subjects in which even the primary reflex will not appear in the toe when the current is strong enough to induce perspiration. Whether this is due to atrophy of the toe reflex through the wearing of shoes, or to some other cause, we have never been able to determine (pp. 96–97).

We may now safely surmise that Watson's "refractory subjects" were simply individuals whose conception of themselves and of what was expected of them in the experimental situation was such that they "voluntarily" refrained from solving either the problem of shock or the problem of fear of shock, by lifting their toe from the metal grill against which it rested between trials. That they conditioned, however—in the sense of reacting emotionally to the conditioned stimulus—can hardly be doubted: " . . . strong enough to induce perspiration."

A number of studies, which the reader will find reviewed by Hilgard and Marquis (1940), have shown that instructions are enormously important in determining what skeletal responses human beings will or will not allow themselves to make to the fear which is aroused by a danger signal. However, comparatively little control over the fear reaction itself is possible. Investigators who have looked for physiological, rather than skeletal, indices of "conditioning," whether in human or animal subjects, have rarely, if ever, failed to find it.

PAVLOVIAN CONDITIONING RECONSIDERED. The present writer and others have criticized the Pavlovian paradigm of conditioning on the grounds that it is really reward learning, i.e., that the subject learns to respond to a signal by salivating, not because the food (of which the signal is premonitory) produces salivation (on a reflex basis), but because the food reduces hunger (Hull, 1943; 5). According to the bifurcated conception of learning which is here under consideration, the Pavlovian paradigm, based as it is on a response (salivation) which involves glands and which is mediated by the autonomic nervous system, would qualify as a conditioned response and would be expected to involve, not effect learning, but association.

Whether salivary conditioning occurs because of the appearance of food in the mouth (and reflex stimulation of salivation) or because of the disappearance of hunger (due to distension of the stomach and associated effects) has apparently not been fully determined. Two experimental possibilities come to mind: (*a*) If a "sham-feeding" preparation were arranged, so that food taken into the mouth and swallowed by a dog would not reach the stomach and so that food could be placed in the stomach without being first in the mouth, differential predictions concerning salivary conditioning would be made on the basis of the two factors mentioned above, i.e., the appearance of food in the mouth vs. the disappearance of hunger. (*b*) If hunger reduction, or reward, is the important element in salivary conditioning, it should be possible to make the salivary response instrumental in the following way. Suppose a dog had been trained to secrete a few drops of saliva in response to a signal that food is about to be presented. Then suppose that conditions were made such that food would materialize *only* if the subject secreted a certain minimum quantity. By successively raising the "production standard," it should be possible, if the reward theory of salivary conditioning is correct, to convert the subject into a veritable "saliva factory."

If the preliminary observations reported by Skinner (1938) and by Mowrer (1938c) are valid, it would seem highly improbable that the salivary response could be made to function in any such instrumental manner. But even though salivary conditioning be true conditioning and not problem solving, as these terms are here defined, Pavlov seems completely to have overlooked what is perhaps the most important function of the conditioned salivary response. Pavlov thought of it exclusively as a physiological preparation for eating; the present analysis would see it as an indicator, perhaps a veritable part of the mechanism, of the secondary motivation known as "appetite." While a good deal is known concerning the role of fear as a motive, we are only beginning to explore the systematic behavioral implications of the appetitive drives.[23]

HULL'S "DILEMMA." In 1929 Hull formulated what he termed "the dilemma of the conditioned defense reaction," as follows:

For a defense reaction to be wholly successful, it should take place so early that the organism will completely escape injury, i.e., the impact of the nocuous (unconditioned) stimulus. But in case the unconditioned stimulus fails to impinge upon the organism, there will be no reinforcement of the conditioned tendency, which means one would expect that experimental extinction will set in at once. This will rapidly render the conditioned reflex impotent, which, in turn, will expose the organism to the original injury. This will initiate a second cycle substantially like the first which will be followed by another and another indefinitely, a series of successful escapes [i.e., *avoidances*] always alternating with a series of injuries. From a biological point of view, the picture emerging from

[23] Cf. Tuttle's remark that "Pavlov died without recognizing the most significant implications of his researches" (1946, p. 270).

the above theoretical considerations is decidedly not an attractive one. . . .

There is thus presented a kind of biological dilemma apparently not at all the product of misplaced ingenuity on the part of the theorist. If experimental extinction operates fully, the organism seems doomed to suffer the injury of the nocuous stimulus periodically in order to renew the strength of its conditioned defense reactions. If, on the other hand, experimental extinction does not operate, the organism seems doomed to dissipate much of its energy reacting defensively to irrelevant stimuli (p. 510). . . . The problem presents a fascinating field for experimental investigation (p. 511).

At this stage Hull was apparently thinking of "reinforcement" entirely in terms of association, or paired presentation of stimuli. As we have already seen, he later came to the position that all reinforcement is ultimately reducible to drive reduction, problem solving, satisfaction. The dilemma outlined above seems to arise, at least in part, from a neglect of the possibility that there are *two* reinforcement processes, one whereby emotions are conditioned and another whereby habits are acquired which reduce emotions (or, in other instances, primary drives). Because the type of reinforcement that is involved in emotional learning fails to occur, i.e., because the *CS* fails to be followed by the *UnCS,* is no reason for saying "there will be no reinforcement of the conditioned tendency," if by the latter one means, as Hull evidently did, not the emotion of fear, but "the conditioned defense reaction." Defense reactions involving the skeletal musculature are "reinforced" if they reduce the emotion of fear which produces them; they are not dependent for their strengthening, in any direct sense, upon the coincidence of *CS* and *UnCS*.

In this situation, as in all situations involving the extinction of a so-called "conditioned defense reaction," we must differentiate between (*a*) the tendency for a danger signal to elicit the emotion of fear and (*b*) the tendency for the fear reaction to produce a skeletal adjustment which has been acquired because it is fear-reducing. Clarity on this score does not entirely resolve Hull's dilemma, but it seems to bring us a step nearer a resolution. A little thought will show that this dilemma is closely related to some of the basic problems in the field of "personality and culture," for example, that of "survivals," or "lag," in culture, and of "fixations" in individuals. These problems have been considered more fully elsewhere (1948b).

A "Vicious Circle" Explained. Another puzzling phenomenon which was brought to the writer's attention a few years ago (by Dr. Judson S. Brown) is the following. If a rat is put at one end of a straight alley about 4 feet long and if, after a period of

10 seconds, the floor of the alley (consisting of a metal grill) is electrified, the rat will soon scamper to the opposite end of the alley and, if a small nonelectrified compartment is available, escape into it. After a few repetitions of this procedure, the subject, as might be expected, will run to the opposite end as soon as placed in the alley, without receiving the shock. What obviously happens is that the rat's fear becomes conditioned to the "danger situation" and, since the running response carries the rat out of that situation, with an attendant reduction in fear, this response is quickly fixated.

Once this response is well established, it will persist for many trials; but the rat will tend to become more and more leisurely in making the run and will eventually delay beyond the ten-second period. If shock is not applied under these circumstances, the tendency on the part of the rat to flee from the end of the maze where it is introduced deteriorates still further; and ultimately the flight response will disappear completely.

This behavior is, of course, in no way surprising, since it conforms perfectly to what is well known concerning the extinction of avoidance reactions. What is surprising, however, is this: If, after a "conditioned" response of the kind just described is well established, the right half of the floor-grill, at the far end of the alley, is permanently electrified so that, in the process of getting from the starting point to the safety compartment, the rat must always receive at least a brief shock, the running response does not extinguish! Even though shock is never again experienced in the left half of the alley, where the animal is introduced, flight from this area continues to occur indefinitely.

When subjected to the first procedure described above, rats behave in a perfectly "normal" and understandable manner. But in the case of the second procedure, their behavior is very surprising, strange, "abnormal"—for they seem to be manifesting a "masochistic trend," a "need for punishment," "pleasure in pain." They continue to cross the electrified segment of the floor-grill and get shocked, whereas if they merely "sat tight" in the first part of the alley, nothing would happen to them. Under these circumstances, the running response obviously gets "punished," and yet, instead of being inhibited by this punishment, it is apparently strengthened by it.[24]

---

[24] Although the experiment just described is not strictly comparable to the situations employed by Meunzinger and Wood (1935) and others in studying the facilitation of learning by means of punishing "right" responses, there is at least an oblique similarity. Perhaps the latter studies can be usefully reexamined with the assumptions underlying the present analysis in mind. [See 12.]

How can this paradox be resolved? The answer seems to be relatively simple on the basis of a two-factor theory of reinforcement. Each time the rat is placed in the experimental apparatus and gets a brief shock on the way to the safety compartment, the part of the alley where the rat is introduced gets "reinforced" as a danger situation (or "conditioned stimulus"), since it continues to be temporally associated with pain.[25] This means that the fear continues to be aroused each time the animal is placed in the alley and this fear is most effectively reduced by the running response, which carries the animal to the safety compartment. The running response, as skeletal behavior, is thereby reinforced (through effect learning); but this behavior is of such a nature that it also provides the kind of reinforcement whereby the fear, or motivation for running, is kept alive.

It is always hazardous to interpret clinical phenomena on the human level in terms of animal experiments, yet there seems to be more than a superficial resemblance between the behavior just described and the "compulsive," "self-defeating," "masochistic" behavior which Horney (1937) and others (15) have discussed under the concept of the "vicious circle." Perhaps the two-factor theory of learning will turn out to have important clinical significance.

By thus sharply differentiating between two types of learning process, or "reinforcement," one is able to resolve the paradox involved in the experiment just described (and possibly also in at least certain types of "vicious circles" found at the human level). Yet a question remains as to what happens to the inhibitory tendency which is undoubtedly created by the fact that the response of running is consistently punished, i.e., regularly followed by electric shock. As a tentative hypothesis, one may assume that this tendency is present but that it is overridden by the reinforcement processes just described.[26]

---

[25] [This analysis is incomplete. See Footnote 26.]

[26] Since the above was written, experimental results obtained by U. E. Whiteis indicate that this hypothesis is well founded. Once the shock on the right side of the grill is removed, the running response quickly deteriorates, reflecting a conflict on the part of the subject between a fear of not running and a fear of running. [Further unpublished work by Whiteis indicates that the reason why the shock on the right half of the alley does not act as an effective "punishment" and thus inhibit the running response is this: Since both halves of the alley are virtually identical visually, the fear produced (by conditioning) in the right half powerfully generalizes, or transfers, back to the left half. It is thus not merely that being in the left, or starting, half of the alley is shortly followed (if the animal runs) by shock, but that this safe half of the alley is *confused with* the right, charged half. That generalization of fear from the right, "shock" half of the alley to the left, "safe" half is of crucial importance in this situation is indicated by the finding that if the two halves of the alley

THORNDIKE ON "PUNISHMENT." In his early statements of the law of effect, Thorndike posited punishment as the antithesis of reward. Rewarding or satisfying consequences of an act were assumed to "stamp in" the connection between this act and the drive which produced it. Punishing or annoying consequences of an act, on the other hand, were assumed to "stamp out" the connection between this act and the drive which produced it. Learning was thus conceived as a reversible process, which was carried in one direction by reward and in the opposite direction by punishment. Whatever it was that learning, under the impact of reward, did, unlearning, under the impact of punishment, supposedly undid.

In later studies, however, Thorndike has taken a different position, based largely on the results of an experiment which was designed to answer this question:

> Other things being equal, does one right response to a certain situation rewarded by the announcement of "Right" strengthen the connection in question more than one wrong response to the situation punished by the announcement of "Wrong" weakens that connection? (1931, p. 38).

From the results thus obtained, Thorndike drew the following conclusions:

> An announcement of "Right" strengthens its corresponding connection much more than an announcement of "Wrong" weakens its connection. . . .
>
> Indeed the announcement of "Wrong" in our experiments does not weaken the connection at all, so far as we can see. Rather there is more gain in strength from the occurrence of the response than there is weakening by the attachment of "Wrong" to it (p. 45).

By way of providing further support for these statements, Thorndike continues:

---

are made visually different, by the insertion of a false interior of distinctive color and pattern into one half of the alley, the "vicious circle" phenomenon disappears. In other words, if the animal is thus enabled to make a sharper discrimination between the two halves of the alley, the *inhibitory* effects of the "punishment" quickly become dominant over the generalized *motivational* effects. However, this analysis does not fully explain why it is that, in the original situation, the generalized motivational effects are dominant over the inhibitory effects (the shock, or "unconditioned stimulus," being, of course, the same in both instances). One possibility is that, since running under most circumstances is *not* punishing, the fear associated in the experimental situation therewith is being continually extinguished in the ordinary life of the animal; whereas, there is no opportunity for extinction of the fear of the right half of the alley, and since the left half is virtually indistinguishable, fear of it, too, is being constantly reinforced, by generalization. Perhaps there are also other factors which are important here but are not at present evident.

Gwinn (1949), in a paper aptly entitled "The effects of punishment on acts motivated by fear," has investigated this same phenomenon; but his experiment seems not to have been so well controlled as that of Whiteis, and his findings are less clear-cut.]

I have studied in the same way the records of the rats, crows, monkeys, and pigs who learned by reward and punishment in the experiments of Yerkes, Kuo, and others. In the case of Kuo's thirteen rats the learning is largely, and perhaps entirely, explainable by the strengthening of the rewarded responses. In the other experiments the relative influence of the rewards and the punishments is not easily measurable, but the former are apparently more potent. I have also supplemented the experiments reported above by additional ones with other subjects and kinds of learning, and have found them fully corroborated (pp. 45–46).

From these findings and Thorndike's remarks concerning them, the inference has sometimes been drawn that there is no such thing as "punishment," psychologically speaking, and that the only kind of learning is reward learning. Thorndike's own, rather guarded, statement on this score follows:

These experiments do not, of course, mean that punishment is always futile. The contrary is demonstrable from general observation and from such experiments with animals as those of Warden and Aylesworth. They need not necessarily predispose us to any change of attitude toward punishment save with such learning and for such learners as I have described. . . . Since in these experiments with these subjects, the wrong connections were simply displaced or nullified by the right ones, not intrinsically weakened, we may properly expect that something similar may happen in many sorts of learning, and we may increase our confidence in positive rather than negative learning and teaching (p. 46).

That there is something amiss with the older conception of punishment, as the antithesis of reward, is clearly apparent; but it does not seem that Thorndike's work has quite brought us to a satisfactory new understanding of this phenomenon. Let us therefore see if the two-factor conception of learning will handle the problem any more effectively.

According to this conception of learning, the first thing to be noted is that "punishment," i.e., a relatively sudden and painful increase of stimulation following the performance of some act, provides the necessary conditions for the establishment of a conditioned fear reaction. The performance of any given act normally produces kinesthetic (and often visual, auditory, and tactual) stimuli which are perceptible to the performer of the act. If these stimuli are followed a few times by a noxious ("unconditioned") stimulus, they will soon acquire the capacity to produce the emotion of fear. When, therefore, on subsequent occasions the subject starts to perform the previously punished act, the resulting self-stimulation will arouse fear; and the most effective way of eliminating this fear is for the subject to stop the activity which is producing the fear-producing stimuli. The cessation, or inhibition, of activity thus becomes the solution to the fear problem and may be expected to be fixated as are other habits.[27]

This analysis agrees with Thorndike's newer view that punishment does not simply cancel out, or "dissolve," the effects of learning which are produced by past rewards; and it also agrees that the inhibition of punished responses comes about because of the learning, through reward, of new responses (such as doing nothing or something else) which are incompatible with the old (punished) ones. What Thorndike's analysis seems to lack is a sufficiently explicit recognition of the role of fear learning and fear reduction. It is apparently fear which constitutes the new problem that instigates responses which, if they prove capable of reducing the fear, become fixated and which, if more powerful, tend to inhibit the older, original responses.

Thorndike's remarks on this score are less explicit but not necessarily incompatible. He says:

> Annoyers do not act on learning in general by weakening whatever connection they follow. If they do anything to learning they do it indirectly by informing the learner that such and such a response in such and such a situation brings distress, or by making the learner feel fear of a certain object, or by making him jump back from a certain place, or by some other definite and specific change which they produce in him. Satisfiers seem to act more directly and generally and uniformly and subtly, but just what they do should be studied with much more care than anybody has yet devoted to it (p. 46).

PUNISHMENT AND CONDITIONING. It is instructive to note that if one uses a noxious or painful stimulus in a conditioning experiment, one does not speak of it as a "punishment," even though one would so characterize it in other circumstances. If it is applied as a result of something which the *subject* has done, then it is a punishment, but if it is applied because of something the *experimenter* has done, i.e., because he has presented a "conditioned stimulus," then it is called an "unconditioned stimulus." One wonders if this somewhat arbitrary terminological distinction is followed by very different consequences in the subject and, if so, what they are. In both

[27] [The only qualification which this statement requires is that "other habits" do not necessarily result in conflict, whereas an "inhibitory habit," which is acquired because it reduces fear, causes some other problem to go unsolved, or at least prevents that problem from being solved in the way that has previously been customary, and thus leads to at least temporary conflict. For a closely similar treatment of the problem of punishment, see Miller and Dollard (1941).]

cases the fear reaction is conditioned, but in the one case it becomes attached to an *external* stimulus which, on one or more occasions, has preceded the noxious event; while in the other case the fear becomes attached to the *internal,* viz., kinesthetic, stimulation which, on one or more occasions, has preceded the noxious event. In the one case the resulting fear may be resolved by *making* a skeletal response and in the other case by *inhibiting* a skeletal response. In both cases the "conditioned response" is fear, but there is a difference in the resulting "problem-solving" behavior.

Perhaps this is one of the striking differences between clinicians and experimentalists: the former are interested in fears that are "cued off" by internal as well as external events, whereas the latter are usually interested only in fears which are elicited by external events. It now appears that each group has much to learn from the other. Clinicians can sharpen their thinking if they familiarize themselves with the work of experimentalists. Experimentalists, on the other hand, have been peculiarly slow to appreciate some of the mechanisms which clinicians understand very well. It is, for example, remarkable that anyone should not have anticipated the conflict which arises if, after an external stimulus becomes capable of arousing a fear reaction and the subject begins to make a skeletal response to it, the experimenter continues pairing the *CS* and *UnCS*. What obviously happens in such cases is that the kinesthetic stimulation resulting from the subject's response begins to elicit fear, and the subject is then motivated both to make and not to make the skeletal response which produces this type of stimulation. Small wonder that Liddell (1944) has characterized such a procedure as "pathogenic" and that it sometimes makes experimental subjects "neurotic"!

Thorndike originally spoke of reward "stamping in" responses and of punishment as stamping them out. It now appears that both reward and punishment "stamp in" responses, but different kinds of responses: reward fixates skeletal responses and punishment establishes the emotion of fear. That punishment serves to inhibit responses which have been established through reward learning is apparently due, not to a direct and antithetical action, but to an indirect process of the kind described.

This line of thought may be extended one step further. There has been much discussion and research on the question of whether pleasant "memories" are more or less durable than unpleasant ones. The results, as is well known, are highly equivocal. Perhaps this is because "memories" are of two kinds—those laid down by effect learning and those laid down by conditioning. An action which is followed by pleasant consequences will be better preserved as one type of "memory," whereas an action that is followed by unpleasant consequences will be better preserved as the other type. This problem needs to be more fully considered with the two-factor theory of learning in mind.

James on the Nature of Emotion. The present analysis, with its recurrent emphasis upon emotion, both as a consequence of learning (conditioning) and as an occasion for learning (problem solving), naturally calls for a clear and explicit statement of assumptions concerning the nature of emotion. In any comprehensive sense, such a statement is not possible in the present paper. However, it is illuminating to consider the present view of the learning process and the significance of the emotions against the background of the James-Lange theory of emotion.

In his *Principles of psychology* (1890), James introduces this theory in the following words:

> The merely descriptive literature of the emotions is one of the most tedious parts of psychology. . . . [The usual descriptive statements] give one nowhere a central point of view, or a deductive or generative principle. . . . [The difficulty is that "emotions" have been too often] set down as so many eternal and sacred psychic entities. . . . Now the general causes of the emotions are indubitably physiological. Prof. C. Lange, of Copenhagen, in the pamphlet from which I have already quoted, published in 1885 a physiological theory of their constitution and conditioning, which I had already broached the previous year in an article in *Mind.* None of the criticisms which I have heard of it have made me doubt its essential truth (pp. 448–49).

James then proceeds, under the heading, "Emotion follows upon the bodily expression in the coarser emotions at least," to state his theory in this way:

> Our natural way of thinking about these coarser emotions is that the mental perception of some fact excites the mental affection called the emotion, and that this latter state of mind gives rise to the bodily expression. My theory, on the contrary, is that *the bodily changes follow directly the perception of the exciting fact, and that our feeling of the same changes as they occur IS the emotion* (p. 449).

This formal statement of the theory agrees well with the conception of emotion upon which the present discussion is based. However, in attempting to explicate the theory, James provided the grounds for a serious ambiguity. In a now famous passage James intimated that it is not that we run because we see a bear and are afraid; it is rather that we "see the bear, and judge it best to run," and then, because we run, we feel afraid. This interpretation is clearly at variance with the present conception of emotion, as a cause of skeletal behavior, but not as a consequence thereof. Paraphrased in the light of this conception, James's illustration would go: We see a bear, we become *physiologically prepared to run,* are afraid, and then may run (or do whatever the fear forces us to do).

That this may, in fact, have been what James meant to imply is suggested by a number of passages, of which the following is typical:

> We may catch the trick with the voluntary muscles, but fail with the skin, glands, heart, and other viscera. Just as an artificially imitated sneeze lacks something of the reality, so the attempt to imitate an emotion in the absence of its normal instigating cause is apt to be rather "hollow" (p. 450).

Although the James-Lange theory has been criticized vigorously and often (Cannon, 1927; Dunbar, 1938), it has shown a remarkable vitality and may only now, more than half a century after its formulation, be coming fully into its own. With the minor reformulation just suggested, it is completely consonant with the present conception of emotion as a conditioned viscero-vascular response which then produces a state of affairs which may motivate any of an infinitely wide variety of skeletal responses and whose reduction may powerfully fixate whatever response brings the reduction about. And equally important is the extent to which it agrees with current formulations concerning the "psychosomatic" disorders (Dunbar, 1938; Wolf and Wolff, 1942). It is now well established that excessively powerful or protracted emotional states may not only produce functional disturbances of an organic nature but may also lead to actual structural pathology, as in the case of stomach ulcers and other comparable conditions.

The whole problem of emotion needs to be rethought from the standpoint of contemporary learning theory, with special reference to the problem of "neurosis" and personality disturbances generally.

THE PROBLEM OF RESPONSE VARIABILITY. Perhaps the most important single difficulty which is encountered in attempting to base the psychology of learning wholly upon the law of effect arises from the phenomena of response variability, or response equivalence. In an earlier study the writer (6) has attempted, and failed, to deal satisfactorily with this phenomenon within the framework of effect theory.

The difficulty, specifically, is this. If, for example, there are several equally good routes whereby a hungry rat or other animal can go from a starting compartment to a food compartment, one might expect, on the basis of the law of effect, that the habit of choice (to speak loosely) which is strongest in the beginning would be progressively strengthened, to the point where, ultimately, that choice would cause the subject to be completely fixated upon one particular route to the goal. What is actually observed is that there continues to be a great deal of vacillation between the various routes. In the case of some subjects a clear-cut "preference" eventually may be established, but in other cases variability continues indefinitely.[28]

The dual learning theory which is here under consideration suggests that in a situation in which two or more equally "effective" responses are possible, the observable alternation of response may be explainable, not on the basis of effect learning, but on the basis of conditioning. As a means of quickly communicating an otherwise rather complex thought the following illustration may be useful. The writer used to eat lunch rather regularly at a particular restaurant. His hunger was seemingly well satisfied by the food he obtained there, and one might have predicted, on the basis of the law of effect alone, that, barring untoward incidents, the writer would continue indefinitely to eat lunch at this restaurant. One day, however, as he started to enter the restaurant in question (and without any identifiable unpleasant experience associated therewith), he experienced an emotion of aversion which was strong enough to cause him to turn about and go to another restaurant, and he has never since returned to the first restaurant.

It would be premature at this point to assume that concomitant emotional learnings, at times perhaps very subtle ones, provide the sole explanation of response variability of the kind under consideration; but such a possibility warrants careful scrutiny. It is, in fact, conceivable that emotional conditioning, of appetites and aversion, provides, respectively, the positive and negative "vectors" which Lewin (1935b) and others have posited as essential parts of "field theory." "Change in cognitive structure" may in many instances

[28] It may be expected that the current researches of Professor J. G. Beebe-Center on taste preferences in rats, in which learning factors are being given special attention, may soon throw new and important light on this problem. Cf. also recent unpublished researches by Dr. R. L. Solomon.

be merely a matter of subtle, or perhaps not-so-subtle, conditioning.

"Field" theorists have made a great deal of "latent" learning and have sometimes cited it as "disproof" of the law of effect.[29] That a hungry rat may learn his way about in a maze without benefit of food does not demonstrate that reward is not involved in such learning. Secondary drives are almost certainly active under such circumstances, and it is therefore possible that their periodic reduction may provide rewards which are no less potent than those provided, for example, by hunger reduction. However, a two-factor theory of learning leaves open another possibility, namely, that some, perhaps most, of the learning that occurs under these circumstances is based on conditioning. Tolman (1935) has offered "sign-gestalt expectations" as an explanation of latent learning. Such "expectations" seem clearly relatable to the results of conditioning, although the details of this relationship have not as yet been worked out. In a recent article entitled "Expectation," Thorndike (1946) has made some interesting suggestions in this connection, among them this, "that what *S-R* psychology has to learn from Tolman's work is the need for a satisfactory account of primitive forms of knowledge, and of how they operate" (p. 281).

"Knowledge" has often been regarded as something "mental" and behavior as something physical. Perhaps the feeling of "knowing" is merely the subjective counterpart of what we objectively perceive as the results of learning. A two-factor theory of learning would then suggest that there might be two basic forms of knowledge. And such a dichotomy is indeed implied by the two idioms, "to know *how*" to do this or that and "to know *that*" this or that is so. An epistemological investigation which was grounded in this type of learning theory might lead to interesting outcomes.

VI. Objections and Difficulties

LABORATORY "CONDITIONING" OF SKELETAL RESPONSES. It will almost certainly have occurred to the reader who is familiar with the technical literature on what has commonly been called conditioning to wonder about the following problem. Hilgard and Marquis (1940) devote considerable space to experiments in which the conditioned stimulus precedes the unconditioned stimulus by a very brief period, commonly 0.4 second. In fact, it is probably

---

[29] For a penetrating experimental analysis of latent learning, see Karn and Porter (1946).

safe to say that this procedure has in the past been the one most typically used in the conditioning of such defense reactions in human beings as the blink, the knee-jerk, the hand-withdrawal, etc. And it is not merely that the conditioning of such responses is *possible* with such a short period intervening between the onset of the *CS* and the *UnCS;* this interval appears to be the *optimal* one for such learning.

At the same time it is well known that one or two seconds, or possibly longer, may be required for the fear reaction to become fully mobilized in human beings, due to the slower rate of response of the autonomic nervous system and of the smooth muscles and glands than of the central nervous system and the skeletal musculature. In view of this fact the question therefore arises: How can a theory which holds that defense reactions, involving the skeletal musculature, are motivated by the conditioned response of fear account for defense reactions which occur before the fear reaction can be effectively mobilized?

No definitive answer to this question is possible at present, but one or two brief comments are in order. It may be noted, first of all, that responses of the kind just described are of comparatively little biological importance. Very little ordinary behavior, whether of men or of lower animals, consists of such hair-trigger reactions. It is probably more important, therefore, that a theory of learning be able to account for the behavior observed in ordinary life than that it account for the behavior observed under the extraordinary conditions of the laboratory.

However, it is by no means certain that the present conception of learning will not accommodate even the special and somewhat artificial "conditioned responses" of the laboratory. By a slight change in one's mode of thinking about the laboratory situation, the dilemma may, in fact, be rather satisfactorily resolved. What one is likely to forget is that it is not merely the specific *CS* that is associated with the noxious *UnCS;* the total experimental situation is similarly associated, and it quickly takes on the meaning: place-where-unpleasant-event-may-occur. Thus, as soon as the subject re-enters the situation (after one or two encounters with the *UnCS*), his apprehension is aroused and he is in a heightened state of vigilance, expectation, readiness. The subject is therefore all "set" to make the response in question, and may do so the instant the specific danger signal appears.

Here we are apparently dealing with a reaction which is comparable to the voluntary reaction of the classical reaction-time experiment. The subject, having been instructed (conditioned?) to behave in a certain way, is given a ready signal, which brings motivation and set to a peak; and he is then given the reaction stimulus —the response to which occurs very quickly (in 0.2–0.3 second) and has many of the characteristics of the type of so-called *CR* which is here under discussion.

This interpretation is made all the more plausible by the commonly observed phenomenon of "pseudo-conditioning," in which the "conditioned response" is tripped off, not by the stimulus which has been previously associated with the *UnCS,* but by some other stimulus which is similar, or perhaps quite dissimilar. Such "conditioned responses" certainly seem more closely related to "false starts" and "startle reactions" than to the conditioned salivary response of Pavlov—or to the conditioned fear reaction.

Curves of Acquisition and Extinction. If the basic distinction which is here under consideration is valid, it will be necessary to reinterpret, and perhaps in some instances discard, many of the curves of acquisition and of extinction which have been widely accepted as model representations of the learning process. If, as this distinction suggests, we are dealing, not with *"the* learning process," but with *two* such processes, then it is essential that data be obtained which will reflect each of these processes in as nearly pure form as possible. Since both types of learning seem to occur simultaneously in living organisms much of the time, it is difficult to fractionate them under ordinary circumstances; and even in the laboratory, the two have commonly been confused. It is clear, therefore, that there is a pressing need for new data in this connection, and that such data may not at first be easy to obtain.

In the writer's laboratory, preliminary attempts have already been made to demonstrate, in strict independence of each other, the two types of reinforcement which are here posited; but although these attempts have not been entirely unsuccessful, neither have they been entirely successful. It is already apparent that these two processes, if two processes they be, are normally coalesced in an intricate manner, that living organisms are normally "set" at all times (save in sleep) to learn in either or both ways, and that controlled separation of the two is no small accomplishment.

Particular attention needs to be directed to the question of the relative permanence of the two types of learning. A few years ago it was commonly assumed (under the law of disuse) that all learning tended to deteriorate with time. Recent research, from both the laboratory and the clinic, suggests, on the contrary, that learning *may* be essentially permanent (cf. earlier discussion of "punishment"). However, there are now grounds for suspecting that the two learning processes may differ in this respect, i.e., that problem solving may be relatively permanent and irreversible, while conditioning may be less permanent and more easily reversed. However, all this is exceedingly tentative and calls for experimental exploration.

PRESENT THEORY AND EXERCISE, EFFECT COMPARED. In another place (15) the writer has excoriated the conjoined laws of exercise and effect as a "vicious convenience," on the grounds that, as between the two, anything can be explained but nothing predicted. To quote:

> The impasse to which the law of effect leads is precisely the one which Freud encountered in trying to explain nonintegrative behavior in terms of the pleasure principle. What contemporary writers, both analytic and academic, tend to do in practice is to invoke the law of effect (pleasure principle) to account for integrative behavior but to resort to the law of exercise ("repetition compulsion") to explain instances of nonintegrative behavior. . . .
>
> We suggest . . . the thesis that to have one principle to account for one set of phenomena which fit this principle (of effect) and another principle (exercise) to account for another set of phenomena which do not, is to rely on a vicious convenience. If we cannot make either of these principles do the complete job it ought to do, we should discard them both and start again, along entirely new and more promising lines (pages 424–25).

In proposing a two-factor theory of learning which posits conditioning and problem solving as separate processes, it may be pointed out, with some justification, that this brings us back to something reminiscent of the exercise-effect formulation. The problem-solving type of learning is patently identical with effect learning (and the pleasure principle); and since conditioning is dependent, not upon satisfaction, but upon the repeated presentation of two (or more) stimuli, the possible relationship to the law of exercise is certainly hinted at. In other words, one must sharply ask: Is not the present formulation merely a subtle reformulation of the old exercise-effect dichotomy?

To this we can reply confidently in the negative. The law of exercise and the law of effect, as originally phrased by Thorndike and widely accepted by others, were supposed to be two principles which applied to the *same* learning process. In the present formulation, two principles are posited, but so, too, are two different types of learning process. There is clearly a "division of labor" between them; and they do not provide the same spuriously easy escape from the dilemma of persistent nonintegrative behavior as did the laws of exercise and effect. As will be seen by perusal of the paper cited above, the present two-factor theory of learning is in strict accord with the more legitimate resolution of this dilemma which is there proposed.

LEARNING THEORY AND LANGUAGE. In the paper just cited, the importance of the connection between learning theory and language theory is repeatedly stressed. However, traditional learning theories have provided only the most tenuous background for the understanding of language and the exquisitely complex processes which it makes possible. If the present formulation has a better claim to validity, it may also have a better chance of articulating successfully with language theory. Whether this is the case remains to be determined.

There is, however, one auspicious omen. In a singularly lucid discussion of language, Russell (1927) has differentiated between language, as *used* and language as *understood*. Used language is obviously behavior and, as such, involves responses of the skeletal musculature and learning according to the principle of effect; whereas understood language, although it almost certainly involves responses of some kind, does not presuppose behavior (in the sense just defined) and may very well be dependent upon conditioning rather than effect learning. Richards (1938, 1942) has stressed the problem-solving character not only of use, but also of understanding, or "interpretation"; and the supporting arguments which he advances are indeed impressive; but in their earlier *Meaning of meaning,* Ogden and Richards (1938) propose a theory of interpretation (see especially p. 11 and p. 21) which is much closer to conditioning theory.

It is too early to tell whether the present reconstituted theory of conditioning, with its emphasis upon feeling rather than upon action, will provide precisely the kind of theory which is needed for a sound psychology of understanding; but it seems fairly certain that this theory comes closer than does that conception of conditioning which includes the acquisition of responses of the skeletal musculature, rather than only those of the visceral and vascular systems.

It is likewise premature to attempt to say whether those learned reactions which we call "perceptions" are acquired through the learning process which is here called conditioning or that which is called problem solving; but the indications are that it is the former. If this should prove to be the case, it would further strengthen the case for the assumption that habits of "understanding" are acquired through conditioning.

LEARNING AND THE PROBLEM OF CONSCIENCE. What is easily the most difficult and probably also most important problem appropriately comes at the end of our explorations. Until comparatively recently, there has been a widespread tendency to assume that however well psychologists, with their "mechanical" laws of learning, might be able to explain the ordinary behavior, or "habits," of human beings (and other organisms), they would never be able to grapple with that ethereal entity, human conscience. And the psychologists, for their part, have often been only too willing to relinquish any claim to tapping the ultimate secrets of personality, and to abjure responsibility for understanding "values," "ethical judgment," "character," and related phenomena.

More recently, however, it has become apparent that we cannot have an adequate psychology of the "total person" until we have lawful scientific principles which will give an equally good account of the "core" of human personality and of its more "peripheral" manifestations. As a part of this movement there is a growing interest in the nature of that psychosocial institution called "conscience" and in the conditions of its successful, and unsuccessful, acquisition. Already there is mounting evidence that conscience is a product of learning; and any theory of learning which makes claim to serious consideration must accept the challenge to provide, ultimately at least, a theory of conscience.

It is obviously beyond the scope of the present paper to undertake such an assignment in any thoroughgoing sense, but one question is of central importance: Is conscience primarily a result of that learning process which is here termed conditioning or of the process of problem solving? It is proverbial that fear and love are conspicuous ingredients of conscience, a fact which would predispose one to the conclusion that conscience is largely, perhaps exclusively, a matter of conditioning. But at the same time there are those who hold that in a really harmonious personality the "ego" and the "superego," or conscience, are fused into a unitary whole, which immediately raises this difficulty: If the ego is the conscious, voluntary, problem-solving part of the total personality, how can functions which by definition are involuntary (reactions of fear and love) become a part thereof?

Perhaps the assumption is wrong and "ego" and "superego" functions never become fully fused. Perhaps, as the writer has elsewhere suggested (19), personal integration is achieved through acceptance by the ego of the demands of the superego which begins as the "voice of the community" (especially parents) and which, though later internalized, seems always to have a more or less foreign, external quality.

There is no problem in the whole psychology of learning, or, for that matter, in the whole of psychology, which seems so likely to repay intensive study. [See later papers in Part II.]

CHAPTER 10

FURTHER EVIDENCE FOR A TWO-FACTOR THEORY OF LEARNING

[This chapter consists of two parts. The first part is an account, written in 1947, of an experiment which was carried out that year jointly with John W. Suter, Jr., and which was designed to test the implications of the two-factor theory of learning as compared with the implications of a one-factor theory of the type advocated by Hull. Also included here are results from an earlier investigation conducted jointly with Alice Traum and Stephen H. Horton. The latter study was factorially designed and throws light not only upon the same issue as that involved in the Suter study, but also upon three other problems which have been previously discussed.

The second part, which is divided into seven sections, represents a miscellaneous collection of arguments and evidence for and against a dualistic conception of the learning process. Naturally these sections, or appendices, are written from the point of view of a partisan; but I have tried to bring together here all the most relevant material which has come to my attention since the publication of the preceding paper.

No part of this chapter has been previously published.]

What are the basic conditions for the occurrence of learning? Pavlov's (1927) answer was that we learn when, and presumably only when, two stimuli—one initially neutral and the other capable from the outset of producing a vigorous reaction of some kind—impinge upon an organism in "temporal contiguity," as the earlier associationists would have said. According to Pavlov, all learning consists of *stimulus substitution,* the process whereby a reaction gets shifted from the stimulus which originally produces it to the new stimulus, which originally did not produce it; and the basic condition for the occurrence of this shifting he assumed to be the mere paired presentation of two stimuli, the conditioned and the unconditioned.

The only other comparably monistic theory of learning is that elaborated by Hull (1943). According to this writer, all learning is dependent upon the reinforcing conditions provided when a drive is reduced, satisfaction experienced, a problem solved. And the principal consequence of learning is seen as *response substitution,* whereby ineffectual or punished responses get replaced by effective, satisfying ones.

Just as Pavlov's conception of learning as conditioning, or stimulus substitution, is in the tradition of associationism, so is Hull's hypothesis a continuation of the line of thought which leads down through the hedonists, the Thorndikians, and the Freudians. According to this latter type of emphasis, it is drive reduction, or pleasure, that provides the basic conditions of reinforcement; and it is the behavior that produces such a state of affairs which ordinarily gets fixated. According to Hull the mere contiguity of stimuli is of only secondary importance, and according to Pavlov drive reduction is irrelevant.

Despite the fact that each of these unitary conceptions of learning has been defended with great vigor and ingenuity, it now seems probable that there are *two basically different types of change,* to both of which we apply the term "learning": the type of change that is involved in stimulus substitution, or conditioning, and the type of change that is involved in response substitution, or problem solving. Pavlov's conceptions account very satisfactorily for the first of these types of learning, as do Hull's for the second. But neither of these writers gives us a sufficiently inclusive theory; neither adequately accounts for *both* of the types of learning just described.[1]

---

[1] In his emphasis on "recency," or lastness-of-response-to-a-stimulus-situation, Guthrie (1935) has propounded another type of monistic learning theory. With truly elegant simplicity, he has insisted that living organisms *learn* what they *do.* The doing terminates, i.e., extirpates the organism from, the "situation," thus leaving it disposed to act (through "openness of pathways") in the same way when the situation recurs. With at least superficial plausibility, this formulation purports to account for both effect (i.e., reward and punishment) learning and for conditioning or redintegrative learning. If an organism is motivated by an internal drive, such as hunger, it is not the fact that eating is pleasurable or rewarding that fixates this response, says Guthrie. This response is learned because it is the *last* thing the organism does in the hunger-situation. Likewise, if an organism is motivated by an external drive ("punishment"), such as electric shock, the response that extricates the organism from this "situation" will, for precisely the same reasons, be learned. And in either case, if there are salient incidental stimuli, "such stimuli . . . tend to become substitute stimuli for the response" (p. 37), thus giving rise to "conditioning" or anticipatory (as opposed to consummatory) reactions. But in order to make the theory really work, it has to be so modified and qualified as to become extremely awkward and topheavy. O'Connor (1946), reviewing the experimental findings concerning "delayed reward," opens a serious breach in the theory which Guthrie (1946) does not satisfactorily repair. And Hilgard (1948), long a student of Guthrie's formulations, has recently listed a number of other difficulties that make it clear that the theory, as such, is not tenable. See II, Section B, below, page 295.

The attempts which have been made to make conditioning theory serve as a universal explanation of learning are manifestly inadequate. For a time it appeared that the subdivision of conditioning into "classical" and "instrumental" conditioning (Hilgard and Marquis, 1940) held promise of integrating all the facts of learning into a single master formula; but it is now evident that so-called instrumental conditioning really involves both conditioning proper *and problem solving* (4, 5). And there is no other conception of conditioning as a universal explanation of learning which does not likewise involve palpable weaknesses.

The attempt to extend problem-solving learning so as to account also for conditioning has been somewhat more successful than has the reverse procedure. In 1938 Mowrer (1938c) adumbrated the possibility that conditioning, or stimulus substitution, might be merely a special application of the reinforcing process provided by drive reduction. If a drive, such as electric shock, impinges upon an organism, we know that whatever response serves to eliminate that drive repeatedly will become increasingly likely to occur when the drive recurs. This, of course, is trial-and-error, or problem-solving, learning in pure form. But we also know that the drive is nearly always accompanied by other, more or less incidental stimuli. It is then but a short step to assume that the response which, through the reinforcing action of drive reduction, gets attached to the drive will have a tendency likewise to become attached to these incidental stimuli. And when this happens, i.e., when the response characteristically made to the drive stimulus begins to occur to these incidental or associated stimuli, then we are likely to speak of conditioning.

This "redintegrative" (cf. Hollingworth, 1928) conception of conditioning is the one which Hull has used as a means of subsuming conditioning under problem-solving learning;[2] but it falls short of being entirely satisfactory. One of its most serious weaknesses is that it contains no provision to account for the fact that a so-called conditioned response often, perhaps more often than not, differs from the so-called unconditioned response. In 1946 Mowrer and Lamoreaux (5) published an experiment in which so-called conditioned responses were produced which were, by design, radically unlike the so-called unconditioned response; and these writers also showed that the emotion of fear has to be introduced as an intervening variable to account for such findings. In situations of this

[2] Although Guthrie's theory of learning, reviewed in the preceding footnote, is couched in a different terminology, it, too, makes use of this interpretation of conditioning.

kind the only response which, properly speaking, may be said to be acquired by conditioning is that of fear; and, once acquired, it is then this emotion, this secondary drive, which elicits the observed outward activities of the subject. From these (at first variable) activities will be selected that response which reduces the subject's fear, and this response may or may not be the same as the one which the subject has found effective in reducing the traumatic stimulus (e.g., shock), for which the conditioned stimulus, or signal, stands. It does not seem possible to account on the basis of the simple redintegrative conception of conditioning for the acquisition of avoidance (fear-reducing) responses which differ markedly from escape (pain-reducing) responses. Fear must be posited as an intervening variable, and the term "conditioning" should be reserved for the process whereby this and other emotional reactions are established; behavioral responses which are then made to the fear are just as much in the nature of problem-solving activity as are the responses made to the original traumatic stimulus with which the danger signal has been associated. In other words, problem-solving learning can occur when the "problem" is either a primary drive (e.g., shock) or a secondary drive (e.g., fear); and conditioning is concerned solely with the process whereby the latter, i.e., the secondary drives, get shifted to new objects or events. Problem solving and conditioning thus are seen as two fundamentally different and distinct processes (9).

I. Two-Factor Theory vs. One-Factor Theory

Statement of Problem. The purpose of the present paper is to report still another line of evidence for believing that what Hull has called the great principle of "primitive reinforcement," which is provided by the advent of drive reduction or problem solving, is not a universally adequate learning principle. We have just seen that behavior may be reinforced, not only by the reduction or elimination of primary drives, but also by the reduction or elimination of secondary drives. Secondary drives we know are capable of being "associatively shifted"; and the crucial issue for a monistic theory such as Hull's is whether this latter type of learning is dependent, no less than is trial-and-error learning, upon drive reduction or whether it may involve a different principle. More specifically the question, as here investigated, is this: Is the learning involved in the associative shifting of the response of fear dependent upon drive reduction ("reward") or upon drive onset ("punishment")?

If the redintegrative conception of conditioning were valid, one would expect responses to become connected most readily to those incidental stimuli which are most nearly contiguous with drive reduction. A stimulus which is contiguous with the *onset* of the drive, e.g., electric shock, but which then disappears, well before the termination of the drive, would be expected to be much less effective as a conditioned stimulus.

Let us put the matter another way. On the basis of any theory of conditioning, it is assumed that the more closely in time a signal

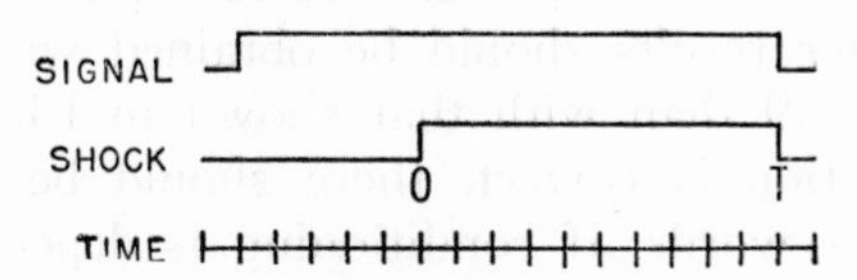

FIG. 49.—Schematic representation of procedure used with Group I subjects. The base line represents time in seconds.

comes to coinciding with the reinforcing state of affairs the better the conditioning. Our concern is to discover *where* the reinforcement involved in conditioning takes place. Hull's view is that this reinforcing state of affairs takes place when the so-called unconditioned stimulus terminates; Pavlov's view, and the one accepted here, is that all that is necessary for conditioning, properly speaking, to occur is that the conditioned stimulus coincide with (or at least approximate) the *onset* of the unconditioned stimulus.

This is a simple, straightforward deduction, but it seems not previously to have been brought to experimental test. Such a test is entirely feasible.

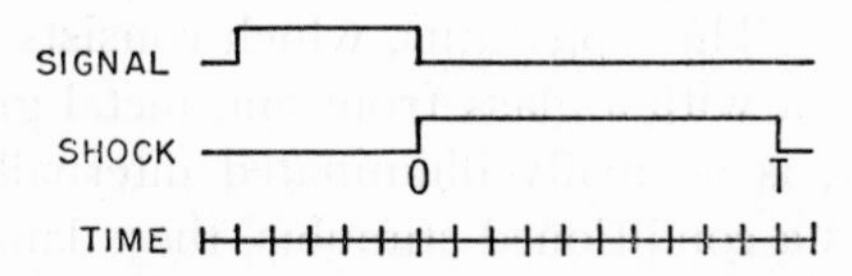

FIG. 50.—Schematic representation of procedure used with Group II subjects. This procedure differs from the Group I procedure solely in the fact that the signal goes off at shock onset instead of lasting until shock termination.

Let us suppose that with one group of subjects we follow the procedure schematically represented in Figure 49. Here the *CS* overlaps and terminates with the *UnCS*. This fact means that the *CS* is present when the primary drive (*UnCS*) terminates and should provide the optimal circumstances for conditioning, according to the redintegrative conception of the process.

By contrast, with a second group of subjects let us follow the procedure represented in Figure 50. Here the *CS* coincides with the onset of the *UnCS* but is not present when the *UnCS* terminates. According to the redintegrative hypothesis, these conditions would be much less favorable for the occurrence of conditioning than are those indicated in Figure 49. But if, on the other hand, one accepts the Pavlovian conception of conditioning, there should be no significant difference in the amount of conditioning obtained in the two cases: in *both* instances the *CS* coincides with the *onset* of the *UnCS*, and it should be of no consequence whether the *CS* is or is not present when the *UnCS* terminates. If Hull's theory of conditioning is valid, *better* results should be obtained with the procedure shown in Figure 49 than with that shown in Figure 50. If the Pavlovian conception is correct, there should be no reliable difference. In other words, if conditioning is dependent upon what happens at *O*, the procedures shown in Figures 49 and 50 should give equally good results, since the *CS* coincides with the *UnCS* at *O* in both cases. But if conditioning is dependent on what happens at *T*, the procedures shown in Figures 49 and 50 *should not* give equally good results, since the *CS* coincides with the *UnCS* at *T* in one case but not in the other.

The following experiment was designed to test this deduction.

SUBJECTS, APPARATUS, AND PROCEDURE. Lashley-strain laboratory rats, about five months of age, were used as subjects in this investigation. Of the 8 animals constituting Group I, 4 were males and 4 females; the same was true of the 8 animals constituting Group II.

In this study the all-purpose demonstration and research apparatus described by Mowrer and Miller (1942) was used, with only slight modification. This apparatus, which consists of an elongated boxlike compartment with a glass front and metal grill floor (which can be electrified), is normally illuminated internally by two small electric lamps. As a conditioned stimulus, these lamps were silently switched off and a third lamp, located immediately in front of the apparatus, was made to flicker on and off at the rate of 4 phases per second. The *CS* came on 5 seconds before the *UnCS*—135 volts of 60-cycle A. C. with a 150,000-ohm limiting resistance—was turned on. In the Group I procedure (Figure 49), the *CS* overlapped and terminated with the *UnCS*. In the Group II procedure (Figure 50), the CS terminated just as the *UnCS* was applied.

In all cases, if the *UnCS* was applied at all, it lasted for 10 seconds. This meant that there was no response on the part of the subjects which would terminate it, and no *skeletal* response which it regularly elicited. The reason for having the *UnCS* of fixed duration, rather than capable of being terminated by some standard response (*UnCR*, so-called) on the part of the subject was that the logic of the experiment required that the interval between the onset and termination of the *UnCS* be kept constant. And the reason that this interval was also made relatively long (10 seconds) was that we wished to make the difference between the Group I and Group II procedures a marked one. If the interval between the onset and termination of the shock had been of fixed but brief duration (e.g., only 1 or 2 seconds) or had been dependent upon how soon the subject made some particular response, then it might have been argued, if the two procedures gave about the same results, that for all practical purposes the *CS* in the Group II procedure coincided, psychologically, with the termination of the *UnCS*, just as much as it did in the Group I procedure. Since the interval between the onset and the termination of the *UnCS* was held at 10 seconds, this argument can hardly be a valid one.

The only question was: What should be our criterion of "conditioning"? According to the writer's view, the response which, in situations of the kind just described, becomes first and most directly attached to the *CS* is that of *fear*. But this reaction is not acknowledged in the redintegrative analysis of conditioning. Instead, the emphasis falls upon some overt, behavioral reaction which serves (at least in "instrumental" conditioning) to avert the impending *UnCS*. In order to meet the redintegrative theory on its own grounds, we therefore used a behavioral index of conditioning, namely, a run to the end of the apparatus opposite to that in which the subject happened to be when the *CS* came on. In both the Group I and the Group II procedures the *CS* was terminated the moment such a response occurred, and the *UnCS* was omitted; but if such a response did not occur during the first 5 seconds after the onset of the *CS*, then the *UnCS* came on and lasted for the fixed interval of 10 seconds, regardless of what behavior the subject manifested. In other words, both procedures were "instrumental" as far as the avoidability of the *UnCS* was concerned, but the *UnCS* was not escapable, once it came on. The two procedures differed only in respect to the overlapping or nonoverlapping of *CS* and *UnCS*.

All subjects received 10 trials (at 2-minute intervals) per day, and the experiment lasted for 10 days.

RESULTS AND DISCUSSION. The results obtained with the Group I animals are shown in Figure 51 by the curve with the open circles and those of the Group II animals by the curve with the filled circles.

The average number of runs made to the *CS* in the first of these groups was 37.875, whereas the average number of runs made to the *CS* in the second group was 37.125. The mean difference be-

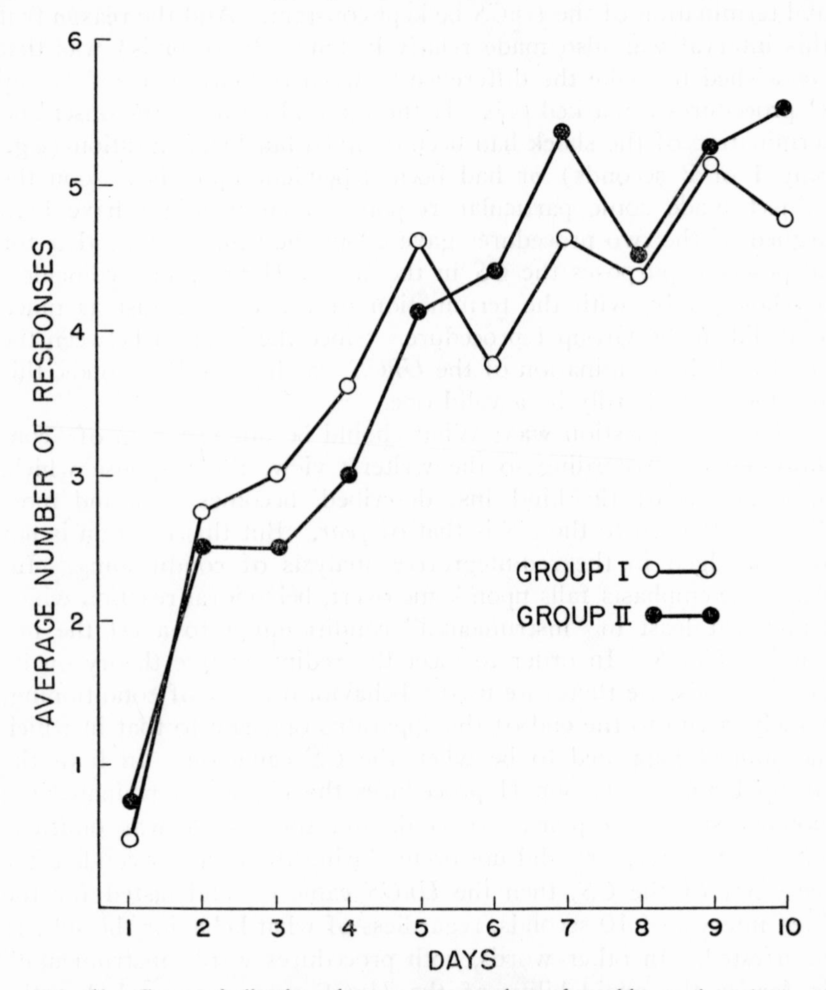

FIG. 51.—Curves indicating the average number of avoidance (running) responses made by two groups of subjects under the experimental conditions represented in Figures 49 and 50. The highly similar nature of the curves is taken as support for a two-factor theory of learning.

tween the number of responses made to the *CS* in the two groups was thus only 0.75, the *t* value of which difference is .043. This means that in 100 repetitions of an experiment of this kind, mean difference of at least this magnitude could be expected in over 90 per cent of the cases if "chance" alone were operating, i.e., if both groups of subjects came from the same "population." The difference is thus completely "nonsignificant," and our null hypothesis—that there is no real difference between the two groups—is not in the least impugned.[3]

Confidence in the findings just reported is increased by the fact that in an unpublished experiment, conducted several years ago by Alice Traum and Stephen H. Horton, very similar results were obtained. In this experiment 32 adult male albino rats were used as subjects, and the criterion of "conditioning" was a vertical leap into the air for half the subjects and, for the other half, a run to the opposite end of the apparatus (which was the same as that used by Suter). When the *CS* (a buzzer) overlapped with the *UnCS* (electric shock), the results shown by the curve (Figure 52) with the open circles were obtained; and when the *CS* did not overlap the *UnCS,* the results shown by the curve with the filled circles were obtained. Here again the difference between means was completely unreliable, being significant at only the .65

---

[3] This sort of finding raises an interesting question concerning the logic of statistical interpretation. Formerly it was common practice to assume that a "critical ratio" (*t*-value) of 3.00 marked the dividing line between "nonproof" and "proof." If a mean difference had a C. R. of less than 3.00, it was said to be "unreliable"; if the C. R. was 3.00 or more, it was assumed that the difference was a "real" one. Today the almost universal procedure in interpreting the difference between two obtained means is to set up, as a *null hypothesis,* the assumption that both means represent samples drawn from the *same* (normally distributed) population and then to ask: How likely is it that in drawing two *random* samples of the sizes in question one would get a mean difference *as large as or larger than* the obtained one? By a very precise logic, it is possible to say that this would occur, on the average, 10 times, 5 times, 1 time, or perhaps only 0.5 or 0.1 time in 100 drawings of two such samples. All of these are meaningful statements, which justify increasing degrees of *disbelief* in the null hypothesis, with no commitment as to the line between "nonproof" and "proof." Stated positively, our new logic tells us that, to the degree indicated, it is probable that the two obtained means represent samples drawn from *different* populations, but it does not answer the question: Different by *how much?* An interesting problem therefore arises when results are obtained which tend, not to discredit, but to "prove" the null hypothesis, i.e., results which give high *P*-values, let us say, of .80 or .90. In order to avoid here the type of difficulty that the older logic ran into, it is apparently necessary to proceed as follows. One sets up, as a new type of "null" hypothesis, the assumption that the two obtained means represent samples randomly drawn from *different* populations; and one then proceeds to ask: How likely would one be to secure a difference *as small as or smaller than* the obtained one if the null hypothesis were true? But it is then immediately evident that in order to give this question the requisite degree of precision, it is necessary to stipulate the *exact amount* by which the true means of these two "different" populations differ. Having done this, it should then be possible to say, quite meaningfully, just how likely one would be to obtain mean differences as small as that in question if one were drawing from two populations which differ by the stipulated amount. In short, it would seem possible, in instances of this kind, to apply the logic of the now conventional null hypothesis "in reverse," and to make quite as reliable and specific inferences about *high P*-values as about low ones. This sort of problem is related to the technique of "sequential analysis," Alpha and Beta types of "errors," fiducial limits, and similar problems which are commanding increasing attention in contemporary statistical literature.

level of confidence. In this instance such small difference as there was was in favor of the overlap procedure; whereas, in the Suter study, the difference was in favor of the nonoverlap procedure.

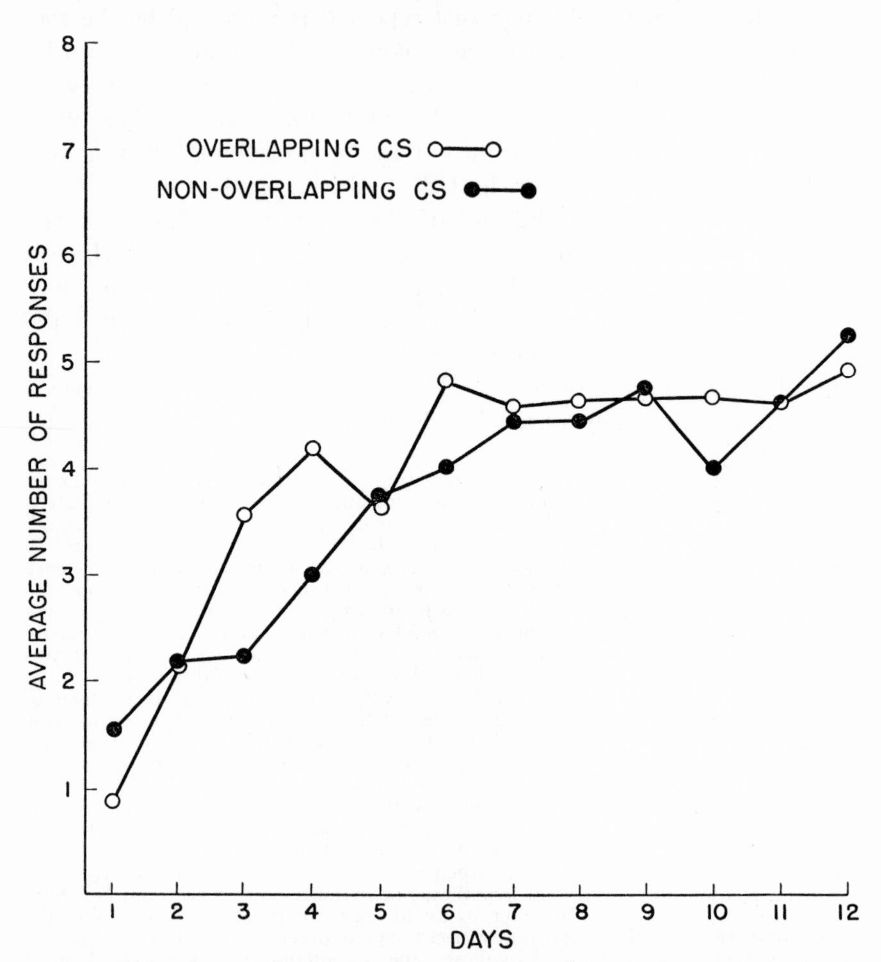

FIG. 52.—Curves indicating the average number of responses made in a factorially designed experiment (Traum and Horton) in which one of the variables was *CS* overlapping with *UnCS* vs. *CS* and *UnCS* not overlapping. With the qualifications indicated in the text, these results are comparable to those shown in Figure 51.

A word needs to be said about the Traum-Horton results: they are not entirely comparable to the Suter results, on two counts. First of all, in the Traum-Horton experiment, in the case of those animals which received an *UnCS* of fixed duration, this duration was for only 2 seconds, as opposed to 10 in the Suter experiment. Moreover, the Traum-Horton experiment was factorially designed, and one of the other variables which was under investigation was an *UnCS* of fixed (2 seconds) duration vs. an *UnCS* of variable duration (depending upon how quickly the subjects responded to it). This meant that in half of those animals in which the *CS* and *UnCS* overlapped, the *UnCS* was of fixed duration and in the other half it was of variable duration. In other words, in the Traum-Horton experiment we have a test of the effect of *CS* and *UnCS* overlapping and not overlapping; but, for the reasons mentioned, it is not as good a test as that afforded by the Suter experiment, in which the *UnCS* was of long (10 seconds) and invariable duration.

The Pavlovian conception of conditioning does not require that nonoverlapping of *CS* and *UnCS* shall produce better results than does overlapping, merely that it shall produce *just as good* results; and this prediction is confirmed by both of the sets of data here reported. Actually one can see a reason why nonoverlapping *might* give better results than does overlapping. If a *CS* is associated both with the onset and with the termination of shock, it might be thought of as having an equivocal significance: in the one case it comes to mean *both* pain (shock onset) and pleasure (shock termination), whereas in the other case it means *only* pain (shock onset). The *CS* might be expected, therefore, to be slightly more potent as a fear producer in the second case than in the first. However, these thoughts are conjectural and have no bearing upon the issue immediately before us, namely: Does a *CS* which overlaps the *UnCS* produce better conditioning (as measured by an overt behavioral reaction) than does a *CS* which does not so overlap? On the basis of evidence from two different sources we have to answer this question in the negative; and the redintegrative conception of conditioning, which calls for a positive answer to this question, is thereby discredited.

We thus find no support for the redintegrative theory of conditioning, since the overlapping of the *CS* and *UnCS* does not apparently result in superior learning, as this theory would demand. But the redintegrative conception of conditioning is open to question at an even more basic level. If avoidance responses are acquired because the reinforcing state of affairs which strengthens the connection between the primary drive and the response which eliminates this drive also strengthens the connection between incidental stimuli and this response, and if, as in the Suter experiment, the conditions are such that the termination of this drive (shock) does not reinforce any particular response, then it is hard to see how the termination of this drive could reinforce the connection between an incidental stimulus and any particular response. This is an involved statement, but all it means is that the redintegrative conception of conditioning would not seem capable of explaining the acquisition of any overt reaction to a signal if that reaction were not also the response which was regularly correlated with the termination of the traumatic stimulus of which the signal forewarned.

If, on the other hand, one assumes that the responses which are acquired through conditioning are exclusively emotional in nature and that all learned skeletal reactions represent problem-solving learning, this difficulty does not arise. A noxious stimulus, such as electric shock, may be depended on to arouse fear, not at its termination, but as its onset. This fear, through simple association, gets shifted to whatever stimuli regularly precede the shock; and once these stimuli become capable of arousing fear, then any overt, skeletal reaction will be learned which is found regularly to eliminate or reduce this fear. Such a problem-solving reaction may be acquired without any reference to the *behavioral* reactions of the subject to the primary drive of shock!

It is true, as has been shown in the earlier study of Mowrer and Lamoreaux (4), that a skeletal reaction will be acquired *more quickly* as the solution to the problem of fear if it is also the solution to the problem, e.g., shock, of which the fear is premonitory. The fact that, in the Suter experiment, there was no overt response which would solve the shock problem probably accounts for the rather low over-all level of learning in both our groups and for the high level of intersubject variability (see Table 6), which a previous study (4) has shown is correlated with degree of learning difficulty. But it is by no means necessary that the solution to the fear be the same as the solution to the shock—or, for that matter, that there be a solution to the shock—in order for the fear solution to be learned.

The redintegrative conception of conditioning—at least the redintegrative conception of the type proposed by Hull—seems to demand that the so-called conditioned response *always* be the same as the so-called unconditioned response and that there must always be such a response. This is due to acceptance of the dubious assumption that skeletal responses can be learned on the basis of conditioning as such. If one assumes that it is only emotional responses which are acquired on the basis of conditioning, then one can speak validly of conditioning as a form of redintegrative learning since, in such cases, the response which gets conditioned always (at least in situations of the type here under discussion) is a re-

TABLE 6

NUMBER OF SO-CALLED "CONDITIONED RESPONSES" (*CR*) MADE BY EACH OF THE 8 ANIMALS COMPRISING GROUP I AND EACH OF THE 8 ANIMALS COMPRISING GROUP II; NUMBER OF RESPONSES MADE DURING THE 10-SECOND PERIOD THAT THE SHOCK WAS ON EACH TRIAL (*SR*); AND THE NUMBER OF INTERVAL RESPONSES (*IR*), I.E., RESPONSES MADE WHEN NEITHER THE SIGNAL NOR THE SHOCK WAS ON

In all cases a "response" consisted of the animal's moving to the opposite end of the apparatus. It will be noted that the two groups are strictly comparable both in terms of *CR*'s and *SR*'s. That the Group I animals showed somewhat more *IR*'s than the Group II animals was due to the behavior of one animal (I-2). With a larger number of subjects in the two groups, it seems probable that all three indices would show virtually identical values.

Subject	Group I			Group II		
	CR	*SR*	*IR*	*CR*	*SR*	IR
1	7	54	38	4	11	75
2	74	12	284	5	3	70
3	3	10	126	28	27	110
4	61	15	105	66	29	169
5	78	32	110	2	20	28
6	4	45	16	44	63	88
7	52	10	128	64	44	89
8	18	25	134	90	13	185
Totals	297	203	941	303	210	814

sponse which the unconditioned stimulus elicits. But in such a case it is a form of "redintegration" that is dependent upon what happens at the time of onset of the "unconditioned" stimulus, not at its termination.

FURTHER BEARING OF THE HORTON-TRAUM EXPERIMENT UPON A TWO-FACTOR THEORY OF LEARNING. As has been already remarked, the Horton-Traum experiment was factorially designed, overlapping *CS* and *UnCS* vs. nonoverlapping being but one of five variables which were under investigation. The other four variables were: *CS* (buzzer) of fixed vs. variable duration; *UnCS* (shock) of fixed vs. variable duration; *UnCS* avoidable vs. unavoidable ("instrumental" vs. "classical" procedure); and the use of leaping into the air vs. running to the opposite end of the apparatus as the so-called "conditioned" response.

The two curves shown in Figure 53 indicate that a variable *CS* gave better results than did an invariable *CS*. This finding (which

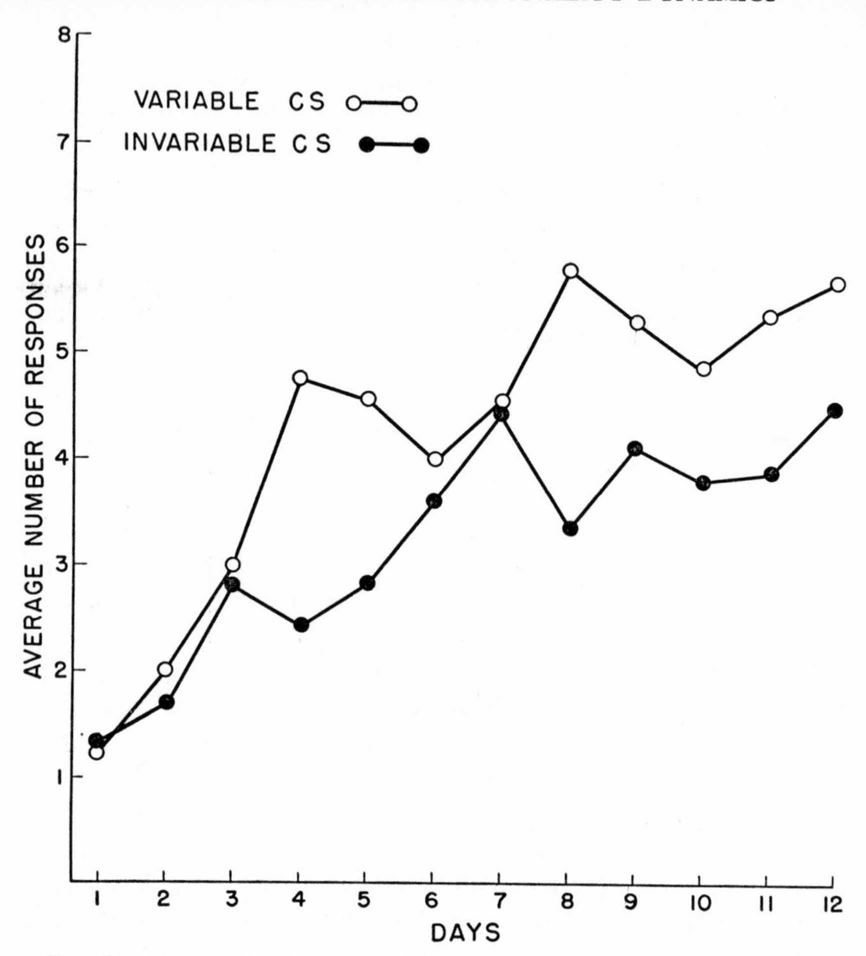

FIG. 53.—Curves showing the incidence of response in the Traum-Horton experiment as a function of the *CS* being variable (going off when the response occurred) or invariable (lasting for five seconds from the time of onset, regardless of how soon there was a response).

is reliable at the .20 level of significance [4]) confirms the same result obtained in the earlier study by Mowrer and Lamoreaux (4).

The two curves shown in Figure 54 indicate that a variable

---

[4] The *t*-values for this and the following differences and their corresponding *P*-values were computed by the same conservative method employed in earlier studies here reported. If, in the present instance, we had used the results for only the last five days of experimentation, the difference between performances of the two groups would have been more highly significant. Although the results for the Traum-Horton study would have been amenable, as a whole, to an analysis of variance, such an analysis has not been carried out. It would have been less sensitive than the *t*-test, and its only unique advantage lies in the fact that it affords a measure of "interaction," which in the present treatment is lacking.

UnCS likewise gave better results than did an invariable *UnCS*. This finding is reliable well beyond the .01 level of significance.

These two findings further verify the hypothesis that a response such as running or jumping is quite as much an instance of prob-

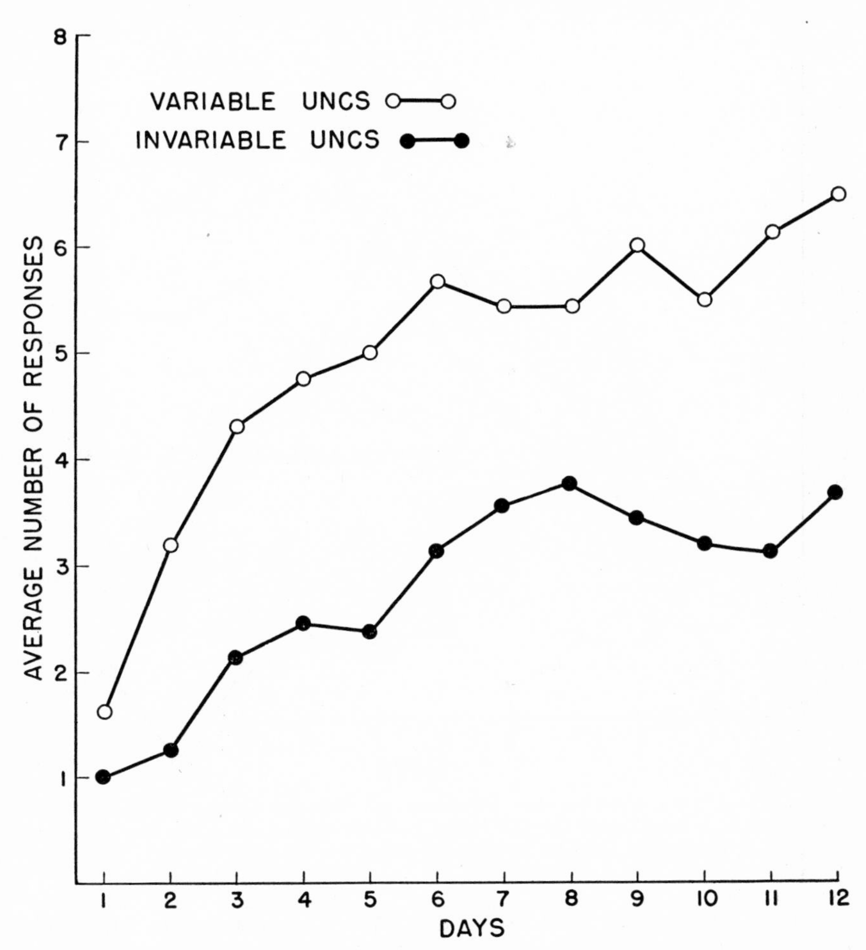

FIG. 54.—Curves showing the effect of having the *UnCS* variable and invariable.

lem-solving behavior when it occurs as a so-called "conditioned" response as when it occurs as a so-called "unconditioned" response. Under both circumstances, such responses are most readily learned when the problem, or drive, which instigates them ends promptly with their occurrence. The indications are, therefore, that they belong to the category of responses which are acquired on the basis of drive reduction rather than through contiguity. Contiguity appears to be responsible for the acquisition of the fear reaction to the *CS* (see Figures 51 and 52), but once this response has been acquired and has begun to function as a drive, what the organism *does* about it is determined by reward-reinforcement.

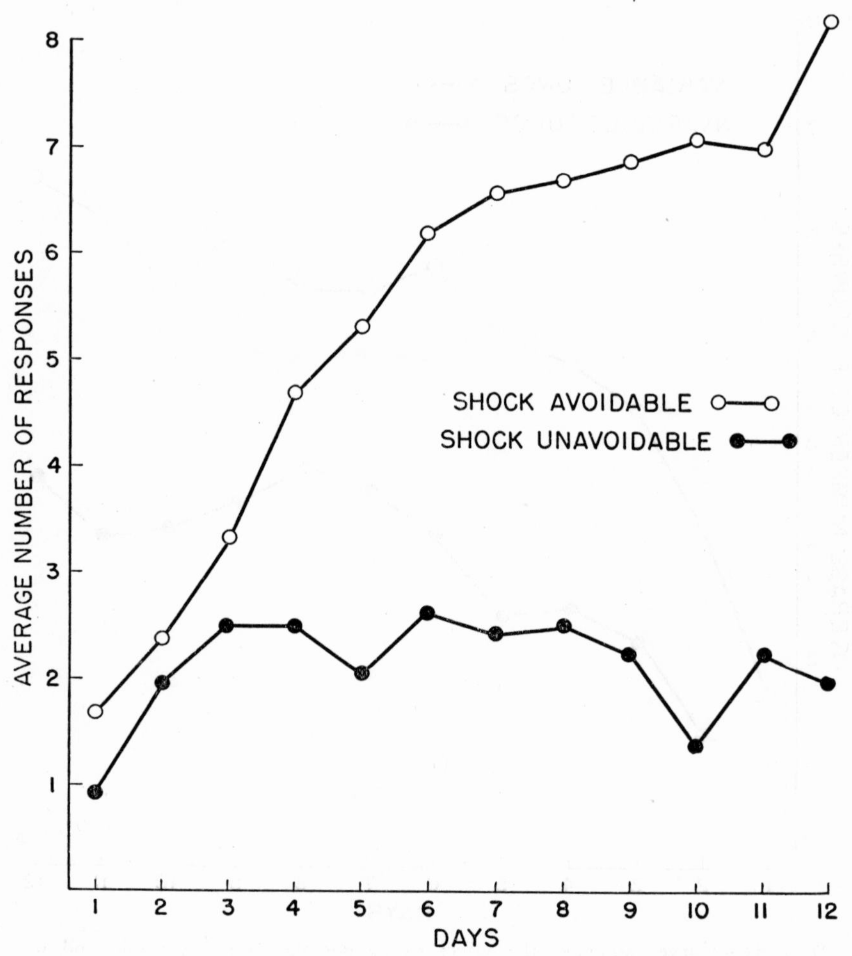

FIG. 55.—Curves showing the effect of having the *UnCS* avoidable and unavoidable.

The two curves shown in Figure 55 indicate that in the Traum-Horton study the responses of running and jumping when the *CS* occurred were learned much better when the *UnCS* was avoidable than when it was unavoidable. This finding is reliable far beyond the .01 level of significance, and dramatically confirms the results of Brogden, Lipman, and Culler which have been discussed in the study by Mowrer and Lamoreaux (see especially the graph reproduced on page 89).

The final variable which was investigated in the Traum-Horton

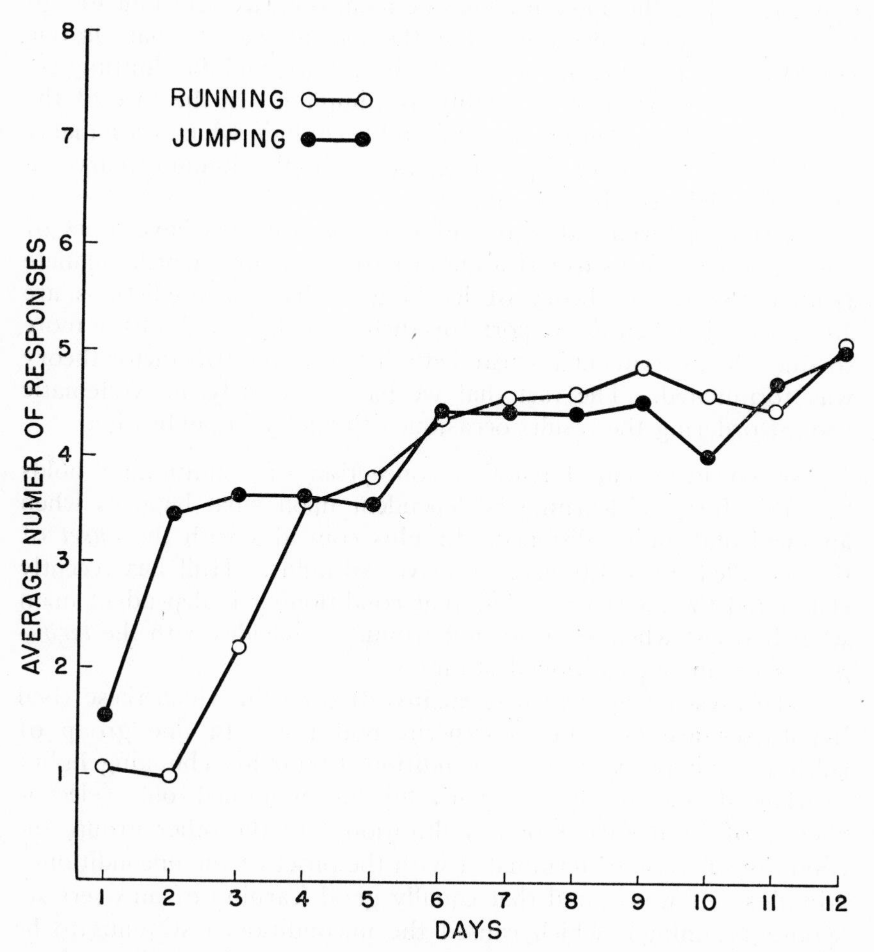

FIG. 56.—Curves showing the relative advantages and disadvantages of employing a running as opposed to a jumping response in the type of investigation under discussion.

study had no great theoretical significance; it was included only as a means of empirically determining, in a systematic and well-controlled manner, whether running or jumping is the better response to use in experimentation of the kind under discussion. The two curves constituting Figure 56 show the results. From the fourth day on, there is a striking similarity in the incidence of these two responses. However, the differences on the first, second, and third days are marked, and probably meaningful. As noted earlier in this volume, the use of the shuttling response predisposes the subjects to a certain amount of conflict—having been driven out of the opposite end of the apparatus on one trial, they are reluctant to "go back there" on the next one; but the indications are that, as one would expect, this conflict eventually disappears, and the shuttling response then occurs just as readily as jumping. In the case of the jumping response, there is no comparable conflict, which presumably accounts for the more rapid acceleration in the jumping curve in the initial days of the experiment.

In this factorially designed experiment, we thus have a set of variables enabling us to test a number of predictions which emanate from a two-factor theory of learning. That the predictions are all verified is taken as support for such a theory—and all the more so since the experiment was carried out before the two-factor theory was formulated. The fact that we had, previously, no systematic way of ordering the results occasioned the delay in publication.

SUMMARY. The Pavlovian conception of conditioning holds that this form of learning is dependent upon what happens when an incidental, or conditioned, stimulus coincides with the *onset* of the so-called unconditioned, or drive, stimulus. Hull has recently elaborated the alternative view that conditioning is dependent upon what happens when an incidental stimulus coincides with the *termination* of an unconditioned stimulus.

The present paper reports an investigation in which these rival hypotheses are brought to experimental test. In one group of subjects (laboratory rats), a conditioned stimulus (blinking light) overlapped and terminated with an unconditioned one (electric shock) of fixed (10 seconds') duration. In the other group, the conditioned stimulus terminated with the onset of the unconditioned stimulus. It was found that equally good learning of an overt response (running), which caused the unconditioned stimulus to be averted, was obtained in both cases. From this, and a related experiment by Horton and Traum, it is concluded that conditioning, properly speaking, is not dependent upon the coincidence of the conditioned stimulus and the termination of the unconditioned stimulus. The Pavlovian interpretation of conditioning is thus confirmed.

Further analysis suggests that one of the reasons for past confusion concerning the basic nature of the reinforcing process in so-called conditioning is that the phenomenon of conditioning has itself been improperly conceived. It is here suggested that "conditioning" be reserved exclusively to refer to the learning of emotional reactions (fear, hatred, disgust, and the appetites), and that the learning of reactions involving the skeletal musculature be termed "problem solving." Justification for this division of learning into two fundamentally different processes has been developed at greater length in another place (9).

II. Other Observations Bearing on the Two-Factor Theory

Section A. The experimental findings which have just been presented appear to raise important difficulties for the system of formal postulates published by Hull in 1943 and more recently (October, November, 1949) distributed in mimeographed form. Postulate III, on Primary Reinforcement (November, 1949, version) reads as follows:

> Whenever an effector activity (R) is closely associated with a stimulus afferent impulse or trace (s) and the conjunction is closely associated with the diminution in the receptor discharge characteristic of a need, there will result an increment to a tendency for that stimulus to evoke that response.

Divested of its semantic formality, this statement says, simply, that responses which solve problems, terminate drives, become more stably connected with these problems, or drives. Provided it is not interpreted as a paradigm for *all* learning, this statement is fully acceptable in the light of contemporary knowledge and logical analysis. However, a statement on *Secondary* Motivation, which purports to stem as a "corollary" from Postulate III, runs counter to the experimental results here presented and is not in harmony with other considerations previously reviewed (9). It reads as follows:

> When neutral stimuli are repeatedly and consistently associated with the evocation of a primary or secondary drive and this drive undergoes an *abrupt diminution,* the hitherto neutral stimuli acquire the capacity to bring about the drive stimuli (S_D) which thereby become the condition (C_D) of a secondary drive or motivation. [Italics added—this statement is new in Hull's system.]

What this statement means, in part, is that when a neutral stimulus is "associated" with the occurrence of a primary drive, such as electric shock, the neutral stimulus will become capable of eliciting a secondary drive or motive—in this case, fear. This much of the statement is manifestly true. However, the implication that the learning here involved is dependent upon an "abrupt diminution" in the primary drive is questionable. The results of the researches just reported indicate that it is drive *onset,* rather than drive "diminution," which is the important event in this kind of learning. Believing that drive diminution is the crucial event in this connection, Hull states that the acquisition of a secondary drive (such as fear) will occur only, or at least optimally, when this diminution is *abrupt.* I predict that experimentation would show that fear conditioning is not significantly influenced by the abruptness, or the lack of abruptness, with which the primary drive (unconditioned stimulus) is terminated. On the other hand, I should expect that fear conditioning *would* be influenced by abrupt vs. gradual *onset* of the primary drive. Confirmation of the first or, more particularly, of both of these predictions would discredit Hull's first corollary. Such confirmation would add support to the assumption that reinforcement in the sense of drive reduction is not relevant to the explanation of secondary-drive acquisition and to the assumption that there are *two* instead of only one type of reinforcement: effect *and* contiguity.

As previously noted in this volume, there is considerable ambiguity in the way in which the term "secondary reinforcement" is currently used. It is sometimes used to denote the reinforcing state of affairs which occurs when a secondary drive undergoes significant diminution or termination. At other times secondary reinforcement is regarded as a kind of "joy" reaction, a conditioned form of primary reinforcement. In order for this latter conception to be satisfactory, the assumption has to be made, not that "primary reinforcement" is simply the name for primary-drive reduction, but that primary reinforcement is a *reaction* of some sort made thereto; otherwise, one could hardly conceive of "secondary reinforcement" as capable of occurring as a *CR.* My preference is for the view that "secondary reinforcement" occurs when and only when a secondary drive is reduced; the conditioning enters the picture as the basis on which the secondary drive is acquired and manifested. I know of no clear-cut evidence that secondary reinforcement can be experienced, as a kind of miniature of primary reinforcement, in the absence of secondary-drive reduction (cf. 9, 12).

Hull's formal statement (Corollary ii) on Secondary Reinforcement implies the view that this phenomenon is a derived form of primary reinforcement, rather than the consequence of secondary-drive reduction. Hull's statement follows:

> A neutral receptor impulse which occurs repeatedly and consistently in close conjunction with a reinforcing state of affairs, whether primary or secondary, will itself acquire the power of acting as a reinforcing agent.

The present writer believes that the empirical fact from which Corollary ii is derived is this, that stimuli which are associated with primary-drive reduction—e.g., the click of the mechanism which delivers a pellet of food to a rat in a "Skinner box"—later prove capable, in the absence of primary drive, of reinforcing behavior (Skinner, 1938; Bugelski, 1938). In the last paper in Part I of this volume, a detailed explanation will be given of how this phenomenon can be accounted for without recourse to the type of assumption adopted by Hull. Here it will suffice to note that if one takes Hull's postulate system at its face value, the same explanation is apparently adduced to account both for *secondary motivation* and for *secondary reinforcement.* In Corollary i "a neutral stimulus" acquires the capacity to elicit a secondary motive, or drive, by virtue of its being "associated with . . . an abrupt diminution" in a primary drive. In Corollary ii, secondary reinforcement is defined as developing when a "neutral receptor impulse" occurs "in close conjunction," i.e., is associated, with a reinforcing state of affairs, which, according to Postulate III, is the same as "an abrupt diminution" in a primary drive.

Either Hull's language is so inexplicit as to lend itself to ready misinterpretation or else he is, in fact, using the same events to account for both secondary drive and secondary reinforcement, which, one would suppose, are *antithetical.* Much of the difficulty appears to come from the fact that Hull's system is predicated on the assumption that learning is a single, unitary process.

Section B. At the end of an article entitled "Association and the law of effect," Guthrie (1940), has made the following statement:

> It will be very unfortunate if we yield to the demand for a double theory of learning, for we shall then content ourselves with superficial generalizations from experiments with reward and punishment, and cease to look for the details of a basic associative process. To my mind the suggestions that two kinds of learning must be recognized will misdirect future research and burden psychology with descriptive categories that conceal the fundamentals of learning rather than aid in their formulation (p. 148).

Here it will be our purpose to examine the logic on which Guthrie based this conclusion.

Guthrie begins his paper by remarking that:

> The notion of conditioning, or a behavioristic use of the principle of association by contiguity, applies directly to the prediction of movements and

not to the prediction of acts as defined by their results. . . . It is this difficulty in extending the movement to significant action that is behind much of the current dissatisfaction with the principle of association or conditioning. . . . It is the search for an act psychology that accounts for the current tendency to distinguish two kinds of association, and for the mistaken notion that there is some sort of opposition between the concepts of association and of the law of effect (pp. 127–28).

After criticizing attempts by Hilgard, Skinner, and Razran to show that there are two types of learning, Guthrie repeats his own well-known monistic formula. For present purposes the essential features of this formula are what Virginia Senders has called the principle of *postremity* and, to borrow Hollingworth's term, the principle of *redintegration*. The first of these principles posits that when living organisms are in a problem situation, they make a succession of responses "until some final movement does away with the situation and leaves the situation faithful to its last associated movement" (Guthrie, 1940, p. 141). When the same situation recurs, Guthrie assumes that the organism will have a tendency to do what it last did in that situation. This, obviously, is but a paraphrase of the older notions of *recency* (Watson, 1914) and *openness of pathway* (Holt, 1931). Because the *last* response to a problem situation is ordinarily also the effective, successful, satisfying one, there is at least a superficial similarity between Guthrie's postremity principle and reinforcement theory as developed by Hull. But there is this notable difference: Hull, by postulating a "gradient of reinforcement," is able to explain how an instrumentally effective response can be learned even though it is not the "last" or even the "next to last" response to a situation, whereas Guthrie's system contains no provision for accounting for this phenomenon (O'Connor, 1946; Guthrie, 1946).

Guthrie's second principle involves the assumption, previously elaborated by Hollingworth (1928), that once a total situation has become connected to a given response, a single significant part of that situation will have a tendency to elicit that response.

How Guthrie puts these two principles, postremity and redintegration, together to explain behavior is indicated by the following example:

So simple an act as sweeping the hearth must have been established by numerous occasions on which the presence of ashes on the hearth has been associated with action. The original motivating stimuli may have been the scolding of another person. In some fashion or other the individual has been often made uncomfortable when ashes were visible. If the situation were invariable, and the ashes always seen from the same initial position, the hearth broom always hanging in the same place, and ashes always in the same place, sweeping the hearth would remain the same stereotyped movement that brought original relief (pp. 146–47).[5]

Thus the original problem situation was, let us say, ashes-on-the-hearth-in-a-particular-room-plus-scolding-mother. Sweeping up the ashes *changes* the situation: ashes-no-longer-on-the-hearth, mother-no-longer-scolding. As a result of the "success" of the sweeping operation, two things happen: (*a*) the same situation will have a strong likelihood of producing the same response and (*b*) the response may also occur to just a *part* of the original situation, i.e., ashes-on-hearth (without mother, perhaps even in rooms other than the original one).

There can be no quarrel with Guthrie's analysis in terms of parsimony: it is exquisitely economical. The question is: Is it *adequate?* At a sufficiently molar level, we may concede that this analysis is adequate, in that it "explains" behavior which is "anticipatory" no less than that which is "consummatory."

However, closer scrutiny raises questions. At the onset of his paper, Guthrie indicates his recognition of the fact that this kind of analysis would lead to the expectation that an "anticipatory" (conditioned, redintegrated) response should be an *exact replica* of its consummatory (unconditioned) prototype. Thus, in the example given, sweeping the hearth in absence of the mother should be exactly the same as sweeping the hearth when mother is present. A study previously reported (5) in this volume shows the untenable nature of this position. On the basis of both commonplace and experimental evidence, we now know that the behavior manifested in response to *signs* may be *utterly different* from the behavior which typically occurs to the total situations which signs represent. This, of course, is the problem which Guthrie has in mind when he speaks of the difference between "movements" and "acts." In the article cited, he tries to deal with this problem in terms of the prior existence of a "hierarchy" (see Hull, 1934b) of more or less equivalent movements which have been previously learned.

Certain types of stimulus situation thus accumulate through association a repertoire of alternative movements which relieve or change the situation. This is what I take Hull to mean by his "habit-family-hierarchy." When we have adequate past observation of the animal and adequate information

[5] Strictly speaking, the concept of "relief" has no place in Guthrie's system; it is simply a shorthand way of designating that a problem situation ("discomfort") has terminated.

of the situation (internal and external) in which it is now placed, we can predict the specific movements that will appear. Lacking these items of information, we shall be limited to predicting that the animal will do one of the things that has given past relief (p. 142).

On an earlier page, Guthrie gives this illustration of the foregoing propositions:

Wickens's (1938) subjects were conditioned to remove the fingers from a metal plate on receiving a signal that had accompanied a shock. Then they turned over the hand and it was discovered that they flexed the fingers at the signal instead of extending as in the conditioning practice. This is not to be wondered at, nor is it a valid reason for rejecting the notion of associated movement. Without any training series whatever most persons, informed that they are about to receive a shock through the metal plate, will make whatever movement is necessary to remove the hand *as it lies* from that contact. This not only indicates that they are intelligent and have insight, but also that they have had varied experiences in getting the hand away from danger. The insight is the result of the experiences, not in itself the cause of the action. They had previously acquired a capacity for an act (p. 138).

Guthrie here lapses from a strictly behavioral analysis and introduces the heretofore unmentioned concept of *danger*. Unless one defines "danger" as some form of peril of which the individual is *not aware,* one must assume that to be "in danger" is to be *afraid.* And once fear has been admitted, then there is no need to try to account the *hard way* for the difference often noted between anticipatory and consummatory behavior. As we have seen, specific adjustments made to fear are commonly very different from the behavior elicited by the thing or situation of which the fear is premonitory; here it is not a question of more or less equivalent members of the same "hierarchy" but of responses to two *different* problem situations.

Although, in the article in question, Guthrie nowhere speaks explicitly of fear, he clearly implies it more than once, as when he says: "Ashes on the hearth evidently become motivating stimuli in their own right and do not require scolding or other incitement" (p. 147).

The issue thus becomes clear: Guthrie must assume either (*a*) that a part-stimulus (ashes) directly produces behavior that was initially produced by the whole situation or (*b*) that the part-stimulus produces, in the immediate and direct sense, *not behavior but emotion.* I believe there is no reasonable option but to choose alternative (*b*). Once one has done so, the problem of "response equivalence," and of response difference, vanishes—but so does the tenability of Guthrie's monism. Evidence from many sources now indicates that fears in particular—and probably emotions in general—are not learned in the same way that skeletal responses are acquired. In the latter case we are dealing with *drive-solution connections;* in the other case we are dealing with *sign-drive connections.* Parsimoniously or not, we have to admit the evidence that solutions, and they alone, are learned on the basis of ending a situation, solving a problem, and that fears are acquired, not because of a principle of lastness, effectiveness, or satisfaction, but purely on the basis of the coincidence of initially neutral stimuli with the *occurrence,* or *onset,* of a problem.

In the final analysis, therefore, the weaknesses that inhere in Guthrie's system are the same as those of Hull's system—a fact which is not surprising since the underlying logic of the two systems is very similar.

Guthrie criticizes a distinction made by Skinner (1938) between *emitted* responses and *elicited* responses. If Skinner had made this distinction more explicit in certain respects, the ineptness of Guthrie's criticisms, and the weakness of his own theoretical system, would have been more apparent still. The key to the ambiguity in Skinner's statements lies in the fact that, as a "behaviorist," he speaks of both the emitted and the elicited responses as *behavior.* It now appears that, with some insignificant exceptions (the "short-latency reflexes"), *behavior* is always *emitted,* i.e., responses involving the skeletal musculature are *always motivated.* On the other hand, the *elicited responses,* i.e., those responses which are produced, not by internal drives, but by external (or internal) signs—are predominantly, perhaps exclusively, emotional and "cognitive." Unlike the "emitted" responses which involve skeletal muscles and perform work, the "elicited" responses involve visceral and vascular tissue and produce motivation, drive, tension—not "action" or "behavior." The action follows upon the occurrence of the tension. Or, in Skinner's terms, elicited reactions (emotions) form a two-link chain with emitted responses (behavior).

Any attempt to base a psychological theory upon a one-link, stimulus-response conception seems doomed to failure. Only by adopting a two-link, stimulus-drive-response conception do we begin to have a satisfactory conceptual framework. And as soon as we acknowledge the distinction between stimulus-drive and drive-response connections and examine them carefully, we see that the evidence impressively favors the view that these two types of connection represent a dual, rather than a single, learning process.

Sheffield's recent reply (1949) to Hilgard's criticism (1948) of Guthrie gives no indication that the latter's present position is substantially different from what it was at the time that the 1940 article, which is here discussed, was written. That the same weaknesses as here noted are still inherent in the system is indicated by the amount of space which Sheffield devotes to an attempted vindication of Guthrie's system with respect to those instances of learning which are associated with "punishment." However, it is apparently impossible to account for the effects of punishment without distinguishing fear learning from overt-response learning; and once one has done this, one is faced by the evidence which indicates that these two phenomena obey quite different rules and serve quite different purposes. No single principle yet conceived will encompass both of them adequately.

SECTION C. As has just been seen, the writings of neither Hull nor Guthrie provide any explicit support for a dual conception of learning; only in terms of the weaknesses of their systems can they be said, indirectly, to increase the plausibility of two-factor theory. It was therefore with considerable interest that the writer noted the title of a paper—"There is more than one kind of learning"—by another major learning theorist, E. C. Tolman, on the program of the 1948 (Boston) meeting of the American Psychological Association. However, when I discovered that by "more than one," Professor Tolman meant no less than *six,* my consolation was short-lived.

The six types of learning—"or rather the learning of at least six kinds of relationships" (Tolman, 1949, p. 154)—which Tolman identifies are:

1. Cathexis
2. Equivalence Beliefs
3. Field Expectancies
4. Field Cognition Modes
5. Drive Discrimination
6. Motor Patterns

Without, I believe, doing injustice to Tolman's thinking, these six categories may be reinterpreted as follows. "Cathectic" learning, which may be either "positive" or "negative," is clearly conditioning, in the sense previously defined (9). Fears and aversions are for Tolman (and for Freud) examples of "negative cathexes" —appetites are examples of "positive cathexes."

The notion of "equivalence beliefs" is less easily understood. Such "beliefs" are related to cathexes but are presumably something more. From the examples given by Tolman, it would seem that the distinctive element is simply secondary motivation and reinforcement. In other words, once cathexes have been established, they operate as motives and their reduction (attainment, fulfilment) operates as a form of reward. Although these phenomena —as stressed throughout this volume—are real enough, they do not seem to involve a new or distinctive learning process, in any fundamental sense.

Tolman's "field expectancies" and his fourth category, "field cognition modes," can, for present purposes, be lumped together: they both involve relatively complex behavioral phenomena, of the type which will be discussed shortly (11) under the headings of "insight" and "deduction." Strictly speaking, these phenomena depend upon learnings that have already occurred, rather than *being* learning.

"Drive discriminations," like discrimination learning in general, represent complex performances, but they can usually be broken down into more basic learnings or shown to involve some type of deduction, reasoning, insight.

Finally, Tolman speaks of the learning that underlies "motor patterns." Here he is referring to trial-and-error learning, or problem solving, in simplest form.

Summarizing, then, Tolman's "six kinds of learning" can be reduced to conditioning ("cathexes"), problem solving ("motor patterns," "field cognition modes"), and deductive processes ("field expectancies," "field cognition modes"). As already indicated, Tolman's "drive discrimination" is apparently a mixed type, involving, in varying degrees, conditioning, problem solving, and deduction.

While Tolman would probably have no objection to this reduction of his classification to two or three more basic categories, he would probably see no advantage in such a procedure, since his whole approach involves a heavy emphasis upon *cognition,* rather than having a more operational and behavioral bias. However, in one major respect, Tolman has been a pioneer in the kind of thinking which the present volume represents: he has long recognized the existence of "intervening variables," between stimulation and overt response. In the second following paper (12), a number of instances will be given of the usefulness of the "intervening-variable," or "mediating-response" concept.

Tolman, too, takes the position that "our familiar theoretical disputes about learning may *perhaps* be resolved, if we can agree that there are really a number of different kinds of learning" (p. 144). Tolman, too, wants to see the pieces put together. Our difference is one not of ends, but of means. I share his doubts about the extent to which his six categories will, in fact, dispel controversy and bring peace on the conceptual front. On the other hand, there is growing evidence that two-factor theory may provide common ground for persons of erstwhile quite different persuasions. It will now be our purpose to review some of this evidence.

SECTION D. A few months after the appearance of the author's paper on the dual nature of learning (9), Cowgill (1948) published—quite independently—an illuminating study on "Variant meanings of the terms 'conditioning' and "conditioned response.' " This author begins his paper with the following remarks:

> It is always disconcerting to the teacher to discover after covering a subject that even the good students quite innocently have construed technical terms differently and hence have been led to different conclusions or to utter confusion. The author has had this experience so frequently with reference to the terms "conditioning" and "conditioned response" that he has been impelled to seek the sources of difficulty and perhaps to contribute to a standardization of scientific vocabulary.
>
> It was evident that some of this difficulty stemmed not from slovenly habits of thought and study, but from divergent usage by teachers and textbooks. In order to discover something of the degree of divergence and identify the specific variations in usage in the latter course, the author has studied definitions and usages in 71 texts or standard references in the fields of psychology, sociology, social psychology, and educational psychology. This approach has revealed a remarkable difference of definition among the various authors and many cases of inconsistency between definition and use (p. 247).

Cowgill then observes:

> From the many variations in usage two stand out both in terms of the number of adherents and because they represent directly opposing positions. These are: (*a*) a strict *substitute stimulus* interpretation, and (*b*) a much broader interpretation which would include any new connections of stimulus and response and would therefore seem to comprehend *all learning* under the banner of the conditioned response (pp. 247–48).

In conclusion this writer says:

> This writer holds no reverence for words. He is fully aware that words are merely symbols which gain content by usage or arbitrary assignment. However, he is concerned with efficiency of communication in

the classroom and the printed page. He is even irked at the necessity of taking time out to clarify his particular usage of a word that might as well be standardized in one form or another. After 30 years of use in the American language it would seem that such standardization is overdue.

The writer would find either of the two major definitions cited above satisfactory if adopted and consistently used. Nevertheless, he ventures the opinion that there is more need for such a unique term in the limited context of the substitute stimulus and sees little necessity for a new term to become a synonym for learning. *The dual aspect of the learning process,* aptly called afferent and efferent modifications by F. H. Allport (1924), is identical with the dual aspect which Bernard (1926) and Young (1930) find it necessary to encompass in conditioning. If these are the essential processes of learning, little seems to be gained by substituting the word "conditioning" for "learning," whereas there is need for terminology to differentiate clearly between the subordinate processes. If used in the substitute stimulus sense, the term "conditioning" has specific analytical meaning; if used in the general sense, other terms must be invented to delineate the specific process to which reference is made.

In the present state of contradictory, inconsistent, and inexact usage, the term has little communicative value (pp. 254–55; italics added).

One of the most interesting passages in Cowgill's paper is the following, in which he speaks of the early history of the over-extension of the term "conditioning":

Watson is probably responsible for this viewpoint and claims made for it. While Pavlov made extensive claims for the conditioned reflex as the key to all learning, his experiments were all of the substitute stimulus variety; and, not being a psychologist, he apparently did not recognize that there was a different type of phenomena to be accounted for. The substitute stimulus concept seemed an adequate explanation for the behavior produced in his laboratory, and there is no evidence that he departed from that restricted conception.

In the hands of Watson, however, the concept was quickly expanded to include response substitution as well as stimulus substitution: "Can we substitute or condition responses? Experiment teaches us that the process of response substitution or conditioning does take place in all animals throughout life" (Watson, 1924). Here the term "conditioning" becomes broad enough to account for all possible new *S-R* connections, not merely

$$\begin{matrix} S & \\ & \searrow \\ & & R \\ & \nearrow \\ S' & \end{matrix}$$

the classical *R* pattern. This conception of the term overlaps and encompasses the pattern of learning emphasized by the trial-and-error school and the experimental data of Thorndike. In short, conditioning is learning and learning is conditioning (p. 251).

As Cowgill indicates, F. H. Allport (1924) was among the first to oppose the monistic trend in Watson's writings:

> As one of the adherents of this viewpoint, Allport is fully conscious of the implications of the position and says significantly: "half of the process of education consists of transferring appropriate responses to new and more finely discriminated stimuli" (p. 39). Thus he does not try to comprehend the whole field of learning under conditioning, but says instead that this is only half of the learning process. By his analysis this is the aspect of learning that has to do with the modification of afferent neural connections:
>
> "The prepotent reflexes are subject to modification by synaptic changes in their central portions. The effects of such changes are: (1) to extend the range and complexity of the stimuli capable of exciting the response, and (2) to refine and specialize the response itself. The first effect, which may be called afferent modification, is brought about by the principle of the conditioned response; the second, resulting in an efferent modification, is due to the selection and fixation of successful random movement in the process of habit formation and thought" (Allport, 1924, p. 56).
>
> Thus, Allport finds the learning counterpart of conditioning in the trial-and-error aspect of behavior. It is only natural that Thorndike should agree with this division of roles, though he would perhaps assign conditioning a less prominent place:
>
> "The *C-R* phenomenon seems much less general than ordinary learning. The phenomena of the conditioned reflex are probably not the archetype of learning in general. . . . They seem, on the contrary, a rather special case" (Thorndike, 1932). (Cowgill, 1948, pp. 248–49.)

In Cowgill's paper we find evidence for a two-factor conception of learning which is all the more striking because the author is a sociologist and may be assumed to have a degree of disinterest and objectivity which those of us who are more closely identified with these problems probably often lack.

Section E. Collateral experimental evidence in support of a two-factor conception of learning is not as yet voluminous, but it is steadily accumulating.

Coppock (1949) has reported the following experiment. Human subjects were divided into two groups. In one group an electric shock of several seconds' duration was administered with a signal coming just before the shock. In the other group the shock had the same duration and intensity, but the signal came just before the shock *went off*. The thinking underlying this experiment was similar to that involved in the investigation reported in the earlier part of the present paper. It was reasoned that if conditioning is dependent, as Hull has maintained, upon the coincidence of the conditioned stimulus with the reinforcing state of affairs which occurs when the unconditioned stimulus—in this case shock—goes off, the conditioned response of fear would occur more readily in the signal-shock-off group than in the signal-shock-on group. On the other hand, if fear learning is dependent upon sheer contiguity rather than the kind of reinforcement stressed by Hull, then fear learning would occur more readily in the signal-shock-on group than in the signal-shock-off group.

Using the galvanic skin response as an index, Coppock found that the signal-shock-on procedure was efficient and the signal-shock-off procedure was inefficient as a means of producing fear learning, thus confirming the view that fear learning, as an instance of conditioning, is dependent upon contiguity rather than drive reduction. It should be emphasized, however, that these results were derived from an experiment which was more exploratory than definitive; and there is also some question about the suitability of the G. S. R. for this type of inquiry.

Dr. E. J. Shoben, in a personal communication, has indicated his intention of repeating the Coppock experiment, using as the index of conditioning heart-rate acceleration rather than the galvanic skin response. To date, however, no results from this inquiry have been reported.

In a letter dated March, 1949, Professor D. D. Wickens has written as follows:

> I have been doing some experimental work in the field of human finger conditioning in which I essentially repeated the procedure you employed in the Mowrer-Lamoreaux experiment [4]. My results were essentially the same as yours. It seems to me that the results could be interpreted along the line of Guthrie's theory as well as in terms of your two-factor theory. I thus ran another group using classical conditioning so that although the response terminated the conditioned stimulus, it did not terminate the unconditioned stimulus. I felt that Guthrie's theory would seem to predict the same result in classical and instrumental conditioning. Actually, the experimental results differ in the two cases. Although the tone termination group is still somewhat better than the nontone termination group in the classical situation, it is not as much better as it is in the instrumental situation. To me, the results are far more in line with the two-factor theory than with a single contiguity theory.

And at the September, 1949, meeting of the American Psychological Association, Wickens, after describing his experiment, concluded with the remark that "The results seem to conform more with prediction from Mowrer's two-factor theory involving the concept of reinforcement than from Guthrie's strictly nonreinforcement theory" (Wickens and Platt, 1949, p. 226). A full report of this investigation has not yet been published.

In a recent paper on "Food-seeking drives, palatability, and the law of effect," Young (1948) arrives at the following conclusion:

> If learning is defined as the acquisition of patterns of behavior through practice, the law of effect is not valid as a law of learning. But if the definition of learning is broadened to include the acquisition of motives (drives and specific food expectancies) as well as motivated behavior patterns, then it can be said that there are two independently variable determinants of such acquisition: (*a*) practice and (*b*) effect (p. 300).

If we substitute "contiguity" for "practice," we find in Young's statement another indication of the growing trend to think about learning dichotomously.

In his paper "Psychotherapy as a problem in learning theory," Shoben (1949) has found the two-factor conception of learning a practical framework in which to analyze the therapeutic process. After describing his conception of therapy, Shoben says:

> Such a scheme seems to harmonize most effectively with a two-factor learning theory of the type most recently developed by Mowrer. Such a theory conceives of skeletal muscle responses as being acquired through the principle of reinforcement, whereas viscero-vascular, "emotional" reactions are acquired according to the principle of contiguity (p. 290).

A recent letter from Professor L. F. Shaffer contains this statement: "During the past few years, I had arrived at an idea very similar to yours, that the law of effect can account for all cases of learning involving tension reduction, but that the principle of conditioning is also needed to account for tension-creating learning."

In his recent book, Maier (1949) has made the following remarks:

> . . . the term *learning* is so general and inclusive that it is applied to noncorrelated activities. Thus Commins, McNemar, and Stone (1932) found no significant correlation between the learning of a platform problem box, a light discrimination problem, and a maze problem. Conditioning and trial-and-error learning scores likewise are unrelated, and the difference in these two functions is not clearly recognized in clinical theory.
>
> . . . problem-solving is frequently considered to be a form of learning. In some instances problem-solving is considered a form of trial-and-error learning; in other instances writers speak of insightful learning. Whether or not insight operates in all learning or whether the appearance of insight introduces another variable becomes a basic question (pp. 3–4).[6]

[6] See (11).

We may also note Postman's (1947) conservative conclusion, following his extended review of the present status of the law of effect, that: "It is safe to say that at the present state of our knowledge the law of effect as a monistic principle explaining all learning has not been substantiated. As *one* of the behavioral facts of learning, it cannot be gainsaid" (p. 550). Whether there is one or more *other* principles of learning this writer does not attempt to say.

Where Hilgard (1948) stands on this issue is not entirely clear. At one place he remarks:

> There are probably a number of different kinds of learning which have emerged at different evolutionary periods, with the more highly evolved organisms using at once several of them. It is quite probable that the different kinds of learning follow different laws.
>
> Learning capacity can be assigned a quantitative meaning only when the several learning capacities are identified. Factor analysis is a useful tool in this direction, although it cannot be used blindly. It may be that some of the primary factors are the results of emphases without our social heritage (p. 330).

A few pages later this writer differentiates between *perceptual learning* and *motor learning* (p. 333). However, it is difficult to say whether by this distinction he means essentially the same as is implied by a two-factor theory, or something different.

The writers who have most recently concerned themselves with this problem are Birch and Bitterman (1949). They begin their paper as follows:

> When Pavlov and Thorndike began their investigations of the learning process, they introduced into psychology two methods of experimentation from which there emerged two diverse conceptions of the mechanisms underlying modifiability. The Pavlovian situation focused attention on the development of stimulus-equivalence. . . . Observations of this sort led Pavlov to the conclusion that contiguity of stimulation is the essential factor in conditioning, which he regarded as a process of afferent modification rather than as a process of stimulus-response connection. . . .
>
> Thorndike's investigations of trial-and-error learning in a sense represented the other side of the behavioral coin. While Pavlov's attention was fixed upon afferent relationships, Thorndike was almost exclusively concerned with action. . . . In order to account for the selection of response appropriate to given motivating conditions and the disappearance of irrelevant responses, Thorndike introduced a primitive need-reduction theory, the now classical law of effect. . . .
>
> The two principles—contiguity and effect—are by no means mutually contradictory, and for some time they were implicitly accepted as comple-

mentary postulates which made it possible to explain, although in an incomplete way, many of the characteristic phenomena of animal learning. However, even the implied conception of qualitatively distinct learning processes did not long remain unchallenged (pp. 292–93).

After singling out Hull as the chief contemporary proponent of an atomistic learning theory, Birch and Bitterman cite a variety of recent writers who have challenged this type of atomism, notably Maier and Schneirla. They also review numerous experimental findings which they believe refute a monistic conception of learning and from which they make inferences such as the following ones:

> These two *kinds* of learning represent qualitatively different processes which may occur successively or concurrently, dependently or independently of each other (p. 299).
>
> These results are directly relevant to the conception of qualitatively distinct processes—stimulus substitution and selective learning—operating in the conditioning situation (p. 300).
>
> The results of the sensory preconditioning experiments require us to postulate a process of afferent modification (sensory integration), the essential condition for which is contiguity of stimulation, and which takes place independently of need-reduction (p. 302).
>
> Maier and Schneirla also suggest that the results obtained in work with decorticate dogs lend support to the distinction between conditioning (sensory integration) and selective learning (p. 304).

In conclusion Birch and Bitterman say, in part:

> Hull and his adherents have attempted to reduce all learning to the establishment and strengthening of stimulus-response connections under the influence of need-reduction. . . . Our analysis of the evidence reveals that stimulus equivalence develops even when neither of these conditions is met. We conclude, therefore, that at least two processes of learning—sensory integration and selective modification of response—must be postulated if the data of conditioning experiments are properly to be understood. Neither of these processes is unique to conditioning, but both may operate in a variety of learning situations (p. 307).

While many of the arguments which these writers advance agree well with the theoretical position here taken, these writers fail to make their analysis maximally convincing because they do not properly differentiate between sign learning and solution learning and wholly neglect the great explanatory power of fear and other emotions as *mediating responses* (see 12). Although the Birch-Bitterman argument is in certain respects incomplete, it is nevertheless compelling and is indicative of the general trend toward acceptance of a basic two-factor conception of the learning process.

In a recent personal communication, Dr. Richard L. Solomon says:

I think you will find, in the writeup I will mail you, that we have some very strong evidence supporting a dual interpretation of learning along the lines that you outlined in your *Harvard Educational Review* paper of 1947. As a matter of fact, the duality of avoidance learning shows up beautifully in our quantitative data on the acquisition of a conditioned avoidance response in dogs, using the shuttle-box situation. Our data show that avoidance learning is not characterized by a smooth change in latency to the danger signal, but is, rather, a two-phase curve which consists of learning to escape followed by learning to avoid. The avoidance appears suddenly and never appears prior to the occurrence of classically conditioned emotional reactions.

As you will see from the report . . . , and also from the forthcoming APA paper, the data on dogs which have been deprived almost completely of autonomic functioning do not support your emphasis on the autonomic nervous system. All of our operated animals acquired a conditioned avoidance response. However, they did require more trials and they did look quite different from normal dogs in many qualitative aspects of their behavior. My tentative conclusion is that there are many important skeletal aspects of emotion which can be classically conditioned in the avoidance situation.

In the unpublished account referred to above, Solomon and his collaborator, Dr. Wynne, report a number of other highly interesting and dramatic findings. An abstract of this work will appear soon (Solomon and Wynne, 1950).

SECTION F. In this section I shall review certain studies which, while not affording direct support for two-factor theory, are in some manner relevant to such a theory.

In their paper on "The role of reward in conditioning theory," Kendler and Underwood (1948) focus attention on the earlier study of Maier and Schneirla, "Mechanisms in conditioning" (1942; also referred to in 9). They say:

Maier and Schneirla have challenged the tendency "to break down the theoretical distinction between the classical notion of conditioning and that of selective or 'trial-and-error' learning," and have emphasized the necessity of distinguishing between these learning situations, not merely in terms of procedure, but also in terms of basic mechanisms of learning which must be postulated. These are, these writers maintain, two qualitatively different forms of learning. They write:

". . . in the *first stage* of the conditioning *procedure* a neutral stimulus develops excitatory value for a response it did not control. The essential condition for this change in the animal is contiguity between the experience of the neutral stimulus and the experience of the unconditioned stimulus. Then a *second stage* may develop. Once the neutral stimulus has become a conditioned stimulus, the response it elicits may be rewarded or punished. Unconditioned stimuli such as food and shock can function in this stage in the same way that 'reward' and 'punishment' function in problem-box learning. Thus during this stage a selective learning is involved; as a result the conditioning procedure ceases to be unique and assumes the psychological characteristics of trial-and-error learning. Then, as in all selective learning, the criterion becomes more and more specific the more effectively it leads to reward or to escape from punishment" (Maier and Schneirla, 1942, p. 131).

From this quotation it would appear that in the classical conditioning set-up sheer contiguity of the conditioned and unconditioned stimuli is the necessary condition for establishing the initial associative connection, with reinforcement by reward (or punishment) playing no role. Once the response anticipates the unconditioned stimulus, however, selective learning by reinforcement takes place which serves to strengthen and perhaps modify the response. . . .

Our analysis of the experimental situations which led Maier and Schneirla to postulate the contiguity stage has in turn led us to believe that such a postulation is not necessary and that Hull's theory of reinforcement is quite adequate to account for the data. The remainder of this paper is an elaboration of this point of view (pp. 209–10).

Here no attempt will be made to review the criticisms which Kendler and Underwood direct against the position taken by Maier and Schneirla. What is important to note is that the latter writers leave themselves open to attack because of their failure to distinguish with sufficient clarity between the nature of conditioned responses and problem-solving response. They are correct in their assumptions as to how conditioning and problem solving occur; but they err in supposing that both of these forms of learning lead to responses in the *behavioral* sense of that term. The criticisms of Kendler and Underwood could, I believe, have been entirely circumvented if Maier and Schneirla had seen that practically all overt, behavioral responses are of the problem-solving type (regardless of whether they "succeed" or "fail") and that the term "conditioned response," as most usefully defined, is a response which is mediated by the autonomic nervous system and involves viscerovascular tissues.

Thus what Maier and Schneirla call a "conditioned response," in the example which Kendler and Underwood select, is really an instrumental avoidance response and, though it is based upon i.e., motivated by, a conditioned reaction (fear), such a response is no different in principle from responses whereby animals run mazes or escape from problem boxes.

It may be that we shall have to extend the process of conditioning to include, along with the emotions, what are now sometimes referred to as the "short-latency conditioned responses," such as the eye blink or the knee jerk. Here, because of the extreme rapidity with which such responses occur, it is not possible to hold that they represent the sequence: signal-emotion-overt response. In some sense, these reactions are directly triggered off by the signal, or *CS*. However, it appears that for this sort of thing to occur, the organism must be actively "primed," or "prepared," by virtue of the fact that it is already in a situation in which the "unconditioned stimulus" is known as likely to occur, with a pre-existent readiness on the part of the organism to respond with the overt response in question. It is as if the conditioned response, properly speaking, i.e., *fear,* has already occurred and has so sensitized the organism that it makes appropriate overt defensive responses trigger-quick.[7] If such an analysis be correct, then we should probably not speak of the stimuli that release such reactions as "conditioned stimuli." The conditioned stimuli are those that prepare the organism for these responses, i.e., those which make up the experimental "situation"; the stimuli which release, or trip them off, should probably be called by some other name—in which event we would no longer be inclined to refer to these responses as the so-called "short-latency conditioned responses."

The foregoing paragraphs lead naturally to some of the considerations which Harris (1946) has discussed in his paper on "Recent developments in conditioning." At an early point he comments:

More and more it is being emphasized that, if conditioning is to be explained, other considerations must supplement what is known as "stimulus-

[7] Support, albeit somewhat indirect, for this interpretation is to be found in the experiment by Passey (1948) in which it was found that "the rate of acquisition of the conditioned eyelid response is a function of the intensity of the unconditioned stimulus. The rate of acquisition bears a direct relationship to the logarithm of the intensity of the unconditioned stimulus. The size of resulting conditioned responses is a function of the intensity of the unconditioned stimulus" (p. 428). Since air puffs "of 7.5, 18, 44, and 88 lb. per sq. in. were used" as the unconditioned stimulus, we may reasonably infer that the different intensities of this stimulus produced varying degrees of generalized apprehension in the subjects (human beings) and thereby produced, in keeping with the analysis suggested above, varying levels in the disposition to make the defensive response of winking when the tone which constituted the so-called conditioned stimulus was presented. An extension of this type of thinking may provide an explanation of pseudo-conditioning (for a review, see Harris, 1944). This phenomenon may be said to occur whenever a "set" to make a given response is so highly developed that the response in question can be elicited by almost any stimulus, like the "false" reactions in the reaction-time experiment. Cf. Coppock and Mowrer (1947).

substitution," the notion that the conditioned stimulus comes merely to act in lieu of the original or unconditioned stimulus in calling out some particular response. In this country, where motor responses have been studied more widely than glandular, it was early noticed that the conditioned response may not closely resemble the unconditioned reflex—may indeed involve movements of the antagonistic muscles (p. 429).[8]

The fact that Harris accepts a questionable definition of conditioning causes him to consider a number of the same issues which Guthrie discusses in the passages quoted earlier in this paper. By refusing to admit "motor responses" into the category of conditioned responses, and by limiting the latter to those reactions of an emotional character which lend themselves so satisfactorily to the role of intermediaries between signals and overt behavior, one has no trouble in disposing of the problem which Harris suggests in the above quotation—and which Guthrie poses as the movement-act paradox.

The second problem to which Harris addresses himself is that of explaining how it is that conditioning can occur without practice, or performance, of the response to be "conditioned." In a section headed "Is movement necessary for learning?" this author says:

No question could be of more theoretical interest than the perplexing one of the role of actual movement in the learning process. Several theories of learning, so-called "peripheral," depend upon a positive assertion, opposed by several which espouse a "central" or even "intracerebral" view. . . .

First work seemed to indicate that actual response was dispensable, when Crisler showed that dogs treated with atropine so that salivation was prevented, and then given conditioning training, salivated to a *CS* when the effect of the drug wore off. This result seemed at the time clear-cut. Moreover, Light and Gantt's experiment agreed with this indication, in that a muscle group whose nerve supply had been interrupted showed, after appropriate training, an appearance of conditioning, subsequent to that nerve's regeneration which made the response possible. Both of these experiments have, however, been subjected to searching criticism. . . .

Kellogg and coworkers (Kellogg, Scott, *et al.,* 1940) have repeated Light and Gantt's study with more extensive notion of bodily activity. They find it very significant that much more happens to a dog when given buzzer-shock training than merely learning to lift a leg. It seems that, although flexion muscles were paralyzed, generalized conditioned responses sometimes actually succeeded in removing the paw from the grid. As they put it, the animal "becomes conditioned 'all over' to the buzzer stimulus. The flexion of the leg is but an element of what ultimately becomes a well-

[8] Cf. the Wickens experiment previously referred to in this chapter.

integrated pattern of response. When experimental circumstances permit, it fits into the rest of the picture."

The early statement of Harlow and Stagner that movement *is* necessary for learning has received recent experimental support—though their experimental work, with curare, perhaps needs re-examination in view of Girden and Culler's description (1937) of the peculiar effects of this drug on conditioning. The latter workers found that a response conditioned under curare could not be elicited in the normal state, and *vice versa.*

Girden has amplified the data on this problem most recently (1943). He confirms Harlow's observation that pupillary responses can be formed under curare . . . but finds that, when given prolonged conditioning training under deep dosage, no striate response whatever appears when the animal makes a partial recovery. At the partial recovery stage, the control was instituted of demonstrating that conditioning training was now capable of producing genuine conditioned responses. That the failure of conditioning under deep dosage was not due to depression of the central nervous system was shown by recordings of autonomic activity which *did* show conditioning at that stage. . . . (pp. 435–37).

Neither the above studies nor others which Harris reviews give a clear-cut, consistent picture. Part of the difficulty may arise from artifacts that are introduced by the experimental procedures (surgery, drugs, etc.) which are employed. But it seems likely that there is also a purely conceptual problem here: the problem of deciding what we are going to mean by the terms "conditioning" and "conditioned response." If we mean by the latter only those learned responses which are mediated by the autonomic nervous system, much of the ambiguity about the experimental results vanishes. As noted in the last paragraph quoted from Harris, curare does not affect the responses mediated by the autonomic nervous system; therefore one may assume that it does not influence the occurrence of conditioned responses *in general,* if these responses are defined as a two-factor theory requires. If one limits or prevents, by surgery, drugs, or otherwise, the occurrence of *skeletal responses* during a conditioning procedure, there is no reason to believe that this would necessarily interfere with the occurrence of conditioning proper. It would not, for example, prevent the development of a fear reaction to a given stimulus; and once the erstwhile inactivated musculature had recovered its motility, an overt behavioral adjustment to the fear might appear on the very first occasion that the fear signal was subsequently presented. But all that this would mean is that an overt response which had previously been connected with the covert response of fear would be elicited now with a new stimulus touching off the fear. In other words, with fear as the mediating response, it is perfectly possible to get signal-fear-behavior sequences as a result of training which has kept the behavior from occurring during the training. This is not to say that such training will necessarily be followed by a particular signal-fear-behavior sequence; it merely indicates the way in which such a development may, under appropriate circumstances, come about.

We thus see that the issue which experiments of this kind purport to settle is not that of "peripheral" vs. "central" learning. Emotions are responses (unless one accepts Cannon's notion of the thalamic nature of emotion), and their attachment to new stimuli may easily *mediate* the occurrence of strictly motor behavior which has been in no direct way associated with the training, but is instead a product of still earlier learning. When such a phenomenon is observed, we are not at all forced to posit "central" learning; and it seems not unlikely that at least some of the incidents which are said to exemplify "insight" are of this mediated nature (see 11).

SECTION G. In this concluding section I shall review three problems which constitute the frontier of thinking about two-factor theory.

The first of these problems has to do with the mechanism whereby conditioned responses, or emotions, are *unlearned*. We know that the common, perhaps the sole, way in which skeletal, problem-solving reactions get eliminated is that of *conflict*. Thus, if a given habit is punished, either by some externally imposed drive or by an increment of fatigue (6), competing response tendencies are initiated which, if sufficiently strong, will outcompete and supersede the original tendencies. But when one starts thinking about the inhibition of emotional responses in the same way, some complications arise. Let us return to the familiar example of conditioned fear reaction. What happens if we try to inhibit it by means of punishment? It is "punishment," in the sense of a sudden increment of drive following a signal, that produces the subsequent occurrence of the fear reaction to that signal. Let us suppose, now, that we *punish this reaction to punishment!* What will happen? Does this mean that fear of punishment can be used to inhibit fear of punishment, that fear can be pitted against fear? Or does it mean that fear is simply added to fear, that the punished response is simply made stronger? Is this what we mean by the Jamesian expression, "fear of fear," and if so, how is this related to the concept of "anxiety" (20)?

It is common knowledge that under circumstances which are

objectively constant, fears may be remarkably stable (see examples given by Hilgard and Marquis, 1940), although even here Miller (1948, 1950) has shown that they can eventually be extinguished. Many writers—for example, three of those already cited in this paper, Sheffield, Shoben, and Tolman—make the assumption that the crucial thing about a "neurosis" is simply a fear which was acquired long ago, under circumstances which no longer exist, but which has failed to extinguish. Therefore, the task of therapy is that of helping the "neurotic" overcome such baseless fears. Shoben has been most explicit in suggesting how this can best be done; and his answer is that we should use the technique of "countercondition," that is, of trying to give the patient pleasurable experiences with an authoritative figure (therapist) to counteract the disagreeable, frightening experiences which he has previously had with parents and others.

This may indeed be the way in which we can best help persons unlearn fears which no longer have a realistic basis; but I am not convinced that this is the situation which we commonly encounter in "neurosis." Here I believe we are dealing with *personal immaturities* and that the fears expressed correspond, often quite accurately, to the disapproval which society has for such characteristics. Therapy, therefore, consists not in trying to banish these fears, but in trying to help the individual grow up to the point that he is no longer "guilty" of the attitudes and actions which society condemns. As Tolman and others have well recognized, the question of fear unlearning is related to certain important clinical problems; but I doubt that this relationship is of precisely the nature which many experimental, and even clinical, psychologists (and psychiatrists) currently believe it to be. However, this is a point of view that need not be elaborated here, since it is discussed at some length in Part II (15, 16, 18–20, 23, 24).

What the preceding discussion should have served to show is that with the redefinition of conditioned responses which is proposed in this book, we need to look again at the question of the process whereby these responses get unlearned. Because the term "conditioned response" has commonly been extended to include responses which are clearly of a problem-solving nature, the results obtained from the study of the extinction of such responses have been confounded and contradictory. As early as 1938 the writer showed (1938c) that a conditioned fear reaction, as measured by the G. S. R., can be "extinguished" and reinstated instantaneously in normal adult human subjects (cf. also 7), provided one uses symbolic mediation; and in therapeutic work one sometimes observes almost equally dramatic changes, as a result of sudden changes (decisions, conversions) which occur within the individual's intellectual life. However, our knowledge in this whole area is fragmentary and unsystematic, and calls for further research.

The next problem which I wish to discuss is this. A group of graduate students at a university where I once discussed the results of the experiment reported in the first part of this chapter raised the following objection to my interpretation of the results. They pointed out that in the experiment which Suter and I performed, the *CS* was associated with the *UnCS* in both our groups. Perhaps, the argument ran, all we had demonstrated was merely that association, as such, is the important thing for conditioning, and that it is unimportant whether the *CS* coincides with the onset or with the termination of the *UnCS.*

It is true that our experimental procedure was such as to be ambiguous on this score, for all we were able to show was that a stimulus which is present both before and during the occurrence of the *UnCS* (shock) produced *no greater* fear reaction than did a stimulus which simply preceded and went off just as the *UnCS* was coming on. These results seem crucial as regards Hull's contention that the *CS* needs to be coincident with the termination of the *UnCS* in order for maximal reinforcement to occur; but they are not crucial with respect to the hypothesis that mere *coincidence* of the *CS* and the *UnCS,* at any point, is the important thing.

Suter and I had actually anticipated this difficulty and had thought of running a group of subjects in which the *CS* would appear a few seconds before the *UnCS* was about to be terminated. According to our hypothesis that association of the *CS* with the *onset* of the *UnCS* is critical, this procedure should have produced very little fear learning. However, our over-all procedure was such that we could not test fear learning under these conditions in the same way we could under the two conditions which we actually employed, i.e., since the *CS* would not precede the *UnCS* we could not measure its efficacy by observing the incidence of anticipatory running responses. However, the experimental procedure used by Coppock (see above) does not involve this limitation (nor does that proposed by Shoben), and the fact that Coppock found a marked differential between the results obtained by pairing a signal with just the onset and with just the termination of the *UnCS* suggests that mere association, or contiguity, as such is not the crucial variable in reinforcement of this kind.

Finally, there is a question which Professor Meredith P. Crawford has raised (in conversation). It goes something like this.

Granted that fear conditioning occurs in the way indicated by the experiment here reported, perhaps other conditioned responses, notably the appetitive reactions, are acquired by the same kind of reinforcement as that which fixates problem-solving responses, namely drive reduction.

The empirical answer to this problem would seem to depend upon the type of experiment previously described (9, see section entitled "Pavlovian Conditioning Reconsidered"). To date this experiment has not been performed, but that it is still desirable is indicated by Tolman's description of it in his (1949) discussion of the question of how "positive cathexes" are formed. He says:

> The sort of evidence one wants could be obtained perhaps for hunger, with a special dog-preparation. If, for example, a dog's esophagus were severed and the upper end brought to the outside so that food taken into the mouth, after chewing and swallowing, would drop out into the open and if also a direct fistula were made into the stomach, so that this food (or other food) could then be reintroduced by the experimenter directly into the dog's stomach, we would have the sort of set-up we need. From this kind of preparation we could discover whether the dog's hunger would become cathected only to those foods which after being chewed and swallowed were reintroduced into the stomach (and hence produced drive reduction) and whether conversely his hunger would not become cathected to or become decathected from foods which in contrast were not reintroduced into the stomach and hence did not produce need reduction. Furthermore, with such a prepared dog the exact quantitative laws relative to frequency of trials, amounts of reinforcement per trial, etc., could be worked out (p. 147).

In the absence of experimental data for this or any similar experiment, we should perhaps for the present leave open the issue which is here at stake.

CHAPTER 11

AN EXPERIMENT EXEMPLIFYING "LEARNING" AS INDUCTION AND "INSIGHT" AS DEDUCTION

[In the two preceding studies we have seen that a number of ambiguities and paradoxes can be cleared up if one assumes that there are two basic learning processes—conditioning and problem solving. In the present paper an attempt will be made to show that still greater orderliness can be introduced by making a systematic distinction between *learning,* as defined by two-factor theory, and a process which is variously known as *insight, reasoning,* or *thinking.* Much of the controversy between the "elementalists" and the "wholists" seems to be resolvable if we assume that each of the contending parties has hold of only a *part* of the proverbial elephant and that both of the parts are real, important, and essential to a sound conception of "the organism as a whole."

The plan of the present paper is as follows: first, a synoptic description of the experiment and its logic (as presented at the 1948 meeting, in Philadelphia, of the Eastern Psychological Association); then a more technical statement of the procedure and the results; and, finally, discussion of the findings in the light of related studies.

Dorothy Kunberger and Kaya Kardash were collaborators in this study.]

Strictly speaking, the experiment here reported concerns the use of secondary reinforcement to facilitate learning which would occur slowly, or not at all, if primary reinforcement were alone operative. With this interpretation there will probably be no disagreement.

A more interesting statement of this experiment and one better presenting the problem is to say that it is concerned with "insight," "deduction," "instruction," "knowledge of results," "identification." Perhaps the tentative, exploratory application of these molar terms in this context will serve to indicate more precisely what they mean —or rather what *we* mean, or may most usefully mean, when we use them.

I think it is not too rash to say that during the last two decades there has been no more important development in psychology than our improved understanding of secondary motivation and reward. For a long while, research into trial-and-error or problem-solving learning was mainly confined to experimental situations in which "the problem," or drive, was a primary, biologically given drive, such as hunger or thirst. And during this same early period our study of the conditioning process almost completely neglected the motivational side of the picture.

Today we know that it is through conditioning that most secondary drives—such as fears, appetites, and aversions—come into existence and that, once such a drive or problem exists, it may serve to initiate and pattern behavior no less than do the primary drives.

A quarter of a century ago, our knowledge of both the genesis and function of the secondary drives was astonishingly meager. In 1919 a past president of the American Psychological Association (Watson) reported experimental results which he interpreted as proving that there was no gradient of primary reinforcement, and from this he argued against the validity of the law of effect, or Thorndikian reinforcement, itself (see also Warden and Haas, 1927).

Not until 1933 was this early failure to demonstrate a gradient of primary reinforcement correctly accounted for. It was then shown, by Roberts, that the earlier results were obtained because the investigator had not recognized and controlled the factor of secondary reinforcement. When this was done, Roberts was able to derive an empirical gradient of primary reinforcement with no difficulty.

During the interim, work with "token rewards" and other forms of secondary reinforcement at Yale,[1] the University of California, the University of Iowa, and elsewhere have established the psychological reality of this phenomenon and suggested its great importance in everyday human affairs (see Miller, 1950).

Parents, for example, make constant use of secondary rewards, in the form of approval, promises, and tokens. By these devices children are often successfully kept at tasks which they would soon desert if one had to depend solely on primary reinforcement (8).

The first purpose of the present experiment was therefore to provide a paradigm of this process of bridging the temporal span between actions and their belated primary reinforcement. Such a paradigm proves surprisingly suggestive as an occasion for thinking about and analyzing such concepts as "insight," "reasoning," etc.

---

[1] It is noteworthy that Wolfe's classical studies on the use of tokens with chimpanzees (1936) was preceded by studies with rats on delayed reward (1934) and what later came to be known as the gradient of reinforcement.

In the present investigation, two randomly selected groups of laboratory rats were trained, by a standard procedure, to come to a trough for a pellet of food whenever a signal was given. They were then subjected to different procedures. In one group, during this second stage of the experiment, the signal was no longer presented by the experimenter but the subject was afforded an opportunity to press a little bar located about 2 feet from the food trough. When the bar was depressed by a standard amount, the signal that food was in the trough occurred.

In the other group exactly the same procedure was followed except that when the bar was pressed the signal did not come on. In both groups an animal got food on going to the trough after pressing the bar; but only in the first group did the signal appear when the bar was pressed.

It will hardly surprise anyone that the "learning" was dramatically superior in the first, or "Experimental," Group of animals. In Figure 57 the solid line with filled circles shows the rate at which the first group of animals learned to press the bar as a means of obtaining food; the solid line with the open circles shows the very much slower rate at which this same performance was mastered by the control animals.

This learning task seems to have been a very difficult one for animals in the Control Group. In our experiment, a few of the animals eventually did fairly well on it, but most of them failed completely; hence the nature of the composite curve shown by the solid line and open circles in Figure 57. Since the time intervening between a rat's pressing of the bar and his chancing to look in the food trough was likely to be fairly great, there was but negligible reinforcement of the bar-pressing response. Unlike the animals in the Experimental Group, which received secondary reinforcement as soon as they pressed the bar, the Control Group animals were rewarded for pressing the bar (by primary-drive reduction) only after what was usually a relatively long interval.[2]

In the language of formal learning theory, the explanation of our results is unambiguous. It is obvious that, in the Experimental Group, the signal served two related functions: (*a*) it provided an immediate secondary reinforcement of the bar-pressing response, and (*b*) it cued off the response of going to the trough for food. Since the animals thus tended to go directly from pressing the bar to the food trough, two important consequences follow: (1) the in-

[2] These animals thus had little or no "knowledge of results." Those in the Experimental Group were "informed" immediately.

terval between bar-pressing and eating was lessened, thus increasing the effectiveness of the primary reinforcement; and (2) since

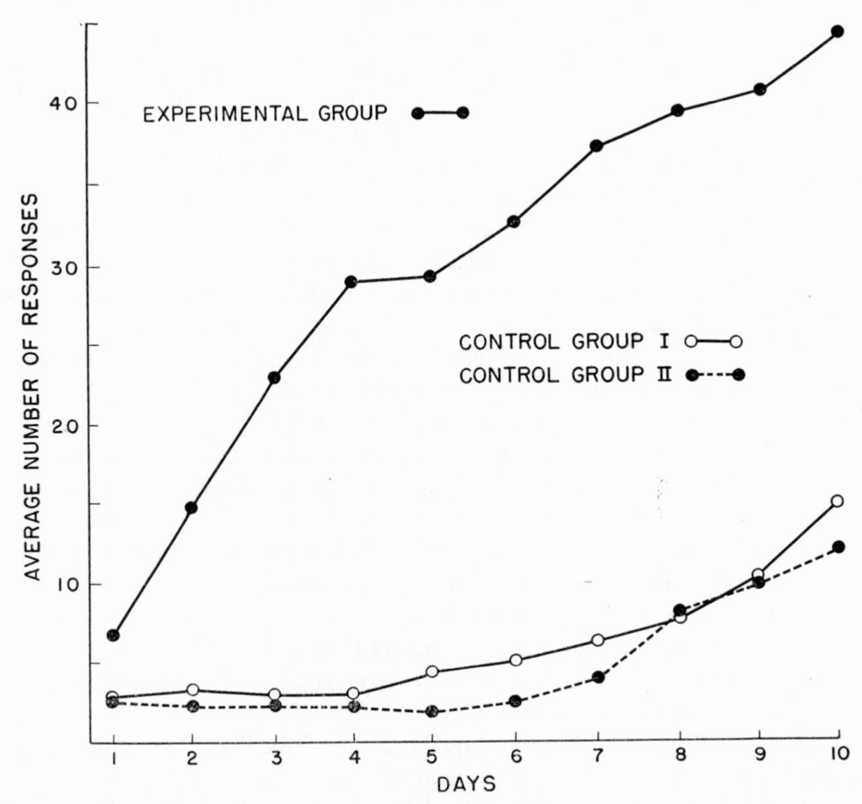

Fig. 57.—Results indicating the effects of introducing a previously learned signal in a problem situation. The "problem" was the hunger drive of the subjects (rats), and the "solution" consisted of pushing a small bar located about 2 feet from the trough into which the food thus won was delivered. The curves indicate the number of times, during a 10-minute test period on each of 10 days, that subjects in the 3 groups pushed the bar and obtained food. In the Experimental Group, each time the bar was pushed the aforementioned signal was given; it was not given in the 2 control groups. Such increment as the 2 lower curves show thus represents unaided, trial-and-error learning; the performance increment represented by the top curve is here interpreted as approximating what is meant by the term "insight." By absolute standards, the performance increment in no case is particularly "sudden," in the sense of requiring only a few trials for perfection; but, relatively speaking, the increment shown by the Experimental Group is much more nearly "sudden" than that shown either by Control Group I or Control Group II. It is believed that this experiment isolates out the variable which crucially differentiates between learning proper and "insight."

the interval between the onset of the signal and eating was thus usually brief, the onset of signal, coinciding with depressing of the bar, retained high secondary reinforcement value.

But now let us ask what these results mean in less rigorous, common-sense terms.

Since "insight" has often been differentiated from more pedestrian forms of "learning" on the basis of the rapidity with which it occurs, we may legitimately ask if our experimental animals did not "have insight." "Insight" means many things to many persons, but one thing which it seems very commonly to mean is that the individual experiences an immediate secondary reinforcement, before the actual instrumental results of an act have occurred (8). Usually this secondary reinforcement is self-administered (as it was in the case of Sultan, 8), but the principle seems much the same if the environment supplies the "O.K.," "That's right," or "That does it!"

One is prompted to speculate on the possibility that when we use the term "learning" we are referring to an essentially *inductive* process, whereas when we use the term "insight" we are referring to an essentially *deductive* process. Perhaps a certain amount of confusion would be removed if we simply recognized both of these processes as real and valid, but different.

I can illustrate this point by translating what happened in the case of our Experimental rats into a syllogism.

The "major premise," built up by the slow inductive process of conditioning, would be: "Signal means that food is in the trough."

The "minor premise" is then "discovered." It is: "Pushing the bar causes the signal to come on."

Then follows the "understanding," "insight," or "conclusion": "Pushing the bar causes food to appear in the trough."

Lacking the opportunity to discover the minor premise, our control rats could not arrive at the "conclusion" deductively. They had to arrive at it, if they got it at all, by the same slow process of induction as that by which they had established the major premise—though this difference is to be noted, that the major premise is built up by the form of learning we call conditioning, whereas the conclusion had to be built up by problem solving or by trial-and-error learning.

The short-cutting of learning which the signal makes possible in this experiment is also suggestive of "instruction" or "teaching." A bright student once defined teaching as the process whereby one organism helps another solve a problem more quickly than it would on the basis of its own unaided, trial-and-error efforts. In the present instance, by virtue of the occurrence of the signal when the bar is pressed, the rat is *told* that the response he has just made was the correct, effective, food-producing one. In this instance it is true that there is a purely mechanical, impersonal relationship between the correct response and the occurrence of the signal; but the signal could just as well have been made by another organism (e.g., the experimenter) and such an action, by the above definition, would qualify as an act of instruction or teaching.

Then there is the possibility of interpreting our results in terms of a *very primitive* form of identification. In the beginning it is the experimenter who makes the signal; later it is the subject that does so. Therefore, in this one limited, specific respect, the rat has learned to *act like,* or "identify with," the experimenter.

This analysis is at variance with the conception of identification as imitation, in which the rat might learn to press the bar because of *seeing* the experimenter (or another rat) do so. However, what is important here is merely that the signal take on a *pleasant connotation,* so that when the subject happens to produce the signal, the response which was effective in producing it will be reinforced.

This line of thought suggests a crude parallel to what seems to be involved in at least the very first stages of human language learning. The human infant hears his parents, particularly the mother, make certain sounds in pleasurable contexts. Thus we may suppose that if the child happens to make or approximate these sounds, he will be secondarily, or "autistically," rewarded and will be inclined to repeat and perhaps perfect them. And in so doing he is identifying with his elders in the quite literal sense of becoming like them. (This line of thought is expanded in Part II, 21 and 24.)

I. Some Technical Details

The study under discussion was performed in the same apparatus as pictured in Figure 22 (p. 94).

All the rats used were of the Lashley strain; they were all males, ranging in age from three to five months. Each of the 2 groups referred to above contained 8 animals.

A standard level of hunger motivation was maintained throughout experimentation by reducing all subjects to 15 per cent below normal body weight, over a period of 5 or 6 days, during which time they learned to eat the small, specially made pellets of Purina Dog Chow and macaroni flour which were used as food reward during experimentation.

The preliminary training was as follows. An animal would be put into the apparatus and allowed to explore about for 2 minutes. Then the signal would be presented. In half the animals (i.e., half of the animals that were randomly selected in advance for the Experimental Group and half that were selected for the Control Group), the signal consisted of a tone of about 800 d.v./s., generated by the oscillator and small speaker constituting a commercial Morse-code practice set. (Unfortunately no precise measurement of the intensity of this tone is available. It might be roughly described, from the standpoint of human hearing, as distinctly noticeable, but in no sense "loud.") In the other half of the animals the signal consisted of an oscillation in illumination pattern such as previously described (5). In all instances the signal was presented and *left on* until the rat had come to the food trough and the experimenter had dropped a pellet into the trough. This procedure of using an auditory signal with half the animals in any given group and a visual signal with the other half was followed throughout all experimentation here reported. However, there was no very reliable or striking difference in the two types of signals as far as our results were concerned. The two types of signals were used simply as a means of having a check on any kind of intrinsic reinforcement value which any one type of signal might be suspected of having.

At least 30 seconds elapsed between successive trials in all cases, i.e., between the termination of the signal on one trial and its onset in connection with the following one. Another rule was that the subject had to be in the right-hand half of the apparatus before the signal was given. This was in order to force the animal to move away from the trough somewhat between trials, instead of allowing it just to sit at the trough continually. This precaution may not have been necessary, but it was thought desirable. Under these conditions the interval between trials was thus 30 seconds *plus* whatever time might be consumed by the rat in getting to, or back into, the right half of the apparatus.

Each animal received 20 trials per day, and the preliminary training lasted 8 days. During this training, the obviously important variable was the time elapsing between the onset of the signal and its termination, as the animal got to the trough and received food. One animal, selected more or less at random, made the following record on the first day of preliminary training: Time, in seconds, intervening between onset of signal and obtaining of pellet: 50, 35, 12, 100, 80, 85, 84, 87, 82, 16, 47, 60, 7, 7, 165, 11, 12, 14, 35. By the eighth day, the corresponding times were reduced to the following: 5, 75, 3, 3, 25, 2, 155, 9, 14, 3, 6, 15, 7, 10, 6, 3, 6, 4, 4, 4. It is thus apparent that the signal had taken on meaning, i.e., that, by the eighth day of preliminary training, it served effectively on most trials to "call" the animal to the food trough.

In the main part of the experiment, the procedure was this.

Each animal was put into the apparatus and allowed to remain a total of 10 minutes. During this time a record was kept of the number of times each of the animals in the two groups pushed the bar and obtained food. The resulting data are presented in Figure 57. The animals (Experimental Group) which had the advantage of having the signal come on as soon as they pressed the bar and remain on until they went to the trough and obtained food were decidedly superior to those which did not have this advantage (Control Group I).[3]

Because the animals in the Control Group tended to be bimodally distributed, consisting of those few animals which became relatively proficient in pushing the bar to obtain food and those which failed more or less completely, a *t*-test of the reliability of the difference between the mean performance of the animals in the two groups was not undertaken. However, inspection of the two curves shown in Figure 57 leaves little doubt as to the reliability of the obtained difference.

II. An Additional Control Group

It is easy to see that the "learning" of the Experimental Group in this study would be facilitated by the occurrence of the previously learned signal whenever the bar was pressed. Though not so obvious, there is also some reason to suppose that the learning of the animals in Control Group I might have been somewhat *depressed* by the *absence* of the signal in the following sense. During the 8-day preliminary training period, these animals had learned to go to the right-hand half of the apparatus and "wait" for the signal. Therefore, during the experiment proper, it might be supposed that the Control I animals would have a tendency to go to the right half of the apparatus and wait, regardless of whether they had or had not pressed the bar, for the signal to occur. It might be supposed that this tendency, if it existed, would serve to make these animals even slower in acquiring the bar-pressing habit as a means of getting food than they otherwise would have been.

In order to check on this possibility a second control group was run, at the same time as were the two groups just described. This second control group has not been previously described, in order to simplify the exposition of what is the primary purpose of the investigation.

---

[3] Unsystematic observations made with some of the animals that served in the Experimental Group indicate that, once the bar-pressing habit is well established, the signal can be discontinued with no detrimental effect on the habit. This finding is in no way remarkable and is mentioned only incidentally.

The animals in Control Group II were treated in the second part of the experiment just as were the Control I animals, but they were not given the previous experience with the signal. Thus, it could not be said that they were deterred in the second part of the experiment by a tendency to wait for the signal. The dotted line with filled circles in Figure 57 shows that the performance of this group was not significantly different from that of the first control group.

By way of summarizing the logic of the three procedures thus far described, we may say: In the Experimental Group the "major premise" that the signal means food is available at trough was *established* and *utilized*. In Control Group I this "premise" was *established but not utilized*. In Control Group II this premise was *not established* and so could not be utilized, but neither could it interfere with learning. In the Experimental Group the preliminary training had a clearly positive influence upon the main learning task—that of bar-pressing to obtain food. In Control I, there was some reason to suppose that the preliminary training might have a *negative* influence upon the main learning task. In Control II, since there was no preliminary training, there could be neither a positive nor a negative influence. The fact that the performance of the two control groups did not differ significantly in the main phase of the experiment suggests that in the case of Control I the preliminary training *did not* have a negative influence.

III. Results Not Due to "Law of Emphasis"

Without additional experimentation the results shown in Figure 57 might be regarded as ambiguous. One possibility of accounting for them is that presented above. But there would be another possibility of doing so on the basis of the so-called law of emphasis (Tolman, Hall, and Brentnall, 1932; Muenzinger *et al.*, 1934–38). It might be argued that the Experimental Group excelled the two control groups, not for the reasons given, but merely because the two types of stimuli (tone and blinking lights) here referred to as "signals" served to *accentuate,* or *emphasize,* the bar-pressing response in the Experimental Group; since these stimuli were absent in the two control groups, they could not act as emphasizers—hence the decidedly poorer performance of these groups.

In a supplementary experiment, the two following procedures were accordingly followed. One group of eight animals was put into the apparatus individually, as previously described, and whenever they pushed the bar, the "signal" (tone in half the cases, lights in the other half) came on and stayed on until the rats went to the trough and got the food. To call these stimuli "signals" now is only a manner of speaking since, at least in the beginning, they had

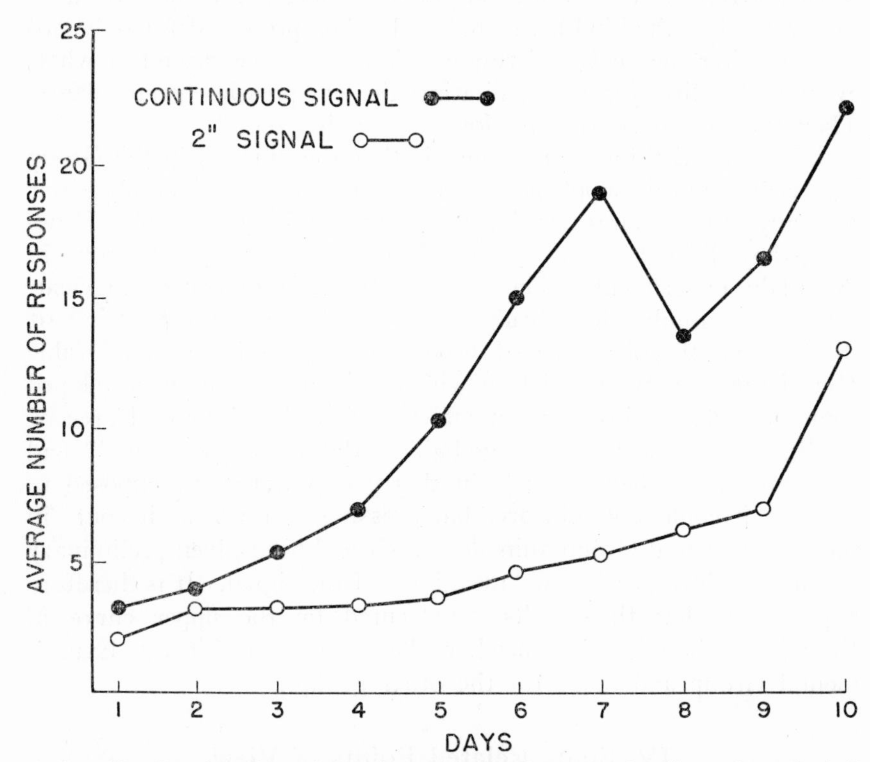

FIG. 58.—Results of a subexperiment designed to test the "law of emphasis." According to the so-called law of emphasis, one might reason that the results portrayed in Figure 57 were obtained, not because of the effects of the previously acquired "signal value" of the stimulus which was introduced in the Experimental Group whenever the correct response (pressing of the bar) occurred, but rather because this stimulus tended, as such, to center "attention" upon this response and thereby fixated it. The results shown above, obtained under conditions described in the text, indicate that this was not the case. (The dip in the top curve was caused by erratic performance on the part of one animal which, for two days, apparently "forgot" all that it had previously "learned." There was no sign of illness, nor could any other explanation be found.)

no particular meaning to the animals, the animals having had no preliminary experience with them. The results are shown graphically in the upper curve in Figure 58.

Another group of 8 animals was treated in exactly the same manner, save that now the "signal" was presented for only 2 seconds after the bar was pressed. The results are shown in the lower curve in Figure 58.

Some instructive relationships are at once evident. First we note that the performance of the Group II animals in this supplementary experiment is strictly comparable to that of the two control groups in the main experiment. There is thus no indication that stimuli of the kind here employed, when presented for only two seconds after the "correct" response is made, have any effect whatever in the direction of facilitating the bar-pressing performance. They do not, in short, function as "emphasizers."

The second thing to be noted is that the animals in the Group I procedure in this supplementary experiment did considerably better than any of the groups mentioned in the preceding paragraph. However, they did not do nearly so well as the Experimental Group in the main experiment. The reasons for this outcome are clear. Since the stimuli which bridged the gap between the pressing of the bar and the obtaining of food gradually took on signal value (by virtue of their association with food), these stimuli developed some secondary-reinforcement effect and produced some degree of facilitation of the bar-pressing habit. But since the "signal" had no such value when the rats in this group were first exposed to the bar, it could not reinforce bar-pressing as much as it could in the Experimental Group animals, which had been given preliminary training with respect to the "meaning" of the signal. It is therefore appropriate that the results represented by the upper curve in Figure 58 should fall somewhere between those for the Experimental Group and those for the other groups.

IV. Some Related Points of View

A. Since the experimentation here described was completed, three investigators have presented points of view which warrant special notice. Writing in 1948, Hilgard remarks:

> The question has been raised, especially by Maier (1931), as to the appropriateness of including processes like reasoning within the same classification as other kinds of learning. My preference is for including them. Leaving them in does not prejudice their explanation. There may be new factors not found in simpler learning, but there is no assurance that all other kinds of learning follow the same principles. Leaving the doubtful processes in simply asserts that a complete theory of learning must have something to say about reasoning, creative imagination, and inventiveness, in addition to what may be said about memorizing and retaining or about the acquisition of skill (pp. 6–7).
>
> The two main theories [of learning] may be designated *association* theories, on the one hand, and *field* theories on the other. Any naming in this

way does some violence to the individual theories, but nevertheless the typical American theories of functionalism, connectionism, and behaviorism have a common underlying logic which permits them to be grouped together, and the other theories, stemming chiefly from Gestalt psychology, have in turn a contrasting common ground. The theories here classified as association theories have been labeled *reflex arc* theories and *stimulus-response* theories. The field theories group together various varieties of *Gestalt, neo-Gestalt, organismic,* or *sign-significate* theories.

The distinctions between the families are not always sharp, and there are agreements and disagreements which cut across lines. That is, on some specific issues it would be possible to find association psychologists on opposite sides of the fence, paralleled by field psychologists divided on the same issue. But the total picture does not present such confusion. Although association psychologists do not comprise a single harmonious family, still any one adherent to that position tends to offer explanations more like those of another than like the explanations of anyone in the field group. Correspondingly, the members of the field psychology family have in common their opposition to associationist conceptions. It is important to understand this basic cleavage, because there are profound differences in outlook, despite efforts of eclectics and mediators to harmonize the opposing camps (pp. 9–10).

The word *insight* is one which the Gestalt psychologists brought prominently into the literature of learning. For most field psychologists something like insightful learning, be it called learning with understanding or learning under cognitive control, is the characteristic form of learning (p. 14).

The preference of the associationist is for the machine model. The uses made of bonds, reflexes, and other isolatable activities which can be integrated into total habit systems more nearly resemble the model of the machine than of the whirlpool (p. 15).

A part of the question involved here is one of semantic taste. One can say that "learning" includes both "learning proper" and "insight." Or, if one prefers, one can separate "learning" and "insight." The point is that there are *two* distinct phenomena, and the question of just what terms can be most satisfactorily used to denote them can remain an open one. The difficulty arises when one takes a position requiring the assumption that it is an either-or matter, that—to use the terms which I favor—there is *only* learning or *only* insight. As Hilgard's analysis indicates, most learning theorists are preoccupied with one or the other of these phenomena. We can assume, if we choose, that one—or perhaps both—of these phenomena is misconceived, unreal; or we can assume that both are real and that it is only when learning theorists take them both into systematic account that we shall have the beginnings of a scientifically adequate and practically effective theoretical structure.

It has long been recognized by philosophers and logicians that there are two routes to "knowledge" or "learning," that of induction or "experience," and that of deduction or "reason." And, what is more, it has been commonly recognized that, in the everyday life of human beings (and perhaps other organisms), these two processes probably occur simultaneously and that they interact in an exceedingly complicated manner.[4] It is therefore only for purposes of analysis that they can be abstracted and given independent status. However, since such abstraction is essential to scientific understanding, it is important that we make the proper abstractions. It is here suggested that the induction-deduction dichotomy is one particularly adapted to this purpose.

Granting the arbitrariness of analysis and the complexity of interaction, we may nevertheless picture what happens in living organisms as something like this: Through the two basic forms of learning—conditioning and problem solving—living organisms develop generalizations (or, if verbally stated, propositions) commonly known as *attitudes* and *habits.* An "attitude" is a generalization that takes this form: *"A* (the *CS*) has been followed by *B* (the *UnCS*) once, twice, three times, *n* times. . . . *A* is *always* followed by *B."* On the other hand, a "habit" is a generalization that takes this form: "This particular response has solved this particular problem once, twice, three times, *n* times. . . . It will *always* solve this problem."

This, of course, is the "Aristotelian logic" of induction, to which Korzybski (1933) and other general semanticists attribute so much of mankind's self-deception and error. They say that it leads us into a psychology of either-or, of truth or not-truth. Certainly modern statistical theory explicitly accepts a relative, or probability, theory of "truth," and so does common sense. It is only a coterie of metaphysicians and theologians who have been seriously misled by the conception of "universals" and "absolutes."

However, when living organisms have experienced either of the types of sequences just described, with a fairly high degree of regularity, they develop a corresponding degree of *confidence* (i.e., attitude- or habit-strength) with respect to the predictability of future events. When, therefore, *two or more* of these confidences, or generalizations, have been established in a living organism, there is a tendency for them to begin to "rub together" and to generate "deductions." Not all generalizations are "related" logically, i.e.,

[4] This position is implicit in the "hypothetico-deductive" approach to science. Hypotheses are inductions, deriving from empirical observation; they are then used to make inferences which are, in turn, subjected to empirical test.

many generalizations can be brought together, or related, psychologically without generating anything. But when *pertinent* generalizations are combined, their combination may be *creative,* and lead to those arresting events which we call "insights," to the having of "an idea."

In the case of the animals comprising the Experimental Group in the present investigation, what, precisely, does it mean to say that they "had insight"? Does it mean that something happened to them which cannot be explained in terms of "learning theory"? If in "learning theory" we include the principles governing secondary reinforcement, then we have already seen that the answer to the latter question is "No." Yet it is obvious that here we are dealing with something over and beyond what is involved in "simple learning," i.e., the rudimentary processes whereby generalizations or confidences (of both kinds) are built up. The distinguishing feature of those situations to which we apply the term "insight" appears to be this, that they always involve what Tolman (1932) has called "intervening variables" or what Osgood (1951) has termed "mediating responses." In the words of Krechevsky (previously quoted, 8), these are the "something" which the organism "contributes to the situation." The organism's "behavior is not something forced upon him by the immediately presented stimuli. He has taken the problem field and has brought to bear upon it all his past experiences" (Krechevsky, 1932b, p. 531).

It would be very neat if the "mediating response" of Osgood should turn out to be the "minor premise" of the logicians. Rather it appears that the mediating response, in the sense of what the organisms "bring to the situation," is the major premise. Thus, to take the familiar syllogism about Socrates, the "situation," the thing that is immediately given is: "Socrates is a man." The thing that the reasoner has to "bring to the situation" is the *major premise,* that "All men are mortal." In like manner, the "something" which the Experimental Group animals brought to the bar-pressing phase of the present study was the generalization, or confidence, that "Signal means food is in the trough." When the immediate situation indicates that "Pressing bar causes signal to occur," then the two propositions can "rub together" and produce the creative leap—"Pushing bar causes food to be in trough." Animals which did not have an opportunity, through lack of preliminary training, to develop the major premise, *or* which did not have an opportunity to discover the minor premise, could not make this leap—and had to arrive at the conclusion—"Pushing bar causes food to be in the trough"—the *hard* way, i.e., by induction.[5]

To take a suggestion from Harlow (see below) and put the matter somewhat differently, learning is a *continuous* process, insight *discontinuous*. Thus again we see the possible dangers and futility in the well-known controversy (see 7) as to whether "discrimination learning" involves continuity *or* discontinuity. Perhaps the reason for the fact that certain experiments seem to support one view and other experiments seem to support the other one is that both continuity ("learning") and discontinuity ("insight") are realities and that the results obtained are, often as not, a reflection of what variables have or have not been allowed, knowingly or unknowingly, to operate in any given instance.

B. Another set of relevant observations is to be found in a recent report by Harlow (1949). His researches indicate that if monkeys are exposed to, and allowed to solve, a *protracted series* of discrimination problems, they show a marked facilitation in their discrimination-learning ability; as Harlow puts it, they seem to "learn to learn":

> The variety of learning situations that play an important role in determining our basic personality characteristics and in changing some of us into thinking animals are repeated many times in similar form. The behavior of the human being is not to be understood in terms of the results of single learning situations but rather in terms of the changes which are affected [*sic*] through multiple, though comparable, learning problems. Our emotional, personal, and intellectual characteristics are not the mere algebraic summation of a near infinity of stimulus-response bonds. The learning of primary importance to the primates, at least, is the formation of learning sets; it is the *learning how to learn efficiently* in the situations the animal frequently encounters. This learning to learn transforms the organism from a creature that adapts to a changing environment by trial and error to one that adapts by seeming hypotheses and insight (p. 51).
>
> It is the purpose of this paper to demonstrate the extremely orderly and quantifiable nature of the development of certain learning sets and, more broadly, to indicate the importance of learning sets to the development of intellectual organization and personality structure (p. 52).
>
> We wish to emphasize that this *learning to learn,* this *transfer from problem to problem* which we call the formation of a learning set, is a highly *predictable, orderly* process which can be demonstrated as long as controls are maintained over the subject's experience and the difficulty of the problems (p. 53).

---

[5] For other studies on related problems, see Maier (1929), Wolfe and Spragg (1934), and Miller (1935).

In a conventional learning curve we plot change of performance over a series of *trials;* in a learning set curve we plot change in performance over a series of *problems.* It is important to remember that *we measure learning set in terms of problems* just as *we measure habit in terms of trials* (pp. 53–54).[6]

Before the formation of a discrimination learning set, a single training trial produces negligible gain; after the formation of a discrimination learning set, *a single training trial constitutes problem-solution.* These data clearly show that *animals can gradually learn insight.*

This terminal performance level is likely to focus undue attention on the one-trial learning at the expense of the earlier, less efficient performance levels. It should be kept in mind that this one-trial learning appeared only as the end result of an orderly and progressive learning process; insofar as these subjects are concerned, the insights are only to be understood in an historical perspective (p. 58).

On the issue of continuity vs. discontinuity in discrimination learning (7), Harlow has the following to say:

The cue afforded by a single trial produces at this point [of sophistication] almost complete discontinuity of the learning process. The only question now left unsettled in the controversy over hypotheses in subhuman animals is whether or not to use this term to describe the behavior of a species incapable of verbalization.

Again, it should be remembered that both the object-quality discrimination learning set and the right-position discrimination learning set developed in a gradual and orderly manner. Only after the learning sets are formed do these phenomena of discontinuity in learned behavior appear (pp. 61–62).

---

[6] I am indebted to my colleague, Professor James E. Hulett, for calling attention to a remarkable parallelism between the above analysis by Harlow and some suggestions contained in an article by Gregory Bateson, first published in 1942 and reproduced in Newcomb and Hartley's *Readings in social psychology* (1947). The following paragraphs are quoted from the latter:

"Let us coin two words, 'proto-learning' and 'deutero-learning.' . . . Let us say that there are two sorts of gradient discernible in all continued learning. The gradient at any point on a simple learning curve (e.g., a curve of rote learning) we will say chiefly represents rate of proto-learning. If, however, we inflict a series of similar learning experiments on the same subject, we shall find that in each successive experiment the subject has a somewhat steeper proto-learning gradient, that he learns somewhat more rapidly. This progressive change in rate of proto-learning we will call 'deutero-learning.'

"From this point we can easily go on to represent deutero-learning graphically with a curve whose gradient shall represent rate of deutero-learning. Such a representation might be obtained, for example, by intersecting the series of proto-learning curves at some arbitrarily chosen number of trials, and noting what proportion of successful responses occurred in each experiment at this point. The curve of deutero-learning would then be obtained by plotting these numbers against the serial numbers of the experiments" (Bateson, 1942, pp. 123–24).

Bateson, in describing deutero-learning, also speaks of "learning to learn" (p. 124).

In summary and conclusion, this writer says, in part:

> The emphasis throughout this paper has been on the role of *the historical or experience variable* in learning behavior—*the forgotten variable* in current learning theory and research. Hull's Neo-behaviorists have constantly emphasized the necessity for an historical approach to learning, yet they have not exploited it fully. Their experimental manipulation of the experience variable has been largely limited to the development of isolated habits and their generalization. Their failure to find the phenomenon of discontinuity in learning may stem from their study of individual as opposed to repetitive learning situations. [Cf. Mowrer, 1939a.]
>
> The field theorists, unlike the Neo-behaviorists, have stressed insight and hypothesis in their description of learning. The impression these theorists give is that these phenomena are properties of the innate organization of the individual. If such phenomena appear independently of a gradual learning history, we have not found them in the primate order (pp. 64–65, italics added).

Although different in respect to subjects and methodology, Harlow's work leads to conclusions which in many ways are strikingly parallel to those which seem warranted on the basis of the present study. In both cases "insight" is seen as a result of an organism's *combining something* in an immediate situation *with something* that is temporally (or spatially) remote. And in both cases, the history of the organism is sufficiently well known so that we can indicate rather specifically what it is that the organism brings to and combines with the significant features of the immediate situation. Though this act of "combining" loses none of its wonder and "creativeness" through our possession of such knowledge, much of the apparent mysteriousness that has characterized past talk about "insight" disappears. As Harlow says, the whole sequence becomes "orderly," and we can begin to study it more scientifically.

Although effective from the standing of quick communication, Harlow's expression, "learns to learn," warrants closer scrutiny. Perhaps a better way of putting the matter is to say that in the course of events such as here described, living organisms *"learn in order not to have to learn."* Learning, in its restricted sense, is a slow process; and in the struggle for existence, speed is often of the essence. Thus, if an organism can develop some substitute for learning, whereby the same ends are served, there is an obvious advantage. "Insight," or "reasoning," seems to provide such a short cut.[7]

One may ask why, if speed is of such importance in the scheme of survival, living organisms do not learn more rapidly. One

[7] Cf. Miller and Dollard (1941) on the function of imitation; also chapter 21.

answer is that if learning were complete in "one trial," living organisms would "know a lot of things that aren't so." Many sequences, both of the stimulus-stimulus and the response-relief kind, are pure coincidences. Thus, learning needs to be something that involves repetition and regularity. In short, "generalizations" have to be built up relatively slowly and cautiously. But if one already has a number of such generalizations, or inductions, which one brings into what appears to be a new situation and if one then "gets a cue" indicating that this situation is really "just a case of this or that," then the tedium of learning proper is bypassed and the individual is said to deal with the situation "insightfully," with "reason."

In its simplest form, deduction is nothing but an instance of the individual's deciding, "This is a case of that." Thus, in the familiar syllogism previously referred to, if we know that "All men are mortal," as soon as we decide or discover that "Socrates is a man," we immediately know that "Socrates is mortal." Socrates may be an entirely new experience to us, as such, but as soon as we can *classify* him, as soon as we can relate him to other members of a category with which we *have* had experience, we can then bring our past learning to bear upon him and properly feel that, in some measure, we "know" him too—and what expectations we may properly have with respect to him. Obviously, this may save us a lot of time and trouble over what would be involved if we had to start afresh with every new organism or situation we encounter.[8]

In this context we gain a new understanding and appreciation of culture, as anthropologists use the term. Culture, most simply defined, is past learning which has been "carried" (by "education") into the present, because it seems likely to help us solve problems—both personal and social problems—more quickly than we, as individuals, can independently *learn* to do so. We are said in this case to learn *vicariously,* from the experience of others; and in so doing spare ourselves time and probably pain. Here, actually, a double saving is involved. By taking over the prior learnings of

---

[8] Learning, in simplest form, seems always to involve generalization in the sense of one's going from the particular to the universal. If *B* follows *A* once, twice, three times, . . . *n* times, we eventually conclude (as noted earlier), "*B* always follows *A*." This is a generalization, or induction, and may be developed both in respect to stimulus-stimulus sequences (sign learning) and response-relief sequences (solution learning). In reasoning, insight, deduction, we move from the universal to the particular. Our major premise is a generalization, derived inductively (either by direct learning or vicariously). The minor premise is a kind of identifying or pointing act. The conclusion is a particularistic statement: "*This* man (Socrates) is mortal." Here, then, we see again the apparently antithetical nature of learning and insight.

others, we gain in terms of the time which we would have to spend acquiring these independently;[9] and, in addition, we are in a position to behave insightfully, reasonably, *humanly*.

It is no accident that Harlow, in the foregoing quotations, ties up his discussion with the problem of "transfer of training." All reasoning, or insight, seems to involve transferring something temporally remote to a current situation which is in some degree *new*. It might be useful to review the relevant facts and concepts in the transfer-of-training literature in the light of this kind of thinking. Perhaps some of the long-existing ambiguities and contradictions could be thereby eliminated.

The problem of latent learning is also worth noting again in this connection. Here there is clearly a kind of transfer of training, and it so happens that those persons who have most stressed latent learning have also been interested in demonstrating the insightful nature of behavior. The Karn and Porter study, previously referred to (8), is especially relevant here in that these investigators were able to analyze, rather fully, one instance of so-called latent learning and show its multivariable nature.

C. A third paper, published independently of either of the two contributions just reviewed, and certainly without any reference to the present investigation, shows much the same type of thinking. It is Yacorzynski's "The postulation of two different but functionally related mechanisms in adaptive behavior" (1949). The author aptly begins by noting:

> Psychological theory at present appears to be oriented towards an integration of various viewpoints, rather than the building of self-consistent systems that characterized the era of the behaviorists, functionalists, gestaltists, and others. Although such a trend in emphasis towards integration is slowly emerging, nevertheless, there are concepts from the various systems which as yet cannot be reconciled. This is true when explanations for adaptive behavior stem from the associationist or Gestalt theories. Even in the present decade these two viewpoints have been considered to be mutually exclusive . . . (p. 111).
>
> A number of factors may be responsible for a controversy of this nature. The possibility exists that one viewpoint is true, that is, from the standpoint of its usefulness as an explanatory system, and the other is false. This is the position held by the strong protagonists in either field. This would mean that a large body of psychologists have been deluded, an idea that may have some grounds for defense and one that may not be too repugnant to many

[9] Of course, there is always the possibility of "cultural lag," i.e., the possibility that what was formerly "so," or effective, is not now. Obviously, there is both security *and danger* in "accepting the culture."

individuals. Another possibility is that both viewpoints are true, and that the apparent discrepancies lie in an inability to find a common denominator of integration which would make both of them acceptable. The latter possibility is the thesis which will be advanced in this paper. I propose, first of all, to marshal data from various sources to show that in the individual's adaptive behavior at least *two functions must be recognized, that of learning and perception.* These two functions will be frequently referred to as mechanisms. In the second place, I wish to discuss the possible reason why confusion exists in the thinking of a large number of psychologists (I reject the group delusion hypothesis) who propose one viewpoint to the exclusion of the other. The main reason for the confusion may lie in the fact that *these two mechanisms are functionally related.* When one is altered a concomitant change occurs in the other (pp. 111–12, italics added).

Yacorzynski takes his definition of "learning" from Hunter (1934): "Learning is taking place whenever behavior shows a *progressive change,* or *trend,* with a repetition of the same stimulation situation, and where the change cannot be accounted for on the basis of fatigue or of receptor and effector changes" (p. 494). Although Yacorzynski makes no attempt to differentiate between sign learning and solution learning, he adopts a definition which, it will be observed, includes both (provided that the word "behavior" is interpreted broadly, to include emotional as well as "action" responses).

His definition of "perception" is more novel. He says:

The term perception is defined as the ability to *see relationships.* Some objections to this definition may be offered in the fact that perception has been used, at least in elementary psychology texts, to cover a whole gamut of data which would not be included in this definition. Nevertheless substituting any other word from the vocabulary of the Gestaltist, such as insight, closure, least action, or using the more popular terms of reasoning, thinking, concept formation, would be inadequate, since these terms are considered as subsidiary concepts in the field of perception thus defined (p. 112, italics added).

The various lines of evidence and logic which this author used to support his case are, to the present writer, cogent and convincing. In summary form they are these:

(*a*) Different parts of the nervous system are involved. . . . (*b*) The early maturation of the two mechanisms differ. . . . (*c*) The peak of development is reached at different times. . . . (*d*) Curves measuring the acquisition or loss of a response differ. . . . (*e*) Individuals are found who have a high development of one mechanism but not of the other (p. 121).

In connection with the last point, the author says:

The curve of learning consists of a *gradual increase in proficiency* with practice. When the problem can be solved by *comprehending relations,* a sudden solution occurs. Gestalt psychologists have called this phenomenon insight. The sudden versus gradual solution of a problem has been subjected to a great deal of controversy by members of the opposing schools. Without entering into this controversy, the plain fact is that problems are often solved gradually *or* suddenly. Even the early experiments of Thorndike on the problem solving of cats in the puzzle box showed this to be true [as Adams (1929, 1931) has indicated]. We must, therefore, grant that the two kinds of solution occur. In such a case, it is not the individual who postulates two different processes for such radically different results who must defend his viewpoint, but the individual who would state that the same process is responsible for both results (p. 117, italics added).

Like Harlow, Yacorzynski finds that the analysis of this kind of problem leads inexorably to a consideration of the organism's *past,* its *learning history* (see 13, 14). In a section entitled "Functional relationships between the mechanisms of learning and perception," he says:

From the standpoint of the experimentalists on learning, there evidently exist good and poor methods in studying this function. The good methods are those which exclude as much as possible any previous experience of the organism with the situation. Thus great care is taken to select nonsense syllables which convey as little meaning as possible either in their written form or when they are spoken. The classical conditioning experiments require complete isolation of the organism from any extraneous stimuli. . . . One need not question the value of these methods in studying learning, but doubt can be cast upon the rationale for their use. It may be that the only thing that these methods do is to *eliminate past learning.* They may, however, also eliminate the appearance of some other function in the solution of a problem. This is exactly the viewpoint maintained by the Gestalists. . . . Using nonsense syllables, the conditioned reflex, and mazes not only eliminates past learning to these situations but the bringing into function of perceptual responses.

The situation as it stands is something like this. The associationists, in studying adaptive behavior, attempt to eliminate from their experimental set-up all possibility of perceptual responses occurring. The Gestaltists, on the other hand, insist that a great deal of learning to the situation must be present in order for the perceptual responses to occur. In other words, to study learning, perception must be eliminated; and to study perception, learning must be included. This course of events must mean only one thing: that in the acquisition of a response in an experimental situation, the mechanisms of learning and perception have a mutual influence upon each other (p. 118).

Those psychologists who maintain a middle-of-the-road position in being neither exclusive advocates of associationism or Gestaltism would in general subscribe to this position. Even the psychologists whose position is more dogmatic take cognizance of this possibility in the way they structure their experimental problems (p. 119).

What value, if any, is derived from postulating that learning and perception are two different but functionally related mechanisms which operate in adaptive behavior?

The immediate result of making this postulate is that the ambiguity and confusion in theory and experimentation which has characterized the approach to the problem of adaptive behavior will be resolved. In the field of theory the oft patronizing or acrimonious attacks, or the disregard of the opposing viewpoints, or the reinterpretation of the results of the opposing school within one's own theoretical framework, will no longer have any meaning (p. 120).

From the present writer's point of view, little is to be added to the foregoing remarks. As already indicated, I believe that a satisfactory conception of learning is one which breaks this phenomenon down into two different processes—conditioning and problem solving; but they are *both* forms of learning. What Yacorzynski has said, and said well, is that learning and what he terms "perception" are different. With this I agree.

CHAPTER 12

A REINTERPRETATION OF FOUR EMPIRICAL STUDIES

[In this paper comments on four different experimental studies are brought together, with a common denominator in the fact that they all lend themselves to reinterpretation in the light of a single hypothesis, namely, that fear is often an overlooked variable intervening between problem situations and the overt, behavioral reactions of living organisms thereto. In all four instances, failure to take cognizance of the role of this "mediating response" has led to theoretical inferences which are either paradoxical or misleading.

Section I reanalyzes experimental results reported by Muenzinger and coworkers concerning the apparent facilitation of discrimination learning by the technique of administrating electric shock punishment for "right" responses. This is done with particular reference to a recent study by Wischner.

In Section II a study by O'Kelly and Heyer is reinterpreted. As is true of Section I, the material in this section is previously unpublished.

Section III is a commentary on an investigation by Estes and has already appeared as a note in the *Journal of Comparative and Physiological Psychology* (1950).

Section IV consists of two parts, both of which deal with certain aspects of Maier's book, *Frustration—the study of behavior without a goal.* Part A has appeared as a book review, in *Science* (1950). Part B is hitherto unpublished.]

I. The Muenzinger-Wischner Results

In a seemingly simple visual discrimination situation, Muenzinger and his students found, contrary to all past evidence and assumption, that "shock for correct responses makes for as efficient learning as does shock for wrong responses. There were no significant differences between a shock-right group and a shock-wrong group in the learning by white rats of a black-white discrimination habit in a T-shaped apparatus, although the latter seemed to be somewhat more efficient than the former. Both shock groups were significantly superior in learning efficiency to a group in which no shock was employed. These data were offered by Muenzinger as a contradiction of that part of the 1911 statement of the law of effect dealing with the after-effects of annoyers and as support for the interpretation that the function of electric shock in discrimination learning is a general one. Shock does not weaken or inhibit the specific response that is shocked, concluded Muenzinger, but rather it makes the animal more sensitive to the cues to be discriminated" (Wischner, 1947, p. 272).

Wischner, in the paper just cited, reports an experiment in which rats were trained in a modified Yerkes-Watson discrimination box, with a procedure similar to that employed by Muenzinger but with this difference. Muenzinger had employed the "correction" method in his training procedure; i.e., when a rat made a wrong choice, it had to return to the choice point and make the right one before the "trial" ended. Wischner, using a noncorrection procedure, failed to get the "Muenzinger effect"; instead he obtained results consistent with the usual expectations generated by the law of effect, i.e., he found that animals which were rewarded for the correct choice and shocked for the incorrect choice learned best; that animals that were rewarded for correct choice and not shocked for either the correct or incorrect choice learned next best; and that animals that were both rewarded and shocked for correct choices learned least well. He therefore concluded that "shock has a specific function with respect to the response that is punished. The animal, very quickly builds up avoidance responses to the cues associated with shock. . . . These results are seemingly in conflict with the findings of other studies that shock administered anywhere after the choice produces a general accelerating effect" (p. 283).

The explanation of the difference in outcome in the two situations may go something like this. In the Wischner experiment, a rat in the shock-wrong group got *doubly* "punished" for making an incorrect choice, i.e., it got no food and received a shock; whereas an animal that made a correct response was doubly "rewarded" in that it got food and avoided shock (escaped from the fear, or danger, of being shocked). Thus, we find highly efficient learning. The situation was clearly "structured"; and preferential, or discrimination, learning took place in an orderly and efficient manner.

In this experiment, rats in the no-shock group showed an intermittent degree of discrimination, for they were *singly* "punished" when they made a wrong response (no food) and singly "rewarded" when they made a right response (food).

Animals that got shocked for right responses showed the poorest discrimination, i.e., the least marked preference, for the reason that while the right responses were doubly rewarded, by escape from hunger and escape from fear, they were also punished, by shock; and the wrong responses received considerable reinforcement by virtue of the fact that they were accompanied by fear reduction (escape from the apparatus without retracing) even though these responses brought no food. Here the situation was poorly "structured," it being a matter of relative indifference whether the animal chose the "right" or the "wrong" response since there was something both right and wrong about each of them.

In summary, then, the first procedure employed by Wischner involved double reward for the correct response and double punishment for the incorrect response; the second procedure involved single reward (food) for the correct response and single punishment (food deprivation) for the incorrect response; and the third procedure involved double reward (hunger reduction and fear reduction) plus punishment (shock) for the right response and a single punishment (food deprivation) and a single reward (escape from fear) for the wrong one. Complicated though the variables be, it is not difficult to understand that the goodness of discrimination, or preference, was in the order indicated.

In the Muenzinger-type experiment, the picture is quite different. It is difficult to tell, precisely, what is involved in all cases, because of the complication introduced by forced correction. But this much seems clear: In the shock-right procedure, once a rat entered the apparatus, it was *trapped*. Only by making the correct response could it get out and end the trial. This meant, one would suppose, that there was no opportunity for the wrong response to get reinforced by fear reduction, since the animal still had to go back, make the right response, and take a shock before getting out of the apparatus. Nor did the wrong response get reinforced by hunger reduction, at least not in any very immediate sense. On the other hand, the right response, though punished by shock, was always followed by escape from hunger *and* escape from fear.

In short, then, in the shock-right procedure as employed by Muenzinger the situation was relatively highly structured: The wrong response was reinforced neither through fear reduction nor hunger reduction, and the right response, though punished, was doubly reinforced. It is not surprising, therefore, that, with forced correction, the shock-right procedure led to about as good discrimination learning as did the shock-wrong procedure, and that the learning obtained in both cases was superior to that obtained with a no-shock procedure, since it, in contrast to the shock-right and the shock-wrong procedures (both of which involved the possibility of double reinforcement), involved a single source of reinforcement, namely hunger reduction only.

Though this type of differential analysis is not made explicit by Wischner, it is implied by certain of his interpretative remarks, as, for example, when he says, with reference to the shock-right procedure:

> This [wrong] response to the dark alley may be rewarding, . . . the reinforcing mechanism being the tension reduction resulting from the escape from the noxious stimulus and termination of the trial. It would appear that the conditions of correction, which "force" the animal to approach the light and thus guarantee reinforcement of this response on each trial, make for a more rapid shift in the relative strengths of the light and dark stimuli to evoke the approach response to light, than do the conditions of noncorrection (p. 282).

And there are other indications that his analysis was moving in the direction of the one here proposed. However, the outstanding accomplishment of the Wischner study is that it squarely identifies what seems to be the variable which has given Muenzinger's findings their striking and seemingly paradoxical character. With this factor identified, it is but a step to the kind of analysis here proposed.

Nor is there anything in Muenzinger's (1948) reply to Wischner or in Wischner's (1948) rejoinder which would contradict the present type of interpretation. However, the phenomenon in question is a complicated one, and the explanation here suggested is, at this point, conjectural, though we have already seen (in the Whiteis experiment, 9) that the assumption that fear can drive rats into the thing feared (shock) as a means of terminating that fear is well founded. Earlier observations on "masochism" (2) are also relevant here, as are some of the findings reported in the concluding sections of this chapter.

II. O'Kelly and Heyer on Water Deprivation, Motivation, and Learning

In an exceptionally well-designed experiment, O'Kelly and Heyer (1948) have shown that the performance of rats in a 12-foot straightaway alley was decidedly better in the case of animals which had undergone 36 hours of water deprivation (Group 36A) than it was in the case of animals which had undergone only 12 hours of deprivation (Group 12A). This finding is in full conformity with common expectation. However, the performance of a third group of animals (Group 36FA) was more remarkable. These animals, having been deprived of water for 36 hours, were given, in the half hour just before being tested, two thirds as much water as was known to be necessary for their satiation. When put into the test alley, these animals appeared to be almost as highly motivated as the 36A animals, although post-test drinking was less than that of even the 12A animals.

The authors describe and interpret their results as follows:

It is important to note that in the case of the 12A and 36A groups, the differing periods of deprivation produced significant differences in performance, the 36-hour animals running significantly faster than the 12-hour animals, and reaching the criterion of learning in 12 trials, whereas the 12-hour group required 16 trials to reach the criterion. It would appear that the usually observed relationship between strength of motivation and speed of performance obtains in our experiment. However, a significant difference also appears between the 36FA group and the 36A. This is a result contrary to what might be expected since a diminution of "tissue need" in the 36FA group did not significantly reduce the efficiency of maze performance (pp. 470–71).

. . . it is to be noted that the 36A animals consumed significantly more water in the reward box [after the test trial] than did *either* the 36FA or the 12A groups. The difference between the 12A and the 36FA animals is significant at the 1 per cent level and demonstrates that the 12A animals consumed *more* water than the 36FA animals in the reward box, yet *less* than the 36A animals. This fact is interesting in the light of the performance scores described above (p. 473).

In the 3-week retention test the 36F group again ran significantly faster than the 12-hour group, but consumed no more water in the reward box. Apparently tissue-need tension at the time of learning is *not* as simply and directly related to habit-fixation as at first seems to be the case. This is further borne out by the comparison between the water consumption of the 12-hour and 36-hour groups on their 3-week retention tests. Here the 12-hour group *ran more slowly* but *drank more*. Thus, although our data do not support Tolman's position with respect to the role of motivation in learning, they also do not lend credence to the assumption of a direct and simple relationship between tissue-need-tension reduction and habit fixation (p. 475).

These results obviously do not substantiate the theoretical position that there is a direct relation between the magnitude of the consummatory response (or need diminution) and habit fixation.

The position taken by Hull (1943, p. 82) that the *termination* of "need-receptor impulse" is the primary reinforcing factor is not congruent with these results. Even though our experiments have demonstrated the significance of the motivational variable, need-reduction has not been proven to be the critical factor. Rather, the deprivation interval itself, irrespective of the local conditions of reward, is the one fact which significantly emerges. This, to use Hull's terminology, would make it appear that the "onset of need-receptor impulse" may possibly be of at least equal importance in habit fixation.

Our results, if verified by subsequent experimentation, would seem to demand a somewhat different theoretical position than those that we have thus far discussed. Any behavior, if it is to have an influence upon later behavior, must exercise this influence through some residual in the behaving organism remaining from the earlier behavior. This *residual* (resulting in the demonstration of habit strength) has been frequently labeled as some sort of "trace." This term has been subject to criticism, but it is, when used in this fashion, as useful as any other term (p. 476).

One of the objects of research in learning is to determine the variables whose mutual interactions constitute the learning trace. Our results appear to indicate the possibility of isolating one of these components, namely, *the interval of deprivation under which previous practices were carried out.* In our experiments the length of water-deprivation during the period of original practice had a clearly measurable influence upon retention performance that was to an extent *independent of the momentary need state at the time of practice, as well as of the number and magnitude of reinforcements.* Indicative of the tracelike character of the deprivation variable is its lessening influence with the passage of time, other factors being equal. The postulation of a "deprivation trace" does not assume, of course, that other factors similar in their manifestations are not also present and contributing in the learning and retention situation (pp. 476–77).

More recent studies by Heyer (1950) have verified the results just described. Using subcutaneous injections of hypertonic saline solution, Heyer has been able to manipulate the "tissue need" for water, *independently of deprivation.* The finding of this investigator which is most immediately relevant is that rats which are relatively suddenly made artificially thirsty in this way do not appear to be as highly "motivated" and do not learn as well as do rats in which thirst naturally develops to the same level (as measured by amount of water required for satiation) over a much longer period of time. Heyer says:

The generalization from these results would seem to be that it is the results of the "time thirsty" rather than the momentary need of the animal which are the relevant motivational variables in influencing acquisition and retention. This is the same generalization arrived at in quite a different way in the straightaway experiment of O'Kelly and Heyer. In that experiment, when the momentary need state was reduced by the predrink method, the animals' performance in learning and relearning was similar to the group with the same deprivation (or time thirsty) but no predrinking, and better than that of animals with objectively the same momentary need state. In the present experiments the momentary need state was increased without altering deprivation time with the result that the animals once more behaved in terms of a manner appropriate to the deprivation time rather than the momentary need state (p. 67).

It will be recalled that Hunt (1941) has shown that chronic food deprivation in young rats results in an increased tendency for these animals to hoard food when later tested under conditions of full satiation. Hunt's explanation of these results is that the food deprivation acts as a kind of trauma, producing hunger anxiety even in the absence of hunger. Although this interpretation has been questioned—see, for example, Miller and Postman (1946) and Morgan (1947)—a strictly analogous hypothesis provides an eminently satisfactory explanation of the O'Kelly-Heyer results. In order to account for their findings, all one needs to do is to assume (see part III of this paper) that, as living organisms experience primary drives such as hunger or thirst, they develop an emotional component which may be called drive-fear, i.e., fear or apprehension of the pain which will be experienced if the primary drive continues unabated or increases. In the O'Kelly-Heyer experiment, we may therefore conjecture that the 36FA animals were only a little less motivated than the 36A animals for the reason that, although their primary drive of thirst had been substantially reduced just before the test run in the alley, their *fear of thirst* had not yet been much diminished, with the result that they were more highly motivated than were the actually thirstier animals which had been without water for only 12 hours, and only a little less highly motivated than the 36-hour deprivation rats which were still fully thirsty, and thirst-frightened.

Although O'Kelly and Heyer do not explicitly make this interpretation of their findings, a number of their comments are in accord therewith. They say, for example, that their findings, "to use Hull's terminology, would make it appear that the 'onset of need-receptor impulse' may possibly be of at least equal importance in habit fixation" (p. 476). The reference here is obviously to Hull's statement of the "law of primary reinforcement" which these authors have previously quoted, to wit:

Whenever a reaction (*R*) takes place in temporal contiguity with an afferent receptor impulse (*s*) resulting from the impact upon a receptor of a stimulus energy (*S*), and this conjunction is followed closely by the diminution in a need (and the associated diminution in the drive, *D*, and in the drive receptor discharge, s_D), there will result an increment . . . in the tendency for that stimulus on subsequent occasions to evoke that reaction (Hull, 1934, p. 71).

What O'Kelly and Heyer are here doing, in effect, is questioning the adequacy of a monistic conception of learning; while acknowledging the reality of effect learning, they are also pointing to the importance of pure conditioning, or contiguity learning. Hence their reference to the "onset of need-receptor impulse" (9, 10). They seem to recognize the *punishing* nature of drives and to be assuming, at least tacitly, that the stimuli associated with such punishment, or deprivation, will have a tendency to reactivate fear in the absence of the primary drive or pain itself. It is also implicit in their argument that a low intensity of drive can have sign value and can cue off the emotional reactions previously elicited only by the high drive intensity.

A further justification for this kind of thinking is the remark of O'Kelly and Heyer about the "lessening influence with the passage of time, other factors being equal" of the residual, or trace, effects of deprivation. We know, of course, that fears tend to extinguish "with the passage of time, other factors being equal"; the empirical results obtained by these investigators on their retention tests are fully in accord with what would be expected if the deprivation of their experimental subjects served not only to make them *thirsty but also afraid:* their thirst could be alleviated with water, but only time would erase the fears which had been set up by the deprivation-produced pain.

III. Estes on "Generalization of Secondary Reinforcement from the Primary Drive"

The growing interest during the past ten years on the part of psychologists in secondary motivation and reinforcement will, one may predict, prove to have been a profoundly important development. Already there are clear indications of its value in integrating, for example, clinical and social psychology with laboratory learning theory. And I believe its importance will be increasingly manifest in other ways (cf. Hilgard, 1949).

Professor Estes' study (1949) therefore falls in a stream of inquiry which deserves the most careful attention and critical analysis. His study is particularly noteworthy for its originality and methodological neatness, but it is misleading in the matter of interpretation.

The problem which was here under investigation is stated by the author as follows:

> Many investigators have demonstrated that a stimulus which repeatedly accompanies the presentation of a primary reinforcing agent (in most cases food) to an organism will subsequently exert a reinforcing effect upon behavior occurring in the same situation *under the same motivating conditions.* The stimulus is said to have become a secondary reinforcer, or secondary reward. . . . This use of the concept needs, however, to be supported by experimental determinations of the extent to which a secondary reinforcer will be effective *under conditions differing from those of original conditioning* (p. 286, italics added).

In essence, Estes' results consist of the finding that an initially neutral stimulus which has been associated (in laboratory rats) with marked thirst reduction will subsequently reinforce a Skinner bar-pressing response when the subjects are no longer thirsty, but are now motivated instead by hunger (but not rewarded by food). Under the particular conditions employed by Estes, the reinforcing effect of the secondary stimulus under test conditions was somewhat *less* when the primary drive was changed than when (in the control groups) it was kept the same; but the effectiveness of the secondary stimulus was still impressive when the prevailing drive was quite different during test conditions from what it had been during the conditions under which the secondary stimulus initially acquired its reinforcing properties.

Estes' study seems empirically sound, and it is conservatively interpreted statistically. It is rather his theoretical position and the interpretation of his findings that invite critical comment.

Fundamentally, my disagreement with Professor Estes is a very simple one. He concludes his paper with this sentence:

> It is suggested that since the effectiveness of a secondary reinforcer clearly is not specific to the original drive, it will not be profitable to define the concept of reinforcement in terms of drive reduction (p. 294).

I am not yet fully convinced that all there is to secondary reinforcement is reduction in a secondary drive such as fear or an appetite. But Professor Estes fails to make the case *against* such a conception in terms that I can find convincing.

There is a line of thought, completely consistent with the reported findings, which the author has neglected. Growing evidence indicates that when an organism is subjected to strong primary drive, there is commonly added to this the secondary motive of *anticipated continuation of the primary drive.* In a paper which reports experimental evidence for this view (17, see also Section II above), I have given the following example:

> One of the commonest yet most dramatic illustrations of this phenomenon is the relief experienced when a physician is consulted. One is ill and suffering from pain and inconvenience. The physician arrives, diagnoses the difficulty, prescribes treatment, and intimates that in a day or two one will be quite hale again. It is unlikely that the examination or the ensuing exchange of words has altered the physical condition of the patient in the least; yet he is likely to "feel a lot better" as a result of the doctor's call. What obviously happens in such instances is that initially the patient's physical suffering is complicated by concern lest his suffering continue indefinitely or perhaps grow worse. After a reassuring diagnosis, this concern abates; and if, subsequently, the same ailment recurs, one can predict that it will arouse less apprehension than it did originally (provided, of course, that the physician's reassurances were valid and his treatment effective) (pp. 472–73).

Applying this same logic to Estes' experiment, we posit that the stimulus which was associated with thirst reduction acquired its reinforcing capacity in the sense that, when subsequently presented, it served as a "promise": since the stimulus, in the past, had been followed by thirst reduction, the "expectation" was established that it would continue to have this significance, thus serving to reduce the subject's fear of continued water-deprivation. Said otherwise, a stimulus which betokens primary drive reduction, but does not actually produce it, may nevertheless produce a reduction in a concomitant secondary drive and thus provide conditions for, often quite powerful, "secondary reinforcement."

The nice feature of the Estes experiment is, of course, the very fact that it shows that secondary reinforcement operated in subjects when fully satiated as far as the thirst drive was concerned. Thus, if there was no thirst, there was presumably *no fear of continued thirst.* Yet the secondary stimulus obviously had reinforcing effects!

This apparent dilemma is readily resolved in a way which is not only plausible but which is empirically supported by Estes' own data. It will be remembered that the subjects which were tested when satiated with water were strongly motivated by *hunger.* Thus, although there was no fear of thirst in them, there was, presumably, now *fear of hunger instead.* It is by no means far-fetched to assume that a stimulus which has become capable of reducing thirst fear will also be capable, through generalization, of likewise reducing hunger fear. Granted these inferences, there is nothing inexplicable about the fact that a stimulus which had previously been associated with thirst reduction was later capable of providing secondary reinforcement, even though the subjects were, at the time, water-satiated.

That drive fear of the kind here posited acted in the Estes experiment as a "mediating response"—thus making possible what the author terms the "transfer" of secondary reinforcement from one condition of primary drive to another—is clearly suggested by the finding that, although the secondary stimulus had a reinforcing effect with water-satiated but hungry rats, this effect was markedly *less* than it was in control groups which were tested when thirsty. This finding is precisely what would be expected on the basis of well-established laws of generalization: since hunger fear is less like thirst fear than is thirst fear, preliminary training with the thirst drive present would be expected to be less effective when later tested with a different primary drive present than with the same one.

On the question of the relative completeness of the "transfer" from the one set of circumstances to the other, Estes has this to say:

> In the absence of any entirely satisfactory method of equating different drives, no definite answer can be given to the question whether the transfer of secondary reinforcing effects from thirst to hunger is complete. In the present experiments, with the two drives equated only in terms of deprivation time, the transfer groups have consistently yielded in the neighborhood of 25 per cent fewer responses during the test periods than the controls. With the animals under 22 hours' deprivation in each case, however, the thirst drive is probably nearer to maximum. Thus it is very probable that conditions could be arranged under which the differences between transfer and control groups observed in these studies could be eliminated or even reversed (p. 292).

The author is correct in indicating that in his study the hunger drive and the thirst drive were not empirically equated. He is probably also correct in predicting that by increasing the hunger drive sufficiently in the test period, the secondary-reinforcement stimulus could be made as effective under "transfer" conditions as under the original (thirst drive) conditions, or even more so. But the critical issue is this: How would the secondary-reinforcement stimulus compare in effectiveness under conditions where the thirst and hunger drives are *empirically equal?* My prediction is that there would be a marked decrement under the "transfer" conditions. The fact that Estes *obtained* such a decrement suggests that the levels of hunger and thirst drive which he employed were, in point of fact, roughly the same.

There are lesser points on which one could quibble with Estes' paper, e.g., the inexplicit and misleading way in which he employs the concept of "conditioning." However, the central issue is the one I have indicated. In my opinion, the author has obviously failed to sustain his contention that "it will not be profitable to define the concept of reinforcement in terms of drive reduction."

As indicated elsewhere (9), I do not believe that drive reduction is the *only* form of reinforcement; I am now persuaded that in some cases (i.e., those involving "conditioning," properly speaking) reinforcement is a matter of pure contiguity. But this is not the issue that Professor Estes raises: he is, by implication, suggesting that drive reduction is *never* the essential condition of reinforcement. Neither his results nor his logic seems compelling on this score.

IV. Maier's "Frustration: A Study of Behavior Without a Goal"

A. This (Maier, 1949) is a significant and exciting book. This is not to say that the book has "all the answers" or that this reviewer necessarily agrees with such putative answers as are given. But it raises the *right problems;* and the attempted solutions, whether right or wrong, are original and challenging.

Quite aside from its special content, this book is noteworthy for the fact that it is written by a man who, though primarily an experimental psychologist, is here concerned with *clinical* issues. The approach to these issues is sympathetic and by no means unsophisticated. The book is, indeed, a kind of model, both in terms of its objectives and its methods, for indicating how experimental and clinical psychology can interact, to the benefit and enrichment of both.

The author has picked out for major consideration what the reviewer regards as the absolutely central and most critical issue in clinical theory no less than in practice: It is the question as to why so-called neurotic behavior is at one and the same time *self-defeating and yet self-perpetuating,* instead of self-eliminating. This is the dilemma which prompted some of Freud's most brilliant speculations; and it is an issue which every serious student in the field must face. Maier attempts to deal with it as follows.

In ordinary trial-and-error learning, says the author, new responses are acquired or old ones eliminated on the basis of their *consequences.* But in other instances, responses persist despite continuously unfavorable consequences. Such an instance Maier and his students have been able to produce experimentally in rats by exposing them to discrimination problems, on a Lashley jumping stand, which are "insoluble." If the problem is soluble, the rats learn to jump to the right or the left on any given trial, according to the nature of the cue stimuli presented on that trial. But if the problem is insoluble, the rats tend to fall into *rigidly fixed patterns,* such as always jumping to the same side.

Maier uses this finding as a basis for postulating that under conditions of *frustration* there is often a breakdown of normal learning and the development of abnormal *fixation.* He thus evolves what might be called the *frustration-fixation hypothesis.* He rejects the Freudian hypothesis that fixated, or "symptomatic," behavior "may serve as a relief for the patient," in favor of the view that once the frustration-fixation mechanism has taken over, the usual principles governing adaptive behavior cease to operate and one sees the occurrence of "behavior without a goal."

The reviewer does not believe that this analysis is satisfactory (cf. Freud's equally *ad hoc* and circular concept, the "repetition compulsion"), but the author does a skilful job of illustrating and defending his thesis, which he states boldly and lucidly.

To many readers the most illuminating part of the book will be chap. viii, in which the author brings his earlier experimental work on reasoning to bear upon contemporary problems in the field of counseling and psychotherapy. Although he largely follows Rogers' analysis of the treatment process, clinical workers of other persuasions will find Maier's discussion of "reasoning as the combination of elements in experience that have not previously been combined" highly suggestive. This part of the book leads to a consideration of some of the most basic issues in the entire field of personality and behavior theory.

B. At an early point Maier differentiates between what happens in a soluble discrimination problem and an insoluble one. He says:[1]

> An animal can readily be trained by this [the Lashley jumping stand] method to develop a preference for one of a pair of cards placed in front of it. The animal expresses its preference by jumping at and striking one of the cards. If the correct card is struck by the animal, the card falls over and the animal lands on a feeding platform where it may eat (reward); if the incorrect card is struck, the card, being securely latched, remains in place and the animal receives a bump on the nose and falls into a net below (punishment).

---

[1] From *Frustration: the study of behavior without a goal* by N. R. F. Maier. Copyright, 1949. Courtesy of McGraw-Hill Book Co., Inc.

When one of the cards is consistently locked and is changed to both the right and left positions on different trials, the animal may be trained to develop a preference for one of the pair of cards so that it consistently chooses the card that leads to reward and avoids the card that leads to punishment, regardless of the side (right or left) on which the reward card is placed. Thus if the black card with the white circle is consistently locked and the white card with the black circle is consistently unlocked the rat learns to choose the latter. The choice of responses is determined by the association of a symbol (appearance of the cards) and the consequence of choices, and responses thus developed will hereafter be called *symbol-reward responses.* This is a common type of selective learning and requires the use of motivation as well as association formation. If the consequences of the choices are reversed, so that the previously rewarded choice is punished and the previously punished choice is rewarded, then we may expect the preference to become reversed. . . .

If, however, the cards are latched in no regular order (i.e., neither a particular card nor a particular position is consistently rewarded or punished), then there is no response that will escape from punishment. In such case the animal normally shows a stage of variability in its choices and soon thereafter it *refuses to jump.* This *resistance to jumping* may be overcome by giving the animal an electric shock at the jumping-stand, prodding with a stick, or blowing a blast of air on it. Under these conditions the animal can be *forced to jump.* We speak of this situation as the *insoluble* or *no-solution problem* and regard it as frustrating both because it is a problem that cannot be solved and because pressure is applied to the animal to force a response. . . .

After a short while in the insoluble problem situation and with pressure applied to force behavior, the animal develops a response to the situation that has *no adaptive value* in the sense that it is adequate to the situation or in the sense that it is superior to any number of other possible responses. Nevertheless, the appearance of the behavior is associated with *a decline in resistance to jumping.* Thus an animal that is forced to respond in the insoluble problem situation may always choose the card on its right, despite the fact that this choice is punished on half the trials. This type of response is not selected by the method with which reward and punishment are used. At the same time it is not a mere random response but is consistently expressed and so must be considered as a response to the situation. . . .

Whether or not such responses differ from the reward-determined responses remains to be demonstrated. If such responses follow the principles of reward learning, then one may assume that the animal is responding to some goal that is not under the experimenters' control. If such responses follow different principles, however, they must be studied as separate phenomena (pp. 25–28, italics added).

On the basis of a large number and variety of experiments, Maier concludes that the behavior resulting from the frustration-fixation sequence is qualitatively different from that governed by the ordinary principles of learning. Thus, he says: [2]

> . . . behavior resulting from frustration is different in kind from that produced by selective reward and punishment training. When the frustration threshold is exceeded, increments of fixation are produced that impose a degree of rigidity upon certain responses and so interfere with learning that demands a response in terms of goals (p. 76).

The plausibility of Maier's analysis is impressive, at least up to a point. Clinical experience clearly indicates that those persons who are known as "neurotic" are individuals who, at an earlier period (notably childhood), have faced conflict situations which to them seemed "insoluble." Under the stress of such situations, they adopt the strategy of conflict resolution through dissociation (or repression) and thus prepare the ground for the sequence of events which we call neurosis. A prominent part of the neurotic picture is that of behavior which is rigid, compulsive, inflexible, seemingly pointless, "without a goal." Maier presented his rats with insoluble problems and got behavior which can be so characterized. What, then, would seem more natural than to assume that he has here isolated the essential features of neurosis?

There are later parts of Maier's book that any clinician will find enlightening; but the same can hardly be said for the first part of the book. Here one encounters what would appear to be a neglect of certain relevant variables and a tendency on the part of the author to emerge with something like an animal parallel of neurosis rather than with a precise analysis of the experimental facts. Fortunately, the later, and most stimulating, parts of the book depend more upon the author's work on "reasoning" than upon his experiments on and thinking about the frustration-fixation sequence.

Let us return to the passages already quoted. We see, first of all, that when a rat is faced with an "insoluble" problem situation, i.e., a situation in which the rat gets punished about half of the time no matter which way it jumps, it "shows a stage of variability in its choices and soon therefore it *refuses to jump.*" The rat, in other words, "leaves the field": because the punishments (bumps on the nose and falls) so greatly outweigh the rewards (opportunities to eat), the animal abandons the problem. The situation is now so negative that, as Maier indicates, rats will sometimes starve rather than continue to try to deal with it (p. 72).

---

[2] From *Frustration: the study of behavior without a goal* by N. R. F. Maier. Copyright, 1949. Courtesy of McGraw-Hill Book Co., Inc.

Fixated, or "neurotic," behavior appears only if the rat can be forced to respond in a situation that is so punishing that responding, even under starvation hunger, has been inhibited. This is done by setting up counter punishment—in the form of "an electric shock . . . prodding . . . a blast of air"—which is directed toward the opposite behavior of *not jumping*. According to Maier, the intensity of the "frustration" experienced by the rat is now stepped up, the frustration "threshold" is exceeded, and one gets behavior—namely, "abnormal fixation"—which transcends the ordinary principles of learning.

Before conceding that this interpretation is justified, we should recall the experiment by Whiteis, reported in an earlier study (9). Here, it will be remembered, rats are put into an alleyway about 4 feet long, with the starting point at the left end and a doorway leading into a safety box at the right end. If the right half of the floor grill is kept electrified, it is no trick to keep the animals off it and in the left half of the alley. But if, shortly after the rat is put into the alley at the left end, that half of the alley is *also electrified,* the rat will run onto the right half of the grill and into the safety box. Moreover, after a few repetitions of this sequence, the rat will soon reach the point that it dashes from the left half of the alley, across the electrified right half of the floor grill and into the safety box, without the administration of shock on the left half of the floor grill. And, once this type of behavior is set up, it may *persist indefinitely.*

In Maier's terms, the rat's frustration threshold is exceeded by virtue of the rat's being exposed to the conflict generated by punishment-if-it-runs and punishment-if-it-doesn't-run; and the running response that develops and persists, despite regular punishment from the right half of the grill, would constitute an "abnormal fixation." As already indicated, this kind of behavior can be quite satisfactorily accounted for in terms of familiar learning principles; and such principles seem equally capable of accounting for the behavior observed in Maier's type of experiment. All one has to do, essentially, is to assume (*a*) that the pain and fear experienced on the jumping stand is greater than that experienced as a result of jumping and (*b*) that the net gain in comfort thus obtained reinforces the jumping response.

This alternative interpretation of the results has evidently occurred to Maier, but he dismisses it on what seem to this writer entirely inadequate grounds. Maier says:

These findings suggest that the abnormal fixation gives the animal a way of responding to insoluble problem situations—a way without which such situations would have remained highly stressful. It must not be supposed, however, that this adjustment value of fixations is a factor in determining the appearance of fixations. Any adjustment accomplished must be regarded as purely incidental and not as a factor that contributes to the development of fixations. This conclusion is supported by the fact that seizure-prone animals are no more likely to develop fixations than stable animals (p. 53).

Patton (1947) has reported that seizures of the kind here alluded to are highly correlated with the presence of middle-ear infection. This finding is substantiated by a more recent study by Kenshalo and Kryter (1949), who conservatively conclude:

The mean percentage for [seizure] susceptible rats with both ears infected was 81.5; for those infected in one ear 50.7; and for those free of infection 36.3. Only the difference between the first and the third is statistically significant.

Apparently, more than half of the albino and hooded laboratory rats suffer from middle-ear infection, and the presence of infection is a factor that must be considered in all experiments in which seizures of the type called sound-induced or "neurotic" is the behavior pattern under investigation (p. 331).

Kenshalo and Kryter used "a 'white' sound field" to test for seizures in their subjects; and Maier finds that the "air blast" (closely approximating "white sound") which he used in his experiments is far more likely to produce seizures than any of the other punishments. At the present time, it would therefore appear that all inferences about psychological conflict derived from the incidence of seizures are of little cogency.

The fact that Maier has observed that "the appearance of the [stereotyped] behavior is associated with a decline in resistance to jumping" (p. 27) is in accord with what would be expected on the basis of a learning-theory analysis of this behavior: after the punishment-for-not-jumping has been applied a few times, the fear generated by the punishment-for-jumping would begin to *generalize back* to the jumping stand, and the rat would have to be *externally forced* to jump less frequently than was necessary before *both* jumping and not-jumping became associated with fear. In keeping with the results of the Whiteis experiment, one might even predict that by a proper arrangement of the variables in the Maier situation, a rat could be *kept jumping* solely on the basis of the fear generated by and generalizing from the punishment connected with jumping. However, as found by Whiteis, this type of effect is dependent upon the ease with which generalization can occur; and it may be that the Maier situation is such that direct (nongeneralized) reinforcement of the fear-of-not-jumping would be at least occasionally necessary.

Maier makes a good deal of the point that the behavior of his fixated animals had no "goal," and he uses this as one of the chief criteria for distinguishing between normal behavior—which always has a "goal"—and behavior which is due to frustration-fixation. This distinction seems to rest upon a lack of proper recognition of the change in the nature of the animal's "problem" as he passes from the "normal" to the "abnormal" type of behavior. As long as the animal's behavior is in large measure dominated by hunger and the prospect of getting food, it is rather obviously goal-oriented: you see the food and you see the animal trying to get to it. However, when the problem of fear becomes so intensified that the hunger drive is dwarfed into insignificance, and when the animal then shows behavior which is no longer directed toward food, it is easy—but hardly justified—to assume that the usual principles of behavior have been suddenly abrogated.

In the one case we are dealing with hunger as a dominant motive, and it requires for its reduction objective substances called food. In the other case we are dealing with fear as the dominant motive, and it requires for its reduction merely that the rat *get off the jumping stand,* even though this involve taking a momentary discomfort (bump on the nose). The fact that the rat is not "going after" anything in this situation which is comparable to what the rat goes after when hunger-dominated is a difference in detail, not in principle. The important consideration is that in both cases the animals are trying to get rid of something—their hunger in the one case, their fear in the other. In this more fundamental sense, the animals in the one case cannot be said to be either more or less "goal-oriented" than in the other.

The only question which Maier's results leave unanswered is why Maier's subjects show less behavior variation when fear-dominated than when hunger-dominated—and this question is not a new one. Several investigations which will be cited in a later study (13) have indicated that living organisms behave less freely, less flexibly when being subjected to punishment than when operating solely under the influence of reward. More recently Farber (1948) has made a special study of this phenomenon, but he does not find anything in his results which he feels compel him to go beyond the established laws of ordinary learning.

PART II
PERSONALITY DYNAMICS

CHAPTER 13

AN EXPERIMENTAL ANALOGUE OF "REGRESSION" WITH INCIDENTAL OBSERVATIONS ON "REACTION FORMATION"

[This paper represents an attempt to "translate" two psychoanalytic concepts in terms of learning theory, and to exemplify them experimentally. Because this paper was written at a time when the author was more of a "behaviorist" than he now is, there is a tendency to emphasize "habit dynamics," i.e., interrelationships between and changes in *overt* response tendencies, with a corresponding neglect of attitudinal changes, or emotional learning. Cognizance is nevertheless taken of the role of fear, and the basic logic of the paper would not be significantly different if it were rewritten with a two-factor conception of learning in mind.

When this paper was originally published, the writer was also more of a "Freudian" than he now is. Here the assumption was uncritically accepted that neurosis arises when the adult route to sexual gratification is blocked ("frustrated") and the individual reverts to earlier modes of sexual adjustment ("fixations"). Because parental disapproval and punishment have been used to dislodge the child from his infantile libidinal (perverse) positions, return to these positions is fraught with a subjective sense of danger. Symptoms emerge, according to Freudian theory, because of the conflict and anxiety thus experienced.

It is true that the experiment here reported provides a rough (nonsexual) analogue of regression as Freud conceived it and, incidentally, an example of reaction formation. But growing experience as a psychotherapist has convinced me of the unsoundness of Freud's position in this connection. "Neurotic" individuals do not seem to be suffering so much from regression as from *immaturities* which they have never surmounted. They are, in other words, individuals who are *developmentally fixated;* but the fixation is not, as Freud supposed, libidinal, save incidentally; it can be more correctly described as "moral." Neurotic persons nearly always report, eventually, childhood or adolescent experiences of a perverse, "shameful" character; but it is not the experience as such that has contributed to their neurosis; it is rather the fact that they have *persisted* in a strategy of secrecy, deception, and dissociation with respect to such experiences (which many "normal" children have also had but have successfully "put behind them," by following a policy of greater forthrightness and fuller communication). In this important sense we regularly find that neurotic difficulties are less a product of the individual's "past" than of the *present.* It is what the individual is and does, here and now, that dooms him to neurotic suffering. His "childhood" is important only to the extent that it is *still with him.*

The issues raised by these introductory comments and by the paper which follows should be reconsidered in the context of later studies (especially 15, 16, 18–21).

The present paper was first published, in 1940, in *The Journal of Abnormal and Social Psychology.*]

I. Fixation, Frustration, and Regression

Two extremely interesting experimental demonstrations of "regression" in the rat have already been published (Hamilton and Krechevsky, 1933; Sanders, 1937), and it may therefore seem unnecessary to report another instance of this same phenomenon. On the basis of evidence already available, there can be scarcely any question of the reality of regression in human beings,[1] or, as the two studies just cited show, of the possibility of its occurrence in animals well below man in the evolutionary scale. Since neither of these studies, however, was apparently conducted with an altogether satisfactory understanding of the theory of regression as it has been developed clinically, they have served in certain respects to obscure rather than to clarify the fundamental nature of regression and the conditions of its occurrence. The present study represents an attempt to eliminate some of this ambiguity. Although animal experimentation along these and related lines may eventually have something new and useful to contribute to human psychopathology, that day apparently still lies in the future. In the meantime, it would seem to behoove those who look forward to making such contributions to acquire the greatest possible familiarity with those theories and principles that have already been derived from careful clinical inquiry at the human level. If clinical concepts are to be taken over and applied carelessly in animal experiments, the results obtained can be expected to be correspondingly confused and meaningless.

Since regression is pre-eminently a psychoanalytic concept and since no one has superseded Freud as a theorist in this field, it is appropriate to turn to him for an authoritative statement of this principle. This writer, it so happens, is not a formal systematist, and it is accordingly necessary to extract his purely theoretical

---

[1] Wells (1916, 1935) and Taylor (1926) have published excellent summaries of the literature on regression in human beings.

views, piecemeal as it were, from the context of his extensive clinical and popular writings. This is not to say, however, that his theoretical formulations are inexplicit, contradictory, or any less comprehensive and complete than the limitations of logic and empirical observation necessitate in a new and difficult field of inquiry.

In a technical paper that appeared in 1916, Freud (1916a) introduced the topic of regression as follows:

> When we investigate psychoneurotic conditions, we find in each of them occasion to comment upon a so-called *temporal regression,* i.e., the particular extent to which each of them retraces the stages of its evolution. We distinguish two such regressions—one in the development of the ego and the other in that of the libido. In sleep, the latter is carried to the point of restoring the primitive narcissism, while the former goes back to the state of hallucinatory wish-fulfilment (p. 138).

At a later point in the same article, Freud also distinguished between "the previously mentioned temporal or developmental regression" and what he then termed "topographical regression" (p. 143). In subsequent writings, however, he has made comparatively little use of this latter term, employing instead the term "repression." Writing in 1920, Freud (1920a) said:

> [In the present discussion] we have not been using the word *"regression"* in its general sense but in a quite specific one. If you give it its general sense, that of a reversion from a higher to a lower stage of development in general, then repression also ranges itself under regression; for repression can also be described as reversion to an earlier and lower stage in the development of a mental act. Only, in repression this retrogressive direction is not a point of any moment to us; for we also call it repression in a dynamic sense when a mental process is arrested before it leaves the lower stages of the unconscious. Repression is thus a topographic-dynamic conception, while regression is a purely descriptive one (pp. 299–300).

As is well known, Freud worked out most of his psychological principles on the basis of observations concerning the sex life of neurotic human beings, but, as in the case of regression, many of his findings have a much wider application. Consequently, it is understandable why it should be in this setting that one finds Freud's most trenchant formulations regarding regression, which, however, because of the dynamic character of all psychoanalytic concepts, are necessarily intertwined with other principles which must also be given at least incidental consideration.

In a paper that appeared in 1912, Freud presented a detailed statement of his conception of regression in the etiology of neurotic illness and posited that its occurrence or nonoccurrence is primarily contingent upon two factors: (*a*) *fixation* and (*b*) *frustration.* According to the view developed at that time and subsequently held with relatively little modification, the erotic life (libido) of civilized human beings passes through several more or less discrete stages in its development from the so-called narcissism of infancy to the genital heterosexuality of normal adult life. Because of the continuing pressure of the socializing and educational forces in modern society (plus the changing needs of the child, produced by physical maturation), each of the intermediate stages is successively achieved and then abandoned for the next higher level of adjustment, until the final adult goal is reached. If, however, for any of several possible reasons, this developmental process does not go forward in the usual way and the individual never advances beyond one of the intermediate stages, there results what may be called *absolute* fixation. This is a phenomenon that actually occurs in the lives of some persons and is assumed to provide the basis for the sexual perversions. But since there is here no question of a *return* from a later to an earlier mode of adjustment, the problem of regression is not, of course, involved.

On the other hand, in the lives of persons who do make the prescribed step-by-step transitions in their sexual development (however falteringly), the habits that are acquired and reinforced at each successive stage necessarily have a certain strength or intensity (cathexis) that is more or less enduring; and it is the varying strength of such habits that determines the extent to which *relative* fixation may be said to have occurred at any given point. This phenomenon, in contradistinction to absolute fixation,[2] is of special significance for the understanding of the mechanism of regression; for it is presumably the specific nature and extent of the relative fixations in an individual's life history which determine the pattern of regression ("choice of neurosis") [3] that will occur if, subsequently, a superimposed mode of adjustment or habit system meets with an insuperable obstacle (i.e., if *frustration* occurs) and if there is relatively little opportunity for further *progression* (i.e., for the development of still other new habits). In other words, the greater the strength of a relative fixation, other things equal, the greater

---

[2] Freud holds that, although sharply distinguishable at the conceptual level, there is in actual practice a continuum between absolute and relative fixations. He says: "There exist, therefore, two extremes—'inhibited development' and 'regression'—and between them every degree of combination of the two factors" (1920a, p. 318). (It should be noted, incidentally, that *absolute* and *relative fixation* are not Freudian terms, but their introduction seems warranted as an aid to clear theoretical exposition.)

[3] Cf. Freud's paper entitled "Types of neurotic nosogenesis" (1912).

the tendency for regression to occur to the level of that fixation when subsequently acquired habits (in the same impulse-need system) are thwarted, punished, or otherwise prevented from functioning effectively and bringing the customary satisfaction.

Of the various passages in which Freud has described the principle of regression, perhaps none is more vivid or instructive than the following, which, for additional reasons that will later become evident, is worth quoting in full:

> The second danger [besides that of absolute fixation] in a development by stages such as [that of the libido] we call *regression;* it also happens that those portions which have proceeded further may easily revert in a backward direction to these earlier stages. The impulse will find occasion to *regress* in this way when the exercise of its function in a later and more developed form meets with powerful external obstacles, which thus prevent it from attaining the goal of satisfaction. It is a short step to assume that fixation and regression are not independent of each other; the stronger the fixations in the path of development the more easily will the function yield before the external obstacles, by regressing on to those fixations; that is, the less capable of resistance against the external difficulties in its path will the developed function be. If you think of a migrating people who have left large numbers at the stopping-places on their way, you will see that the foremost will naturally fall back upon these positions when they are defeated or when they meet with an enemy too strong for them. And again, the more of their number they leave behind in their progress, the sooner will they be in danger of defeat (1920a, pp. 298–99).

The writer goes on to say that a clear conception of the relation between fixation and regression is fundamental to the understanding of the psychoanalytic theory of the neurosis, for, as already indicated, regression or a tendency to regression is assumed to lie at the basis of all symptom formation. When, under the stress of a need that has been denied its customary form of gratification, regression occurs or is in danger of occurring, anticipation of the penalties that were originally effective in bringing about the required habit progression to this particular level of gratification is, according to psychoanalytic theory, sure to be reactivated;[4] and it is precisely this reactivation of old anticipations of punishment which provides the anxiety that is so constant and so conspicuous a feature of every neurosis. It is for this reason that regression is so likely to be pathogenic. In this connection, Freud says:

---

[4] The connection between punishment (or threat of punishment) and education (habit progression) has been discussed at length in a previous publication (Mowrer, 1938d). It is here taken for granted and will be given only incidental consideration in the subsequent pages of this paper.

I think that you will be soonest reconciled to this exposition of fixation and regression of the libido if you will regard it as preparatory to a study of *aetiology* of the neuroses. . . . People fall ill of a neurosis when the possibility of satisfaction for the libido is removed from them—they fall ill in consequence of a "frustration," as I called it. . . . This of course does not mean that every frustration in regard to libidinal satisfaction makes everyone who meets with it neurotic, but merely that in all cases of neurosis investigated the factor of frustration was demonstrated (1920a, p. 301).

The libido is [thus] blocked, as it were, and must seek an escape by which it can find an outlet for its cathexis (charge of energy) in conformity with the demands of the pleasure principle: it must elude, eschew the ego. The fixations upon the path of development now regressively transversed . . . offer just such an escape. In streaming backward and re-"cathecting" these repressed [abandoned] positions, the libido withdraws itself from the ego and its laws; but it also abandons all the training acquired under the influence of the ego. It was docile as long as satisfaction was in sight; under the double pressure of external and internal frustration it becomes intractable and harks back to former happier days (1920a, p. 314).

You see that this escape of the libido under the conditions of conflict [frustration] is rendered possible by the existence of fixations. The regressive cathexis (with libido) of those fixations leads to a circumventing of the repressions [inhibiting anxieties] and to a discharge—or a satisfaction—of the libido, in which the conditions of a compromise have nevertheless to be maintained. By this detour through the unconscious and the old fixations the libido finally succeeds in attaining to a real satisfaction, though the satisfaction is certainly of an exceedingly restricted kind and hardly recognizable as such (1920a, p. 315).

In thus retrogressively resorting to earlier modes of gratification, the individual, however, commonly re-encounters *old* anxieties; and it is the coexistence of *both* pain- and pleasure-giving functions in the symptomatic acts of the psychoneuroses that gives them much of their apparent mystery, unintelligibility, and tenacity. The paradox is rendered all the more dramatic by the fact that the individual in whom old sources of pleasure are being reactivated is likely to know nothing, consciously, of this aspect of the process and to experience only the painful component. As Freud says, "the person concerned is unaware of the satisfaction and perceives this that we call satisfaction much more as suffering, and complains of it" (1920a, p. 319).

Taken, then, in its most general, abstract form, regression—or, to use a somewhat more descriptive term, habit regression—is a relatively simple concept. As the preceding discussion shows, it is merely the converse of habit *progression,* which may be defined as the development of a new mode of need gratification as a consequence of disruption of or interference with a previously established mode of adjustment. If, after habit progression has occurred, the more recently acquired mode of adjustment is in turn disrupted, one of two results may be expected: (*a*) still further habit progression or (*b*) return to an earlier mode of adjustment, i.e., habit *regression.*

In contrast to its conceptual simplicity, regression as it actually occurs in the case of any given human being is likely to be a relatively complicated affair. First of all, the behavior that appears when a given level of adjustment is regressed to is almost never exactly the same as the behavior that occurred previously, before this level of adjustment was abandoned. Changes in physical size and appearance, altered status in the community or family, acquisition or loss of habits not directly affected by the regression, rearousal of anxieties that were used to produce habit progression, and a number of other factors may so confuse any given instance of regression as to render it almost unrecognizable as such. Yet another complication arises from the fact that in many cases neurotic symptoms appear, not because regression has actually occurred, but because it is merely in danger of occurring. Finally, regression at the human level is not something that ordinarily transpires before the eyes of the clinical observer but has to be reconstructed on the basis of the testimony of the affected individual or of other persons.

From the point of view of exemplifying the concept of regression and of giving it objective specificity, it is, therefore, a real advantage to be able to produce instances of this phenomenon under the controlled and reproducible conditions of the laboratory. Beginnings have been made in the study of experimentally induced regression in children (Barker, Dembo, Lewin, 1937), but such work, whether with children or adults, has severe limitations.[5] Animals can, of course, be much more freely manipulated and modified from the point of view of their basic behavior in an experimental setting than can human beings, and their use in this connection is clearly indicated. At the present stage, however, the usefulness of animals in such research is probably mainly pedagogical, in the sense that it provides a more general opportunity for first-hand contact with clinically discovered phenomena than does the clinic itself and supplies paradigms that may be especially useful as aids to the clearer conceptualization of the psychological principles involved. Special care should apparently be exercised at present not to interpret such experimentation as constituting "tests" of the

[5] Cf. studies by Hovland and Sears (1938), and Siipola (1938) on "habit reversions" in conflict situations.

validity of the concept of regression, or of any other psychological principle derived from clinical investigation at the human level. If comparable findings are obtained in animals lower than man, a certain presumption is established in favor of the validity of the observations at the human level; but, on the other hand, failure to obtain comparable findings does not demonstrate the invalidity of the human observations. It is, therefore, as an "analogue" of human regression that the animal behavior reported in the next section is presented and not as a rigorous, experimental attempt to determine whether the theory of regression, as developed psychoanalytically, is "true or false."

II. An Experimental Analogue of Regression

During the course of an investigation undertaken for a different purpose, it was discovered that by slightly altering conditions, something analogous to human regression could be produced in the white rat. The apparatus being employed at that time and later taken over without modification for the present study, consisted of a box-like compartment, 5 x 10 x 36 inches, the front side of which was made of glass, with the floor consisting of a grill of transverse stainless steel rods (0.084 inch in diameter), spaced ⅜ inch apart. The top was hinged so as to act as a door through which rats could be put into and taken out of the apparatus. At the right-hand end of the compartment thus formed was a brass pedal, 2 x 4 inches, hinged at the bottom and normally held in a vertical position by a spring attached to an arm that extended horizontally in the rear. This arm made an electrical contact that was broken whenever the pedal, which moved very easily, was pressed. By means of a 5,000-ohm, wire-wound potentiometer, the sliding arm of which could be slowly rotated by a constant-speed motor and an electromagnetic clutch arrangement, an alternating current (60 cycles, 115 volts at source) could be impressed on the steel rods forming the grill. This current built up linearly from zero intensity until, at the end of 2.25 minutes, it reached a maximum intensity, after which it remained constant until the pedal was pressed, at which time the potentiometer would reset (due to release of the clutch) and the current on the grill would drop to zero. As soon as the pedal was allowed to return to normal position, the current would again automatically build up.[6]

---

[6] In order to protect the rat from receiving a tetanizing shock in the event of a marked drop in bodily resistance (as, for example, due to its feet becoming moist with urine), a 10,000-ohm fixed resistance was placed in series with the grill and

A

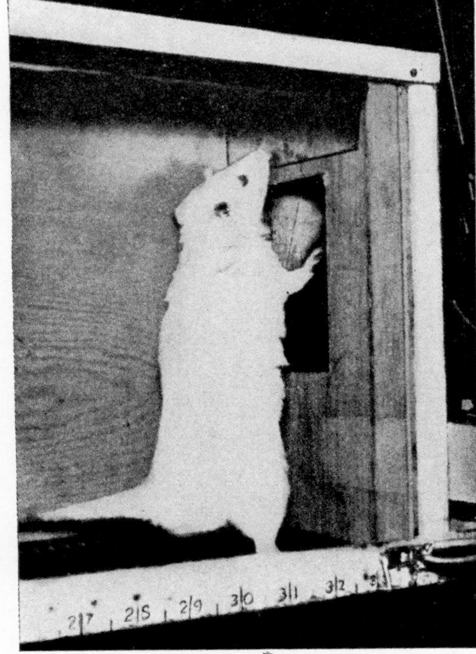

B

Fig. 59.—Two modes of adjustment to a common stimulus situation (electric charge on grill): habit *A* and habit *B*. Habit *A* consists of sitting quietly on the hind legs, which has the effect of diminishing the subjective intensity of the shock. Habit *B* consists of pressing a pedal that causes the charge on the grill to drop to zero.

When a rat (never before subjected to shock) was placed in this apparatus for the first time and the alternating current was allowed to build up, there was usually an initial period of about 60 seconds during which the shock appeared to be subliminal. There then appeared minor signs of agitation, such as sniffing at the grill, lifting of individual feet, "sitting up," moving the head to and fro, and so forth. As the current became stronger, the agitation became progressively more violent, culminating in jumping, squealing, biting at the grill, clawing at the walls, and random running about. Under these circumstances the average rat would, through chance, hit the pedal and thereby turn off the shock within 3 to 6 minutes after its onset. This first, wholly fortuitous escape from shock created a noticeable tendency for the animal to stay at the pedal end of the apparatus; and when the shock next became liminal,[7] the resulting agitation consequently occurred primarily in this vicinity. On the second trial, the animal usually hit the pedal within 2 to 4 minutes and very commonly "froze" as soon as it did so, in precisely the position that it happened to be in at the instant when the shock went off (reminding one of the game of "Statue" played by children). On the third presentation of the shock, the amount of random movement that occurred before the pedal was pressed and the shock terminated was relatively limited. Learning, in other words, was fairly precipitous. By the time an animal had had 10 presentations of shock, random agitation had virtually disappeared and the pedal-pressing reaction had become prompt and specific. The position typically assumed by the rat in pressing the pedal is shown in Figure 59*B*. Between trials, after the pedal habit was well established, the rat would usually sit (often on its haunches facing the pedal) in a position that was expeditious for making the next pedal reaction.

In the early stages of learning, escape from shock by pressing the pedal would often be immediately followed by several additional, highly energetic repetitions of this act, not infrequently accompanied by biting of the metal frame surrounding the pedal. This behavior naturally delayed the shock from building up again.

---

the leads from the potentiometer. The strength of the current impressed on the grill when the motor-driven potentiometer was at maximum setting was adjustable by means of a second (manually operated) potentiometer of the same specifications, in tandem with the first, which, however, was set so as to give the type of behavior described in the following paragraph and was not changed during the course of the present study.

[7] On the second and for a few subsequent presentations of the shock, the limen seemed to be considerably lowered, agitated behavior being observable as soon as 30 to 40 seconds after the current started to build up. This "sensitization" effect has been studied quantitatively and will be discussed separately.

Reactions that seemed to be definitely anticipatory also occurred occasionally, some seconds after the last pedal reaction was made but before the shock had again actually become liminal (as judged by other behavior). These reactions likewise caused the shock-presenting apparatus to reset at zero, but they were not counted as learning trials. In order for a reaction to count as a trial, a minimum of 30 seconds had to elapse between reactions.

In the present study, 5 Wistar albino male rats, six months old and experimentally naïve, were subjected to 10 learning trials daily for 3 successive days under the conditions just described. These animals will be referred to collectively as the Control Group and designated individually as C_1, C_2, C_3, C_4, and C_5. Complete records of learning performance were kept for each of these rats, but they are of no special relevance here and need not be reproduced.

Five comparable animals, constituting the Experimental Group (E_1, E_2, E_3, E_4, and E_5), instead of being treated as were the members of the Control Group, were first submitted to the following procedure. On each of 6 successive days they were put individually into the apparatus, with the shock-terminating pedal covered with a metal curtain. The shock was then allowed to build up to maximum intensity and remain there for 15 minutes. At the end of this time the shock was turned off by the experimenter and the rat removed from the apparatus. Under these conditions all the animals discovered that if they sat quietly on their hind legs, holding their fore-paws well above the grill, they received comparatively little shock.[8] The result was that after 2 or 3 15-minute sessions in the apparatus, the rats would take this position as soon as the shock became sensible and would maintain it, with only occasional interludes of random activity, until the shock was turned off. This reaction of sitting quietly on the hind legs in order to lessen (though not entirely escape) the shock will be designated as Habit *A,* in contrast to the pedal-pressing reaction, which will be designated as Habit *B.*

On the day following the 6 days of training in Habit *A,* the animals in the Experimental Group were put into the apparatus, with the metal curtain removed, and the pedal therefore made available to them for the first time. Within 10 minutes or less time

---

[8] The relatively low voltage of the current made this effect possible. If a much higher voltage had been used, such that the total amount of current flowing through the rat would have remained approximately constant regardless of changes in the rat's resistance, then the smaller the area of contact with the grill the greater the concentration, or density, of current in the affected areas and the greater the subjective intensity of the shock. Under the latter conditions, sitting on the hind legs would have been more, instead of less, painful than crouching on all fours.

some of the animals showed enough random activity to result in their pressing the pedal. But some of the animals persisted in Habit *A* so consistently that they did not press the bar in this length of time and had to have their toes pinched slightly by means of a slender rod that was inserted below the grill, in order to break up the Habit *A* type of adjustment and bring about a renewal of random activity. In this way all the animals in the Experimental Group were eventually made to press the pedal, after which Habit *B* (the pedal habit) was learned fairly rapidly, though not so rapidly as it had been learned by the Control Group. This difference was obviously due to the lingering tendency on the part of the former group to meet the shock situation by means of Habit *A,* a tendency which was not present in the Control Group; but since Habit *B* was a definitely superior mode of adjustment (permitting the rat to escape the shock completely instead of only partially), it eventually superseded Habit *A* in all cases. By the end of three days of training in Habit *B* (30 trials in all), the animals in the Experimental Group were quite as proficient in executing it as were the animals in the Control Group. That is to say, after equal amounts of training in Habit *B,* the animals in the 2 groups behaved in an indistinguishable manner in this situation. This fact, nevertheless, does not mean that they no longer differed. As will be shortly noted, the fact that their historical antecedents were different caused them to act differently under changed conditions.

To summarize the procedure up to this point, the 5 animals in the Control Group and the 5 animals in the Experimental Group were given equal amounts of training in Habit *B,* with only this difference, that the latter were first required to learn Habit *A* and were then made to abandon it and *progress* to Habit *B,* whereas the animals in the former group learned *only* Habit *B.*

On the day following the completion of training in Habit *B,* the animals in both groups were put into the apparatus with the pedal accessible as usual, except for the fact that whenever they touched it they received a slight shock from its surface.[9] This new element in the situation created a type of conflict. In order to terminate the mounting grill shock, the rat, in other words, had to submit to at least a momentary additional shock from the pedal. Instead of Habit *B* now functioning without hindrance, as it previously had, a definite obstacle was placed in the way of its free performance. Under these conditions, the animals in the

[9] The current used to produce this shock was derived from a Muenzinger-Walz constant-current apparatus (1934) and was adjusted to 0.03 milliampere.

Control Group continued to execute Habit *B* for 10 trials (cf. Section V). On the other hand, 4 of the 5 animals in the Experimental Group promptly "regressed" to Habit *A* (see Figure 59*A*). The difference in behavior in this connection is clearly shown in Table 7, which, taken with the accompanying legend, is self-explanatory.

TABLE 7

LENGTH OF DELAY IN PRESSING ELECTRICALLY CHARGED PEDAL OBSERVED IN TWO GROUPS OF RATS

The entries represent the time (in seconds) that the individual members of two groups of rats delayed, after the onset (at zero intensity) of a gradually increasing electric charge on the grill on which they stood, before pressing a pedal to cause this charge to drop to zero, the pedal being also for the first time in their experience electrically charged. It will be noted that the pedal-pressing reaction to the grill shock, referred to as Habit *B*, persisted in all the rats in the Control Group for all 10 trials, despite the "frustrating" shock on the pedal. On the other hand, in 4 out of 5 of the animals in the Experimental Group, Habit *B* was abandoned after 1 to 3 contacts with the pedal (a delay of 300 seconds being the criterion of abandonment). Upon abandoning Habit *B*, the rats in the Experimental Group "regressed" to Habit *A*.

Trials	Control Group					Experimental Group				
	C_1	C_2	C_3	C_4	C_5	E_1	E_2	E_3	E_4	E_5
1	59	87	98	92	95	73	186	149	88	73
2	64	94	116	95	75	45	128	277	(300)	108
3	75	91	128	90	101	157	(300)	102		78
4	125	74	124	108	120	(300)		(300)		78
5	120	110	121	111	69					63
6	92	134	160	137	86					108
7	123	141	86	118	153					75
8	124	118	121	107	75					84
9	113	90	82	98	182					69
10	120	65	105	118	83					108

III. Freudian and Other Theories of Regression Compared

Before discussing the supplementary observations on "reaction formation" made in connection with the experiment just described, it is desirable to consider the behavior here reported in somewhat greater detail. It is believed that the basic psychological mechanisms underlying this behavior are comparable in all essential respects to those involved in the phenomenon of regression as it is defined psychoanalytically and that by making this parallelism explicit certain problems can be seen somewhat more clearly than when viewed only against the complex background of clinical observations.

Upon first encountering a given form of noxious stimulation (grill shock),[10] the rats in the Experimental Group in the present study made a characteristic adjustment to it (Habit *A*). This adjustment represented a *first fixation.* It was not, however, an entirely adequate solution to the problem, and when a new, more completely satisfactory type of adjustment was made available, the animals (in some instances with a little prodding) fairly quickly *progressed* to it. This new adjustment (Habit B) constituted a *second fixation.* Now, however, when an "external obstacle"[11] (shock on pedal) was placed in the way of this latter type of behavior, i.e., when a *frustration* was introduced, the impulse to terminate the grill shock by means of Habit *B* was thrown into *conflict* with the impulse to avoid the pedal shock. Since the margin of advantage that Habit *B* had previously had over Habit *A* was now eliminated (in four of the five animals), Habit *A* became the preferable (less "painful") mode of adjustment and was reverted to. In manifesting this regressive change, moreover, the behavior of the rats here employed further paralleled the behavior commonly observed in human beings under similar circumstances in that a very elementary type of "symptom" (reaction formation) also emerged. This feature of their behavior will be returned to subsequently.

The first major point to be emphasized in the present connection is that the regressive behavior here reported was *historically* determined. Since the animals in the Control Group did not abandon Habit *B* when its previously unhampered execution was interfered with, it follows that the animals in the Experimental Group did so, under externally identical circumstances, solely for the reason that their *past experiences* had been different.[12] In other words, because they had first learned, and later abandoned, a given type of adjustment (Habit A), they were *predisposed* to return to it, in a way that the animals in the Control Group were not, when the subsequently acquired adjustment (Habit *B*) was interfered with.[13]

---

[10] This may be thought of as analogous in function to libido (erotic drive) in Freud's discussion of regression in human beings (Section I).

[11] Cf. the quotation from Freud (1920a, pp. 298–99) in Section I.

[12] It can scarcely be supposed that this dissimilarity of behavior was due to "constitutional" differences. Genetically these animals, coming from a highly inbred strain, were practically identical, and the two groups were, moreover, formed by purely random selection.

[13] This finding may seem to have an obvious moral for education. If "stable personalities" are desired, then let children be taught only one mode of adjustment to any given need. In other words, "bad habits," if allowed to form, not only have

As the passages cited in Section I indicate, this view of the historical determination of regression is completely consonant with psychoanalytic theory. Freud has unremittingly stressed the role of prior fixations in the causation of regression, and the term itself carries a similar implication. A person cannot "go back" to something with which he has had no previous experience.

In a challenging paper, Lewin (1937) has, however, taken the position that regression is not historically determined. He says:

> The theory of regression indicated [here] is entirely unhistorical. According to it, the regressive behavior would occur under the described circumstances even if the person in question were created as an adult Golem. In other words: even a person without childhood who never experienced childlike behavior should regress to childlike behavior not very different from what has actually happened in the history of the individual (1937, p. 209).[14]

According to this writer, the personality of a normal adult is "more differentiated" than that of a child. This so-called differentiation ("number of subparts within the person") tends to break down under "high pressure," i.e., the personality becomes less complexly structured. "In other words: a person under pressure should 'regress' to a more 'primitive' level at least as far as his degree of differentiation is concerned" (1937, p. 208). Lewin adds that this "primitivation" occurs not because of the continuing latent existence of specific habits or patterns of adjustment (fixations) that have been overt at an earlier point in the individual's life history, but because the personality is more or less destructured, as a result of a traumatic factor (abnormal "tension," "high pressure," or some other strain within the personality). If, for example, a bunch of toy blocks is arranged so as to form a house and if the house is then pushed over, the resulting unstructured mass of blocks is more "primitive"; this change in complexity of organization represents "regression," even though the blocks had never before been in such a disorganized state. According to Lewin, it is sheer coincidence that the personality of the child and of the

---

to be overcome before "good habits" can be established, but they more or less permanently weaken the "good habits." Therefore, establish the "good habits" in the first place. Although this is good advice in so far as it is practical, the fact is that human needs and human abilities do not develop hand in hand. The infant has most of the basic needs that the adult has, but he has vastly different potentialities for fulfilling these needs in "good" (i.e., socially approved) ways. He must, therefore, necessarily be allowed to develop and engage, often for months or even years, in habits that are "bad" in the sense that they must ultimately be given up for "better" ones. This is a dilemma that must be kept constantly in mind in the training of children [Mowrer, 1938d; see also (14)].

[14] Cf. the discussion in Section I.

adult who has "regressed" is, in both cases, relatively undifferentiated.[15]

In his study of reasoning in schizophrenic human adults, Cameron (1938) concludes that the intellectual changes occurring in this type of mental disorder involve simple "disorganization" and "confusion" rather than regression, as many writers currently believe. This conclusion agrees with Lewin's redefinition of regression in ahistorical terms, but Lewin's views in this connection are not supported by the main body of clinical observation, nor by the findings of the present, admittedly analogical investigation. Personality destructuralization, of the kind posited by Lewin, may indeed occur, but it seems dubious to propose that the behavioral changes of the kind that are commonly referred to as "regressive" and believed to be historically determined also fall into this category. [See 20.]

In addition to the question as to whether regression is or is not historically conditioned, yet another issue arises here. In the two studies cited at the outset of this paper, Hamilton and Krechevsky (1933) and Sanders (1937) have taken the position that regression represents "a reversion to an earlier, well-established mode of behavior, and persistence in that mode despite the relative inefficiency of that behavior in solving the problem confronting the organism. Further, regression has been assumed to arise when the individual is placed in a strong emotional situation" (Hamilton and Krechevsky, 1933, p. 238; Sanders, 1937, p. 494). These writers thus indicate, first of all, their acceptance of the orthodox psychoanalytic view that regression is a function of past experience. Their second point, that the mode of behavior regressed to in any given case is relatively "inefficient," involves assumptions that will be returned to in the next section. For present purposes, major interest attaches to their contention that the *precipitating* cause of regression (as contrasted to the predisposing cause, i.e., fixation) is a "strong emotional situation." This latter proposition conforms to the popular notion that "mental breakdowns" are caused by severe emotional experiences or "shocks," but it is not in keeping with the analytic view in such matters, according to which the precipitating cause of regression is *frustration,*[16] which in turn is defined as a relatively specific interference with an established mode of need fulfilment. In other words, "emotional situa-

---

[15] See McGill (1938) for a critique of Lewin's theory of the ahistorical character of psychological causation in general (especially pp. 530–31). Cf. also Boring (1933, chap. v).

[16] Cf. Section I.

tions" are pathogenic, i.e., lead to regression, only when they constitute such an interference. Failure to make this essential distinction impairs the relevancy of the otherwise admirably designed experiments of the writers cited.[17]

In the experiment reported by Hamilton and Krechevsky, rats first learned that they could obtain food either by turning to the right or to the left at the choice point on a simple T-maze, but that they could do so more quickly (due to a shorter path) by turning to the right. When this *right*-turning habit was well established (occurring in 90 per cent of the trials), conditions were altered so that a *left* turn now resulted in their getting to the food more quickly. The right-turning habit consequently began to disappear and to be superseded by a new left-turning habit. At this stage the animals were divided into a control group and an experimental group, and in the case of the latter animals "a strong electrical shock was administered at a point just before the bifurcation" (1933, p. 234). "Upon introduction of shock the experimental group, *as a group,* showed a decided tendency to revert to its former right-turning behavior" (1933, p. 245). The control group, on the other hand, continued, as might have been expected, to show left-turning behavior with gradually increasing regularity. The shock just before the choice point was regarded in this experiment as providing a "strong emotional situation"; and since it resulted in a reduced tendency to perform a subsequently acquired habit, this change was taken as evidence of the statement that regression occurs "when the individual is placed in a strong emotional situation."

The inadequacy of this analysis is indicated by the experiment reported by Sanders. In her study rats were trained to run down an initial common path, take a U-shaped detour to either the right or the left, and then come back into a final common path, at the end

---

[17] In reporting a series of studies aimed primarily at other problems, Miller and collaborators have assigned frustration its proper role in relation to regression as psychoanalytically conceived. They have secured evidence demonstrating: (*a*) that interference with a thoroughly established maze habit through nonreward results not only in a retrogressive change from few to many errors (blind-alley turns) but also in a reversion to the particular *patterning* of errors observed early in the initial learning period (Miller and Miles, 1936); (*b*) that interference, through nonreward, with the habit of running down a straight alley for food reinstates an earlier gradient of speed of running (Miller and Miles, 1935); and (*c*) that this type of frustration also produces a return of earlier random activity (sniffing about, grooming, etc.) accompanied, however, by a form of "energization" (aggression?) that makes this activity more vigorous than it originally was (Miller and Stevenson, 1936). Although the role of frustration in the production of regression is demonstrated admirably in these studies, it is didactically unfortunate that the particular situations employed were of such a nature that the role of fixation was not also clearly illustrated.

of which they obtained food. Definite preferences were shown by individual rats for one or the other of the alternative routes, which preferences were assumed to be "unlearned," "ontogenetically lower," possibly "inherited." This "natural tendency" to select a given route was then strengthened by introducing a differential temporal delay in the final common path, consisting of only 5 seconds if the preferred path were taken but of 90 seconds if the nonpreferred path were taken. Training was continued until 36 of 40 trials were "in the direction of the natural tendency." At this point the procedure was reversed, the long delay in the final common path occurring if the previously preferred path were taken and the short delay occurring if the previously nonpreferred path were taken. The latter procedure was continued until all animals had altered their behavior to the extent of now selecting the formerly nonpreferred path in 36 of 40 trials. At this juncture an electric shock was introduced just before each animal reached the choice point, near the end of the initial common path. As a consequence, all 5 of the rats used in this study reverted to the originally preferred route, although this route was now not "adaptive by any objective standard" since it continued to involve the longer delay in the final common path. On the basis of this finding, Sanders concluded that "regression has an emotional basis," although a second experiment with the same animals showed that if they were shocked in an unrelated compartment, but immediately before they were put into the maze, no regression occurred. The latter finding leads Sanders to add the qualification that although "regression has an emotional basis, . . . this emotionality must be very closely integrated with the situation" (1937, p. 510).

Martin (1937), using the same type of apparatus previously employed by Hamilton and Krechevsky, has likewise recently reported failure to obtain regression by shocking rats outside the experimental situation proper, thus giving further grounds for the inference, suggested by Sanders' findings, that electrical shock (emotional disturbance) per se does not produce this phenomenon.

It is impossible to say precisely why it is that in both the Hamilton and Krechevsky experiment and the Sanders experiment, regression occurs only if shock is administered just before the choice point, not if administered in a spatially unrelated situation; but the present writer suspects that this fact is in some way dependent upon the character of the *anticipatory reactions* in progress as the animal approaches this point. Anyone who has watched rats run a familiar maze has observed their tendency to hug the wall on the side of their next anticipated turn. Such a tendency is probably one of the best objective measures in animals of what is known in human beings as "intent." It is well established that if a person (especially a child) is punished merely for *intending* to do something, the punishment may be quite as effective in inhibiting the intended act as is punishment administered during or after the act. On the other hand, if a person is simply subjected to a painful type of stimulation before a given intention is formed (and if no connection is established through the speech process), such a penalty will have no specific deterring effect. Similarly in the case of rats in a maze: if they are shocked before a given "intention" has formed, i.e., before certain anticipatory reactions are in progress, there will be no inhibition of the act for which the anticipatory reactions are appropriate.[18] Although it is realized that this hypothesis, when applied to the experiments in question, raises certain unsettled issues, it points the way for further investigation and serves as a tentative means of bringing the results of these experiments into line with the conception of regression which holds that its precipitating cause is a *specific frustration* (habit interference) rather than a generalized emotional disturbance.

IV. Regression and "Efficiency"

In the experiments just cited, the authors take as one criterion of regression the "relative inefficiency" of the habit that is reverted to. If, as in these experiments, the habit reverted to involves the use of a spatially or temporally longer path to food than does the abandoned habit, it may appear that there is indeed an objective basis for comparing the "efficiency" of the two habits. As various writers have pointed out, however, the concept of "efficiency" always has an ultimately subjective reference. In what sense can a shorter pathway connecting two points in space be said to be "more efficient" than a longer pathway, except in the sense that the margin of gains over losses is greater *for the rat* in one case than in the other? Under the simplest conditions, the loss would be locomotor effort (increased fatigue stimulation) and the gain would be food (reduced hunger stimulation). With amount of food obtained per run (on either path) constant and with the effort exerted unequal, then the short path is, in this *subjective* sense, more "efficient." Theoretically, if none of the factors in this

[18] Evidence presented by Miller (1935) in another connection lends strong support for this assumption [cf. also 12, Section I].

situation was altered, the habitual use of the short path would never be abandoned.

The fact is, however, that at a particular point in both of the investigations under discussion the short path *was* abandoned. How did this change come about? According to the present analysis, it could have occurred only because the margin of gains over losses was altered in such a way as to make it "more efficient," in the subjective sense, for the rat to take the long path. In these investigations the food received at the end of a run remained constant, and the relative lengths of the two pathways remained constant. What changed? As already indicated, it is the writer's conviction that in order to obtain the effect reported by the authors cited, the short pathway must have taken on anxiety-arousing potentialities (due to the electric shock) which it did not formerly possess and which were not acquired (at least, not in the same degree) by the long path. If such can be assumed to be the case, the advantage in using the short path would thereby have been destroyed, and it would have then become "more efficient" to take the longer path; i.e., the margin of gains over losses would have been reversed, with a corresponding shift in behavior, which was "regressive" but not "inefficient." Only by arbitrarily restricting interest to the food-getting function can the regressed-to behavior be characterized as "inefficient." Such an atomistic approach is obviously unrealistic and can be pursued to no advantage.[19]

When the results of the experiment described in Section II of the present study were first publicly reported (Mowrer, 1937), Dr. Saul Rosenzweig raised the question as to whether the abandonment of Habit *B* (pedal-pressing) and the return to Habit *A* (sitting on the hind legs) was really a regression, or simply an "intelligent, adaptive reaction to a change in external circumstances." He emphasized the view that real regression always involves giving up one mode of adjustment that is relatively "good" for one that is "not so good." He summarized his point by saying that had he been a rat in the experimental situation described, he would have done just what the rat did but that he would not have felt that he had "regressed." Dr. Rosenzweig did not, in other words, consider the habit that was reverted to any less "efficient" than the habit that was abandoned, and suggested that the change was not, therefore, genuinely regressive.

---

[19] The writer is assuming no one will hold that the regression observed in these experiments had a "structural" basis, i.e., was produced by differential damage to the neural mechanisms mediating the two habits.

The writer fully agrees, as may be surmised from the preceding discussion, that it was *not* less "efficient" for the rats (Experimental Group) that had learned Habit *A,* as well as Habit *B,* to revert to Habit *A* when an electric charge was put on the pedal (thereby interfering with Habit *B*); but it is not so easy to concede that this change in behavior cannot, for this reason, be legitimately regarded as a regression. As already pointed out, this type of change seems to possess all the essential attributes needed to qualify as regression in the traditional psychoanalytic sense; and it may help in clarifying the issue to recall that one of the distinctive contributions of psychoanalysis has been to break down the dichotomy between "normal" and "abnormal," "adaptive" and "maladaptive." According to psychoanalysis, all behavior—including even the most rampant and maddest of psychoneurotic symptoms—is adaptive in the basic sense that the individual who is doing the behaving is trying to diminish his discomfort and tensions, thereby obeying the all-inclusive "pleasure principle" (Freud, 1911).[20] Living organisms do what they have to do and can; from the point of view of their own psychic economy every act represents the most "efficient," most "adaptive" behavior that is psychically possible under the circumstances.[21]

It is not difficult to see why there should be a strong inclination to assign a negative value judgment to regressive behavior. Human regressions are commonly in a direction *opposite* to that of the educational, socializing forces of the group; regression, under these conditions, is antisocial (countercultural) [22] and as such is regarded *by other persons,* as "bad," i.e., from their point of view "undesirable." This fact may prompt the group to take such retaliatory action toward the regressing individual (social disapproval, segregation, etc.) as will prevent the regressed-to mode of adjustment from being as satisfactory as it otherwise might be; but it is still the "lesser of two evils," from the individual's standpoint. If such were not the case, the regressive adjustment would be abandoned.[23]

---

20 *Vide infra,* Footnote 24.

21 This somewhat dogmatic statement raises a recondite psychological problem. How does one account for such apparent violations of the pleasure principle as "deliberate" postponement, or even permanent renunciation, of gratifications that are immediately available (in the objective sense) and the self-infliction of injury or the solicitation of such treatment from others? This issue has, however, been dealt with in two other papers (Mowrer, 1938; 2) and will not be discussed at this time.

22 Cf. Dollard (1935). [See also 15, 18.]

23 "Better" adjustments than the one regressed to may, of course, be theoretically possible in a given situation, but the actual behavior of any particular human being is always limited, not by an all-wise Providence, but by that individual's own perceptions, knowledge, and intelligence, i.e., by his existing habit systems and his

If, therefore, in the experiment described in Section II, the mode of adjustment (Habit *A*) that was regressed to when Habit *B* (pedal pressing) was interfered with was necessarily "better" from the rat's point of view, and if it is scarcely meaningful to speak of a rat's behavior as being either "good" or "bad" in the social sense (particularly in a situation that did not simultaneously involve other rats), then there would appear to be no grounds for holding that this adjustment was in any psychologically significant sense inferior, considering the changed character of external circumstances. It was, to be sure, a less-preferred adjustment *before* the shock was put on the pedal, a fact clearly shown by the alacrity with which the rats "progressed" from Habit *A* to Habit *B* when the pedal was for the first time made available to them (without shock on it). The mere fact, however, that in one situation a given type of adjustment (Habit *A*) may be inferior to another (Habit *B*) does not mean that, with altered circumstances (shock on pedal), the former may not become superior. In the field of *habit dynamics,* functional values are relative, not absolute; and much confusion can apparently be avoided if this fact is kept continually in mind.

In the light of the foregoing discussion, the supplementary experiment, reported below, may seem superfluous—and in the writer's estimation it is, in so far as the validity of this discussion is concerned; but it was nevertheless carried out, mainly as a matter of curiosity, and also partly in the hope that it might further point up some of the issues previously raised. It will be recalled that Dr. Rosenzweig questioned the justification for calling the reversion from Habit *B* to Habit *A* in the above experiment a "regression," on the grounds that, with the alteration in external circumstances (introduction of shock on pedal), Habit *A*, which had previously been abandoned for Habit *B,* ceased to be an inferior type of adjustment and became the superior adjustment; and going from an inferior to a superior adjustment was not to be regarded

---

capacity and opportunity for new learning. (To take an example at the animal level, it was theoretically entirely possible in the conflict situation described in Section II, with electric shock on both the grill and the pedal, for the rat to turn over and lie on its fur-covered back, thereby completely escaping all shock. But this behavior is not in the reaction repertoire of ordinary rats and did not, therefore, come within the range of adjustmental alternatives in this situation.) The essence of many types of psychotherapy consists of an attempt to enlarge the patient's repertoire, or range, of relief-bringing (satisfying) behavior, either by "advice" (instruction) or by placing him in situations in which new learning is demanded (occupational therapy, change of environment, etc.). The psychoanalytic approach, on the other hand, rests on the assumption that most behavior limitations (neurotic incapacities) are due, not so much to simple habit deficits, as to internal conflicts (inconsistent habits) involving anxieties that are not "realistic" (1). The therapeutic goal of analysis, therefore, is to remove these anxieties and thereby free the individual for effective, satisfaction-bringing action. [Cf. 18–22.]

as a "regression." The writer's reply has been, in effect, that behavioral changes are always *progressive* in the dynamic sense [24] and that regression has meaning, therefore, only in the *genetic* sense; and since Habit *A* was genetically prior to Habit *B*, then the change noted *was* a regression.

The supplementary experiment here referred to was carried out as follows.[25] Five experimentally naïve rats were put individually into the apparatus previously described, and the electric shock on the grill (floor) was allowed to build up. The pedal at the end of the apparatus was available from the outset as a means of escape from the grill shock, but it was also kept continuously charged with the same intensity of electric current previously used to produce regression in the experiment already reported. Under these conditions 4 of the 5 rats readily acquired the pedal-pressing response (Habit *B*), despite the presence of shock on the pedal, and executed it with relatively little evidence of conflict for 10 trials per day on each of 3 successive days. At the end of this time the experiment was discontinued, with no indication that the picture would have changed had it been carried on indefinitely. The fifth animal hit upon and then abandoned the Habit *B* type of response to the grill shock after 2 trials on the first day and manifested instead a Habit *A* type of adjustment. On the second day this animal completed 10 Habit *B* responses, but on the third day, after 4 Habit *B* responses, again resorted to Habit *A*. In short, the results thus obtained show that in 4 of the 5 rats tested, the Habit *B* type of adjustment was consistently preferred to the Habit *A* type of adjustment, under the conditions stated, while in one animal the choice was unstable.

These results indicate, in other words, that for rats with no previous training ("fixation") in the performance of either Habit *A* or Habit *B*, the latter is the favored adjustment. This finding might, therefore, be taken as an answer to Dr. Rosenzweig's query

---

[24] This statement must be qualified in two respects. In the first place, it applies only to behavioral changes that are relatively stable, that involve, that is, at least a temporary dynamic equilibrium. It obviously does *not* apply to behavioral changes that involve mere random, unorganized, unrewarded striving. (Cf. Valentine, 1938, p. 214). The second point is that although regression is most clearly definable in the genetic sense, it may also conceivably be defined, in the dynamic sense, as a disruption (due to failure of reward or conflict) of a patterned, well-organized type of adjustment to the given situation, with ensuing recourse to random, unorganized behavior. But since random behavior is always a prelude (save in *Gestalttheorie*) to the establishment of a stable habit, regression, defined in this dynamic sense, is also a genetic regression. Cf. Wells' discussion of the *genetic, dynamic* and *social* aspects of regression (1935).

[25] The writer is indebted to Dr. Neal Miller for proposing the particular form of this experiment.

as to whether the reversion from Habit *B* to Habit *A* under the conditions previously described was indeed regressive, in the sense of involving a change from a "good" to a less "good" habit. Have we not, in the experiment just described, a 4-to-1 vote in favor of the "goodness" of Habit *B,* as judged by 5 "unbiased" rats? Was not, therefore, reversion from Habit *B* to Habit *A* in the other experiment an instance of "true" regression, in that the rats which manifested this behavior did something that 4 out of 5 other rats, by the testimony of their own behavior, branded as "crazy," i.e., opposed to the self-interest of "right-thinking" rats in general?

The dilemma is easily resolved by making explicit some of the implied steps in this line of reasoning. In the experiment last performed, what was done, in effect, was to try to set up a social standard by which to judge the "normality" of rat behavior in a given situation. Instead of using a *human* social norm, which would have been patently unwarranted, a *rat* norm was established instead; and then the behavior of other rats was compared and contrasted therewith. Since the behavior of these other rats was found to be *different,* it was judged, therefore, as "abnormal," in this case, "regressive." What was overlooked here—but is fortunately well known because of the experimentally controlled character of the situation—is that the life histories of the two groups of rats were different in one important detail, namely, that one group had been previously fixated on Habit *A* whereas the other group had not. The characteristically different types of reaction on the part of the two groups of rats in externally identical situations were, therefore, neither more nor less "normal" for one group than for the other.[26] The difference merely shows, again, the force and cogency of the argument previously advanced, that regression is historically conditioned (by the presence or absence of prior fixations) and that it is primarily in the *genetic* sense that this concept has greatest usefulness and meaning.[27]

---

[26] In another study (19) the point has been stressed that apparently the sole basis for calling many types of behavior "abnormal," in both human beings and the lower animals, is that they are simply not understood by the observer. The problem is rendered especially acute in human beings by virtue of the fact that their life histories are so exceedingly variable, and yet these variations are rarely well known to the observer (or even to the individual himself).

[27] It goes without saying, of course, that in the experiments here reported the picture would have been very different had a sufficiently intense shock been used on the pedal to have prevented *all* rats from pressing it in order to escape the grill shock. Naturally, the intensity of the shock used was standardized somewhat below this point. The relation of intensity of shock in this situation to the type of reaction produced further emphasizes the relativity of effects in the study of habit dynamics. In passing it may be mentioned that the nature of the results obtained in a situation of this kind can also probably be significantly influenced by

V. An Experimental Analogue of Reaction Formation

As early as 1908, Freud alluded to the principle of "reaction formation," yet it is only within relatively recent years that he and other psychoanalytic writers have particularly stressed its significance. This state of affairs has been part of a more general shift of emphasis in analytic theory, the outcome of which has been to elevate anxiety to a position of pre-eminent importance as "the fundamental phenomenon and the central problem of the neurosis" (Freud, 1936, p. 111). According to this latter conception, all symptomatic acts are to be viewed as serving in one way or another as "mechanisms of defense" against this phenomenon. Representing a return to a theoretical position tentatively advanced in 1894 and then abandoned, this interpretation was revived by the elder Freud in 1936 and has recently been further elaborated by Anna Freud (1937). The latter lists ten "mechanisms of defense," as follows: regression, repression, isolation, undoing, projection, introjection, turning against the self, reversal, sublimation, and reaction formation. It is therefore in this setting, as one of a variety of related mechanisms, that reaction formation will be discussed and exemplified (19).

Like all other psychoanalytic principles, reaction formation is regarded as pathological only when it functions with unusual force or frequency. In its simplest, least dramatic forms, it involves nothing more, for example, than the tendency on the part of a student who is especially fond of playing bridge to avoid his bridge-playing friends at the time of an impending examination. The paradox is that he avoids them precisely for the reason that he likes them, but the paradox disappears when it is realized that he also fears the consequence of indulging his liking, at least at this particular time. The student's avoidance of his friends under these circumstances thus represents an attempt to minimize the prospect of failing in the examination; it is, in short, a "defense" against anxiety. The tendency for an inebriate to make wide detours in order to avoid passing a familiar bar when trying to support a resolution to be temperate is another illustration of the same mechanism.

Of the various passages in which Freud refers to reaction forma-

---

the relative amount of training given in the performance of particular habits (strength of fixation) and, somewhat less certainly, by the age of the animals employed. The possible role of age was only hinted at in some preliminary experimentation and has not been definitely established. [Cf. "What is normal behavior?" (Mowrer, 1948b).]

tion, the following, constituting an incidental comment on the infantile neurosis of a five-year-old boy, sets forth the essential features of this phenomenon perhaps most clearly.

Thus we have a conflict springing from ambivalence—a firmly founded love and a not less justified hatred, both directed against the same person. His [little Hans'] phobia must be an attempt to resolve this conflict. Such conflicts due to ambivalence are very common; we are acquainted with another typical outcome of them in which one of the two contending trends, usually the tender one, becomes enormously augmented, while the other disappears. Only the excessiveness of the tenderness and its compulsive character betray the fact that this attitude is not the only one present, and that it is ever on its guard to keep the contrary attitude suppressed, making it possible to construe a train of events which we describe as repression through *reaction formation* (1936, p. 38).

The element of conflict in such a situation emerges, not only from the love-hate ambivalence per se, but also from the knowledge (often unverbalized) that overt expression of hostility would result in "loss of love" (punishment, deprivation, isolation, etc.). Anticipation of such a loss arouses anxiety, and in the attempt at "defense" against the latter the most elaborate efforts may be made to conceal and deny the component of hostility. How can the defense be managed better than by continual testimony, in word and act, of affection and solicitude? But the trained eye detects this subterfuge, this intensification of one type of behavior by the very strength of an opposing impulse.[28] Anna Freud describes as follows the form that reaction formation may take in a little girl who is highly ambivalent toward her mother:

A child who has been aggressive toward her mother develops an excessive tenderness towards her and is worried about her safety; envy and jealousy are transformed into unselfishness and thoughtfulness for others. By instituting obsessional ceremonials and various precautionary measures she protects the beloved person from any outbreak of her aggressive impulses, while by means of a code of exaggerated strictness she checks the manifestation of her sexual impulses [which would be disapproved by the mother no less than aggression] (1937, p. 51).

Particularly common as the basis of compulsive behavior in both children and adults, reaction formation is not, however, always easy to demonstrate convincingly from clinical material. Although (like regression) relatively simple as an abstract concept, it is likely

---

[28] The Queen in *Hamlet* (Act III, Scene II, line 240) shows a nice appreciation of this mechanism in her famous remark: "The Lady doth protest too much, methinks."

in any actual case—save in such elementary examples as first given above—to seem complicated and obscure, especially in situations in which other interpretations are logically possible. It is all the more fortunate, therefore, that what seem to be good experimental analogues of this phenomenon as it appears in human beings can be produced by the use of animals in the laboratory.

It has already been remarked that instances of reaction formation were observed in connection with the study of regression reported in Section II. It will also be recalled that after the animals in the Experimental Group had acquired Habit *A* and then abandoned it for Habit *B,* a shock was put on the pedal involved in executing Habit *B;* and that the shock, after a few (one to three) repetitions of the pedal response under these conditions, caused Habit *B* to be in turn abandoned, with a reversion to Habit *A.* This breakdown of Habit *B* and regression to Habit *A,* although relatively precipitous, did not, however, occur without evidence of conflict in these animals. Even more pronounced in the animals in the Control Group, this conflict took the following form. After Habit *B* was well established in these animals, they customarily sat very near the pedal after pressing it, in readiness for the next presentation of shock from the grill. When, however, shock was put on the pedal, their behavior was noticeably altered. After discovering that the pedal was charged, these animals would frequently *retreat* from the pedal end of the apparatus soon after they began to feel the grill shock, i.e., as soon as they began to have an impulse to press the pedal. In effect, they were thus *running away from the pedal because they wanted to go toward and touch it;* they were, in other words, manifesting a simple but presumably genuine type of reaction formation. A more precise, though less dramatic, statement of the causal sequence here involved would be that these rats ran away from the pedal because of anxiety, which was aroused by the tendency to touch it. In this sense the reaction formation was indeed a defense against (flight from) anxiety. But since the grill shock continued to mount, its motivational value soon exceeded that of the anxiety and overcame the rat's "pedal phobia," driving the animal back to the pedal and compelling it to press it.

In other words, in this situation a state of conflict, or "ambivalence," was generated, in which there were recurrently competing impulses, the one an impulse to approach and press the pedal (and thereby escape the grill shock), the other an impulse *not* to press the pedal (and thereby avoid an additional shock from it). In the absence of grill shock, there was no impulse to press the pedal, nor fear of it, and therefore no need to flee from it. As the grill

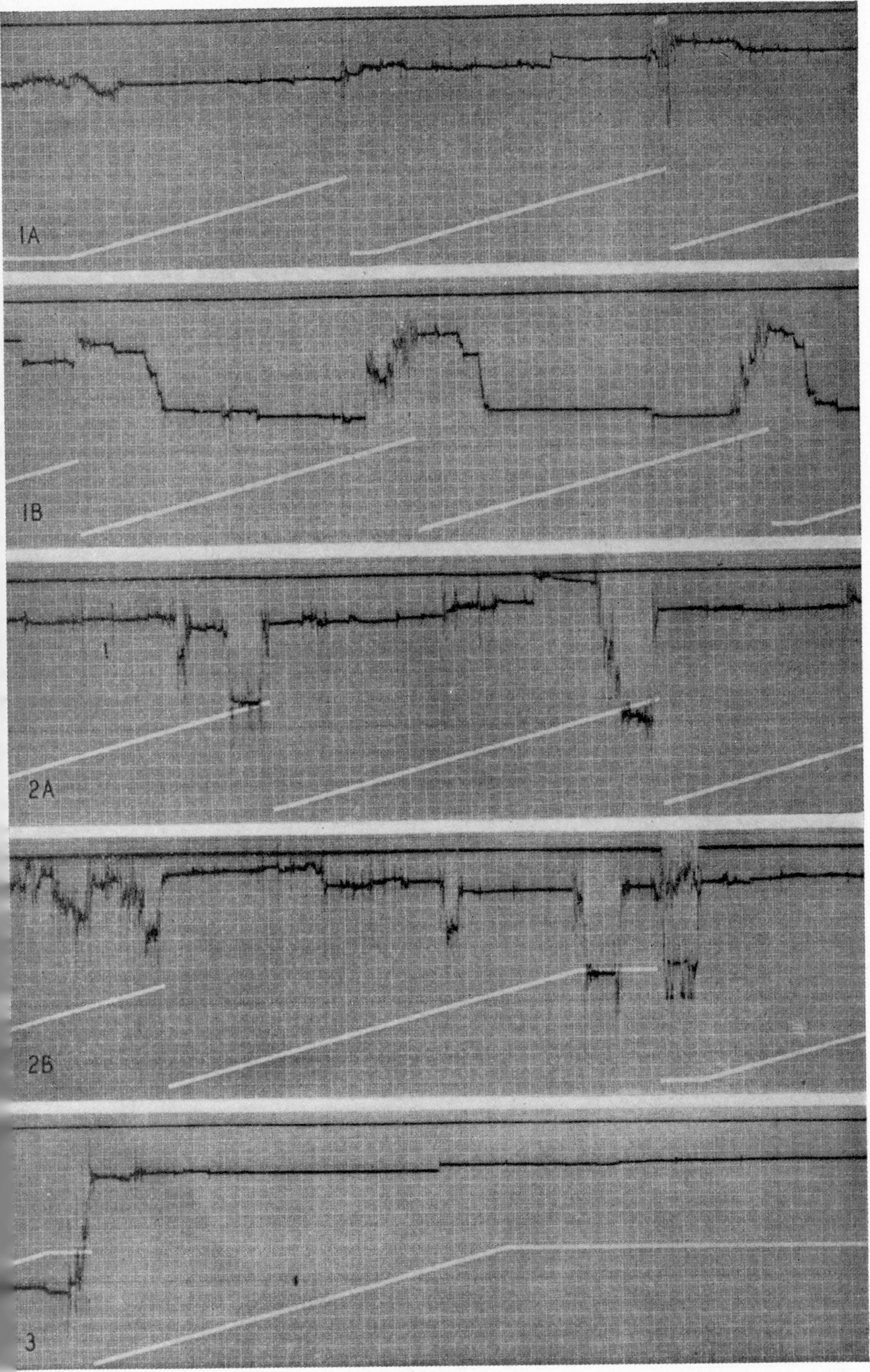

FIG. 60.—Records showing instances of "reaction formation" in a conflict situation in rats. 1A and 1B are continuous, as are 2A and 2B, and were cut only for convenience in mounting.

shock mounted, however, this fear of the pedal recurred, and the animal sought to dissipate it by running away from the pedal; but since complete escape was impossible and since the grill shock continued to mount, the fear of the pedal was eventually exceeded by the intensity of the grill shock, and the animal (having no Habit *A* to regress to) was forced to return to and press the pedal.

The records reproduced in Figure 60 show some interesting instances of this type of behavior. Before these records can be completely intelligible, however, a brief explanation is due as to how they were obtained. First of all, it should be mentioned that the grill constituting the floor of the apparatus used in this work was "free-floating," to the extent that the two metersticks forming the side-rails of the grill were extended approximately another meter at the left-hand end and were there pivoted on a fulcrum, while the right end, not similarly extended, was supported by a system of springs. A thread connected to the right end of the grill communicated with an optical lever which caused a beam of light to register on a piece of moving photographic paper any significant movement on the part of a rat while on the grill. If the rat was at the right end of the grill (near the pedal), the beam of light was deflected toward the left side of the paper (upper side in Figure 60), and, if the rat moved to the opposite end of the grill, the beam moved to the right (lower) side of the paper. Agitated behavior at any one location on the grill registered simply as rapid transverse oscillations of the beam. The recording system was critically dampened to prevent after-vibration. The transverse white lines on the records represent seconds, with 5-second intervals accentuated by somewhat wider white lines.

Records 1*A* and 1*B* in Figure 60 are continuous and show the step-by-step development of reaction formation in one of the animals (*C*4) used in the Control Group in the experiment on regression during the session in which shock was for the first time placed on the pedal. It will be noted that the first depression of the pedal, with resulting elimination of the grill shock (represented by the sudden drop of the oblique white lines, indicating grill-shock intensity), occurred without any apparent agitation on the part of the rat (see the irregular black line, made by the light beam controlled by the vertical movements of the grill). The second pedal-pressing reaction was preceded by a slight amount of agitation, as indicated by the oscillations of the light beam just before the shock indicator drops to zero. Before the third reaction, the rat moved away from the pedal a little distance (slight drop in the black line at beginning of record 1*B*), and then, after a pause, returned to the pedal and pressed it. This was the first of a series of responses that seemed to involve unmistakable instances of reaction formation. As the grill shock built up a fourth time, the rat retreated from the pedal end of the apparatus relatively early and remained at the opposite end until the shock had reached an unusually high intensity, at which point the rat returned to the pedal and, after considerable conflict, pushed it. Almost exactly the same thing happened on the fifth presentation of the shock. Somewhat similar behavior also occurred on the five following presentations of grill shock (not shown).

Records *2A* and *2B,* obtained from another member (*C*3) of the Control Group, show a slightly different pattern of behavior, but the phenomenon of reaction formation is no less clearly manifested. On the presentation of grill shock first shown in record *2A* (which had been preceded by two initial trials), this animal remained at the pedal end of the apparatus until the shock had become quite intense, then fled to the opposite end of the apparatus, remained there in some conflict for 8 or 10 seconds, but finally returned to the pedal and pressed it without ado. This pattern of behavior is duplicated, with minor variations, on the three subsequent presentations shown in these two records. On the last of these the rat showed considerable intermittent agitation as the shock built up, but it stayed at the pedal end of the apparatus (save for an incomplete excursion toward the opposite end) until the shock reached maximum intensity (indicated by the flat, nonascending portion of the white line). At this point the animal dashed to the other end of the apparatus, remained there for a brief period, returned to the pedal, hesitated a while longer, and then finally pushed it. But that action did not end matters. For some reason, perhaps because of the unusual duration and intensity of the grill shock on this trial, the rat continued violently to push and bat at the pedal for a considerable time after the grill shock was turned off. This is indicated by the failure of the grill shock to start building up and also by the break in the black line at the top of the record (made by a beam of light reflected from a second optical lever attached to the pedal).

Record 3 portrays the behavior of one of the rats (*E*1) in the Experimental Group at the point when it "regressed." At the extreme left of this record, the grill shock is seen approaching maximum intensity, with the rat at the nonpedal end of the apparatus (indicating reaction formation). After the shock had reached and maintained maximum intensity for 10 or 12 seconds, the animal came, somewhat falteringly, toward the pedal and pushed it. This, however, was the animal's last pedal reaction. It is to be noted that as the next presentation of shock built up to and then remained at maximum intensity, there was not the slightest tendency toward reaction formation. It was as if the rat had "decided" not to push the pedal again but instead to sit on its hind legs and "take" the shock, i.e., to "regress." Since the pedal was dangerous only when there was a temptation to touch it, there was now no reason to fear or flee from it.

These more or less fortuitous observations on reaction formation are, so far as the writer is aware, the first that have been published concerning this phenomenon in animals.[29] Other instances have undoubtedly been noted in prior experimentation and can probably be multiplied indefinitely by specifically planned attempts to produce them.

Summary

The five major divisions of this paper may be characterized as follows:

Section I reviews the concept of "regression" as it has been developed psychoanalytically and restates it in the terminology of the psychological laboratory.

Section II describes an experiment in which "frustration" of one mode of adjustment, Habit *B,* caused regression in one group of rats to a previously practiced ("fixated") mode of adjustment, Habit *A,* but did not lead to regression in another group of rats that had not practiced Habit *A* before acquiring Habit *B.*

In Section III the hypothesis that regression is "historically conditioned" (by the presence or absence of prior fixations) is supported and contrasted to an ahistorical interpretation of this phenomenon; the view that "emotional disturbance," rather than specific frustration, is the precipitating cause of regression is also discussed and criticized.

Section IV considers the social, dynamic, and genetic implications of regression. It is concluded that from the definitional standpoint the genetic aspect of this phenomenon is basic.

In Section V the psychoanalytic concept of "reaction formation" is defined and exemplified by human illustrations and by behavior manifested by rats in connection with the study of regression.

[For more recent discussions of the topics covered in this paper, see Sears (1943) and Farber (1948); also Whiting and Mowrer (1943).]

---

[29] It should, however, be noted that Miller (1937) has previously prepared and publicly exhibited a motion picture of reaction formation in rats.

CHAPTER 14

ENURESIS—A METHOD FOR ITS STUDY AND TREATMENT

[The preceding study has dealt with habit progression and regression as experimental problems, with animal subjects. In the present paper we turn to the analysis of a human developmental task, and our approach becomes largely clinical.

Here the molar concepts of personality theory and the more limited hypotheses of learning theory are brought together, to produce a method which has practical applications while also providing an opportunity for further inquiry. One of the most striking, and quite unexpected, scientific by-products of the method is the light it throws upon dream work, both as it applies specifically to enuresis and more generally.

In this introduction I wish to emphasize again that in proposing the technique here described for the treatment of enuresis, there is no tendency to ignore or deny the manifold ramifications of the problem. While the method itself is based upon a fairly atomistic—some might say "mechanistic"—training procedure, it is proposed with full cognizance of the fact that enuresis, like many other persisting immaturities, nearly always involves some disturbance in the identification of the child with his elders (see the last paragraph of Section IV and Footnote 19; also 21). Where identification with the same-sexed parent is powerful and has taken place easily, I suspect that the wish to *grow up* and *be like* that parent is ordinarily enough to insure the development of urinary continence at a normal age. However, since the failure of this progression may serve to worsen, rather than improve, existing relationships with parents, there seems—theoretically and empirically—to be no danger (if certain safeguards are observed) in the use of this highly specific approach.

This study, carried out jointly with Dr. Willie Mae Cook Mowrer, was originally published, in 1938, in the *American Journal of Orthopsychiatry.* At the end of the paper the reader will find a brief note on more recent related studies and reference to an improvement which has been made by Dr. H. Wright Seiger in the form of the apparatus employed.]

I. History of the Problem

Despite unremitting efforts, dating from antiquity,[1] to develop a specific form of therapy, nocturnal enuresis continues to be generally regarded as an unsolved problem. A review of the several hundred titles constituting the earlier literature on this topic reveals a remarkable array of proposed curative measures, ranging from patent superstitions and magical nostrums to a wide assortment of allegedly scientific methods. Innumerable drugs and hormones;[2] special diets (including fresh fruit, caviar, and colon bacilli); restriction of fluids; voluntary exercises in urinary control; injections of physiological saline, sterile water, paraffin and other inert substances; real and sham operations (passage of a bougie, pubic applications of cantharides plasters, cauterization of the neck of the bladder, spinal punctures, tonsillectomy, circumcision, clitoridotomy, etc.);[3] high-frequency mechanical vibration and electrical stimulation of various parts of the body; massage, bladder and rectal irrigations; Roentgen and other forms of irradiation; chemical neutralization of the urine; sealing or constriction of the urinary orifice; hydrotherapy; local "freezing" of the external genitalia with ice or "chloratyl"; elevation of the foot of the patient's bed; sleeping on the back; not sleeping on the back; and the use of a hard mattress: these are some of the methods which were commonly recommended and resorted to. In the hands of a limited number of individuals, virtually every method which was proposed seemed to produce cures; but the inability of other persons to obtain equally good results by what appeared to be precisely the same objective procedures eventually made it clear that the effectiveness of these methods was more a function of subtle psychological influences than of the particular physical praxis involved.[4] Following this realization, hypnotism and other forms of suggestion (including various kinds of placebos) were widely employed for a time; but the results were neither much better nor worse than those obtained by earlier methods, and the search for a truly ra-

[1] Goldman (1934–35 X, p. 247) says: "The ancients were much concerned about the problem [of enuresis] as attested by Pliny, the famous historian, in his *Natural History*. He relates: 'The incontinence of urine in infants is checked by giving boiled mice in their food, in fact, this would appear to be the most common folk remedy for this condition. Other remedies are that the child should wear a clean smock at baptism, that the godparents should keep their money in their pockets, and among other remedies is the consumption of wood lice and the urine of spayed swine.'"

[2] Cf. Zappert (1920) and Kanner (1935).

[3] For an especially barbaric form of surgical mutilation, see Davis (1908).

[4] Cf. Davidson (1924).

tional therapeutic approach to the problem of enuresis continued.

Recent writers in this field are inclined to believe either (*a*) that enuresis (which can properly be said to occur only in children who are at least three years old) is merely a continuation, due to inadequate training, of the so-called physiological incontinence of infancy or (*b*) that it is caused by certain unconscious (or conscious) emotional needs which are not finding appropriate satisfaction during the child's waking hours.[5] Neither of these hypotheses can be lightly dismissed; each seems to provide the correct understanding of a certain class of cases, while in still other instances of enuresis both of these causal mechanisms are probably concurrently operative.

Learning to awaken to the relatively vague and not very intense pressure created by a filling bladder, while successfully ignoring many other potentially disturbing stimuli, must be for the young child something of a feat, especially in view of the pre-existence of a strictly reflex, subcortical neural mechanism for the automatic relief of this need. That children do, in fact, require special assistance in the acquisition of this particular mode of control at the early age at which this is demanded of them in our culture is attested by the common practice of periodically arousing them from sleep in anticipation of the need to urinate.[6] That some children

[5] The present discussion is restricted to so-called "uncomplicated" enuresis, in which no organic etiology is demonstrable. Writers in this field agree that all enuretic children should have the benefit of a thorough physical examination before any form of psychotherapy is initiated, although it is the consensus of opinion that at least 95 per cent of all children presenting this problem are medically negative.

[6] This practice is apparently not found among primitive peoples (and to only a limited extent among the lower classes in our own culture). In the relatively few published anthropological studies which make any reference to toilet training in children, it is usually stated or implied that sphincter control during sleep is not expected of primitive children until a much later age than it is in civilized societies. Kidd (1906), in writing on childhood among the Kaffirs, says: "The mat on which the child has slept from infancy is burnt by the mother when the child begins to cut its second teeth. Up to that period the child has not full control of its natural functions during sleep; but as soon as the second teeth begin to appear it is supposed to have full control of itself" (p. 85). Rattray (1929) reports that Ashanti children are not fully trained in this regard when they cease to be suckled (at about three or three and a half years), that it then becomes the father's responsibility, in the case of male children, to complete this training. "Should the child at first wet the sleeping-mat during the night, the father will not flog him, but will call in small boys and girls about his son's own age and tell them to come and catch this boy and make him dance a dance called *nonsua bono*. He will be tied up in his bed-mat, taken to 'the bush' and dressed in *nsansono* (a kind of nettle); water will be thrown over him and the boys will sing: 'You wash your sleeping-mat in the night; you wash your cloth in the night.' . . . Sometimes a child who has not a strong *sunsum* (spirit) will die after such ridicule. . . . We have here an example at an early age of the use of the strongest of primitive sanctions, i.e., ridicule" (p. 12). It would appear from these and other reports that, although not subjected to the insistence upon cleanliness at the early age that this demand is made of children in our culture, primitive children are by no means always spared in this

should naturally respond more readily than others to this form of training and that the intrinsic adequacy of this training should vary from family to family seems inevitable, with a certain percentage of children consequently failing to acquire the dry-bed habit as soon as is normally expected. On the basis of this reasoning, the rational treatment of these so-called enuretic children would seem to lie, therefore, in the direction of supplementing, and if possible making more specific, the training in urinary control which has previously been given to them but without producing the desired results.[7]

The fact that methods of treatment—such as some of those mentioned at the outset of this paper—which are painful or at least disagreeable to the child, but which have no specific relationship to the real problem involved, should be capable of "curing" enuresis in some cases is not, of course, inconsistent with the assumption that enuresis is due to a specific habit deficiency. Efficient learning presupposes an adequate degree of motivation; and if in the enuretic

---

respect when they become somewhat older. (As an illustration of especial leniency, Whiting (1938) cites an incident of bed-wetting by a Waskuk, New Guinea, girl, age eight years, in which the only adult disapproval expressed seems to have been occasioned solely by the fact that the incident occurred in the house of a stranger, being thus regarded as a mark of disrespect.)

Although regular awakening of children during the night as a method of training in bladder control is apparently rare or quite unknown among primitive peoples, it cannot be assumed, however, that specific conditioning in this respect is entirely absent. Mead (1935), in describing the Arapesh, reports that "when an infant urinates or defecates, the person holding it will jerk it quickly to one side to prevent soiling his or her own person" (p. 41). The widespread practice among primitive peoples of allowing the infant to sleep until a fairly advanced age in intimate contact with the body of the mother (usually nude) would also presumably tend to insure some response of the mother and consequent disturbance of the child whenever elimination occurs in the night, although even this cannot be assumed to occur universally; for Ford (1938) has observed that Fijian mothers, when themselves awake and holding sleeping children, are usually careful not to arouse them if they should urinate or defecate, instead merely removing or wiping away the excreta with leaves or bunches of grass.

That human infants, if left strictly alone as far as toilet training is concerned, would sooner or later acquire sphincter control during sleep as well as at other times seems almost certain. No healthy member of any other mammalian species, once past the stage of genuine infantile helplessness, ordinarily soils itself during sleep; it is, therefore, of especial interest to inquire why this practice should be so common and sometimes persist so long in human children in modern civilized societies. An attempt to account for this anomaly will be made in subsequent pages.

[7] It does not follow, however, as some writers have assumed, that the way to prevent enuresis from existing at later ages is to begin toilet training earlier and make it more intensive than is ordinarily done; probably as much or more harm is done by premature and too insistent toilet training than by delayed and lax training. Voicing the view of a large school of pediatricians and psychiatrists, Markey (1932) has stated: "The longer the beginning of baby training is put off, the more fixed does a conditioning to recumbent elimination become. These joys are given up more reluctantly the longer they are allowed to last, and enuresis is prolonged as a natural result of the urge for pleasure" (p. 271). For a similar point of view, see Hamill (1929).

child this has been lacking, the desire to escape an odious form of "treatment" may conceivably bring about the formation of the required habit. But, at the same time that many cases of enuresis seem analyzable in terms of defective habit formation, the understanding of other instances of this disorder appears to require a different approach. In some children a change of surroundings or the alteration of other factors having no superficially discernible relation to enuresis will unexpectedly effect a dramatic "cure"; likewise, children in whom toilet habits have already been well established sometimes begin wetting the bed with distressing regularity for no immediately apparent reason. That enuresis in such cases is indicative of some basic frustration in the impulse life of the child and represents an attempt to obtain indirect or substitutive gratification of the thwarted needs or desires seems most likely; but it is often a difficult matter to determine precisely what these frustrated impulses are and how they can be provided with other, less devious avenues of expression.

II. Enuresis, Sex, and Dreams

Freud's dictum that "whenever enuresis nocturna does not represent an epileptic attack it corresponds to a pollution" (1916b, p. 51) epitomizes the view held by one group of writers.[8] As Sadger (1910) has put it, urinary eroticism "is the model for all the later developing sexual acts" (p. 117) and is not distinguished by the young child from sexual feeling proper; urination, especially when it occurs during sleep and is accompanied by fantasies which would presumably be repressed during full consciousness, is thus believed to be richly charged with pleasure-giving potentialities. Marcuse (1924–25) recalls the common observation that in boys and men a full bladder is likely to produce an erection during sleep and that in male infants the onset of urination even during waking hours is often accompanied by marked tumescence; sexual pleasure in many normal adults is said to be increased by a full bladder, and urinary sensations have been reported to replace sexual feeling proper in certain neurotic states. This functional relationship, Marcuse believes, "is to be seen as an expression of the original anatomical and physiological connection of the urinary and genital apparatus: their differentiation in the central nervous system first

[8] For a more recent and somewhat modified statement of this view, see Fenichel (1934), who begins his discussion of enuresis with the remark that "Infantile nocturnal enuresis still offers many unsolved problems for psychoanalytic investigation" (p. 25).

occurs much later, on the average at puberty,[9] although both systems remain in close interdependence" (p. 230).

Campbell (1918) has reviewed a mass of evidence from children and psychotic adults suggesting that in at least some individuals urination takes on and retains—conjecturally because of unusually severe repression of genital sexuality—a definitely sexlike pleasure and meaning which may be experienced either directly or symptomatically. When urination thus becomes so highly libidinized, it can scarcely be doubted that the affected individual will tend to show extraordinarily strong resistance to the imposition of the usual urinary restraints and limitations. But urination, it must be remembered, is itself an *intrinsically pleasurable biological function;* and there seems to be no very reliable way of determining when this form of pleasure has been augmented by having been invested with substitutive capacities for sexual gratification and when it has not. So vigilant are the efforts usually made to repress genital sexuality in children in our culture that one might reasonably expect a widespread prevalence of urinary eroticism, but the writers believe that this type of libidinal displacement is actually not very common. While recognizing the difficulties of making definitive observations in this connection and at the same time acknowledging the significance of isolated cases of enuresis, such as those reported by Angel (1935), and Hale (1914), we do not believe that a sexual etiology can be justifiably attributed to this disorder in more than a limited portion of children who manifest it. In only one child known to the writers has enuresis seemed due to so-called urethral eroticism, and even here the facts are not entirely unequivocal.

Perhaps the most significant evidence obtainable in this connection is that afforded by the dreams which commonly precede or accompany bed-wetting in children. Freud (1920b) has repeatedly called attention to the tendency in dreams for the sleeper to interpret potentially disturbing stimuli in such a way that they cease to

---

[9] This assumption would seem to be more in keeping with the common folk saying that bed-wetting will disappear spontaneously at puberty than with careful scientific observation. According to Ackerson's data (1931), obtained from "248 boys and 108 girls formerly enuretic (beyond their third birthday) for whom the ages at which enuresis ceased was noted" (p. 180), enuresis shows "steadily diminishing incidence from about 3 to 17 years" (p. 178). When presented in graphic form, these data give an almost perfectly straight line (with a slight tendency to become asymptotic at higher ages). There is nothing, therefore, in these or any other data known to the writers to support the common supposition concerning the advent of puberty and the spontaneous cessation of enuresis. Addis (1935) is inclined to the view that "the beginning of puberty may have a specific effect [upon enuresis] . . . and many indications suggest that enuresis is often connected with a sex factor" (p. 178); but this writer's statistics are unfortunately presented in such a way as not to show whether this actually is or is not true.

be regarded, at least for the time being, as a necessary cause for awakening. As an illustration of this process, Freud cites the case of "the sleepy [medical] student, who was awakened by his landlady with the admonition that he must go to the hospital, and then sleeps on, with the following account of his motives: "If I am already in the hospital, I shan't have to get up in order to go there. The latter is obviously a dream of convenience. . . . In a certain sense all dreams are dreams of convenience. *The dream is the guardian of sleep, not the disturber of it*" (p. 197).

As another example of a dream of convenience, Freud recalls the following personal experience: "On this occasion I became thirsty before going to bed, and emptied the glass of water which stood on the little chest next to my bed. Several hours later in the night came a new attack of thirst, accompanied by discomfort. In order to obtain water, I should have had to get up and fetch the glass which stood on the night-chest of my wife. I thus quite appropriately dreamt that my wife was giving me a drink from a vase. . . . Love of comfort is really not compatible with consideration for others. . . . Such dreams of convenience were very frequent with me in the years of my youth" (pp. 104–5).

Initially unaware of a number of earlier observations (Janet, 1890; Marcuse, 1924–25; Ochsenius, 1923; Schwarz, 1915; Weissenberg, 1925–26; Zappert, 1920) to the same effect (which were apparently also unfamiliar to Freud), the present writers independently discovered before proceeding far with their investigations that enuretic children very often have the most vivid "dreams of convenience" just before or during the act of urinating in bed. Under these circumstances, the sleeping child, instead of awakening to the stimulation produced by a distended bladder, fancies himself in a toilet, swimming in a pool, at the beach, alone in the forest or in some other secluded place where urination, which he now indulges in, would be allowable; in this way the child dismisses the otherwise disturbing fact that he is in bed and avoids the discomfort of awakening and really going to the toilet.[10] Adults who as children were enuretic can usually recall recurrent dreams of this kind. The writers have found that "toilet dreams" are often so convincing to children that upon being awakened immediately after the onset of

[10] Weissenberg (1925–26) believes that so-called "toilet dreams" occur not as an exception but as a regular accompaniment of bed-wetting. He was able to elicit an account of dreams of this kind in a high percentage of the children whom he studied: and the fact that dreams of this kind were not reported by other children does not mean that they did not occur. English and Pearson (1937) report a limited number of dreams in which urination during sleep had a more or less veiled sexual significance, but more frequently they find aggressive implications (see Section IV).

urination (by a method to be described later in this paper), they can be persuaded only with the greatest difficulty that they have not already made a trip to the bathroom. Not infrequently a smaller child when aroused under these conditions and told to go to the bathroom to finish urinating will defiantly insist that he has "just been in there!"

That the child who dreams he is in the toilet and then proceeds to urinate in his bed is following what Freud has called the "pleasure principle," to the extent that he is seeking to avoid the discomfort of exertion, exposure to cold, or possible accidents while groping about in the dark, is obvious; but that there is anything specifically sexual in this act for most enuretic children seems improbable. What is more likely to be true is that the child in whom "dreams of convenience" of this kind can successfully operate is simply at an intermediate stage of toilet training in which a certain amount of the nervous excitation originating in the bladder goes to the cerebral hemispheres (instead of immediately discharging reflexly) and produces a disturbance there, which, however, is not yet sufficiently compelling to produce awakening. Some types of neurotic children, who are in more or less chronic flight from the reality of waking life, may be unusually sound sleepers, with resulting failure to be awakened by a degree of stimulation which would suffice to produce this reaction in a normal child. In such cases it is perhaps justifiable to refer to enuresis as a neurotic "symptom"; but in the majority of children, bed-wetting is probably to be explained along other lines.[11, 12]

---

[11] Contrary to popular belief, enuretic children have not been found to sleep more soundly on the average than nonenuretics (Courtin, 1923).

[12] [Although this is not the place to enter into a detailed discussion of dream theory, I wish to report that during the decade which has intervened since this paper was written I have noticed an increasing tendency to dream when and only when it is time for me to wake up, and that this type of dream is clearly designed to terminate rather than preserve sleep. I could give many examples of this; the most recent one will suffice. *It seemed that I was teaching a course. In some rather undefinable way things were not going well. It seemed that the course was going to be taken away from me and given to someone else.* I wakened and discovered that it was my regular rising time. Immediately the import of the dream was clear: That evening I was to hold a seminar for a group of social workers on the subject of psychotherapy. At the last meeting of the group, a week earlier, I had felt that I had not been sufficiently prepared and that things had not gone well. The dream was a way of saying to myself, though asleep, that it was time for me to get up and begin thinking about and preparing for the seminar so that it would not be "taken away from me." Such a dream obviously follows the reality principle much more than the pleasure principle; and it is more aptly thought of as a "conscience dream" than as a wish-fulfilment. One is thus forced to question the general validity of Freud's statement that "The dream is the guardian of sleep, not the disturber of it." I wonder if further investigation will not show that the type of dreams one has is an index of his position on the immaturity-maturity axis—the immature, pleasure-dominated, reality-evading person using dreams to preserve sleep and the more reality-oriented person using them in the interests of terminating

III. Enuresis: Consequence or Cause of Personality Difficulties

Another prevalent theory holds that enuresis is an hysterical manifestation, whereby deep-seated anxieties are "converted" into a physical dysfunction. According to this view, it is always dangerous to attempt to eliminate enuresis directly, lest in so doing the underlying anxieties be reactivated and freed to produce some still more serious disturbance. Although apparently valid as an explanation in isolated cases of enuresis, this theory can scarcely be upheld as universally applicable. Certain writers (Davidson, 1924; Ochsenius, 1925; Weissenberg, 1925–26) have reported an increase in enuresis among children during World War One in countries in which there was great social unrest, deprivation, and general apprehension.[13] But one need not invoke the concept of conversion hysteria to account for loss of sphincter control in children under emotional stress. If excitement and nervous tension can produce lapses in this respect in children, as we know it can, even during the waking hours, how much more readily fearful dreams and nightmares might have a similar effect, when central control of the bodily functions is lessened due to sleep. There is, however, another possible way of accounting for the fact that children seem prone to react to deprivations and thwarting with enuresis, without positing the involvement of any specific element of fright; this point will be returned to shortly.

Fearfulness has often been assumed to be a primary cause of enuresis, and it may indeed be in some cases; but what would seem to be more frequently true is that enuresis is the primary condition and fearfulness a *consequence,* arising from the threats and punishments which are often resorted to by adults in attempting to eliminate this condition. Many children have been so harshly dealt with in connection with toilet training that they live in real terror of nocturnal lapses; and once the disgracefulness of bed-wetting, as reflected by the attitudes of adults, is accepted by the child and "internalized," a kind of vicious circle is often set up, the enuresis creating greater shame and apprehensiveness, which in turn may further aggravate the enuresis. In such cases it seems reasonable

---

sleep when it is expedient to do so. The reality-testing function of dreams which French (1937) has described, and which I have commonly seen in neurotic patients, may represent an intermediate step between these two levels of dream work.]

[13] This seems to have been especially true in Germany. Postwar American tourists have reported that German hotelkeepers often took it for granted that any child born between 1914 and 1918 would be a chronic bed-wetter, and acted accordingly.

to infer that the enuresis can be eliminated or at least materially helped by relieving the child of his old anxieties; but this is usually a long, tedious process. The writers have found that the simpler procedure is to give the child special training of the kind shortly to be described, which allows him to bring the urinary function under surer control and thus eliminate the cause for his previous anxiety. The stigma of being a bed-wetter weighs heavily upon a great many children; and the writers have noted that the elimination of this difficulty, when accomplished by rational, unemotional measures, comes as a distinct relief in such cases, making for better social attitudes and improved adjustment in general.[14] A "vicious circle" of the kind just described can undoubtedly be broken in some instances by attacking the emotional problems as basic; but this seems often to be a rather inverted method of approach, although in using other, more direct approaches the problem of motivation cannot be overlooked.

IV. Enuresis and Frustration Theory

Various writers (Davidson, 1924; Fuchs and Gross, 1916; Hoffman, 1919; Uteau and Richardot, 1916) have observed that enuresis seems to be unduly common among soldiers.[15] Discounting the not inconsiderable number of cases of malingering, where bed-wetting is deliberately resorted to in an attempt to obtain a disability discharge or at least to escape active service, veritable epidemics of real enuresis occur from time to time. If these outbreaks were reported only among men who are actively engaged in combat or who are in training for imminent service, the logical assumption would be that anxiety is here the prime etiological factor. The fact that enuresis may also be either recurrent or more or less chronic in barracks during times of prolonged peace suggests a different explanation, namely, that the discipline and arbitrary treatment which forms so large a part of military training may reinstate in young men attitudes of hostility and resentment which they felt as children toward parental authority but which they may have been

[14] By the elimination of enuresis, the attitude of parents toward a previously afflicted child is often radically changed, sometimes shifting the balance from near rejection to real acceptance.

[15] Hernaman-Johnson (1921) has raised the question as to whether this may not be due to the fact that many cases of enuresis in the population at large do not ordinarily come to professional attention. No definitive data are apparently available on this point, but observations cited below suggest that this writer's supposition is not entirely correct.

able to express only in such a roundabout way as being seemingly unable to acquire or retain the dry-bed habit.[16]

The veritable barrage of prohibitions and injunctions constituting the socialization of the growing child in our culture is inevitably frustrating; and, to make matters worse, the natural reaction to frustration (Dollard, Doob, Miller, *et al.,* 1939), namely, acts of outright defiance or attack upon the frustrating person or persons, is rigorously forbidden. It is not surprising, therefore, that resentments and hostilities which are thus forced underground crop up in strange places and in weird guises. A great many instances of constipation, eating idiosyncrasies, backwardness in speech, so-called reading disabilities and other problems commonly presented by modern children can be fully understood only when viewed in this light. Denied the luxury of undisguised aggression toward frustrating parents and teachers which children in many primitive societies are encouraged to express quite openly (Mead, 1930, 1935), the child in our culture is driven to such devices as feigned incapacities and passive noncooperation as the only means available of defending his individuality and warding off the too rapid encroachment of ways of life which to him seem unreasonable and foreign. Slowness in the acquisition of socially approved habits of elimination and periodic lapses in the exercise of these habits seem to be a form of self-assertion and retaliation by the infantile personality. The child who has discovered how effectively he can outrage the surrogates of the culture who are assigned to him in the form of his father and mother by the act of nocturnal enuresis, an act which is committed while he is asleep and therefore one for which he is usually not held fully accountable, has at his disposal a peculiarly effective outlet for his resentments: in this act he achieves real retaliation and at the same time tends to avoid the consequences which would follow if he committed an equally annoying act during his waking hours.[17] As McGuinness (1935) has aptly said:

Sometimes enuresis is an aggressive act in a very submissive child. It may arise from such strong emotions as fear, hatred, jealousy and inferiority. A child is at once at a disadvantage in the presence of adults in that he is physically unable to meet them on an equal ground. No matter what the

---

[16] Cameron (1924) has remarked, "In [English] schools, if punishment were meted out or other boys became critical, the disorder [enuresis] could become epidemic. Sometimes the hysterical suggestion extended to the bowel, and incontinence of faeces was added" (p. 48).

[17] The fact that there is a certain similarity between this and the so-called secondary gain from neurotic illnesses does not, of course, warrant the inference that, because of this, eneursis must be symptomatic of a neurosis.

adult may do, however, the child is the sole master of his function of elimination, and he can always employ this route for voicing his protest (p. 289).

In 2 of the 30 children on whom the present study is based, enuretic behavior had a conspicuously aggressive connotation; in various other members of the group a smaller or larger element of hostility seemed likewise to be involved. In such cases it is obviously essential that the child's attitude toward parents or parent substitutes be changed from one of ambivalence in which negative feelings predominate to one in which positive feelings are stronger.[18] Then and only then can specific educational procedures be expected to produce permanently satisfactory results. In fact, it seems to be a sound generalization that in order for child training of any kind to proceed smoothly and effectively and to be enduring, the love of the child for the adult in the situation must be strong enough to counteract, or at least hold in bounds, the negative impulses which are certain to be engendered by the educative process (Aichhorn, 1936). With this principle clearly in mind one is justified in seeking for improved educational techniques as such; but without proper recognition of this basic personal equation, otherwise satisfactory methods are likely to miscarry sadly.[19]

V. A Conditioned-Response Rationale

The first requirement, therefore, for the establishment of satisfactory toilet habits in children is the existence of thorough confidence in and respect and affection for the adults who are commissioned to carry out the requisite training. Moreover, the acquisition of bladder control during sleep being something of a feat for

[18] Goldman (1934–35) reports that, after a negative physical examination, he routinely refers enuretic children to the psychological clinic. "Here both child and parent are studied and treated from the standpoint of functional derangement. . . . Enuresis is a problem of both the physician and the psychologist" (p. 293).

McGuinness (1935) says: "It is necessary to keep certain principles in mind [which are]: Making friends with the child; gaining the child's confidence and interest, and allowing him more chance to develop new channels of activity and self-expression. The re-education of parents is important and usually difficult" (p. 293).

[19] Not only is the establishment of a strong affectional bond between child and parent essential for the elimination of hostility as a possible cause of enuresis, but it is also known from a variety of investigations (mostly psychoanalytic) that developing love for parents (object-choice, as contrasted to the narcissism of infancy) is an important factor in suppressing infantile sexuality and bringing about the so-called latency period. To the extent, therefore, that enuresis is a form of persistent infantile eroticism, it is also important that the child-parent relationship be taken into account in enuresis therapy. It is not without significance to note that the incidence of enuresis in orphanages, where children do not enjoy normal parental relationships, is often alleged to be exceptionally high (Fordyce and others, 1924; Markey, 1932; Weissenberg, 1925–26).

the young child, he should not be motivated to a higher level of performance than he is capable of attaining in the light of his age and specific capacities, lest anxieties be developed which will retard the real training process and perhaps lead to disturbances in other departments of the child's life. Further study of this problem is desirable, especially in the way of comparing the manner in which children react to the different total patterns of training given in various cultures, before definitive conclusions can be reached in this field; but it seems to be a safe assumption that at least one helpful step could be made toward the solution of this problem in our own culture if the training which we employ with children in order to aid them in the acquisition of bladder control during sleep could be made *more specific and precise. If this could be done, the severity of methods used to motivate this type of learning in the child could presumably be reduced, with an improvement in the general parent-child relationship and with less emotional stress upon all concerned. This procedure, coupled with an appreciation of the aggressive implications which enuresis sometimes has, should constitute a distinct step in advance of the bungling, hit-or-miss methods which have been traditionally employed.*[20]

In so far as the most common method of training in bladder control during sleep may be said to rest upon any definite psychological theory, it would appear to be this, that if the child is repeatedly awakened at a time when the bladder is partially filled, but not so distended as to produce reflex emptying, the attendant bladder stimulation will eventually become specifically associated with the response of awakening, before the point has been reached at which voiding tends to occur automatically. On the assumption that this interpretation is substantially correct, there now arises this important question: would it not be advantageous from the point of view of most efficient habit formation if the awakening could always occur at a time when bladder distention is maximal and only at such a time, instead of at more or less arbitrarily determined intervals during the night, when bladder-filling may be at any of various stages? If some arrangement could be provided so that the sleeping child would be awakened *just after the onset of*

---

[20] Certain writers have taken the position that enuresis has nothing to do with adequacy of habit formation, holding instead that it is *entirely* dependent upon personality dynamics. Hamill (1929), for example, states that "The sleeper responds [by awakening] to the stimulus [of a full bladder] if he wants to. . . . The histories in all the improved cases contain conclusive evidence of one fundamental conclusion: these children can stop [wetting the bed] if and when they wish to." It is suggestive that, using as therapy clinical interviews based upon the foregoing assumption, Hamill obtained cures in only 40 of the 80 cases so treated.

urination, and only at this time, the resulting association of bladder distention and the response of awakening and inhibiting further urination should provide precisely the form of training which would seem to be most specifically appropriate.[21] This conception of an improved habit-formation sequence can be schematically represented as follows:

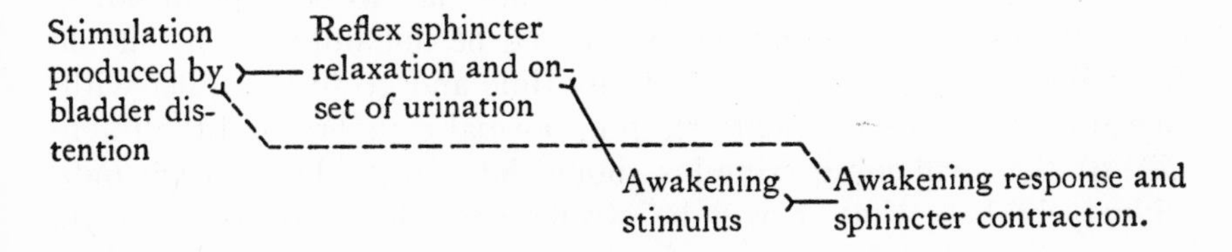

By the well-known conditioned-response principle of Pavlov, an increasingly strong functional connection (dotted line) would be expected to develop between the stimulation arising from the distention of the bladder and the responses of awakening and contracting the bladder sphincter. Soon this connection should become sufficiently well established to cause the awakening response and the contraction of the bladder sphincter to "come forward" in time and occur actually in advance of the onset of urination, instead of afterwards. The conditioned contraction of the sphincter in response to bladder distention would thus tend to inhibit the occurrence of reflex sphincter relaxation during sleep and to lead to awakening when bladder pressure finally becomes sufficiently great. We thus have a theoretical basis for the expectation that soon the subject would not only cease to urinate reflexly during sleep but would also become capable of retaining his urine longer than had previously been possible, without necessarily awakening. This, as we know, is the ideal state of affairs and the one actually attained when the conditions of "bladder training" have been favorable; not only does the successfully conditioned child refrain from urinating reflexly in bed, but he is also able to sleep through the night without having to awaken and go to the toilet more than once, if at all.

---

[21] Schacter (1932), one of many writers (reviewed by Anderson, 1930, pp. 603–604) who have expressed the view that enuresis commonly reflects a habit deficiency, believes that it "represents a weakness in the development of cortical dominance of the urinary function during sleep; more especially of a deficiency of inhibitory control over an essentially automatic function." But his proposal that the child with this difficulty be taught to set an alarm clock to awaken him at fixed intervals has the same disadvantages as periodic awakening by the parents, except that it is more convenient for the latter. For a discussion of the mechanics of habit formation in this situation, see also Bott, Blatz, Chant, and Bott (1928).

VI. Instrumentation

If regular awakening of the enuretic child immediately after the onset of urination was to be rendered possible, it was obvious that this would have to be accomplished by means of some automatic mechanical arrangement.[22] In attempting to devise such a mechanism, four important considerations had to be kept in mind: the child's freedom of movement should be unhampered, he should be at liberty to get out of bed at any time and go to the toilet without aid, he should be able to sleep in normal comfort, and the intensity of the awakening stimulus should be adjustable for each individual child so that it will be strong enough to arouse him yet not so strong as to produce fright or any other traumatic effect. The most satisfactory way of meeting these requirements seemed to be to take advantage of the electrolytic properties of urine so as to allow it, upon escaping from the child, to complete an electrical circuit which would then bring about the presentation of whatever stimulus might be selected to produce arousal. To this end a special type of pad has been developed, consisting of two thicknesses of heavy absorbent cotton fabric (28 by 32 inches) which serve as a separator between two equally large pieces of #16 bronze screening, with the top piece of the screening covered by a third thickness of the fabric. This combination is quilted together and is light in weight, durable, and not uncomfortable for the child to sleep on. As long as the pad is dry, there is no electrical contact between the two pieces of screening; but as soon as urine strikes the pad, it quickly penetrates the fabric and forms a contact. By having the two pieces of screening which are contained in the pad connected (by means of flexible, insulated wires) in series with a small battery and a sensitive relay, it is thus possible to cause the short-circuiting of the pad to activate the relay which in turn can be made to complete a second circuit which causes the waking stimulus to be presented. After some experimentation, a common electric doorbell has been selected for this purpose; this, together with a rheostat for controlling its loudness, the relay, and the necessary batteries can be compactly mounted in a small metal box with a telephone jack installed at one end for insertion of a

[22] Under primitive conditions, where mother and child sleep in close physical contact, with little or no clothing separating them, urination by the child is likely to produce a reaction on the part of the mother which would tend to have much the same effect as the inanimate device here proposed (see Footnote 5). The present proposal is, therefore, nothing but an attempt to provide the modern civilized child with an advantage which children have doubtless enjoyed for countless ages under primitive life conditions.

plug attached to the two wires (twisted lamp cord) communicating with the pad on which the child sleeps. A pad of the type described usually short-circuits within 2 or 3 seconds after urine strikes it, which means that the interval between onset of urination and the presentation of the waking stimulus is thus relatively brief.[23]

It is possible that the accidental escape of saliva from the mouth of a sleeping child might short-circuit the pad if the saliva came into contact with it; but this is easily avoided by placing the pad under only the lower part of the child, with the head well above its upper edge. In very humid weather a pad may absorb during the day sufficient moisture from the atmosphere to render it inoperative; but a short period of drying on a radiator or over an electric lamp before being put on the child's bed will restore its usability. If a child tends to perspire excessively during warm weather, his covering should be reduced to a minimum, and the sensitivity of the relay can be diminished somewhat so the sweat which is taken up from the child's body will not activate it and cause the presentation of the awakening stimulus. There is the further possible complication that, in the case of adolescent boys, the pad may be short-circuited by nocturnal emissions. Whether this would indeed occur and if it did occur whether it would have any untoward consequences are questions which can be answered only by empirical observations which have not as yet been made.

VII. Related Studies

A review of the literature on the topic of enuresis extending back two decades (which was conducted in November, 1935, at the time that the present method of treatment was first undertaken by the writers at the New Haven Children's Center) revealed no record of a similar method having previously been reported. Several references to methods of treatment were discovered which entail interference with, or obstruction of, normal urination by means of clamps, rubber sacks, and so forth;[24] and it seems likely that some of these methods—notably those which actually prevent the passage of urine—may operate somewhat like the present method of treatment in that they would conjecturally tend to produce awakening

[23] The construction of the pads and apparatus essential for the application of this method of treating enuresis has been described in detail elsewhere (Mowrer, 1938a) and will not be considered further in the present report. It should be mentioned in passing that the electrical currents used to operate this apparatus are very weak and cannot come into contact with the child so as to produce a shock.

[24] See, for example, Glaser and Landau (1936), Baretz (1936), and Bonjour (1931).

immediately after the onset of attempted urination. But they also have certain features which make them considerably less satisfactory than the present method, even though good therapeutic results have been reported from their use in several instances.

Some months later (May 4, 1936), the *Baltimore Sun* published the following statement as a legend beneath an Associated Press photograph:

Sverdlovsk, U.S.S.R.—Russian science has just announced this gift to Soviet motherhood—a light which flashes when baby needs changing. Wires from batteries are attached to strips of tinfoil in a special packet beneath the infant. Cloth sandwiched between the tinfoil becomes a conductor when dampened and, presto, the light goes on. The system is already in use in a hospital here.

Subsequently a survey of the literature prior to 1915 showed that in 1904, Pfaundler, the German pediatrician, described an arrangement very similar in principle to the one more recently developed in Russia which was originally designed for precisely the same purpose. However, instead of having a light which flashed on and signaled the infant's need of changing, Pfaundler arranged his apparatus so that an electric bell would ring. When an enuretic child was admitted to the children's ward of his hospital, Pfaundler later made a practice of having its bed equipped with one of these devices and was surprised to find that, if used continuously for a month or so, the method—which he had merely hoped would serve to inform the nurses that the child was wet and needed changing —was likely to have distinct therapeutic consequences. He reports that in some cases just the knowledge that urination in bed during the night would cause a bell to ring henceforth inhibited this act (an observation which the present writers can corroborate).

Following the announcement of Pfaundler's accidental discovery of this method of treating nocturnal enuresis, Genouville and Rémy-Roux published, respectively in 1908 and 1910, papers dealing with the application of Pfaundler's method, which they reported as giving good results. Genouville says:

Rapidly, at the end of a few nights, accidents become rarer and rarer. Finally they cease, due to the education of the sphincter through sudden awakening by the bell. It is nevertheless necessary, as experience has shown, to continue the use of the apparatus somewhat longer, which is a simple matter since, the accidents having ceased, the bell remains henceforth silent (p. 101).

[In using this method, which he termed "suggestion without words," Genouville found, as have the present writers, that the sound of the bell will almost always inhibit further urination, even though it does not at first produce awakening; and he concluded that] It is therefore because it produces useful contractions of the sphincter and especially because it produces them at the desired physiological moment, with a precise physiological relevance, that the application of our apparatus is capable of giving good results (p. 106).

And Rémy-Roux pertinently adds:

The effect is not the same, as Genouville has rightly said, if the parents awaken the child at fixed hours and have it urinate. We have all seen this method, commonly employed by families, fail: there is a great difference between a child's being awakened at times when the need to urinate is perhaps not even being felt and his being suddenly aroused by the bell, exactly at the instant when involuntary micturition is in the act of occurring. In the first case, it is as if one were in reality trying to habituate the child to urinating during the night, which is superfluous; in the second case, on the other hand, the child's mind is sensitized and the bell, which sounds when he is fully asleep, at the same instant that the bladder is emptying, suddenly stops the stream of urine by a vigorous contraction of the sphincter (p. 339).[25]

Although Genouville and Rémy-Roux both reported rather dramatic success with Pfaundler's method of treating enuresis, the technique apparently did not come into widespread use; but this is thoroughly understandable when one notes the cumbersome, inefficient design and construction of the Pfaundler apparatus. One major defect was that in order for the apparatus to operate, a sufficiently strong electrical current to ring the bell directly had to pass through the moistened area of the pad on which the patient slept. This had numerous disadvantages, most serious of which were the relatively great amount of urine (Genouville says 20 to 30 c.c.) which had to be voided before an adequate contact was established and the fact that the electrical current, when it did begin to flow in sufficient amount to ring the bell, tended to produce rapid oxidation of the two metal screens contained in the pad. These difficulties are obviated by the interpolation of a sensitive relay between the pad circuit and the bell circuit. One other complication was that, with the Pfaundler method, the pad on which the child slept was not permanently quilted together, but consisted instead of two loose pieces of screening, with a removable piece of linen (Rémy-Roux used a layer of absorbent cotton) sand-

[25] In 1916, Uteau and Richardot reported having developed a method of recording the time during the night at which bed-wetting occurred in soldiers who were under suspicion of malingering. If the wetting (which stopped a specially constructed clock) occurred just before the subject got up in the morning, instead of earlier in the night, malingering was assumed to have been established. Although their method was technically very much like that originally developed by Pfaundler, Uteau and Richardot made no attempt to apply it as a therapeutic measure.

wiched between, the resulting combination being then placed under the bottom sheet of the child's bed. The type of pad developed by the present writers is obviously more convenient and efficient.

VIII. Application of Method

In using their method of treating enuresis, the writers have found it expedient to observe certain rules and principles, which have been formulated and supplied to other persons who have employed the method, as follows:

Instructions

The distinctive feature of this method of treating nocturnal enuresis or bed-wetting is that it provides a means of causing the sleeping child to be regularly awakened immediately after the onset of urination, thus tending to establish a specific association or connection between the need to urinate and the act of awakening. With careful observation of the following rules, excellent results may be expected within four to eight weeks in children whose enuresis is not complicated by serious personality difficulties or by organic illness. In children in whom physical or serious emotional complications are suspected, this method of treatment is not recommended, except when applied under psychological or medical supervision. Neither is this method recommended, except under professional guidance, for use with children under three years of age.

Before treatment is begun the child should be fully apprised of the general nature of the method. If desired, a small amount of water (with a little table salt added) may even be poured on one of the pads on which the child is to sleep in order to indicate to him what will happen when he urinates on the pad during the night. He will see that the only thing which occurs is that the bell in the box on the floor rings and that there is no reason to be apprehensive or fearful. It should also be mentioned to older children that there is no possibility of their receiving an electrical shock.

The child should sleep in a bed that can easily be gotten into and out of, in a dimly lighted, moderately warm room from which the bathroom is conveniently accessible. Upon being put to bed each night, the child should be admonished to awaken and jump out of bed and go to the toilet the moment he hears the bell begin to ring. He should also repeatedly be urged to get up and go to the bathroom alone every time he awakens in the night, even though he feels no specific urge to do so. Once the use of this method has been commenced, all routine arousing of the child should be discontinued. In the beginning the ringing of the bell may not awaken the child. In this event the child should be aroused by the attending adult as speedily as possible *while the bell is still ringing*. After the child is on his way to the bathroom, the plug at the end of the piece of lamp cord attatched to the pad should be withdrawn from the receptacle in the end of the box, a dry pad placed on the bed and connected with the box, and the wet pad dried, either on a radiator or over (but not too close to) one or two electric lamps.

It is essential that the child under treatment for enuresis by this method be required to sleep nude below the waist. He should wear only a jacket or short shirt of some kind. Otherwise a very considerable amount of urine may be voided and absorbed by the lower part of his clothing before sufficient urine reaches the pad to cause the bell to ring. The child sleeps, of course, directly on the pad, with the requisite amount of covering over him but not with a sheet or anything else between him and the pad. A rubber sheet may be used under the pad on which the child sleeps as a protection to the mattress, but this is merely a precaution rather than a necessity as there is ordinarily not enough urine voided to pass through the pad and wet anything below. Usually the ringing of the bell will inhibit further urination on the pad, even though it does not awaken the child. (If the child persistently makes a spot larger than two or three inches in diameter, it suggests that the wetting is being engaged in intentionally, after the child is already awake.) The size of the wet spot thus being ordinarly small, drying is a quick, simple process. If, after continued use, a pad becomes slightly offensive, it can be washed by immersion in a solution of warm water, soap, and ammonia. After being thoroughly dried (preferably out of doors in the sunshine), it is again ready for use. With proper care a pad will give continuous service for at least two years.

Once the present method of treating enuresis has been undertaken, all other therapeutic devices aimed specifically at the enuresis should be discontinued. There should, for example, be no restriction of diet or fluid intake. In older children (of five years or over), we have in fact found it desirable to recommend the following practice. After the child has gone seven consecutive dry nights on the pad with normal fluid intake, his fluid intake is increased somewhat (by the amount of one or two cups of water) just before retiring. This practice should be continued until the child has again gone seven successive nights without wetting. The extra water and the use of the pad should then *both be discontinued.* In the case of younger children, our recommendation is that they be trained to the criterion of seven consecutive dry nights with normal fluid intake and the method then be discontinued. No additional incentive or reward other than the privilege of ceasing to sleep on the pad should be employed in any case. Once the use of the method has been undertaken, it should not be interrupted except for the most urgent reasons until the treatment is completed. Relapses following this method of treatment are relatively rare, but if they should occur, the treatment should be resumed and continued until the child once more succeeds in having seven successive dry nights, with or without an increased fluid intake, depending upon the age of the child.

The electrical apparatus required for the use of this method is relatively simple, but the box in which it is contained is kept locked as a protection against possible damage. If the apparatus ceases to operate, the physician or psychologist who is supervising its use should be notified. Ordinarily this apparatus will give perfect service for many months without any readjustment or attention.

IX. Results

Although careful individual records and case histories have been kept on the 30 children (ranging in age from 3 to 13 years) who have thus far been treated for enuresis by this method, it does not seem necessary to present any of these at this time. Suffice it to say that elimination of enuresis, to the criterion stated above, has been achieved *in all cases,* the maximum time required to accomplish this in any child being two months. The promptness of the therapeutic effect depends, of course, upon the age of the child, his eagerness to overcome his difficulty, and a number of other variables. We have naturally refrained from using this method with highly neurotic and psychotic children, just as one would refrain from making otherwise normal physical demands on children who are physically ill or genuinely incapacitated. One feeble-minded child with an I.Q. of approximately 65 was, however, included in the group treated and responded satisfactorily. It will be interesting to determine the extent to which this method can be used to cope with enuresis in children with even lower intelligence.[26]

Personality changes, when any have occurred as a result of the application of the present method of treating enuresis, have uniformly been in a favorable direction. In no case has there been any evidence of "symptom substitution." Our results, therefore, do not support the assumption, sometimes made, that any attempt to deal directly with the problem of enuresis will necessarily result in the child's developing "something worse." Although the majority of the children with whom this therapeutic procedure has been employed were, at the time of treatment, under observation at the New Haven Children's Center and consequently living under as favorable conditions as could be provided, the method has also proved its applicability in private homes, when used by parents (under professional supervision), without any special alteration in the child's normal surroundings. Home situations will undoubtedly be encountered in which this procedure will not work; but our findings to date suggest that there is probably a relatively large group of enuretic children who can be successfully dealt with in this way. In fact, some of the most dramatic cures of enuresis which have

---

[26] The method is now being tested, under the direction of Dr. Anthony J. Mitrano, with a large group of defective children at the Vineland Training School, Vineland, New Jersey. To date Dr. Mitrano reports uniformly favorable results. The method is also being successfully used under the direction of workers at the Psychological Clinic of Northwestern University.

thus far been obtained have occurred in children treated under normal home conditions.

Relapses have sometimes occurred a few weeks or a few months after treatment, but this has usually happened in children who have had to return to an intolerable home situation, where emotional stresses are too great and newly acquired habits give way to old ones. Other children, however, have now maintained the new behavior resulting from treatment for as long as two and a half years, and the usual expectancy is that the cure will be permanent. Even if there were no therapeutic gain whatever in certain cases, the application of this method would nevertheless have some advantage, even in these instances; for the opportunity which it affords of preventing the enuretic child from urinating more than a few drops, which occurs on a pad that can be quickly exchanged and dried, and of then having the child complete the act of urination in the bathroom, is in itself an advance over the situation in which the child floods the whole bed, which then has to be completely changed.

The fact that this method of dealing with enuresis involves an automatic mechanical arrangement and is therefore less dependent upon the particular personality traits of the individuals applying it has numerous advantages, but it also has some conceivable disadvantages which should be mentioned. The method makes it possible for intimidation, physical punishment, and tense emotional tactics in general to be dispensed with and, in effecting an eradication of enuresis, incidentally eliminates what is often a source of serious friction between parent and child. Since the method is thus relatively automatic, it gives promise of being useful in the hands of a wider percentage of persons than other less specific methods have been found to be. We must again warn against the assumption that the method can be made to function in an entirely impersonal manner in all cases; and we wish to re-emphasize the importance of its being applied only under the supervision of psychologically trained persons who are capable of detecting and dealing with emotional tensions between the child and the surrounding adults when these seem likely to delay or prevent the achievement of therapeutic success. In the hands of vindictive, sadistic persons this method can, to be sure, become just another means of assaulting the privacy and individuality of the enuretic child; but even in such circumstances the application of a technique from which the child is likely to obtain a specific and useful form of training seems decidedly preferable to the innumerable other procedures which are always available to brutal parents and other persons who are more intent upon obtaining gratification of displaced aggressive impulses than they are interested in helping children really overcome their difficulties.

One further point remains to be considered in this connection, namely, whether the present method of treating enuresis should be used to supplement or replace the usual methods of early toilet training. Despite certain similarities, there is this important difference between the problem of terminating the so-called physiological incontinence of infants (under three years of age) and that of eliminating the behavior which is more or less arbitrarily distinguished in older children as enuresis. In the older child, all the capacities necessary for the development of approved toilet habits are assumed to be present; here the problem appears to be primarily one of providing a specifically appropriate type of training. In the case of the infant, however, the possibility of establishing continence is directly contingent upon certain maturational factors: not only must cortical functioning have reached a relatively advanced stage of development, but the physical ability on the part of the child to get out of bed and go to the toilet unaided, or the verbal capacity to call and make his needs known, must also be taken into account. In the infant, therefore, pressure for the establishment of approved toilet habits at night must not be too insistent, and the methods used must be suited to the level of the child's physical and mental development. Since the method of treating enuresis which is described in the present paper presupposes that the child is old enough and well enough developed physically to get out of bed alone and attend to his toilet routine unassisted, it would probably be inadvisable to try to use this method with younger children in whom these abilities are not yet present. It may, however, prove helpful to use a pad of the kind described above with infants, merely as a means of signaling to the attending adult (e.g., by means of a light or a remotely located buzzer) that the child has urinated and is in need of attention, so that he will become accustomed to being dry instead of lying for long periods in wet clothing. Aside from this possible modified application, we do not at present recommend that the technique which we have developed for dealing with enuresis in older children be used with subjects under three years of age, except possibly in special cases where expert psychological observation and guidance can be maintained. Although we cannot afford to go too far in emulating the leniency with which children are treated in many primitive cultures, lest we undermine the very foundation of the adult type of personality which we value in civilized society, we are inclined to be unnecessarily exacting of our children and can doubtless go a long way in the direction of greater leniency in many situations, of which toilet training would appear to be one. Given the assurance of having at their disposal a reliable and effective method of dealing with the problem should it persist unduly long, parents will perhaps find it less imperative to push toilet training as feverishly as they are now inclined to do and will be able to become somewhat more casual in this connection, with salutary effect.

X. Enuresis: Symptom or Habit Deficit?

The writers anticipate that their method of dealing with enuresis will be in some quarters characterized, despite the favorable character of the results thus far obtained and the qualifications and warnings given against an oversimplified view of the problem, as "symptomatic therapy." Not so much in defense of this method—which can stand or fall on its own merits—as in an attempt to indicate some of the generally uncritical thinking which has come over into the field of child training and education in the form of careless medical analogies, we are impelled to make a few concluding remarks on this score. Illustrative of the view which has gained currency among a large group of writers regarding the meaning and management of all forms of so-called "problem" behavior in children is the following statement by Beverly (1933) concerning enuresis:

> [Enuresis] must be considered as a symptom—analogous to a fever. The chief concern should be to determine the other symptoms and attempt to find the underlying cause of the difficulty. Just as we are more concerned about the cause of the fever and other symptoms, so we should primarily be concerned with the cause of the incontinence and other symptoms. Just as we no longer treat the fever primarily, but its cause, so we should no longer treat the incontinence primarily, but its cause. Just as the fever disappears when its cause has been eradicated, so the incontinence disappears if the underlying cause can be eradicated (p. 723).[27]

The common criterion as to whether a given item of child behavior is or is not a "symptom"—in so far as attention is usually given to this problem—seems to be whether somebody who is important in the life of the child objects to it. Let us suppose that a three-year-old child eats peas with a spoon instead of a fork and that someone does object to it; this item of behavior becomes a

[27] A colleague once expressed disapproval of our approach to the problem of enuresis on the grounds that if one succeeds in eliminating a child's enuresis by such direct methods, one often "loses one's barometer" and is henceforth unable to tell whether there is really anything wrong with the child, psychiatrically.

"symptom," and as such it must not be dealt with directly; training the child by straightforward methods to use a fork instead of a spoon would be "symptomatic therapy." What one must do is to eliminate, once and for all, the "underlying cause," which in this case is presumably the child's hunger. This reasoning is made none the less fallacious by the fact that it is implicit in the commonly recommended practice of restricting the fluid intake of enuretic children: no one can deny that a child does urinate *because* he drinks water.[28]

But let us suppose that the position now be taken that a given item of behavior, such as eating peas with a spoon instead of a fork, really becomes a "symptom" only after ordinary methods of training and disapproval have failed to eliminate it. The "underlying cause" of this behavior will now be said to be either feeble-mindedness or negativism, stubbornness, hostility, or some other attitude implying thwarting and frustration. Assuming that the methods employed in the situation have been reasonably adequate (which is not always true of training for bladder control during sleep), the perverse behavior can supposedly be dealt with only by eliminating some of the basic dissatisfactions in the life of the child; punishment, while perhaps eradicating the specific behavior at which it is directed, is said only to increase the child's smoldering resentments, which will erupt sooner or later in some other form.

---

[28] The loose way in which the term "symptom" is commonly used in the field of child conduct implies little more than that the behavior to which it refers is *caused;* such an affirmation has, of course, no significance or value. In physical diagnosis a *symptom* is usually defined as any subjectively experienced phenomenon which a patient reports and complains of to the physician, for whom it then becomes a *sign* of a disease process. In the great majority of instances, so-called "behavior problems" in children are certainly not symptoms in this sense; for it is usually some *other person,* not the child himself, who reports and complains of them. In his psychoanalytic writings Freud has used the terms "symptom" and "symptom-formation" in a restricted, technically defined sense; for him they always imply anxiety, repression, and regression, occurring in a special sequence and pattern. It is the writers' impression that much would be gained if these terms were used only in this delimited and explicit manner.

It is indeed true that enuresis *may* be a symptom in the strict sense; but like so many other items of childhood behavior, it is impossible to determine from its sheer form whether it represents real psychopathology or merely reflects faulty education and training. When urinary continence has been established and maintained for some months or years and is then lost, there is a strong presumption that the resulting enuresis is, in fact, a symptom; but otherwise, in the case of children who have never ceased to show nocturnal incontinence, which is regarded as normal during infancy, how is one to know from the incontinence alone that it is a symptom rather than simply a reflection of pedagogical inadequacy on the part of nurses and parents? And when does persisting behavior of this kind suddenly cease to be normal and become a symptom? As pointed out above, the age at which bladder control during sleep is expected of children varies enormously in different cultures and can therefore scarcely be regarded as a valid criterion for judgment in this respect. The problem clearly warrants more careful consideration than has been accorded it.

The writers have repeatedly stressed in this paper their belief that, in a situation where an enuretic child is under the control of parents or parent substitutes whom he hates more than he loves, it will materially facilitate the treatment of his difficulty if the child's affective valences can be altered in a positive direction. But what must not be overlooked is that all education is more or less frustrating and that even the best-loved of children have periods of resentment when they show behavior which is either directly or indirectly retaliatory. If we insist, therefore, whenever behavior of this kind appears, that the only *safe* way of dealing with it is to remove the underlying frustration, we unavoidably repudiate our responsibility for the education and socialization of our children. Not only education but life itself is frustrating, and unfortunate indeed is the child who does not learn to tolerate this type of experience and to readjust accordingly.

The issue here involved is, in reality, a focal point of the perennial variance between clinician and educator (parent, teacher, or clergyman). The specialist who is engaged exclusively in therapeutic work sees mainly the bad effects of education and is likely to reach the conclusion that education in general is mainly bad.[29] The educator, on the other hand, sensing his position as the authorized agent for perpetuating the accepted values and traditional ways of the culture, is inclined to hew close to the traditionally prescribed line, letting the chips, in the form of distorted, broken personalities, fall as they may. The charge by the clinician that the educator is "brutal" and "sadistic" and the countercharge by the educator that the clinician is "unrealistic" are perhaps but the displaced expressions of a common dissatisfaction with the tense, ruthlessly competitive conditions of civilized life as we know it, which neither the educator nor the clinician usually cares to criticize, much less take active steps to change. Dollard (1935) has brilliantly set this problem, and the reader is referred to his paper for a discussion of its further implications. Present purposes will have been served if these remarks but call attention to the futility of the guerrilla warfare which continually occurs between the clinician and the educator, which could be so profitably turned into a joint attack upon the problems of "social engineering" and the creation of a culture giving greater promise of "maximal gratification of the instinctual life of individuals while guaranteeing the security of all in the pursuit of their aims" (Dollard, 1935, p. 433).

[29] It must be said, to their great credit, that both Sigmund Freud (1935a) and Anna Freud (1928) have carefully sought to avoid this error.

Summary

A survey of the literature on the topic of nocturnal enuresis shows that most modern writers in this field are inclined to believe either (*a*) that enuresis is merely a continuation, due to inadequate training, of the physiological incontinence of infancy or (*b*) that it is caused by certain emotional needs which are not finding appropriate expression during the child's waking hours. Those writers who subscribe to the latter view may be subdivided according to whether they believe: (1) that enuresis is a substitutive form of gratification of repressed genital sexuality, (2) that it is a symptom of deep-seated anxieties and fears, or (3) that it is a disguised expression of hostility toward parents or parent substitutes which the victim of the enuresis does not dare to express more openly.

There can now be scarcely any doubt that one or more of these emotional factors are of predominant etiological significance in isolated cases of enuresis and that they are contributing factors in a much larger group of cases; but they do not, in the opinion of the present writers, provide a fully satisfactory and comprehensive explanation of enuresis in general. On the basis of a variety of evidence which is cited, it appears that there is a relatively large group of enuretic children in whom faulty habit training is the predominant, perhaps exclusive, causal factor and that it is an important contributing factor in many instances of enuresis where emotional considerations are also involved.

In many primitive societies the young child spends much of its waking as well as sleeping life in intimate contact with the body of the mother, with little or no clothing between them. Under these circumstances, the onset of urination by the child is likely to produce an immediate response on the part of the mother, which tends to check the urination and produce awakening, thereby providing psychologically efficient conditions for the development of bladder control in the child during sleep. But conditions are very different in our own culture; and if a child in civilized societies is to have the benefit of this more specific form of conditioning, it is clear that some automatic mechanical arrangement will have to be provided. Such an arrangement is described in the present report.

The method of approach to the problem of enuresis here proposed, combined with an appreciation of the aggressive implications which this form of behavior commonly involves, has produced therapeutic success in all of the 30 children with whom it has so far been employed. In no case has there been any indication of "symptom substitution," such personality changes as have resulted from its application being uniformly in a favorable direction. It is concluded that the widespread view that enuresis is always a "symptom" and must not be dealt with directly represents the misapplication of a concept illicitly borrowed from adult medicine and psychopathology.

[Shortly after this paper was published, Dr. Joseph J. Michaels (1939) prepared a critique thereof, which also appeared in the *American Journal of Orthopsychiatry.* At about the same time Morgan and Witmer (1939) published, independently, an account of the results obtained from the use of a similar method. In 1946, Dr. H. Wright Seiger announced an improvement in the type of "pad" on which the child sleeps. Persons interested in obtaining this newer and simplified form of the apparatus may communicate with Dr. Seiger. More recently Davidson and Douglass (1950) have described still another version of the apparatus, with which highly satisfactory results have also been obtained.]

CHAPTER 15

TIME AS A DETERMINANT IN INTEGRATIVE LEARNING

[In the laboratory, the effects of reward and of punishment are usually studied separately. If, however, we create a situation in which a given type of behavior has consequences which are both rewarding *and* punishing and if, moreover, we vary the *temporal relationship* of these consequences both with respect to each other and with respect to the act which they follow, we approximate a degree of complexity comparable to that encountered by living organisms in ordinary life. In the experimental paradigm which is here described, questions arise which transcend those customarily considered in learning research and which approximate those with which human beings are concerned in their everyday existence.

Elsewhere, Mowrer and Kluckhohn (1944) have proposed a systematic distinction between *adaptation* and *adjustment,* the former being the process whereby living organisms become organically modified, generation to generation, in such a way as to make for surer survival and the latter being the process whereby living organisms become behaviorally or functionally modified in such a way as to reduce discomfort and increase pleasure. In the present paper the concept of *integration* is added as a third major frame of reference, in which the chief concern is with *conflict resolution,* with the harmonizing of competing adjustments (habits) in such a way as to insure the greatest *long-term* satisfaction and security to both the individual and his society. It is clearly in this latter area that such problems as morality, personal freedom, will power, and failure to integrate (neurosis) lie.

Although not called by this term, it is in this paper that the author first discusses the "neurotic paradox," which receives more extended treatment in a subsequent study (18). Here also to be found are adumbrations of views on anxiety which will be presented later (19) and dissatisfactions with certain fundamental aspects of Freudian theory which are likewise more fully treated in the latter part of this volume (17, 20, 21, 23, 24).

This study was conducted jointly with Albert D. Ullman and was first published in the *Psychological Review* (1945).]

Each of the three great schools of contemporary psychology has made distinctive contributions to the better understanding of the integrated functioning of living organisms. Gestalt psychology has particularly stressed the view that behavior is always a product of the total psychological situation.[1] From its inception, psychoanalysis has been indirectly concerned with the phenomenon of integration through its antithesis, namely, psychological conflict; and, more recently, analytic writers have dealt increasingly with the "synthetic functions of the ego," whereby the competing demands of id, superego, and external reality are somehow reconciled (A. Freud, 1937; S. Freud, 1922, 1935b). Even stimulus-response or "objective" psychology, though preoccupied with a more segmental approach to the study of behavior, has fostered many researches on the "complex learning processes."[2]

Yet a basic problem remains unsolved. It is a familiar fact that living organisms sometimes manifest behavior which is chronically *nonintegrative,* i.e, behavior which is consistently *more punishing than rewarding.* This fact constitutes a major theoretical paradox and is the outstanding characteristic of neurosis and criminality. The present paper attempts to show that the factor of *time* is of special significance in this connection and that only by taking it into explicit account can the problem of persistent nonintegrative behavior be satisfactorily defined and a hopeful way to its theoretical solution be indicated.

I. Gestalt Theory, Psychoanalysis, and Stimulus-Response Psychology Compared

While stressing "organization," "insight," "configuration," and other integrational concepts, Gestalt psychologists have had little to say about integration *failure.* Perhaps the main reason for this neglect is the fact that writers of the "wholistic" persuasion tend to regard integration as an automatic consequence of organic maturation or "growth" which can be used as an explanatory device instead of being something which is an outcome of psychological processes and which must itself be studied and explained. For Gestalt writers, integration tends to be an unanalyzable ultimate,

[1] See Hopkins (1937), Redfield (1942), Howells (1940), and Smuts (1926) for an indication of the widely diverse fields into which Gestalt conceptions of integration have permeated.

[2] See, for example, the chapter by Heron in Moss's *Comparative psychology* (1942). Cf. also the chapters on "problem-solving behavior" and "thinking" in Woodworth's *Experimental psychology* (1938).

without antithesis.[3] This tendency is illustrated by the fact that a well-known book in this field (Koffka, 1928) lists 25 separate index references to "configuration" but not one to "conflict." A more recent book by another Gestalt writer (Katona, 1940) contains 38 index references to "organization" but none to "disorganization" or any equivalent concept. Of the 45 articles reprinted in Tomkins' source book on *Contemporary psychopathology* (1943), only 3 have a Gestalt, "organismic," [4] or "field theoretical" orientation, and Hunt's handbook on *Personality and the behavior disorders* (1944) has but 2 such chapters in a total of 35. Goldstein (1939) has been much interested in comparing "ordered" and "disordered" behavior, but the examples of the latter which he cites, while instructive in their own right, have their origin in cortical damage and hardly give us a theory of integration failure applicable to organisms whose nervous systems are structurally intact. Lewin has used the terms "dedifferentiation" (1935) and "regression" (1936) to characterize nonintegrative behavior and has explicitly recognized the problem of conflict (1935), but his insistence upon an ahistorical, spatial type of analysis seems to the writers to impose serious limitations upon his otherwise very suggestive system.[5] And, despite the statement that "this [Gestalt] viewpoint has theoretical importance for psychodynamic theory as well as practical importance for psychotherapy" (1940, p. 147), Brown's *Psychodynamics of abnormal behavior* is actually highly eclectic and draws far more tellingly from psychoanalysis than from *Gestalttheorie.*

In short, we need not multiply evidence to show that Gestalt psychology has not particularly concerned itself with problems of abnormal, nonintegrative behavior and is probably not inherently well suited to this task.[6]

---

[3] In conversation, Professor George Hartmann has suggested that the antithesis which is probably implicit in Gestalt theory is the Greek contrast between cosmos and chaos. This, however, is more of a metaphysical than a psychological conception, as is the whole-part dichotomy.

[4] To the extent that "organismic" means the psychosomatic or psychobiological unity of living organisms and thus ends the mind-body dichotomy, it is taken for granted by all modern scientific schools of psychology and psychiatry. It is only when living organisms are said always to "act as totalities"—thus logically excluding the possibility of conflict—that "organismic" takes on the distinctive connotations with which it is here used.

[5] However, some of the incidental observations he has made concerning "psychological lifetime" and "levels of reality and irreality" (1935, 1942) are highly instructive and will be referred to later. [Cf. MacKinnon's (1950) paper on the application of Lewinian concepts to the field of psychotherapy.]

[6] For Gestalt-like approaches to the problem of nonintegration, see Werner (1940) on "rigidity," Korzybski (1933) on "loss of conditionality," and Kretchevsky (1935) on impairment of "behavior plasticity." Under the heading of "disturbances of integration," Angyal introduces the concept of "bionegativity," which he defines as "a personality constellation in which one or more part processes disturb the total

The psychoanalytic movement has stemmed from the historic discovery of Breuer and Freud that neurotic symptoms have not only symbolic meaning, but also dynamic "purpose," i.e., are motivated and satisfying (wish-fulfilling). This arresting hypothesis stands in direct opposition to the common perception of only the painful and embarrassing consequences of neurotic behavior, but the pragmatic usefulness of this view has gradually won for it widespread support. However, the hypothesis that abnormal behavior always involves some degree of reward, as well as punishment, does not solve the *quantitative* aspect of the problem. If the over-all gain, or satisfaction, resulting from a given form of behavior *exceeds* the over-all loss, or pain, such behavior would seem to be conforming very acceptably to the so-called pleasure principle and would scarcely be deemed "abnormal." But if behavior consistently results in *less* gain than loss, it is almost certain not to be judged "normal" and is very troublesome, both practically and theoretically. Analytic writers are generally agreed that repression is a *sine qua non* of neurosis, but since the pleasure principle is supposed to operate no less in the unconscious than in the conscious regions of the personality, the question remains: How is it that any pattern of action, if predominantly painful in its consequences, may nevertheless persist indefinitely?

In his later years, Freud attempted to solve this dilemma in a most extraordinary manner. He began his attack by asking if there are any known types of behavior which do indeed conform to the common conception of neurotic phenomena which had prevailed before his and Breuer's original discovery, i.e., types of behavior which are not merely predominantly, but *exclusively*, painful. The recurrent anxiety dreams of persons suffering from traumatic neuroses, the seemingly pleasureless repetitive play sometimes seen in children, and the painful "transference" of analytic therapy seemed to Freud, upon reexamination, to fill this description.[7] He therefore felt justified in postulating what he had already begun to suspect on the basis of the commoner neurotic symptoms, namely, "that there really exists in psychic life a repetition compulsion, which goes beyond the pleasure principle [and which is] more primitive, more instinctual than the pleasure principle which is displaced by it" (1922, pp. 24–25).

This positing of a repetition compulsion which supersedes the

---

function of the organism" (1941, p. 329). This is an acceptable description of non-integration, but it is hardly an explanation or theory. (Cf. 19.)

[7] Elsewhere (1933a) Freud has discussed the "economic problem of masochism," but it apparently played no direct part in his thinking in the present connection.

pleasure principle did indeed resolve the paradox of behavior which has consequences consistently more punishing than rewarding, but it did so at great cost: it was a repudiation, or at least a subordination, of the one principle which had previously dominated all psychoanalytic thought and theory. As Kubie remarks:

> This concept presents a more revolutionary challenge to accepted psychoanalytic premises than any which Freud, or even any dissenter, has heretofore formulated. Implicitly, by denying to the pleasure principle a central and determining position in the dynamics of human behavior, it strikes at the very foundations of the libido theory and of our basic conceptions of the dynamics of neurosis (1939, p. 390).

At first stunned and bewildered by such a pronouncement on the part of a trusted leader, most analysts were slow to react to the full implications of Freud's repetition compulsion (and its correlative speculations concerning the death instinct); but a rising tide of skepticism and dissent is now evident, of which the following comment, again by Kubie, is representative:

> Thus we are finally forced to conclude that there is neither any need nor any evidence for a "repetition compulsion"—and that the phrase itself has become a mere descriptive epithet, a psychoanalytic version of the word "habit," that the virtue of the concept is purely descriptive, and that it can never be called upon . . . to explain a single neurotic phenomenon (1939, p. 402).

However, in disavowing the repetition compulsion, one does not solve the problem which prompted Freud to advance this hypothesis; instead, one merely revives it. Today there is more and more discussion in analytic circles of "ego psychology," which contains certain intimations of a solution to this problem along more acceptable lines. But as a distinguished American analyst has recently pointed out, much of the current work on ego psychology is still far from satisfactory from a scientific standpoint in that it tends to personify *the ego* instead of deriving systematic principles whereby the so-called ego or integrative functions are carried out.[8] Later we shall return to some of the most promising suggestions which have been advanced in this connection, but in the meantime it will be instructive to review briefly the efforts which have been made to deal with

---

[8] T. French, "The integration of social behavior," paper read before the Boston Psychoanalytic Society, January 21, 1944. We feel that the same criticism is to some extent also applicable to a recent paper by G. W. Allport (1943). However, we are in complete agreement with Allport that the concept of "ego," vague as it is, covers an important and much neglected area in contemporary academic psychology.

the problem of persistently nonintegrative behavior in terms of stimulus-response psychology.

In making repetition or "exercise" the unitary law of learning, William James accepted the logically necessary implication: namely, that "not only is it the right thing at the right time that we must involuntarily do, but the wrong thing also, if it be an habitual thing" (1890, p. 114). For such a theory, the persistence of "wrong," i.e., nonintegrative, behavior is no problem. Since each repetition of a response is assumed to strengthen the tendency to repeat that response, any response, regardless of its consequences, tends automatically to become more and more strongly fixated. Habits are thus like avalanches, which, once started, cannot be stopped. Or, one might say, habit formation is a kind of perpetual motion with constant acceleration. But such a theory leaves unexplained the not unusual case in which behavior with mainly undesirable consequences, instead of being reinforced by each occurrence, does indeed get eliminated, stopped. In order to account for this latter phenomenon, James had to abandon what he termed the scientific or "mechanical" frame of reference and invoke "the will." This, he said, was the force which transcends the law of habit, by means of which it was supposedly possible (if "the will"—compare current references to "the ego"—were "strong" enough) to restrain a "wrong" or "disadvantageous" habit until "disuse" had had an opportunity to obliterate the hypothetical neural pathways which "use" had originally established.

It was an obvious advance when Thorndike (1900), a few years later, formulated the law of effect as a supplement to James's law of exercise. In fact, subsequent developments have shown that of the two the supplement is actually the more fundamental, since increasing evidence suggests that the mere repetition of a response, as distinct from its effects, probably has little or no significance in determining its fate (6; Thorndike, 1931). However, Thorndike's law of effect runs squarely into the paradox of persistent nonintegrative behavior. Thorndike divided his law of effect into two subprinciples which we may refer to as the principle of reward, according to which responses with pleasurable consequences get "stamped in," and the principle of punishment, according to which responses with painful consequences get "stamped out." By implication, a given act should be "stamped in" or "stamped out" in direct proportion to the extent to which its consequences are predominantly rewarding or predominantly punishing. Without emendation, such a theory obviously cannot account for the "stamping in" of responses whose consequences are *predominantly punishing.*

The impasse to which the law of effect thus leads is precisely the one which Freud encountered in trying to explain nonintegrative behavior in terms of the pleasure principle.[9] What contemporary writers, both analytic and academic, tend to do in practice is to invoke the law of effect (pleasure principle) to account for integrative behavior but to resort to the law of exercise ("repetition compulsion") [10] to explain instances of nonintegrative behavior.

---

[9] French (1933) and Mowrer (1938c) have both previously commented on the parallelism between Thorndike's law of effect and Freud's pleasure principle. However, without a word of explanation this parallelism is likely to be disputed, or at least misunderstood. The psychological theory of "pleasure" which is best known in our culture today is that of the English hedonists or utilitarians, who held that: "Every pleasure is *prima facie* good, and ought to be pursued. Every pain is *prima facie* evil, and ought to be avoided" (Bentham, 1934, p. 59). Thus, the pursuit of pleasure and the avoidance of pain become, in Bentham's words, the "two sovereign masters" of mankind (1780). Although we know that Thorndike read and was impressed by Bentham and, in his earlier writings, even used a somewhat similar terminology, he has recently stressed the difference between hedonism and the law of effect: "The general consequences of the action of reward are very different from those assumed by the pleasure-pain psychology of Bentham, Spencer, Bain, or their followers. Human beings are not propelled by pleasure and repelled by pain in any such uniform ways as these hedonists assumed" (Thorndike, 1943, p. 39). Instead, says Thorndike, living organisms are "propelled" by motives (drives, "pain" in the most general sense), and it is the reduction of these sources of discomfort that provides pleasure.

Superficially, it may seem that Freud's pleasure principle is pure hedonism, and there are indeed passages which seem to imply as much; but Freud's more considered formulations make the same distinction as does Thorndike. Thus, says Freud, "we take it for granted that the course of mental processes is automatically regulated by 'the pleasure principle': that is to say, we believe that any given process originates in an unpleasant state of tension and thereupon determines for itself such a path that its ultimate issue coincides with a relaxation of this tension, i.e., with avoidance of 'pain' or with production of pleasure" (1922, p. 1). At a later date, in discussing the psychoanalytic theory of drives ("instincts"), Freud says, "The source is a state of excitation, within the body, and its aim is to remove the excitation . . . which is experienced as satisfaction" (1933b, pp. 132–33).

It is clear, therefore, that Thorndike's law of effect and Freud's pleasure principle both differ from hedonism in essentially the same manner: for the hedonists, pleasure was a motive, whereas for Freud and Thorndike it is always "pain" or "tension" which is the motive, and pleasure is a product—one might almost say by-product—of drive reduction or problem solution. It is true that Thorndike has made a more explicit connection between the law of effect and "learning" than Freud ever proposed, but if we translate "determines for itself such a path that its ultimate issue . . ." as "learning," we see that such a connection was at least implicit in Freud's formulations.

[10] The similarity between the law of exercise and the repetition compulsion has been noted by Kubie, who says: "The 'repetition compulsion' is here given a power in human affairs directly comparable to the power attributed to 'habit' in popular lay psychologizing. It is looked upon as an explanation beyond which one need seek no further" (1939, p. 395). And Hendrick similarly remarks, "The repetition compulsion includes the traditional concept of habit, but Freud's emphasis on its unconscious dynamics, its presence from the very earliest experience of infancy, and its relationship to instinct theory, involves more than the renaming of a general observation" (1939, p. 103). It is interesting to note that although the "repetition compulsion" appeared relatively late in Freud's writings, it was actually present in nascent form in the much earlier notion of "fixation." A somewhat similar conception of behavior perpetuation without a dynamic element of satisfaction is involved in Allport's first formulation of what he has termed "functional autonomy"

It is interesting to find that psychoanalysis started with the pleasure principle and later turned to repetition compulsion, whereas learning theory started with the law of exercise and was later forced to posit the law of effect. Superficially, this crisscrossing of two great streams of psychological thought might be interpreted as proving that both these "laws" are really necessary for an adequate and comprehensive theory of behavior. But we suggest instead the thesis that to have one principle to account for one set of phenomena which fit this principle and another principle to account for another set of phenomena which do not, is to rely on a vicious convenience. If we cannot make either of these principles do the complete job it ought to do, we should discard them both and start again, along entirely new and more promising lines.

It now appears that the solution to this problem is to discard one of these principles altogether and revise and expand the other in such a way as to make it really adequate to its task. Both clinical and experimental evidence is now available which seems to argue definitively against the law of exercise and the "repetition compulsion." At the same time other data are at hand which make it possible to extend the law of effect in such a manner as to resolve the paradox of persistent nonintegrative behavior.[11] This we shall attempt to do in the next section.

II. The Calculus of Consequences

It is not necessary to trace recent developments concerning the problem of whether there is both a "law of reward" and a "law of

(1937, but see also 1940). Later we shall see that an integrated personality does indeed have a kind of "autonomy" which gives it a certain limited immunity to the law of effect; but this will be found to differ significantly from the law of exercise, the repetition compulsion, and functional autonomy as originally put forward.

[11] [What does this argument mean when recast in terms of a dualistic conception of learning? Since the law of effect and the law of exercise were both supposed (by Thorndike) to apply to the acquisition of overt, skeletal responses, the two-factor theorist would say that the latter is unnecessary and invalid. However, in so far as the so-called law of exercise is thought of as a law of repetition or frequency of stimulus-stimulus associations, then there is an important place for it (as conditioning) in two-factor theory. Actually, as the beginning paragraph in the following section indicates, the law of effect as formulated by Thorndike is double-barreled, involving both a "law of reward" and a "law of punishment." With the first there need be no quarrel; it is the second that causes trouble. For Thorndike "punishment" was an event which has an effect (stamping out) that is antithetical to the effect of reward (stamping in). According to two-factor theory, punishment is a more complex affair, having two major stages: (1) the conditioning of fear to certain cues associated with the punished response; and (2) the inhibition of that response because the fear reinforces responses which are incompatible with it. Fortunately, the central argument of this paper is not critically dependent upon a monistic ("reinforcement") conception of learning; it could very simply be recast in terms of two-factor theory, with no loss of cogency.]

punishment," or only a "law of reward" from which the facts subsumed under the "law of punishment" can be derived. This problem has been considered elsewhere (Mowrer, 1941a; Mowrer and Kluckhohn, 1944). But there are two well-attested empirical phenomena which are of the utmost significance in this connection. Extensive experimental evidence as well as common experience shows that if a response is immediately followed by a rewarding state of affairs (drive reduction), the tendency for that response to occur in the same problem situation in the future is reinforced more than if there is a temporal delay between the occurrence of the response and the reward. This functional relationship has been termed the "gradient of reinforcement" (Roberts, 1930; Hull, 1943; Hilgard and Marquis, 1940; Miller and Dollard, 1941). It is also well known, though less fully documented experimentally, that if a response is immediately followed by a punishing state of affairs (drive increase), the kinesthetic and other stimuli resulting from the making of this response become more strongly conditioned to the emotional response of anxiety [fear] than if there is a delay between the occurrence of the response and the punishment (Hilgard and Marquis, 1940; Kappauf and Schlosberg, 1937).

Any thoroughgoing analysis of the problem of persistent nonintegrative behavior must, I believe, start with these two facts. From these facts it follows that the consequences of a given act determine the future of that act not only in terms of what may be called the quantitative aspects of the consequences but also in terms of their temporal pattern. In other words, if an act has two consequences—the one rewarding and the other punishing—which would be strictly equal if simultaneous, the influence of those consequences upon later performances of that act will vary depending upon the *order* in which they occur. If the punishing consequence comes first and the rewarding one later, the difference between the inhibiting and the reinforcing effects will be in favor of the inhibition. But if the rewarding consequence comes first and the punishing one later, the difference will be in favor of the reinforcement.

In either instance the resulting behavior would be nonintegrative. Logically, two events which are equivalent if simultaneous should still be equivalent if successive; but psychologically this is not the case. In our example, if the reward comes first, the tendency to perform the act in question will be more reinforced than inhibited, and if the punishment comes first, the act will be more inhibited than reinforced. Whereas, from a strictly "reasonable," integrative standpoint, the inhibitory and the reinforcing effects should exactly cancel each other.

One can think of this problem in terms of a physical analogy. If two weights of equal mass are placed at equal distances from the fulcrum of a lever, they will, of course, exactly counterbalance each other; but if either of these objectively "equal" weights is placed further from the fulcrum than the other, it has a mechanical advantage which enables it to tip the balance in its favor. In the functional sense, the weights are no longer "equal," and a state of "disbalance" results.[12] In this physical analogy, *spatial distance* from the fulcrum provides the advantage, whereas in the psychological situation it is *temporal nearness* to the rewarding or punishing state of affairs that is the deciding factor. In this sense the analogy is not an entirely happy one, but it will suffice to illustrate the point that in a dynamic (conflict) situation, the outcome is determined not alone by the absolute magnitude of the causal forces but also by their relational (in the one case spatial, in the other case temporal) properties.[13]

At this point the two following objections should be briefly considered:

1. It may seem that an analysis such as the foregoing one is too "mechanical" and that it does not sufficiently recognize the extent to which normal adult human beings are able to make "reasoned judgments" which neatly transcend the behavioral dilemmas into which the temporal factors just discussed would seem to lead. We acknowledge that normal adult human beings do possess truly remarkable powers in this respect, but we feel that the present analysis has the double advantage of calling attention to the basic problem which human "rationality" has to solve and of providing a useful avenue of approach to a clearer understanding of just how these capacities are mediated. Most clinical writers agree that it is precisely the mechanical, rigid, stereotyped, inflexible, irrational aspect of nonintegrative behavior that distinguishes it most sharply from integrative behavior. It is scarcely a disadvantage if an analysis of the problem of nonintegrative behavior accommodates this fact.

[12] It is scarcely necessary to remind the reader that not only can one weight in this manner "outweigh" another of equal mass; by the same principle, a small weight can balance or even outbalance an objectively very much heavier one. The same seems to be true of the psychological effects of reward and punishment. . . . Since the above was written we have discovered Magoun's engaging little book, *Balanced personality* (1943), in which the same physical analogy is used. However, it is enlivened by picturing "Dottie Desire" on one end, "Connie Conscience" on the other, with "William Wisdom" in the middle, ready to lean now one way, now the other, as a means of keeping a proper equilibrium between these two opposing forces. This dramatization of the Freudian conception of Id, Superego, and Ego may be compared with the conflict situation described in the following section.

[13] This, we suppose, is a form of "field theory," but one which is to us much less nebulous than many of the formulations which currently pass under this heading.

2. The other most likely criticism of this line of thought is that it is unrealistically simple and that an experimental verification is a waste of time. We do not wish to underestimate the complexity of human or even infrahuman behavior. Later we shall, in fact, stress some of the complications that arise even at the experimental level. We are also aware that actual human conflicts do not consist of neatly arranged pairs of contending forces but may involve a multitude of motivations, as shown by the mechanism of "over-determination" in dreams, neurotic symptoms, and even in the normal decisions of daily life. Our excuse for deliberately simplifying our experimental situation and for using subjects which are incapable of many of the behavioral complexities found in man is that we wish merely to demonstrate a principle, in its clearest and least ambiguous form. Once agreed on the principle, we should be prepared to return to the level of actual human behavior with improved understanding and discernment.

III. An Experiment on Integrative Learning

The apparatus used in this study has been described in detail elsewhere (Mowrer and Miller, 1942). Here we need mention only that it consisted of a box-like compartment, 33 inches long, 20 inches high, and 6 inches deep, with a glass front and a floor consisting of a metal grill from which electric shock could be administered. Food, in the form of a small cylindrical pellet of Purina Dog Chow (¼ inch long and ⅛ inch in diameter), could be made available in a small trough at the left end of the apparatus.

The subjects were 21 black female rats, five months of age. After each animal had been reduced to 15 per cent below normal body weight by living on a restricted diet over a period of several days, it was put into the apparatus and taught to go to the food trough whenever a buzzer was sounded. The buzzer lasted for 2 seconds, and just as it terminated a pellet of food was dropped into the trough. Buzzer and food were presented at regular minute intervals, 20 times per day over a period of 5 days. All animals soon learned to run to the food trough as soon as the buzzer sounded, in much the same way that a dog or cat learns to come when called. By the end of these 100 preliminary training trials, the average time elapsing between the appearance of food and its being seized and eaten was less than 1 second.

At the end of this preliminary training, the experimenters made a "rule," which was that the subjects were henceforth not to touch the food for a period of *3 seconds* after it appeared in the trough.

One may think of this as a kind of rat "etiquette," according to which it was not "polite" to eat until the prescribed length of time had elapsed. We could not, of course, "tell" our subjects about this rule, but we established conditions which were calculated to teach it to them. On the day immediately following the 5-day training period just described, each of the 21 rats was put into the apparatus as usual; but the conditions were now such that if a rat took the food within the forbidden 3-second interval, it received 2 seconds of shock (0.06 milliampere) from the floor of the apparatus. In other words, the rats were "punished" for eating within the tabu period but were free to eat, without punishment, if they waited a minimum of 3 seconds after the food appeared.

The problem which the animals had to solve was how to get the food without also getting the shock. The essential aspects of this problem have already been described, but two additional conditions must now be mentioned. At the end of the preliminary training procedure, before the experiment proper started, the 21 subjects were randomly divided into three equal groups, which will hereafter be designated as the 3-second Group, the 6-second Group, and the 12-second Group. All these groups were treated in exactly the same way except in the matter of *how soon* the shock was administered as a result of an animal's violating the rule against taking a pellet within the 3-second tabu period. In the case of the 3-second Group, the punishment came immediately after the tabu period ended, i.e., 3 seconds after the food was presented. For the 6-second Group, the punishment came 3 seconds after the tabu period had ended, i.e., 6 seconds after the food was presented. And for the 12-second Group, punishment came 9 seconds after the tabu period had ended, i.e., 12 seconds after the food was presented. This arrangement allowed us to make a systematic comparison of the degree of difficulty encountered by our subjects in solving the problem of how to get the food without getting shocked as a function of the length of time by which the punishment for eating within the tabu period was delayed.

The other special condition to be mentioned is that, with all three groups, the buzzer, which during the preliminary training had the single function of calling the animals to the food trough and which terminated just as the food appeared, now remained on, in all cases, until the end of the tabu period. If the animal did not take the pellet during this period, the buzzer was then turned off; this meant that its termination served as an "all-clear" signal. On the other hand, if an animal erred and took the food during the tabu period, the buzzer remained on throughout this period *and* until the shock was administered, i.e., the buzzer stayed on until the shock had been applied for 2 seconds. The buzzer and shock then went off together. We shall later explain the reason for this particular use of the buzzer, but suffice it now to note that during the second phase of the experiment the buzzer had a more complicated "sign function" than during the preliminary training period. It formerly meant "come and get the food"; but in the second stage of the experiment, it meant "the food is in the trough but don't take it until the buzzer goes off." If this warning was violated, the buzzer remained on until the punishment had been applied.

In the phase of this experiment which has just been described, each animal received 10 trials per day over a 10-day period. The interval between successive trials was regularly 60 seconds.

There were three obviously possible ways in which an animal could react in this experiment: (1) it could take the food within the danger period and get shocked; (2) it could avoid the shock by not eating at all; (3) it could wait the 3 seconds and then eat, thereby avoiding the shock but getting the food. Without attempting at the moment to justify these terms, we shall refer to the first of these patterns of behavior as "delinquent," the second as "neurotic," and the third as "normal." We shall also characterize the first and the second of these patterns as "nonintegrative," and the third as "integrative."

Figure 61 shows the average incidence of these 3 patterns of behavior in the 3-second Group throughout the 10-day experimental period. On the first day, "neurotic" and "delinquent" responses predominated, but from the third day on "normal" responses were increasingly in the ascendancy. In other words, the 7 animals comprising this group learned to deal with this conflict situation in a predominantly *integrative* manner.

Although the differences between the curve for "normal" responses and the curves for "neurotic" and "delinquent" responses are conspicuous upon inspection, the question of how reliable these differences are, statistically, presents some interesting complications. In order to make these complications more apparent, we reproduce in Table 8 the number of "normal," "delinquent," and "neurotic" responses made by each of the 7 subjects in this group throughout the 10-day experimental period. The total number of "normal" responses made by all 7 animals was 469, which is very much larger than the number of either "delinquent" or "neurotic" responses, which totaled 123 and 108 respectively. Dividing each of these 3 totals by 7, it would be a simple matter to obtain the corresponding averages; and it then might seem appropriate to apply the familiar *t*-test to the differences between these averages. If these averages represented the performances of three separate groups of subjects, the *t*-test would, of course, be in order; but the values

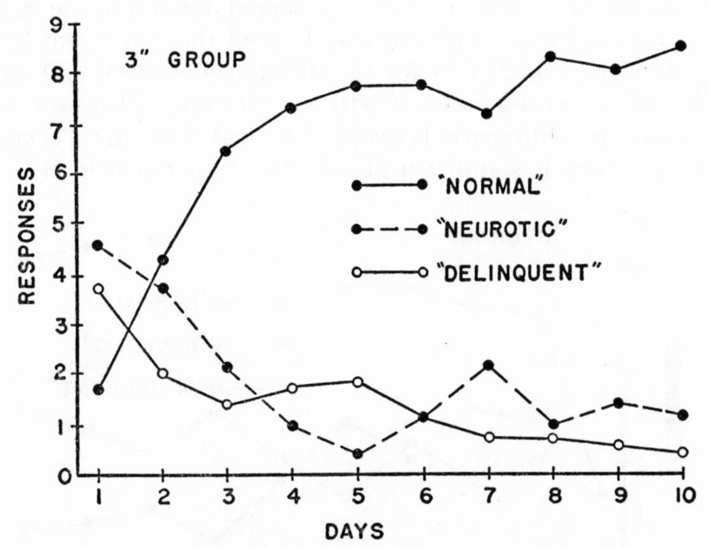

FIG. 61.—Curves showing the average incidence of 3 different patterns of response made by the 7 rats comprising the 3-second Group. Each animal was given 10 trials a day, and the experiment lasted 10 days.

shown in Table 8 and in Figure 61 represent performances which have a *reciprocal* relation to each other and are for a single group of subjects. These facts violate the assumptions on which the valid

TABLE 8

INCIDENCE OF 3 DIFFERENT KINDS OF RESPONSES MADE BY EACH OF THE 7 RATS IN THE 3-SECOND GROUP

Animal	No. 1	No. 2	No. 3	No. 4	No. 5	No. 6	No. 7	Totals
"Normal" responses	69	74	77	68	54	51	76	469
"Delinquent" responses	15	21	9	21	12	30	15	123
"Neurotic" responses	16	5	14	11	34	19	9	108
Totals	100	100	100	100	100	100	100	700

use of the *t*-test is based. Fortunately the method of chi square is quite specifically suited to deal with this sort of problem.

Applying the general chi-square formula (see, for example,

Snedecor, 1938, chap. i), we obtain a value of 202.22 for the difference between 469 ("normal" response) and 123 ("delinquent" response) and the number of each of these two types of response which would be expected if they occurred randomly, on a 50–50 basis. This value is significant far beyond the 1 per cent level, as is the chi square of 225.86 for the difference between 469 and 108 ("neurotic" responses) on a strictly 50–50 ratio. However, the chi square for the difference between 108 and 123 and "chance" is only 0.97, which is significant at only the 40 per cent level.[14]

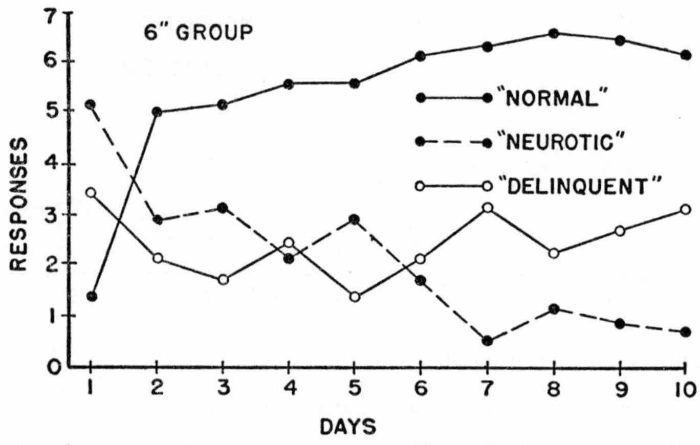

FIG. 62.—Average incidence of "normal," "delinquent," and "neurotic" responses made by the 7 animals comprising the 6-second Group.

Figure 62 shows comparable data for the 7 animals in the 6-second Group. Here the general picture is much the same as in Figure 61, except that these animals made relatively more "delinquent" and fewer "normal" responses. The integrative solution to this type of problem is obviously harder in this situation, where punishment is delayed 3 seconds, than in the situation in which it comes immediately after the tabu period. The chi square for the difference between 381 (total number of "normal" responses made by all 7 animals) and 172 (total number of "delinquent" responses) and the number of such responses which would be expected on the basis of a 50–50 hypothesis is 78.99. The chi square for the difference between 381 and 147 (total "neurotic" responses) and the hypothetical expectation is 103.70. Both of these values are significant well beyond the 1 per cent level. The chi square for 172 and

[14] The chi-square test could, of course, be applied to the results obtained on any of the 10 days of experimentation, as well as to the over-all results. But since the course of learning is so clear from the curves shown in Figure 61, this procedure does not seem necessary.

147, on the same hypothesis, is 1.96, which is significant only at the 18 per cent level.

In Figure 63 the trend noted in going from Figure 61 to Figure 62 becomes more striking: the incidence of "normal" responses not only starts but remains lower than the incidence of "delinquent" responses. Under the conditions represented by the curves in Figure 63, i.e., with the punishment for violating the tabu delayed 9 seconds after the tabu period has ended, nonintegrative behavior is the rule

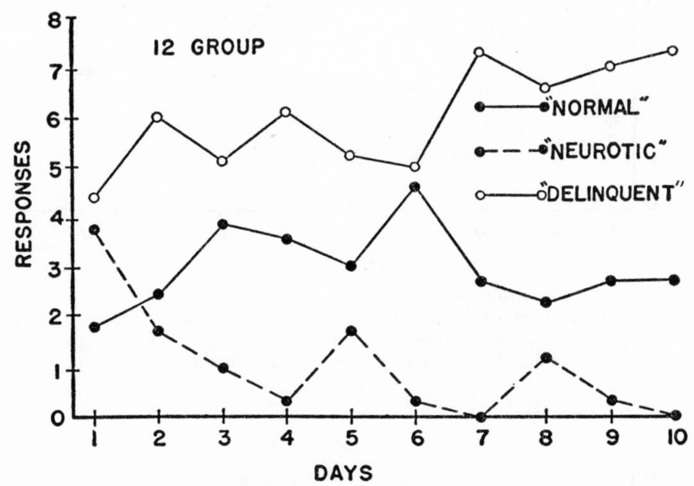

Fig. 63.—Average incidence of "normal," "delinquent," and "neurotic" responses made by the 7 animals comprising the 12-second Group. Note that in this group "delinquent" responses predominated throughout the experiment.

rather than the exception and becomes increasingly so with successive trials. It will be noted, however, that the nonintegrative pattern is of the "delinquent" rather than of the "neurotic" type. As a matter of fact, the animals in this 12-second Group actually made fewer "neurotic" responses than did those in either the 3-second or the 6-second Group.[15]

This 12-second Group made a total of 208 "normal" and 421 "delinquent" responses. These numbers depart from what would be expected on the basis of a 50–50 hypothesis by a chi square of 72.12. The chi square for 208 and 71 ("neurotic" responses) is 67.27, and for 421 and 71 is 448.98. All these values are significant beyond the 1 per cent level.

Figures 64, 65, and 66 show the same 9 curves as have just been

[15] In all groups the number of "neurotic" responses could almost certainly have been increased and the number of "delinquent" responses decreased by using a more intense punishment.

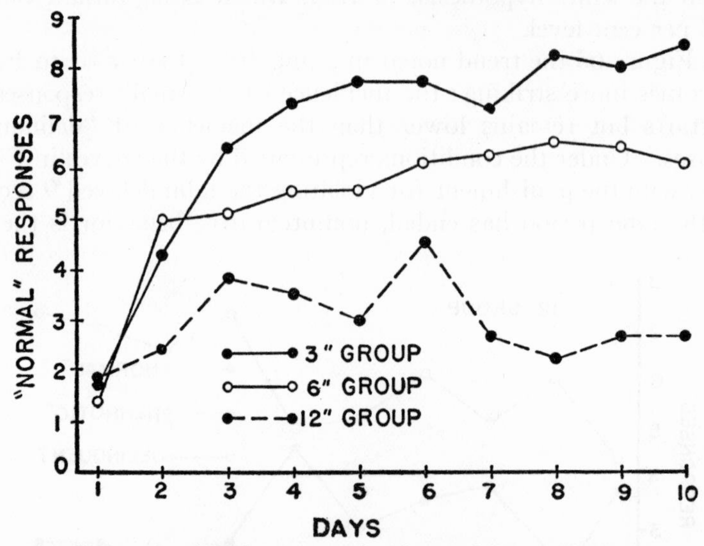

FIG. 64.—Curves showing the average incidence of "normal" responses made by the 7 animals constituting each of the 3 experimental groups. These curves have already been presented, separately, in Figures 61, 62, and 63; they are here brought together in order to make possible a more direct comparison.

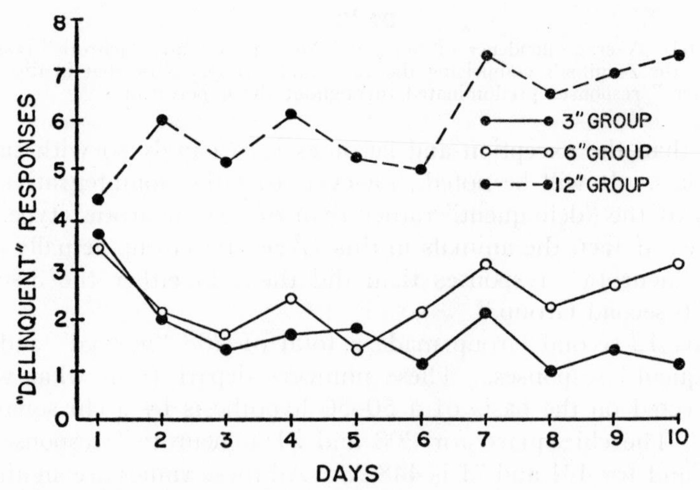

FIG. 65.—Average incidence of "delinquent" responses made by the 7 animals constituting each of the 3 experimental groups.

discussed, but here they are so arranged as to make possible a more direct comparison of the number of "normal," "neurotic," and "delinquent" responses made by each of the 3 experimental groups.

Figure 64 shows how close a connection there was in this experiment between the promptness with which "punishment" was applied for a "wrong" act and the readiness with which the "right" ("normal") type of behavior was learned. Under the conditions of this experiment, time is obviously an important factor in determining the outcome of what we have termed "integrative learning."

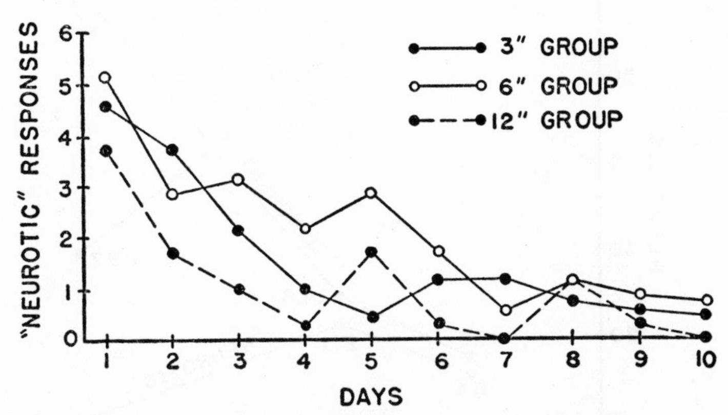

Fig. 66.—Average incidence of "neurotic" responses made by the 7 animals constituting each of the 3 experimental groups.

The average number of "normal" responses made by the 7 animals in the 3-second Group, during the entire 10-day experimental period, was 67.0; for the 7 animals in the 6-second Group, 54.3; and for the 7 animals in the 12-second Group, 29.7. The difference between the first and second of these averages has a *t*-value of 1.755 and is reliable at only the 10 per cent level; but the differences between the second and third and between the first and third have *t*-values of 3.219 and 6.016, respectively, both of which are reliable at the 1 per cent level or better.

Figure 65 shows the relative incidence of the "delinquent" pattern of response in all 3 groups. The animals in the 3-second Group made the fewest (17.6) of these responses on the average, those in the 6-second Group slightly more (24.6), and those in the 12-second Group a great many more (60.1). The first two of these means differ at only the 25 per cent level of significance, but the first and third and the second and third differ at the .01 level or better.

Figure 66 shows that the 3 experimental groups did not differ very markedly in terms of the number of "neurotic" responses made. Typically, this was a form of behavior which appeared early in the experiment in all groups but then gave way either to the "normal" or to the "delinquent" pattern. This change, like the others already noted, presumably represents a form of true learning rather than a shift in either of the primary motivational de-

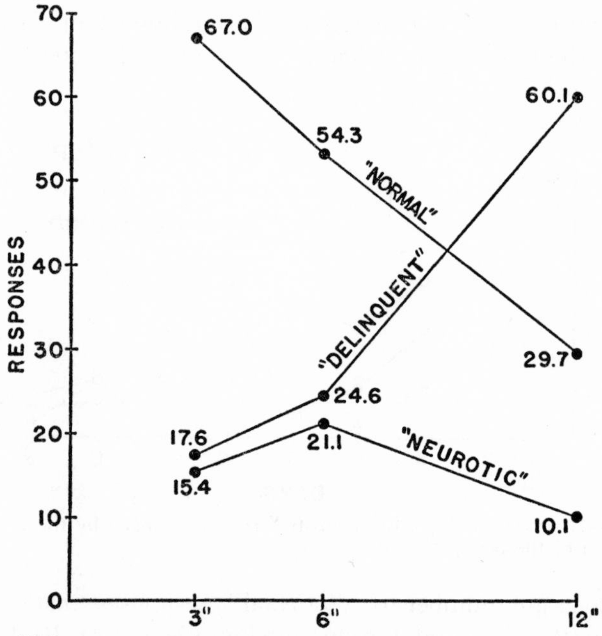

Fig. 67.—Values representing the average number of each of the 3 different kinds of responses made by each of the 3 experimental groups. These 9 values give in summary form the data shown in the 9 "learning" curves which are presented in various combinations in the preceding graphs.

terminants, since both hunger and shock were held objectively constant throughout the experiment (as inferred in the one case by body-weight and in the other by readings of the milliammeter).

The average number of "neurotic" responses made by the 7 animals in the 3-second Group was 15.4; for the 7 animals in the 6-second Group, 21.1; and for the 7 animals in the 12-second Group, 10.1. The difference between the 3-second Group and 6-second Group means is reliable at only the 45 per cent level and that between the 6-second and 12-second means at only the 40 per cent level. However, the difference between the 6-second and 12-second means approaches significance, at the 8 per cent level. These data indicate (and Figure 67 will show even more clearly) that in so far as the obtained differences are trustworthy, the 6-second Group was most disposed toward a "neurotic" solution of the conflict, the 12-second Group least so, and the 3-second Group intermediate. This outcome is understandable in the light of the fact that the "normal" solution was found relatively easily by the 3-second animals and the "delinquent" solution was the one most readily adopted by those in the 12-second Group; being caught in the middle, so to speak, the 6-second animals were more disposed toward a "neurotic" solution.

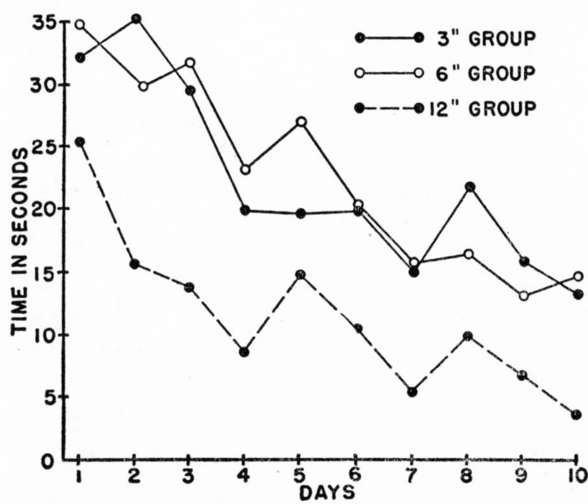

FIG. 68.—Length of time for which the 7 animals in each of the 3 experimental groups delayed, on the average, before taking food on each of the 10 days of experimentation.

The trends and relationships shown in Figures 61–66 are presented in a more abstract, condensed form in Figure 67. The numerical values reproduced near each of the points on the 3 curves refer to the average number of responses of the kinds indicated which were made by the 3-second, the 6-second, and the 12-second Groups throughout the entire 10-day experimental period. In other words, these values may be thought of as over-all "scores" made by homogeneous groups of subjects under different experimental, or "test," conditions. The curves show particularly clearly how significant is the temporal factor in determining the outcome in a conflict situation of the kind here presented.

Careful record was kept of the point in the 60-second interval between successive trials at which each animal ate the pellet of food which was always presented at the beginning of this interval. Figure 68 shows these data in summary form. The relatively short average eating latency of the 12-second Group is explicable in terms of the great number of "delinquent" responses made by this group, i.e., since the punishment for immediate eating was considerably delayed, it had relatively little inhibitory influence. On the other hand, the animals in the 3-second and 6-second Groups, being punished more promptly for eating within the tabu period, tended to favor a "normal" solution, which involved a postponement of eating for both groups. The fact that the average eating latency starts relatively high in all 3 groups and gradually declines is consistent with the similar downward trend noted in the incidence of "neurotic" responses in all 3 groups (see Figure 65). It also suggests that as the experiment progressed the animals learned to make their "normal" responses more promptly, instead of waiting unnecessarily after the tabu period had ended.

There is little point in attempting to present the latency data for the 3 different types of response. By definition, a "neurotic" response always involved a latency of 60 seconds, and a "delinquent" response never involved a latency of more than 3 seconds. Therefore, in neither case would the latency data be of any interest. In the case of the "normal" responses there was undoubtedly a decrease in average latency as the experiment progressed, but this fact is sufficiently evident from the data presented in Figure 68 to make a separate graph unnecessary.

IV. Symbols, Emotion, and Reason

The results described in the preceding sections of this paper indicate that punishment which is belatedly administered for the occurrence of a forbidden act is much less effective in enabling rats to work out an integrative solution to the type of conflict situation employed in this investigation than is punishment which is more promptly administered. Or, to put the matter differently, our results show that the capacity of the rat to compare and "balance" the good and bad consequences of an act is very dependent upon the temporal order and timing of these consequences. Thus, if the reward (hunger reduction) for engaging in a given act comes at once and the punishment (electric shock) shortly thereafter, the rat is able to resolve the conflict integratively ("normally"), but if the punishment is delayed by more than a few seconds, the rat is likely to become confirmed in a nonintegrative ("delinquent" or "neurotic") pattern of behavior.[16]

[16] It should be noted that the experiment here reported deals with only one of the two dilemmas described in Section II, namely, that arising from having a small reward occur first and a larger punishment later. One could also investigate, with

In fact, the capacity of the rat to engage in integrative problem solving is even more circumscribed than would at first appear on the basis of the experimental findings so far reported. In the course of exploratory work, we found that if, during the second stage of the experimental procedure, we continued to turn the buzzer off at the moment the food was presented (as we did during the first stage of training), our rats could not learn to behave integratively, regardless of whether the punishment came relatively soon or late. Under this regime, rats sometimes made "normal" responses, but they did not show any improvement in the frequency with which they made them. Various researches (Anderson, 1932; Brown, 1939; Yarborough, 1921) have suggested that under at least certain circumstances rats are capable of making fairly accurate temporal discriminations; but our exploratory findings indicate that, under the particular conditions which we employed, it was apparently impossible for them to learn to discriminate, purely on the basis of the stimulus trace produced by the buzzer (Hull, 1943), between the first 3 seconds (the tabu period) and the later portion of the trace (the safe period). In the main experiment, as it was eventually carried out, we therefore allowed the buzzer to continue to sound throughout the tabu period, thus providing our subjects with a cue which was sufficiently conspicuous to enable them to make the necessary discrimination, at least under the more favorable circumstances of relatively prompt punishment.[17]

It will be recalled that we not only allowed the buzzer to sound throughout the tabu period but also, in the event of violation of the tabu, until the electric shock had come and gone. This latter provision was introduced as a means of helping our subjects "make the connection," or "bridge the gap," between what happened in the tabu period and what happened later by way of punishment.[18] The impressive thing is that, even with these aids, the time factor was still so crucial in determining whether our subjects hit upon the

---

a slightly different experimental setup, the effects of having a small punishment come first and a large reward later. Presumably the temporal factor would be no less important in producing nonintegrative behavior in the second case than our results show it to be in the first.

[17] Several months after our experimentation was completed, Miss Babette Samelson raised the question as to whether animals which had learned, with the aid of the buzzer, to solve the dilemma with which we confronted them could have continued to behave integratively thereafter, without the help of this external cue. As yet we have not had an opportunity to check on this interesting point.

[18] This arrangement was based upon the fact, demonstrated by Pavlov (1927) and others, that "delayed" conditioned responses are more readily established than "trace" conditioned responses. For an instructive demonstration of the role of "tokens" in helping span relatively long periods of time between the performance of a response or "work" and reward, see Wolfe's experimentation with chimpanzees (1936).

integrative solution to the experimental problem or adopted a nonintegrative adjustment. Unaided, the rat seems to be almost completely at the mercy of the gradient of reward and the gradient of punishment. If a given response has two (or more) consequences which are separated by any appreciable time, this organism is evidently quite helpless, without external aids of the kind we supplied, to cope with the situation in anything but a stereotyped, nonintegrative manner. And even with such aids, the time factor is still of critical importance in determining the outcome.

The contrast between the "stupidity" of our rats and the quite extraordinary talents of normal adult human beings for integrative behavior is so great that it may seem a waste of time to attempt to study this phenomenon in so simple an organism. However, one must keep in mind that an altogether too large number of adults in our society are not "normal," i.e., have not achieved an optimal integration.[19] Perhaps a searching analysis of the reasons for integration failure in the rat will throw some light upon the cause of integration failure at the human level.

So long as the unique human capacity for integrative behavior was regarded as a divine gift, just so long was integration failure regarded as a demoniacal curse, beyond which no further explanation or understanding could be sought. Attempts to deal with this problem along naturalistic lines have almost universally stressed the role of something called "reason," but usually without giving any very satisfactory definition of this faculty. In the midst of many empty and contradictory assumptions, there is nevertheless one that has seldom been disputed, namely, that reason is intimately associated with articulate (predicative) language.

Many lower animals can respond to and even make *signs* (signals and cues), by means of which "communication" is said to occur; but in order for an organism to "reason," it must be able to do something more: It must be able to use signs as *symbols,* i.e., it must be able to make signs *and then respond to them.*[20] The

---

[19] As this statement implies, we do not accept the "cultural" definition of "normality," i.e., we do not identify normality with social conformity. If a culture is itself badly integrated (Lynd, 1940; Mead, 1942), a high degree of conformity will, in fact, automatically insure a low degree of personal normality in our sense. In such a culture the individual's only hope of achieving integration must lie in some degree of culture repudiation and nonconformity. This is not to deny, however, that the ideal situation is one in which social conformity and personal integration maximally coincide. [Cf. Mowrer, 1948b.]

[20] A response which thus serves as a basis for producing or guiding further behavior has been aptly referred to by Hull as a "pure stimulus act" (1931). And Miller and Dollard (1941) have spoken of emotions as "response-produced drives." The relationship of symbols and emotions will be considered in greater detail below. [See Mowrer, Palma, and Sanger, 1948; also 23 and 24.]

capacity to engage in this latter process, which one might call "self-communication," seems to be the essence of what we mean by "having reason."

Let us look more closely at this process. In the chapter on "Language and Symbolism" in Yerkes' book, *Chimpanzees* (1943), reference is made to an experiment in which a chimpanzee was tethered in the middle of a large room and allowed to watch the experimenter deposit food in one of four boxes which were located in the four corners of the room. The chimpanzee was then led back to its living quarters. A few minutes later the animal was returned to the experimental room and allowed to select one of the four boxes. If the box containing the food was left in its original position, the ape could respond appropriately, even after relatively long delays. But if, in the ape's absence from the room, the box containing the food was replaced by one of the other boxes of a different color and put where this other box had originally been, the animal persisted in looking for the food on the basis of position in the room rather than color of the box. Since chimpanzees are known to have excellent color vision, their failure to solve such a problem seems most remarkable. Yerkes says:

> This behavior differs so strikingly from our own that it seems amazing. . . . To us it seems almost incredible that with both boxes before it, but interchanged in position, the animal should go where the food had been concealed, in spite of the altered appearance of the box, and there search persistently for its expected reward. Under like circumstances a person would notice at once the changed appearance of the food box and look about for the original box. . . . We were finally forced to admit that our subjects [failed in this experiment] because they lacked a symbol or representative process comparable with our word "green" (1943, pp. 178–79).

Yerkes's experiment shows that the chimpanzee is capable of carrying away with it from a situation of the kind just described some inner change or state which "stands for" the response which it will later make when it re-encounters the same situation.[21] But as Yerkes points out, this symbolic capacity is evidently limited to the *spatial* aspects of the situation. We should not be surprised, therefore, at the rat's inability to behave integratively in a situation in which the problem lies in the *temporal* dimension.

---

[21] It will be remembered that, in his original work on "delayed response," Hunter (1912) concluded that the capacity to respond to cues long after they have disappeared involved the maintenance of fixed bodily postures or sets. The experiment by Yerkes as well as other research indicates that this is probably not the case, although we still do not know precisely how this feat is accomplished. When this problem is solved, we should have a better understanding of so-called one-trial learning and certain forms of "insight." (See 11, 12.)

But neither should we conclude that the rat is totally without skill in the use of symbols. A number of experimenters have noted that, at the choice point in mazes, rats are likely to engage in what Tolman (1938) has called "vicarious trial-and-error behavior," i.e., the rat will turn tentatively in one direction, then in the other, and so back and forth until it finally "decides" to take one of the paths rather than the other. Muenzinger and Gentry (1931) have commented on the occurrence of a similar type of behavior in rats when confronted by an auditory discrimination problem, but in the maze it can hardly be such a problem that the animal is trying to solve, since this behavior also occurs when auditory (and even visual) cues are minimal or lacking altogether. Closer analysis suggests that these little motions are a form of symbolic exploration, or "reasoning." In turning the head to the right or to the left, it is as if the animal were trying to anticipate, or "feel," the consequences of actually going in that direction. A type of comparison or "discrimination" may indeed be taking place, but it is a comparison of *emotions,* not visual cues. "Deciding" or "willing" to go one way rather than the other would thus seem to be determined on the basis of which "pure stimulus act" aroused the strongest anticipation of reward and the least anticipation of punishment.[22]

This is not the place to elaborate such an hypothesis, but it is interesting to compare Freud's theory of human thought. He says:

> Thinking is an experimental dealing with small quantities of energy, just as a general moves miniature figures about over a map before setting his troops in motion. In this way, the ego anticipates the satisfaction of the questionable impulse, and enables it to reproduce the painful feelings which are attached to the beginning of the dreaded danger-situation. Thereupon the automatic mechanism of the pleasure-pain principle is brought into play and carries through the repression of the dangerous impulse (1933b, p. 124).

Perhaps the commonest cause of our failure to fathom the nature of human "reason" has been the tendency to contrast it with

[22] It would appear that the failure of our rats to solve the experimental conflict with which we confronted them is due, not to a complete absence of symbolic capacity, but rather to the fact that they had no pure stimulus act by means of which to re-present the impending electric shock. It is interesting to ask what the limits of integrative ability might be in both the rat and the ape if they were put through a course of training in the use of symbols comparable to that which human beings receive. As Lewin has pertinently remarked: "An education for the present seems here to be in no sense necessary. The pedagogical task seems, rather, to be precisely the opposite extension of the narrow horizon of the present in spatial (including social) and temporal dimensions. For today Goethe's saying is still valid—'Who cannot give an account of three thousand years remains in the darkness of inexperience, can live only from one day to another'" (Lewin, 1936, pp. 172–73). See also Lewin (1942b).

"feeling." If the foregoing analysis be sound, we must come to see "emotion," not as the antithesis of "intellect," but as an indispensable ingredient and adjunct thereto. In its primitive and most basic form, reasoning seems to consist of a succession of pure stimulus (symbolic) acts whereby the remote as well as immediate consequences of an impending overt action are brought into the psychological present, in full force, so to say, and balanced and compared in a manner that is quite out of the question in an organism which has to rely solely upon the gradient of reward and the gradient of punishment. In this way human beings have been able to develop the capacity of "moral judgment," "planfulness," or "rationality," in a way that sets them well apart from all other animals. Or in other words, skill in the use of symbols is at the basis of certain forms of "memory," "attention," "interest," "imagination," and other forms of higher mental processes which are uniquely human. Let us see, now, if this assumption is of any assistance in understanding what it means to "lose one's reason," i.e., to suffer an impairment of the integrative functions, at the human level.

But first let us ask what circumstances may prevent an organism from developing "reason." These may be listed as follows: (1) We must immediately acknowledge the fact that infrahuman organisms are congenitally limited in the matter of brain complexity and capacity; only man has a sufficiently elaborate nervous system to allow the development of at least the highest forms of symbolic functioning. (2) Human beings differ among themselves in this connection; and in the extremes of feeble-mindedness, the capacity for symbolic functioning may be well below that of the so-called lower animals. (3) Nor do we find "reason" even in perfectly normal human beings at birth; it is a capacity the development of which is dependent at once upon continuing neural maturation and a complicated process of tuition. (4) That "reason" is a product of such tuition is indicated in an especially decisive manner by the fact that if certain sensory avenues are blocked (notably vision and hearing), the individual remains, unless given very special training, little better than a "dumb animal." (5) We do not know precisely what sort of individual a human being would become if he grew up in complete social isolation on the proverbial desert isle; but our knowledge of feral children suggests that without contact with human culture, the human animal does not even remotely approximate the average level of socialized mentality.

Loss of "reason" or reasoning ability may most obviously result from brain damage. Of special significance in this connection is the work of Goldstein on the psychological effects of head injuries sustained by German soldiers during the first World War. This writer reports that the most characteristic consequences of cortical lesion is an impairment of "abstraction," i.e., the ability to "transcend concrete (immediate) experience." Goldstein remarks that whenever an individual with such a deficit has to "refer to things in an imaginary way—then he fails. . . . Or we might point to the patient's inability to emancipate and withhold himself from the world, the shrinkage of his freedom, and his greater bondage to the demands of environment. The most general formula to which the change can be reduced is probably: The patient has lost the capacity to deal with *that which is not real—with the possible*. . . . Depending on which of these manifestations of the basic disturbance has been brought into focus, they have been named respectively: disturbance of *'symbolic expression'* (Head), of the *'representational function'* (Woerkom), of *'categorical behavior'* (Gelb and Goldstein)" (Goldstein, 1939, pp. 29–30).[23]

In a suggestive paper entitled, "Emotion as Relative Functional Decortication: the Role of Conflict," Darrow (1935) has called attention to the familiar "disorganizing" effects of "excited emotion" and has shown that heightened blood pressure is the most characteristic physiological accompaniment. The cause of such emotion he finds in "dynamic conflicts" which threaten the individual's "accepted patterns of thinking and acting and their corresponding patterns of cortical activity. Most often the accepted and established patterns which are threatened in excited emotion are those which have habitually represented and furthered the physical safety and comfort, the intellectual and social dignity and integrity of the individual. . . . The hypothesis we set forth is that active conflict in the normal individual is frequently the essential condition for the release of the primitive autonomic subcortical mechanisms of *excited* emotions" (1935, p. 572).[24]

Here we see an example of a *temporary* impairment of the "ego" or integrative functions which provide an intermediate link between those instances of integration failure due to structural defects already reviewed and the type of integration failure found in the purely functional process of repression. It is perhaps stretching Darrow's argument to say that the mental blocking that often occurs in strong emotion is designed to *protect* the very functions which are temporarily obliterated thereby, but in repression the

[23] The results of psychosurgery, as recently reported by Freeman and Watts (1942), present an essentially similar picture.

[24] Cf. Lewin's description of the experiment by Dembo on the "experimental simplification of the structure of the person" (1935, pp. 265–67).

process seems to be precisely of this nature. Freud has repeatedly remarked that repression of an impulse or memory characteristically occurs when it arouses effects which are so strong that they threaten to overwhelm the "ego." To this extent repression is definitely a "defensive" mechanism, but the resulting advantages usually prove to be achieved at a great cost. Repression is effected by excluding the symbolic representative of certain impulses from consciousness, i.e., from the dominant integrative center of the personality. Although repression thus brings a temporary peace, the process is likely to be pathogenic for the reason that energies which formerly submitted themselves to the management of, and thereby strengthened, the "ego" are now withdrawn and left free to seek—through those habits called "symptoms"—their own irresponsible, nonintegrative paths to gratification. This is why Freud has characterized repression as a reversion from the "reality principle" to the more primitive "pleasure principle," from the "ego" (consciousness) to the "id" (the unconscious).

By way of summary of this section, it may be said that living organisms which are unable (for any of several possible reasons) to employ symbols versatilely are doomed to relative fixity of response, which, in the case of responses which have both remote and immediate consequences, is almost certain to result in a failure of "integration." Such a failure of integration was noted in the animal experiment here reported, and results which have been reported by others show how limited the capacities of infrahuman organisms in general are in this respect.[25] Goldstein remarks that the "performances which the patient [with cortical injury] can carry out, and to which he always tends to cling, have the character of stereotype and exhibit little variation" (1939, p. 42). Korzybski (1933) maintains that a loss of "conditionality" of response is the essence of abnormality in human beings. Murray (1938) has similarly commented on the loss of flexibility as a key problem in abnormality. And Kubie has said that "the nuclear problem in the neurosis is the repeativeness of its phenomenon" (1941, p. 23). "The flexible repeativeness which is an inescapable part of the life of the normally developing child becomes its rigid and inflexible neurosis" (1941, p. 28).

The common denominator in all these forms of nonintegrative behavior seems to be the inability to use symbols appropriately as a means of bringing remote as well as immediate consequences into

---

[25] For a more extended review see Everall (1935). Cf. also Robinson (1940), and Morgan and Lannert (1941) on the problem of "perseveration" at the human level.

the present in such a manner that they may exert an influence proportional to their objective importance.

V. The Vicious-Circle Concept

Although it is evident that the temporal factor has not been sufficiently emphasized in the analysis of nonintegrative behavior, neither has it been entirely overlooked.[26] In one of the papers already cited, Kubie makes the following allusion to the time element:

> . . . the rigid ultimate forms of these repetitive patterns seen in neuroses have been reached only after a long process of trial and error, during which many and varied patterns of neurotic effort have appeared and been abandoned. The neurotic pattern which finally persists, and which becomes most repetitive and which has so often been characterized as manifestations of a "repetition compulsion," proves invariably to have been the one that served the largest amount of neurotic demands, or which gave the patient the greatest *temporary relief from tension* (1939, pp. 399–400). (Italics added.)

In a later paper this author similarly remarks:

> With the acquisition of the power of abstract thought and fantasy, the repetitive tendencies of both normal and pathological phenomena are increased immeasurably. . . . Like all substitutive symptom formations, fantasy adds fuel to the fires it is supposed to quench, and kindles expectations which it cannot gratify. . . . Only during the actual moment of fantasy is there a *passing illusion of relief,* followed at once by a sharpened sense of deprivation and an increased yearning (1941, pp. 33–34).[27]

Freud's most explicit references to time as a factor in integration occur in the context of his discussions of the reality principle

[26] Israeli (1941, 1936), Frank (1939), Lewin (1935), Murray (1938), and others have discussed some of the implications of time for general personality theory. However, it has not been as explicitly related to the problem of conflict as would seem indicated. The most systematic discussion of conflict which has appeared to date is that of Miller (1944), in which the temporal dimension is omitted almost completely.

[27] Italics added. The quotations invite attention to a tremendously important but difficult problem. If symbols are essential to the kind of integrative problem solving which we call "reason," they are probably also the vehicle of hallucination and delusion. It is obviously useful to be able to anticipate remote rewards and punishments and to compare these with the more immediate consequences of behavior; but when the imaginative functions become hypertrophied, so to speak, we approach the realm of psychosis. In this paper we have thus far conceived of symbols wholly as a means whereby the individual's relation to reality is improved; but if the individual learns to use symbols as ends in themselves, i.e., as a way of obtaining emotional satisfactions which are independent of reality, they lead to an escape from rather than a mastery of the external world. The psychology of psychosis is still but poorly delineated, but it becomes increasingly clear that better understanding in this area will presuppose a more penetrating analysis of symbolism and semantics.

as opposed to the pleasure principle and of the "ego" as opposed to the "less well organized" parts of the personality. The following excerpts, drawn from various of Freud's writings, summarize his views in this connection.

The processes of the system *Ucs* (unconscious) are timeless; i.e., they are not ordered temporally, are not altered by the passage of time, in fact bear no relation to time at all. The time-relation . . . is bound up with the work of the system *Cs*.

The processes of the *Ucs* are just as little related to reality. They are subject to the pleasure principle; their fate depends only upon the degree of their strength and upon their conformity to regulation by pleasure and pain (1915b, p. 119).

The transition from the pleasure principle to the reality principle is one of the most important advances in the development of the ego (1935a, p. 312).

We know that the pleasure principle is adjusted to a primary mode of operation on the part of the psychic apparatus, and that for the preservation of the organism amid the difficulties of the external world it is *ab initio* useless and indeed extremely dangerous. . . . It is replaced by the "reality principle," which without giving up the intention of ultimately attaining pleasure yet demands and enforces the postponement of satisfaction, the renunciation of manifold possibilities of it, and the temporary endurance of "pain" on the long and circuitous road to pleasure (1922, p. 5).

It would seem but a short step from these formulations to the theory of persistent nonintegrative behavior which we have sketched; but, as indicated in Section I, Freud instead fell back upon the dubious doctrine of the "repetition compulsion." This retrogressive move on the part of the leader of psychoanalysis has meant that progress along these lines has had to come from analysts who, to some extent, have deserted Freud's leadership. Thus, we find that the concept of "vicious circle," while wholly compatible with and a logical extension of earlier Freudian theory, has actually been evolved as an alternative of the "repetition compulsion" by analysts of a slightly renegade complexion. Horney says:

F. Kuenkel in *Einfuehrung in die Charakterkunde* has drawn attention to the fact that the neurotic attitude calls forth a reaction of the environment, by which the attitude itself is reinforced, with the result that the person is more and more caught, and has greater and greater difficulty in escaping. Kuenkel calls this phenomenon *Teufelskreis* (1937, p. 68, footnote 1).

The formation of a vicious circle is typical not only in the context in which it has been discussed here; generally speaking it is one of the most important processes in neuroses. . . . The formation of vicious circles is the main reason why severe neuroses are bound to become worse, even though there is no change in external conditions. Uncovering the vicious circles, with all their implications, is one of the important tasks of psychoanalysis (1937, p. 138).

And Maslow and Mittelman have similarly remarked:

This sequence, which is a "vicious circle," is one of the most important factors in the persistence and recurrence of abnormal psychological manifestations. The concept implies that the patient takes certain measures to enable himself to function or to escape catastrophe, but that these measures renew his difficulties if he fails and even, to some extent, if he succeeds (1941, pp. 183–84).

The child who resorts to enuresis as a means of venting resentment toward indifferent or harsh parents and thereby elicits still more rejection and loss of love; the businessman who, when faced by the prospect of failure, becomes alcoholic and thus incapacitates himself for taking what might have been effective recuperative measures; or the woman who jealously nags her husband and in so doing destroys such residual affection as he may have for her—these are everyday examples of the self-defeating, short-sighted, nonintegrative strategy which constitutes the "vicious circle" and which seems to be a common feature of all the psychoneuroses.

It is true that, in the laboratory study of nonintegrative behavior which has been reported in this paper, we do not have a perfect analogue of a "vicious circle." That is to say, in trying to reduce their hunger by eating the food as soon as it appeared, our "delinquent" rats did not cause their hunger to be accentuated later; instead, they encountered a different form of drive increase, namely, electric shock. Likewise, in trying to reduce their anxiety by not eating the food at all, our "neurotic" rats did not cause their anxiety to be subsequently increased; instead, they simply experienced a growing hunger. However, it is clear that in our experiment, as in a situation involving a "vicious circle," the critical consideration is the time element. The fact that a given action often has not only immediate but also remote consequences and that, without the skilful use of symbols, the former tend to outweigh the latter is the basic condition of persistently nonintegrative behavior in both cases.

It would be a relatively simple matter to design an experiment which would provide at least a rough paradigm of the "vicious circle." Let us suppose, for example, that rats were first taught to press a bar as a means of turning off an electric shock administered through the grill on which they stood. Suppose that, after this bar-pressing response had become prompt and specific, the experimenter decided to try to break this habit by means of punishment consisting of a reapplication of the shock a few seconds after this particular shock-eliminating response had occurred. The animal would, of course, react to the punishment by making precisely that response for which the punishment was applied.[28] This response would terminate the shock but would insure its reappearance a little later. Since the relief obtained by pressing the bar would be immediate and the punishment remote, such behavior might be perpetuated indefinitely. The only way for the rat to escape from such a "vicious circle" would be to stop making the bar-pressing response and begin searching for a new way of eliminating the shock without at the same time precipitating its recurrence. The difficulty obviously is that, with the automatic effects of reinforcement operating so powerfully to perpetuate this nonintegrative act, it is a question whether there is any stronger mechanism that could come to the rat's rescue and save it from this continued self-torture.[29]

This discussion throws into relief the need for what seems to us to be a very important terminological distinction. Psychological writers commonly use "integration" and "adjustment" as if they were strictly equivalent concepts. This, we believe, is a major cause of theoretical confusion. For example, Shaffer (1936), following Hamilton (1916), has given wide currency to the expression "persistent nonadjustive behavior" as a synonym for neurosis. "The core phenomenon of the generalized psychoneurosis," he says, "is a persistent nonadjustive emotional reaction to baffling personal difficulties" (1936, p. 253). Although this usage drives Shaffer into the awkward necessity of acknowledging the "adjustive value of nonadjustment" (1936, p. 257), he neglects the way out of the difficulty which seems to us most clearly indicated. The distinguishing characteristic of both neurosis and criminality is not that they are *nonadjustive*; if modern experimental and clinical inquiry shows anything it is that all persistent behavior

[28] Not realizing that thumb-sucking and other forms of so-called infantile eroticism are frequently a response to anxiety (Erickson, 1940), parents frequently treat such behavior in a way which still further undermines the child's security and thereby aggravates the very tendency which the parent is intent upon eliminating. Punishment and rejection displayed in this context may lead to chronic disharmony and destructiveness in the child-parent relationship. Much school "discipline" probably also follows this pattern.

[29] Is this the basic pattern of masochism? In so far as all neuroses are said to represent a "masochistic trend," the answer is probably yes; but the behavior which this term is used to designate more specifically seems to follow a different pattern, namely, one in which there is severe "guilt" which can be dissipated only by soliciting—directly in sexual masochism, indirectly in moral masochism—some form of punishment which will afford at least temporary relief. Cf. Freud's discussion of "criminality from a sense of guilt" (1915a); also Fenichel (1934, pp. 463–64).

is in some sense adjustive (drive reducing). What should be stressed instead is their *nonintegrative* character; and this, as we have tried to show, is mainly a function of a failure properly to compare and balance consequences which are unevenly distributed along the time dimension. If we could but abandon the practice of using the term adjustive (nonadjustive) where we should say integrative (nonintegrative) and vice versa, it should aid materially in sharpening our theoretical perceptions.

VI. Learning Theory and Character

We anticipate that the foregoing analysis of integration and integration failure will not carry much conviction for some readers. They will point out that we have based this analysis upon the law of effect and will advance a common, and to them, a fatal objection thereto. The law of effect holds that behavior is determined by its consequences and that if these consequences are rewarding the behavior is reinforced, whereas if the consequences are punishing the behavior tends to be inhibited. Yet it is fully apparent that behavior often develops without any ostensible reward and may even survive for an astonishingly long time in the face of what seems to be nothing but pain and adversity. In fact, the capacity to display a certain amount of "autonomy" in this respect is a mark of character and good "morale" in this culture, just as too great dependence upon comfort and pleasure is looked upon as a sign of personal weakness. How, if at all, can these facts be reconciled with the theory?

One important source of confusion arises from a tendency to equate "reward" and "award." No supporter of the law of effect has ever held that actions can be reinforced only by situations in which the actor receives something—food, money, praise, or whatever—from the outer world. Everyone knows that human beings (and probably even lower animals to some extent) are normally capable of and do in fact very often engage in self-rewarding processes (see 8, 12). Thorndike (1943) has explicitly acknowledged as the "confirming" or "okay" reaction what passes more commonly as "knowing when one is right." The supposition is, therefore, that habits which sometimes seem to develop and persist without benefit of reward are simply habits in which the reward is subtly self-administered, either with or without the subject's conscious knowledge.

The fact that certain habits or "traits of character" may persist in the face of consistent punishment raises a more difficult problem. One possibility is that the punishment, which is observed, is offset by self-administered reward, which is not observed. The approval of one's own conscience may, for example, be quite as powerful in a positive sense as its disapproval (in guilt, depression, etc.) may be in the negative sense. But there may be more to the problem than this. Personal integration is a precious thing, and once a satisfying, harmonious personality pattern has been achieved, the "strength of the total ego" seems capable, in ways which have not yet been clearly analyzed, of being mobilized in support of any single part (habit) for which the going is particularly hard. In this sense we may grant to well-developed human personalities a certain type of "autonomy"; but this is not to say that punishments, if they are real in the sense of causing genuine inner pain and tension increase, do not automatically put a strain upon "the person." Shakespeare remarked long ago that "every man hath his price" in the moral sense, and the experiences of the current war [World War II] (in concentration camps as well as combat) seem to be showing that every man likewise has his breaking point, psychologically [cf. Boder, 1949]. The results of Dollard's (1943) recent survey show unmistakably that hunger, thirst, fatigue, fear, and other discomforts tend automatically and inevitably to drive men out of battle. Integration, ideology, morale, or whatever one wishes to call it can withstand varying amounts of such punishment without "cracking," but there is no absolute immunity.[30]

Whiting and Mowrer (1943) and Mowrer and Kluckhohn (1944) have recently described an experimental paradigm of personality development which emphasizes the view that socialization is always an uphill business and that there is continuous danger of regression to lower, easier forms of adjustment which have existed earlier. This analysis obviously draws heavily upon the works of Freud, particularly the thesis put forward in his *Civilization and its discontents* (1930). But it now appears that something has been lacking, or at least insufficiently stressed, in this type of analysis. To say that growing up and being trained for adult responsibilities in any society is one great, joyous adventure is surely more sentimental than sensible. But is it not possible that the perpetuity of human resistance to and resentment of culture has been somewhat exaggerated by psychoanalytic writers? That life in a human society, even a relatively bad one, is better than social isolation is

[30] Apparently no one has noted that it is in the psychotic that "autonomy," in the sense of imperviousness to reality demands, is most nearly approximated. Cf. Freud's concept of narcissism (1935a); also Footnote 27. [For the bearing of this discussion on anxiety theory, see 19.]

attested by the whole course of history. And it now seems probable that although induction into such a life is begun without the small child's consent and carried on for a considerable time against it, a point is eventually reached, in "normal" cases, at which something very momentous happens: the individual becomes aware of "what it is all about" and begins to line up, willingly, on the side of morality and social order.

The delinquent or criminal obviously fails to make this transition, or makes it very imperfectly; whereas the neurotic makes it only at the expense of partial psychic self-destruction (repression). For the more fortunate type of individual, this "conversion" [31] gives him the strength and stability to labor, deny himself, and to have a concern for others which marks the difference between the pleasure principle and the reality principle, between a well-socialized man and a beast. This, in short, is the highest that has been attained in terms of personal integration and the Good Life; but if we deny that it is based upon the same elemental principles that govern "lower" forms of behavior, whether human or infrahuman, we cut ourselves off from the broader type of understanding for which science ever strives.

We anticipate one other source of objection. There can clearly be no adequate human psychology which does not give a satisfactory account of neurosis and criminality. This, as we have seen, demands that we be willing to consider the problem of integration, which, in turn, leads straight to questions of social ethics and value. In the Middle Ages all behavior disturbances were frankly interpreted in religious terms.[32] Then there followed an interlude in which biological and even chemical explanations were in vogue. We are now swinging back toward the "spiritual" type of explanation, but with an obstacle imposed upon us by an historical coincidence. In attempting to become a science, academic psychology set a serious delimitation upon itself. Traditionally, interest in and the quest for personal unity have been regarded as the proper concern of religion and ethical philosophy, of which the new science was to have none. It was perhaps unavoidable that psychology should go through such an adolescent revolt on its way to maturity and self-sufficiency. But has not the time come when we can drop our defensiveness and self-imposed delimitations and turn energeti-

---

[31] Adolescence is the period recognized in most societies as the beginning of the "age of accountability." It is also the time of most frequent religious conversion in our society and of initiation rites among primitive people. Cf. Freud on the normal dissolution of the "Oedipus complex" (1924).

[32] See, for example, Freud (1934, pp. 436–72).

cally to this important area of human concern? If we can, the following decades should mark an unparalleled advance in social applications and systematic unification of our science.

Summary

Persistent nonintegrative behavior, i.e., behavior which has consequences which are usually more punishing than rewarding, remains one of the important unsolved problems of psychology. The law of exercise ("repetition compulsion") accommodates the fact that behavior sometimes persists despite predominantly painful consequences, but it provides no basis for explaining why such behavior, more commonly than not, gets eliminated. The law of effect ("pleasure principle"), as traditionally formulated, accounts well enough for the elimination of nonintegrative behavior, but it breaks down in those instances in which such behavior persists.

There are three alternatives:

1. We can continue to resort, now to the law of exercise, now to the law of effect, depending upon which seems most expedient at the moment; but this *ad hoc* procedure will never lead to a science with high predictive power.

2. We can abandon the attempt to deal with behavioral phenomena along conventional scientific lines and resort to a "wholistic" approach; but the danger here is that we will merely revert to prescientific voluntarism.

3. Or we can repudiate the law of exercise (a step well justified on empirical grounds) and see if the law of effect can be so refined and elaborated as to resolve the paradox of persistent nonintegrative behavior.

An experimental paradigm with rats as subjects shows that the tendency for a given action to be perpetuated or inhibited is influenced not only by the nature of the consequences ("effects") of that action but also by the *temporal order* or *timing* of these consequences. Thus, if an immediate consequence is slightly rewarding, it may outweigh a greater but more remote punishing consequence. And equally, if an immediate consequence is slightly punishing, it may outweigh a greater but more remote rewarding consequence. Living organisms which are not skilled in the use of *symbols* are severely limited in their capacity to resolve behavioral dilemmas of this kind and may, as a result, continue indefinitely to manifest so-called nonintegrative behavior. But by introducing the time element (and the notion of reinforcement "gradients"), it is possible for us to escape from the dilemma which such behavior presents from a theoretical standpoint.

The prodigious capacity found in normal adult human beings for using symbols, i.e., for "reasoning," seems to have what is perhaps its greatest utility in enabling the individual to bring the remote as well as immediate consequences of a contemplated action into the *psychological present* and thereby compare and balance the probable (anticipated) rewards and punishments in a manner which enormously increases the chances that the resulting behavior will be integrative. Such behavior is properly termed *rational,* in contradistinction to the *prerational* behavior seen in lower animals.

Neurotic and criminal behavior may be said to represent either a fixation at or a regression to the prerational level of functioning. In psychosis, conflict is resolved in the opposite direction, by an overelaboration of the rational (symbolic) processes: hence, the term "irrational." As Angyal has remarked, "The conscious self, by overstepping the realm of its legitimate influence, may become a destructive factor. The relative autonomy of the symbolic realm within the total organism is the most vulnerable point of the human personality organization" (1941, p. 123).

Until comparatively recently the dominant note in European and American psychology was rationalism. However, animal experimentation on the one hand and clinical observations on the other have equally revealed its inadequacies. The present paper attempts to locate rationality in a larger conceptual setting, midway on a continuum between the prerational and the irrational adjustive processes.[33]

---

[33] Compare Edna Heidbreder's paper (1945). Contrast Lewin's distinction between "learning through motivation" and "learning through cognition" (1942a).

CHAPTER 16

DISCIPLINE AND MENTAL HEALTH

["Many parents and teachers today half believe that if they discipline children it will make them neurotic in later life. The thesis of the present article is that although discipline without love rarely achieves its intended ends, neither can love and unconditional acceptance, without discipline, lead to normal character development and mental health. It is not, therefore, a question of whether we shall or shall not discipline our children. 'It is probably as fallacious,' says the author, 'to assume that a child can develop into a psychologically and socially normal adult without discipline as it is to assume that a society can exist without it.' 'The important consideration in dealing with children is to see to it that the child's experience with discipline teaches him to look upon it, not as something capricious, stupid, and malevolent, but rather as something which is consistent, wise, and beneficial.'

"This paper was initially prepared for a conference on 'Freedom and Security' which was held on Star Island in the summer of 1947, under the auspices of the Unitarian Church. The position taken in it has been more comprehensively developed in a number of other, more technical writings by Dr. Mowrer."

These paragraphs are quoted from the editor's introduction to this paper as originally published in the *Harvard Educational Review* (1947). Although prepared for a nonprofessional audience, this paper is included here because it brings together and illustrates, at the level of practical application, a number of the principles which have been dealt with more abstractly and technically in preceding studies; and it also anticipates, briefly, many of the problems which are considered in subsequent papers.]

I. Conflicting Trends in Child Rearing

Most parents are today confused about the problem of discipline. Intuitively they feel that certain ways of dealing with their children are necessary and proper, but they are often also convinced, on intellectual or so-called "scientific" grounds, that just the opposite courses of action are the correct ones. These conflicting tendencies need to be carefully scrutinized. Perhaps we will find it possible not only to understand but also to reconcile them. Perhaps we will find that our scientific knowledge, from the clinic and the laboratory, is catching up with common sense. We have come to distrust common sense, even though it represents the essence of thousands of years of human experience. Perhaps we will find it more valid than we have sometimes recently supposed.

There are many reasons for the current distrust of common sense when it comes to dealing with our children. Modern medical research has demonstrated the fateful potency of germs, vitamins, hormones, and other agencies which are unknown to direct experience. These developments alone were enough to shake the confidence of parents in their own knowledge. But there are other changes, of a revolutionary technological nature, going on concurrently. What the "old folks" know is not always what the youngsters need to know. This fact has made children bold and their parents timid, hesitant to press their ways and values upon their offspring. And parents themselves have had crises to face. They have seen the faith of their fathers vanish as the mists of morning under the impact of the penetrating rays of science and the winds of modern materialism. Small wonder they lack confidence and conviction when it comes to teaching their young the way of life!

But these are only background facts as far as our immediate problem is concerned. The most powerful and direct influences which have served to topple traditional concepts and practices in child training are those which have emanated from the clinical study of sick souls. The basic writings of Sigmund Freud lie on the living-room table (or in a dresser drawer) in thousands of American households, and his apostles are the prophets of child guidance and adult psychiatry in hundreds of American communities. This man and his many followers have exerted an enormous influence upon our conception of human mentality and its management. It is here that we find the most disturbing attacks upon traditional views and values with respect to childhood discipline.

II. The Freudian Syllogism

In his *General introduction to psychoanalysis,* and recurrently in his more technical writings, Freud has stressed the pivotal importance of *frustration* in the causation of neurosis. Human beings, he says, become mentally ill because they experience greater emotional deprivation than they can tolerate. Their pentup, repressed energies and impulses, lacking full satisfaction, force themselves into consciousness and thereby produce anxiety—the common coin of neurosis.

From this conception of neurosis it takes no expert to draw the inference:

> Frustration causes neurosis.
> Discipline involves frustration.
> ∴ If you don't want your child to be neurotic, don't discipline him!

Few, if any, parents wish their children to become mental cripples. And so, granted the original Freudian premise, parents have found themselves in a position in which they seemed either to have to repudiate the established conception of parental responsibilities or else to go against the dictates of what they take to be scientific gospel. If and when, in a fit of desperation, they do resort to disciplinary measures with their children, it is often with guilt and self-accusation. This half-heartedness and confusion are, of course, often sensed by the child and are taken as meaning that something fraudulent is being done to him, instead of something that is valid, clear in its purpose, and wholesome in its effect.

That the position in which many modern parents thus find themselves is an intolerable one goes without saying. But it is less easy to discover—and, once discovered, to apply—the remedy.

III. Discipline Necessary and Constructive

First we must examine the conclusion which seems to follow so inexorably from our premises. Perhaps, after all, it is true that children *can* be properly, and more hygienically, reared without frustration, without discipline. Perhaps our recourse to discipline, to warnings, to penalties, to punishments is more of a reflection of our own weaknesses and perversity than it is of any need on the part of the child. To say that a child has a "need for discipline"—in the sense that he has a need or wish for food, warmth, security, etc.—is, of course, clearly unwarranted. No child, at least in the beginning, *wants* to be disciplined. In what sense, then, if at all, can we say that the child needs this kind of control and training?

The need here involved is obviously something that is experienced *as a need,* not so much by the child as *by society.* Most adult human beings are uncomfortable if children, whether their own or those of others, are allowed to grow like Topsy. They are likely to be uncomfortable, first and most directly, because of the inconsiderate, disorderly, and often destructive and dangerous things which undisciplined children do. But adults are made perhaps even more uneasy by the prospect of what would happen if all children were allowed to remain unmannerly and unruly. Society cannot be made up of adults who know no restraint, no control, no discipline. And the adult who fails to cooperate in training children in the ways of restraint, responsibility, and adulthood generally is, in effect, confessing his skepticism concerning the worth of organized human society. Few persons, even in this hectic day, are so disillusioned and pessimistic as this!

Anthropologists who have studied other societies, both primitive and civilized, tell us that they know of no society in which adults do not, at least on occasion, find it necessary to use relatively drastic measures with their young. They may not spank their children as we sometimes do. They may hit them with the open hand or fist between the shoulder blades. Or they may not strike them at all. Perhaps, instead, they hold them under a smoke-filled blanket or tell them of witches and demons. But, in one way or another, they find it necessary to use fairly stringent means to impose upon the young the will and ways of adult society.

Obviously, this is not to say that punishment, in and of itself, is a good thing. Nor do we have any facts to justify sadistic, brutal, stupid treatment of children. The control of children without punishment should be an ideal; and when a parent finds that he is having to make frequent use of this type of discipline, he can be sure that something is radically wrong with his approach to and relationship with his child. But if, on occasion, he finds that some type of physical chastisement is necessary, he need not feel that he has failed as a parent or that the child will be irreparably damaged by it.

From this survey, brief as it is, we see more clearly what many have vaguely felt all along, namely, the illicit character of the conclusion that we can and ought to raise children without disciplining them. Unless we wish to go counter to the bulk of human experience, we must assume what our feelings confirm, that this conclusion is not true.

In passing, it ought to be said that few of even the most slavish of Freud's followers have ever *said* that we should never discipline children; but it is an inference which many have been quick to draw from psychoanalytic doctrine and one which Freud and his followers have been slow to repudiate. Tacitly, and sometimes explicitly, it has had their approval.

But useful as it may be to identify a false conclusion, the problem goes further; we need to search out and understand the reasons why the conclusion was ever drawn and believed.

IV. Frustration and Neurosis

If we asked a logician to look at the syllogism presented above, he would say that the conclusion is not necessarily false, but that it is *indeterminate*. By this he would mean that, logically speaking, the conclusion may be either true or false. And he would probably diagnose the difficulty as lying in the major premise: "Frustration causes neurosis." He would want to know if frustration always causes neurosis, or only sometimes. He would want to know also if neurosis can be caused by anything other than frustration. For the major premise to be perfectly explicit and the conclusion completely determined, it ought to read: "Frustration, and it alone, causes, and always causes, neurosis."

Turning to Freud we find him saying that in all the patients he ever treated he never found one in whom frustration was not at least the *precipitating* cause of neurosis and in many cases also the *predisposing* one. But he does not say that frustration always and inevitably produces neurosis. Sometimes it does and sometimes it does not. However, Freud was vague and vacillating in what he had to say on this latter score. Why frustration does not *always* end in neurosis was a mystery which he never solved, even to his own satisfaction; and so it is not remarkable that we find him speaking most often of those persons in whom frustration does, rather than does not, appear to produce neurosis. They are the persons he saw and studied; his method did not give him comparable data concerning normal persons.

Strictly speaking, the logician is right in pointing out that, because of the inexplicit nature of the major premise in our syllogism, the conclusion that we should never discipline our children is indeterminate; but this is not to say that the argument has been any the less effective with the logically unsophisticated. And, at most, all the logician is able to tell us is that the conclusion *may* be untrue—not that it necessarily is, or why it is.

V. The Conditions of Effective Discipline

What, then, of the minor premise?—"Discipline involves frustration." The soundness of this proposition seems to justify no suspicion of doubt. Only with a wild distortion of the common meaning of terms would it seem possible for discipline not to be frustrating. Discipline always involves a penalty, actual or implied; and to say that discipline need not be frustrating would seem tantamount to saying that punishment is rewarding, that black is white. Wise discipline, as we shall presently see, is useful and helpful to the child *in the long run;* but for the moment it can hardly fail to be perceived, one would suppose, as disagreeable, objectionable, thwarting, frustrating.

Oddly enough, there is a sense in which discipline may also be satisfying. In clinical practice one commonly encounters the paradox of persons, both adults and children, who out of a sense of guilt will sometimes court punishment as the only means they know of escaping from their intolerable self-accusatory feelings. This is a dynamism which every parent ought to understand for his efficient functioning both as a parent and as a person. But for present purposes the important consideration is this: that which is perceived by others as punishment may be experienced by the recipient as satisfying. When this happens, the disciplinary effect is, of course, nullified. In this event the discipline ceases to be discipline and is no longer frustrating and, by implication, does not contribute to neurosis (though it serves to satisfy a neurotic strategy).

Only when would-be discipline has an over-all effect which is more objectionable than it is gratifying is it truly discipline, and in such an event it is surely also frustrating.

We are still vague about many aspects of the psychology of discipline. In fact, we do not always use the term itself precisely and consistently. But this much now seems established: in order for would-be discipline to have the desired effects, i.e., to be genuinely disciplining, the frustration, the penalty, the punishment thereby imposed must be ultimately accepted by the child as wise and proper. The actions and attitudes of the parents must, in other words, be *internalized* by the child and accepted as his own. The conditions under which this fortunate outcome is achieved are still far from certain. But we have reason to believe that this internalization does not occur (*a*) if the parents make no demands whatever upon the child or (*b*) if they make too great or unreasonable, inconsistent demands upon him. Only when discipline is far-seeing and just and when it is underwritten by love and basic security in the child-parent relationship is it genuinely "discipline," in the sense that it leads to normal character development, responsibility, and conscience, i.e., to the capacity for self-discipline.

John Dewey has remarked that a teacher can no more teach unless there is a learner that learns than a seller can sell unless there is a buyer that buys. Paraphrasing this thought, we may say that discipline is discipline only if it "takes." Otherwise, it is sheer lost motion, useless at best and at its worst very bad indeed.

VI. Biological or Moral Frustration?

Still we seem remote from our objective. We appear hardly nearer to an understanding of our basic problem than we were at the outset. Let us try, therefore, yet another approach.

The major premise of our syllogism is that frustration causes neurosis. Certainly neurosis appears to be universally associated with frustration. Human beings can experience frustration without being necessarily described as neurotic. That is to say, they may be temporarily thwarted by prevailing life circumstances; but the person who is chronically frustrated, continually unhappy, unable, as we say, to adjust to life—these are surely but synonyms for neurosis. There is thus little doubt that frustration and neurosis somehow go together, and yet we have reason to believe that there is something spurious about the proposition that frustration causes neurosis. Perhaps the key to the riddle lies in the special way in which Freud conceived of *frustration.*

It is well known that the frustrations from which Freud and his followers believe people fall ill are mainly frustrations of the sexual impulse and of the impulse of anger, hostility, hate. These are the two impulses which human societies have found most difficult to subdue, and it is with respect to these impulses that the most severely punitive measures are likely to be used. Freud saw these facts with a new clarity, and he was impressed with the difficulty which human beings, as biological organisms, experience in tolerating the renunciations which society asks of them in respect to these two impulses. Human beings are disciplined with special rigor in regard to the impulses of lust and hatred; and it is because of the resulting frustration, the resulting limitations upon full gratification of these primordial needs that human beings become anxious and neurotic. So goes the logic of Freud.

On the basis of his own clinical experience, the present author has come to see the situation somewhat differently. Most neurotics are not less "expressive" than are normal persons, either in the matter of sexuality or in that of aggression. In most instances neurotics present a history of more rather than less self-indulgence than does the average person, and it is only by an extraordinary feat of tortuous interpretation than one can see their troubles as stemming from too little gratification of either the sexual or the aggressive "instinct."

Yet the neurotic presents a picture of unhappiness, anxiety, confusion, frustration. Whence does it come?

The answer may be surprisingly simple, but none the less true because of its simplicity. Neurotic suffering seems not to come from the intensity of unsatisfied sexual or aggressive needs. The driving force of neurosis is an aggrieved conscience which, in the final analysis, means a fear of community disapproval or reprisal. Our biological impulses, while often imperious, are never intense enough to kill us; but an outraged community may! It is not surprising, therefore, if the internalized voice of the community, i.e., conscience, has a force proportionate to the external dangers which it reflects.

It is not possible here to give all the evidence upon which these statements rest; nor is it possible, for that matter, to present fully even the theoretical position from which the foregoing remarks are drawn. Suffice it to say that, from the author's point of view, frustration does indeed cause (or at least universally accompanies) neurosis, but it is not a sexual or aggressive frustration; it is instead moral frustration. Neurotics are persons who are ethically stunted. They are personally immature, and yet within them are forces driving them toward maturity. It is precisely the conflict between these forces and the conscious wishes and tendencies of the individual that constitute his neurosis. In the language of psychoanalysis this newer point of view says that anxiety, guilt, depression, feelings of inferiority, and the other forces of neurosis stem, not from an id-ego conflict, but from an ego-superego conflict. The trouble, in other words, is between the individual's conscious self and the values implanted in him by his social training, rather than between the conscious self or ego and the biologically given impulses of lust and hostility.

VII. Discipline, Conscience, and Neurosis

All this, no doubt, still seems very obscure and complicated, but we are nearing the more enlightening part of our analysis. As a means to that end, let us turn back now to the question of the relation between neurosis and discipline.

According to the Freudian view—stated, to be sure, in a somewhat oversimplified manner—discipline produces inhibition, inhibition produces frustration, and frustration means neurosis. The contrasting point of view which we are here exploring may be stated most simply—though again somewhat overly so—by saying that human beings become neurotic not because they have been overdisciplined but because they have been disciplined too little and *unwisely.*

Such a statement immediately calls for amplification. We have all known individuals who were disciplined very severely in childhood and yet who turned out as adults to be either neurotic or perhaps frankly criminal. And yet the assertion has just been made that failures of adult personality stem from too little discipline. How can this seeming contradiction be reconciled?

Let us remember, first of all, that we are here conceiving of a neurotic as a person in whom there is more or less serious disharmony between ego and superego, between the conscious, executive "self" and "conscience." The ego distrusts and disdains the superego, and, as the superego attacks with its characteristic weapons of guilt, anxiety, and depression, the ego fights back with such defensive devices or "symptoms" as it may have at its disposal. The neurotic struggle is revealed with particular clarity in alcoholism: here the ego counterattacks the superego with a form of chemical warfare, and the fact that the alcohol, if enough is consumed, eventually knocks out the ego as well as the superego is purely coincidental. Other neurotic strategies show variation in form and detail, but the basic mechanism is much the same: they are all devices for "neutralizing" conscience, but they are devices which are so costly in their over-all consequences that we rightly refer to them as neurotic symptoms rather than as normal habits.

In therapy the major objective is to help the neurotic to reconstruct and understand the genesis of his distrust and hatred of conscience and then to help him learn to do business with his conscience instead of having continually to fight with it. Here the objective is not a mere truce or compromise solution, but rather a genuinely cooperative arrangement in which conscience comes to be seen as protective and helpful instead of arbitrary and mean. But our present concern is with prevention rather than with treatment. So let us view the problem of discipline in the light of the causation rather than the cure of neurosis.

If the core of neurosis is a distrust on the part of the ego of the internalized surrogate of external authority, then it readily follows that the best prophylaxis is to see to it that external authority, or discipline, is presented in such a form that it proves wise and helpful. If this is done, the inner residue of that authority, namely conscience, will be similarly regarded, as something necessary and useful, something to be accepted, relied upon, and perhaps even cherished.

Let us say this a little differently and in somewhat greater detail. From the standpoint of insuring personal normality and mental health in adult life, the important consideration in dealing with children is to see to it that the child's experience with discipline teaches him to look upon it, not as something capricious, stupid, and malevolent, but rather as something which is consistent, wise, and beneficial. When the authoritative persons in a child's environment, i.e., his disciplinarians, display these latter traits, external authority is perceived as helpful and the internalized representation of that authority, conscience, is harmoniously integrated with the rest of the personality. In fact, it is not too much to say that in this fortunate event, ego and superego become more or less as one, at peace and unified.

When external authority is patently foolish, vacillating, and unsympathetic, there is likely to be little or no internal conflict because this authority is so completely rejected that no internalization occurs. This is the type of situation that leads to adults with criminal tendencies or to persons who simply are said to have "no character." But when there are force and determination in external authority, and yet blindness and perhaps malice as well, that authority tends to get internalized, but it is *not accepted.* It rails against the rest of the personality, but to this railing the ego turns, as it were, a deaf ear. Such a spurned and distrusted superego causes feelings of personal inadequacy, anxiety, and depression; but because of the ego attitude of rejection, there can be no synthesis, no harmony, but only conflict, antagonism, neurosis.

VIII. The Argument in Review

At this point let us take our bearings and see what we have thus far accomplished and what remains to be done. We have seen that the disciplining of children is not only a social necessity; it is equally essential for the development of a normal, happy, adult human being. And we can no more abandon the responsibility for this training of our young than we can renounce the whole human enterprise. Adult neurosis, we have seen, is not an inevitable consequence of discipline but is instead an expression of discipline applied unwisely, without love and understanding. Every normal individual, in passing from infancy to adulthood, goes through a transitional period, or perhaps several periods, in which there is skepticism, conflict, and even rebellion with respect to authority; but, at some point along the life line, the individual discovers the greater satisfactions and contentments of the mature way of life—he has, as we are likely to say, a "conversion"—and he usually remains firmly anchored in that way of life. By contrast, the neurotic is the person who in at least certain areas of his personality continues to be infantile, or at least adolescent, well into his adult years. He is not, as has sometimes been implied, a person in whom the socialization process has been overdone. The less flattering but more accurate characterization of the neurotic is of a person who is undersocialized and immature and who, at the same time, has learned to protect himself against the forces which are pushing him toward genuine adulthood.

If, now, this conception of human development, sketchy as it is, seems basically correct, we are in a position to look with new eyes upon the problem of discipline. No longer is it a question of to discipline or not to discipline. No longer can we blame discipline, as such, for our adult vagaries. Instead it is *bad* discipline that is to blame, and it is now our task to learn to tell bad discipline from discipline that is valid and useful. Of what is good and what is bad in discipline folk-belief has many, though often contradictory, things to say; and there is no want of advice on every hand. Let us here take a somewhat different and more systematic tack.

Let us ask what are the basic functions of discipline. In the most general terms we have already answered this question. One function of punishment, and discipline generally, is to make it possible for adult human beings to tolerate the human young in their midst; but over and beyond this is the necessity of training them so that they may ultimately take over the responsibilities which their elders have previously carried and thus perpetuate the way of life which their society has found good.

IX. Five Functions of Discipline

However, we can be much more specific about the problem than this. Discipline, we discover, serves at least five basic functions:

1. Surely the first of these is obvious enough to everyone. When we put the question by asking why we punish children in-

stead of letting them learn by the *natural* consequences of their actions, the most immediate answer is that the natural consequences of some acts are lethal. Instead of learning from the consequences of such actions, children are likely to be killed or at least severely injured. We scold and warn and sometimes physically punish small children in connection with all manner of dangers—fire, traffic, wild animals, irresponsible adults, disease. "Learning by doing" by directly experiencing such dangers is simply too costly, and we provide artificial social consequences, namely punishment, instead.

There is much that parents might learn about allowing their children to experience the natural consequences of their actions under carefully controlled circumstances and then teaching them to transfer the wisdom and reliability of their parents' warnings from these relatively safe situations to really dangerous ones, so that the necessity for physical punishment under the latter conditions is greatly reduced. The wise parent will also often withhold privileges as a means of discipline rather than administer physical punishment. But these considerations do not lessen the necessity, in at least some situations, for parents to be prepared to administer, personally, some form of pain to children in place of the greater injury which might otherwise be experienced.

2. Another use of punishment derives from the fact that the natural consequences of some acts are so remote in time that the child cannot, unaided, learn from them. A child does not learn from consequences which kill him; and neither does he learn from consequences which come so belatedly that he fails to "see the connection." Many children would be quite willing not to go to school. As Pinocchio discovered, the world offers many more alluring pastimes than does school. Furthermore, the *natural* consequences of ignorance are likely to be so remote temporally that they are experienced only after the opportunity for school learning is past. Hence, our tendency to attach immediate social consequences to childish indolence and truancy.

Some educational theorists would have us believe that if schools were only run properly, no external compulsion would be needed. We are not here excusing those schools which are really run badly, of which there is certainly no scarcity; but what we are saying is that no school on earth can make formal education sufficiently attractive so that, without the pressure of parents, contemporaries, and conscience, children would attend it spontaneously. The consequences of illiteracy and innocence of school learning generally are simply too remote to impress the child himself.

3. The third function of discipline in childhood is more subtle than the two just mentioned but not less important. Let us put it as simply and directly as possible by saying that one of the major functions of parental discipline is so to sensitize children to social disapproval that in adult life they will respond to and be modified by the merest tokens or semblances of punishment. Good neighbors can, as we say, "take a hint," and good citizens will stop on hearing a policeman's whistle, instead of having to feel the impact of his nightstick.

It is doubtful if children who are not disciplined by parents or appropriate parent-surrogates are likely to grow up with this kind of sensitivity and responsibility. By our standards, some primitive peoples are surprisingly indulgent with their children prior to puberty, but then they come down hard, with initiation rites which we are likely to regard as unnecessarily brutal and stupid. However, closer study seems to indicate that, if you postpone the disciplining of the human animal until puberty, you then have to strike with double force if you hope to convert him into an adult member of society who is responsive to the will of the group and a cooperative member thereof. In knocking out an adolescent boy's tooth or otherwise mutilating him, it is as if the adult members of certain primitive societies were saying to him: "This is just a sample of what will happen to you if you don't behave yourself now and don't do what is expected of you." In most instances comparatively mild reminders keep him in line the rest of his life.

Whether they do it by relatively mild measures in infancy or by more radical methods in adolescence, the adults of every society must bring oncoming generations into accord with the established ways of the group. Only in this way can the group continue to be a group.

4. The fourth function of discipline is closely related to the third one, and yet there is enough difference to call for separate mention. Adult human beings must not only be "good" in the sense of behaving themselves; they must also be "good" in the sense that they are industrious, productive, ambitious, effective. They must value and know how to achieve the approval of their group, not only because of the things they don't do but also because of the things they do do and of the skill with which they do them.

Ambition, as the clinical practitioner knows only too well, *may* be a morbid and destructive force, but this is not to say that it has no place whatever in a healthy personality. Ambition may be based upon neurotic anxiety, and the psychoanalysts have suggested that in other instances it represents, in sublimated form, the disguised outcroppings of sex and hostility. Without attempting to debate the justification of these interpretations, we may safely assume that in most instances ambition represents substitution, not sublimation. Instead of being exclusively dominated by sex and aggression, the mature adult learns to find his major satisfactions in other directions, notably in the clear conscience that comes from a sense of the day's work well done, of obligations honorably discharged. This is not to say that a man does not work to have a wife and children nor that we may not strive to best a business or professional rival. But in the emotionally healthy man or woman, the sustaining force behind his or her labors is the satisfaction that derives from self-approval and from the feeling that one has done all that other members of one's group could well ask of one under the circumstances.

The individual who was wisely disciplined in childhood finds it easier as an adult to work productively and satisfyingly than do those individuals who were not. It is no accident that the neurotic and the criminal characteristically show disturbances and inhibitions in their work habits and attitudes.

5. The fifth and final function of discipline which we propose to consider here has to do with what we may call the realistic value of restraint and postponement. Human beings begin life under the full sway of what Freud has appropriately called the pleasure principle. Their wishes and impulses are imperious and brook no interference or delay. Only gradually and with difficulty do the human young learn that renunciation today may be the best way of insuring plenty tomorrow. When or where our remote ancestors first discovered the advantage in not eating all their maize or beans during the lean winter months in order to have seed for the coming year we cannot say; but it involves a principle which has made a deep imprint on the mind of mankind.

So deeply has this principle of giving up as a means of gaining in the long run impressed human beings that today we sometimes seem to assume that there is virtue in renunciation as such. How often we see parents, for example, who try to teach their children to save by forcing them to amass an ever increasing sum of money. We now suspect that children learn most quickly to save if they are allowed to experience the *function* of saving, namely that by saving one can do things, make purchases, and experience satisfactions which one cannot do without saving. The child who is most likely to save his first dollar spontaneously is the one who has previously learned to save pennies so that he had a nickel to spend, and nickels so that he could purchase things that cost a quarter.

The wisely disciplined child learns to make both the renunciations which are in his own individual interest and also those which are in the interest of his group. If renunciation is a virtue, it is also a part of wisdom and—need we add?—an attribute of the mature, happy, and healthy personality.

X. Personal Freedom and Social Responsibility

In recent decades it has been unfashionable to speak up in support of discipline, responsibility, and duty. Self-expression, freedom, and personal liberty have been the popular rallying cries. Merely because we have discovered the unhealthy after-effects in the lives of some unfortunate individuals of stupid and brutish discipline, we have jumped to the conclusion that it is discipline as such which is to blame. On both theoretical and pragmatic grounds we now know that discipline, properly conceived, is not only necessary for the maintenance of group life but that it is also necessary for the normal development and adult happiness of the individual.

In an era when fascism, with its fanatic emphasis upon discipline and obedience, has led to so many hateful and tragic events, it is easy to assume that discipline and the democratic way of life are antithetical. Let us not be misled: The parental discipline of children which leads to maximal self-discipline and personal maturity in later life is an absolute prerequisite for the healthy functioning of a democracy. The fascist state extols discipline and adult obedience precisely for the reason that it wishes to keep the adult population personally immature, the better to exploit and enslave it.

So let us face up to the admittedly difficult but essential task of disciplining our young. We are, of course, intent upon not employing would-be disciplinary methods which make for resentment, rebellion, or apathy in children and thus alienate them from rather than align them with organized society. But on the other hand, it seems equally misguided to assume that merely because disciplinary endeavor can go wrong, we can or should abandon it altogether. It is probably as fallacious to assume that a child can develop into a psychologically and socially normal adult without discipline as it is to assume that a society can exist without it. Complex group life is a human invention and one that is maintained only with vigilance and continuous effort. No society can long exist that makes no demands on its adult members and exacts no toll of those who do not meet these demands. And any education which does not prepare the young for the restraints and responsibilities of such an existence is failing in its manifest function.

In the foregoing pages comparatively little attention has been given to questions of what-to-do-when. Perhaps the most common type of inquiry which one hears from parents is of this variety: What should I do when Johnny won't eat his spinach? How should I act when Mary is rude to guests? And so on and on. The reason parents seem so helpless in the details of child management is that they are confused at the level of underlying assumptions.

In the preceding pages we have tried to deal with basic principles and fundamental attitudes and values. When one is clear about the essential logic of child training and is free from emotional confusion, one usually finds the will and the way for dealing with specific problems. And all the advice in the world on how to handle this or that specific situation does not give parents the genuine competence for which they seek nor their children the training and trust in their parents which they need.

In the preceding pages it may appear to some that punishment has been emphasized too much and the importance of love stressed too little. Again let us point out that only those parents who love their children deeply and devotedly can discipline them properly. To the child who feels rejected by his parents, even the most severe of physical punishments or deprivations may serve only to confirm his feelings of resentment and his desire for retaliation. But for the child who is secure in his parents' abiding affection and who cherishes a similar love for them, for such a child a mere disapproving look or warning word may be profoundly more effective as discipline than any amount of physical chastisement.

A rich store awaits someone who will make a careful study of the Bible, not from the standpoint of theology, but from the standpoint of psychology. Here let me call your attention to but one passage, which neatly presents the principle involved in the dynamic relationship between discipline and love: "For I say unto you, That unto every one which hath shall be given; and from him that hath not, even that he hath shall be taken away from him" (Luke, 19:26). The parent who has little love for his child is likely to have still less as a result of his disciplinary efforts. In terms of the modern psychological clinic, a "vicious circle" is created. Whereas, in the case of a parent whose love is great and abiding, the effects of discipline are likely to be such that his love will be made stronger still, thereby creating what may be called a "beneficent circle."

This discussion of discipline and mental health is manifestly incomplete and raises, perhaps, far more questions than it answers. But it will have served its primary purpose if it but indicates the fallacy of the widespread contemporary belief that discipline is the specific cause of mental disorder and that the latter can be prevented only by some fantastic policy of child training that involves no discipline.

CHAPTER 17

AN EXPERIMENTAL ANALOGUE OF FEAR FROM A SENSE OF HELPLESSNESS

[The experiment here reported shows in a surprisingly clear-cut manner that living organisms fear not only painful events but also *fear itself*. It shows, moreover, that one of the best ways of generating this "fear of fear" is to subject an organism to a painful situation over which it has no control.

Perhaps we have isolated here, in prototype, one of the central reasons why human beings so universally prize *freedom* and why threats to freedom, under a totalitarian regime, are anxiety-producing. Perhaps we also have here at least a partial explanation of the effectiveness of procedures such as those used in the Cardinal Mindszenty "trial" (Swift, 1949) and which, on a lesser scale, characterize "third-degree" methods generally (cf. Boder, 1949; May, 1950).

The present study was conducted jointly with Peter Viek and was first published in the *Journal of Abnormal and Social Psychology* (1948).]

A painful stimulus never seems so objectionable if one knows how to terminate it as it does if one has no control over it. Presumably the reason for this is that in the one case one's discomfort consists almost solely of the primary drive of pain, whereas in the other case there is the same element of pain but to this is added a fear that the pain may persist indefinitely. In a situation in which the pain can be terminated at will, there is presumably little or no admixture of such fear.

One of the commonest yet most dramatic illustrations of this phenomenon is the relief experienced when a physician is consulted. One is ill and suffering from pain and inconvenience. The physician arrives, diagnoses the difficulty, prescribes treatment, and intimates that in a day or two one will be quite hale again. It is unlikely that the examination or the ensuing exchange of words has altered the physical condition of the patient in the least; yet he is likely to "feel a lot better" as a result of the doctor's call. What obviously happens in such instances is that initially the patient's physical suffering is complicated by concern lest his suffering continue indefinitely or perhaps grow worse. After a reassuring diagnosis, this concern abates; and if, subsequently, the same ailment recurs, one can predict that it will arouse less apprehension than it did originally (provided, of course, that the physician's reassurances were valid and his treatment effective).[1]

Probably the same mechanism operates in the case of children who get spanked by their parents. Some parents seem to make a practice of stopping a spanking as soon as the child cries lustily, the assumption being that the spanking has then done its work. Other parents, by contrast, seem to have a preconceived notion of the amount of punishment that is needed and proceed to administer it without much regard for the child's protestations. Although there are apparently no empirical data on this score, it is a safe guess that spankings of the latter kind are more dreaded, even though they last no longer and involve no more actual pain than do the former.

Freud (1936) has commented at length upon the relation between fear (or "anxiety") and the feeling of helplessness, which he equates to trauma. The following passage gives a representative summary of his views:

> Having developed this series: anxiety—danger—helplessness (trauma), we may summarize the matter as follows: The danger situation is the recognized, remembered and anticipated situation of helplessness. Anxiety is the original reaction to helplessness in the traumatic situation, which is later reproduced as a call for help in the danger situation (p. 150).

Child play, Freud believes, is often motivated by a desire to master anxiety through a reproduction in miniature of a situation which was, in reality, traumatic but is now, through play, brought under control. He says:

> The ego, which has experienced the trauma passively, now actively repeats an attenuated reproduction of it with the idea of taking into its own hands the direction of its course. We know that the child behaves in such a manner toward all impressions which he finds painful, by reproducing them in play; through this method of transition from passivitity to activity the child attempts to cope psychically with its impressions and experiences. If this is what is meant by "abreacting a trauma," no objection can be made to it (p. 150).
>
> "Spoiling" young children has the undesirable result that the danger of object loss—the object being the protection against all situations of helpless-

[1] Obviously we are here dealing with at least one of the phenomena commonly subsumed under the term "suggestion." It is probably no accident that apprehension and suggestibility are frequently perceived as being in some way related.

ness—is overemphasized in comparison with all other dangers. It therefore encourages persistence in the childhood state of which both motor and psychic helplessness is characteristic (p. 151).[2]

Another plausible conjecture is that fear from a sense of helplessness is one of the very powerful motives for the learning of language. Even though an infant can indicate discomfort by crying, he cannot indicate *which* discomfort; and it must be with an enormous sense of relief that the small child discovers the wonderful power of language as a means of controlling the intensity of his drives. The muteness of the infant seems to dispose him to a pervasive insecurity, and the unique value of language in reducing this insecurity is suggested by the way in which the child, once he has caught the trick of speech, is enchanted by this new skill and exercises it, at least for a time, almost incessantly (Mowrer and Viek, 23; also 24).

Many other examples, of both a causal and clinical nature, could be adduced to show that fear is commonly correlated with a sense of helplessness, but so far as the authors are aware no attempt has previously been made to demonstrate this correlation experimentally. It was surprising to discover how easy it is to reproduce this phenomenon under controlled conditions, in even so lowly an organism as the laboratory rat.

I. Apparatus and Subjects

The subjects used in the research here reported were 20 male rats (Lashley strain), approximately 5 months of age. On a random basis they were divided into two equal groups, the Shock-Controllable (*S-C*) Group and the Shock-Uncontrollable (*S-UnC*) Group. Each of the 10 animals in the *S-C* Group was then, again randomly, paired with one of the animals in the *S-UnC* Group; and the resulting 10 pairs of animals received the same general experimental treatment, except that the 2 individuals constituting each of the pairs were differentially treated in the manner indicated below.

The apparatus used in this investigation has been described in detail elsewhere (Mowrer and Miller, 1942). In essence, it is a

[2] In at least certain types of psychodrama, it seems likely that one of the principal gains comes from the opportunity thus afforded the individual to acquire some degree of competence and mastery in a "pretend" version of a situation which has previously been or is expected to be "traumatic." This is perhaps only an extension of the not uncommon practice of "briefing" both children and adults concerning new or hazardous situations which they are about to enter. If realism can be engendered, "role-taking" or "acting out" may carry this form of preparatory learning a step further than does mere verbal rehearsal.

rectangular box-like cage, the front of which is a piece of window-glass and the bottom of which is a metal grill which can be electrified so as to administer a shock to the feet of an animal standing upon the grill. The shock used in this study was supplied by 130 volts of 60-cycle alternating current, with a 200,000-ohm limiting resistance in series with the grill and subject (see Mowrer and Miller, 1942).

Before the experimentation was started all subjects were reduced to and were then held for the duration of the experiment at 15 per cent below normal body weight. A small amount of food was obtained during the procedure described below, but most of the animal's food was obtained in individual feeding compartments, after they had been taken from the experimental apparatus but before they were put back into their common living quarters.

II. Procedure and Results

Once each day for a period of 15 days, each of the 10 animals constituting the *S-C* Group was put into the experimental apparatus. After a standard interval of 20 minutes, each animal was offered a bit of food (moist Purina Dog Chow) on the end of a small stick. This was inserted upward through the floor grill, directly in front of the subject, wherever the latter happened to be. If, within a period of 10 seconds after the food was presented, the animal ate, this was regarded as a *response,* and the shock was applied 10 seconds after this reaction occurred. The shock was then left on until the subject had, in the course of trial-and-error behavior, leaped vertically into the air. Usually such a leap carried the animal upward several inches, although all that was required was that the animal get all four feet off the grill simultaneously. If an animal did not eat the food within 10 seconds after it was presented, this was regarded as an *inhibition* and the food was withdrawn; but the shock was applied 10 seconds thereafter, just as if the animal had at that point eaten. In either case, i.e., regardless of whether the animal responded or inhibited, it was left in the apparatus for 20 minutes after being shocked and was then taken from the experimental apparatus and fed in the manner described above.[3] Each animal thus received only one experimental

[3] The reason for the protracted (20-minute) period in the apparatus both before and after each daily trial was that in this way the fear-producing properties of the apparatus, as such, could be kept to a minimum. If, immediately upon being put into the apparatus, the food were presented and the shock administered, being put into the apparatus would itself become a danger signal and would activate pervasive fear, thus causing the inhibition of the eating response in all cases. However, by

"trial" per day, and this consisted, in essence, of the offering of food and of the administration of shock, both when the food was and was not taken. The shock could in either case be terminated by the subject's leaping into the air.

The procedure used with the experimental "twin" of each of the animals in the *S-C* Group was as follows. Each of these animals was put into the apparatus, left for 20 minutes, and then offered food, in the manner just described. And again, regardless of whether the animal ate or inhibited, it was shocked after a delay of 10 seconds, but with this difference. Instead of the shock remaining on until the subject leaped into the air, the shock was left on for a predetermined length of time, without any reference to what the subject did in response to it.

However, in order to insure that each animal in the *S-UnC* Group would receive the same amount of shock as its counterpart in the *S-C* Group, a special procedure was followed. This can be most quickly grasped by referring to Table 9. Here it will be seen that on the first day of experimentation it took animal No. 6 of the S-C Group 14.3 seconds to leap into the air after the shock was applied. Therefore, this was taken as the length of time which animal No. 6 of the *S-UnC* Group should be shocked on the first day. And the same procedure was followed on the remaining 14 days of experimentation.

In Table 9 the rows labeled "Eating delay" give the time in seconds by which these 2 animals delayed in eating the food which was offered to them. If an animal delayed by 10 seconds, the food was then removed, which accounts for the fact that no delay which is longer than this period is recorded in Table 9. It will be seen that the *S-C* animal "inhibited" only twice in the course of 15 days, whereas the *S-UnC* animal, having received exactly the same amount of shock, inhibited 12 times.

That the results shown in Table 9 are more or less typical of those obtained with the other 9 pairs of animals is indicated by the data shown in Table 10. Here the number of "inhibitions" for each day of experimentation for each of the 2 groups is indicated, along with the total number of inhibitions for the whole experiment for both groups. The difference between the 16 inhibitions (mean = 1.6) for the *S-C* Group and the 85 inhibitions (mean = 8.5) for the *S-UnC* Group is significant at the .002 level by Fisher's *t*-test.

---

postponing the "trial" for a considerable period after the rat was put into the apparatus, this act took on no special significance; and fear was not specifically aroused until the food was presented. With this procedure the inhibition of eating became a much more discriminating index of the amount of fear which was associated with the appearance of food.

TABLE 9

ILLUSTRATIVE RESULTS FOR ANIMAL NO. 6 *S-C* AND ITS EXPERIMENTAL TWIN, NO. 6 *S-UnC*

Results		Successive Days															Total Inhibitions
		1	2	3	4	5	6	7	8	9	10	11	12	13	14	15	
Animal No. 6 *S-C*	Eating delay	0.0	0.0	0.0	0.0	0.0	8.0	0.0	10.0	10.0	5.0	8.0	0.0	0.0	0.0	0.0	2
	Shock duration	14.3	1.5	1.2	1.0	1.7	2.2	8.5	3.9	1.4	2.4	2.8	3.3	1.1	2.0	2.4	
Animal No. 6 *S-UnC*	Eating delay	0.0	0.0	0.0	10.0	10.0	10.0	10.0	10.0	10.0	10.0	10.0	10.0	10.0	10.0	10.0	12
	Shock duration	14.3	1.5	1.2	1.0	1.7	2.2	8.5	3.9	1.4	2.4	2.8	3.3	1.1	2.0	2.4	

TABLE 10

NUMBER OF RESPONSE INHIBITIONS OBTAINED IN GROUP *S-C* AND GROUP *S-UnC*

Group	Successive Days															Total
	1	2	3	4	5	6	7	8	9	10	11	12	13	14	15	
Group *S-C*	0	0	1	0	2	2	2	3	1	1	1	1	1	1	0	16
Group *S-UnC*	0	1	3	5	5	5	6	6	7	7	8	8	8	8	8	85

There is, of course, the possibility of analyzing these data, not in terms of "inhibitions," but in terms of the total amount of delay which the animals in each group displayed before taking food or having it withdrawn. When this is done, the difference between the mean delay for the animals in the 2 groups is significant at the .006 level.

By either of these modes of analysis, it is evident that the animals for which the shock was of fixed duration were much more "punished" by the shock than were the animals for which the duration of shock was under their control. These results provide surprisingly direct confirmation of the less rigorous types of observation reported at the outset of this paper.

III. Discussion

Another way of describing the phenomenon here referred to as fear from a sense of helplessness is to say that living organisms are capable of being inhibited, not only by fear of physical punishment, but also—perhaps even more so—by *fear of fear*. Objectively there was no difference in the amount of *physical* pain experienced by the two groups of animals in the experiment just described, but those animals in which the physical pain was accompanied (presumably) by an element of fear found the total experience much more "punishing" than did those animals in which the physical pain was accompanied (presumably) by little or no fear.[4] Here, then, would seem to be a clear-cut experimental paradigm of the concept of "fear of fear" about which William James used to talk and which Franklin D. Roosevelt made a household byword.[5]

In an earlier publication (1) one of the present authors has taken the position that fear is a "conditioned form of the pain reaction." It now seems sounder to assume that fear tends to

---

[4] For a discussion of the manner in which punishment is here conceived to operate, see chapters 5 and 8.

[5] This phenomenon is important not only in the field of social psychology but also in clinical psychology. Neurotic individuals are commonly said to "overreact," to be "unstable," to respond to objective situations with "disproportionate affect." It now seems well established that the reason the neurotic often reacts so strongly to a seemingly trivial incident is that he has to face not only the realistic consequences of the incident but also the onslaught of pent-up recriminations from conscience. Thus the individual may become inhibited with respect to certain performances which the normal individual sees through with equanimity. In other words, actions which are only slightly annoying or humiliating to the normal individual may be profoundly punishing to the neurotic because he fears not only the objective realities but also the fear (anxiety, depression, self-condemnation) which his conscience generates. Cf. (18).

occur as a direct reaction to pain itself, which may then be transferred, through conditioning or associative shifting, to any stimulus which is premonitory of the pain (9). But if this assumption be sound, the question must be asked how it is possible for organisms to react to objectively identical pain stimuli with very different amounts of fear (and thus show different amounts of anticipatory fear) when a signal of this pain—in this case, food on a stick—is presented.

Up to this point we have spoken of this problem only in very general and loose language, saying, for example, that a painful stimulus is less objectionable or punishing if one "knows how" to terminate it. But what, precisely, does this "knowing how" involve, and how does it affect the fear? At the human level the effect is probably achieved by some such process as the following: The subject says, "There is that disagreeable stimulus again, but I need not be too much disturbed about it because I can stop it when I wish. I 'know' that I can do this because I have done so repeatedly in the past." That such complex symbolic reactions can take place in the rat seems most improbable; but if something in the nature of a rudimentary equivalent does not occur, it is difficult to see how otherwise to explain the experimental findings here reported.

Let us begin with the first response to shock, following eating, in the case of animals No. 6 *S-C* and No. 6 *S-UnC*. In both cases the shock lasts for 14.3 seconds, and in neither case, on this first trial, does the subject "know what to do about it." Both animals engage in trial-and-error behavior; both animals presumably experience the same amount of fear; and in both cases the shock eventually terminates. On this first trial the subjects have no way of "knowing" that in the one case the experimenter turned the shock off because of what he saw the subject do (i.e., leap into the air) and in the other case because of what he saw a stopwatch do (i.e., register 14.3 seconds).

But on the second and ensuing trials, the experiences of the two rats become quite different. When rat No. 6 *S-C* reproduces the response (jumping) he made just before the shock went off on the preceding trial, he finds that the shock again goes off; but when rat No. 6 *S-UnC* reproduces the response (unrecorded) which occurred just before the shock went off on the preceding trial, *nothing happens:* the shock (probably) continues.

Intuitively we can see at once that rat No. 6*S-C* will soon begin to have a "better attitude" toward the shock than will rat No. 6 *S-UnC*. Rat No. 6*S-C* will begin to be less frightened when the shock comes on and probably also less frightened *lest* it come on. But why, precisely, should this be the case?

We conjecture that the answer may go something like this. In the case of rat No. 6*S-C,* leaping soon becomes something that the rat is awfully glad he can do! Said less loosely, the leaping response gets connected with the experience of relief (from shock and fear), with a feeling of rather profound satisfaction. Now—and here is the hazardous step—if the rat can be assumed to have some *symbol for leaping,* a look upward, a tensing of certain muscles, or the like, we can then infer that when, on subsequent occasions, the rat is afraid (whether before or during shock), the making of this symbolic response, this equivalent of leaping, will somewhat alleviate his fear. By thus "thinking" of how the shock can be gotten rid of, the rat can presumably lessen the attendant fear of the shock.[6]

If this reasoning is sound, we see that rat No. 6*S-C* will be less afraid when the shock is actually on, and less afraid lest it come on, than is rat No. 6*S-UnC,* which has no such "faith" in jumping (or any other response) and no comparable way of "reassuring" itself that "everything is under control." It follows, therefore, that objectively the same shock will be more punishing (as measured by its capacity to inhibit the eating response) in the case of rat No. 6*S-UnC* than in the case of rat No. 6*S-C*.

From one point of view it might be supposed that a rat which had been taught to jump in response to the shock might be more readily deterred from eating than a rat which had not been taught to make any particular response to shock. It might be supposed, in other words, that the leaping response would be more likely to "interfere," or "compete," in some rather inexplicit way, with the eating response than would no such response. But our results show that things come out in just the reverse way: the animal which acquires a satisfactory technique for dealing with the shock is also the animal which is freest to make the response which enables him likewise to deal with his hunger. This finding seems clearly to support the interpretation suggested above, that the animal which is best able to cope with the shock has less fear, both during and

[6] In a communication received by the senior author after the above was written, Dr. Viek remarks: "In reading over the paper . . . I began to regret that I had not made more accurate observations during the trials concerning possible 'symbolic movements' in the *S-C* rats which might serve to alleviate their fear. I do recall that the behavior of the *S-UnC* animals throughout the experiment was more generalized, and involved much motion. The *S-C* rats in many instances would sit on their haunches and get ready for the leap. It seems to me to be rather a reasonable step than a hazardous one to suppose such a symbolic leaping." [Cf. Coppock and Mowrer, 1947.]

in anticipation of the shock, and is therefore less deterred from performing an action which has been followed by shock.

It is interesting to note a special feature, not heretofore mentioned, of the data presented in Table 10. It will be seen that the number of inhibitions per day for the *S-C* Group started at zero on day 1, rose to 3 on day 8, and then subsided again to zero on day 15. In the *S-UnC* Group, on the other hand, the pattern is quite different: the number of inhibitions for day 1 was, likewise, zero; but it rose rather steadily during the first week and remained high (around 7 or 8) until the end of the experiment. Thus we have another indication that an electric shock which can be controlled is much less fear-producing (and "punishing") than is the same amount of shock administered in such a way that it cannot be controlled. That is to say, not only is there a striking difference in the *total number* of inhibitions in the two groups; there is also a suggestive difference in the *day-to-day incidence of inhibitions.*[7] The fact that the *S-C* animals show no inhibitions on the last day, while the *S-UnC* animals showed 7, suggests that a kind of confidence or security based on "know-how," had developed in the former case, but not in the latter.

It may occur to the reader to ask this question: Are the results here reported obtainable only if one uses an inhibitory index of fear? Should not the basic pattern also be demonstrable in a more "active" manner, as, for example, through the learning of a defense reaction of some sort? Elsewhere (Mowrer and Viek, 1951) we have indicated that, in principle, it makes little difference whether one uses as an index of fear the fact that the subject does not do something which he otherwise would have done or the fact that the subject does something which he otherwise would not have done. But for the present purposes the first of these procedures possessed important advantages over the second. It will be recalled that if, in the present experiment, a subject refrained from eating the food which had been offered, shock followed anyway. We did not, in other words, provide an opportunity for the subject to avoid the punishment by being "good." This somewhat paradoxical procedure was dictated by the fact that if we allowed a rat to avoid getting shocked by refraining from eating, then we would no longer be able to insure that the 2 animals constituting each of the 10 experimental "teams" would get exactly the same amount of shock each day and during the experiment as a whole; for, with this

[7] We are indebted to Ulysses E. Whiteis for calling our attention to this difference.

latter procedure, whenever one animal inhibited and the other did not, we would have had to shock the other and not the one.

From a wide variety of studies, we know that if one uses, not inhibition, but overt reaction as an index of fear, and if, under these circumstances, one does not allow the subject to avoid the traumatic stimulus whenever the reaction indicating the fear appears, then this reaction soon falls under inhibition (cf. the work on so-called "classical" conditioning) and is no longer a valid fear indicator. This difficulty seems to be less serious (though probably not altogether absent) when one is using an inhibitory index of fear. Furthermore, for reasons discussed in another connection (19), inhibitory indicators are probably, in general, more sensitive and subject to better experimental control.

Summary

Both clinical and commonplace observations suggest that the fear aroused by a physical pain is a function of whether the pain is or is not under the subject's control. A painful stimulus which is not controllable tends to arouse an apprehension that it may last indefinitely or get worse, whereas objectively the same stimulus, if subject to termination at will, arouses little or no such apprehension. The apprehension experienced in the former case is appropriately termed "fear from a sense of helplessness."

An experimental paradigm of this phenomenon is here reported, with laboratory rats as subjects. Using the inhibitory, or "punishing," effects of objectively equal electric shocks as an index of the subjects' anticipatory fear of these shocks, we have found that fear is much greater in rats which cannot terminate the shock than in rats which can do so. By a special experimental procedure it was possible to insure that the animals receiving these two treatments experienced not only the same intensity but also the same duration of shock. It was surprising how strikingly different the fear was in the two cases.

Another way of characterizing this "fear from a sense of helplessness" is to say that it represents what William James referred to as "fear of fear." Our results seem clearly to indicate that *anticipatory* fear, and the resultant inhibitory capacity, of a physically painful stimulus is markedly influenced by the amount of fear which *accompanies* that stimulus. It is thus apparent that we may come to fear not only physical pain but also fear itself.

CHAPTER 18

LEARNING THEORY AND THE NEUROTIC PARADOX

[Approximately a year after the publication of this paper, Freud's remarkable posthumous volume, *An outline of psychoanalysis* (1949), appeared. On reading this book, the author discovered that in it Freud had moved appreciably nearer to the position which is taken in the present paper and the two following ones. Formerly, he had identified neurosis as a condition in which a too severe superego or conscience overwhelms the ego and enforces a repression of certain id forces, notably those of sex and aggression. In the work just cited, the older point of view is not explicitly repudiated; but one senses a distinctly friendlier and mellower attitude with respect to the superego and its functions.

On the side of the older, more strictly biological type of theory, we find Freud repeating such phrases as the following:

> The power of the id expresses the true purpose of the individual organism's life (p. 19).
>
> The holding back of aggressiveness is in general unhealthy and leads to illness (p. 22).
>
> The superego may bring fresh needs to the fore, but its chief function remains the *limitation* of satisfaction (p. 19).
>
> In consideration of its origin, we term this portion of the id *the repressed* (p. 43).

On the other hand, as one moves through the pages of this small book, the references to the superego become less and less hostile—and in the end, almost reverent. Thus:

> In so far as the superego is differentiated from the ego or opposed to it, it constitutes a third force which the ego must take into account (p. 16).
>
> An investigation of normal, stable states, . . . in which the superego is not distinguished from the ego because they work together harmoniously—an investigation of this kind would teach us little (p. 46).
>
> So long as the ego works in complete agreement with the superego, it is not easy to distinguish between their manifestations; but tensions and estrangements between them become very plainly visible. The torments caused by the reproaches of conscience correspond precisely to a child's dread of losing his parents' love, a dread which has been replaced in him by the moral agency. On the other hand, if the ego has successfully resisted a temptation to do something that would be objectionable to the superego, it

feels its self-respect raised and its pride increased, as though it had made some precious acquisition. In this way the superego continues to act the role of an external world toward the ego, although it has become part of the internal world (p. 122).

Here is the most positive statement Freud ever made as regards the role of the superego within the total personality; here he clearly asserts that conformity to the demands of conscience can be a source of satisfaction (formerly he had viewed the id as the ultimate source of "happiness"); and he indicates equally clearly that "tensions and estrangements" between the ego and superego can be a source of neurotic suffering (not merely conflicts between the ego and the id).

On the next page Freud quotes two lines from Goethe which, when translated, read: "What thou hast inherited from thy fathers, acquire it to make it thine." After which he says:

Thus the superego takes up a kind of intermediate position between the id and the external world; it unites in itself the influences of the present and of the past. In the emergence of the superego we have before us, as it were, an example of the way in which the present is changed into the past. . . .

Here the book abruptly stops—and remains unfinished. It was not that Freud was too old or too ill to go on with this task to its completion; rather does it seem that at this point he reached some kind of *internal* obstacle, became dissatisfied with what he had written and had no heart for trying to go on with it. This conjecture gains credence from the facts simply presented in the first paragraph of James Strachey's Preface:

Freud began writing this unfinished *Abriss der psychoanalysis*—his last work of any considerable length—in London on July 22, 1938. A few weeks later he broke it off at a point where, to all appearance, it cannot have been very far from completion. He never returned to it, but, in the following October, started upon a similar project, to which he gave an English title, *Some elementary lessons in psycho-analysis.* This second version, however, included in Vol. V of Freud's *Collected papers,* extends to only a few pages (p. 7).

This singular train of events suggests that when Freud attempted to bring together and systematize, in brief compass, his far-flung theories and speculations, he was struck by internal inconsistencies which called for drastic revisions. Had he been a younger man at this point, and thus able to undertake the extensive task thus indicated, the author believes the basic logic of analytic experience would have driven him to something not greatly unlike the position which is here presented.

• • •

Since the above was written, Volume V of Freud's *Collected papers* (Freud, 1950) has been published, and in it we find an interesting confirmation of the foregoing conjectures. The last chapter of this volume consists of the beginning pages of the *Elementary lessons,* referred to above; here there is nothing novel or surprising. But the next to last chapter, entitled "Splitting of the Ego in the Defensive Process," dramatically supports the view that, at the very end of his life, Freud was grappling with a major theoretical reorientation. He begins the article in question with these words:

I find myself for a moment in the interesting position of not knowing whether what I have to say should be regarded as something long familiar and obvious or as something entirely new and puzzling. But I am inclined to think the latter (p. 273).

Freud then puts the problem thus:

Let us suppose, then, that a child's ego is under the sway of a powerful instinctual demand which it is accustomed to satisfy and that it is suddenly frightened by an experience which teaches it that the continuance of this satisfaction will result in an almost intolerable danger. It must now decide either to recognize the real danger, give way to it, and do without the instinctual satisfaction, or to repudiate reality and persuade itself that there is no reason for fear, so that it may be able to retain the satisfaction. Thus there is a conflict between the demand of the instinct and the command of reality (p. 372).

Throughout his professional lifetime, Freud had proceeded on the assumption that if conflicts of this kind are terminated pathogenetically, i.e., by means of repression with subsequent symptom-formation, it is always the "instinctual satisfaction" rather than "reality" which is repudiated. Since the reality to which Freud refers in his example is a *social reality*—the child "was soon caught at it by his energetic nurse and was threatened with castration"; and later Freud speaks of similar threats by the father—repudiation of this reality, which is the prototype of the superego, is tantamount to *superego repudiation.*

It is therefore not surprising that Freud shortly remarks that this way of thinking "seems so strange to us." He seems never to have considered previously the possibility that repression frequently, or perhaps somewhat regularly, goes in the direction of the superego rather than in the direction of the id. And when Freud did at length reflect on this possibility, he found himself, once more, unable to complete the discussion on which he had embarked. The last, unfinished paragraph of this remarkable article is worth quoting in full.

This way of dealing with reality, which almost deserves to be described as artful, was decisive as regards the boy's practical behavior. He continued with his masturbation as though it implied no danger to his penis; but at the same time, in complete contradiction to his apparent boldness or indifference, he developed a symptom which showed that he nevertheless did recognize the danger. He had been threatened with being castrated by his father, and immediately afterwards, simultaneously with the creation of his fetish, he developed an intense fear of his father punishing him, which it required the whole force of his masculinity to master and overcompensate. This fear of his father, too, was silent on the subject of castration: by the help of regression to an oral phase, it assumed the form of a fear of being eaten by his father. At this point it is impossible to forget a primitive fragment of Greek mythology which tells how Kronos, the old Father God, swallowed his children and sought to swallow his youngest son Zeus like the rest, and how Zeus was saved by the craft of his mother and later on castrated his father. But we must return to our case history and add that the boy produced yet another symptom, though it was a slight one, which he has retained to this day. This was an anxious susceptibility against either of his little toes being touched, as though, in all the to and fro between denial and acknowledgement, it was nevertheless castration that was finding the clearer expression. . . . (p. 375).

Thus, while the paper which follows and the three ensuing ones represent what is in some ways a radical departure from traditional psychoanalytic thought, they constitute rather what the author regards as a logical extension and correction of a theoretical system which is still intrinsically Freudian.

The present paper, in abridged form, was given as an address before the 1948 meeting of the American Orthopsychiatric Association and appeared, in full, in the *Journal* of the Association a few months later. The essential argument of the paper is contained in Sections VII and VIII; the earlier sections are mainly historical and documentary.]

Informed and forward-looking psycho-clinicians today are generally agreed that the most important and exciting future advances in the understanding of personality and in psychotherapy will come from the mutual modification and blending of learning theory and psychoanalysis.[1] Notable steps have already been made toward such a synthesis,[2] and one can foresee still greater activity and accomplishment in this area in the decades immediately ahead.

Here I invite you to consider what, in many respects, is the abso-

[1] To express my own views accurately, "learning theory" should be thought of as including "culture theory." Habits and attitudes are to an individual what culture is to a society. In common speech we recognize this perception when we say, "He is a learned man, a man of much culture." An adequate statement should also acknowledge the contributions, actual and potential, of social structure theory.

[2] See, for example, the recent paper by Shaffer (1947).

lutely central problem in neurosis and therapy. Most simply formulated, it is a paradox—the paradox of behavior which is at one and the same time self-perpetuating and self-defeating! Ranging from common "bad habits" through vices and addictions to classical psychoneurotic and psychotic symptoms, there is a large array of strategies and dynamisms which readily fit such a description but defy any simple, common-sense explanation.

Common sense holds that a normal, sensible man, or even a beast to the limits of his intelligence, will weigh and balance the consequences of his acts: if the net effect is favorable, the action producing it will be perpetuated; and if the net effect is unfavorable, the action producing it will be inhibited, abandoned. In neurosis, however, one sees actions which have predominantly unfavorable consequences; yet they persist over a period of months, years, or a lifetime. Small wonder, then, that common sense has abjured responsibility in such matters and has assigned them to the realm of the miraculous, the mystical, the uncommon, the preternatural.

I. Freud's Early Attempts to Resolve the Neurotic Paradox

In Western European culture, Sigmund Freud was the first man with the requisite talent and courage to contend that the neurotic paradox could be resolved in a completely naturalistic manner. One of his initial attempts to deal with it involved the concept of erotic fixation. He believed that because of early libidinal attachments either to another person (often of an incestuous nature) or to the self (as in narcissism), some individuals were arrested in development and, in consequence, persevered in abortive, self-defeating actions which a free, unfixated person would soon abandon.

Later, as a result of World War I, there came to Freud's attention individuals who were likewise fixated upon senselessly repetitive, self-defeating behavior. These persons gave a history, not of too powerful libidinal attachments, but of experiences which were so traumatic that they could not be fully assimilated.

Thus in *erotic fixation* on the one hand and in *traumatic fixation* on the other Freud offered two possible explanations of the basic feature of neurosis. Yet a question remained. Ordinarily, dangers which are clearly past, however grave they may have been at the time, gradually lose their affective force, and pleasures which no longer please are similarly given up. This is the verdict of common sense, and it is also supported by results from the learning laboratory.[3] Why, then, do neurotics provide an apparent exception?

[3] See Sections V–VIII.

Freud's emphasis upon fixation did not really solve the problem. He had posited that fixation was largely dependent upon the *quantitative* factor. In the course of development, everyone experiences trauma in some degree and is likewise more or less fixated libidinally. Freud suggested that it was perhaps the *intensity* of the trauma or the fixation which decided the issue. Yet some persons show themselves capable of surviving equally severe trauma or of surmounting equally strong fixations without becoming neurotic. Confronted by these facts, Freud was sometimes reduced to positing constitutional factors as the determining ones, but he did not rest comfortably with such thinking.

As if recognizing the impasse to which these early formulations brought him, Freud remarks: "Here . . . we leave the path we have been following. At the moment it will take us no further, and we have much more to learn before we can find a satisfactory continuation of it" (1920a, p. 244). His next theoretical step was one which he made very confidently. It was to propose that psychic forces may be unconscious and still powerfully active in the economy of the total personality. "We challenge anyone in the world to give a more correct scientific explanation of the matter," he said, and then added that neurotic symptoms "show the way unmistakably to conviction on the question of the unconscious in the mind; and for that very reason clinical psychiatry, which only recognizes a psychology of consciousness, can do nothing with these symptoms except to stigmatize them as signs of a special kind of degeneration" (pp. 245–46).

There then follows a feat of intellectual penetration and conceptual analysis which has seldom been equaled in psychological literature. It will be my task to show, however, that Freud's theoretical scheme is correct only up to a point, and to maintain that the revision and correction of this scheme is one of the great scientific challenges and responsibilities of our time.

Let us begin with Freud's formulation of what I have called the neurotic paradox. He says (1920a):

> When we undertake to cure a patient of his symptoms he opposes against us a vigorous and tenacious *resistance* throughout the entire course of the treatment. This is such an extraordinary thing that we cannot expect much belief in it. . . . To think that the patient, whose symptoms cause him and those about him such suffering, who is willing to make such sacrifices in time, money, effort, and self-conquest to be freed from them—that he should, in the interests of his illness, resist the help offered him. How improbable this statement must sound! (p. 253).

Freud then comments upon the "highly varied and exceedingly subtle" forms which neurotic resistance may take. Even the first rule of analysis, that of free association, arouses opposition and reservation: "We do succeed in extracting from the patient a certain amount of obedience for the rule of the technique; and then the resistance takes another line altogether" (p. 255). The resistance may now assume the form of logical opposition to analytic theory. Or it may masquerade as a great thirst for knowledge and eagerness to be instructed and advised; or it may take the form of complete overt acceptance coupled with covert doubt.

But these resistances, serious as they may seem, are relatively superficial; it is only with the emergence of the "transference" that the really "decisive battle begins." Here Freud remarks:

> If the patient is a man, he usually takes his material from his relationship with his father, in whose place he has now put the physician; and in so doing he erects resistances out of his struggles to attain to personal independence and independence of judgment, out of his ambition, the earliest aim of which was to equal or to excel the father, out of his disinclination to take the burden of gratitude upon himself for the second time in his life. There are periods in which one feels that the patient's desire to put the analyst in the wrong, to make him feel his impotence, to triumph over him, has completely ousted the worthier desire to bring the illness to an end. Women have a genius for exploiting in the interest of resistance a tender, erotically tinged transference to the analyst; when this attraction reaches a certain intensity all interest in the actual situation of treatment fades away, together with every obligation incurred upon undertaking it (p. 256).

Nothing is empirically better founded than these observations of Freud concerning neurotic resistances. No clinician with even a modicum of awareness of what transpires in the therapeutic situation has failed to sense these strategies; indeed at times he feels all but overwhelmed by them. As data, as phenomena, they are among our most certain and most important. We can fully agree with Freud when he says that "the overcoming of these resistances is the essential work of the analysis, that part of the work which alone assures us that we have achieved something for the patient" (p. 257). The question is one of theoretical explanation and adequate conceptualization. To this end he continues:

> I have given such a detailed consideration of this point because I am about to inform you that our dynamic conception of the neurosis is founded upon this experience of ours of the resistance that neurotic patients set up against the cure of their symptoms (p. 257).
>
> In what way can we now account for this observed fact, that the patient struggles so energetically against the relief of his symptoms and the restora-

tion of his mental processes to normal functioning? We say that we have come upon the traces of powerful forces at work here opposing any change in the condition; they must be the same forces that originally induced the condition. . . . As we already know from Breuer's observations, it follows from the existence of a symptom that some mental process has not been carried through to an end in a normal manner so that it could become conscious; the symptom is a substitute for that which has not come through. Now we know where to place the forces which we suspect to be at work. A vehement effort must have been exercised to prevent the mental process in question from penetrating into consciousness, and as a result it has remained unconscious; being unconscious, it had the power to construct a symptom. The same vehement effort is again at work during analytic treatment, opposing the attempt to bring the unconscious into consciousness. This we perceive in the form of resistance. The pathogenic process which is demonstrated by the resistance we call *repression* (p. 259).

This quotation contains a theoretical insight which, in my judgment, has not been sufficiently appreciated. Even Freud did not fully exploit it. What it says, in effect, is that a neurotic is a person in whom there is a kind of inner debate, or conflict, which has been partially resolved by repression of one of the contending parties. When such a person comes into therapy, it is as if the therapist is invested by the patient, slowly or quickly, with the attributes of the repressed part of his personality. The debate which has previously gone on between the two contending factions within the one individual *is now externalized as a struggle between the patient and the therapist.*

Freud called this phenomenon "transference" and he knew two very important things about it: (1) that the patient's neurotic suffering and symptoms are often dramatically alleviated by the development of transference (thus showing that symptoms and resistances are in some way equivalent); and (2) that it is through the handling or "working through" of the transference that permanent immunity to neurosis is achieved, if at all.

Again there can be only agreement with Freud.[4] Empirically his contentions are well founded, but from the standpoint of theory much remains to be desired. It is surely obvious that the most

---

[4] Therapists of the so-called "nondirective" school may take issue with this statement. They maintain that the activation of transference represents a technical error, which they strive to avoid. In some instances, where the personality problem is not very deep-seated or where the therapeutic relationship remains a relatively casual one, it is perhaps correct to insist that transference does not take place. However, it seems probable that in more serious treatment situations, even the nondirective or, more accurately, the noninterpretative approach arouses strong transference and that the chief difference is in the method of handling it, though even this distinction may not prove to be as marked as is sometimes maintained.

pressing question is: whence comes this internal struggle which besets every neurotic and which is then converted into the interpersonal conflict which one sees in therapy? From the use of the term "transference" and from the statements made in the excerpts already quoted, one would suppose that the inherent logic of the situation would have driven Freud to assume that neurosis is but the internalization, or introjection, of the early conflicts which exist between the child and his principal socializers. Transference would thus be nothing more nor less than a social struggle between a relatively immature person and a more mature one, a struggle which initially existed in childhood, had been introjected, and then, in therapy, is again made external.

The next question would then be: What is it about the socialization of some children which leads to conflicts which are internalized and thus provide the basis of neurosis, whereas in other cases these conflicts are worked through in the child-parent relationship and the intrapsychic development of the child proceeds with relative harmony?

But these were not the questions Freud asked. Possibly because of his preoccupation with dream interpretation, possibly because of deeply rooted forces within his own personality, he turned his theoretical analysis at this point into a direction which prevented his ever reaching the conclusions toward which his work otherwise so clearly points—a direction which has done much to mislead and retard both the conceptual and therapeutic endeavors of others.

The story of this fateful turn in Freud's reasoning is soon told. Freud pictured the mental anatomy of neurotics and normal persons alike, as follows:

> The unconscious is a large anteroom, in which the various mental excitations are crowding one another, like individual beings. Adjoining this is a second, smaller apartment, a sort of reception room, in which consciousness resides. But on the threshold between the two there stands a personage with the office of doorkeeper, who examines the various mental excitations, censors them, and denies them admittance to the reception room when he disapproves of them. . . . The doorkeeper is what we have learned to know as resistance in our attempts in analytic treatment to loosen the repressions.
>
> Now I know very well that you will say that these conceptions are as crude as they are fantastic and not at all permissible in a scientific presentation. . . . Still, I should like to reassure you that these crude hypotheses, the two chambers, the doorkeeper on the threshold between the two, and consciousness as a spectator at the end of the second room, must indicate an extensive approximation to the actual reality (pp. 260–61).

According to this conceptual scheme, impulses which are objectionable to the censor are kept imprisoned, as effectively as possible, in the antechamber; i.e., in the unconscious. They are, in short, repressed. To this Freud adds: "We know that the symptom is a substitute for some other process which was held back by repression" (p. 262). Like a dream or a Freudian error, the symptom represents a repressed impulse which, by means of the strategy of disguise, escapes into consciousness and finds a route, however devious, to gratification.

What, then, are these imprisoned impulses most likely to be? To this Freud replied:

> Every time we should be led by analysis to the sexual experiences and desires of the patient, and every time we should have to affirm that the symptom served the same purpose. This purpose shows itself to be the gratification of sexual wishes; the symptoms serve the purpose of sexual gratification for the patient; they are a substitute for satisfactions which he does not obtain in reality (p. 263).

All this, of course, is very familiar to the present audience. I again bring it to your attention only as a means of high-lighting a point which may previously have escaped your scrutiny. You will recall that in the excerpts here quoted, Freud begins by posing what I have termed the neurotic paradox, the paradox inhering in the fact that neurotic symptoms are both self-defeating and yet self-perpetuating. We must now ask: Does Freud, in the work from which these quotations come, resolve this paradox? He certainly does not do it explicitly. It is as if he becomes so absorbed in discussing repression and symptom formation that he loses sight of and never returns to this basic issue. However, by implication he may be assumed to say something like this: The reason neurotic symptoms cause suffering and are thus disadvantageous is that the censor objects to them; and the reason they are self-perpetuating is that to another part of the personality they are gratifying, relieving, pleasurable.

Superficially this may appear to be a very satisfactory resolution, but let us look deeper. If a person refrains from gratifying impulses which involve an objective danger, we need hardly refer to him as neurotic. A person would presumably be termed abnormal only if he inhibited sexual or other impulses when, in reality, the way was open for their gratification. Much effort on the part of Freudian analysts has always been directed toward trying to get their patients to "see the difference" between then and now—between childhood, when gratification of certain impulses was indeed hazardous, and adulthood, when the individual's status is realistically different.[5] The essence, then, of neurosis would consist of the tendency on the part of the afflicted individual to continue to act as though the conditions of childhood, now past, still prevailed.

This formulation does not resolve our basic dilemma; it only restates it. The findings of laboratory experimentation, as well as common sense, lead us to believe that there is in all living organisms a tendency which pushes them in the direction of "reality testing." If an organism, out of fear, does something it would otherwise not do, or if it refrains from doing something which otherwise it would do, there is at least a recurrent disposition to "feel out" the situation, to see if the danger is "still there." But according to the earlier Freudian views, this tendency is for some reason lost by neurotic individuals—which is why they are neurotic—and it is presumed to be recoverable only through the process of psychoanalytic therapy.

Here the mystery is only pushed back a step, not removed. In Freudian terms one must say that in the normal person the censor is normally flexible, whereas in the abnormal person the censor is abnormally inflexible, rigid, severe. In other words, *a person is abnormal because his censor is abnormal.* This is an obvious piece of question-begging, particularly since no attempt was made in that period to explain how the censor "got that way." By implication one might infer belief in a traumatic explanation of such inflexibility, such unrealism, such severity on the part of the censor; but this would again be falling back on a concept which, as Freud himself remarked, "will take us no further." As of 1920, the date of publication of *A general introduction to psychoanalysis,* we must therefore conclude that the basic neurotic paradox was still almost as far from a satisfactory resolution as ever.

II. Freud's Ill-fated Venture Beyond the Pleasure Principle

As if recognizing his earlier failure to resolve the central paradox of neurosis, in 1922 Freud published his highly speculative and controversial work, *Beyond the pleasure principle.* Taking the traumatic neuroses, anxiety dreams, certain monotonously repetitive games played by children, data drawn from the transference neurosis, the apparent inability of some persons to escape from a kind

[5] In the light of this logic, therapy then becomes essentially a matter of helping the patient correct overly extended generalizations by means of appropriate discriminations. This conception of neurosis and its treatment will be discussed more fully in Section IV. [Cf. Miller and Dollard, 1950.]

of unrelenting "fate," and certain forms of masochism as points of departure, Freud concluded:

> In the light of such observations as these, . . . we may venture to make the assumption that there really exists in psychic life a repetition compulsion, which goes beyond the pleasure principle . . . and this seems to us more primitive, more elementary, more instinctive than the pleasure principle which is displaced by it (pp. 24–5).

Elsewhere (15) I have reviewed some of the principal arguments which have been advanced by others against this conception and have added some of my own. Here it need only be remarked that the repetition compulsion was obviously an attempt—one might almost call it an act of desperation—to deal with the basic neurotic paradox. But that Freud himself was by no means satisfied with the result is indicated by the fact that with the publication of his *New introductory lectures* in 1933(b), he reverted to a conceptual scheme only slightly different from the earlier one.

III. Freud's Second "Topography" and the Neurotic Paradox

Freud's first topographic or spatial conception of personality involved the unconscious, the conscious, and the censor. His second system likewise involved a tripartite division of personality: the ego, superego, and id. Superficially, the id corresponds to the earlier conception of the unconscious, as "the various mental excitations . . . crowding one upon another, like individual beings"; the ego corresponds to the conscious part of personality; and the superego corresponds to the censor. But in his second formulation, Freud develops the second and third of these three conceptions so much further than in his first formulation that it is important, in any attempt to unravel the fundamental paradox of neurosis, to examine the second formulation in some detail.

Just as the best statement of his earlier views is contained in the two chapters on fixation and on resistance and repression in the *General introduction,* so one finds the fullest elaboration of his later conceptions in chap. iii, "The anatomy of the mental personality," in the *New introductory lectures.* "Here," says Freud, "I am giving you a supplement to the introduction to psychoanalysis which I started fifteen years ago. . . . " He begins this chapter by announcing that psychoanalysis has advanced beyond the stage of being merely a psychology of the unconscious and now encompasses something new, which he calls "ego psychology." "At last we had got so far that we could turn our attention from the repressed to the repressing forces, and we came face to face with the ego. . . ." Almost at once he takes up the task of describing the superego, which he conceives as being a specialized portion of the ego.[6] It will be recalled that one of the major weaknesses of Freud's earlier formulation was that in it he had little or nothing to say about the origin and developmental history of the censor, a weakness which left the neurotic paradox unresolved.[7] As if determined to make good this neglect—"psychoanalysis could not study every part of the field at once"—he gives an account of the superego which contains some of the most penetrating insights shown in any of his writings.

After alluding to the tendency of psychotics to be preoccupied with violent self-criticism and delusions of observation and persecution, Freud says:

> Under the strong impression of this clinical picture, I formed the idea that the separating off of an observing function from the rest of the ego might be a normal feature of the ego's structure; this idea has never left me, and I was driven to investigate the further characteristics and relations of the function which had been separated off in this way. The next step was soon taken. The actual content of the delusion of observation makes it probable that the observation is only a first step towards conviction and punishment, so that we may guess that another activity of this function must be what we call conscience. . . . I will henceforward call this function in the ego the "superego" (pp. 85–86).
>
> The role which the superego undertakes later in life is at first played by an external power, by parental authority. The influence of the parents dominates the child by granting proofs of affection and by threats of punishment, which, to the child, mean loss of love, and which must also be feared on their own account. This objective anxiety is the forerunner of the later moral anxiety;[8] so long as the former is dominant, one need not speak of superego

---

[6] It is not surprising to find Freud conceiving of the superego in this manner, for in the passage from his earlier writings already quoted the censor was "a personage with the office of doorkeeper, who examines the various mental excitations, censors them, and denies them admittance to the reception room" where consciousness resides. Clearly, such a doorkeeper would be "in the employ" of consciousness. It is understandable, therefore, that in the later formulation the superego is seen as a specialized development of the ego.

[7] Freud answers those who had attacked his earlier theoretical system on the grounds that it neglected the "nobler" side of human personality, by saying sarcastically: ". . . psychoanalysis was met by illuminating criticisms to the effect that man is not merely a sexual being but has nobler and higher feelings. It might have been added that, supported by the consciousness of those higher feelings, he often allowed himself the right to think nonsense and to overlook facts" (p. 82). It is not that Freud ever overlooked the self-critical, moral forces; he acknowledged them from the beginning. Rather the problem comes from the way in which he evaluated them and the role he attributed to them in personality pathology. We shall return to this point later.

[8] For purposes of later discussion it is well to note Freud's use here of the terms "objective anxiety" and "moral anxiety." As he indicates in various other places,

or of conscience. It is only later that the secondary situation arises; the external restrictions are introjected, so that the superego takes the place of the parental function, and thenceforward observes, guides, and threatens the ego in just the same way as the parents acted to the child before (p. 89).

To this Freud adds that he cannot say as much as he would like about just how it is that the authority of parents becomes incorporated into the child as superego; but he gives to this process the appropriate term "identification."[9] In summary he remarks: "For us the superego is the representative of all moral restrictions, the advocate of the impulse towards perfection, in short it is as much as we have been able to apprehend psychologically of what people call the 'higher' things in human life" (p. 95). Elsewhere (1930) he refers to it as the "internalized voice of the community."

It is also important to note that in this discussion Freud was taking issue with the traditional view that conscience is something innate, inborn—the "voice of God speaking within us."[10] "Conscience," said Freud, "is no doubt something within us, but it has not been there from the beginning. In this sense it is the opposite of sexuality, which is certainly present from the very beginning of life, and is not a thing that only comes in later. But small children are notoriously amoral" (p. 89). Here he was certainly on solid ground, for those who contend most loudly for the innateness of conscience are usually among the strongest advocates of training calculated to produce conscience!

We have dwelt thus at length upon Freud's views concerning the superego for the reason that the resolution of the whole neurotic paradox hinges upon the way in which this part of the personality is perceived. We shall later revert to this topic, but first let us review Freud's characterization of the ego proper and its manifold functions as he conceived them.

---

the first of these terms meant for him simply the reaction to objective danger, namely fear; and it is also clear that by the latter he meant what is commonly referred to as conscious guilt or "pangs of conscience" (p. 109). "Neurotic anxiety," by contrast, he thought of as something quite different. The question of the origin and ultimate nature of the latter is of crucial importance for the main thesis of this paper.

[9] The highly important question as to precisely how it is that the learning which underlies identification takes place, or fails to take place with ensuing character disturbances, is still unanswered. However, laboratory studies now in progress (21, 24) seem likely to throw light upon the problem.

[10] It is interesting to note how easily many theological statements containing the term "God" can be rendered into perfectly intelligible naturalistic statements if this term is translated as "mankind" or "the community." Such a rendition would leave Freud differing with traditional views about conscience mainly on the score of whether it is innate or learned.

One can hardly go wrong [says Freud] in regarding the ego as that part of the id which has been modified by its proximity to the external world and the influence that the latter has had on it, . . .[11] This relation to the external world is decisive for the ego. The ego has taken over the task of representing the external world for the id, and so of saving it; for the id, blindly striving to gratify its instincts in complete disregard of the superior strength of outside forces, could not otherwise escape annihilation. . . . On behalf of the id, the ego controls the path of access to motility, but it interpolates between desire and action the procrastinating factor of thought, during which it makes use of the residues of experience stored up in memory.[12] In this way it dethrones the pleasure principle, which exerts undisputed sway over the processes in the id, and substitutes for it the reality principle, which promises greater security and greater success (1933, p. 106).

The ego advances from the function of perceiving instincts to that of controlling them, but the latter is only achieved through the mental representative of the instinct becoming subordinated to a larger organization, and finding its place in a coherent unity. In popular language, we may say that the ego stands for reason and circumspection, while the id stands for the untamed passions (p. 107).

The proverb tells us that one cannot serve two masters at once. The poor ego has a still harder time of it; it has to serve three harsh masters, and has to do its best to reconcile the claims and demands of all three. . . . The three tyrants are the external world, the superego, and the id (p. 108).

In this way, goaded on by the id, hemmed in by the superego, and rebuffed by reality, the ego struggles to cope with its economic task of reducing the forces and influences which work in it and [of imposing upon them] some kind of harmony; and we may well understand how it is that we so often cannot repress the cry: "Life is not easy." When the ego is forced to acknowledge its weakness, it breaks out into anxiety: reality anxiety in face of

---

[11] It may seem a self-contradiction that Freud should speak of the superego as a "split off" portion of the ego and then characterize the ego itself as a modified part of the id. The seeming contradiction is strengthened when one recalls that the id is for Freud that which is innately given in personality and the superego is acquired by the process of identification. We must remember that he is here attempting to deal with a very difficult problem of conceptualization. It would perhaps have been more exact to speak of the id as comprising what modern learning theorists call the *primary drives* (and probably their attendant appetites) and of the superego as the socially acquired *secondary drives*. Since fear and love are believed to be the two principal ingredients of conscience, such a distinction seems particularly apt.

[12] It is virtually impossible to determine whether Freud meant the term "ego" to subsume the superego or to imply only the ego proper. There is no explicit reference to the superego function; but conscience, representing the culture (wisdom and virtue) of one's society, might well be thought of as "the residues of experience stored up in memory." The voice of community and conscience certainly restrains the pleasure principle and "substitutes for it the reality principle" as a condition of the social, moral way of life as opposed to the solitary, amoral type of existence. Here, as elsewhere in Freud's writings, one senses a tendency to glorify the eighteenth century conception of reason. Freud refers approvingly to "the Logos," at the expense of that which has come down to us as mere tradition, however much human suffering and learning it may reflect (Section VIII).

the external world, moral anxiety in face of the superego, and neurotic anxiety in face of the strength of the passions of the id (pp. 109–10).[13]

Little need be added here concerning the nature of the id, in part because it is not very different from Freud's earlier conception of the unconscious and in part because it is inherently uncomplicated. In summary, he remarks: "Naturally, the id knows no values, no good and evil, no morality. The economic, or, if you prefer, the quantitative factor, which is so closely bound up with the pleasure principle, dominates all its processes. Instinctual cathexes seeking discharge—that, in our view, is all that the id contains" (p. 105; see also pp. 103–4).

We are now finally in a position to return to our central task, that of understanding the dynamics of neurosis and, if possible, defining the logic of its treatment. Already a theory is implicit in the passages quoted from Freud; and it will now be our purpose to try to make this theory more explicit. However, we must be prepared to find here a structure which is far from complete and, in certain respects, manifestly unsatisfactory.

Briefly, Freud's theory is that human beings "fall ill," psychologically speaking, because they experience neurotic anxiety. This, it will be recalled, is the anxiety which an individual feels when forces in the id, having been repressed, threaten to erupt into consciousness. He says:

> From the very beginning our view was that men fall ill owing to the conflict between the demands of their instincts and the internal resistance which is set up against them; not for a moment did we forget this resisting, rejecting, and repressing factor, which we believe to be furnished with its own special forces, the ego instincts, and which corresponds to the ego of popular psychology (p. 83).
>
> The resistance can only be a manifestation of the ego, which carried through the repression at one time or other and is now endeavoring to keep it up. And that too was our earlier view. Now that we have posited a special function within the ego to represent the demand for restriction and rejection, i.e., the superego, we can say that repression is the work of the superego—either that it does its work on its own account or else that the ego does it in obedience to its orders (pp. 97–98).

The objective of psychoanalytic therapy is easily inferred from these passages: it is to strengthen the "poor" ego so that it can ward off the restrictive demands of the superego and thus allow the forces of the id to find suitable outlets to gratification. Says Freud: "We must admit that the therapeutic efforts of psychoanalysis have chosen

[13] See Footnote 8.

much the same method of approach. For their object is to strengthen the ego, to make it more independent of the superego, to widen its fields of vision, and so to extend its organization that it can take over new portions of the id. Where id was, there shall ego be."

On this platform psychoanalysis has done a prosperous business. It has attracted a world-wide following among those who purport to do psychotherapy; and its philosophy, expressed and implied, has permeated popular thought in almost every civilized country. To the social historian of the future will fall the task of determining why analytic therapy and philosophy have so caught the imagination of contemporary mankind. Our task is a simpler one: merely to ask if analytic theory has or has not succeeded in giving a rigorous explanatory account of the fundamental neurotic paradox.

In an earlier section we have seen that the only solution Freud proposed to this problem in terms of his first topographic system was to suggest that abnormal human beings have abnormal "censors," thus leaving unanswered the question as to what determines whether the censor itself will be normal or otherwise. So far we have found nothing in Freud's second topographic formulation which would carry us further; all it has said is that persons become abnormal or "fall ill" because their superegos are unduly harsh, strict, demanding, and otherwise behave in an unreasonable manner. And it is this unreasonableness which causes the impulse life of the individual to be unduly restricted, thereby predisposing him to anxiety and symptom formation.

Nor, says Freud, can these "neurotic" superegos be accounted for solely in terms of the harshness with which parents deal with their children:

> If the parents have really ruled with a rod of iron, we can easily understand the child developing a severe superego, but, contrary to our expectations, experience shows that the superego may reflect the same relentless harshness even when the upbringing has been gentle and kind, and avoided threats and punishments as far as possible. We shall return to this contradiction later, . . . (p. 90).
>
> It follows from our account of its origin that it [the superego] is based upon an overwhelmingly important biological fact no less than upon a momentous psychological fact, namely the lengthy dependence of the human child on its parents and the Oedipus complex; these two facts, moreover, are closely bound up with each other. For us the superego is the representative of all moral restrictions, the advocate of the impulse towards perfection, in short is as much as we have been able to apprehend psychologically of what people call the "higher" things in human life. Since it itself can be traced

back to the influence of parents, teachers, and so on, we shall learn more of its significance if we turn our attention to these sources. In general, parents and similar authorities follow the dictates of their own superegos in the upbringing of children. Whatever terms their ego may be on with their superego, in the education of the child they are severe and exacting. They have forgotten the difficulties of their own childhood and are glad to be able to identify themselves fully at last with their own parents, who in their day subjected them to such severe restraints. The result is that the superego of the child is not really built up on the model of the parents, but on that of the parents' superego; it takes over the same content, it becomes the vehicle of tradition and of all the age-long values which have been handed down in this way from generation to generation (pp. 94–95).

Mankind never lives completely in the present; the ideologies of the superego perpetuate the past, the traditions of the race and the people, which yield but slowly to the influence of the present and to new developments, and, so long as they work through the superego, play an important part in man's life, quite independently of economic conditions (p. 96).

What, more concretely, does all this come to? Everyone is now conversant with the concept of "culture lag." Like habits and attitudes in an individual, the traditions and values of a society tend to have momentum of their own which causes them to persist somewhat beyond the period of their actual usefulness.[14] But unrealistic habits and attitudes in an individual are ordinarily self-correcting. Why is this not also true of the habits and attitudes which constitute a neurosis? Far from being self-correcting, they tend to be self-exacerbating. What is the fateful differential? Freud, astute observer that he was, concluded that the answer is not a purely quantitative one, since the severity of the superego does not seem wholly or even mainly a function of the actual severity of the treatment which parents accord to their children.

Finally we extract a hypothesis on which Freud apparently pinned his last hope of accounting for the enigma of neurosis. This hypothesis, referred to as that of the "timelessness of the repressed," he sets forth as follows:

Conative impulses which have never got beyond the id, and even impressions which have been pushed down into the id by repression, are virtually

---

[14] Both the cultural functionalists, such as Malinowski and Radcliffe-Brown, and anthropologists of the "historical" school, such as Smith and Boas, would admit this much. However, the former would maintain that "lag" is never very great, whereas the latter would maintain that it may last for hundreds or perhaps thousands of years. Present-day anthropologists are tending to agree that in those instances where there is what appears to be a protracted lag the apparent autonomy of the culture can be accounted for in terms of "secondary gains"; i.e., emotional satisfactions which have become dissociated from the economic or "practical" functions originally served.

immortal and are preserved for whole decades as though they had only recently occurred. . . . It is constantly being borne in upon me that we have made far too little use of our theory of the indubitable fact that the repressed remains unaltered by the passage of time. This seems to offer us the possibility of an approach to some really profound truths. But I myself have made no further progress here (p. 105).[15]

But this suggestion obviously does not resolve the difficulty. The problem which Freud's theoretical system poses is not how to explain the durability of repressed impulses; it is rather the rigidity and immutability of the represser—the superego—which calls for explanation. Although Freud came to believe that parts of the superego and even parts of the ego may be "unconscious," it would have made little sense for him to speak of the superego repressing itself, and thus producing the effect of "immortality." It is hardly remarkable that he admits to "no further progress here" and later refers to his attempt to resolve this paradox as "exhausting and perhaps not very illuminating" (p. 110).

If it appears an unduly harsh verdict, then, to say that Freud never succeeded in advancing a satisfactory answer to the most basic problem in neurosis theory, let him again speak for himself. In *The problem of anxiety* (1936) Freud asks:

Why are not all neuroses merely episodes in the individual's development which become a closed chapter when the next stage of development is reached? Whence comes the element of permanency in these reactions to danger? Whence springs the preference over all other affects which the affect of anxiety seems to enjoy in alone evoking reactions which we distinguish from others as abnormal and which in their inexpediency obstruct the stream of life? In other words, we find ourselves abruptly confronted once again by the oft-repeated riddle: What is the source of neurosis, what is its ultimate, its specific, underlying principle? After decades of analytic effort this problem rises up before us, as untouched as at the beginning (p. 120).

IV. The Conditioned Reflex and Neurosis

The first great name among those who have attempted to resolve the enigma of neurosis on the basis of learning theory is that of Pavlov. His observations concerning disturbances in the behavior of the dogs which he and his coworkers used in studying the con-

[15] Here one is, of course, reminded of Jung's speculations concerning the "racial unconscious." But it is not easy to see how such a concept really advances our clinical understanding of or control over neurosis (cf. Footnote 14). For further discussion of the relationship between time and the unconscious, see Freud (1936), pp. 94–96, 109, 123–24, and 128–29.

ditioned salivary reflex are now very widely known, and deservedly so. His books continue to offer challenging and instructive data for the serious student of dynamic psychology. But Pavlov himself was not such a student. He abhorred any concept so subjective as drive or motivation or satisfaction, and he was able to think only in terms of that particular conception of learning which stresses stimulus substitution, or, more familiarly, associative learning. Having observed behavior disturbances in his experimental subjects under a rather wide range of conditions, he concluded that there are two possible sources of such disturbances—conflict and trauma. Thus, "All these experiments clearly bring out the fact that a development of a chronic pathological state of the hemispheres can occur from one or other of two causes: first, a conflict between excitation and inhibition which the cortex finds itself unable to resolve; second, the action of extremely powerful and unusual stimuli" (1927, p. 318).

In the one case the "chronic pathological state" was to be thought of then as due to a "clashing" of excitatory and inhibitory processes, while in the other it was regarded as a product of overexcitation. But in both instances Pavlov conceived of the resulting "disturbance of the higher nervous activity" as involving definite injury of or damage to the brain cells. A neurosis was thus reduced to a "pathological" state (implying structural or at least "physiochemical" derangement) of cortical mechanisms, which stood in contrast to the "normal" or "physiological" state of these mechanisms. This same type of view was, of course, held by many psychiatrists who were Pavlov's contemporaries; but he seems to have found a special reason for accepting it in the fact that the "neurotic" behavior of his experimental animals was relatively permanent. He says: "From some of these disturbances the animal recovers gradually and spontaneously under the influence of rest alone, on discontinuance of the disturbing experiments; in other cases the disturbances are so persistent as to require special therapeutic measures" (p. 284).

Though Pavlov looked upon these disturbances as being "of a purely functional origin, and not due to surgical interferences or trauma," he did not believe that the disturbance itself was "purely functional." If such disturbances had been merely the products of learning, then he would have expected them to be temporary. All learned behavior, according to Pavlov, consisted of conditioned reflexes, and all conditioned reflexes are temporary, provisional, i.e., become "extinguished" unless they are periodically reinforced by the paired presentation of the "conditioned" and the "unconditioned" stimuli which were initially involved in the establishment of the new stimulus-response connection. Since behavior which he termed "neurotic" often appeared and persisted for a remarkably long time without any evident reinforcement of this kind, Pavlov inferred that such behavior could not have been learned and was therefore due to "pathological" brain changes.

This conclusion had two very important consequences. In the first place, it caused Pavlov to stress the constitutional factor in determining individual susceptibility to neurosis. He says: "The pathological state of the hemispheres in different individual animals [resulting] from the action of injurious influences varies greatly. One and the same injurious influence causes severe and prolonged disorders in some dogs; in others the disorders are only slight and fleeting; while yet other dogs remain practically unaffected" (p. 284).

These observations led him to a rather elaborate classification of temperament types in dogs, to the almost exclusive neglect of what may be termed life-history factors. He seems to have had little or no conception of the extent to which what is learned in one situation is often very powerfully influenced by what has been learned in *past* situations. Said otherwise, the *meanings* of situations differ as a function of prior experience. Although the constitutional factor cannot be arbitrarily excluded as a determinant of neurosis, the fact that Pavlov completely failed to control the surely equally potent factor of prior experience goes far to nullify the force of his conjectures in this connection.

Pavlov's second inference which is of importance here may be said to go something like this: if neurosis is a matter of brain damage, however minute, then therapy might be expected to follow more or less traditional medical lines—sedation, rest, diet, and healthful living generally. In his last book (1941) Pavlov elaborated his conceptions of diagnosis and treatment, but the results sounded strangely outmoded and futile. His fame will hardly rest upon this labor of his declining years.

Many other investigators sought to confirm and extend Pavlov's observations and theories. Prominent among these may be mentioned Anderson and Liddell. They believe that any of several experimental procedures may "strain an animal's nervous system to the breaking point" (1935, p. 332). They believe that the conditioned-reflex type of training is especially trying for the reason that it involves a drastic restriction, both mechanical and psychic, of spontaneous movement and a resulting accumulation of nervous tension which would normally be kept dissipated in a situation permitting complete freedom of movement. The agitation of their "neurotic" sheep they interpret as representing a "neuromuscular outlet which has been closed through previous training [but which] now opens because of actual damage to the nervous system to prevent any further rise of tension. The nervous movements of the leg, and, in a more exaggerated form of the neurosis, the tremors observed in the rest intervals between stimulations are to be regarded as the protective operation of the neuromuscular system to prevent the nerve cells of the higher centers from being subjected to further strain" (p. 352). Although differing in detail, this line of thought obviously follows the same channels laid down by Pavlov.

Another rather different way of thinking about these problems which was inspired by Pavlov's work is that of Korzybski (1941) and his associates. This writer believes that the original Russian words which Pavlov used for "conditioned" and "unconditioned" have been misinterpreted and mistranslated. He prefers to render them as "conditional" and "unconditional." Thus a *conditional* response is one that is flexible, shows discernment of circumstances, varies with conditions; whereas an *unconditional* response is one that is headlong, blundering, undiscriminating. The former are normal and serve to keep us out of trouble, whereas the latter are abnormal and get us constantly into trouble.

It is true that for Pavlov an unconditioned response was one with a kind of invariability about it; but he regarded such a response as invariable or reflexive because it is invariably or at least very generally useful. Thus, if a dog shows an "unconditioned" salivary reflex when food is placed in the mouth, this was hardly taken by Pavlov as defining a state of abnormality. Although Korzybski may be justified, on a strictly linguistic basis, in retranslating the Russian words used by Pavlov in this connection, he is clearly not justified otherwise, for such a reinterpretation radically alters the whole sense of Pavlov's experiments and theory.[16]

Even if Korzybski's claims were in this respect justified, he would still have to face the task of resolving the neurotic paradox. Specifically, in his terms, it is the problem of explaining what makes one individual characteristically behave conditionally (normally,

---

[16] Elsewhere (9) the writer has adduced evidence for believing that there are two basically different learning processes—problem solving and conditioning. Pavlov's experiments with the salivary reflex give instances of conditioning in pure form, but one can meaningfully interpret Korzybski's "conditional" responses only if they are viewed as products of that type of learning here termed problem solving. The shift in assumptions required by Korzybski's reinterpretation of Pavlovian conditioning will become clearer as the distinction between these two types of learning is elaborated in later sections of this paper.

rationally) and another behave unconditionally; or what makes one and the same individual sometimes behave in the former manner and at other times in the latter manner. With a grand sweep, Korzybski identifies the villain of the piece as something which he calls "Aristotelian logic." By this he seems to mean two things: (1) the tendency to look upon truth as absolute rather than relative and (2) the tendency to continue to use, in a scientific age, language which was developed in a prescientific age.

There can be no question that Korzybski has been a pioneer in the kind of thinking which has recently attained its most precise expression in that form of statistical interpretation which holds that experimental or other evidence never *proves* or *disproves* the ultimate and final truth of a proposition; it only renders the proposition increasingly *probable* or *improbable.* It is also true that in certain types of persons seen clinically there is a tendency to think about their own and other's behavior in terms of categorical imperatives or absolutes, rather than functionally, genetically, causally. But we also find neurosis in persons who do not show this type of mentality; we cannot escape the conclusion that thinking of this kind is by no means a universal cause of neurotic difficulties, and one suspects that even in specific cases it is probably not causal in any very basic sense.

Korzybski's concern about the misleading effects of prescientific language—such, for example, as speaking of the sun "rising" and "setting" when we know well enough that it does not do either—may be regarded even more lightly. I do not think my colleague, Professor I. A. Richards, will mind my quoting a recent apposite remark of his on this score to the effect that these ambiguities "never cause anyone any trouble. They are taken in a kind of Pickwickian sense, not seriously at all." [17] Certainly in my own clinical experience I have yet to find anyone who appears to be seriously or even mildly neurotic because of confusions of this kind, although, to be sure, a neurotic person may *worry* about such things, along with almost anything else.

A still different approach to the basic neurotic paradox which stems from Pavlovian thinking is suggested in a recent work by Hull (1943). In his eariler writings, this author took a systematic position similar in most essential respects to that of the Russian investigator. But in the work cited, he shifted his conception of the reinforcement process from that posited by Pavlov to one much more nearly like that long advocated by Thorndike. For Pavlov,

---

[17] Cf. Richards (1938).

as we have seen, the essential conditions for learning, or reinforcement of new stimulus-response sequences, are provided when a stimulus which already has the power to evoke a given reaction is preceded by or combined with a stimulus which has formerly been neutral or ineffective in this respect. Thorndike, by contrast, has held that new "connections" are formed or old ones strengthened when, in the course of the random or variable behavior which an organism shows in a problem situation, the problem is resolved and the organism experiences relief, satisfaction, reward. The resulting learning consists, then, of a strengthening of the "connection" between problem or drive and the response which solved this problem and so reduced the drive.

Taking this Thorndikian conception of reinforcement, which is particularly designed to explain problem solving or so-called trial-and-error learning,[18] Hull has sought to extend it so as to account also for associative learning. Since drives are reduced and problems solved not in a vacuum but in concrete situations involving many other stimuli, Hull has proposed the hypothesis that the reinforcing effect provided by drive reduction will strengthen the connection, not only between the drive and the particular response bringing about this fortunate state of affairs, but also between accompanying stimuli and this response. And, as Hull points out, one would expect this incidental form of learning to occur quite as readily with respect to irrelevant elements in the situation as to the relevant ones; that is:

> Since organisms have no inner monitor or entelechy to tell them in advance which stimulus elements or aggregates are associated with the critical causal factor or factors of reaction situations [i.e., factors which determine whether a given response will or will not produce the desired result], the *law of reinforcement, other things equal, will mediate the connections of the non-critical stimulus elements to the reaction quite as readily as those of the critical ones* (1943, p. 258).
>
> As a result of the largely random flux of events in the world to which organisms must react, it inevitably comes about that they will often be stimulated by extensive groups of conditioned-stimulus elements, *none* of which is causally related to the critical factor or factors in the reinforcement situation. In such cases, if the stimuli evoke the reaction it will not be followed by reinforcement. This, of course, is wasteful of energy and therefore unadaptive. The necessarily unadaptive nature of the appreciable portion of the habits set up by virtue of the law of reinforcement naturally raises the question of how organisms are able to survive under such conditions. The

[18] Richards has suggested that we might better call it "trial-and-triumph"!

answer is found in the behavioral principle known as *experimental extinction* (p. 259).

Following these remarks Hull goes on to elaborate a theory from which it is an easy inference that "neurosis" is simply a loose way of referring to the fact that a human being or lower animal has a number of response tendencies which do not show an appropriate degree of discrimination. Simple-minded as such a thesis may sound, it is no more so than (*a*) the Freudian notion, previously discussed, that a "neurotic" is a person who fails to see the essential difference between conditions which existed in his childhood and those prevailing today (especially the castration complex) or (*b*) Korzybski's contention that a neurotic is a person who behaves "unconditionally," fails to distinguish between situations which *are* alike and those which *appear* to be.

Reduced to its lowest common denominator, we have here a conception of neurosis which appears perhaps more commonly than any other in the speculations of writers with very different backgrounds and preconceptions. What such a conception says, in effect, is that neurosis comes about as a result of overgeneralization, overlearning, which causes the affected individual to exhibit habits and attitudes which are no longer appropriate, or are still appropriate in some circumstances but not in others. In this way one can seemingly account for all "parataxia" (Sullivan, 1947) and the "disproportionality of affect" which are so characteristic of persons whose behavior is said to be "neurotic," or, in more extreme cases, "crazy."

Certainly the learning requirements which are set for the human young are very great, and the zeal and determination manifested in this connection by the adult members of society are impressive. What could seem sounder, simple as it is, than to suppose that a neurotic is simply a person in whom this socialization or educative process has overshot its mark? As a friend of the author once remarked, it looks as if the neurotic is a person in whom the culture has "taken all too well." Certainly the neurotic is a person manifesting striking inhibitions and incapacities; and there are still other observations which seem to justify the verdict that the basic difficulty of such a person is that his superego, or censor, is "too severe."

This perception of the situation, as we have seen, still leaves unanswered the fundamental problem as to why some individuals become neurotic, i.e., fail in their discriminative functions, whereas others do not. Freud considered but discarded the possibility that the difference lay in the severity with which children are actually treated by their parents. Pavlov threw most of the burden of proof back upon biological heredity. Korzybski has posited as a purported explanation something which might be referred to as "social heredity," namely, that element of our culture which he terms "Aristotelian logic." Few of us will rest easy with either of these latter interpretations.

Nor do the results commonly obtained through would-be psychotherapy look as if we had thus isolated the active and specific virus of neurosis. Schisms and schools flourish with respect to therapeutic theory,[19] and the general public turns eagerly but vainly to those who are supposed to be experts in such matters for a meaningful philosophy of life and a guiding principle in practical affairs.

Does it seem too bold to suppose that the time has come for us to examine and, if necessary, discard some of our most entrenched beliefs and interests? In the following sections, I shall indicate a mode of thought and action which may hold some promise of extricating us from our present plight.

V. An Experimentally Produced "Vicious Circle"

Laboratory findings provide very little support for the view that neurosis consists simply of overlearning of habits and attitudes which were acquired in circumstances wherein they were more or less appropriate but which now persist under altered circumstances in which they are no longer appropriate. Experimental studies (Hull, 1943, 6; Youtz, 1938) have shown over and over that habits which formerly produced desirable outcomes but no longer do so will undergo the process of extinction.[20] There is equally impressive evidence for believing that attitudes, and emotions also, tend to disappear if the signal which arouses them is no longer really significant; that is, if it is no longer followed by the event or situation with which they have previously been associated (Hull, 1943;

---

[19] In another connection the author has recently circularized thirty members of the American Orthopsychiatric Association concerning their perception of contemporary theory concerning psychotherapy. The most common evaluation was "chaotic."

[20] Allport (1937) has suggested that habits and attitudes may sometimes continue to function even though the original circumstances which brought them into existence have long since ceased to exist. To this hypothetical phenomenon he has given the term "functional autonomy." However, in the light of ensuing criticism, Allport has been obliged to concede that in cases of apparent autonomy it is probable that although the original source of reinforcement no longer exists, the habit or emotion in question continues to be reinforced in some new or subsidiary manner (1940). As Mowrer and Ullman (16) have pointed out, the concept of functional autonomy as originally formulated by Allport is not much different in principle from Freud's repetition compulsion.

Kingsley, 1946; Pavlov, 1927). In other words, it makes no difference whether we are working with the form of learning commonly known as problem solving (habits) or with that form known as conditioning (attitudes, emotions): if the conditions of reinforcement—reward in the one case and, in the other, contiguous occurrence of the signal and the significate—no longer hold, there will be a disintegration, sometimes slow but ultimately certain, of the learned connection.

The assumption that a reinforced occurrence of a habit or attitude increases its likelihood of recurrence and that unreinforced occurrence decreases its likelihood of recurrence has recently been brought into question by a series of experiments initiated by Humphreys (1939a; 1939b; 1940). This investigator found that learning which has been established by means of alternately reinforced and unreinforced "trials" is more resistant to extinction than is learning that has been established under conditions of unfailing reinforcement. However, satisfactory explanations of this phenomenon are now available (Hull, 1943, 7), and it is to be noted that the procedure involving alternate reinforcement and nonreinforcement does not give rise to habits and attitudes which do not extinguish but merely to habits and attitudes which are somewhat *slower* to extinguish.[21]

Employing the same general methods as those used by Pavlov to produce and study "experimental neuroses," a number of later investigators have likewise been able to produce in animal subjects disturbances of behavior and attitude of relatively permanent character. But the most plausible interpretation of these results is not that they represent either overlearning which fails to extinguish or organic brain damage; instead they seem to involve *a rupture of the basic relationship between the subject and the experimenter.* The researches of Liddell and others (Gantt, 1944; Hull, 1943; Liddell, 1944) indicate that it is only by first gentling and "petting"

[21] In a personal communication, Dr. L. C. Wynne recently informed me of experimental results which indicate that if laboratory rats are sometimes punished and sometimes not for performing a "forbidden" act, the inhibition produced in this manner is more enduring than that established by consistent punishment. Superficially this finding may look like the Humphreys effect "in reverse," but actually it is a straightforward application thereof. Since the fear produced by intermittent punishment is more resistant to extinction than a fear produced by continuous reinforcement, the inhibitory effects in the one case will be expected to be more enduring than those observed in the other. Within the limits of Dr. Wynne's experiment, the inhibitions produced by discontinuous reinforcement did not, in fact, appreciably lessen under conditions of nonreinforcement. However, it can be confidently predicted that they, too, would ultimately disappear if the extinction procedure were carried far enough. It therefore seems again unlikely that the Humphreys effect will provide a solution to the neurotic paradox.

an animal that one can later produce a "neurosis." And the latter condition apparently involves an impairment of the subject-experimenter relationship, produced by the way the experimenter subsequently treats the subject. If nothing is done to re-establish such a damaged relationship, it will hardly be surprising if the "neurosis" persists.

It is also worth noting that the criteria of "neurosis" used by animal investigators have not always been altogether satisfactory. Sometimes it has appeared that the capacity for self-mystification on the part of the experimenter was the principal desideratum. If as a result of a particular laboratory procedure animals behave in a manner which to the experimenter is unaccountable or "crazy," this behavior has often been dubbed "neurosis." We should, of course, insist upon a definition of neurosis that is a function of the subject's experience and personality, not of those of the experimenter.

The fact that much of the research which has thus been done with animals fails to throw any new light on the basic neurotic paradox does not mean that it is impossible to produce in such subjects behavior which is genuinely paradoxical. Here I want to speak of two such instances of behavior which seem to take us at least a little nearer to an understanding of the fundamental nature of neurosis.

Some years ago Dr. Judson S. Brown told me of a remarkable incidental observation he had once made. Later, on two separate occasions, students of mine reconstructed Dr. Brown's experimental conditions and reported the same observation. I am therefore highly confident of its reliability. The observation is this:

Let us imagine that a rat is put at the left-hand end of an alley about 4 feet long, with high sides and ends. The rat is allowed to explore for 10 seconds, then an electric charge is put on the entire length of the grill constituting the floor of the alley. The rat is thrown into rather violent trial-and-error activity, in the course of which it discovers an opening at the extreme right-hand end of the alley, leading into a small compartment where there is no shock. There the animal is left for 2 or 3 minutes, and is then returned to the left-hand end. Again, after a period of 10 seconds, shock is applied to the grill and the rat is driven, now much more quickly, into the safety compartment. On the third trial, the rat is likely to be sufficiently frightened to run immediately to the opposite end of the alley and into the safety compartment before the shock is applied. On subsequent trials the rat will gradually slow up in this behavior until, failing to get into the safety compartment within the period of grace, it again gets the shock and is thereby driven into the compartment. After a few "reminders" of this kind, the rat is likely to become highly reliable in its behavior, that is, it will continue for a great many trials, upon being put into the apparatus, to run directly to the safety compartment and in this fashion avoid receiving any electric shock. Although the number of runs which an animal will thus make between shocks tends to get greater and greater, yet there is an enduring tendency to "reality test," which serves the function of keeping the animal informed as to whether the shock is "still there," thus enabling it to avoid making an endless series of responses which are not necessary.

By a very simple procedure, all this can be dramatically altered. After a rat has been well trained to avoid shock by running to the safety compartment within the 10-second period of grace, let us arrange the apparatus so that the right half of the grill is *permanently* charged. This will mean that in order for the rat to get from the left-hand end of the alleyway to the safety compartment, it must always cross a section of grill which is charged. On first thought, one might suppose that the shock thus received by the rat in the process of running from the left-hand end to the safety compartment would act as a punishment and would soon inhibit the running response. But nothing of the kind occurs. Instead, upon being introduced into the alleyway, the rat will run *even more promptly* to the safety compartment. And more remarkable still, this behavior goes on and on for hundreds of trials, although shock is never again administered in the part of the apparatus where the rat is introduced!

Here, surely, is crazy behavior. An observer viewing such a performance for the first time and without knowledge of the background of the experiment might well be moved to diagnose the rat's behavior as "masochistic." Now that the shock has been permanently withdrawn from the left-hand end of the grill, all the rat would have to do to avoid both the shock and the effort involved in running would be to sit still in that part of the apparatus where it is introduced. But instead the rat "prefers" to keep running across the charged grill, thus "punishing" itself hundreds of times. In fact, the indications are that if the experimenter but had the patience to continue observing such a stereotyped, monotonously regular performance, this behavior would go on indefinitely.

Let us now ask how, if at all, this rather striking performance is related to the basic neurotic paradox. The behavior involved meets the requirement of being self-defeating and yet self-perpetuating. And it has the additional advantage—which carries us beyond anything which Freud proposed in this connection—of qualifying as a vicious circle, as Kunkel and Horney have used that expression. Horney describes this phenomenon as follows:

> The formation of a vicious circle is typical not only in the context in which it has been discussed here; generally speaking it is one of the most important processes in neuroses. Any protective device may have, in addition to its reassuring quality, the quality of creating new anxiety. A person may take to drinking in order to allay his anxiety, and then get the fear that drinking, too, will harm him. Or he may masturbate in order to release his anxiety, and then become afraid that masturbation will make him ill. Or he may undergo some treatment for his anxiety, and soon grow apprehensive lest the treatment harm him. The formation of vicious circles is the main reason why severe neuroses are bound to become worse, even though there is no change in external conditions. Uncovering the vicious circles, with all their implications, is one of the important tasks of psychoanalysis. The neurotic himself cannot grasp them. He notices their results only in the form of a feeling that he is trapped in a hopeless situation. This feeling of being trapped is his response to entanglements which he cannot break through.[22] Any way that seems to lead out drags him again into new dangers (1937, pp 138–39).

Let us repeat the key sentence in the foregoing quotation: "Any protective device may have, in addition to its reassuring quality, the quality of creating new anxiety." Certain aspects of this mechanism are well illustrated in the experiment just described. The rat becomes afraid of the experimental situation as soon as put into it; this fear drives it to the safety compartment where it is relatively fear-free; the running is thus powerfully reinforced as a form of problem-solving behavior; but in performing this act the animal also gets shocked; shock serves to reinforce the fear of the apparatus; and when the animal is again put into the apparatus, its fear prompts it to repeat the same cycle.

Implicit in this analysis and in much of what has been said previously is the assumption that there are two basic learning processes: problem solving and conditioning. It is by the first of these that overt actions or habits are acquired; these serve to reduce drives, solve problems, provide pleasure. And it is by the second of these basic learning processes that the emotions or secondary drives—as opposed to the primary drives which are biologically "given"—are themselves acquired. In the experiment under discussion, fear of the apparatus is reinforced every time the rat gets shocked therein; and the habit of running in response to this fear is reinforced by

---

[22] Cf. (18).

the fact that the running, though resulting in a momentary exposure to the shock, leads to a relatively enduring reduction in the secondary drive of fear. Only by positing these two basic, but basically different, learning processes does it seem possible to make a clear-cut analysis of a vicious circle of the kind just described and to resolve a number of other important dilemmas which have been discussed in detail elsewhere (9).

Some disturbing problems still remain. Horney speaks of a vicious circle as involving behavior which (*a*) serves more or less directly to reduce anxiety, but which (*b*) has the indirect or delayed effect of increasing it. In the paradigm just described we have spoken, not in terms of anxiety, but in terms of fear. Although in the passage quoted Horney seems to be equating anxiety and fear, she indicates elsewhere (1937, chap. iii) that she agrees with Freud and most other clinicians that there is an important difference. However, in the experimental paradigm of a vicious circle we probably have no justification for speaking of anxiety, only of fear; and since there is general agreement that it is anxiety, not ordinary objective fear, which is "the fundamental phenomenon and the central problem of neurosis" (Freud, 1936, p. 111), serious doubt is raised as to whether our paradigm is very illuminating so far as the neurotic paradox is concerned.

Moreover, assuming that such an experiment does provide a valid paradigm of neurosis, it would imply a conception of psychotherapy which experience shows is much too simple. In order to "cure" a rat of unnecessarily running away from a part of the apparatus which is no longer dangerous, all that is necessary is to block the entrance to the safety compartment, thus forcing the animal to retreat from the charged half of the grill back upon the uncharged half. Finding that this half of the grill is now permanently free of shock, the rat is perfectly willing to stop the unnecessary flight from it. If neurosis in human beings were due to a fundamentally similar mechanism, instruction in the changed realities of the situation or, in more extreme cases, spontaneous or forced "reality testing" might be expected to produce equally dramatic results. Clinical experience does not confirm such an inference (cf. 9, Footnote 26).

VI. Time and Integration Failure

Implicit in the passage previously quoted from Horney is another possible explanation of vicious circles. She speaks of an activity which provides a means of first reducing anxiety "and then" of increasing the individual's insecurity. In other words, she tacitly introduces the *time factor* as a variable in the vicious circle. In an experiment previously reported (15), this factor has been explicitly investigated and found to be a potent one indeed.

Common sense teaches us and laboratory studies have confirmed that both rewards and punishments are more effective if they follow an action immediately than if they occur more remotely in time. This fact—subsumed under what is more technically referred to as the gradient of reinforcement for problem solving and the gradient of reinforcement for conditioning—provides the basis for a paradox which, if not precisely the same as the neurotic paradox, carries us at least a step nearer its understanding. Actions which have exclusively rewarding consequences tend to be "stamped in," and actions which have exclusively punishing consequences naturally tend to get "stamped out." But more common are actions whose consequences are mixed, some rewarding and some punishing. If these consequences are equally distant in time from the action producing them, that action will be inhibited or reinforced roughly in proportion to the degree to which these consequences are predominantly punishing or rewarding. The net result is in no way paradoxical. But the instant that multiple consequences of an act become unevenly distributed in time, the possibility is opened for paradoxical outcomes.

In the experiment cited, hungry rats were taught to come to a little trough for a pellet of food whenever a buzzer was sounded. After all the subjects had stably acquired this behavior, an arbitrary "rule" was made by the experimenters to the effect that it was not "nice," or "proper," for a rat to take the pellet of food immediately upon its presentation. The "correct" behavior was to wait 3 seconds after the food had appeared and *then* take it. Since a full minute was allowed between successive trials, the rats did not have to take the pellet *precisely* at the end of the 3-second delay; any time after this lapse of time was all right. The point was that they were not to take the food *within* the tabu period. This rule was enforced by punishment in the form of electric shock.

All "offenders" received a shock of the same intensity and duration (2 seconds), but the subjects were divided into different groups with respect to *how soon* the punishment was administered. In one group of subjects the punishment came immediately after the tabu period. Most of the rats in this group quickly learned to behave integratively; i.e., they learned to wait at least 3 seconds before taking the pellet of food, thus avoiding the shock and having the satisfaction of eating. But the groups in which the shock was delayed (for 3 and 9 seconds, respectively) gave different results. The animals in these groups were inclined to behave nonintegratively in one of two ways: they were inclined either to persist in taking the pellet of food within the forbidden period and thus get regularly shocked somewhat later or to give up altogether the attempt to eat in the experimental situation. The first of these patterns involved getting the food but also getting the shock, and the second involved getting no shock but likewise getting no food.

In our original report of this experiment we labeled the rats which were more or less completely inhibited with respect to eating as "neurotic"; the animals that persisted in eating within the tabu period and being persistently shocked we labeled "delinquent" or "criminal." But this was probably because our conception of neurosis was then still largely dominated by Freud's view that a neurotic is an individual with an overly severe superego, one in whom attempts at control and restraint have been "all too effective," an individual in whom the problem is, in short, one of *overlearning.*

Presumably the rats that resolved the conflict between eating and getting shocked by not eating were not very pleased about the situation, just as human beings are not pleased by the renunciations and disappointments they must endure. But Freud's emphasis upon the thwarting of impulse and desire in the etiology of neurosis [23] now seems to have been a seriously misplaced one. As I have said elsewhere (19), I believe the indications are that human beings fall victims of neurosis, not because of what they would do but cannot, but because of what they have done and would that they had not. If this thesis, to which we shall return shortly, is valid, we should expect to find a more nearly valid paradigm of neurosis in those rats which persisted in taking food during the tabu period despite the continuing punishment.

It was not inappropriate that we should previously have referred to these animals as delinquent or criminal. Whatever else the criminal is or is not, he is surely a person who is not so much deterred as is the ordinary person by certain objective punishments

[23] "... I will now add another piece of information which throws further light upon the significance of the symptoms. A comparative examination of the situations out of which the disease arose yields the following result, which may be reduced to the formula—namely, that these persons have fallen ill from *privation* (*frustration*) which they suffer when reality withholds from them gratification of their sexual wishes. . . . The symptoms can serve the purpose both of sexual gratification and of its opposite, namely, anxiety reduction. They are in fact, as we shall see, the effects of *compromises* between two opposed tendencies, acting on one another; they represent both that which is repressed, and also that which has effected the repression and has cooperated in bringing them about. . . . The symptom is then a double one and consists of two successive actions which cancel each other" (Freud, 1920a, pp. 264–65).

or the prospect thereof. In the past we have had a tendency to contrast the criminal and the neurotic by saying that the criminal is undersocialized, undertrained, whereas the neurotic is supposedly oversocialized, overtrained. But for reasons which I have advanced in another connection (Mowrer, 1948b), I believe that the neurotic character lies much closer to the criminal character than we have commonly thought. The differential here would seem to consist mainly in the extent to which the function we call *conscience* has been developed in the two cases. Both the criminal and the neurotic have a tendency to behave immaturely, irresponsibly, antisocially. But unlike the pure criminal, the neurotic has a conscience which is strong enough to "bother" him. Like the normal person, the neurotic has a conscience, often a very powerful one; but the normal person "does business" with his conscience, whereas the neurotic distrusts, spurns, and represses conscience. However, this conscious repudiation of conscience does not mean that its forces are nullified. Instead they are merely muted, so that their signals to the ego become distorted and delayed. Instead of being experienced promptly and explicitly as conscience guilt, they appear in the form of depression, anxiety, and self-derogation. Since these states are thus dissociated from the circumstances and events that occasion them, they appear to be alien to the personality, unrealistic, irrational, abnormal, and it becomes exceedingly difficult if not impossible for the ego to make realistic, adequate adjustments to them.

Returning now for a moment to the experiment just described, let us ask if any of our subjects were truly neurotic. The answer is, probably not. The rats which persisted in taking food despite the delayed though inevitable punishment were presumably not as comfortable in the experimental situation as they would have been if they had worked out an integrative solution to this conflict. But we can hardly say they were neurotic. We must keep in mind that these rats had not been taught from earliest childhood to believe that this was a conflict which any proper, self-respecting rat would resolve integratively. They did not, in other words, live in a society with a culture which demanded this kind of achievement. And they did not, therefore, have a conscience which condemned them for their failure. They suffered only from the objective discomfort and fear of the shock. To this was not added the forces of self-condemnation, and without this subjective increment to the objective realities we cannot appropriately speak of neurosis.[24]

---

[24] At another time I shall further elaborate upon the implications of these remarks. They provide, I believe, an answer to the question as to why neurotics are

However, by thus pursuing the logic of this and other animal studies, I believe we are led to a clearer perception of the nature of neurosis as we know it at the human level. We are brought to realize that Freud and many others have, indeed, erred precisely in the sense of trying to account for human neurosis in terms of what we may call, in the words of Allport (1947), an "animal model," and that it is only by going beyond this predominantly biological type of preoccupation and facing man in terms of his spectacular uniqueness that we come to intimate grips with the essence of neurosis.

VII. Negativism, Neurosis, and Resistance

In this paper we have followed a long and in certain respects disappointing historical course. We have traced the successive formulations of one of the most brilliant and original minds of modern times and found, in the end, no satisfactory resolution of the basic problem of neurosis. Then we turned to numerous other investigators who have approached the problem both from related and from radically different angles, but still there is no clear-cut answer. At this point we again might well exclaim with Freud, "After decades of [scientific] effort this problem rises up before us, as untouched as at the beginning." But our labors have not been wholly unrewarding. They give us a perspective which earlier investigators lacked. They enable us to see more clearly the outline of the maze in which these gifted and intrepid explorers have struggled; they enable us to see what now appears to have been a fateful error, an early mistake in choice of paths which led to the discovery of much new territory but which has not led to the desired goal—a precise understanding of and a specific therapy for the psychoneuroses.

From Section I of this paper it will be recalled that one of Freud's first and most basic discoveries was that the neurotic is a person who has at some prior stage in his life cycle resolved a powerful psychic conflict by means of repression. Freud also saw with singular clarity that the forces behind the resistance which meets our therapeutic efforts are the same that have produced and subsequently maintain the original repression. And he saw that the struggle that ensues between therapist and patient is but an externalization of the inner struggle which is the heart of neurosis.

---

said to be "unstable" and why the emotions of the neurotic are commonly characterized as "disproportionate" (19).

But to the end of his long career, Freud carried with him one highly doubtful assumption which thwarted his theoretical endeavors and blighted the therapeutic accomplishments of the school which he founded. For Freud the neurotic conflict originates in the fact that the great power and disciplinary efforts of parents are pitted against the biologically given drives of the small child. This may be said to have been his major premise, and one which we must reiterate and fully accept. But his minor premise, if we may continue this analogy from formal logic, was that because the child is so completely and protractedly dependent upon his parents, the latter's demands are relatively quickly and powerfully introjected. Freud believed that once this has happened there ensues a pitched battle between the superego and ego, on the one hand, and the id on the other. This battle he called the Oedipus complex. He believed it was characteristically resolved by repressions—repressions which bring infantile sexuality and aggression under control during the so-called latency period but which, in the normal instance, are largely abrogated in adolescence. But, said Freud, if these repressions are initially too strong or overdone, they are not sufficiently undone in adolescence and may persist on into adult life, with the pathological consequences which we refer to as neurosis.

What could be clearer, then, as the duty of the therapist than to set about undoing, belatedly, these too-strong repressions, weakening the severity of an oversevere superego, counteracting disciplinary efforts of parents which have "taken" only too well? The disturbing fact remains that this conception of neurosis and of the therapeutic task has not led to very happy practical outcomes. It has not pointed the way to a more hygienic program for the early training of children, and it has not provided for human beings generally a more competent and satisfying life philosophy. The question which therefore presses in upon us is: What is it that is so tragically wrong with the system of thought which, on the whole, is so obviously right?

From our vantage point today we may see clearly what our predecessors discerned dimly or not at all. Standing on the shoulders of giants of the past, to borrow a phrase from Robert Burton, we may succeed where they failed. For Freud and innumerable followers neurosis was the consequence of repression which the ego and superego have turned against the forces of the id, but it is today increasingly evident that neurosis is rather the product of id and ego functioning in league *against the superego*. As Freud himself fully recognized, the human infant is in the beginning "all id," and as the ego evolves it is predominantly a pleasure ego, an id-ego.

It is during the period of intensive socialization, between the years of two and six in European and American societies, that serious conflict first arises. However, it is at first mainly an external conflict, the conflict between the child and his would-be socializers. Characteristically or at least recurrently refractory, disobedient, and uncooperative, the child is commonly said to be in the *negativistic* stage. In the fortunate instance, as conscience is forged from an admixture of love and fear of parents, this early rebellion is replaced by a more or less harmonious synthesis of id, ego, and superego. But in the less fortunate case, conscience is formed but not accepted, and the unresolved struggle between the child and his socializers lives on as deep conflict between the id-ego of infancy and the now internalized but *unassimilated* psychic representative of parents and community, namely, the superego

Sometimes small children may be observed stopping their ears with their fingers when their parents criticize or admonish them. The older child or adolescent cannot shut out the voice of his conscience by so simple an expedient, but by means of repression a similar result may be produced. The internalized criticisms and admonitions of parents and community are now muffled and no longer heard clearly and explicitly, but they are still capable of breaking through into consciousness as depression, anxiety, and inferiority feeling. Symptoms are then formed as means of dealing with these distressing affects, and the afflicted individual is a full-fledged neurotic. Sooner or later, as one anxiety-reducing strategy after another is tried and found to be only partially effective, the individual may come to therapy, with the two great energy systems of his personality in a seemingly hopeless stalemate.[25]

At this point two options are open to the therapist, though in the past it has seemed to many that there was only one. The whole force of the Freudian tradition has disposed the therapist to assume that the patient's superego was too severe; if this were indeed the case, the therapist had no choice but to join forces with the (presumably repressed) id and thus attempt to woo the ego away from its allegiance to and domination by the tyrannical superego, to a

[25] Since the above was written, a friend has given me the following quotation: "Let us note that in every one of us there are two guiding and ruling principles which lead us whither they will; one is the natural desire of pleasure, the other is an acquired opinion which is in search of the best; and these two are sometimes in harmony and then again at war, and sometimes the one, sometimes the other conquers" (Plato, *Phaedrus*). To this we need only add, "and sometimes they remain indefinitely deadlocked." [Cf. Freud's posthumous volume, *An outline of psychoanalysis* (1949), in which we read: "The ego has been weakened by the internal conflict; we must come to its aid. The position is like a civil war which can only be decided by the help of an ally from without" (p. 63).]

more friendly accepting relationship with the id. As Alexander and French (1946) have recently observed, this strategy often results, not in curing the patient, but in producing "a deep narcissistic regression" in which he luxuriates during the course of treatment, but from which he emerges with no fundamental change in his basic personality structure. The probable explanation of this untoward outcome is to be found in the mistaken belief that neurosis rests upon a conflict in which the ego and superego are aligned against the id. If we assume that this conflict is one in which the ego is far more powerfully allied with the id than with the superego, we see at once why orthodox Freudian treatment serves in many cases only to propitiate and prolong a neurosis rather than cure it.

If we proceed on the assumption that the neurotic's basic conflict is between an id-dominated ego and an unassimilated or repressed superego, we are fully prepared, both conceptually and practically, for the externalization of this conflict which occurs in therapy. Freud called this remarkable phenomenon "transference," and it is most aptly conceived as an action whereby the patient now "extrojects" his superego and invests the therapist with the mantle of parental authority and social sanctions. The ensuing resistance is thus nothing but the unresolved negativism of early childhood which has gone underground for a more or less extended period but is now once again brought out into the open.[26] So long as this conflict was internalized, there was little opportunity for it to be resolved, since the individual thus protects himself from the behests of conscience and from the continued learning that is involved in growing up. It is precisely the fortunate fact that neurotics tend in the therapeutic situation to resume the unresolved fight with their parents and with society that offers the greatest

[26] The terms "symptom" and "defense" are commonly used as if referring to essentially the same phenomena. It may be an aid to greater explicitness and more exact conceptualization if the term "symptom" is used to refer to habits which an individual develops as means of dealing with the anxiety which results from inner neurotic conflict and if "defense" is used to refer to habits which an individual uses as means of fending off the demands for change which the therapist (like the parent of an earlier era) makes of the patient. Defenses, thus defined, tend to be similar to—in some instances identical with—the tactics learned in childhood as means of resisting parental and other socializing pressures. We also see why it is that symptoms tend to disappear in therapy, long before the neurotic structure of the patient's personality is fundamentally modified. As the internal neurotic conflict is transformed back into a social conflict, symptoms are converted into defenses and the patient takes one of two courses: he either concludes that he doesn't need treatment—since his symptoms have disappeared—and breaks off the therapy, often in a "huff" with the therapist; or the patient enters into a relational struggle from which, if correctly handled, he will emerge a more mature and better integrated individual.

therapeutic opportunities. Freud correctly regarded "transference" as having highly important therapeutic potentialities. It now appears that greatest therapeutic progress is made, not by assuming that parents produced too much learning in the childhood of the neurotic adult, but by making the opposite assumption—that the parents produced too little learning. Therapy may then be conceived as an attempt, not to reverse the earlier influences of parents, but to take up and resume the unfinished business of the parent-child relationship; namely, that of making the human animal into a normal, mature, morally and socially accountable human being. Neurosis is thus seen as a kind of ignorance rather than illness, and therapy becomes, explicitly and integrally, a part of the total educative enterprise, not an antidote for what is presumed to be too much education.

Learning theory again comes to our aid at this juncture and enables us to picture normal and neurotic development with special lucidity. Repeatedly in this paper there has been reference to the two basic learning processes—problem solving and conditioning. I have elsewhere (9) pointed out a number of other dichotomies which more or less precisely parallel this twofold division. We know that problem-solving behavior is mediated by the central nervous system and the skeletal musculature, and that the conditioned reactions are mediated by the autonomic nervous system and by smooth muscle and visceral tissue. We know that the former is appropriately referred to as response substitution (or trial-and-error learning), the latter as stimulus substitution (or associative shifting), that the one is under direct voluntary control and that the other is not.

What is of special relevance here is that it is through our problem-solving behavior that we exert our *effects* upon the world about us, and it is through conditioning that the world *affects* us. The normal person is in more or less continuous interaction with his environment, modifying it, being *effective,* but being in turn modified by it, *affected.* "Give and take" is the maxim of the mature, well-integrated, undefensive individual. In Figure 69, at the right I have attempted to indicate diagrammatically the relationship of such an individual to his environment and something of his internal structure. The arrow extending from the individual across to the world represents his problem-solving behavior, his impact upon the world; and the arrow extending from the world back to the individual represents the conditioning process, the impact of the world upon the individual.

Examining the normal individual more closely, we find a differentiated area of the id labeled "E" for ego and another area labeled "C" for conscience or superego, which is the introjected form of the world, particularly the social world. Because of the harmonious relationship which the individual-as-a-whole has with his environment, the ego is on correspondingly good terms with the con-

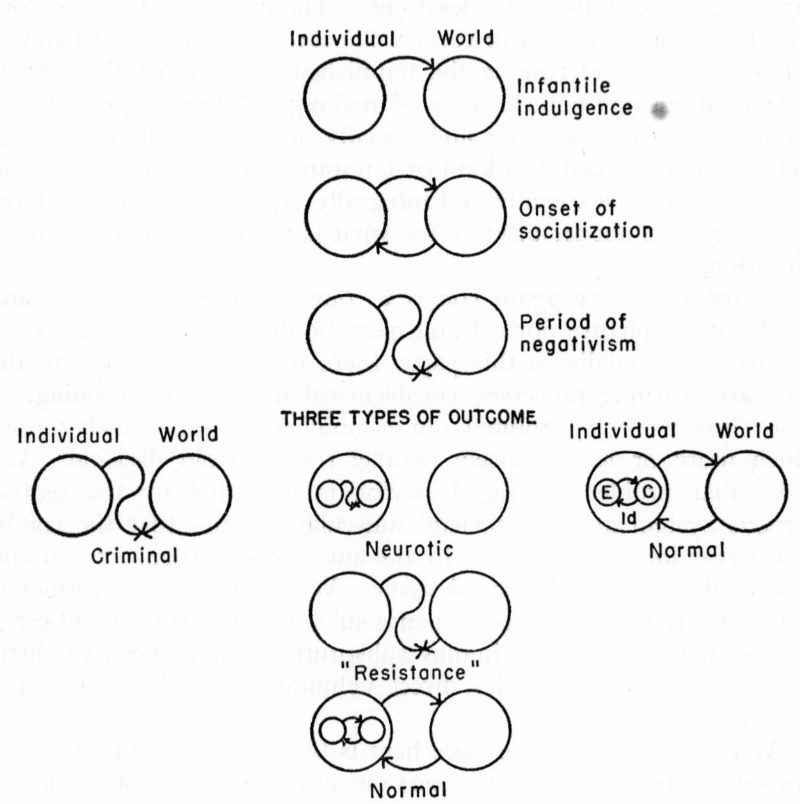

FIG. 69.—Diagrammatic representation of the vicissitudes of human socialization.

science. As common sense fully recognizes, such an individual's outward behavior is heavily influenced, not only by prescriptions that are currently enforced by the external world, but also by the dictates of conscience. Such a person is said to have "good character" and is characterized by *self-control,* which is to say that controlling agencies in the environment have been internalized, incorporated, and accepted as a part of the total self. Such a person has, in short, strongly *identified himself* with his society.

But such admirable and ideal personalities are not born, nor do they develop automatically. They are the hard-won products of successful socialization. Using the same mode of graphic representation, we may depict the situation genetically, beginning with the diagram at the top of Figure 69. During the period of "infantile omnipotence," to borrow Freud's apt phrase, the individual is indulged, waited on, "babied." His needs and wishes are gratified as fully as possible, and no demands are made of him other than that he be comfortable and thrive physiologically. But eventually a time must come—early in some societies, later in others—when this indulgence and irresponsibility must end. We begin to say, "You are no longer a baby. You are a big boy (or girl) now," and we begin to enforce demands for the renunciation of infantile pleasures and for obedience and responsibility. This is the onset of socialization, and it marks the first serious attempt that is deliberately made to condition the child, i.e., to create in him social attitudes and emotions which we hope will lay the basis for good character.

Previously, of course, there will have been in the normal family situation a good deal of affectional learning. Because the mother and other responsive persons have mediated comforts and reliefs, the baby will already have developed strong dependence upon and love for them. This cushion of positive feeling seems to be of the utmost importance in later taking up the shock and in making more acceptable the demands and impositions of active socialization. But even at best a good deal of resistance and resentment can be expected. As already noted, the period between the ages of two and six is commonly referred to as the period of "negativism." Normally, this is gradually worked through, and by the time the individual is a young adult, we have a reasonable approximation of the ideal pictured at the right in Figure 69.

Unhappily the end results are not always of this type. Sometimes the opposition to authority and social sanctions which is aroused in the early attempts at socialization is continued, relatively unmodified, on into later life. When this occurs we encounter a criminal, an individual whose inner personality structure remains relatively little differentiated, whose ego is almost indistinguishable from the id and whose total energies are directed toward attacking, exploiting, and resisting the social order in which he finds himself. This conceptualization is admittedly greatly oversimplified and does not at all do justice to the complexities of criminal psychology, but it serves to indicate the position in our schematization of the criminal personality-type and the extreme in socialization failure.

Between the criminal on the left and the normal individual on the right lies an intermediate type of personality, the neurotic.[27]

[27] For a detailed defense of this way of conceptualizing these three major personality patterns, see Mowrer (1948b).

Such an individual, as previously noted, has internalized many of the demands and obligations imposed by his socializers, but these demands—collectively known as conscience—are not inwardly accepted. The internal picture is now essentially a replica of the outward struggle which characterized the period of negativism. Childish refractoriness has become neurosis, and the individual is so preoccupied with this internal drama that he more or less withdraws, both effectively and affectively, from the real environment (symbolized in Figure 69 by the absence of interconnecting arrows with the "world").

We may quickly recapitulate what has already been said in detail. When such an individual comes into therapy, this internal conflict is again externalized; he develops "transference," becomes "resistant," regresses to childhood negativism.[28] In Figure 69 this stage is shown as leading only to normality, but theoretically there are the same three possible resolutions that have previously been indicated in connection with the period of childhood negativism: normality, criminality, and more neurosis. Actually, it seems that much would-be therapy leads, in practice, to all three types of result. Our task, clearly, is to discover why this should be the case and to increase the incidence of the ideal outcome.

I believe that, in general, too little and technically improper attention has been given to the defensive interpersonal strategies which emerge in psychotherapy. I had originally planned to report some recent research findings and some illustrative excerpts from electronically recorded therapeutic interviews. This material will have to be reserved for a later presentation, at which time a number of matters pertaining both to practice and theory will be discussed. Since we are here primarily concerned with what I have called the neurotic paradox, I shall now try to bring together what has already been said and to show its bearing upon this formal theoretical issue.

VIII. A Proposed Resolution of the Neurotic Paradox

As defined at the outset of this paper, the neurotic paradox lies in the fact that human behavior is sometimes indefinitely perpetuated despite the fact that it is seriously self-defeating. Freud's major attempt to resolve this paradox involves the assumption that in

[28] As Freud long ago pointed out, one of the distinguishing differences between neurosis and psychosis is in the capacity for relationship, in the ability to develop transference. The work of Sullivan (1931), Fromm-Reichmann (1939), and others shows that this capacity is not altogether absent in the psychotic but that it can be activated but slowly. Whether this is merely a quantitative difference or one involving a distinctive type of dynamism is one of our great unsolved problems.

neurosis there are acts and feelings which have been appropriate at one stage of the individual's life history but are no longer so. More specifically, Freud believed that it was the superego which, as a result of too zealous childhood training, retained its overseverity into adult life despite altered circumstances and in this way produced the distressing, hampering effects seen in neurosis. But this approach to the problem goes counter to one of the best-established principles in the psychology of learning, which is that all learning tends to undergo extinction unless it is at least periodically reinforced.

Recognizing this difficulty in Freud's formulations, Horney and others have sought to rectify it by positing that the wasteful, self-defeating habits and attitudes which constitute neurosis do indeed become periodically reinforced through the operation of so-called vicious circles. But here again neurosis is conceived as a *learning excess,* and it is assumed that if one can but stop the cyclic sequence of events which keeps this learning reinforced, neurosis will be self-correcting.

Against these and similar attempts to resolve the neurotic paradox, we have posited the view that neurosis is not a learning excess but a *learning deficit.* Because of resistances which the infantile ego sets up against the socializing forces and because of the opposition which it later exerts against the internalized agent of these forces, namely the superego, the ego remains immature, asocial, id-dominated.

That such an ego continues to experience anxiety is in no way surprising since it is still at war with the superego, which is constantly being kept alive and vigorous by the very nature of the social realities which it represents. We do not ask why the criminal continues to be a fearful individual. There is the ever-present danger that he will be apprehended and punished for his rebellious, antisocial behavior. And much the same is true of the neurotic. It is not that he is suffering from unreal or "childish" fears. He, too, faces a real danger, the danger of having his immaturities and "delinquencies" discovered—the danger, as one patient expressed it, of being "unmasked"—and of having to resume the painful task of renouncing the pleasure principle of infancy and accepting the reality principle of adulthood.

The problem, then, is not to explain why the neurotic does not *unlearn;* it is rather to account for the fact that he does not *learn.* We have already touched upon some of the reasons why small children resist primary socialization and why in later life the ego of the neurotic continues to fight with the superego. And we have also seen the way in which this intrapsychic struggle again becomes externalized in therapy and to what extent the transference behavior is essentially defensive, defensive in the sense of trying to avert the learning involved in further "growing up."

Having thus established the thesis that the neurotic is an "underdone" human being, in some respects not unlike the criminal, rather than an overdone, superhuman sort of creature, we must now turn and make an important modification of an earlier statement. We have repeatedly characterized the neurotic as a victim of underlearning, immaturity, ignorance; but this underlearning is of a special kind and is vouchsafed by what is, in one respect, "overlearning." Preston (1940) has remarked that mental health is a matter of attitudes, and it is with respect to *attitudinal learning* that the neurotic is most deficient. To say that an individual is neurotic is not to say that there is anything deficient about his problem-solving learning ability. Indeed, it is the very fact that he has been so skilful in parrying the early attempts of his elders, and later of his conscience, to socialize him that has kept him neurotic. The essence of the difficulty is precisely that, through problem-solving learning or the primitive pleasure principle he has learned how to keep from learning in the sense of being conditioned, i.e., changed emotionally and attitudinally. To put this matter somewhat paradoxically but succinctly, the neurotic is an individual *who has learned how not to learn.*

In therapy it is therefore true that there is a kind of unlearning that must occur—unlearning of the "skills" and strategies by which conditioning, whether by society or by conscience, has been warded off. These strategies must be activated in the therapy, but they must then be shown to be ineffective and, indeed, unnecessary. The way is then opened for the more basic kind of emotional learning against which past problem-solving behavior has served as a protection. Religious leaders are fond of saying that a sinner can be saved only if he "opens his heart to God." Perhaps we can appropriately paraphrase this statement by saying that a neurotic can be cured only if he "opens his heart" to the great moral teachings and emotional values of his society. Then and only then does it seem possible for the erstwhile neurotic to become a whole man or woman, at peace with himself and his fellow-men.

There is a strange and basic contradiction in Freud's theoretical thinking. In 1911 he showed a penetrating grasp of the reason why human development is always difficult and uncertain in outcome. He pointed out that the infant is at first completely under the sway of the primitive pleasure principle, whereas the normal, mature adult follows what he designated as the reality principle. The progress from the one to the other he saw as dependent upon the slow and painful development of the capacity to forgo immediate satisfactions and to submit to labor and other ordeals as means of achieving greater long-term gains and averting future suffering. Freud correctly insisted that the reality principle does not involve a repudiation of the pleasure principle but rather a refinement and "safeguarding" of it. The difficulty lies precisely in the fact that in making the transition from the one to the other, the individual has to learn to move at least temporarily away from satisfaction and comfort toward discomfort and pain, as a means of ultimately finding the route back to more assured, stable, long-term satisfactions. Human development is fraught with the repeated necessity for making *detours* of all kinds, and it is the individual's resistance or willingness in these paradoxical developmental steps that draws the fateful line between the neurotic and the normal personality.

All this Freud saw clearly. But a strange bias prevented him from assigning to it the real significance it appears to have in a total theory of personality. His bias was that he regarded the superego as a more or less archaic relic of childhood and the traditions, values, and morality of the race as equally outmoded carry-overs from earlier stages in the history of the race. For Freud, human culture as transmitted from generation to generation was not in the least concerned with insuring and promoting human happiness; its sole function and objective was to insure the survival of the group. As he says in *Civilization and its discontents,* society provides man with greater security than he can achieve in a solitary mode of existence, and because of this, man barters "some part of his chances for happiness" for this security (1930, p. 92). He does this very reluctantly and with a sense of the "cultural privation" which "dominates the whole field of social relations between human beings" (p. 63). We rightly find fault, said Freud, "with our present state of civilization for so inadequately providing us with what we require to make us happy in life, and for the amount of suffering of a probably avoidable nature it lays us open to . . . " (p. 92).

Because the superego is but the "internalized voice of the community," it is not surprising, therefore, that Freud expressed a low opinion of it:

In our investigations and our therapy of the neuroses we cannot avoid finding fault with the superego of the individual on two counts: in commanding and prohibiting with such severity it troubles too little about the happiness of the ego, and it fails to take into account sufficiently the difficulties in the way of obeying it—the strength of instinctual cravings in the id and the hardships of external environment. Consequently in our therapy we often find ourselves obliged to do battle with the superego and work to moderate its demands. Exactly the same objections can be made against the ethical standards of the cultural superego (p. 139).

These highly dubious and arbitrary asseverations have, perhaps more than anything else, prevented a fruition of Freud's otherwise often profound and insightful theorizing. They drove him to a conception of normal personality as fantastic as it is pessimistic, according to which the ego stands alone, beleaguered on all sides by the contradictory, hazardous, and often unrealistic demands of the world, the id, and the superego. The goal of psychotherapy, stated most abstractly, was therefore to strengthen the ego in order that it might better endure and perhaps in some measure coordinate the divisive forces to which it is constantly exposed.

Clinical experience and other sources of evidence justify us in taking a radically different point of view. A less partisan examination of the facts suggests that human culture, far from being indifferent to human suffering and unhappiness, is eminently concerned with them, and that traditions and social values represent some of our soundest guides to psychological and social reality. In other words, it is increasingly evident that individual development from the primitive pleasure principle toward the reality principle, as Freud early conceived them, importantly involves the assimilation and acceptance of the great fundamental edicts of culture and conscience, not a distrust of and a standing apart from them as Freud was led to conclude.

Freud explicitly equated happiness to pleasure in the sense of instinctual pleasure. He was strangely blind and obdurate to the very apparent fact—apparent at least to individuals who have been able to take full advantage of developmental opportunities available within the established framework of their society—that there is such a thing as conscience pleasure, and that in the long run happiness is far more securely founded upon this than upon instinctual pleasure. Freud wrote voluminously about a highly questionable process which he termed *sublimation.* Since man cannot, because of what Freud termed "cultural privation," find happiness in the free and complete gratification of his instinctual desires, his only hope of attaining even a modicum of happiness is achieved by eking out more limited and indirect gratifications of these impulses. A more felicitous conception is that of *substitution,* the process of replacing immediate, infantile, organic pleasures by the more enduring satisfactions which come from a sense of full and responsible observation of the rules and principles governing the activities of family, community, state, nation, and of the human enterprise generally. In so accepting these rules and principles, one wins back to a fuller and more assured satisfaction of even the instinctual needs than seems possible in any other pattern of existence.[29]

Briefly, let us see if we can more sharply focus the principal implications of this discussion. We have seen that a neurotic is a person who has proceeded quite a long way on the road toward becoming a mature, socially responsible adult but who at some point has gotten "stuck," "bogged down." By processes which we are only beginning to understand, the neurotic has earlier taken into himself the basic values and attitudes of his particular society and of his particular subgroup within that society. But what he has *not* done is fully to come to terms with and harmoniously assimilate these basic values and attitudes into the fabric of his total personality. Such a step the neurotic is unable (unwilling?) to make, and thereby hangs the mystery.

If the neurotic cannot go forward on life's pathway, neither can he go backward. To go backward is to become less human, more like an animal, and it is constantly being borne in upon us that we cannot escape the fate of *being human beings.* The force that thus pushes us onward is not therefore some childish whimsy, a vagary of an eccentric upbringing, but one of the most powerful and pervasive of our total contemporary experiences.

With progress blocked and retreat cut off,[30] the neurotic characteristically feels trapped, helpless, impotent. He cannot, in other words, either move forward, go back to where he came from, or stay where he is. The "road" seems hopelessly uphill in both directions, and yet he can find neither peace nor rest in pausing!

---

[29] For a somewhat similar view, see Maslow (1948); also Hollingworth (1949).

[30] Perhaps the most basic difference between the neurotic and the psychotic is that, for the latter, the road back to childhood and infancy is less completely closed. This, presumably, is because parts of the prepsychotic's personality or "mind" are still very "primitive," as Fromm-Reichmann has suggested. But even here there are powerful pressures, within and without, pushing the individual toward adulthood and full humanity.

[Clinical experience which has intervened since the above was written inclines me to the belief that the basic difference between the neurotic and the individual with psychotic tendencies is this: In the neurotic we always have a person who has faced a strong conflict as to which of his parents he should identify with; but there has been no question but that he wanted to be a human being—it was simply a matter of *which kind.* For the individual with psychotic tendencies, however, the dilemma has been a more basic one: Does he wish to be a human being *at all?* Animal identifications in children who have been neglected and mistreated are not uncommon and become all the more intelligible when we study the process by which human identification on the part of animals can be made to occur. (See 21, 22, 24.)]

Growing up and becoming "normal," in the sense of measuring up to standard specifications for being a human being and fulfilling the expectations which are placed upon us, is something no one can do without help. Human socialization involves learning things, of both a technical and moral nature, which took the race millions of years to work out. Unaided, alone, isolated from other human contacts, no single individual would ever learn more than a tiny fragment, a minuscule beginning, of the totality which we call human culture. In the protective yet ever expectant atmosphere of the home and, later, the school, through a precious admixture of love and fear, the human animal is little by little prepared for and initiated into this great enterprise. But sometimes, for various reasons, individuals grow up physically and leave family and school without having learned quite all that they should have learned in those settings. It is such persons who often find themselves confused, trapped, brought to a standstill. And it is only by the fortunate accident of their being able to resume, under more auspicious circumstances, a child-parent relationship with a second "father" or "mother" that some of the unlearned lessons are completed and the individual is able to move on and take his proper place among his fellows.

Thus it is that we come to see that neurosis involves, basically, a learning deficit rather than a learning excess, but one which the individual is often unable to correct, spontaneously and unaided.

When we see the development of human personality in this light, not only is the neurotic paradox formally resolved; we are also enabled to conceive the task of therapy, not as that of attempting to stay or actually reverse the process whereby the human animal is converted into a full-fledged member of his society; rather do we see therapy as the more promising venture of reinstituting and, if possible, in some measure completing the education of the laggard learner.

CHAPTER 19

THE PROBLEM OF ANXIETY

[This chapter consists of four parts. Section I was delivered as an address at the 1947 (Chicago) meeting of the American Association for the Advancement of Science. Sections II and III are excerpts from a long unpublished manuscript on anxiety. Section IV was written expressly for this volume.]

I. A "Guilt" Theory of Anxiety

For a number of reasons, some of which we shall explore in this paper, human beings have found it difficult to conceptualize the experience of anxiety. This can hardly be due either to the rarity or to the recency of the experience. On both theoretical and historical grounds, we can safely surmise that predisposition to and recurrent consciousness of anxiety date back to the time when *Homo sapiens* first began to live in well-organized social groups, some hundreds of thousands of years ago; and we have no reason to suppose that any group has subsequently existed in which the experience was unknown. Yet the fact is that we are only now learning how to talk and think about this phenomenon in a reasonably explicit and systematic manner.

It will not be possible here to indicate, save in an exceedingly sketchy fashion, the nature of the evidence for believing that anxiety is such an old and pervasive experience as I have indicated. The data, actually, are not at all unfamiliar; but we have not understood their meaning. Only now are we beginning to know how to interpret and evaluate them; but as our knowledge of contemporary man's methods of managing—and mismanaging—anxiety grows, we become increasingly impressed with the extent to which ancient and even prehistoric man was probably also preoccupied with this psychological problem.

There is, for example, good basis for believing that anxiety is the principal reason for modern man's addiction to alcohol, tobacco, and numerous other less common intoxicants and narcotics. The antiquity of these substances and their use needs no documentation here; nor does the fact that certain other types of addictions or "vices"—such as gambling, sexual monomania, and gluttony, which, as we now know, derive their main reinforcement from the relief of anxiety they afford—date far back into human history.

Addictions and vices, so-called, are likely to require material artifacts, and thus they leave a record that can be read, albeit often obscurely, by posterity. But there are other forms of behavior which are likewise largely motivated by anxiety but which do not necessarily involve physical accouterments. We have few remnants from early man from which we can decide whether he, like his modern counterpart, occasionally engaged in behavior which made his fellows look upon him as "strange," "alien," "mad," or not. But we do know that holes were sometimes trephined in the skulls of persons who lived thousands of years ago; and this and similar practices seem most reasonably explained as primitive psychiatry. (The modern practice of psychosurgery will perhaps suggest that psychiatry is still primitive, or else that trephining was not primitive at all, in the sense of being backward and irrational, but very advanced indeed!)

The common use of magic as a means of coping with anxieties arising from a variety of causes is certainly well authenticated in our nonliterate contemporaries; and we can plausibly conjecture that it occupied a similar place in the lives of prehistoric peoples. And there are still other techniques, ceremonies, and practices that make it appear that man has been having and trying to get rid of the experience of anxiety for an incredibly long time. However, none of these techniques which I have or might have mentioned is more interesting or important than one about which we must now say at least a word, namely, formal religion.

Again we have to reconstruct; for prehistoric and even ancient man did not explicitly tell us, or probably even himself, that in his religious rites and practices he was attempting to allay anxiety; but many students of the problem agree that the management of anxiety is a very important and basic function of religion. What traditional religions have specifically offered to the devout is the promise of "peace" and "salvation"; and although the word "anxiety" is rarely mentioned, it is easily inferred that it is this experience from which "salvation" is promised and in exchange for which "peace" is given.

Although I am unable to find the word "anxiety" anywhere in the King James version of the Old Testament (and a less careful check indicates that it is also exceedingly uncommon in other great religious documents),[1] it is surely obvious to a modern reader that the anguish of the human soul with which many of the Old Testament writers were concerned was none other than anxiety and its related states of depression and guilt. Elsewhere I have recently reviewed the writings of the Psalmist, David, and nothing could be clearer than that his beautiful poetry—and, incidentally, shrewd psychologizing—is concerned with only one theme: the story of a human being, cast down and anxious, who found himself in the Lord and was thenceforth joyous and at peace.

Blessed is he whose transgression is forgiven, whose sin is covered. Blessed is the man unto whom the Lord imputeth not iniquity, and in whose spirit there is no guile. When I kept silence, my bones waxed old through my roaring all the day long. For day and night thy hand was heavy upon me: my moisture is turned into the drought of summer. I acknowledged my sin unto thee, and mine iniquity have I not hid. I said, I will confess my transgressions unto the Lord; and thou forgavest the iniquity of my sin. . . . Thou art my hiding place; thou shalt preserve me from trouble; thou shalt compass me about with songs of deliverance (32:1–5, 7).

One finds this same theme of misery and despair, confession and repentance, and joy and salvation occurring over and over again in the Psalms; but at no place is it more succinctly or explicitly formulated than in the following:

I will bless the Lord at all times: His praise shall continually be in my mouth. My soul shall make her boast in the Lord; the humble shall hear thereof, and be glad. O magnify the Lord with me, and let us exalt his name together. I sought the Lord, and he heard me, and *delivered me from all my fears* (34:1–4, italics added).

Christian writers, to my way of thinking, handled the problem of anxiety much less well, psychologically speaking, than did those of the Old Testament. In the Middle Ages theology almost wholly replaced anything that might be called psychology, and the naturalism which one finds in David and other Hebrew writers was superseded by a rampant supernaturalism. In the interest of brevity but at the risk of appearing dogmatic, one may say that the first twelve or fifteen centuries of the Christian era were definitely retrogressive with respect to precise knowledge concerning the experiences of anxiety (and psychological matters generally). Only with the

[1] The *Shorter Oxford English Dictionary,* 1933 edition, reports that usage of the word "anxiety" dates from 1525, "anxious" from 1623. With the publication of the King James version (1611), these terms were therefore either new or unknown, their meanings being rendered by such expressions as "wild with care," "take thought of," etc. In modern versions of the Bible, the words "anxiety" and "anxious" appear relatively frequently.

Renaissance did the capacity for naturalistic analysis of the problem return; and even then it was not until the early part of the nineteenth century that this rebirth of free inquiry produced a man whose writings on the topics are intelligible and stimulating to a modern reader. This man was the prodigious and inspired, but only recently acclaimed, Søren Kierkegaard.[2]

How much of a voice in the wilderness Kierkegaard's was is suggested by his remark, "One almost never sees the concept of anxiety dealt with in psychology," and then he adds one of his many penetrating observations, "and I must therefore call attention to the fact that it is different from fear and similar concepts which refer to something definite" (1824, p. 38). Anxiety, for Kierkegaard, was a fear of "nothing." Small wonder that the human intellect had previously had difficulty in placing such an experience in the scheme of orderly knowledge!

Not only do we find that Kierkegaard anticipated Freud in an astonishing number of ways. We shall shortly see that in his discussion of the problem of anxiety he was in one important respect more correct than Freud. But it is as if Freud had to live and write before Kierkegaard's work, with which Freud evidently had no contact, could be understood and appreciated. We shall therefore confine our attention for the time being to Freud and then later return briefly to Kierkegaard (cf. Section 3).

It is impressive that Freud, no less than Kierkegaard, was struck by the conceptual difficulties which anxiety presents. Thus, remarked Freud:

> I speak purposely of "hypotheses." This [the problem of anxiety] is the most difficult task that has been set us, but the difficulty does not lie in the incompleteness of our observation, for it is actually the commonest and most familiar phenomena that present us with such riddles; . . . No, it is genuinely a question of hypotheses; that is to say, of the introduction of the right abstract ideas, and of their application to the raw material of observation so as to bring order and lucidity into it (1933, p. 113).

For present purposes we may posit that Freud contributed three great hypotheses concerning anxiety, the first of which has to do with the dynamics of *symptom formation,* the second with the phenomenon of *repression,* and the third with the ultimate nature of *anxiety* itself. These three hypotheses are all so interrelated that it is difficult to discuss one without presupposing the others. But let us begin with symptom formation.

---

[2] For a scholarly history of thought concerning anxiety, see May (1950).

Freud tells us that early in his psychoanalytic investigations he "noticed a very important connection between anxiety development and symptom formation. It was that the two are interchangeable" (1933, p. 116). This relationship he illustrates as follows:

The agoraphobiac, for example, begins his illness with an attack of anxiety in the street. This is repeated every time he walks along the street again. He now develops a symptom—a street phobia—which can also be described as an inhibition or a functional restriction of the ego, and thus he preserves himself from anxiety attacks (pp. 116–17).

With this discovery Freud laid one of the central pillars upon which the modern understanding of neurosis is based. As Hendrick (1939) has remarked, "This theory of symptom formation as a protection against anxiety . . . is at present universally accepted by analysts; for it seems to explain adequately a great many related phenomena observed by them" (p. 171).

This theory is especially important in that it provides a means of simply and precisely defining the term "neurosis." On the basis of this hypothesis one can say that a person "has a neurosis," or "is neurotic," to the extent that he engages in behavior which serves to reduce anxiety directly (symptomatically) but does not alter the realities *which produce the anxiety.* Freud repeatedly referred to anxiety as a kind of "signal," a premonition of impending danger, an indicator that something is not going well in the life of the affected individual. The neurotic is thus a person who attempts, knowingly or unknowingly, to neutralize this signal, this indicator, without finding out what it means or taking realistic steps to eliminate the objective danger which it represents. He is, in other words, like a person who stops up his ears to keep from hearing an air-raid siren or who, let us say, mans an antiaircraft gun and aims it at the siren rather than at the approaching enemy.[3]

[3] This definition of neurosis as any type of behavior which serves to reduce anxiety without affecting its fundamental causation has the important theoretical advantage of explaining why it is that such a "symptom" is at one and the same time both self-perpetuating and self-defeating. It is self-perpetuating because it is reinforced by the satisfaction provided through the resulting anxiety reduction; and it is self-destructive in that it prevents the individual from experiencing the full force of his anxiety and being modified by it in such a direction as to eliminate the occasion for the anxiety. (For a discussion of the dilemma of persistent non-integrative behavior, see 15 and 21.) Simple and precise as this definition is, one continually reads and hears controversy over the meaning of the term "neurosis." Part of the difficulty seems to arise from a tendency on the part of many to take much too narrow a view of "neurotic" behavior. According to the foregoing conception, any *persistent* behavior which reduces anxiety without rectifying its cause is "neurotic," regardless of whether this behavior falls into one or another of the diagnostic categories of traditional psychiatry or is something quite different and perhaps entirely commonplace.

This analogy serves two purposes: it gives us a paradigm for conceptualizing more accurately what we mean when we speak of "neurosis," and it also leads logically to the second hypothesis of Freud which we wish to discuss. Having seen that anxiety represents a kind of danger, to which the neurotic reacts unrealistically, Freud understandably wanted to know the exact nature and source of this danger. Undoubtedly he, like many puzzled physicians, priests, and others before him, *asked* the neurotics who consulted him what it was that made them so anxious; and we may be certain that they consistently said they did not know. Convinced that this reply was not only universal but honest, Freud was thrown back upon his own intellectual powers, and he eventually evolved the hypothesis that in anxiety the true source of danger is excluded from consciousness by the process which he came to refer to as *repression.* Thus, concluded Freud, anxiety differs from ordinary fear in that in fear we know the object or situation of which we are afraid; we are afraid of something definite; but in anxiety there is no object; our "fear" is wholly indefinite; it is as Kierkegaard aptly remarked, a fear "of nothing." [4]

I have just said that Freud "eventually" developed the idea that in anxiety the true source of danger is excluded from consciousness, i.e., is repressed. I say "eventually" because in his first theoretical pronouncements on this score, Freud emphasized not so much the factor of danger as that of dammed-up sexual energy or so-called libido. In individuals who were sufficiently frustrated or inhibited sexually, said Freud, the accumulated sexual tension, no longer capable of being restrained, erupted into consciousness, not as lust or passion, but as anxiety. It was, he said, as if the libido was itself directly "transformed" into anxiety.

But this formulation was unsatisfactory on a number of counts, and Freud later advanced an alternative hypothesis. In this he posited the following sequence: The individual, commonly as a child, engages in some forbidden act, usually sexual or aggressive in nature, and is punished for it. He then tries alternative or substitutive means of satisfying the same need but is again punished. This opposition from the social environment sets up a powerful internal conflict between the original impulse and the fear of punishment. Finally, in at least some instances, this conflict is resolved by the fateful device of repression: the impulse or wish is denied,

[4] Others had, to be sure, previously spoken of "mind" that was unconscious; but this fact does not detract from the great importance which attaches to Freud's emphasis upon the connection between repression and anxiety.

the temptation and therefore the fear are eliminated, and inner peace is restored.

But, said Freud, these repressive solutions are psychologically expensive for the individual and are maintained only with great difficulty and effort. Sooner or later, the condemned impulse will attempt to reassert itself; the forces of repression will be strained; and the individual, thus threatened with a "return of the repressed," feels *anxiety*. This experience is really *fear of* the inhibited, rebellious impulse; but since only the fear and not the impulse gets into consciousness, the individual suffers, not from fear in the ordinary sense, but from anxiety.

By way of recapitulation let it be said that we are here fully accepting the basic theory of Freud concerning the nature of *symptom formation,* i.e., that a neurotic symptom, so-called, is any habit which resolves anxiety but does not lessen the ultimate, realistic problem which the anxiety represents. And we are also in complete accord with Freud's contention that *repression* is necessary to an adequate theory of anxiety; without this concept a really satisfactory account of anxiety is apparently quite impossible. But it now appears, on both pragmatic and logical grounds, that Freud never succeeded in fully apprehending the essential nature of anxiety itself.

It is not possible at this time to give at all completely the evidence on which this statement is based. But what can be indicated, at least briefly, is the direction in which Freud's analysis needs to be modified. In essence, Freud's theory holds that anxiety comes from evil wishes, from acts which the individual would commit if he dared. *The alternative view here proposed is that anxiety comes, not from acts which the individual would commit but dares not, but from acts which he has committed but wishes that he had not. It is, in other words, a "guilt theory" of anxiety rather than an "impulse theory."*

Stated in its most concise but abstract form, the difference between these two views is that the one holds that anxiety arises from repression that has been turned toward the *id;* whereas the other holds that anxiety arises from repression that has been turned toward the *superego* or *conscience.* A few neo-Freudians have recently suggested that anxiety *may* arise from repression that goes in *either* direction, toward the id *or* toward the superego;[5] but for Freud and most of his followers the overwhelming emphasis has been upon anxiety as a product of repressed impulses, not upon anxiety as a product of repudiated moral urgings—and the thera-

[5] See, for example, Fenichel (1945) and Fromm (1947); see also Jung (1938).

peutic efforts of Freud and his followers are well marked by this conceptual bent: they have been in the direction of trying to "reduce the severity of the superego." It now appears that in most, if not all, neurotics the problem is to help the individual "grow up" to the demands of his conscience, not to try to whittle down or dilute those demands.[6]

The reformulation of anxiety theory here proposed raises a host of theoretical as well as practical issues, but the results to date of exploring these have been highly encouraging. First of all, it brings scientific anxiety theory into fundamental agreement with the implicit assumptions of the great religions of the world concerning anxiety, namely, that it is a product, not of too little self-indulgence and satisfaction, but of too much; a product, not of overrestraint and inhibition, but of irresponsibility, guilt, and immaturity (cf. the earlier references to the writings of David). It gives us a more hopeful and healthier conception of the nature of psychotherapy and of the educative process generally. And above all, it suggests that the ethical accomplishment of untold past generations, as imbedded in the conscience of modern men and women, is not a stupid, malevolent, archaic incubus, but a challenge and guide for the individual in his quest for self-fulfilment and harmonious integration.

From the more technical point of view, this reformulation of anxiety theory has a number of interesting implications, only two of which we can here mention. In the first place, it throws light upon the question—much debated in psychoanalytic literature—as to whether repression should itself be regarded as a symptom or whether it should instead be looked upon as the prerequisite of symptom formation, a primal pathogenic act—partly conscious and partly unconscious—which provides the background conditions for true symptom formation. In one respect repression is indeed like a symptom: it is unrealistic. But the problem toward which this unrealism is directed, while in one sense the same, is in another sense different. A true symptom is directed toward the banishment of anxiety, whereas repression is aimed at a different psychological condition, namely fear, particularly moral fear or guilt. But though

[6] It is seriously misleading if I seem to imply here that this alternative formulation is new. A common and certainly very old precept of religion is: Be good and you will be happy. Or, as Archbishop Tillotson more eloquently said, "To be happy is not only to be freed from the pains and diseases of the body, but from anxiety and vexation of spirit; not only to enjoy the pleasures of sense, but peace of conscience and tranquillity of mind" (quoted from *Johnson's Dictionary,* 1876 edition). Rather have I simply attempted to state an old hypothesis, but scientifically phrased, without the theological overtones.

experientially different, these two states are ultimately the same; for, if the foregoing analysis is valid, anxiety is merely fear which has been converted into anxiety by the act of repression. Or, more precisely said, anxiety is merely fear (anticipation of punishment, guilt, bad conscience) which has been repressed as such and which, incapable of being kept completely repressed (by the forces of the ego and id), periodically breaks forth into consciousness, there to be experienced, not as what it is, namely social fear and guilt, but as anxiety.[7]

The second and final point to be made in this connection is one that follows from what has just been said. Previously we have noted that Freud's first theory held that anxiety is simply dammed-up sexual energy which, as it bursts into consciousness, undergoes a qualitative transformation: instead of being experienced as lust, it is experienced as anxiety. We now see that the revised theory of anxiety which has been proposed in the present paper is in one important respect much closer to Freud's first theory of anxiety than to his later one. What we have here proposed is that instead of dammed-up libido, it is "dammed-up" moral force and guilt which, as they erupt into consciousness, undergo the qualitative transformation and are experienced, not as guilt, but as anxiety.

With this formulation we are now able to return to our earlier remark to the effect that in one important respect Kierkegaard was more nearly right in his theory of anxiety than was Freud. With uncanny insight, Kierkegaard referred to the "qualitative leap" whereby "objective dread" or guilt is transformed into "subjective dread" or anxiety proper. He saw with amazing clarity—though he did not use the modern phraseology—that it is with this "leap" that a person passes from normality to neurosis; and he also implied that it is by a similar "leap," but in the reverse direction, that the individual ceases to be neurotic and becomes normal.[8]

Nothing could be truer in the light of my own clinical, as well as personal, experience than the proposition that psychotherapy must involve acceptance of the essential friendliness and helpfulness of anxiety, which, under such management, will eventually again become ordinary guilt and moral fear, to which realistic readjust-

[7] Cf. the position suggested in the last section of this chapter.

[8] One can hardly regard it as other than mischievous that so many modern writers stress the view that there is a "continuum" between normality and abnormality, that there is "no sharp dividing line" between the two. It seems more nearly true that the ego attitudes of the neurotic and of the normal person are as different as night and day; and the change from one to the other is often so dramatic that, as Alexander and French (1946) suggest, one can justifiably speak of it as a "conversion." Cf. Sheen (1949).

ments and new learning can occur. This, I submit, is in marked contrast to the Freudian imputation that anxiety is an impostor—foreign, unfriendly, and destructive.[9] This, it appears, is precisely the view of the patient; and it is hardly surprising, as Alexander and French (1946) have recently pointed out, that orthodox psychoanalytic treatment only too often leads to a "deep narcissistic regression" rather than to the growth in personal maturity, social adequacy, and happiness which one has a right to expect of a really competent therapy.

With these remarks it becomes apparent that in thus revising basic anxiety theory, we are not engaging in an idle intellectual exercise; nor are we merely proposing a different approach to psychotherapy and education. Instead we are suggesting the need for a radically changed attitude, generally, toward social authority, toward the internal representative of that authority, and indeed toward the validity and vitality of the whole human enterprise. Freud often asserted that psychoanalysis had nothing to do with philosophy, that it was science, pure and simple. It now appears that Freudian psychoanalysis not only involved philosophy but, in some respects, bad philosophy; and it was the failure to recognize where his science ended and his philosophy began that led Freud and his followers to some of their most grievous and fundamental errors.

II. Kierkegaard on Anxiety

The most comprehensive historical treatment of the problem of anxiety is that recently published by May (1950). In this we see again that anxiety is by no means a twentieth-century phenomenon nor one that is of interest only to psycho-clinicians. Niebuhr and Tillich are cited as typical of the contemporary theologians for whom anxiety is of central importance, and reference is made to the literary treatment accorded to it by such writers as Auden and Kafka. However, for present purposes, the most important feature of May's work is his review of writers prior to the present century who have touched upon the anxiety problem. Only with the Renaissance, says May, do we get an intellectual climate which was favorable to explicit consideration of this problem. This may have been due to an actual increase in the prevalence and intensity of anxiety, rising out of the greater emphasis upon "freedom" and "liberty" for the individual and an accompanying

[9] For a statement of Freud's attitude toward organized society and, implicitly, toward the intrapsychic representative thereof, namely, conscience, see *Civilization and its discontents* (1930).

loss of the personal security which is said to have characterized life in the Middle Ages. Or it may be that only in the Renaissance did writers have sufficient intellectual curiosity and daring to deal with an experience which was by no means new to their generation.

In any event, it was not until the seventeenth century that anyone ventured even near the problem of anxiety. May briefly alludes to Pascal in this connection, and then has this to say about Spinoza: "At several points in his analysis Spinoza stands on the threshold of the problem of anxiety, as, for example, when he defines fear in juxtaposition to hope, but he does not cross the threshold into the problem of anxiety itself" (p. 4).

Writers of the eighteenth century contributed little to the problem of anxiety, but the nineteenth century produced, in the person of Søren Kierkegaard, a writer who seems likely to become more important in this century than he was in his own time. Kierkegaard has been "discovered" by American readers only since 1940, as indicated by the fact that it is within this period that his major works have been issued in English. In ways which cannot be fully indicated here, it seems that his contributions to anxiety theory are second in importance only to those of Freud. Freud had the advantage of being completely naturalistic in his thinking, where Kierkegaard was still operating on the basis of strong theological presuppositions; yet in ways which will be apparent later, Kierkegaard seems to have been nearer the truth in certain respects than was Freud. But, paradoxically enough, Freud had to live and write before the earlier work of Kierkegaard could be correctly understood and appreciated.

Because of the difficulty which the human race has experienced in developing the concept of anxiety, many of Kierkegaard's writings must have been thoroughly incomprehensible to his contemporaries, as they are likely still to be to a modern reader who is not familiar with Freud. But to one who knows Freud, Kierkegaard suddenly appears as an inspired genious who lived before his time.

Kierkegaard now appears to have been the first of the modern "depth" psychologists. As Lowrie remarks in his introduction to *The concept of dread* (1946),[10]

---

[10] The title of this book might have been more appropriately translated as *The concept of anxiety*, but was instead translated as *The concept of dread* for the following reasons: "The very title of this book reveals a serious lack in our language: we have no word which adequately translates *Angst*. In the first translations of fragments of S. K., published by Professor Hollander in 1924, he used the word 'dread,' and everyone has agreed to continue it after a desperate search for something better. The Spanish translation uses *angustia;* Unamuno, writing in French, spoke of *agonie;* it has been seen that both the French translators use *angoisse*. The words rightly indicate the distress of the moment, but do not suggest what is

This work and *The sickness unto death*—the only books expressly described as psychological,[11] though by no means the only ones in which this interest is prominent—are sufficient in themselves to insure to Søren Kierkegaard a prominent and peculiar place among psychologists. A very peculiar place indeed, for in his time, and still more in ours—even when it does not decline to admit that there is such a thing as a psyche—psychology has been content to remain so much on the surface that there is not much to distinguish it from histology, and even the so-called "deep psychology" of Freud and Jung and Adler does not delve deep enough to discover soul (p. xi).

With only slight charity of interpretation one can, indeed, say that Kierkegaard in many rather specific ways anticipated Freud. That he anticipated Freud's emphasis upon *ambivalence* or conflict is evident in more than one place. He speaks repeatedly about the "ambiguity of dread" and specifically refers to an individual who with respect to dread both "loves it and flees from it" (p. 4). And at greater length he speaks of this "ambiguity" in such a way as strongly to suggest what Freud came to refer to as *reaction formation.*

For dread is a desire for what one dreads, a sympathetic antipathy. Dread is an alien power which lays hold of an individual, and yet one cannot tear oneself away, nor has a will to do so; for one fears, but what one fears one desires. Dread then makes the individual impotent, and the first sin always occurs in impotence (p. xii).

Like Freud, Kierkegaard also saw an important relationship between sexuality and anxiety, for he opens one chapter with the statement, "With sinfulness was posited sexuality. That same instant the history of the race begins. Since sinfulness moves by quantitative increasements, so does dread also" (p. 47).

In passages which are too long to reproduce here, it seems likely that Kierkegaard understood what Freud characterized as the "return of the repressed," and many similar parallelisms might be cited. But perhaps the most striking similarity is in what may be called the psychic anatomy, or topography, which the two writers

essential to the experience S. K. deals with, that it is an apprehension of the future, a presentiment of a something which is 'nothing' . . . " (pp. ix–x). Early translators of Freud encountered the same difficulty. For example, in *Social psychology and the analysis of the ego* (1921), the word "dread" is used throughout in place of "anxiety," which appears in later translations. Since, in their original writings, both Kierkegaard and Freud used the German word *Angst* and since it is clear that they were talking about the same phenomenon, it will be assumed that whenever in the ensuing discussion the word "dread" appears the reader will automatically interpret it as meaning "anxiety," in the modern technical sense of the term.

[11] The subtitle of *The concept of dread* is *A simple psychological deliberation oriented in the direction of the dogmatic problem of original sin.*

set up for theoretical purposes. Kierkegaard summarized his assumptions in this connection thus:

> Man is a synthesis of the soulish and the bodily. But a synthesis is unthinkable if the two are not united in a third factor. This third factor is the spirit (p. 39).

Clearly the bodily component corresponds to what Freud characterized as "id." The "soulish," or psychic, factor corresponds equally well to Freud's "ego." And from the way in which Kierkegaard uses the term "spirit" in a number of different contexts, it is not too much to suppose that for him it was roughly equivalent to "superego" or conscience.

That these two writers, working independently,[12] should emerge with closely similar notions ceases to be remarkable when one realizes that both of them were using essentially the same method, the method of clinical psychology. Although Freud used introspection and self-analysis—cf. the analysis of his own dreams (1913) and his autobiography (1935); Sachs (1944) remarks that he used his own mind as his "laboratory"—Freud derived most of his data from the study and treatment of other individuals who were suffering from various forms of neurosis. Kierkegaard, by contrast, was not a clinician in the formal sense, but he was deeply involved in the quest for self-understanding and in the process of self-analysis. Thus, as Lowrie remarks,

> S. K., because he was intent upon psycho-analyzing himself, his own ego, could not well forget that he was dealing with a soul, a synthesis of soul and body; and because spirit is not obviously and inevitably present in this synthesis, he was compelled (in the best sense of the word) to revert to the Greek and New Testament trichotomy: body, soul, and spirit.
>
> It will not do to dispose of S. K.'s psychology by remarking that his own soul, the soul he chiefly studied, was a sick soul. For not only could he reply that all souls are sick, and that the notion that one has a "healthy-minded" soul is the most perilous of all sicknesses; but all pathologists will agree with him that the study of abnormal states is essential for the understanding of normal health. If it is true that few men have had so sick a soul to deal with as had S. K., and also that no one of them has ever probed so deeply into his sick soul, with such intellectual competence, we may reasonably expect to learn something from his psychology (p. xii).

Perhaps the best place to begin the study of Kierkegaard's explicit treatment of the anxiety problem is with his understand-

[12] Kierkegaard could not have been influenced by Freud because of antedating him; and Freud's writings and information derived from his associates give no indication that he was at all aware of Kierkegaard.

ing of the fact that for persons of his day he was dealing with an unfamiliar concept, for he says: "People have often explained the nature of original sin, and yet they lacked a primary category—dread, which really is its determinant" (p. xii). And elsewhere he says:

> Dread is a qualification of the dreaming spirit, and as such it has its place in psychology. . . . One almost never sees the concept dread dealt with in psychology, and I must therefore call attention to the fact that it is different from fear and similar concepts which refer to something definite, whereas dread is the reality of freedom as possibility anterior to possibility. One does not therefore find dread in the beast, precisely for the reason that by nature the beast is not qualified by spirit (p. 38).

Three aspects of the excerpt call for comment. "Dreaming spirit" may at first seem but a vague, poetic metaphor; but we have a cue to its interpretation in the earlier suggestion that for Kierkegaard "spirit" was equivalent to what "superego" was for Freud. And if we translate "dreaming" to mean "sleeping," "dormant," or "repressed," we arrive at the statement: Dread is a consequence or manifestation of a repressed superego (cf. Section I).

Next it is instructive to note Kierkegaard's clear perception of the fact that anxiety is not the same as fear and that the reason for this difference is that ordinary fear is fear with a conscious object, a fear *of* something; whereas anxiety is a fear without a conscious object, a fear or dread of "nothing." Poe called it "that nameless terror" (22). And Freud has differentiated it from fear in a number of different ways, of which the following are the most important:

> In my opinion, *anxiety* relates to the condition and ignores the object, whereas in the word *fear* attention is directed to the object . . . (1935, p. 343).

> Anxiety is undeniably related to expectation; one feels anxiety *lest* something occur. [Translator's note: That is, the German usage is: *Angst vor etwas*—literally, anxiety *before* something, instead of *of* something.] It is endowed with a certain character of indefiniteness and objectlessness . . . (1936, pp. 146–47).

Using a somewhat different terminology, Freud elsewhere makes this distinction as follows:

> We then started from the distinction between objective anxiety [fear] and neurotic anxiety [anxiety proper], the former being what seems to us an intelligible reaction to danger—that is, to anticipated injury from without—and the latter altogether puzzling and, as it were, purposeless (1933, p. 114).

Finally it should be noted that in observing that one does not "find dread in the beast, precisely for the reason that by nature the beast is not qualified by spirit," Kierkegaard is apparently showing his awareness of the fact that in lower animals conscience is much less highly developed than in man. By implication he may also be saying that because lower animals use symbols much less extensively than does man they are less aware of "possibility" and therefore less expectant, less anxious.

In view of the preceding discussion, it is interesting to note that Kierkegaard makes a distinction between "objective dread" and "subjective dread." Though vague and colored by theological considerations, this distinction is noteworthy as an adumbration of another one of Freud's theses. In discussing the transition from the one to the other of these states, Kierkegaard says:

> Thus dread is the dizziness of freedom which occurs when the spirit would posit the synthesis, and freedom then gazes down into its own possibility, grasping at finiteness to sustain itself. In this dizziness freedom succumbs. Further than this psychology cannot go and will not. . . .
>
> This may be expressed by saying that nothing which is the object of dread becomes, as it were, more and more a something.
>
> We shall now consider a little more particularly that *something* which the nothing of dread may signify in the latter individual (pp. 56–57).

Consider now the following sentences from Freud:

> A *real* danger is a danger which we know, a true anxiety [i.e., fear], the anxiety in regard to a known danger. Neurotic anxiety [anxiety proper] is anxiety in regard to a danger which we do not know. . . . By bringing into consciousness this danger of which the ego is unaware, we obliterate the distinction between true and neurotic anxiety and are able to treat the latter as we would the former (1936, pp. 147–48).

Instead of saying, with Freud, that therapy is accomplished when anxiety is converted into objective fear, Kierkegaard states that "It is only at the instant when salvation is actually posited that this dread is overcome" (p. 48) and that "The ambiguity lies in the relation; for so soon as guilt is posited, dread is gone, and repentance is there" (p. 92). The words are different, but the underlying thought is clearly the same. However, this similarity prevails only so long as both authors keep on a relatively high level of abstraction. When they descend to details and means, their teachings come into sharp contrast. The most striking and fundamental difference is that for Kierkegaard anxiety is a constructive, "saving," "educative" experience, whereas for Freud it is destructive, pathogenic, and alien to the best interests and aims of the affected individual. From the standpoint of psychotherapy and many other practical considerations, this issue is of such central importance that it needs full elaboration. As a first step to this end, the following section will be devoted to a systematic statement of Freud's basic assumptions concerning the nature of anxiety.

III. Freud's "Two Theories" of Anxiety

Many conjectures have been made as to why Freud's formulations have proved so controversial. Freud himself attempted to interpret the opposition he encountered as a form of "resistance," comparable to that which he had learned to expect in the neurotics who came to him for treatment. This interpretation involves two assumptions: (1) that Freud was right and the patients wrong and (2) that Freud was right and the world wrong. He conceded that he had "disturbed the sleep of the world" and felt that, although he received small immediate thanks for his efforts, the future would vindicate him.

Here let us consider a different explanation of the mixed feelings which Freud's pronouncements have aroused, namely the possibility that some of these are profoundly right, thus generating support, and that some of them are profoundly wrong, thus leading to rejection. At first a proper sorting and evaluation were impossible. But now, at a greater distance, we may be able to come nearer to success in this venture.

It seems likely that the future will support Freud in respect to two of his most daring hypotheses. He seems to have established for all time the proposition that neurotic actions, or "symptoms," differ from ordinary "habits" primarily in that the former are motivated by and are perpetuated because they lessen the drive of anxiety, whereas "normal" habits are motivated by and are perpetuated because they lessen other drives, such as hunger, thirst, cold, fatigue, sex, fear, etc. In terms of modern learning theory, anxiety is *the problem* and the symptom is the "habit" or *solution.* Nor is the scope of this explanation limited just to the psychoneurotic symptoms, narrowly conceived. As we have seen in earlier sections, this hypothesis brilliantly accounts for a wide variety of so-called "addictions," "vices," and common "bad habits."

It seems likely that the second great insight for which Freud will receive everlasting credit is that anxiety itself can be properly conceptualized only by invoking the dynamism of *repression.*[13] We

[13] For a qualification of this point of view, see Section IV.

have just seen the extent to which Kierkegaard was disadvantaged because he lacked an adequate understanding of this phenomenon; and the writings of King David, otherwise so astute, show a similar defect. It is the phenomenon of repression that enables us clearly to differentiate between fear and anxiety; and it is the elimination of this phenomenon which is seen as essential for anxiety to be transformed back into fear and for the neurotic to become normal. Without the concept of repression, anxiety is as meaningless and puzzling intellectually as it is experientially.

It is only when we come to the question of the ultimate nature of anxiety that Freud's inferences appear to have been unsound. His conceptual ineptitude in this area did much to counteract the practical gains which might otherwise have resulted from his formulations concerning the nature of symptom formation and repression. In an earlier section Freud has already been quoted as saying of anxiety that "It is genuinely a question of hypotheses; that is to say, of the introduction of the right abstract ideas. . . ." It becomes increasingly apparent that Freud never succeeded in capturing the "right abstract ideas" concerning anxiety and that as a consequence psychoanalytic theory has failed to provide a really adequate psychology of personality and that it is for the same reason that psychoanalytic therapy has remained at best only partially efficient, even in the seemingly most favorable cases.[14]

It is difficult to determine how much confidence Freud felt in his postulations concerning anxiety. In certain passages, such as the one just alluded to, it would seem that his views were very tentative indeed; but further study of his writings suggests that this display of finely suspended judgment may have been merely one of the numerous rhetorical devices which he used so skilfully. In his earlier papers Freud expressed a conviction, verging on dogmatism, that anxiety was undischarged sexual excitation. To quote:

> In all the cases I have analyzed it was in the sexual life that a painful affect . . . had originated. It is easy to see that it is precisely in regard to the sexual life that unbearable ideas [which then get repressed] most frequently arise (Freud, 1894a, p. 67).
>
> Why does the nervous system under such conditions—of psychical incapacity to master sexual excitation—take on the particular affective state of anxiety? . . . *The nervous system reacts to an internal source of excitation with a neurosis, just as it reacts to an analogous external one with a corresponding affect* (1894b, pp. 101–2).

---

[14] For attempts to evaluate the therapeutic accomplishments of psychoanalysis, see Dollard (1944), Hendrick (1939), and Bibring (1937). Cf. Freud (1935).

Phobias do not occur at all when the vita sexualis is normal, that is, when the specific determinant is absent; by this specific determinant we mean a disturbance of the *vita sexualis* by deflection of the somatic away from the psychical field (1895, pp. 120–21).[15]

In referring to this theory many years later, Freud (1933), characterized it as follows:

[My original theory held that] the most frequent cause of anxiety neurosis is undischarged excitation. A libidinal excitation is aroused, but is not satisfied or used; in the place of this libido which has been diverted from its use, anxiety makes its appearance. I even thought it was justifiable to say that this unsatisfied libido is transformed into anxiety (p. 115).

The first attempt of Freud to formulate a theory of anxiety can hardly be said to have been a success. It held, in essence, that anxiety occurs whenever "libido," the all-powerful and pervasive sexual instinct, is frustrated. According to this hypothesis, anxiety *is,* in fact, merely transformed libido: what is normally experienced as pleasurable becomes, under the pressure of frustration, tormenting and painful.

Eventually Freud realized that this theory of anxiety raised more problems than it settled, and he discarded or at least amended it. Frustration, he maintained in his second theory, was still the condition of anxiety, but the mechanisms were different. A repressed impulse, usually sexual but perhaps aggressive, presses forward for gratification; this impulse arouses an anticipation of external disapproval and punishment; and the resulting feeling is that of anxiety. Since the impulses which arouse this particular species of fear are *internal* and *unconscious,* anxiety has the peculiar quality of "nameless terror" which distinguishes it from ordinary, objective fear. Anxiety, said Freud, is thus a "signal" that a dangerous impulse is about to erupt into consciousness and serves automatically to strengthen the forces holding this impulse

---

[15] Other clinicians have confirmed Freud's observation that neurotics tend to show impairments in their sexual functioning and that individuals who are leading a normal sex life rarely turn up in the clinician's consulting room. But the inference which Freud drew from this observation is not the only one which might logically be justified. His conclusion was that the impaired sexual functioning was the *cause* of the neurosis; therefore therapy, he felt, should be directed toward overcoming the specific sexual impairment or "inhibition." Equally plausible—and dynamically better founded—is the inference that sexual impairment and neurosis are simply different aspects of the same personality disorder and are common consequences of a basic disturbance in the individual's human relationships. In other words, according to the latter view, the person who is capable, in marriage and elsewhere, of *good personal relationships* has the double reward of good sexual adjustment and of freedom from neurosis, so-called. A person who, in such relationships, does not have basically good interpersonal skills tends to suffer the joint consequences of sexual impairment and *other* neurotic difficulties.

under repression. As a corollary, therapy consists in weakening the forces of repression and allowing the imprisoned impulses to come into full consciousness and to achieve appropriate gratification.

The following excerpts give in Freud's own words what, for present purposes, are the essential features of this second theory of anxiety:

> The division of the mental personality into a superego, ego and id, which I spoke about in the last lecture, has forced us to take up a new position with regard to the problem of anxiety. In assuming that the ego is the only seat of anxiety, and that only the ego can produce and feel anxiety, we have taken up a new and secure position, from which many facts take on a new aspect (1933, pp. 118–19).
>
> I cannot tell you all the individual steps of an investigation of this kind; let it suffice to say that, to our astonishment, the result was the reverse of what we had expected. It is not the repression that creates the anxiety, but the anxiety is there first and creates the repression! But what sort of anxiety can it be? It can only be fear of a threatening external danger; that is to say, objective anxiety. It is true that the boy is afraid of the demands of his libido, in this case of his love for his mother; so that this is really an instance of neurotic anxiety. But this being in love seems to him to be an internal danger, which he must avoid by renouncing his object, only because it involves an external danger situation. And in every case we have investigated we have obtained the same result. It must, however, be confessed that we were not prepared to find that the internal instinctual danger was only a halfway house to an external and real danger situation (1933, pp. 119–20).

This second theory is an advance over Freud's first one.[16] It is not only more intelligible from the standpoint of common sense; it also has the advantage of being easily translatable into the concepts of modern learning theory. Such a reformulation may be thought of as going somewhat as follows: A child experiences an impulse and, after the necessary trial and error, discovers behavior which results in gratification. Sooner or later, however, this behavior is apprehended by adults, who disapprove and punish it. The resulting conflict between desire and dread of punishment (Freud's "objective anxiety") may not be readily resolvable by means of other, socially acceptable modes of gratification, so the

---

[16] It is difficult to tell to what extent Freud regarded his second theory as really distinct from the first one and to what extent he regarded it as merely an extension or revision of the first. Although he speaks in the above quotation of having "taken up a new and secure position" with respect to the problem of anxiety, he has elsewhere (1936) remarked that the second theory merely "differs somewhat" from the first (p. 139) and that the first theory was not necessarily wrong but is now "of less interest to us" (p. 143).

child's only recourse may be to *repress* the dangerous impulse. The act of repression brings a kind of psychic peace, but the repression may not be strong enough to enforce this peace permanently. And it is precisely this periodic failure of repression that accounts, by this theory, (*a*) for the recurrent character of anxiety and (*b*) for the often relatively permanent nature of neurosis (cf. 19).

From the formal, theoretical standpoint, this formulation leaves little to be desired. It is certainly explicit, clear, and plausible. It is not, therefore, without a sobering sense of the seriousness of the obligation involved when one questions its correctness and proposes an alternative formulation. But we must also note the weaknesses of Freud's theory. It does not, for example, easily explain why many of the seemingly "freest" people, including the frank libertine, are often among the most anxious. It does not give a ready understanding of inferiority feeling and depression, which, intuitively, seem so intimately related to anxiety and which one tends increasingly to see clinically these days, instead of the more blatant "symptoms" which Freud mentioned most often.[17] Nor does it give a form of therapy which has much to recommend it, either on the basis of its popular reputation or on the basis of the scientific attempts which have been made to validate it. Conceptually and practically, the Freudian theory of anxiety leaves much to be desired.

IV. Fear and Anxiety, Normal and Neurotic

By way of summing up, let us recall that Freud posited (1) that neurotic symptoms are attempts on the part of human beings to diminish or avert anxiety and (2) that anxiety can be understood only if we link it dynamically with the process of repression. Freud further posited (3) that the direction of repression is always toward socially tabued impulses, notably those of sex and aggression. According to his "first theory," anxiety is simply unexpressed, unutilized "libido" which in bursting the bonds of repression erupts into consciousness, not as recognizable passion or lust, but in a different state which gives the experience of anxiety. In his "second theory," Freud no longer held that anxiety was merely transformed libido, but rather regarded it as an anticipation of

[17] In order to account for depression, suicide, and "masochistic" phenomena generally, Freud was impelled to go beyond his theory of anxiety and advance other hypotheses of a most involved and questionable nature. See Freud's *Beyond the pleasure principle* (1922) and his paper "Mourning and melancholia" (1917). Cf. Horney's strictures on this score (1939).

social condemnation or punishment which is tripped off whenever repressed impulses (of sex or aggression) threaten to return to consciousness and demand expression. However, since the immediate cause for the alarm thus experienced is internal and consciously unidentified, the resulting affect has the peculiar quality of anxiety.

The alternative view which has been put forward in Section I of this chapter holds that it is rarely, if ever, a repression of primal impulses which initially predisposes human beings to anxiety; instead it is a repression of the socially inculcated drives of fear, gratitude, and obligation that fall under repression and which, in the act of threatening to break through and again become conscious, produce anxiety.

The distinction here involved and its clinical importance could be readily illustrated by means of psychotherapy recordings, but such examples would be complicated and lengthy. The two following incidents from the author's own experience have the virtue of both simplicity and brevity.

While working on a monograph a few years ago, it became necessary to give the final examination in a large introductory course. The writer personally proctored the examination, during the course of which he felt a mounting tension, verging on anxiety. This feeling continued on into the evening, at which point he discussed it with his wife. As a result of this conversation, it became apparent that the tension represented a previously unrecognized conflict between (*a*) the wish to push ahead with the monograph and (*b*) the obligation to get the examination papers marked quickly and the grades for the course to the proper authorities. As soon as this conflict was fully acknowledged and the decision made to read and mark the papers as quickly as possible, the tension lifted completely.

A few months later the writer was en route by train to a professional meeting. He had just returned from the diner, about eight o'clock in the evening, and had read only a few pages in a technical book when he had a rather sharp thrust of anxiety. This was a very puzzling and punishing experience. The writer had only the most agreeable anticipations of the meeting, and there seemed to be nothing else that might justify the anxiety. If one were inclined to try to deal with anxiety along Freudian lines, one would begin to look either for repressed sexual or aggressive impulses. In the present instance one might say something like this to one's self: "Now when I was in the diner or returning therefrom, did I, by any chance, see some woman toward whom I had unrecognized desires, and is this what is making me anxious? Or, does the conductor on this train remind me of my father and did I hate my father, and am I trying to express aggression toward the conductor—but instead feel anxiety?" The actual resolution of the mystery went as follows. For a number of years the writer has made it a rule never to work in the evenings save under circumstances of special urgency. There was no urgency about the present situation; yet he was reading a technical book—and it was evening. As soon as this simple insight had occurred, there was immediately an experience of relief, the book was put away, and there was no more anxiety.

In both these illustrations it is clear that, under pressure of competing drives, conscience functions had been briefly dissociated, repressed. In both instances genuinely "neurotic" anxiety was involved, but the repressions were light; the conflict which had led to the repression was easily reconstructed; and a normal, fully conscious resolution was easily substituted for the dissociative, neurotic one. I would have searched long and unprofitably for a Freudian explanation of these two anxiety experiences; and in clinical practice, in general, I have found the Freudian approach far less efficient than is the one here proposed. The salient difference, as already noted, is that in the one instance we proceed to look for repressed "wishes," whereas in the other we look for a conflict which has been solved dissociatively, with the element which has fallen under repression being some kind of obligation, or "ought."

Sometimes the question is raised as to whether it is not possible for repression to go in *either* direction. I do not say that impulse repression is impossible; but my clinical experience indicates that this type of repression, if it occurs at all, is uncommon and probably unimportant. It is true that neurotics frequently complain of sexual impairments and give other indications of lowered self-expressiveness; but in all instances the manifestations turn out to be secondary effects rather than primal causes. The *basic* difficulty is personal immaturity, in the sense of an inability or unwillingness to face those forces, both internal (conscience) and external (social sanctions), which push us in the direction of social responsibility and moral adequacy.

The objection is also sometimes advanced that neurotics, far from being on bad terms with their consciences, let themselves be dominated by moral scruples only too completely; and in support of this argument, persons are pointed to who are obsessively clean, thrifty, punctual, honest, or overconscientious in some other way. However, such behavior is invariably a "smoke screen," which is designed to deflect suspicion from the individual's real weaknesses and characterological "soft spots."

It is not, therefore, these or related problems that constitute the real difficulty from the standpoint of formulating a sound anxiety theory. Nor is there any difficulty in differentiating anxiety as clinically encountered from ordinary fear: fear has an identifiable object and is perceptually specific, whereas clinical anxiety is pervasive and its cause "nameless." But what of "normal" anxiety—the anxiety which everyone occasionally has and to which we give the term "anxiety" no less than to the forms which are seen clinically? This is the situational "nervousness" which almost everyone has experienced, without regarding himself or being regarded by others as in any sense "neurotic."

Freud often spoke of "objective" or "normal" anxiety; but these terms were usually just synonyms for "fear." Nowhere, to my knowledge, did he ever discuss the problem of normal anxiety as a state which is qualitatively different from fear but yet is not neurotic anxiety.[18] In the following passage, I have previously touched tangentially on the problem:

> Personal integration is a precious thing, and once a satisfying, harmonious personality pattern has been achieved, the "strength of total ego" seems capable, in ways which have not yet been clearly analyzed, of being mobilized in support of any single part (habit) for which the going is particularly hard. In this sense we may grant to well-developed human personalities a certain type of "autonomy" . . . (15, p. 451).

But I am indebted to Dr. Rollo May for bringing the problem of normal anxiety to my attention with the emphasis which it deserves, first in conversations and later in the manuscript of his recently published book, *The meaning of anxiety* (1950). The following quotations will indicate the way in which Dr. May has approached this problem:

> The nature of anxiety can be understood when we ask *what* is threatened in the experience which produces anxiety. The threat is to something in the "core" or "essence" of the personality. *Anxiety is the apprehension cued off by a threat to some value which the individual holds essential to his existence as a personality.* The threat may be to physical or psychological life (death, or loss of freedom), or it may be to some other value which the indi-

[18] Recalling Freud's paper of 1908, "'Civilized' sexual morality and modern nervousness," I have reread it with the thought in mind that here he might have been using the term "nervousness" to refer to normal anxiety, as distinct from neurotic anxiety, or "neurosis." But from the explanation which he advanced (repressed sexuality), it is clear that for him "nervousness" was but a popular term for neurosis.

vidual identifies with his existence (patriotism, the love of another person, "success," etc.). . . . The occasions of anxiety will vary with different people as widely as the values on which they depend vary, but what will always be true in anxiety is that the threat is to a value held by that particular individual to be essential to his existence and consequently to his security as a personality (p. 191).

The diffuse and undifferentiated quality of anxiety refers to the *level* in the personality on which the threat is experienced. An individual experiences various fears on the basis of a security pattern he has developed; *but in anxiety it is this security pattern itself which is threatened.* However uncomfortable a fear may be, it is experienced as a threat which can be located spatially and to which an adjustment can, at least in theory, be made. . . . But since anxiety attacks the foundation (core, essence) of the personality, the individual cannot "stand outside" the threat, cannot objectify it, and thereby is powerless to take steps to meet it. . . . The fact that anxiety is a threat to the essential, rather than to the peripheral, security of the person has led some authors to describe it as a "cosmic" experience (Sullivan) (pp. 191–92).

Sullivan has remarked that the self-dynamism is developed in order to protect the individual from anxiety; the converse is as true, that mounting anxiety reduces self-awareness. In proportion to the increase in anxiety, the awareness of one's self as a subject related to objects in the external world is confused (p. 192).

Since anxiety threatens the basis of selfhood, it is described on the philosophical level as the realization that one may cease to exist as a self. This is phrased by Tillich as the threat of "nonbeing." One is a being, a self, but there is at any moment the possibility of "not being." The normal anxiety associated in the minds of most people with death is one common form of this anxiety (p. 193).

As an example of normal anxiety, let us consider an illustration which is pieced together from what persons who have existed under totalitarian governments have reported to the present writer.

A prominent Socialist was living in Germany when Hitler came to power. Over a period of some months he knew that some of his colleagues were being imprisoned in concentration camps or taken off to other unknown fates. During this period he existed in continual awareness that he himself was in danger, but he never could be certain *if* he would be apprehended, or, if he were, *when* the Gestapo would come, or, finally, *what* would happen to him if he were arrested. Throughout this period he experienced the diffuse, painful, and persistent feelings of uncertainty and helplessness which we have described above as characteristic of anxiety. And the threat confronting him was not merely that of possible death or inconvenience and discomfort of the concentration camp; it was a threat to the meaning of his existence as a person, since the freedom to work for his beliefs was a value which he identified with his existence. This individual's reactions to threat had all the essential characteristics of anxiety, yet it was proportionate to the actual threat and could not be termed neurotic.

Normal anxiety is, like any anxiety, a reaction to threats to values the individual holds essential to his existence as a personality; but normal anxiety is that reaction which (1) is not disproportionate to the objective threat, (2) does not involve repression or other mechanisms of intrapsychic conflict, and, as a corollary to the second point, (3) does not require neurotic defense mechanisms for its management, but can be confronted constructively on the level of conscious awareness *or* can be relieved if the objective situation is altered (pp. 193–94).

. . . Every individual experiences greater or lesser threats to his existence and to values he identifies with his existence in the course of his normal development as a human being. But he normally confronts these experiences constructively, uses them as "learning experiences" (in the broad and profound meaning of that term), and moves on in his development (p. 195).

In dealing with persons in situations with which their age and objective capacities fit them to cope adequately, a handy distinction between normal and neurotic anxiety is *ex post facto,* i.e., how the anxiety is used; normal anxiety being that which is used for a constructive solution to the problem which causes the anxiety, and neurotic anxiety being that which results in defense from and avoidance of the problem (p. 199).[19]

In discussing the relationship between anxiety and fear, May remarks:

Until recent years the distinction between fears and anxiety has been frequently overlooked in psychological studies, or the two affects have been

[19] The problem which May here poses is an exceedingly interesting one. Sometimes an attempt is made to differentiate between normal and neurotic anxiety solely on the grounds that the one is "situational" whereas the other is "characterological." Put a little differently, this distinction holds that normal anxiety is a product of the present; neurotic anxiety, a product of the past. Although useful as a first approximation, this distinction is not ultimately satisfactory for the reason that, as previously noted in this volume, neurotic anxiety, upon analysis, always turns out to represent personality immaturities which are present, here and now, and which always involve objective or "situational" factors, namely the reactions of other significant persons if they were to know the full facts of the case. Nor does the "proportionality" or "disproportionality" of anxiety satisfactorily differentiate between the normal and neurotic varieties. Upon analysis, neurotic anxiety turns out to be no less "proportionate" than normal anxiety. The really distinctive thing about neurotic anxiety is the element of *dissociation* (or repression) which is always involved, and it is this peculiarity which, by causing anxiety to occur *out of its natural context,* gives it its appearance of disproportionality. This, then, as I see it, is the essential consideration—not what the person *does* about anxiety. One can, very clearly, behave either constructively or destructively with respect both to normal anxiety and to neurotic anxiety. The constructive or normal response to normal anxiety needs no illustration (see May, pp. 223–32). On the other hand, one may react destructively (symptomatically) with respect to normal anxiety, e.g., by getting intoxicated, gambling, or overeating, just as one may in response to neurotic anxiety. Finally, one can react constructively or "normally" to neurotic anxiety, i.e., one may seek professional help and allow the anxiety to keep one motivated to do the work of therapy. It is apparent, therefore, that we need not only the distinction between normal and neurotic anxiety, but also a distinction between constructive (normal) and nonconstructive (abnormal, pathological) *ways of dealing* with *both kinds* of anxiety.

lumped together on the assumption that they have the same neurophysiological base. But this failure to make a differentiation confuses the understanding of both fears and anxiety. The reactions of an organism in times of fear and of anxiety may be radically different, due to the fact that these reactions occur on different psychological levels of the personality.

It is now possible to answer the question: What is the relation between anxiety and fears? The capacity of the organism to react to threats to its existence and to its values is, in its general and original form, anxiety. Later, as the organism becomes mature enough neurologically and psychologically to differentiate specific objects of danger, the protective reactions can likewise become specific; such differentiated reactions to specific dangers are fears. Thus anxiety is the basic, underlying reaction—the generic term; and fear is the expression of the same capacity in its specific, objectified form. . . . If one is to speak of either emotion as derived, it is fear that is derived rather than anxiety. In any case, the customary procedure of subsuming the study of anxiety under fear, or trying to make anxiety intelligible through a study of fear, is, the present writer believes, illogical. The understanding of fears hinges upon the understanding of the prior problem, anxiety (pp. 204–5).

We speak of anxiety as "basic" not only in the sense that it is the general, original response to threat, but also because it is a response to threat on the basic level of the personality; i.e., it is a response to a threat to the "core" or "essence" of the personality rather than to a peripheral danger. Fears are the responses to threats before they get to this basic level. By reacting adequately to the various specific dangers which threaten him (i.e., by reacting adequately on the level of fears), the individual avoids having his essential values threatened, avoids being threatened at the "inner citadel" of his security system. If however he cannot cope with dangers in their specific forms, he will be threatened on the deeper level which we have called the "core" or "essence" of personality (p. 205).

I confess that for a long time I was at a loss to know how to evaluate so-called normal anxiety and how to fit it into a comprehensive theory, along with fear and neurotic anxiety. We know a great deal about fear, about the circumstances under which it is acquired, and how it then functions as a drive or motive (see Part I). And there is likewise growing clinical support for the view that neurotic anxiety arises when a social fear, having been repressed as a means of ending a conflict, threatens to return to consciousness. Thus far, we need only the familiar principles of stimulus-response psychology in order to account for these phenomena; but such a psychology has no place in it for such a concept as "normal" anxiety. In order to accommodate the latter, it is necessary, as May has found, to go to some form of *Gestalttheorie* or "ego psychology"; and in so doing we begin to see the possibility of developing a really unified type of theory, one that satisfactorily accounts for *all three*—fear, neurotic anxiety, and normal anxiety—alike.

Whatever else the "ego" or "self" may be, it is *a system, an organization.* Just as the physical body has an organic unity, so does the mind have a *psychic unity.* When the integrity, or unity, of the body is threatened, by injury or disease, the body registers *physical pain.* Analogously, may we not suppose that when the integrity or unity of the "self" is threatened by *severe conflict,* it registers *psychic pain* or *normal anxiety?* As May has indicated, fear is a reaction to or perception of external danger, which is mediated by the ego, very often with little or no "ego involvement." The ego structure is simply the vehicle for the fear reaction, just as it is for many other types of reactions and perceptions. But when the ego—the structure, the vehicle, the mechanism itself—is under stress, there is a resultant tension, or "pain," which is properly termed *anxiety.*[20]

A somewhat similar type of analysis is to be found in the volume by Syngg and Combs (1949). In a chapter entitled "People under threat: the anatomy of maladjustment," these authors say:

> We have described the basic need of the individual as the maintenance or enhancement of his phenomenal self (p. 115).
>
> It is this highly stable complex of differentiations which each of us is constantly attempting to preserve and enhance (p. 128).
>
> As a result [of threat] the person shows signs of tension arising from the threat he perceives. . . . This type of threatening situation is sometimes described as "conflict" (p. 131).

Syngg and Combs acknowledge the influence of Lecky (1945) and of Rogers (1942):

> Lecky first discussed this concept of an adequate self as a self-consistency. Rogers (1947, p. 364) later expanded on this concept and has stated the case as follows: "It would appear that when all of the ways in which the individual perceives himself—all perception of the qualities, abilities, impulses, and attitudes of the person, and all perceptions of himself in relation to others—are accepted into the organized concept of the self, then this achievement is accompanied by feelings of comfort and freedom from tension which are experienced as psychological adjustment. . . . The definition of adjust-

[20] Whereas fear is a "conditioned reaction," anxiety is "unconditioned," primitive, reflexive. Fear is learned, anxiety unlearned—an inherent property of a "self-system" (Sullivan, 1947) under stress. Miller and Dollard (1941) may be said to have foreshadowed this type of analysis with their reference to "the stimulation produced by conflict" (p. 41).

ment is thus made an internal affair rather than dependent upon an external reality" (pp. 135–36).

While a definite kinship of thought is to be recognized in the foregoing passages from Syngg and Combs, a truly remarkable parallelism is to be found in an unpublished paper by Dr. Camilla M. Anderson which has only recently, and largely accidentally, become available to me. Dr. Anderson (1949) says:

> Anxiety is psychic pain—in contrast to somatic pain. Every individual has a character structure or psychic anatomy, only partially known to himself. This psychic anatomy we shall call the psychological image, and it is comparable to the individual's concept of himself as a physical image. . . . Anxiety arises in any situation where (1) there is a threat to the integrity of an individual's image; and (2) where the individual maintains his image intact but experiences some disturbance in the function of any of his component parts. Automatic screening or compulsive selection of behavior is universal, perpetual, and normal and is carried out in order to keep the unity of the structure-function concept of the physical image intact (p. 3).

Although the influences of Freud, Sullivan, Rank, Rogers, and perhaps others can be detected in Dr. Anderson's paper, the composite has novelty, consistency, and, I believe, explanatory potential which the author has not at all fully exploited.

And Erikson (1943) succinctly puts the same point of view when he says: "Anxiety is for the personality what pain is for the body: a sign that coherence and integration are endangered by what is happening to one part or function" (p. 421).

Conceptually useful and empirically valid as the foregoing interpretation of normal anxiety seems to be, there is however an ambiguity that easily arises. Because this form of anxiety represents ego involvement and threat-to-self, because it indicates that something is "wrong," out of balance, unadjusted, there is a tendency to gloss over the really profound difference between this kind of anxiety and *neurotic anxiety,* and to treat them both as roughly equivalent.

Let us take a hypothetical individual who is in deep conflict but who is fully and painfully conscious of the elements in the conflict. Let us suppose that this individual is an adolescent boy who has just gone through puberty and that his conflict revolves around the problem of masturbation. Thus one factor will be the intensity of his sex drive and the other will be the feeling, instilled by parents and others, that it is unmanly, disgraceful, "wrong" to masturbate. Here we have a typical id-conscience type of debate, a social fear or guilt-feeling pitted against a powerful impulse or "wish." Here, we should expect, the individual's self-image will be under threat and he will experience considerable anxiety—but of a type which probably accompanies all major developmental phases. It betokens a personality *in crisis,* but it does not mean that there is as yet true psychopathology—or that there need be. A crisis is a decision-point, a kind of crossroads; and it is the nature of *the response thereto,* rather than the crisis itself, that determines whether the outcome will be destructive or will lead to greater strength of character and a higher personal synthesis.

If, in the example before us, the boy can communicate to others the nature of the dilemma which confronts him, new learnings will occur which will have the effect of modifying his earlier, childish conception of himself and permitting him to move forward on his march toward maturity. He will develop certain "principles" which will resolve his conflict and lessen his anxiety—but which, if subsequently violated, will reactivate his earlier confusion and suffering. From such crises, constructively resolved, comes adult "character."

But not all individuals have the requisite skills and courage—and social opportunity—to deal openly and realistically with their conflicts. Their first move toward dissociation involves deception and denial with respect to others; from these it is but a step, under the pressure of continuing anxiety, to deception and denial with respect to the self, i.e., repression. In the example under discussion, we may be sure that the repression will be in the direction of the moral reservations rather than in the direction of the sexual impulse—with an ensuing change in personality which is likely to be outwardly manifested as rebellion against authority and more or less elaborate rationalizations concerning the bogus character of morality and social conventions.

As a result of this strategy of dissociation and denial, the individual may succeed in banishing his anxiety, that is to say, the *normal anxiety* which is associated with a conflict in which the contending forces are consciously recognized; but in its stead there will now be a susceptibility to *neurotic anxiety,* i.e., a tendency for the dissociated parts of the personality to press forward for readmission into consciousness and in so doing to revive the old conflict; but since these forces are now "outlawed" and "nonexistent" as far as the conscious self is concerned, the tensions, apprehensions, and alarms which they produce can only be perceived as thoroughly mysterious and incomprehensible.

Whereas the techniques of counseling or ordinary wise, informed conversation are usually adequate for dealing with the anxiety which accompanies conflicts in which there have been no major dissociations, once the latter have occurred and become consolidated we pass over into the domain of psychotherapy proper. Said otherwise, normal anxieties can be dealt with at the level of ordinary common sense; but neurotic anxieties call for more specialized, technical treatment. The clear recognition of this distinction between essentially normal and pathological anxiety will, I believe, do much to help define the nature of training in various professional fields and draw lines of demarcation with respect to proper divisions of labor.

This is not the place to enter into a detailed discussion of depth therapy, but certain high lights should be noted. The major tool of the psychotherapist is *interpretation,* which means that after he has listened at length to the accounts and complaints of the patient, he begins to have associations, to "see connections" which to the patient are forbidden, barred. By expressing his thoughts, the therapist brings back into consciousness for the patient the conflicts which have been eliminated by means of repression. These acts of interpretation, or reassociation, relieve the patient's neurotic anxiety but they reactivate normal, situational anxiety. This the patient does not like, and there follows the familiar picture of resistance and negative transference. The patient wants the therapist to dissipate his neurotic anxieties forthwith. The therapist knows that the most he can do is to help the patient exchange his neurotic anxieties for normal ones, from which he may then move on to a degree of maturity which will vouchsafe the tranquillity that he seeks. It is therefore precisely this refusal of the therapist —or more correctly his inability—to help the neurotic sufferer find peace with immaturity that is responsible for the pyrotechnics of the transference. As Alexander Leighton once remarked to the author, "People come to a psychiatrist and ask him to relieve them of their symptoms, without being willing to alter their fundamental style of life." Kierkegaard long ago observed that anxiety is, or at least may be, *educative.* Neurotic anxiety is educative when it causes the afflicted individual to develop, not more symptoms, but habits which involve going to a therapist and doing the work of therapy; and when, as a result of therapy, the neurotic anxiety is converted into normal anxiety, the way is open for still further learnings of a developmental nature.

What, then, in summary can be said about the relationship between fear, neurotic anxiety, and normal anxiety? First we may observe that a normal person can have fear without anxiety. Secondly, we have seen that fear may be one leg of a conflict which will be so profound as to reach anxiety proportions, but this will be *normal* anxiety. If, now, in an attempt to get rid of the normal anxiety the afflicted individual represses the fear-element (usually it is a *social* fear), the conflict may be brought to a conclusion, but it will be at the price of leaving the person disposed to outcroppings of *neurotic* anxiety. In psychotherapy, the objective is to *replace dissociations by associations,* to substitute normal anxiety for neurotic anxiety, on the assumption that then and only then are the ordinary developmental processes able to operate and bring the individual's conflicts to a constructive rather than pathological conclusion.

CHAPTER 20

BIOLOGICAL VS. MORAL "FRUSTRATION" IN THE CAUSATION OF PERSONALITY DISTURBANCES

["The contemporary schools of psychology have in common a scant respect for the fundamental human experiences known as conscience, the sense of obligation, the feeling expressed by 'ought.' Personality and character tend to be analyzed into their elements, and motivation is reduced to the operation of reflexes or the activity of instincts. Psychology as now taught makes little endeavor to provide the student with opportunity or encouragement to consider a design for living. This book indicates some of the ways in which improved insight into the meaning and origin of moral obligation may contribute toward the attainment of happiness as well as toward a revision of psychology" (pp. v–vi).

"Experience with the personal adjustments of college students has shown that many of their problems hinge on moral dilemmas. Perhaps because of the declining vogue of philosophical studies, these students have little skill and less practice in the logical analysis of their difficulties. Nevertheless they have achieved a degree of freedom from such dogmatic codes as may have been impressed upon them in childhood. Now they find themselves with no satisfying principles of moral guidance except imitation and safety" (p. vi).

"Except perhaps for the extremes in each case, happiness is equally possible for young and old, poor and rich, dull and bright, ignorant and learned, employees and employer, followers and leaders, the man with the hoe and the man with the white collar. Its liveliness may be the same on widely different levels of health, talent, intelligence, power, resources, and responsibility" (p. 161, Hollingworth, 1949).

"People holding views like this may even venture to support them by consulting numerous textbooks of academic psychology. They will find it easy to gather an impressive list of such books in which the word *conscience* is not even mentioned in the index. When it is mentioned the topic may be glossed over in a sentence or two as if the writer were reluctant to devote more space to problems so essentially inscrutable" (p. 274).

". . . much of man's trouble is rooted in a troubled conscience. It is as important for the mental hygienist to understand the workings of conscience as it is for the garage mechanic to understand the mechanism of the carburetor" (p. 275).

"Another way of approaching these aspects of personality is to ask how does the child learn to behave in terms of 'I ought' as opposed to his unlearned 'I want' " (p. 288).

"In other words, the ideal of an integrated personality calls for the harmonious functioning of ego impulses in terms of the rules of the game as accepted and understood by the super-ego. When ego and super-ego cooperate like the members of an efficient team, *personality integration* has been achieved" (p. 296, Klein, 1944).

This paper is reprinted from the January, 1949, issue of *Progressive Education,* having been delivered in November, 1948, as an address at the YMCA Faculty Forum of the University of Illinois as the first of a series of presentations by various speakers on the topic "Stable Truths in an Unstable World." It extends the clinical and social points of view which have been expressed in the preceding chapters.]

In the domain of physical disease, it has been the usual experience to find that when causal factors are genuinely understood, both prevention and treatment improve dramatically. That the indices of personality disorder in our time—alcoholism and other addictions, financially ruinous gambling, invidious extravagance, marital failures, psychosomatic illness, lowered personal efficiency, and chronic unhappiness, not to mention the more spectacular diagnoses of criminality, neurosis, and psychosis—that these indices of personality deficiency and disorder continue to mount, with no discernible prospect of leveling off or dropping, suggests that in *this* area we are still groping for first principles.

The very term "neurosis" (or "nervousness") identifies a bias which was prevalent during the closing decades of the last century, namely that personality problems were due to neural weakness, degeneration, or infection—an "osis" of the nerves. Then followed a view which holds sway to the present day: the view of Sigmund Freud and his many followers that neurosis and related manifestations appear when there is a too complete holding in, because of parental discipline and social tabus, of certain biologically given impulses, notably those of sex and aggression. This inhibition or frustration of the animal drives is believed by the Freudians to produce *anxiety,* and it is in attempting to derive some measure of relief from this distressing emotion that the afflicted individual develops the bizarre and self-defeating habits or "symptoms" referred to above.

In the light of clinical experience, the plausibility of the Freudian position is impressive. It has given us at least a partial understanding of areas which were formerly mysterious and terrifying, and it has provided some useful scientific concepts and categories for thinking about problems which formerly baffled reason fairly completely. Yet the stubborn fact remains that Freudian thinking has failed to generate either a more hygienic social philosophy (thus leading to the more effective prevention of personality difficulties) or a highly efficient curative procedure. There are even indications that Freudian thought has in some instances actually aggravated, both at the individual and social level, the very conditions it is supposed to correct.[1]

The argument may be advanced that Freudian doctrine is still so new, relatively speaking, and has had so little chance to prove its worth on a really broad front that judgments should be suspended for some decades to come. There can be no unbiased denial that Freudian concepts have contributed powerfully to the development of a great intellectual ferment, but the objective evidence likewise suggests that Freudian theory and practice have not given us final solutions. As a method of treatment, Freudian analysis has led to outcomes which range from moderate successes to spectacular failures. Also noteworthy is the fact that when formal educational programs are founded explicitly on this basis, the results have often been little short of catastrophic.[2] And unsystematic but extensive evidence suggests that when parents have attempted to fashion their home management of children along what they take to be Freudian lines, they have frequently had occasion to regret the outcomes (16).

In some respects the tenets and practices of Progressive Education are reminiscent of Freudianism. There is in both cases a deep distrust of the purely traditional and a near glorification of what is biologically given. Just as Progressive Education (in pristine form) was "child-centered" (as opposed to society-centered), so did Freudianism emphasize the body and its pleasures and depreciate those parts of human personality which are socially derived, cultural, "spiritual." [3]

---

[1] For substantiation of this statement from very different points of view, see F. Alexander and T. M. French (1946); F. J. Sheen (1948); (18).

[2] The best example of this sort of thing has been reported by Willie Hoffer (1945). Anna Freud (1935) refers to experiments of this kind but gives no indication of outcomes. The institution described by August Aichhorn in *Wayward youth* (1936) was eventually closed by the Austrian government, in part because of community dissatisfactions. On one occasion the writer has seen psychoanalytic philosophy applied to the management of an institution for adolescent girls, with explosive consequences.

[3] For a good historical survey of the Progressive Education Movement, see Carleton Washburne's book (1926). The more recent history of the movement is indicated by articles published in *Progressive Education.*

Yet, despite this parallelism, the indications are that Progressive Education is not a lineal descendant of Freudianism. Instead they both appear to have sprung from common roots and seem destined to share a common fate.

A brief historical survey promises to provide useful information concerning the social and intellectual forces that gave rise to both these modern movements and to place them in a perspective that may point more clearly to hopeful future trends.

I. Emergence of the Culture-Idea

By 1850 Western Europe and America did not yet have the concept of *culture,* in its modern sense. In its place stood God's will and wisdom. The flesh was subordinated, at least as an ideal, to the values of the spirit; and conscience, as God's voice speaking in man, was taken as a reliable guide in both philosophy and practice.

But then, in 1859, appeared Darwin's *Origin of Species,* and an era came to an end. For increasingly large numbers of literate persons it was no longer credible that man was created, physically and mentally, in the Garden of Eden in 4004 B.C. Mounting evidence, particularly from geology and paleontology, showed that man's body is the product of organic evolution extending back millions of years. And if man's body has this type of development, then, asked a growing chorus of voices, is it not probable that his "mind," too, has had a similar history? No longer did it appear likely that social and moral truths had been miraculously revealed to man. Instead, it seemed ever more probable that the solutions to the problems of group life and individual conduct evolved, slowly and painfully, out of long human experience, no less than did the more prosaic knowledge of how to hunt and domesticate animals, how to plant and harvest, how to build houses and sail ships.

This newer perception was vividly set forth a quarter of a century ago in historian James Harvey Robinson's book *Mind in the making.* But even earlier, anthropologists had started operating their new science on the assumption that the ways, beliefs, and values of human societies are, in most instances, exceedingly old and that they represent, not revelation, but evolution—the hard-won residues of long, often heroic, trial-and-error learning. In fact, it was less than a score of years after Darwin published his great work that the English anthropologist, E. B. Tylor, gave the modern scientific definition of culture—and the God concept has been losing ground ever since. Functionally, the God idea and the culture idea are singularly similar, differing principally in that the one implies a supernaturalistic personification of the Good and the Useful, while the other does not. It would appear that one of the reasons for the widespread personal confusion and philosophic dislocation in our time is the abandonment by large numbers of persons of the God idea and their inability to replace it as yet with the more abstract, impersonal concept of culture.

II. Cultural Relativism and Personality Disorders

Against this background, a number of twentieth-century social developments and psychological dilemmas become intelligible. Prior to Darwin, moral values and social restraints had supernatural sanctions. But, with the decline of the God idea or theism, the old justifications and rationalization fell away. And what the new science of anthropology had to offer as a substitute was meager indeed. One of the first anthropological notions to gain general popularity was that of *cultural relativism:* all questions of ethics and values are relative to one's particular society and culture. To many persons, this view of the human situation meant that morality, as conventionally conceived, was a hoax or—to use an expression of the 1920's—"the bunk"; and moral expediency became for many the order of the day.

It was no accident that a Freud appeared in this era. In an earlier day, the common faith had been: "Be good and you'll be happy," i.e., normal, not neurotic. Now goodness became a hollow thing, and the only possibility of happiness that seemed to remain was something that had previously been disparagingly referred to as the "pleasures of the body." Granted his major premise, Freud's deduction was logical enough:

> Human happiness derives, directly or indirectly (i.e., through sublimation), from organic needs and satisfactions.
>
> Neurosis is a form of unhappiness.
>
> Therefore, neurosis must involve some unusually strong blocking of or interference with biological impulses.

Because medicine is pre-eminently an applied biological science, this "biologizing" of "mental disease" had a strong appeal in medical circles. Today Freudian thought is easily the dominant fashion in American psychiatry. But however congenial it may be to the medical mind, we again recall a perdurable reality: personality disturbances are increasing, *pari passu,* with the spread of Freudianism. Whatever its triumphs in other fields, modern medicine has not solved the riddle of the unhinged soul. Today civilized man is increasingly afraid of his anxieties. Since World War II, particularly energetic and, in some respects, revolutionary steps have been taken to stem the tide of neurotic suffering and personal disorganization. While continuing to support medical endeavors to cope more adequately with the problem of mental health, great national agencies, such as the Veterans Administration and the United States Public Health Service, are turning increasingly to psychology and the social sciences for leadership and new vision in these matters.

Although the public and its elected representatives have not been able to tell us precisely what to do or how to do it, their clear mandate is: Do something! Present indications are that our best hope of meeting this crisis lies in the direction of conceiving personality disorders, not as an outcome of biological frustration, but as an expression of *moral frustration.*

III. Personality Disorders and Moral Frustration

Elsewhere (19) I have elaborated upon the foregoing statement. Reduced to simplest terms, what it means is this:

Freud advanced three great assumptions, which underlie the contemporary medical approach to mental disorder. Two of these are sound, the third unsound and misleading.

One of Freud's earliest and most revolutionary contentions was that symptom therapy is futile. He believed that neurotic symptoms are essentially habits which the disturbed individual acquires as a means of reducing or avoiding anxiety. Thus by means of suggestion, authoritative command, or other procedures, it may be possible to make a compulsive hand-washer or an agoraphobiac give up his particular eccentricity, but the underlying problems remain and substitute symptom formation is very likely to follow. This is a principle which is today almost universally accepted in psychiatry and psychology.

Freud's second great insight was that anxiety, which is a peculiar form of fear characterized by vague dread and objectless apprehension, can be scientifically comprehended only if we posit a process which Freud called "repression." The consideration which sets anxiety apart from ordinary fear is that in the latter condition we speak of being afraid *of* this or that; we know *why* we are alarmed and can usually take more or less effective steps to deliver ourselves from the danger that threatens us. But in anxiety the situation is very different. We feel baffled, caught, trapped, and all the more terrified because our feelings seem so unaccountable. I believe it is again correct to say that all modern students of the problem of anxiety—and some ancient ones too—accept Freud's proposition that anxiety is simply fear the object of which has been lost from consciousness through a dynamic process known as repression (cf. 19).

But here the agreement ends. Freud went beyond these two generally accepted principles and made a special assumption about the nature of repression. As already indicated, he believed that it is almost always impulses either of lust or of hostility that get pushed below the threshold of consciousness and that it is when these impulses press against the repressing forces and threaten to erupt back into consciousness that the experience of anxiety is characteristically felt.

On the basis of evidence which I cannot easily reproduce here, I have come to feel that Freud was in error on this latter score. It now seems highly probable that although Freud was right about the nature of symptoms and the necessity of repression for the occurrence of anxiety, he was wrong in his assumption concerning the *direction* of repression. Many sources of present evidence indicate that most—perhaps all—neurotic human beings suffer, not because they are unduly inhibited as regards their biological drives, but because they have disavowed and repudiated their own moral strivings. Anxiety comes, not from repressed sexuality or pentup hatred, but from a denial and defiance of the forces of conscience.

I cannot begin to set forth the clinical evidence on which I base this point of view. Other, more extended papers will have to serve this function. Here it is more appropriate to indicate how this position fits in with a number of other types of observation.

IV. Some "Stable Truths" in Culture Theory

On an earlier page I noted a historical trend, extending now over almost a century, toward repudiation of the God idea. Since conscience is said to be the voice of God speaking in man, is it not reasonable to suppose that God and conscience have tended to fall into disrepute simultaneously, with an increasing disposition toward anxiety and its sequelae?

If I can read the signs of our time aright, one of the great tasks which confronts us in our quest for peace of mind and more meaningful existence is the *rediscovery of ethics*. For historical reasons which we have already examined, morality and personal responsibility have become unfashionable. A woman student recently phrased the situation aptly when she said, "I think my grandmother probably used the word *duty* at least ten times as often as I do." Because duty has traditionally been associated with a kind of religious logic which many persons can no longer assimilate, there has been a widespread tendency to reject duty as such, along with the supporting rationalization. Today it seems probable that human experience had shown the validity of the Ten Commandments long before Moses purportedly brought them down from Mount Sinai, and it seems equally likely that most if not all the social wisdom they contain will prevail even though the trek up Sinai be universally relegated to mythology.

It is at this point that we touch most vitally upon the problem of "Stable Truths in an Unstable World." As you know, my paper today is the first of a series of discussions which will approach this topic from a number of different angles. The first general impressions which we received from the budding science of anthropology suggested that truth itself was as unstable as "the world." But it is interesting, and reassuring to those who believe in the validity of a scientific attitude toward life, to find that anthropology is today in the process of isolating from the welter of contradictions and contrasts certain great social—if you will, *moral*—principles which are universal, stable, enduring. Here let me indicate three examples.

No successful and surviving society has ever been found in which considerable store is not set by the trait of personal consistency—the ninth commandment: "Thou shalt not bear false witness." Human beings simply cannot work and live together efficiently if they do not make their words match reality with reasonable fidelity, if they do not keep their agreements, and do not appear at appointed times and places.

No society can be a going concern unless there is some form of political authority. We sometimes make the mistake of thinking of aggressive behavior as being exclusively antisocial. We must remember that there is also such a thing as *prosocial* aggression, and that it is an essential element in parental discipline and in community control. This is by no means all there is to discipline and control, but it is apparently a universal ingredient thereof.

Finally I would mention the universality of belief in education. Every healthy society believes in itself, in its ways and values. These it insists upon perpetuating. Transmission of the culture may take place informally and incidentally, as in most nonliterate societies, or it may also take place formally and self-consciously, as in a great modern university such as this one; but the variations in process should not keep us from seeing the ubiquity of the purpose and goal.

I am sure that a well-informed anthropologist or broadly trained historian could adduce many other instances of "stable truths" in the realm of man's relationship with man. But perhaps the three illustrations I have given will suffice to show that science can and indeed does point the way to universal and abiding ethical principles, for the person who is minded to look for them.

If our particular era seems to be one of special confusion and instability, we must remind ourselves that within a comparatively short space of time we have come up against the problem of "one world." Space and time have been foreshortened to such a degree that we shall probably be involved for decades to come in working out solutions to the emergent problems. But even this, when seen in proper historical perspective, seems capable of being interpreted optimistically, rather than necessarily as a cause for despair and a tomorrow-we-die philosophy.

V. Religion, Medicine, or a Middle Ground?

If, in the preceding paragraphs, our discussion has taken a somewhat speculative and abstract turn, this has been an inadvertence. My principle concerns here today are very concrete, specific, earthy. I am asking with you this question: What can be done to stem the rising tide of mental disorder in our time? Historically, medicine and religion have failed to give the answer—medicine because of its biological biases, religion because of its otherworldly, mystical biases. Yet between the two of them, medicine and religion seem to come close to encompassing the whole truth. Perhaps we can say that each of them contains *half* the truth: the modern medical approach is right in that it is scientific, naturalistic, empirical; and religion is right in its contention that the problem of personal happiness and normality is inextricably bound up with the moral nature of man. Perhaps it is not too gross an oversimplification to suggest that our best hopes for improved happiness and better mental health lie in the direction of a *new* discipline, one that will combine a concern for *both* empiricism and ethics. If only the world can hold together politically for another generation, I think we will see very significant progress made along these lines.

As many of you will already know, psychiatrists and representatives of organized religion have recently been involved in a good deal of controversy over the cause and treatment of personality problems. Last summer the International Congress on Mental

Health, meeting in London, saw this issue debated more vigorously than perhaps any other. Some of the representatives of both sides of the argument are convinced that there can be no peace, no compromise. Others are inclined to feel that some sort of reconciliation and division of labor are possible.

Among the representatives of organized religion who take the latter position is Monsignor Fulton J. Sheen. In his booklet, *The modern soul in search of God* (1948), he makes the following statement:

> To prevent being misunderstood, let it here be stated unequivocally: (1) There is nothing wrong, but even something commendable, about a psychological method which cures mental disorders by making the unconscious conscious. (2) Not every mental disorder has an ethical or moral foundation. For that reason, medical science has a vast area in which it can legitimately operate. We wish to commend those genuinely scientific psychiatrists who, finding a spiritual disorder in patients, send them to a spiritual director, just as we, finding a mental disease in our spiritual patients, send them to a good psychiatrist (p. 35).

Time Magazine, in a feature story about Dr. William C. Menninger, current president of the American Psychiatric Association, president of the American Psychoanalytic Association, and chairman of the Group for the Advancement of Psychiatry (G. A. P.), published the following:

> The carefully reassuring statement, approved by the entire membership of the G. A. P., stated flatly that there is no conflict between psychiatry and religion, and concluded: "In the practice of his profession, the competent psychiatrist will therefore always be guided by this belief." [This pronouncement was made in part in response to Sheen's charge that medical psychoanalysis is based on "materialism, infantilism, hedonism, and eroticism."]
>
> Dr. Will's own position: "The psychiatrist deals with unconscious difficulties. To do this, he must often try to remove a sense of guilt. But, remember, neurotic guilt is not the same thing as real guilt. The minister . . . deals with . . . a *real* guilt over transgressing explicit moral laws, not the irrational guilt of the emotionally disturbed patient." [4]

This compromise is artificial and forced, but it is probably the only one that medicine and religion can make without one or the other ceasing to be what it necessarily must be. Monsignor Sheen's position is ambiguous in that he assumes that the unconscious, or repressed, part of the neurotic personality can be made conscious

---

[4] *Time,* Oct. 25, 1948, pp. 70–71.

without raising any moral, but only medical, issues. If, as now seems increasingly likely, what most often gets repressed are man's moral rather than his biological strivings, then the undoing of repressions is pre-eminently a moral enterprise, and no amount of doubletalk can make it a medical problem in the strict sense.

And Dr. Menninger is on equally unsafe ground when he speaks of purely neurotic or imaginary guilt. Very often neurotics torture themselves (and others) with excessive virtues of various kinds—in the confessional these persons are known as "the overly scrupulous"—but in all cases (save where the difficulty has a *purely organic basis,* such as a brain tumor or the like), I believe that this sort of behavior is but a smoke screen which is designed, consciously or unconsciously, to deflect suspicion from areas of real interpersonal and social immaturity and deficiency. The difficulty—and what Monsignor Sheen has quite properly objected to—is that most medical analysts proceed on the explicit Freudian assumption that anxiety arises because the "superego" or conscience is "too severe" and make it their business to try to soften it, weaken it, water it down, whereas the real problem is that the neurotic individual is himself trying to do this, too. Valid treatment should instead lie in the direction of helping the individual grow up, emotionally and socially, to the point where the demands of conscience and community are understandable and acceptable.

I know that the line of thought we have followed here today raises many questions, but I am yet to be convinced that any of them are necessarily unanswerable. I believe that public and governmental steps now being taken to expand and invigorate research, training, and treatment in the area of personality problems are sound, and I believe that psychology and the related social sciences are in a uniquely favorable position to render an important service in this connection.

Clinical psychologists are being trained in large numbers today who are well founded in the biological disciplines most closely related to their own field; and traditionally there has been a close connection between psychology and the fields of philosophy and religion. Psychology thus appears to occupy precisely the intermediate ground between medicine and religion on which a new and, let us hope, more effective discipline for attacking the manifold aspects of modern man's emotional and ethical suffering can be most solidly built.

CHAPTER 21

IDENTIFICATION: A LINK BETWEEN LEARNING THEORY AND PSYCHOTHERAPY

[In abridged form, this paper was given as an address in connection with the ceremonies dedicating the new Psychology Laboratory of the University of Southern California (June, 1950). It deals with a topic which seems likely to occupy an increasingly central place in personality theory and to prove highly fruitful from a research standpoint. This topic is alluded to in other chapters of this book (11, 18, 22, and 24).

The author is indebted, especially in respect to Section III, for stimulating suggestions received from the doctoral dissertations of two former students, Dr. Winifred S. Lair and Dr. Douglas P. Courtney. I am also grateful for useful comment on the part of Margaret P. Reeves.]

I remember hearing many years ago a story about a farmer who, having lived for a long time alone, decided to get a parrot for company. When the bird was at last obtained, the farmer set out to teach it to call him "Uncle" and devoted many long evenings to repetition, in the bird's presence, of the phrase, "Say 'Uncle.' " When, at length, the farmer's patience had worn thin because of no response from the bird, he got a stick and would hit the bird after each refusal to respond as commanded. But the latter procedure proved no more effective than the first; and finally the farmer, completely exasperated, grabbed the bird, carried it to the nearby chicken house, and tossed it inside.

The end of the story is not hard to anticipate: later the farmer heard a commotion in the chicken house and, upon investigation, found that the parrot was beating the chickens over the head with a stick and shouting, "Say 'Uncle!' Say 'Uncle!' "

This story, as is often the case with folklore, contains a number of subtle insights and was to prove prophetic of scientific developments which have occurred within the last two or three decades.

I. Imitation and Learning Theory

There has been no lack of awareness throughout recorded history of the fact that children learn the ways of their social group, not only as a result of their elders' conscious efforts to teach them, but also through a less conscious but often very powerful process that has been most often denoted by the term "imitation." Miller and Dollard (1941) attribute to Aristotle the "distinction of having first ascribed an important role to the fact of imitation"; and they quote him as saying that man "is the most imitative of living creatures, and through imitation learns his earliest lessons" (p. 311).

Plutarch's *Lives* was written in order to provide inspiring adult models for Greek youth to emulate; and the importance of "example" has been stressed by many religions. Pestalozzi shows an especially sensitive understanding of the fact that children develop their most basic traits of character, not as a result of rule-of-thumb *training,* but by virtue of actively reaching out for and taking into themselves essential aspects of the personalities around them.

In more recent times humanists, philosophers, and social theorists have written extensively upon this theme but without any unifying principle or coherent theory; for they lacked a *method* which would discipline speculation and rigorously order facts. Therefore, as the techniques of exact experimentation which had yielded such prodigious returns in the physical and biological sciences were applied to problems of human and animal behavior, there was widespread readiness to seize upon new "laws," however imperfect or partial, and to try to put them into practical operation.

The three American writers who probably exercised the greatest influence upon both popular and scientific thought in such matters during the first third of the present century are William James, John B. Watson, and E. L. Thorndike. James regarded *exercise* as the "great law of habit"; Watson stressed the Pavlovian concept of *conditioning;* and Thorndike propounded the law of *effect.* These writers and many of their followers have been intent upon discovering the first, most basic principles of learning and have either ignored *social learning* or have given advice to parents, teachers, and others which was limited in purview and not correlated with the profound, though unsystematized, insights which had been derived through long human observation and experience. In the fields of pediatrics and child care, "scheduling" and "habit training" emerged as deductions from these "scientific learning principles"; and teacher-training and classroom methods have likewise felt the impact of premature application of theories which were insufficiently elaborated.

An attempt to build upon and refine rudimentary learning theory which deserves special attention here was made by E. B. Holt in 1931 in his book *Animal drive and the learning process.* Holt saw imitation as having crucial importance in social psychology and personality development and made an attempt to understand it in terms of conditioning or contiguity learning. Holt noted that most of the responses made by a human infant *stimulate the infant himself,* as well as others. The infant *feels* changes in bodily posture, he *sees* his hands and legs move, and he *hears* his own vocalizations. Holt posited that the neural pathways involved in making a given response are still "open" when the response-produced stimulation occurs and that the resulting neural excitation will tend to flow back into these pathways, again producing the response in question. In this way Holt derived the concept of the "reflex-circle," by means of which he sought to explain the repetitive or "iterative" behavior commonly seen in infants.

Babbling and other vocal activity in infants provide good examples of this process. Let us assume that an infant makes the sound "da." While the motor outlets involved in making this response are still "open," the sound is heard: the resulting neural impulses flow into the same channels and again prompt the infant to say "da." The externally observed consequence is a succession of sounds: "Da, da, da, da, da." As this sequence occurs, the stimulus, "da," acquires an ever greater capacity to elicit the response involved in making such a sound. Therefore, when a parent or other person subsequently says, "Da, da, da," to the infant, this stimulus is likely to trip off the same response; and we say, "The baby *imitates* us!"

Holt's analysis had two great merits: (1) it was a challenge to those who had held that imitation occurred on a nonlearned, instinctive basis; and (2) it pushed learning theory beyond the point of making all social learning dependent upon active, self-conscious, deliberate training on the part of "the other-one." However, as Miller and Dollard pointed out a decade later, Holt's theory had various shortcomings, one of them crucial: The theory contained no satisfactory provision for the ultimate "damping" of reflex-circles, once they were set going. Unamended, this theory would seem to make living organisms into perpetual-motion automata, wholly lacking in the precision, variability, and spontaneity which they in fact display.

Absent in Holt's analysis is any systematic use of drive and drive reduction as significant psychological variables, despite the fact that "drive" appears in the title of his book. Holt tried to be a consistent monist and to make contiguity learning the sole and sufficient basis for his theory.

Struck by the inadequacies in Holt's treatment of the problem of imitation, Miller and Dollard undertook a no less monistic analysis but one based upon reward theory. They say:

The weakness in the Holt theory seems to be that he assumes that the connection between [for example] the vocal response and the auditory stimulus will be strengthened by mere temporal contiguity of these two events. This simple assumption does not adequately interpret the facts. A temporal relationship is undoubtedly one condition of establishing a connection between a stimulus and a response—a response to a cue must occur before it can be learned—but this does not seem to be the only condition essential to learning. It is urged in this instance, as elsewhere throughout this book, that reward is essential to the strengthening of a connection between response and stimulus, and that, without reward, extinction will occur regardless of temporal contiguity of stimulus and response (p. 276).

The theory of imitation developed by Miller and Dollard is, in essence, as follows: One organism happens to be doing what another organism is doing at the moment that some drive is reduced, some problem solved, a reward experienced. The situation, or stimulus-pattern existing just before the reward occurs is thus drive-plus-stimulation-coming-from-behavior-of-other-organism; and it is therefore the connection between this total *constellation* and the response which gets strengthened by the ensuing reward. If the response in question is regularly followed by reward when the "cue" provided by the behavior of the other organism is present, and only at such times, then this response on the part of the first organism will tend to occur only, or at least predominantly, when the same response is being made by the second organism. When this point is reached, we are inclined to describe the behavior of the first organism as "imitative." The authors give the following example:

Two children . . . were playing in their bedroom, which was adjacent to the family kitchen. The kitchen opened upon a back stairway. It was six o'clock in the evening, the hour when father usually returned home, bearing candy for the two children. While playing in the bedroom, Jim heard a footfall on the stairs; it was the familiar sound of father's return. The younger child, however, had not identified this crucial cue. Jim ran to the kitchen to be on hand when father came in the back door. Bobby happened on this occasion to be running in the direction of the kitchen and behind Jim. On many other occasions, probably many hundreds, he had not happened to run when Jim did. He had, for instance, remained sitting, continued playing with his toys, run to the window instead of the door, and the like; but on this occasion, he was running behind his brother. Upon reaching the kitchen, Jim got his candy and Bobby his.

On subsequent nights with similar conditions, the younger child ran more frequently at the mere sight of his older brother running. When he ran, he received candy. Eventually, the behavior, under pressure of continued reward, became highly stabilized, and the younger child would run when the older ran, not only in this situation but in many others where time and place stimuli were different. He had learned in this one respect to *imitate* his older brother, but he had not learned to run at the sound of his father's footfall (pp. 94–95).

To this type of imitation Miller and Dollard gave the name *matched-dependent behavior*—"matched" in the sense that the behavior of the one organism is *like* that of another and "dependent" in the sense that the former is *cued off* by the latter. These authors distinguish matched-dependent behavior from *same* behavior, i.e., similar or identical behavior engaged in simultaneously but independently by two or more organisms (as, for example, the hand-clapping of members of an audience). Such behavior they do not classify as imitative. On the other hand, they regard *copying* as the most highly evolved form of imitation, an extension and elaboration of matched-dependent behavior in which there is a deliberate attempt on the part of the subject, and perhaps also on the part of the model, to make the subject's behavior approximate, in some specific way, ever more closely to that of the model.

The underlying dynamic of imitation, say Miller and Dollard, is that it helps living organisms find the solutions to problems more quickly than they would on the basis of their own, unaided, trial-and-error efforts. From the standpoint of a small child, an adult human being is a paragon of efficiency, power, and know-how. He is richly laden with those "answers" and "solutions" which constitute human *culture,* and the young of the species soon find that by observing and emulating their elders they can often dramatically short-cut the tedium and hazard of independent search-and-discovery. Parents in every society spend some portion of their time consciously educating their offspring, and in some societies the formal task of training and instruction is so involved that, beyond a point, it has to be delegated to persons who specialize as *teachers.* But it is probable that in all societies the most basic human skills, e.g., those of walking and talking, are acquired quite informally, as a result of a kind of "hunger" on the part of the child which makes him "go after" these skills, as exemplified by parents and other adults, in a highly active, aggressive, spontaneous, independent fashion.[1] To a degree the child may thus

[1] Miller and Dollard further emphasize this distinction when they remark: "While Negroes in America, for instance, have learned some of the social habits of Western civilization under direct reward and punishment, they have learned much more by matching and copying the superordinate whites" (p. 191). To this may be added the reflection that teaching and imitation are, in a sense, the two sides of the same coin: *teaching* is the process whereby the adults in a society try to speed up the learning of the young by giving them "the answers" (which are the essence of culture), and *imitation* is the corresponding attempt on the part of the young to speed up their learning. Both represent attempts to short-cut inde-

be said, with respect to his "education," to have "taken matters into his own hands." It is here that an adequate theory of imitation and of the related phenomenon of identification is most urgently needed, although the underlying mechanisms probably continue to function to some extent throughout life.

II. A Two-Factor Analysis of Imitative Learning

Holt fell short of deriving a convincing explanation of imitation from the principle of contiguity learning. Aware of the weaknesses of Holt's approach, Miller and Dollard based their analysis upon the premise that learning occurs when and only when a drive is reduced, a reward experienced. They say:

> The learner must be driven to make the response and rewarded for having responded in the presence of the cue. This may be expressed in a homely way by saying that in order to learn one must want something, notice something, do something, and get something. Stated more exactly, these factors are drive, cue, response, and reward (p. 2).

This formulation makes reward a crucial condition for the occurrence of reinforcement or learning; but it tacitly acknowledges the *fact* of contiguity learning, i.e., it posits that if a "cue" is present when a "drive" evokes a response which is rewarding, the cue will tend to become independently connected with that response. Although the terminology is different, the phenomenon is clearly the same as that which Pavlov called "conditioning" and Thorndike called "associative shifting." The "cue" is equivalent to the "conditioned stimulus," the "drive" is equivalent to the "unconditioned stimulus," and the response is "unconditioned" or "conditioned" depending upon whether it is elicited by the drive or by the cue.[2] The only fundamental difference is at the level of *theory:* Pavlov held that contiguity of stimuli provided the necessary and sufficient circumstances for learning, whereas Miller and Dollard emphasize *reward.*

As we have seen, Holt failed to develop a satisfactory explanation of imitation on the basis of contiguity theory. How adequate is the alternative type of explanation adduced by Miller and Dollard? As I shall attempt to show shortly, their explanation, while in some respects an advance over that of Holt, likewise suffers from a crucial defect. If Holt erred in excluding reward as a relevant variable in

---

pendent trial-and-error learning, i.e., learning "by experience." Imitation may thus be said to be the non-verbal equivalent of *studying.*

[2] Cf. Mowrer (1938c), Hull (1943); also Mowrer and Lamoreaux (1951).

learning,[3] Miller and Dollard appear to have weakened their analysis only slightly less by denying contiguity as an independent principle. Elsewhere (9, 10) I have advanced detailed evidence for believing that a comprehensive conception of learning does not rest upon the question of contiguity *or* reward but must instead embrace *both* principles and attribute to each its special functions. When this is done, one arrives at an explanation of imitation which seems to possess all the advantages of both the Holt and the Miller-Dollard approaches and none of the attendant disadvantages.

Recently, more by accident than by design, the author's own researches have taken a turn which brings one face to face with the problem of imitation. In the hope of learning something new and useful about the psychology of language, the author acquired birds of several species which are known to be capable of learning to "talk" and began to study the means by which this remarkable performance can be brought about. From the writings of bird fanciers—there has been no scientific literature in this area—and from his own experience, he soon discovered that the indispensable precondition for a bird's learning to talk is that you must make him *like* you; you must, in other words, make a "pet" of the bird, which implies in more than a purely figurative sense that you *adopt* him. You, personally, must feed, water, and otherwise care for the bird and spend a good deal of time in its presence; and as you thus attend to its wants and interests, you utter the words or phrases which you want the bird to learn to say. In essence there is nothing more to the *procedure* than this; but the *mechanism* whereby the auditory stimuli which thus impinge upon the bird are converted into responses which reproduce these stimuli is apparently more complex than earlier theorists have supposed.

[3] Holt did not overlook the fact that when a strong stimulus or drive impinges upon an organism, the organism commonly engages in a succession of random movements and that the last of these tends, with repetition of the sequence, to become stably connected with the drive. But instead of seeing here the operation of an independent principle, Holt attempted to adduce this type of learning from contiguity theory. Thus, "Learning by trial-error-and-success is very different from the previously considered cases of learning by reflex-circles, although the physiological principle involved is the same in both cases (neuro-biotaxis or Pavlov's law)" (p. 97). Again, "I believe not only that avoidance responses are acquired more tardily on the whole than adient responses [cf. evidence to the contrary cited on p. 42 of Holt's book], but also that a tolerably *well-adapted* response can be acquired only on the basis of some previously acquired adience, and that the precision of the former will depend on the precision of the latter" (p. 103). Although Holt speaks in one place of a "relief-giving" group of muscles (p. 95), he does not list either "relief" or "reward" in the Index. Of contemporary learning theorists, the one whose position is closest to that of Holt is probably Guthrie (see 10); certainly the emphasis by both writers on lastness-of-response and their monistic position with respect to contiguity is striking.

Certainly the author's observations give no support for the view that birds imitate "instinctively." A wild bird that is treated impersonally never talks, a fact which indicates that we are here dealing with a form of *social learning*. Holt's theory would lead us to expect that this learning is dependent entirely upon "iterative" reflex-circles; but experience has consistently shown that reward in the presence of the trainer is in some way basic to the process, a fact which increases the plausibility of the Miller-Dollard hypothesis. However, it will be recalled that this hypothesis, in its most basic form, holds that imitation develops as a result of one organism's making a particular response and getting rewarded at the same time that it notices a second organism making the same response. As it applies to a bird's learning to talk, the difficulty with this hypothesis is that it assumes the very thing which is to be explained, namely, how it is that a bird ever manages to make a response so unlikely as a word! For example, according to the Miller-Dollard analysis, the only way a bird could learn to say "Hello" imitatively would be to *say it* while noticing another bird (or person?) saying the same thing—and getting rewarded. The question is: How is the bird going to learn to make this highly improbable sound in the first place? A two-factor analysis of the process of word learning resolves this difficulty.

As has already been pointed out, the first requirement in training a bird to talk is that the trainer personally administer such primary rewards as hunger reduction and thirst reduction, in much the same fashion that a parent bird normally does with its fledglings. As a result of this procedure all the stimuli which are incidentally associated with the person of the trainer—particularly his appearance and the noises he characteristically makes—take on positive sign value. Soon the bird reaches the point at which it is obviously "glad to see" and equally "glad to *hear*" the trainer. Said otherwise, the trainer's sights and sounds take on secondary-reward value for the bird. And all this, we now believe, occurs through pure contiguity learning.[4]

Now the second stage, which involves trial-and-error or reward learning, appears to go as follows. Since the appearance of the

[4] It is true that these positive, appetitive attitudes toward the trainer are acquired in the context of drive-reduction or reward, but evidence which cannot be reviewed here (9, 10) suggests that reward reinforces only overt, skeletal behavior (or its symbolic equivalents) and that even in those situations where reward is present, the attendant acquisition of viscero-vascular (emotional) reactions depends solely upon the principle of contiguity. It is now well established (10) that fear is learned by virtue of the coincidence of a signal and the *onset* of a painful stimulus. Reward is apparently irrelevant. When, on the other hand, a sign appears in conjunction with the *termination* of a drive and there is attendant appetitive learning, we can hardly say that reward is here likewise "irrelevant"; but it is relevant in a way, as yet not well understood, which is *different* from its role as a reinforcer of overt, skeletal behavior.

trainer has, by the process just described, taken on secondary reward value,[5] we have every reason to suppose that, if the bird could, it would reproduce the visual stimuli associated with the trainer. This the bird is not able to do. The bird cannot reproduce the trainer by drawing or painting a likeness of him; and even if the bird could make itself look like the trainer, there would ordinarily be no way for the bird to see this resemblance and thus be rewarded by it.[6]

But with the *sounds* the trainer makes it is different. The bird, provided it belongs to one of the "talking" species, can make a great range and variety of sounds; and if one of these happens to resemble, even slightly, one of the trainer's sounds, that sound will, by the principle of generalization, have some secondary-reward value; and the response involved in making it will be somewhat reinforced. In this way the basis is laid for automatic trial-and-error learning which will bring the sound-producing response to an ever higher level of perfection, with no immediate or direct intervention on the part of the trainer. Because the reward underlying this kind of learning is thus self-administered, I have called this theory of word learning *autistic.* It differs mainly from Miller and Dollard's formulation in this respect, that by positing contiguity and reward learning as two separate and distinct processes, we escape the awkward necessity of having to suppose that the bird "just happens" to say a word in the trainer's presence as a precondition to learning to say it "imitatively," i.e., regularly whenever the trainer says a word.[7]

Once a bird begins to reproduce fragments of human speech on a purely autistic basis, there is then the possibility that its vocalizations will have overt, instrumental value; for example, a bird may find that its trainer will spend more time with it and be more responsive when it utters recognizable words and that it can perhaps attract the atten-

[5] For a discussion of alternative views regarding the exact nature of secondary reward (or reinforcement) see 9, 10, 12, and 17.

[6] An interesting experiment could be performed in this connection by providing a talking-bird-in-training with a opportunity to peck a button which would exhibit a silent motion picture of the trainer, or, more simply, cause the trainer to appear in person. The hypothesis presented above would require that such a response on the part of the bird would be thus reinforced and fixated.

[7] Another way of putting this is to say that, by virtue of the conditioning procedure described, the bird develops a kind of *image* of the trainer's sounds and then, quite independently, can work at reproducing, or *copying,* them. By the use of this construct we circumvent the awkward necessity of assuming that the bird has to *say* a word before the bird can "learn" it. A word, it appears, is "learned" in three stages: By conditioning it is acquired as an image; on the basis of secondary reinforcement it is acquired as an autistic response; and, finally, it may come to function as an instrumental response in the objective sense. (See 24 for a more detailed discussion of these three stages of language learning.) To a considerable degree Miller and Dollard may be said to have foreseen the possibility of this type of analysis (see 24), but they made no systematic use of it. This may be because such an analysis calls for a dualistic conception of learning.

tion of other human beings as well. But this is a later stage and should be carefully distinguished from the more basic process whereby the bird first learns to reproduce the trainer's sounds without the immediate presence or mediation of the trainer.

Elsewhere (24) the author has advanced further evidence in support of the foregoing account of imitative learning in birds and for believing that essentially the same type of explanation is applicable to the early stages of language learning in human infants and that it has still wider applicability.

III. Imitation and Identification

Not long ago the author described the researches on word learning by birds to another audience and during the course of the presentation used the term "identification" freely and (he now suspects) rather loosely. He suggested, for example, that word learning by birds was perhaps the prototype of what is known clinically as "identification" and went on to say that birds might offer an opportunity for more exact study of this phenomenon than is possible with human beings. He may even have made the somewhat flippant comment that birds learn to "talk" because, by virtue of the intensive emotional reconditioning to which they are exposed, they get so mixed up that they probably think they *are* human beings!

In the discussion period which followed, a member of the audience said something like this: "You have used the term 'identification' extensively and 'imitation' hardly at all. We used to think we knew what we meant by 'imitation,' but then the psychoanalysts made it fashionable to use 'identification' instead. I wonder if we know what we mean by *that* term."

In his recent paper on identification, Stoke (1950) has suggested that the proper definition for this term is as follows:

Identification is a term which has crept into the literature of child development and mental hygiene from Freud. Its meaning may be derived from a few quotations: ". . . and here we have that higher nature, in this ego-ideal, or superego, the representative of our parents. When we were little children we knew these natures, we admired and feared them; and later we took them into ourselves." ". . . identification endeavors to mold a person's own ego after the fashion of the one that has been taken for a model." "It is easy to state in a formula the distinction between identification with the father and the choice of the father as an object. In the first case one's father is what one would like to *be,* and in the second he is what one would like to *have.*" From the wealth of context in which the term is used it is usually implied that a child gives its emotional allegiance to one of its parents and attempts to duplicate in its own life the ideas, attitudes, and behavior of the parent with whom it is identifying. There are occasional uses of identification in Freudian literature aside from the above, but this is the chief usage and the one with which we shall be concerned (p. 163).

In his book *A general introduction to psychoanalysis* (1920), Freud uses the term "identification" in three different ways. In describing the analysis of a woman with a compulsion which dated back to an embarrassing incident which occurred on the first night of her marriage, Freud speaks of identification in the first sense. He says:

It was clear, first of all, that the patient identified herself with her husband; in imitating his running from one room into another she acted his part. To keep up the similarity we must assume that she had substituted the table and table-cover for the bed and the sheet (p. 232).

Here Freud uses "identification" and "imitation" interchangeably. The reproduction of another's behavior is employed in this instance as a kind of pantomime, a means of communicating by "acting out" rather than by explicit verbal statement. The symbolic significance, or meaning, of the compulsive behavior was at length made clear by the patient herself. In acting as her husband had acted, she was indeed identifying with him in the sense of becoming, in a very limited way, identical with him. Fenichel (1945) makes a distinction between identification at this purely imitative level and identification in the more profound sense when he says:

Any imitation, whether conscious or unconscious, presupposes a kind of identification, that is, an alteration of one's own ego which follows the pattern of an object model. However, the identification at the basis of imitation, as contrasted to other types of identification, is a superficial, limited, capricious one, employed for one definite purpose only (p. 222).

Freud's second use of the term "identification" stems from a period when he was preoccupied with "libido theory" and probably has no enduring theoretical significance; but it should be mentioned in order to put it in proper historical perspective and to differentiate it from the third, more significant sense in which he employed the term. The second meaning of the term is given in the following passage:

As with paranoia, so also with melancholia (under which, by the way, very different clinical types are classified), it has been possible to obtain a glimpse into the inner structure of the disorder. We have perceived that the self-reproaches with which these sufferers torment themselves so mercilessly actually relate to another person, to the sexual object they have lost or whom they have ceased to value on account of some fault. From this we conclude that the melancholic has indeed withdrawn his libido from the object, but that by a process which we must call "narcissistic identification" he has set up the object within the ego itself, projected it on to the ego (p. 370).

In this quotation it is apparent that Freud is referring to a phenomenon which goes further than anything ordinarily implied by the term "imitation." The frame of reference is no longer purely behavioral; instead it takes one into the realm of "ego psychology." Although this is a conception of identification which Freud had previously developed in some detail in a paper entitled "Mourning and melancholia" (1917) and one which he subsequently alluded to (see, for example, *The ego and the id,* p. 36), it appears to have been a conceptual makeshift which he developed because certain peculiarities of his major theoretical formulations made it difficult for him otherwise to account for depression and related phenomena (19, 20).

The third and most instructive sense in which Freud used the term "identification" is revealed by the following passage, again taken from *A general introduction to psychoanalysis:*

From analysis of the delusion of observation we have come to the conclusion that in the ego there exists a faculty that incessantly watches, criticizes and compares, and in this way is set against the other part of the ego. In our opinion, therefore, the [delusional] patient reveals a truth which has not been appreciated as such when he complains that at every step he is spied upon and observed, that his every thought is known and examined. He has erred only in attributing this disagreeable power to something outside himself and foreign to him; he perceives within his ego the rule of a faculty which measures his actual ego and all his activities by an *ego-ideal,* which he has created for himself in the course of his development. We also infer that he created this ideal for the purpose of recovering thereby the self-satisfaction bound up with the primary infantile narcissism, which since those days has suffered so many shocks and mortifications. We recognize in this self-criticizing faculty the ego-censorship, the "conscience"; it is the same censorship as that exercised at night upon dreams, from which the repressions against inadmissible wish-excitations proceed. When this faculty disintegrates in the delusion of being observed, we are able to detect its origin and that it arose out of the influence of parents and those who trained the child, together with his social surroundings, by a process of identification with certain of these persons who were taken as a model (p. 371).

At the time the foregoing passage was written, Freud had not yet coined the term "superego," but the concept was already well developed; and it is evident that he had also grasped the possibility that this part of the personality is acquired by a remarkable, but somewhat mystifying, process which he called "identification." With the emergence of the superego concept, the tripartite division of the mind into id, ego, and superego became complete; and identification, in the third sense in which Freud used the term, took a permanent place in the new system as the process whereby the superego is acquired. As Freud points out in his posthumous volume *An outline of psychoanalysis* (1949), the id represents an individual's *biological heritage* and is genetically given; the superego represents an individual's *social heritage* and is acquired by means of identification; and the ego, largely a product of independent experience, strives to mediate, reconcile, and integrate the competing demands of these energy systems.

In the present section of this paper our attention is centered upon the question of precisely how it is that those functions and faculties denoted by the term *superego* are acquired. Theologians have sometimes held that the superego or conscience is innately given; it has been called "God's voice speaking in man"; and at other times it has been equated to "the soul." Freud, on the basis of clinical observation, vigorously repudiated all nativistic conceptions of the superego; but he was never able to be very explicit in describing the precise process of superego formation. After what was perhaps his most penetrating discussion of this problem, in the chapter entitled "The anatomy of the mental personality," which appeared in *New introductory lectures on psychoanalysis,* one finds Freud exclaiming, "What would one not give to understand these things better?" (p. 105).

The following paragraph gives the gist of Freud's conclusions on this score:

> But let us get back to the superego. We have allocated to it the activities of self-observation, conscience, and the holding up of ideals. It follows from our account of its origin that it is based upon an overwhelmingly important biological fact no less than upon a momentous psychological fact, namely the lengthy dependence of the human child on its parents and the Oedipus complex; these two facts, moreover, are closely bound up with each other. For us the superego is the representative of all moral restrictions, the advocate of the impulse toward perfection, in short it is as much as we have been able to apprehend psychologically of what people call the "higher" things in human life. Since it itself can be traced back to the influence of parents, teachers, and so on, we shall learn more of its significance if we turn our attention to these sources. In general, parents and similar authorities follow the dictates of their own superegos in the upbringing of children. Whatever terms their ego may be on with their superego, in the education of the child they are severe and exacting. They have forgotten the difficulties of their own childhood, and are glad to be able to identify themselves fully at last with their

own parents, who in their day subjected them to such severe restraints. The result is that the superego of the child is not really built up on the model of the parents, but on that of the parents' superego; it takes over the same content, it becomes the vehicle of tradition and of all the age-long values which have been handed down in this way from generation to generation. You may easily guess what great help is afforded by the recognition of the superego in understanding the social behavior of man, in grasping the problem of delinquency, for example, and perhaps, too, in providing us with some practical hints upon education. It is probable that the so-called materialistic conceptions of history err in that they underestimate this factor. They brush it aside with the remark that the "ideologies" of mankind are nothing more than resultants of their economic situation at any given moment or superstructures built upon it. That is the truth, but very probably it is not the whole truth. Mankind never lives completely in the present; the ideologies of the superego perpetuate the past, the traditions of the race and the people, which yield but slowly to the influence of the present and new developments, and, so long as they work through the superego, play an important part in man's life, quite independently of economic conditions (pp. 94–96).*

In his books *The ego and the id* (1921), *Group psychology and the analysis of the ego* (1921), *Civilization and its discontents* (1930), and *Totem and tabu* (1918), Freud further develops the implications of identification and its relation to superego formation; but throughout there is an implied dilemma. The forces of the id are assumed to be innately given and require no other explanation. The ego consists of those habits and habit systems which have been acquired as solutions to problems presented either by the id, by the superego, by the external world, or by some combination thereof. Here the principle of learning through problem solving, or the law of effect, gives at least a rudimentary explanation of ego development (8, 15). But the superego presents a more difficult problem: it is not innate but neither can one easily see how it can be acquired on the same problem-solving basis as is the ego. The superego, at least in the most immediate sense of the term, is not problem solving but *problem making,* since it contains the emotional forces which underlie injunctions, restraints, and obligations. Fenichel (1945) recognizes this problem when he remarks: "Affects may be projected, that is, perceived in someone else, to avoid perceiving them in one's self. [However], the idea of an introjection of an affect seems to make no sense" (p. 164).

Without using the same terminology, Freud has explored the possibility that the superego is a product, not of problem-solving

[* From Sigmund Freud, *New introductory lectures on psychoanalysis* (New York: W. W. Norton & Co., Inc., 1933), pp. 94–96. Copyright by Sigmund Freud. By permission of W. W. Norton & Co., Inc.]

learning, but of conditioning. In the chapter on "The anatomy of the mental personality" already cited, he says:

The role which the superego undertakes later in life is at first played by an external power, by parental authority. The influence of the parents dominates the child by granting proofs of affection and by threats of punishment, which, to the child, means loss of love, and which must also be feared on their own account. This objective anxiety is the forerunner of the later moral anxiety; so long as the former is dominant, one need not speak of superego or of conscience. It is only later that the secondary situation arises, which we are far too ready to regard as the normal state of affairs; the external restrictions are introjected, so that the superego takes the place of the parental function, and thenceforward observes, guides and threatens the ego in just the same way as the parents acted to the child before (p. 89).

In a very literal sense all conditioning can be regarded as a type of "introjection." For example, in the familiar laboratory paradigm of conditioning, a signal is presented to the subject and is then followed by a painful stimulus, such as an electric shock. After one of two paired presentations of signal and shock, the signal becomes capable of eliciting an emotional reaction of *fear*. The latter may appropriately be regarded as an internal reproduction, or introjection, of the externally applied shock. Under favorable circumstances, the fear will adaptively motivate the subject to engage in behavior which will avert the shock.[8]

[8] Fear learning, like conditioning in general, may thus be said to take on problem-solving implications: if by experiencing fear in a dangerous situation one is prompted to engage in behavior which circumvents the feared event, then, in a sense, the having of the fear becomes "rewarding," or at least highly "useful." Under these circumstances one may be tempted to posit that even conditioning, in the final analysis, depends upon the same principle as does problem solving, namely the factor of drive reduction or reward. But we have elsewhere (9) seen that the avoidance of an impending noxious stimulus, such as an electric shock, can be rewarding only in the sense that such avoidance is accompanied by a reduction of, or escape from, fear. Pursuing this logic, we then arrive at the startling conclusion: Fear is reinforced by fear reduction! This would hardly make sense biologically, and experimentally and clinically we know that fears which are followed by reassurance and fear abatement, rather than by at least periodic recurrence of the thing feared, tend, not to be strengthened, but to extinguish. We can most readily resolve this difficulty by recalling the distinction, elaborated elsewhere (16), between the concept of adaptation (survival) and adjustment (satisfaction). To *have* a fear is (very often) *adaptive,* but to get rid of it is *adjustive*. The acquisition or having of fear depends, it would seem, upon one learning principle, viz., that of conditioning; and the diminution of fear sets the stage for the second form of learning, namely that form which results in the strengthening of overt, problem-solving behavior. Let us try to put the problem somewhat differently. Through the process of introjection, what was initially *external discipline* becomes *internal discipline,* our conscience now "speaks for" our parents. Loosely stated, we "trouble ourselves" in order that others will not later trouble us (more?). Thus, at a high level of abstraction, we may say that the punishing function of conscience is "rewarding." This, of course, is not to say that the "pangs" of conscience are no longer painful; instead it implies that, with sufficient personal maturity, an individual may come to respect, accept, and value these reactions and to

But as the following passage indicates, Freud's observations did not support the view that the superego is nothing but the precipitate of parental and other social conditioning of the child. Freud says:

> The superego, which . . . has taken over the power, the aims and even the methods of the parental function, is, however, not merely the legatee of parental authority, it is actually the heir of its body. It proceeds directly from it, and we shall soon learn in what way this comes about. First, however, we must pause to consider a point in which they differ. The superego seems to have made a one-sided selection, and to have chosen only the harshness and severity of the parents, their preventive and punitive functions, while their loving care is not taken up and continued by it. If the parents have really ruled with a rod of iron, we can easily understand the child developing a severe superego, but, contrary to our expectations, experience shows that the superego may reflect the same relentless harshness even when the upbringing has been gentle and kind, and avoided threats and punishment as far as possible (pp. 89–90).[9]

In other words, Freud was not able to establish to his own satisfaction that the superego is acquired either as a product of emotional conditioning or, on the basis of the pleasure principle, as a solution to some felt need or problem. Yet he was firm in insisting that it was in some manner a product of social interaction and learning.

The next major theoretical attack upon this problem was made by Anna Freud in her book *The ego and the mechanisms of defense* (1937). Here, in a chapter entitled "Identification with the aggressor," she takes the position that the type of identification which we have just been discussing arises from the following circumstances. A child experiences severe anxiety because of conflict between his own infantile desires and the injunctions and prohibitions of parents and other moral authorities. Under the pressure of this anxiety, the child searches, as in any trial-and-error learning situation, for a means of reducing his anxiety. In many, perhaps we can say all, normal instances, the child hits upon this solution. If he consciously aligns himself *with* the aggressive, punitive socializer or, more exactly, pretends that he *is* that person, the child then has no more reason to fear him, the conflict disappears, and anxiety abates.

---

act *upon* rather than *against* them, i.e., he satisfies, rather than represses, conscience (see 15, 16, 18–20, and 22). Although the drives produced by conscience go contrary to the primitive pleasure principle (adjustment), they are in the service of the reality principle (long-term pleasure) and permit the individual to behave with a high degree of *integration* and *integrity*.

[9] Anna Freud (1935) has taken a different position in this connection: "Thus the old relation between the child and the parents continues within the child, and the severity or mildness with which the parents have treated the child is reflected in the attitude of the superego to the ego" (pp. 86–87).

Anna Freud gives a number of apt illustrations of this mechanism, one of which—a very simple but dramatic one—will suffice.

My readers [she says] will remember the case of the little girl who tried by means of magic gestures to get over the mortification associated with her penis-envy. This child was purposely and consciously making use of a mechanism to which the boy [in another example] resorted involuntarily. At home she was afraid to cross the hall in the dark, because she had a dread of seeing ghosts. Suddenly, however, she hit on a device which enabled her to do it: she would run across the hall, making all sorts of peculiar gestures as she went. Before long, she triumphantly told her little brother the secret of how she had got over her anxiety. "There's no need to be afraid in the hall," she said, "you just have to pretend that you're the ghost who might meet you." This shows that her magic gestures represented the movements which she imagined that ghosts would make (pp. 118–19).

Since the ghosts that children typically speak of represent an intermediate link between their parents and the establishment of their own internalized moral authority or superego,[10] we see in this illustration the process of identification caught, as we may say, in mid-flight.

Later Anna Freud further remarks:

By impersonating the aggressor, assuming his attributes or imitating his aggression, the child transforms himself from the person threatened into the person who makes the threat. In *Beyond the pleasure principle* the significance of this change from the passive to the active role as a means of assimilating unpleasant or traumatic experiences in infancy is discussed in detail. "If a doctor examines a child's throat or performs a small operation, the alarming experience will quite certainly be made the subject of the next game, but in this the pleasure gain from another source cannot be overlooked. In passing from the passivity of experience to the activity of play,

---

[10] In his poem, "Seein' Things," Eugene Field (1850–1895) shows a nice understanding of this stage of development. The third of the five stanzas of this poem runs as follows:

> Once, when I licked a feller 'at had just moved on our street,
> An' father sent me up to bed without a bite to eat,
> I woke up in the dark an' saw things standin' in a row,
> A-lookin' at me cross-eyed an' p'intin' at me—so!
> Oh, my! I wuz so skeered that time I never slep' a mite—
> It's almost alluz when I'm bad I see things at night!

Compare the patient whose presenting symptoms are described in Section V as "generalized anxiety, sexual inhibitions, and a complaint of *imaginary figures* who lurked behind bushes at night and furtively slipped along behind the patient in the street." One of the rather numerous ways in which he was currently being "bad" involved the fact that he was "knocking down" in a restaurant in which he was then employed as a student waiter. However, unlike the little boy in Field's poem, he did not realize there was any connection between his "badness" and the "things" he saw.

the child applies to his playfellow the unpleasant occurrence that befell himself and so avenges himself on the person of this proxy" (pp. 121–22).

In the following section an attempt will be made to draw together these observations by the two Freuds and give the theory of identification a more systematic formulation than has emerged from the foregoing discussion.

IV. Identification (Developmental and Defensive) and the Concept of Mediation

It is evident from the preceding section that identification and imitation are closely related, but the exact nature of that relationship is not as yet fully clear. Perhaps this is in large measure due to the fact that the concept of identification has never been defined with precision and rigor. Lair (1949) has recently addressed herself to this task, with highly useful results. Much of the confusion arises, apparently, because of the failure to distinguish between *two* forms of identification, forms which Lair designates as *developmental* identification and as *defensive* identification.

Developmental identification turns out to be the same phenomenon as that described in Section II in connection with the discussion of language acquisition and other "imitative" performances of an *autistic* nature. In the talking-bird paradigm, we have assumed that the bird (or baby) utters its first words as a means of reproducing a bit of the beloved and longed-for trainer. Lair, in presenting one instance of this type of identification, refers to ". . . the early hallucinatory wish mechanism used by the child in the first half of the first year to bring back or recall the nurse who had sole charge of her, and was a substitute mother" (p. 255). Later Lair quotes from Anna Freud and Dorothy Burlingham (*Infants without families,* 1944) as follows:

> After one of the father's visits, Tony did his best to keep his image alive by imitating him. He developed a morning cough because his father had coughed in the morning. At breakfast he stirred his corn flakes with a spoon for a long time saying: "My daddy did this when we had breakfast together. All the children should do it like my daddy." His last demand every evening before falling asleep was "A story about daddy" (p. 112).

And again as an instance of developmental identification, Lair quotes Blanco (1941) to this effect:

> When, for instance, a child is being subjected to the violent frustration of the absence of the mother, he can deal with it by means of an imaginary

putting of the mother inside himself and thus having her, as it were, handy in order to provide for all these needs . . . (p. 30).

Although the phraseology is different, it is clear that the type of identification connoted in the preceding paragraphs is the same phenomenon as that considered in Section III under the heading "A Two-Factor Analysis of Imitation." The fact that it is called "developmental" identification is in no way inconsistent with the fact that it often leads to at least transitory reproduction of such "functionless" behavior as that involved in the little boy's coughing and stirring his cereal as his soldier-father did. At the most primitive level of identification with which we are now dealing, parts of the personality of the beloved parent or parent-substitute are satisfyingly reproduced *without regard to objective utility;* but in this way some types of behavior will come into existence which, though in the beginning having only autistic value, will soon prove valuable in an external, instrumental sense. Speech is the prime example of this (see 24).

In Lair's terminology Anna Freud's "identification with the aggressor" becomes equivalent to "defensive identification" and seems to be different from anything which has been denoted by the term "imitation." The following quotations which have been collected by Lair further depict and conceptualize this phenomenon:

With this defense, if you are identified with a force of which you are afraid, you can no longer be hurt, because you are the force (Witmer, 1947, p. 247).

The meaning of it is as follows: if I cannot withstand the enemy in any way, I will ally myself with him and so render him harmless (Nunberg, 1931, p. 31).

By way of introducing the following quotation from Murray (1947), Lair (p. 265) says:

An example of defensive identification reported in a normal child by Dr. John M. Murray shows this process more clearly. Dr. Murray's young son came home from the hospital following a bout with pneumonia. After being put to bed he kept getting out and wandering around in his bare feet. Worried that the boy might have a relapse, the father went upstairs to insist that he stay in bed. He tells his experience, and the conclusions he drew, as follows:

"I said, 'Come on now, Jim. If you do that again I'll smack you; I don't want you to get sick again.' I went downstairs and pretty soon feet were going along the corridor in just the same way. So I went out and cut a little switch from a bush in the yard. As I went upstairs, my Jim heard me coming and he headed for the bed. I gave him one quick clip with the switch across his bare feet. Then he hopped into bed and began crying. He cried for a while and I went downstairs. He cried some more, and then about ten minutes later his mother, who was upstairs, heard him talking to himself, and this is what he said, 'Now you be a good boy and stay in bed. If you don't, I'll sock you.'

"What I want you to get out of that story is this: that lad was a different lad from the one he had been before he got hit. He had taken an infinitesimal part of me inside himself. This experience of being frustrated and of being hurt a little caused the reaction, and his response was to take a part of me inside himself. If he would follow that part of me, he would be spared further conflict along this line" (Murray, pp. 86–87).[11]

Later Lair remarks:

In conclusion . . . one might say, then, that identification may be descriptively classified into two types, developmental and defensive, but that the fundamental mechanisms are the same. That is, the infant or child reacts to tension or frustration by an attempt to master the object of frustration and by identification with it (Lair, p. 277).

It is true that in both developmental and defensive identification the subject is "frustrated," but the different nature of the frustration in the two instances is noteworthy. In the one case it arises from a sense of helplessness and loneliness: the parent or parent-person is *absent,* and the infant wishes he were *present.* In the other case, the frustration arises rather from interference and punishment: the parent or parent-person is *present,* and the infant wishes he were *absent.* But the latter wish brings the average child into intolerable conflict: while he hates the parent for his disciplinary actions, he also loves the parent and experiences acute anxiety at the prospect of his really being separated, physically or emotionally, from him (or her).

Developmental identification, we may suppose, is a milder and simpler experience than is defensive identification, which has a violent, crisis-like nature. The one is powered mainly by biologically given drives ("fear of loss of love," in the analytic sense) and the other by socially inflicted discomforts ("castration fear" or, less dramatically, simply fear of punishment). The first presumably in-

[11] This account reminds one of the relatively common experience of observing a small child, two or three years old, say "No, no!" to himself in situations in which this has been said to him by others and perhaps enforced by punishment. Here behaving like the "aggressor" is highly functional, both subjectively (it inhibits the contemplated behavior and reduces fear) and objectively (it nullifies the likelihood of punishment). What was originally a two-person event now becomes a one-person event, but "the person" now has a new and higher degree of complexity. Instead of two persons communicating with each other, the communication is now between *two parts* of the same person.

volves relatively little conflict; but in the latter case, conflict and attendant anxiety are outstanding. The distinction here made between developmental and defensive identification does not, of course, imply that events connected with the latter are not also "developmental." They may deserve to be regarded as such in a very profound and important sense. They, more than anything else, may cast the mold of character and set an enduring life style. However, the two terms are convenient and convey something of the essence of the two processes to which they refer.

All this becomes further clarified if one invokes Courtney's (1949) concept of "mediation." He says:

> Learning as used here is restricted explicitly to social learning: i.e., learning involving interpersonal interaction (p. 152).
>
> The second step toward a human, social learning theory is the inclusion of human organisms in the PROBLEM-SOLUTION sequence. There is a striking quality in human behavior that needs clearer recognition. It is that most human problems are not solved by the person in whom the problem (the internal disequilibrium) is felt. They are solved by another person—a mother, a father, a teacher, a lover, in short, an *agent*. A psychology or learning theory that is limited to an *S—R* learning unit seems, per force, to restrict the stimulus and the response to a given person. In human, social learning employing a PROBLEM-SOLUTION structure, it is quite feasible to have one person involved in the problem and additional persons or agents involved in the problem solution (pp. 177–78).
>
> Those who write about children make much of the child's dependence and the parent-child relationship, but they have not integrated these things with learning theory. The culture-transmission approach to education places the agent at the center of the transmission process; but, even here, the function of the agent has never been explored thoroughly in a tight, logical learning pattern (p. 179).
>
> The point intended here is that the agent *is* the solution to an infant's first problems. Later differentiation places the agent in the secondary-solution or anticipated-solution role. Providing the anticipation of a solution [secondary reinforcement], the agent conversely reduces the anticipation that there will not be a solution, i.e., reduces anxiety (p. 181).

Courtney's concept of mediated problem solving is depicted in Figure 70. Let us assume that an infant experiences a simple organic need or stimulus, S_o, which leads to a distress response, R_d, such as crying and violent random movements. The latter provide sensory stimulation, S_s, for the parent-person, who is usually the mother. This stimulation produces certain emotional reactions, R_e, which in turn produce emotion tensions, S_e; and these prompt the mother to engage in relief-giving behavior, R_r, behavior which reduces or eliminates S_o and thus stills the whole cycle of infant-mother interaction until S_o or some other drive is again active.

Because the infant's response, R_d, is followed by relief and reward, the response is reinforced according to the principle of problem-solving learning with which we are already familiar (9, 10). But this is not all that happens: because the infant also sees, hears, feels, and perhaps smells the mother while she is caring for him, these stimuli acquire, on the basis of conditioning, secondary reinforcement

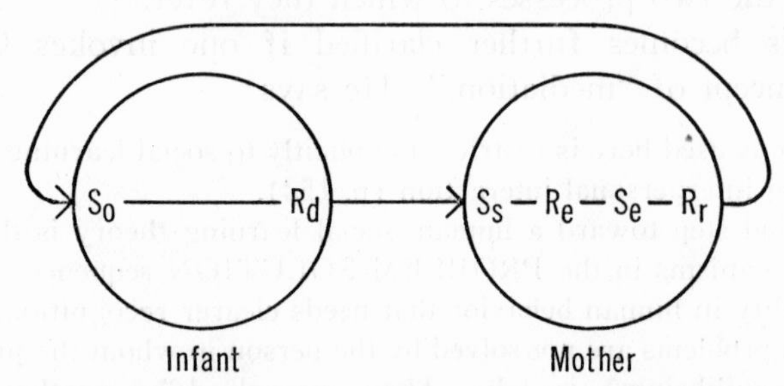

FIG. 70.—Schematic representation of the period of infantile indulgence. The "good mother" is one who is constantly attentive to the infant's expressions of distress (R_d) and who reacts in ways which are designed to reduce the sources of distress (S_o). The infant is almost completely helpless, and the mother, or mother-person, becomes an indispensable link, or *mediator,* between the infant's wants and their satisfaction. At this stage the accent is upon *care* of the infant; little or no attempt is as yet made to control him. It is at this stage that *developmental identification* begins to occur, whereby skills, such as walking and talking, are acquired which will carry the infant toward greater self-sufficiency. (Cf. Mowrer and Kluckhohn, 1944, p. 70 and p. 76.)

properties (9, 10). The stage is now set for the occurrence of identification of the "developmental" variety.

As a result of the care which the mother thus mediates and administers, two things happen to the infant: he grows physically, and he develops emotionally and with respect to skills. No longer is he helpless—and harmless. He can now cause trouble, actual and potential, and his parents begin to "discipline" him. This second state of affairs is represented in Figure 71. Because of drives that can now be either organically or emotionally based, the small child engages in behavior which is socially disapproved, R_{sd}. This behavior may stimulate parents in either of two ways: it may give them direct organic discomfort (as when a child hits, bites, or kicks) or it may produce emotional discomfort, because of the parents' anticipation of what will ultimately become of the child if his misbehavior and immaturities are not modified. Either of these forms of discomfort may prompt the parent to engage in behavior which is directed toward the child in the form of punishment, R_p.

In Figure 70 it will be noted that the parent-agent's behavior is directed to what may be called the stimulus side, or felt needs, of the child, whereas in Figure 71 the parent-agent's behavior is directed toward the response side, or behavior, of the child. That these two types of mediation produce very different reactions in the child becomes clear when we note that in the first case the parent's approach to the child brings comfort and his nonapproach brings distress, whereas in the second case the parent's approach brings distress and

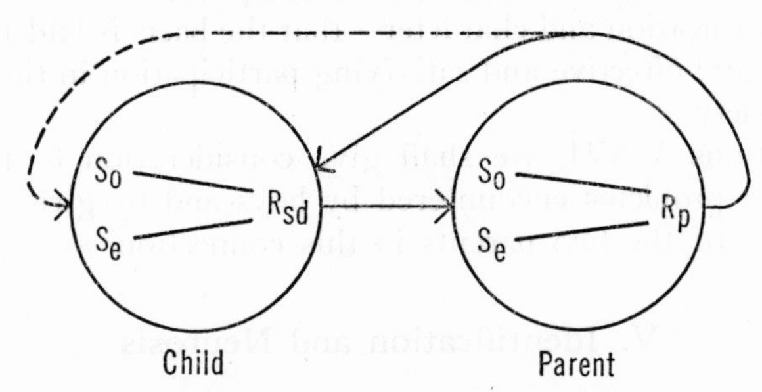

FIG. 71.—Schematic representation of childhood discipline. As the child grows, develops, and becomes more independent, the attention of parent persons shifts from care to *control,* from indulgence to discipline. Mediation is now more in the direction of trying to present to the child, in attenuated form, the consequences which socially disapproved behavior, if not curbed, will bring in later life. However, it should be noted that the caring, nurturing function does not entirely disappear (dotted line). With the transition from infantile indulgence to discipline, ambivalence, conflict, and anxiety arise. These lead to the occurrence, in normal instances, of *defensive identification* and to the establishment of the child's basic character structure.

his nonapproach brings relief, or at least no distress. That *ambivalence,* in the sense of conflict and anxiety (19), arises in this second stage is not surprising; and, as has been shown in another connection (18), it leads to momentous consequences.

Courtney summarizes his discussion and draws an interesting implication in these words:

> Agents traditionally carry out two roles. The first is a supporting, helpful "mother" role. The second is a punishing, thwarting, directing "teacher" role. One is essentially problem solving. The other is essentially problem making. The outstanding historical example of the switching of these roles is that period when mothers were urged to be "scientific" in the feeding of their babies. This "science" consisted in arbitrarily timed feeding schedules. It placed the "mother" prematurely in the role of "teacher." Before she was well established as the "problem solver" she was converted into the "problem maker." The pendulum has now swung back and mothers are resuming their traditional "helping" function (pp. 183–84).

If a child were cared for but never disciplined, he would presumably show only developmental identification and would develop skills but not character; if, on the other hand, a child were poorly cared for or cared for quite impersonally (perhaps by some sort of machine) but were thoroughly disciplined, he would probably not develop either skills or character, as we commonly conceive them (16). It is probably only by allowing early experience to be divided into two stages—loving care and indulgence, which leads to developmental identification and skills; and discipline, which leads to defensive identification and character—that the basis is laid for normal personality and effective and satisfying participation in the adult life of one's society.

In Sections V-VII, we shall give consideration to the special development problems encountered by boys and by girls and to the unique roles of the two parents in this connection.

V. Identification and Neurosis

Other writers have not failed to comment upon the relationship between identification difficulties and the predisposition to neurosis; but they have not, the author believes, sufficiently stressed the importance of this connection or given a proper indication of its generality. It has been the author's experience that neurotics, almost without exception, have had a father and mother who were poorly matched maritally and that as a result of the disharmony in the household the natural course of development by means of identification with the same-sexed person was disturbed.

In the ideal family constellation, a little boy finds it very natural and highly rewarding to model himself in his father's image. The father is gratified to see this re-creation of his own qualities, attitudes, and masculinity; and the mother, loving the father, finds such a course of development acceptable in her son. Tentative explorations, conscious and unconscious, in the direction of being "like mother" quickly convince the boy that this is not his proper or approved destiny; and he speedily reverts to his identification with father. In the well-ordered, psychologically healthy household, much the same picture, in reverse, holds for the little girl.

But where there is parental disharmony, all this is changed. If there is chronic antagonism between husband and wife, the boy discovers that if he identifies with his father it is at the price of losing his mother's love and approval; if she is antagonistic toward and disapproving of the husband, she will feel scant enthusiasm for seeing her son become "just like *him.*" If, on the other hand, the boy tries to take his mother as a personal model, he will almost certainly incur his father's displeasure and also risk the general opprobrium connected with being a "sissy."

For the little girl in such a household, very much the same type of dilemma arises. To be like her mother is to take a critical, unloving attitude toward her father; and if she tries to resolve her difficulties by being like father, she will lose the mother's support and possibly that of women generally.

In the face of such an identification dilemma, three possibilities are open, at least in principle, to a child. If, despite the complications mentioned, a child succeeds in identifying strongly with the same-sexed parent, he is not likely to become neurotic. Loss of the affection and support of the opposite-sexed parent during childhood and youth undoubtedly has a negative, impoverishing influence upon personality development; but this influence does not seem to predispose the affected individual to neurosis. If, on the other hand, the child has been completely alienated with respect to the same-sexed parent and if his affection and respect have gone entirely to the opposite-sexed parent, as an adult he will be disposed, not to neurosis, but to perversion. The *neurotic,* it appears, is a person who, as a consequence of the kind of family pathology described, has failed to make a full-fledged, whole-hearted identification with the same-sexed parent but who, at the same time, has not fully identified with the opposite-sexed parent.

On the basis of clinical observation we can, indeed, go further and say that the neurotic is typically a person who, as a child, was inclined to prefer and side with the opposite-sexed parent at the time of marital quarrels but who, at the same time, was sufficiently attached to the same-sexed parent and sufficiently sensitive to the stigma attached to cross-sex identification that he or she was never able to align himself or herself completely with either sex.

The evidence, derived from psychotherapy, on which this conclusion is based is relatively extensive; but it will be possible to reproduce here only one brief excerpt from a recording by way of illustration. The patient, a young engineer, came into therapy with presenting symptoms of anxiety, depression, and work inhibition; but he shortly revealed that he also suffered from congenital testicular atrophy and for years had been supposed to take regular doses of a male hormone preparation. He was puzzled by the fact that he could bring himself to do this only intermittently and half-heartedly. The following material is from the thirteenth interview.

Patient: I remember that sometimes I was quite confused, bewildered by the fact that my father and mother quarreled, occasionally. It was mostly nagging on the part of my mother, and my father was one of these people who could never remember to be home on time—and would stop to chat with people. He would go out to get a quart of ice cream and arrive home an hour later, having forgotten the ice cream, and so forth. Little squabbles like that. Most of these things we weren't supposed to hear; but I was often a very interested onlooker from the top of the stairs, when I was supposed to be in bed, I think.

I remember one time there was a very considerable "row," with all the attendant tearfulness, and so forth, because my father had been having a small affair with one of the maids we had. Mother had gone through all the business of threatening to go home, and so forth. This I don't think my parents ever knew, that my sister and I knew, but again we heard some commotion and stood at the top of the stairs and listened. It was a very unpleasant experience, hearing parents quarrel.

It's a very funny thing about that incident, that I didn't remember it until years and years and years later—I never consciously remembered it. I don't think I remembered it, perhaps, until four or five years ago. It must have happened fifteen years ago. . . . At one time I wondered if my sister remembered it, a couple of years ago; so I asked her. She said, "Yes," she remembered it. I don't know why I should have wondered if she remembered it or not, unless it might have been of some importance to me.

Therapist: After that long period of forgetfulness, or repression, it may have been that you were a little distrustful of your memory, perhaps some feeling that you may have just dreamed it up.

P.: Yes, that's— I probably might have been, because there's many things I don't know whether I remember or whether I dream them—hazy things. (*Pause.*)

I think perhaps I took my mother's side in a great many of these arguments. Although I said nothing whatsoever, I think probably, in my mind, I took my mother's side, all along realizing that she wasn't blameless either. She nagged pretty thoroughly and pretty hard.

It's unfortunate that she died, because one thinks of a person who is dead in a more respectful way, I think. So I don't know whether I can view my opinions of her objectively or not.

T.: Mmm-uh. But that same subjective distortion would also tend to lessen your opinion of your father, perhaps, in that, saying it very grossly: He killed her!

P. (*showing excitement*): Which, of course, is nonsense; but I suppose there is some of that attitude. I think my respect for him probably *was* lessened when mother died. Then there may have been to this business, "He killed her," there may have been some connection there also because she died during a double operation, or after a double operation she had for displacement of some organ or other which occurred during childbirth; and so

I may have connected that, too. It was a thing they should have had something done about a long time before they did, and didn't.

T.: Well, maybe we're coming back to our old problem, from a new angle here: maybe one of the reasons why you have had difficulty with your medication is that you're not sure you want to be a man, not sure you want to be like father, not sure you want to be—a woman-killer.

P.: I don't know; I don't think I've ever had those thoughts. It might be.

If, as the author has attempted to show elsewhere (16, 18, 19, 20, 22), neurosis consists of an ego-superego conflict (rather than an ego-id conflict, as Freud maintained), it is understandable that an identification dilemma of the kind just portrayed is likely to be pathogenic: a disturbed, highly ambivalent relationship between a child and the same-sexed parent is the forerunner of the later internal struggle between ego and superego, which is the core of neurosis. This conception of neurosis and its implications for therapy will be further developed in the following section.

Here, somewhat parenthetically, the author would like to call attention to a slightly different picture which one sees clinically, namely, that wherein familial pathology consists, not so much in interparental conflict, as in a relatively well accepted dominance inversion on the part of the husband and wife. Both of these abnormalities are recognized by Seward (1946) in the following passage:

Sex typing of personality and privilege becomes an important means of social control, and infractions of the code are severely punished (Davis, 1941). The individual is trained to his sex role from the moment of birth when girls are placed in pink, boys in blue bassinets. Awareness of sex-appropriate conduct makes its early appearance in life through observation and imitation of models in the home (Ferguson, 1941). Some unpublished observation by one of the writer's students shows an increasing awareness of sex roles between the ages of two and three. . . . Sex models in the home must be appropriate *as long as society persists in stereotyping sex roles.* Domineering mothers and ineffectual fathers are likely to produce a younger generation of tomboys and sissies (Ferguson, 1941; Henry, 1934). Deviant sexual orientation in later life may originate in the child's inability to identify himself with his like-sex parent (Hamilton, 1939). Absence of the father or fear of him frequently results in a passivity in boys and tendency on their part to imitate the attitudes, interests, and manners of the mother. Converse attachments may be built up in girls. In either sex, cross-parent identifications are often the cause of maladjustment in sex role and heterosexual inadequacy in adult life (Oltman and Friedman, 1938, 1940). . . . Not only does the family have the responsibility of providing the child with appropriate sex models; it also provides him with his first tryouts of his sex role. Frank points out that the little boy should be able to play up to his mother and have his attentions appreciated. If she makes him feel that the male's interest in sex is repulsive to women, she may block his psychosexual development. . . . The girl in turn learns how to be womanly through her early relationship with her father. His approval and admiration of her as a young woman help her to take a positive attitude toward her sex membership (Frank, 1944) (pp. 153–55).[12]

It is the author's tentative impression, supported by somewhat similar observations on the part of clinical colleagues, that an adult reared in the inverted type of household is a less good therapeutic prospect than is an adult who has been reared in a conflicted type of household. Perhaps in the latter cases the husband and wife are at least trying to be masculine and feminine, whereas in the other situation they have largely renounced these roles for the opposite ones. In any event, we think we understand the type of patient who emerges from the conflict home better than we do the other type and will confine the ensuing discussion to the problems which the former presents.

VI. Identification, Neurosis, and Psychotherapy

The occurrence of resistance and transference phenomena in psychotherapy has made it clear that the patient is here reactivating and reliving old problems, old relationships, which were previously experienced with the parents. But it is only by seeing these problems as prominently involving an identification dilemma of the kind discussed and illustrated in the preceding section that one has a correct perception of his role and responsibilities as a therapist.

By observing the technical rules of therapy—and here I am speaking of analytically oriented therapy—one enables the neurotic patient to engage in what the author has sometimes called "therapeutic regression," i.e., to return to his childhood dilemmas and revive, recon-

[12] This quotation could easily be misconstrued, distorted. It might be interpreted as suggesting that it is a good thing if a little boy is permitted to show specifically sexual behavior with respect to his mother. This, I believe, is not the author's intention at all. Rather is she saying that a mother must respect and reward the masculinity strivings of her boy children. She must respect their tentatives at being men, their attempts to be manly. And by the same token Seward is saying that, for normal development, a little girl needs a father who will respect her femininity, who will not ridicule and belittle things womanly but who will take the position with his girl children that they have a "future" which is every bit as important and worthwhile as that of boys. Just as the mother will naturally not feel that she, herself, can provide a model for masculinity, neither does the father expect to guide his daughters, in any specific sense, in the ways of womanhood; but in both instances the parent of the opposite sex can give a child the feeling that he or she, in identifying with the same-sexed parent, is doing an important and proper thing.

sider, and resolve them in a new way. Personality development involves many "choice points," and the child, if he adopts a wrong strategy, takes a misleading, self-defeating path at a crucial stage of his development, has to go back to that stage, at least at the level of thought and feeling, and, with the help of the therapist, find another avenue of development which will lead, smoothly and certainly, to the goal of adult adjustment and personal maturity.

Freud was eminently right in stressing anxiety as the basis of all neurotic symptomatology and in maintaining that anxiety—or at least that type which leads to symptom formation—arises only when there has been a prior act of repression. But clinical experience continues to provide new and ever stronger evidence that pathogenic repression goes not in the direction of the primal, biologically given impulses of sex and aggression, as Freud supposed, but in the direction of the socially derived drives which constitute conscience. The neurotic is, without exception in the author's experience, a person who has done things of which he was ashamed but who, instead of avowing and forsaking his immaturities, has tried instead to deny, repudiate, and repress his own self-condemnation, shame, and guilt. Freud conceived the neurotic as a person in whom the superego has overwhelmed the ego and enforced a repression of important id forces. The picture which the author consistently sees in neurotic patients is that of a person whose ego functions have continued to be largely id-dominated, as is typical and normal in infancy but pathological at the adult level.

In the normal individual, parental authority has been both internalized as superego and assimilated by and integrated with the ego. In the neurotic, parental authority has been internalized but has not been assimilated. The superego is thus a kind of incapsulated, walled-off foreign body which succeeds in exerting an influence upon the conscious life of the individual only in the form of neurotic anxiety, depression, and inferiority feeling. To oversimplify what occurs in therapy, we may say that in the transference relationship the neurotic's unaccepted, unassimilated superego is "extrojected" out upon the person of the therapist, and when this occurs we see the patient repeat and relive the problems which he encountered but did not successfully resolve in his childhood relationship with his parent. Therapy thus provides a kind of second childhood and a second chance at the "unfinished business" of growing up.

Again we must greatly telescope the actual events of therapy, but in outline what happens is this. The therapist, by virtue of his special technical training, is able to meet the assaults and strategies of the transference without manifesting countertransference, i.e., without reacting in the highly personalized, emotional way in which the patient's own parents behaved with him. This behavior on the part of the therapist has two important consequences: (1) it enables the patient to work through his anxieties and guilts in connection with all the "bad" impulses and habits which are revived in the transference and to achieve, perhaps for the first time in his experience, a defense-free, honest, and comfortable relationship with another human being; (2) it dissolves old expectations, strategies, and habits sufficiently so that the patient can consider alternative modes of adjustment, and since the therapist has already established himself as a helpful, competent individual in the eyes of the patient, the patient, in the later stages of therapy (the so-called "positive transference") tends to identify with the therapist.

This latter phenomenon is so common and so typical that the available examples of it are manifold; however, the following will usefully serve for present purposes. The patient, in this instance, was a male graduate student specializing in commercial art, who came into therapy because of generalized anxiety, sexual inhibitions, and a complaint of imaginary figures who lurked behind bushes at night and furtively slipped along behind the patient in the street. The interview from which this excerpt is taken was the twenty-seventh. The patient began by apologizing for being a few minutes late and complained of unusual fatigue.

Patient: I'm just beat. I'm absolutely exhausted. I ought to go home and go to sleep.

(*Laughs.*) You know, it's a funny thing, but this friend of mine whom I was with—the fellow I've been telling you about the last few sessions, the one whom I had made some judgments on—and, it's a funny thing; and I've been listening to him talk. I've been doing a lot of listening lately. And I hear him say some of the same things I've always said. "I don't know. Well, I don't know. I just don't get it. It doesn't figure." And, it's funny. I wouldn't like the great indecision he's in. And, its interesting, though, some of the questions he brought up.

The things he talks about, make it seem—it seems as if the problems which I had when I came here are so, well, common problems, in that I hear him saying so many of the things that I used to say, some of the phrases—"Where're we gonna go? What is— If there's nothing more than all this—" It's like a guy with forty paths—which one to take? "Where should I go?"

He has such a fantastic preoccupation with what is truth and what is right and what is wrong, which indicated to me, very much, that he's having a problem about right and wrong himself.

He said, "If I could only—" We were riding in the truck this morning, and he said, "If I could only separate that part of me which is emotional from that part of me which is rational—" And I said to him (*laughs*)—I use, I used a Mowrer, ah, idea; and I said, "Well, isn't it possible that you're trying to say that maybe we, if you could only bring those two things together—?"

And he said, "Yeah, I guess maybe you're right." The reason I'm bringing all this up is that I find it so akin to all the things, all the things I've been thinking about all these months, and I realize that his problems are so very much like mine, and so many of my friends must have problems which are so much, very much like mine.

Therapist: All right, I'm going to make a comment a little earlier today than I usually do. I think what you've just been saying is a kind of unit and is fairly clear in its meaning. I think that if I'd been right bright I'd have seen some of this one or two interviews back.

This is the man, I believe, that you reported some conversation about to a woman, a girl. [P.: Yeah.] And you gave her some kind of advice about this man. [P.: Yes.] Now, I think that many of the things you have been saying are just what they, just what they seem to be. That is to say, we want to look at the reality factors first and acknowledge them. But I think there's rather interesting evidence here, that there's a little evidence here of something over and beyond the purely reality factors. I think there's a little psychological drama going on here that we (*P. laughs*) want to notice.

I notice that you laughed a little bit just now—

P.: Yeah, I was— You're right. I've been trying to say it, you know. There— I have a big guilt feeling about this whole thing. [T.: Mmm-huh.] Not a big guilt feeling. It's not even an anxiety. It's just—it's a bewilderment, you know. I'm sort of lost in a maze of emotions and ideas and concepts, you know. I've gone ahead and done something, and I wonder if I've done the wrong thing, after talking to him, that maybe I've, why should I have destroyed anything for him? I'd probably have no right to—probably should have just kept my goddamned mouth shut and minded my business and let him go on with his life, and let all these other people conduct their lives the way they want to. And who am I to stick my nose into it? And I went and did it, and I'm sorry; I'm very, *very* sorry. And I feel very *badly* about it.

T.: Well, I don't believe you've got that one quite right yet. I think the guilt is there, but I don't think you have identified the source of the guilt right yet. I think the guilt comes, very simply, from your having attempted to be like me.

P.: Me?

T.: Yes.

P. (*laughs*): Yeah? I see what you mean.

T.: And you, you— There's been an attempt here— Uh. First of all, you see, there's been the quandary: "What am I going to do? I don't know what I'm going to do now [that I'm getting my degree]." And, I don't know whether this has been unconscious or just partly conscious—I'm sure it hasn't been fully conscious; but it's a very natural thing, and commonly happens in the last stages of therapy, that the person goes through a period of feeling, "Well, golly! If I could just be like Pop, like the Old Man, maybe the answer to my life problems is to become a psychologist, too. [P. (*laughs and says*) : I see what you mean.], and I think you're, you're living through something like that now. It's as if, somewhere down the line, you got the idea that you could not be like your biological father; and what you're exploring now is the possibility of being like this sort of second, or substitute, father—and seeing how I'll feel about it, seeing if I think you might do it, or would I *let* you do it. Do you dare lay claim to such a (*P. laughs*), such a *high* thing? And I think that's where the guilt comes. You had guilt last time and you had guilt again today, uh, because you were afraid that I would say, "You preposterous, you presuming young jackanapes! How *dare* you think you can be a man too?"

P.: I see— Yes, this is—this is— (*laughs*). I guess I've repressed [i.e., not told Therapist] a lot of things. A lot of people talk about dreams now, you know, sort of discussion about dreams, and truth, discussion among college people, especially among many of my friends. I've used so many of your concepts, really; and I think I, I think you're right. In fact, I know that you're very right, that I have been (*laughs*)—but I never realized that that's why I felt guilty.

P.: I have something very interesting to say right now. You know I'm not tired.

T.: That's interesting.

. . . . .

T.: I think your fatigue was a kind of converted guilt or apprehension. It was almost as if you came in and said, "I'm all beaten down today; don't you hop on me."

P.: Better than that! You know what happened? When I was riding down, I was, I almost wanted to say, I, I fantasied this, just for a split second, you know one of these quick, a quick think you see. As if to say, "I'm tired today. Do you mind if I don't come in?" You know what I mean? Calling up and saying, "Gee, I'd just like to take a nap today. I hope you don't mind. I'll come in tomorrow." 'Cause you know, I didn't want to face you, the rod, the wheel. And I got more tired as I thought about it.

You know, I gotta say this and—uh, I realize so much and also in these last few minutes that so many of the things that I've always wanted are so much nearer to me. I don't mean practically but emotional and rationally.

You don't know how I feel right now. Remember when I used to come and sit in this chair and feel numb? [T.: Uhhuh.] Well, I don't feel numb now. . . . It's like someone just lifted a great weight out of my head.

Although identification with the therapist is a common occurrence in the later phases of therapy, we can perhaps take comfort in the fact that this identification is likely to be transitory. Again greatly telescoping what actually happens, we may say that, as a result of having worked through the negative transference, the patient develops a feeling of gratitude and trust with respect to the therapist, with resulting changes in ego attitudes toward authority figures which prepare the way for a more accepting and conciliatory orientation toward the superego. In other words, by virtue of the "therapeutic regression," the patient extrojects his unassimilated conscience upon the person of the therapist; works through, on an interpersonal basis, the conflicts which he could not resolve intrapsychically; and then, with changed ego attitudes toward the therapist (as a symbol of authority), begins to identify with the therapist as a preliminary to reintrojecting conscience and terminating therapy.

This discussion leaves many interesting questions unanswered; but here we can speak only synoptically and must leave these problems for another time.[13]

VII. Identification and Object Choice

Freudian theory presents a basic dilemma in that it posits two fundamental patterns of human relations, that of *identification* and that of *object choice,* but it fails to indicate explicitly the circumstances under which each of these develops. The normal individual is assumed to have identified with the parent and other persons of the same sex and to have taken opposite-sexed persons as love objects. The pervert has identified with the opposite sex and takes same-sexed persons as love objects.[14] And, in Section IV, evidence

[13] One of the most intriguing of these is the question of the relationship between the sex of the therapist and that of the patient. At first it might appear that, if the foregoing analysis is correct, the patient and therapist should always be of the same sex; but this does not follow as a matter of theory, and practice further indicates that it is not true, at least not in any categorical sense. One possible explanation of the fact that both men and women therapists, if properly trained, can do good work with both male and female patients is that some of the conflicts which have to be worked through in treatment are "pre-Oedipal," i.e., have to do with conflicts and identification dilemmas which antedate the period (from three of five) during which sex typing and training are most intensive. Another possibility is that every good therapist, whether man or woman, has a clear image and active appreciation of both masculinity *and* femininity, and can thus promote growth along whichever line of development is appropriate for the patient (see Footnote 12). However, this is an issue which has been but little explored and should be reserved for fuller discussion at a later date.

[14] Such a person is said to be "homosexual." This expression shows how largely biological and how little psychological our thinking is in this field. In the psychological sense, one may conjecture that there is no such thing as "homosexuality": presumably a person always selects as a love object a person of the sex opposite to that with which he (or she), at least for the time being, most strongly identifies. In this sense everyone is "heterosexual." In other words, the fact that the genitalia of two persons are the same (anatomical, or biological, sameness) does not at all mean that, in the psychological sense, they are "like-sexed." Or, it may be that the so-called homosexual is a person who has not yet made the differentiation (to be discussed below) between personal models and love objects. Research with birds (24) suggests a tendency for them both to become sexually attached to and to identify with their trainers. One can hardly suppose that we yet have definitive answers in such matters.

has been advanced that the neurotic is a person who is partially identified with *both* sexes, caught somewhere in between—confused, insecure, unstable, guilty, anxious.

All this is clear enough. The question is: What, precisely, are the factors or experiences which decide whether a child will tend to identify with or take as a sex object the parent-person of one sex or the other?

All theorists seem agreed that both identification and object choice depend upon a positive, affectional relationship between the individuals concerned. In order for a boy to want to be like his father, he must *like* his father; and in order for the boy to like women in general, he must, we assume, like his mother. But what, we must ask, is the exact nature of this "liking" in the two cases which leads to such very different outcomes?

One possibility is to assume that there are two different forms of liking, or loving, and that the child learns, at an early age, to direct one of them toward persons of one sex and the other toward persons of the opposite sex. Clearly the difficulty here is circularity; for we are assuming what remains to be explained; namely, why and how this type of learning occurs.

Another possibility—and the one implicitly adopted by Freud—is to assume that there is only one basic form of love, namely, sexual love, that this determines object choice, and that identification follows as a derivative, or consequence. If, for example, a boy becomes sexually, or libidinally, oriented toward women, then automatically he tends to become a real man, for men, at least all proper men, are so oriented. The boy in making such a choice comes closer to manhood, closer to being like men, closer to being identified with them.

In spite of the great emphasis which Freud, in the passages quoted in earlier sections of this paper, placed upon identification, it is clear that he regarded it as subsidiary to and dependent upon object choice. Nowhere is this more apparent than in one of his later papers, published in 1931, with the title "Female Sexuality." He begins this paper with the following significant paragraph:

In that phase of children's libidinal development which is characterized by the normal Oedipus complex, we find that they are tenderly attached to the parent of the opposite sex, while their relation to the other parent is predominantly hostile. In the case of boys the explanation is simple. A boy's mother was his first love-object; she remains so, and, as his feelings for her become more passionate and he understands more of the relation between father and mother, the former inevitably appears as a rival. With little girls it is otherwise. For them, too, the mother was the first love-object; how then does a little girl find her way to her father? How, when, and why does she detach herself from her mother? We have long realized that in women the development of sexuality is complicated by the task of renouncing that genital zone which was originally the principal one, namely, the clitoris, in favor of a new zone—the vagina. But there is a second change which appears to us no less characteristic and important for feminine development: the original mother-object has to be exchanged for the father. We cannot as yet see clearly how these two tasks are linked up (p. 252).

Freud is correct in noting the difficulties connected with this view of psychosexual development, but he never made what would seem to have been a most natural alternative assumption, namely, that the love a child first develops for his parents is such as to lead to identification and that object choice *follows as a secondary result.* Thus, when a little boy begins to experience libidinal impulses he will, if already he has become firmly aligned with his father and with men in general, be strongly disposed to direct these impulses toward women, in keeping with the model provided by his father; and the little girl, in identifying with her mother, will tend, like mother, to take men as sex objects.

One of the important implications of this alternative view can be brought out by reconsidering the problem posited in the paragraph just quoted from Freud. Because Freud assumed that object choice is primary and identification derived therefrom, he believed that the psychosexual development of boys is simpler than that of girls, since boys can at an early date take women as sex objects and retain them as such throughout life; but girls, Freud conjectured, having, like the boys, taken the mother as the first sex object, must later abandon this object choice in favor of men and assume instead an identification relationship with the mother and with women generally. The alternative hypothesis here suggested holds that the situation is the reverse. Because the infant's first experiences of care and affection are with the mother, we infer, for reasons which have been considered at length in Section II, that there will be a tendency for children of *both* sexes to identify (see Section IV) with the mother. This provides a path of development which the female child can follow indefinitely; but the male child must, in some way, abandon the mother as a personal model and shift his loyalties and ambitions to his father. Once the boy and the girl are securely aligned with the mother and the father, respectively, *in terms of their basic character structure,* then, as specific sexual needs arise, they can be handled along lines prescribed as correct and proper for members of their particular sex.

However, we must not neglect to consider the question of how it is that the boy, whose primal identification is ordinarily with the mother—for example, mothers almost certainly play a greater role in their infants' learning to walk and talk than do their fathers—how it is that the boy eventually abandons the mother as his personal guide and takes instead the father. Here we have few facts to guide us, but we may plausibly conjecture that the first identification which infants make with mother figures is *undifferentiated.* By this I mean that the small child probably first comes to perceive the mother, not as a woman who is distinct from men, but simply as a human being, different in no systematic way from other adult figures in the environment. The personal characteristics which are acquired through identification with, or imitation of, the mother during this period are characteristics or accomplishments which are appropriate to *all* persons, male and female alike. It is only at a later stage, presumably, that the child becomes aware of the partition of mankind into two sexes; [15] and it is then that the father, who has played a somewhat subsidiary role up to this point, normally comes forward as the boy's special mentor, as his proctor, guide, and model in matters which will help the boy eventually to achieve full adult status in his society, not only as a human being, but also in the unique status of a *man.* This, we note, involves two things: (1) being a man in the sense of being honorable, reliable, industrious, skilful, courageous, and courteous; and (2) being a man in the sense of being masculine, i.e., sexually oriented toward members of the opposite sex.

For the girl child the mother is teacher and model, not only during the undifferentiated infantile period, but also during the later stages when she is acquiring her training along sex-typed lines. While there may be some economy in this arrangement of being able to keep the same identification model throughout the whole of early life over the one which is necessary for the male child, the difference is probably not particularly fateful in the normal, emotionally healthy family constellation. At any rate, it is an arrangement that has seemed to

[15] Children are often surprised at this discovery and may be incredulous regarding it. These observations are consistent with the view that during the infantile period (from birth to the age of two or three), mothers are probably perceived as differing in no systematic way from all other persons, who drift vaguely about in the background. The discovery of sexual differentiation, as indicated not only by the genitals but by secondary sexual characteristics, dress, and occupation, plus the realization on the part of the child that he (or she) must somehow fit into this scheme of men and women, can hardly fail to be important, and in some children perhaps to take on crisis-like proportions. Freud, as is well known, made these events the basis for the "castration complex," from which he drew far-reaching inferences along other lines.

work, after a fashion, for a long time and will probably not be soon abandoned.

The difference between the Freudian point of view and the one here presented is simply illustrated in the series of diagrams shown in Figure 72. Figure *72a* represents the prenatal period, when both

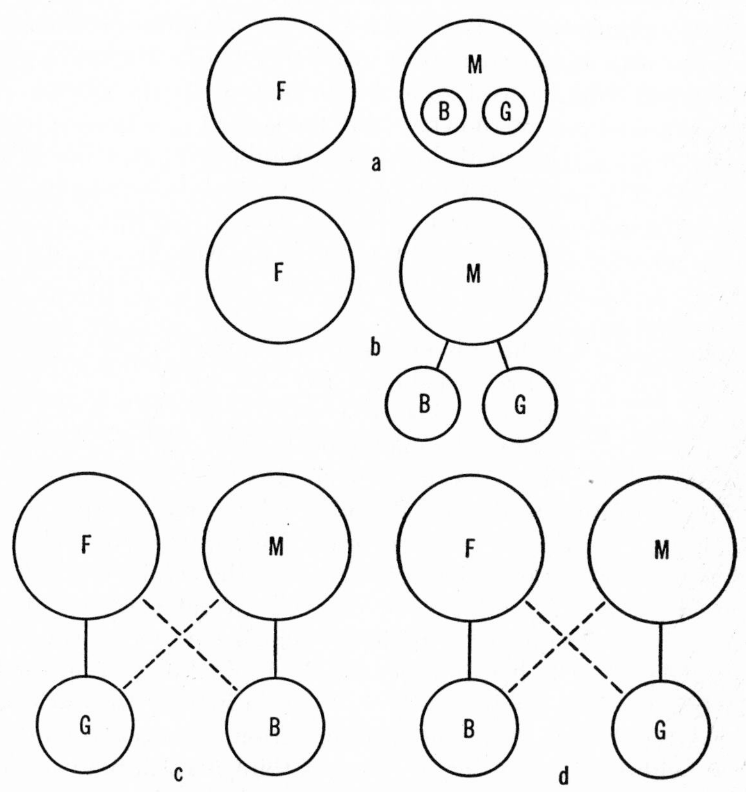

FIG. 72.—Four diagrams designed to illustrate two conceptions of the relationship between object choice and identification. The Freudian conception is shown by the sequence *a, b, c*. The alternative conception here proposed is shown by the sequence *a, b, d*. For details, see text.

the boy and the girl child are *anatomically attached* to the mother and live within her body. In the postnatal, infantile period (Figure *72b*), children are still powerfully "attached to" and dependent upon the mother; but the attachment or relationship is now largely one of *mediation* (Section IV), although in the act of nursing there is again a "connection" which approximates that provided by the umbilical cord. According to Freud, the emotional conditioning which develops in connection with the stage represented by Figure *72b* leads, in the case of male children, directly into an enduring libidinal attachment (Figure *72c,* solid line) to the mother, and later to women in general. In some rather inexplicit way, loving women sexually "makes a man" of the boy and brings about masculine identification (broken line). Even less clear is the mechanism whereby the little girl's major sexual interests (solid line) become invested in the father and, through him, in men generally. Nor is it evident how what was initially a kind of primitive sexual attachment to the mother becomes converted into identification (broken line).

The more nearly correct view, I believe, is shown in Figure *72d.* Our underlying assumption here is that the type of relationship which an infant normally has with his or her mother disposes the infant first of all to a relationship with the mother which is best referred to as developmental identification. In the case of the girl, this can continue relatively uninterruptedly (solid line), with the sexual interest in men developing at appropriately later stages and derivatively (broken line).

In theory at least, the only problem which arises is that of getting the boy's affection and regard shifted from the mother to the father in sufficient degree so as to insure a transfer of the identification trends from the female to the male model. The answer here seems to lie in actual practice. When a boy child is three or four years of age, the good father tends to "take him on," to accept responsibility for him in a way that he does not do for his little girls. The boy becomes *my boy, my son;* the father permits the child to accompany him in his work, if possible, and otherwise creates special opportunities for excursions and experiences which the mother could not well provide. The father, in other words, begins to open up for the child a glimpse into "man's world." Even in infancy toys will have been sex-typed, but now the differentiation becomes even more marked, with the boy getting as presents things which unmistakably resemble or replicate the father's possessions and tools. At the same time the good mother begins to "wean" her son, to cut the "apron strings," and to urge him gently to "follow," both literally and figuratively, his father. When this process is successful, the major emotional attachment shifts to the father (solid line), and the first step has been taken toward establishing a sexual orientation (like father's) toward woman (broken line).[16]

[16] See Stoke (1950) for some excellent examples. Although little boys and girls associate freely and, later, come back together again for purposes of adolescent courtship, it is striking how strong are the tendencies toward isolation during the period designated by Freud as latency. Does this isolation represent reaction formation against submerged sexual interests, or is this period rather seized upon as a time when consolidation of masculinity and femininity is being sought in peer groups, as well as with the same-sexed parent? This phenomenon in our

The position here taken that identification is the basic fact of child-parent relationships and that sex-object choice is a later and derivative phenomenon has a number of illuminating implications. First of all it gives a possible explanation of the fact that parents have traditionally attempted to preserve with their small children a kind of myth of asexuality as far as their personal lives are concerned. Realizing intuitively, if not otherwise, that a too vivid demonstration of adult sex life may, through identification, create a precocious concern on the part of the child with erotic matters, parents usually conceal and sometimes even deny their own activities in this connection. Indirectly and by implication the child often "suspects," and at a little later period he gets still stronger intimations from stories, movies, and like sources. Perhaps we may even say that the "Oedipus complex" in the strictly Freudian sense is precisely what this behavior on the part of parents is designed to avoid and that this complex, when present, is an expression of familial pathology rather than an inevitable stage of development.

During World War II the expression "momism" came into existence as a means of denoting a type of personality commonly encountered in young men in which there is an excessive dependence upon and attachment to the mother, with but feeble attachment to the father and no very clear image gained through him of man's estate. Bach (1946), Sears (1946), and others have commented upon the probable roots of this phenomenon, namely the absence, both physically and psychologically, of the father from many American urban homes. Because of the conditions of contemporary economic and social life, many fathers have neither the opportunity nor the inclination to "take on" their sons in the way that was common, for example, in the days of the guilds and still occurs in many rural families.

The position here taken that identification is the basic fact of child-parent relationships and that sex-object choice is a later and derivative phenomenon has special bearing on the question of "homosexuality." The Freudian view, which holds that object choice is basic and identification derivative, has long presented a puzzling picture with respect to the genesis of homosexuality. The precondition for its development in the male was supposed by Freud to be an excessively strong "mother attachment" or "mother fixation" with the intimation that this attachment was strongly libidinal or erotic

society might be usefully studied in relation to the practice in many primitive societies of sending boys and girls to live, sometimes for several years, in separate "houses" or camps.

in character. While it is universally recognized as undesirable for boys to develop and retain a too lively or too active sexual interest in their mothers, it is not immediately evident how such an interest would necessarily drive them in the direction of homosexuality. Indeed, one might suppose that it would orient them all the more powerfully toward heterosexuality. It is far simpler and probably more nearly correct to suppose that it is the boy who remains "attached" to his mother, not as a sex object but as an identification model, who is later predisposed to perversion. If mother (like women in general) is sexually oriented toward men and if the boy's strongest personal alignment remains with her, then he, too, as a consequence of his persistent mother identification, will tend to be sexually oriented toward men.

Because male children have to make an identification shift from mother to father if they are to avoid homosexuality and since no such shift is normally required of girls, it might be inferred that the hazard of homosexuality would be greater in men than in women. If this prediction is not confirmed by the facts, it may indicate either that other factors, e.g., economic conditions, enter as complications or that the shift, as already suggested, is not ordinarily difficult to make.

There is also a curious contradiction between the Freudian view that character formulation is dominated by libidinal forces and the manifest fact that effective psychotherapy can be done without any conscious effort to redirect or recondition these forces. There are, it is true, psychiatrists and clinical psychologists who apparently operate on the assumption that what a neurotic patient needs most is instruction, encouragement, and guidance in obtaining new and different forms of sexual gratification. But the sounder position is that if, in the transference relationship, one works through old interpersonal problems which are largely nonsexual in nature, the patient will develop a more positive and firmer identification with members of his own sex and will, as a secondary and indirect consequence, make appropriate readjustments in the specifically sexual area. Obviously the skilled and ethical therapist does not set out to cure a neurosis by sexual re-education, any more than a good parent would stress the sexual experience of his children to the exclusion of all other facets of their existence; but this is the course of action which might seem dictated by Freud's emphasis upon the primacy of object choice in determining personal normality or abnormality.

If it should appear that in this concluding section we have unduly emphasized or possibly distorted Freud's position with respect to the relative importance of identification and object choice, doubt on this score will be dispelled by the following quotation, taken from the latter part of the article on female sexuality already cited:

> A study of the analytic literature on this subject makes evident that it already contains everything that I have said here. This paper would be superfluous were it not that in so obscure a field of research every account of any worker's direct experience and the conclusions to which he personally is led may be of value. I have, moreover, I think, defined certain points more precisely and shown them in stricter isolation than has hitherto been done. *Some of the other writings on the subject are confusing because they deal at the same time with the problems of the superego and the sense of guilt.* This I have avoided . . . (p. 269, italics added).

It will be recalled that Freud developed the concept of identification as a means of accounting for superego formation; and his insistence that other writings which introduce this topic are "confusing" leaves little question as to whether, in Freud's mind, it was sex or character which is the more basic to the understanding of personality problems. Yet in more than one place in the same article, Freud himself confesses to confusion and uncertainty. Throughout the article one finds such phrases as:

> But possibly I have received this impression because . . . (p. 254). Very possibly this account . . . will strike the reader as confused and contradictory. This is not altogether the writer's fault. A description which fits every case is in fact almost impossible (p. 261). I know this sounds quite absurd, but perhaps only because the idea is such an unfamiliar one to us (p. 267).

One may, therefore, with good reason doubt the validity of Freud's emphasis upon specifically sexual factors in the etiology of neurotic difficulties and build instead upon leads which are provided by his brilliant but incomplete formulations regarding the phenomenon of identification and its vicissitudes. In this and the immediately preceding sections of this paper, we have attempted to show that these formulations provide the basis for a more consistent and more unified conceptual system than do the inferences which Freud made from so-called libido theory.

VIII. Summary

A. IMITATION AND LEARNING THEORY. Folk wisdom and common sense have long recognized the importance of parental example as well as precept in the training of children. But modern learning theorists, in their search for lawful simplicity, have stressed principles which have not been sufficiently elaborated to account for the intricacies of *imitation* and other complex forms of *social learning.* Using the principle of association through contiguity, Holt was the first to make a concerted attack, in terms of learning theory, upon the problem of imitation; and Miller and Dollard, a decade later, followed with an approach to the same problem which relied heavily upon a theory of learning that stresses the importance of *reward.* While both of these analyses have important features, neither is entirely adequate.

B. A TWO-FACTOR ANALYSIS OF IMITATIVE LEARNING. Contemporary investigations have indicated that no single principle will accommodate all the facts of learning but that by positing both *conditioning* and *problem solving* as distinct processes, many otherwise puzzling phenomena can be accounted for. Experimentation with "talking birds" has revealed that both of these learning processes are importantly involved in the imitative behavior of these subjects. By the process of conditioning, the spoken words of the trainer become "good sounds" to the bird, with secondary reinforcing value. When, subsequently, the bird itself makes vocal responses which are somewhat similar to those made by the trainer, these responses are subjectively reinforced, repeated, and perfected. This *autistic* conception of imitation differs in important ways from the earlier theories of Holt and of Miller and Dollard.

C. IMITATION AND IDENTIFICATION. "Imitation" and "identification" are sometimes used as distinctive terms, sometimes as synonyms. "Identification" was introduced by Freud to denote that remarkable process whereby the human young acquire, not simply imitative motor skills such as walking and talking, but those attitudes and convictions which make up the *superego* or *conscience.* Discussions of imitation had not usually included this aspect of personality development. While the fears and loyalties which constitute the basic stuff of conscience are probably acquired on the basis of conditioning, acceptance of the attendant social and moral responsibilities by the ego or executive part of the personality can probably be accounted for only by means of an "ego psychology" which emphasizes *conflict* and *anxiety.* Full and final acceptance of the restrictive, coercive dictates of parents and other social authorities ("conversion") seems to come about as a means of resolving the conflict-produced anxiety which would otherwise be experienced. Hence comes the striking phrase, first employed by Anna Freud, "identification with the aggressor."

D. IDENTIFICATION (DEVELOPMENTAL AND DEFENSIVE) AND THE CONCEPT OF MEDIATION. It now appears that there are two importantly different forms of identification: developmental identification, representing an attempt on the part of the infant to reproduce bits of the beloved and longed-for parent; and defensive identification, based upon an attempt to resolve intolerable conflict produced by the disciplinary action of parents. The first of these includes much of what has previously been referred to by the term "imitation"; and the second is synonymous with Anna Freud's expression "identification with the aggressor."

Another way of making this distinction is to say that developmental identification is based upon the personal mediation of parents which is directed toward the "stimulus side" or *needs,* of the infant, whereas defensive identification comes about when the personal mediation of parents is addressed to the "response side," or *behavior,* of children.

E. IDENTIFICATION AND NEUROSIS. *Personal normality* presupposes that an individual has assimilated not only those values and ideals which are regarded as necessary and proper for all persons, but also those values and ideals which are uniquely appropriate to one's *sex role,* as a man or as a woman. Where identification has occurred predominantly with the opposite-sexed parent rather than with the parent of the same sex, the individual is disposed to homosexuality. Where there is a confused, divided sexual identification, the resulting personality is likely to be *neurotic.* An excerpt from a recorded therapeutic interview illustrates the type of identification dilemma which is often the prelude to neurotic difficulties.

F. IDENTIFICATION, NEUROSIS, AND PSYCHOTHERAPY. By observing the necessary technical rules, a competent psychotherapist creates a situation in which *therapeutic regression* takes place and the patient is able to reactivate the old childhood conflicts which resulted in identification confusion and ambivalence toward the same-sexed parent. Through proper management of the resulting negative transference, the basis is laid for a new and firmer alignment on the part of the patient with persons of his own sex and a more assured, secure, and satisfying relation with members of the opposite sex. Very often, in the later stages of therapy, the patient will pass through a transitory *identification with the therapist.* A verbatim fragment from a therapy recording illustrates this phenomenon.

G. IDENTIFICATION AND OBJECT CHOICE. Although it was Freud who originated the concept of identification as a basic process underlying character formation, he has repeatedly given it an importance secondary to *sex-object* choice. Freud's view was that the libidinal experiences of the infant (particularly those of nursing and fantasy) dispose it to take the mother as its first love object. Boys, reasoned Freud, are able to retain their initial sexual orientation toward the female sex; but girls, in some manner, have to shift their major libidinal "cathesis" from the mother to the father and hence to men in general, if they are to avoid perversion. The present writer's position is that identification normally precedes and, later, dictates object choice. Thus, the first stage of identification, which in principle is probably no different from what is properly called imitation, is ordinarily with the mother, as the most familiar, most responsive, most loving parent. Later, when *sex-typing* of the child becomes important and the more *restrictive aspects of culture* have to be transmitted, the boy is encouraged to take his father as a personal model, whereas the girl can retain the mother as a model. Some of the implications of these two points of view are briefly considered.

CHAPTER 22

THE LIFE AND WORK OF EDGAR ALLAN POE—A STUDY IN CONSCIENCE-KILLING

[In the opening sentence of his essay "The Poetic Principle," Poe remarks that in it he has "no design to be either thorough or profound." I may make a similar disclaimer with respect to the paper which follows. Certainly I lay no claim to thoroughness—I have not read all Poe's own works, much less all that has been written about him. This paper is little more than a collection of work-notes, which I hope eventually to bring into more finished form. But a psychotherapist uses interpretations—made with an appropriate degree of tentativeness—both as a means of treatment and as a means of inquiry and exploration; what I have to say here is in the nature, then, of an interpretation, rather than a final "diagnosis."

And as to profundity, it is not, I believe, necessary to the task at hand; for the hypothesis which I wish to propose, and in some degree test, against the background of Poe's life and the general tenor of his writings is a relatively simple one. If this hypothesis has not been proposed by critics and interpreters of Poe during the nineteenth century, it was because of the nonpsychological character of their thought. And if it has been overlooked during the first half of the present century, it is because the only psychology which has evolved with sufficient scope to deal with problems such as Poe presents has been characterized by a conceptual one-sidedness which has often obscured plainer truths.

Biographers and others who have written about Poe fall into two categories: those who believe that his writings and the facts about his life can be explained on a purely "rational" basis and those who hold that such an explanation is impossible and that we must have recourse here to the principles of "depth" psychology. While belonging to the latter group, I am aware that not everything which Poe wrote was "of the soul"; some of it was written largely for effect—and some of it merely for money. Our data are therefore in some measure "contaminated," but there remains much which is subjectively valid and for which we find intriguing possibilities of explanation in the principles which have been discussed in preceding chapters.

This paper, in substance, was presented as an address before the Psychological Association of Quebec, in February, 1949, but has not been previously published.]

I. Introduction

Almost all who have sought to untangle the enigma of the life and works of Edgar Allan Poe have been ready enough to acknowledge the failure of others in this respect. Joseph Wood Krutch, for example, remarks:

> Three quarters of a century have passed [he was writing in 1926] and the bibliography of writings about Poe is longer, perhaps, than that devoted to any other American writer except Whitman, and yet from this mountain of matter has emerged no solution of his mystery and no generally accepted estimate of either his work or his character (p. 9).

Perhaps it is the vanity of each succeeding writer to think that he can succeed where others have failed; but it is to be noted, entirely objectively, that prior to the turn of the century we had no naturalistic frame of reference in which to think about problems such as Poe presents. It will not be surprising, therefore, if contemporary writers progress further than did those of the last century who, though closer to Poe in time, were worlds removed from him in logic.

Since during the whole of his life (he died at forty) Poe was, by present-day standards, severely neurotic and, near the end, probably psychotic, and since *scientific* study in these areas has prospered only for the last half-century, it is not surprising that earlier analyses seem incomplete and superficial. But the science of personology is still in the making, and Krutch's study, however much an advance it was for its day, leaves many questions unanswered.

Because few acutely neurotic persons—prior to the development of electronic recording of therapeutic interviews (and much of this material cannot yet be used)—have left such voluminous, and none so eloquent, a record of their sufferings as did Poe, his writings and the historical facts about him provide a useful proving ground for current hypotheses. Since the author has a hypothesis to test, Poe comes conveniently to hand.

Poe once registered his opinions of those "gray-beards" who write on "history, philosophy, and other matters of this kind" by remarking, in "The Short Story," "These grave topics, to the end of time, will be best illustrated by what a discriminating world, turning up its nose at the drab pamphlets, has agreed to call talent." Such barbed lines may reflect Poe's secret love of the academic life, which he aspired to but never attained (having been expelled, with much bitterness on the part of all concerned, from the University of Virginia early in his student career there—and later from West Point—although "he always passed for one of the best scholars in America"[1]). Or in these lines he may be warning those with an inquiring turn of mind who were to come after him not to examine too closely his own works of "ambitious genius."

In "The Philosophy of Composition," Poe tried to beat the critics and the analyzers to the draw by reporting how and why he wrote his best-known poem, "The Raven"; but this effort, like that of others, leaves Poe's secret—if it may be said ever to have been "his," save in an unconscious sense—essentially untouched.[2]

In a series of papers (18, 19, 20), I have recently elaborated a theory of anxiety and neurosis which seems to penetrate the artistic façade of Poe's writings and to order them so naturally that, once one sees them in the light of this hypothesis, they become structured, like a complex visual figure whose *pattern* is for the first time suddenly apprehended. The thesis of this paper is that many of Poe's most successful literary contributions conform neatly to this theory and that it is the *psychological reality* of Poe's "best" works that accounts for their goodness and their popularity.

The plan of the paper will be as follows: a brief review of the psychological hypothesis under discussion; an analysis of the production in which Poe most nakedly exposes the theme of unsuccessful conscience-repudiation as the basis of anxiety; an analysis of the production in which the same theme is clearly implied but partially disguised; an analysis of Poe's most famous and, superficially, enigmatic poem, "The Raven"; then a re-evaluation of Basler's analysis of "Ligeia" and of Bonaparte's discussion of "The Black Cat"; and finally a summarizing section.

One reason for this particular plan is that Poe's writings, like the productions of other neurotics, have to be viewed in juxtaposi-

---

[1] This quotation is from page xii of the biographical introduction which James Hannay prepared for the collection of Poe's works which he published in London in 1853, four years after Poe's death. Stern (1945) refers to "the intellectual and analytical part of Poe's versatile mind" (p. 507). Krutch, on the other hand, expresses a lower opinion of Poe's scholarship. In one of many similar passages, we find him remarking: "To say with Andrew Lang that Poe had a scholar's taste without a scholar's training is to forget that he lacked absolutely the humility which is a necessary part of the scholar's temperament and that his pretentiousness was enough, taken merely by itself, to suggest much more easily the perfect charlatan" (p. 95). Of all the Poe critics, Campbell (1933) appears to have gone to the most pains to examine the facts pertaining to Poe's scholarly competence; and the list of accomplishments which he adduces is impressive, although he, too, observes that Poe "did not scruple to twist or garble a quotation when he felt that this would serve his purposes" (p. 8).

[2] T. S. Eliot, in his small volume, *From Poe to Valéry,* gives his readers the option of interpreting "The Philosophy of Composition" as "a hoax, or a piece of self-deception, or a more or less accurate record of Poe's calculations in writing the poem" (pp. 29–30).

tion if one is to discern the red thread of meaning that runs through them. Viewed in isolation, their meaning is often too subtle ("delicacy is the poet's own kingdom") [3] for conscious detection, but when the same motif appears recurrently, it rises above the threshold of perception and may be explicitly noted—i.e., "interpreted."

II. Anxiety and Superego Repression

It is to Freud's great credit that he clearly discerned and had the courage to demonstrate that the behavioral manifestations which we now call "symptoms" are not the essence of neurosis and that the modes of treatment that are aimed at their direct alleviation are as ill-considered theoretically as they are futile practically. Throughout his long career as a practicing psychotherapist, Freud maintained that *anxiety* is "the fundamental phenomenon and the central problem" (1936, p. 111) and that symptoms are but the "defenses" which the afflicted individual develops as means of coping with this tormenting experience. In terms of modern learning theory, anxiety is the *drive* and the symptoms are the solutions or "habits" which, though possessing real disadvantages for the individual, persist because, with respect to this powerful source of discomfort, they are relieving, *drive reducing*. Today this conception of the surface manifestations of neurosis is very generally accepted among psychoclinicians; and it is the first leg on which the theory of anxiety here accepted stands.

Almost equally well established is Freud's second assumption concerning anxiety, namely that it is an experience which occurs only when there has been a prior act of repression.[4] "Repression" implied, for Freud, that something once conscious gets more or less permanently cut off from voluntary recall but that, though it is now "unconscious," it retains its "psychic energy," which is to say that it continues to influence thought, feeling, and action. This assumption has been a point of much controversy; but Freud's contention, bizarre as it seems to common sense, has gradually gained acceptance and can be validated to the satisfaction of anyone who will examine the clinical evidence.

This, then, is the second leg; and our theory of anxiety is almost ready to walk. But there is an important question of *direction:* Shall the legs carry us forward or backward?

We have posited, with Freud, that anxiety, not what a person

---

[3] *On Poets and Poetry.*

[4] Here the term "anxiety" implies "neurotic anxiety." Cf. the earlier discussion of the relationship between neurotic and normal anxiety (19).

does about it (i.e., his "symptoms"), is the central problem in neurosis and that anxiety exists only when it has been preceded by repression. The critical question now is: "What is it that gets repressed and, in attempting to return to consciousness, produces anxiety?"

Although Freud's formulations on this score varied somewhat over the years, he was steadfast in holding that whereas the ego (or executive part of the personality) and the superego (conscience) are the forces that bring repression about, the *what* of repression is always some biologically given impulse which falls under the ban of social (and later, the individual's own) disapproval. A child (adolescent or adult) in striving to be "good" finds himself tormented by "evil" impulses, characteristically those of sex or hostility. A seemingly insoluble conflict is thus created, but at length it may be terminated by a half-voluntary, half-automatic act of renunciation. By this act the impulse is disowned, repudiated, dissociated so completely that it is no longer a part of the conscious self at all. It is no longer experienced, and intrapsychic peace prevails once more.

But the peace is likely to be short-lived. The repudiated impulse retains its vitality; and, at periods when the impulse is particularly strong or the repressing forces somewhat weakened, it may break through the "membrane" separating it from consciousness, not with sufficient force to be fully recognizable but far enough to arouse great fear. And since this fear is experienced without knowledge of what caused it (the "villain" having escaped without identification), the fear is nameless, objectless, mysterious, terrifying—that is to say, *anxiety.*[5]

---

[5] An analogy will help clarify this conception of anxiety. Let us imagine a medieval walled city in which the inhabitants have been accustomed to passing freely in and out of the portals and thus enjoying access to both the city itself and the countryside. But now a serious civic disturbance breaks out, and it is decided that the offending individuals shall be cast out of the city and the city gates closed to them. They clamor to be readmitted, but ineffectively. The "dissociation" is "successful," and the remaining inhabitants congratulate each other on their felicity. However, as time passes, they become increasingly inconvenienced by their repressive strategy, grumbling grows, and, to preserve order, more persons have to be banished. This cyclic process continues until the strength and number of the excluded persons approximate that of the persons remaining within the city. When this point is reached, the city is so weakened by its own methods of dealing with internal conflict that it falls under constant threat of a "return of the repressed." Naturally the outcasts, in trying to get back into the city, employ various ruses and disguises. In this way they become the causes of mysterious troubles and anxious times. If, ultimately, the outcasts are successful in reentering the city, not gradually and relatively peaceably (as in psychotherapy) and at a rate which will make their assimilation possible, but suddenly, by total assault, then the original government and social structure of the city (the ego) may be completely disorganized, with resultant panic and confusion (psychosis).

This was Freud's conception of anxiety. It was couched in naturalistic terms, it is logically sufficient, and it has had an enormous vogue in both professional and lay circles. But there are growing indications that it is nonetheless incorrect in one important respect. Clinical experience shows that it is not usually—perhaps never—the biologically given impulses that fall under repression and then erupt as anxiety; it is instead *conscience* which, when faced by a hostile, immature, impulse-dominated ego, proves unequal to the struggle and loses its place in the court of consciousness. Guilt is the form in which conscience is normally represented, and it is my thesis that anxiety is experienced when there is "unconscious guilt," i.e., *repressed, dissociated guilt,* which is pressing forward for recognition but which is not recognized as such.[6]

Various attempts, some of which will be reviewed later, have been made to interpret the life and works of Poe in the light of Freud's impulse theory of anxiety. Far more satisfactory, I believe, is an analysis which is based upon the assumption that it is not repressed "wishes" but *repressed regrets* that underlie anxiety (19).

III. "William Wilson"

The first three productions by Poe to which I invite special attention—"William Wilson," "The Black Cat," and "The Raven"—were written in the sequence in which I shall discuss them, in 1839, 1843, and 1845, respectively; but their familiarity and fame would place them in the reverse order. Indeed, it is as if they represent, in turn, increasingly skilful elaborations upon, and concealment of, a common theme. Krutch indicates that Poe seemed to recognize "The Raven" as his masterpiece as soon as he had finished it; and it is true that the year 1845 marked the climax of Poe's creativity, and was followed by what many regard as a disintegration of his total personality.

As a schoolboy I read and was required to memorize "The Raven," but although I subsequently dipped occasionally into Poe's writings, I did not until recently read "The Black Cat," although

[6] If Freud had employed the analogy suggested in Footnote 5, the people who stayed within the city would have been viewed as "good" and those excluded as "bad." Thus, much could be said for the technique of exclusion, and its ultimate failure would seem a great tragedy. But if we take the alternative position that it is the "good" people—i.e., those who are loyal to and compatible with the inhabitants of the state or nation as a whole, then the situation takes on a different coloring.

I knew it by name; and as for "William Wilson," I did not even know of its existence until much later.[7]

The story opens with the author—"Let me call myself, for the present, William Wilson"—darkly condemning himself for his "unparalleled infamy." He then speaks of his family, his temperament, and of his having been spoiled as a child. Only in thinking of a particular school (Manor House School, which Poe actually attended in England, between the ages of six and eleven) does his past afford him any comfort.

> It gives me, perhaps, as much of pleasure as I can now in any manner experience, to dwell upon minute recollections of the school and its concerns. Steeped in misery as I am—misery, alas! only too real—I shall be pardoned for seeking relief, however slight and temporary, in the weakness of a few rambling details (p. 59).[8]

In the elaborating of these "rambling details," Poe remarks that:

> . . . the ardor, the enthusiasm, and the imperiousness of my disposition, soon rendered me a marked character among my school-mates, and by slow, but natural gradations, gave me an ascendancy over all not greatly older than myself;—over all with a single exception. This exception was found in the person of a scholar, who, although no relation, bore the same Christian and surname as myself. . . . (p. 62).
>
> Wilson's rebellion was to me a source of the greatest embarrassment;—the more so as, in spite of the bravado with which in public I made a point of treating him and his pretensions, I secretly felt that I feared him, and could not help thinking the equality which he maintained so easily with myself, a proof of his true superiority; since not to be overcome cost me a perpetual struggle (p. 63).

It further develops that the other William Wilson, by a "remarkable coincidence," had entered the school on the same date and

---

[7] Upon acquiring the Viking Portable Library collection of Poe's works, with an introduction by Philip Van Doren Stern (1945). No clinical psychologist can read Stern's introduction to this volume without having his interest piqued, and the fifty-four pages of "Letters" which follow will still further stimulate his curiosity concerning the psychodynamics of Poe's character. The next part of this collection is devoted to "Tales of Fantasy," of which "William Wilson" is the first. I must have read very hurriedly the editor's brief preface, and I seem to have attached little significance to the lines with which Poe introduces the story:

> "What say of it? what say of conscience grim,
> That Spectre in my path?"

For I had more than half finished the story—I remember reading it piecemeal—when its symbolic significance began to dawn on me.

[8] In this and the two following sections, the quotations from Poe, unless otherwise indicated, are from the Stern edition; page references are thus to this volume.

had the same birth date. Between these two boys a singular ambivalence developed, which Poe describes as follows:

It may seem strange that in spite of the continual anxiety occasioned me by the rivalry of Wilson, and his intolerable spirit of contradiction, I could not bring myself to hate him altogether. We had, to be sure, nearly every day a quarrel in which, yielding me publicly the palm of victory, he, in some manner, contrived to make me feel that it was he who had deserved it; yet a sense of pride on my part, and a veritable dignity on his own, kept us always upon what are called "speaking terms," while there were many points of strong congeniality in our tempers, operating to awake in me a sentiment which our position alone, perhaps, prevented from ripening into a friendship. . . . To the moralist it will be unnecessary to say, in addition, that Wilson and myself were the most inseparable of companions (pp. 64–65).

If there is any doubt at this point that the other William Wilson is conscience, the next passage dispels it:

[But] my rival had a weakness in the faucial or guttural organs, which precluded him from raising his voice at any time *above a very low whisper*. Of this defect I did not fail to take what poor advantage lay in my power (p. 65).

Who other than conscience is it that merely "whispers" to us? And note that this being is now identified as a *rival,* albeit one toward whom there was also some feeling of friendship.

I have already more than once spoken of the disgusting air of patronage which he assumed toward me, and of his frequent officious interference with my will.[9] This interference often took the ungracious character of advice; advice not openly given, but hinted or insinuated. I received it with repugnance which gained strength as I grew in years. Yet, at this distant day, let me do him the simple justice to acknowledge that I can recall no occasion when the suggestions of my rival were on the side of those errors or follies so usual to his immature age and seeming inexperience; that his moral sense, at least, if not his general talents and worldly wisdom, was far keener than my own; and that I might, today, have been a better, and thus a happier man,[10] had I less frequently rejected the counsels embodied in those meaning whispers which I then but too cordially hated and too bitterly despised (pp. 67–68).

As time passed the relationship became increasingly strained, until at length, "an altercation of violence with him [marked] the

---

[9] The correspondence between Poe and his foster father, John Allan, which was carried on while Poe was a student at the University of Virginia, is full of mutual recrimination, bitterness, and lack of sympathy and understanding. It is from his father that a boy gets much of his "conscience," and here again, as in the case of the two William Wilsons, these two persons have "the same name."

[10] Observe that Poe here reflects the common perception of his day concerning the relation between being good and being happy. (See 21.)

day of the last conversation I there held with my singular namesake" (p. 68).[11]

At this point, then, conscience was at least partially repudiated, but not wholly so, for just after the quarrel, the first Wilson decided to play a practical joke upon the second, and went to his room where he lay *sleeping,* at which time he was seized with an attack of anxiety, which Poe knew how to portray superbly.

> I looked;—and a numbness, an iciness of feeling instantly pervaded my frame. My breast heaved, my knees tottered, my whole spirit became possessed with an objectless yet intolerable horror.[12] Gasping for breath, I lowered the lamp in still nearer proximity to the face. . . . Awestricken, and with a creeping shudder, I extinguished the lamp, passed silently from the chamber, and left at once the halls of the old academy, never to enter them again (pp. 69–70).

After having thus left his conscience behind, "asleep" (repressed), Wilson went to Eton where (now "all id") he entered upon a life of "soulless dissipation" and "delirious extravagance." Once, during the course of a particularly violent revel—"madly flushed with cards and intoxication"—Wilson was accosted by a "stranger" who "whispered the words 'William Wilson!' in my ear." This apparition "struck my soul with the shock of a galvanic battery. . . . But in a brief period I ceased to think upon the subject [reinstated the repression]; my attention being all absorbed in a contemplated departure for Oxford" (p. 72).

At Oxford, "my constitutional temperament broke forth with redoubled ardor, and I spurned even the common restraints of decency in the mad infatuation of my revels." Here, though in affluent circumstances, he began to practice "the vile arts of the gambler by profession" (p. 73). Having duped a fellow-student by the name of Glendinning in a particularly despicable and ruinous

---

[11] Under date of January 3, 1830, Poe wrote to his foster father (from West Point), in part, as follows: "As to your injunction not to trouble you with further communication, rest assured, Sir, that I will most religiously observe it. When I parted from you—at the steam-boat—I knew that I should never see you again" (Stern, p. 7). John Allan had already made it clear to Poe, as a result of earlier disagreements between them, that he had no intention of including him as an heir to his estate.

[12] At another time I hope to discuss at length Poe's allusions to anxiety. Here a few phrases will suffice: " . . . a certain nameless awe. . . . " (*The Masque of the Red Death*); "A feeling, for which I have no name . . . will admit of no analysis . . . " (*Ms. Found in a Bottle*); " . . . a year of terror, . . . feelings more intense than terror for which there is no name upon the earth" (*Shadow—A Parable*); " . . . an anomalous species of terror . . . intolerable agitation of soul" (*The Fall of the House of Usher*); " . . . terror, deadly and indefinite . . . inconceivably hideous . . . " (*The Premature Burial*).

manner one night, Wilson again encounters his "double," in a highly dramatic way:

> The wide, heavy folding doors of the apartment were all at once thrown open, to their full extent, with a vigorous and rushing impetuosity that extinguished, as if by magic, every candle in the room. Their light, in dying, enabled us just to perceive that a stranger had entered, about my own height, and closely muffled in a cloak (p. 76).[13]

The stranger announces that Wilson has won Glendinning's money by cheating!

"In a perfect agony of horror and of shame," Wilson left the chambers of his host, and fled to Paris, Rome, Naples, Egypt, but "the hated and dreaded rival" imperiously followed. Wilson gave himself up more and more to wine, sensuality, and other "symptoms." When these strategies failed, he at length did violence to his pursuer (and thus committed suicide):

> It was at Rome. . . . I had indulged more freely than usual in the excesses of the wine table. . . . I was anxiously seeking (let me not say with what unworthy motive) the young, the gay, the beautiful wife of the aged and doting Di Broglio.[14] . . . At this moment I felt a light hand placed upon my shoulder, and that ever-remembered, low, damnable *whisper* within my ear.
>
> In an absolute phrenzy of wrath, I turned at once upon him to have thus interrupted me, and seized him violently by the collar. . . .
>
> "Scoundrel!" I said, in a voice husky with rage, while every syllable I uttered seemed as new fuel to my fury, "scoundrel! imposter! accursed villain! [15] you shall not—you *shall* not dog me unto death! Follow me, or I stab you where you stand!"—and I broke my way from the ball-room into a small ante-chamber adjoining—dragging him unresistingly with me as I went.
>
> Upon entering, I thrust him furiously from me. He staggered against the wall, while I closed the door with an oath, and commanded him to draw. He hesitated but for an instant; then, with a slight sigh, drew in silence, and put himself upon his defense.
>
> The contest was brief indeed. I was frantic with every species of wild excitement, and felt within my single arm the energy and power of a multitude. In a few seconds I forced him by sheer strength against the wainscot-

[13] This passage will hardly fail to recall to the reader the passage quoted earlier (18) in which Freud uses the analogy of adjoining rooms to represent the conscious and unconscious (repressed) parts of personality. For other instances of the use of this same imagery, see Sections V and VI.

[14] For references to Poe's awareness of the Oedipus relationship, see Footnote 23, Section V.

[15] This outcry may remind the reader of lines which Poe was to write some six years later: " 'Prophet!' said I, 'thing of evil!—prophet still, if bird or devil!— . . . ' " Like the Raven, Poe was occupied with an all-engrossing theme.

ing, and thus, getting him at mercy, plunged my sword, with brute ferocity, repeatedly through and through his bosom (pp. 80–81).

A large mirror,—so at first it seemed to me in my confusion—now stood where none had been perceptible before; and, as I stepped up to it in extremity of terror, mine own image, but with features all pale and dabbled in blood, advanced to meet me with a feeble and tottering gait.

It was Wilson: but he spoke no longer in a whisper, and I could have fancied that I myself was speaking while he said:

"You have conquered, and I yield. Yet, henceforward art thou also dead—dead to the World, to Heaven and to Hope! In me didst thou exist—and, in my death, see by this image, which is thine own, how utterly thou hast murdered thyself" (p. 82).

This story is replete with psychological implications, but let us at this point follow only one of them. As we have noted earlier, there is a striking resemblance between many of the things Poe is known actually to have said or written to his foster father, John Allan, and the words which William Wilson hurls at his double. As Stern remarks,

The story is autobiographical, not only in its material—the school is the one Poe attended at Stoke Newington—but also in its inner meaning. Of all his stories it tells us most about its author and gives us the greatest insight into the secret workings of his mind (p. 55).

And in one of the passages quoted, we get a further intimation of the Oedipus theme: the murder takes place at the point at which Wilson is about to keep a rendezvous with "the young, the gay, the beautiful wife of *the aged and doting* Di Broglio."

Freud has emphasized but one facet of the tragedy by Sophocles: the unholy lust of a man for his mother and the lengths to which this fateful passion may lead him. Poe illuminates the other, more important side of the picture: he indicates that in killing one's father one kills an indispensable part of one's self, or, *per contra,* in killing conscience one is killing his father—and the host of other forebears of whom the conscience is representative.

If Poe *knew* all this, as he must have to write "William Wilson," the question inevitably arises: Why did he, personally, become more and more severely neurotic throughout his life? If he had the correct "insight," why did it not save him? To attempt an answer to this question now would be to anticipate a discussion which is better left until the end. But this much can here be said: Although Poe understood well enough what "the moralist" has to *say* about these matters, his own deepest beliefs and emotional convictions were to the contrary. As the following sections will further indicate, Poe's stories never have a real moral. Although he would pay lip-service in them to morality, the course of *action* which his heroes pursue is always in the reverse direction. Poe was certainly conscious of this, too, for in "The Imp of the Perverse," he says:

> I am not more certain that I breathe, than that the assurance of the wrong or error of any action is often the one unconquerable *force* which impels us, and alone impels us to its prosecution. Nor will this overwhelming tendency to do wrong for the wrong's sake admit of analysis, or resolution into ulterior elements. It is a radical, a primitive impulse—elementary (Cameo Edition of Poe's complete works, Vol. V, p. 191).

For the present, we can do no more, then, than to note the discrepancy between what Poe knew, intellectually, and how he *felt* and what he *did*. "He has great intellectual power, but no principle—no moral sense" (quoted by Poe, himself, in a letter to Mrs. Whitman, under date of October 18, 1848).

IV. "The Black Cat"

In passing from "William Wilson" to "The Black Cat," let us pause long enough for a glance at "The Tell-Tale Heart" and "The Imp of the Perverse." "William Wilson," as previously noted, appeared in 1839; and "The Black Cat" was published four years later, in 1843. Of the two other stories just mentioned, the first appeared in 1843, and the second in 1845. Psychologically, however, they both fall in between "William Wilson" and "The Black Cat."

Like "William Wilson," "The Tell-Tale Heart" is clearly an account of conscience-killing. It begins with the well-known lines:

> True!—nervous—very, very dreadfully nervous I had been and am; but why *will* you say that I am mad? . . .
>
> It is impossible to say how first the idea entered my brain; but once conceived, it haunted me day and night. Object there was none. Passion there was none. I loved the old man. He had never wronged me. He had never given me insult. For his gold I had no desire. I think it was his eye! yes, it was this! He had the eye of a vulture—a pale blue eye, with a film over it. Whenever it fell upon me, my blood ran cold; and so by degrees—very gradually—I made up my mind to take the life of the old man, and thus rid myself of the eye forever (p. 290).

Having smothered the old man in an "uncontrollable terror," the author then concealed the body under the floor "so cleverly, so cunningly, that no human eye—not even *his*—could have detected anything wrong."

There was a police investigation, but the author was serene and smiling—"for *what* had I to fear?"

The officers were satisfied. My *manner* had convinced them. I was singularly at ease. They sat, and while I answered cheerily, they chatted of familiar things. [The peace of mind that is achieved by means of repression?] But, ere long, I felt myself getting pale and wished them gone. My head ached, and I fancied a ringing in my ears: but still they sat and still chattered (p. 295).

The denouement—the return of the repressed—occurs shortly. The ringing in his ears ceases to be *in* his ears; it is shortly converted into an hallucination, an external, objective noise:

I felt that I must scream or die! and now—again!—hark! louder! louder! *louder!*

"Villains!" I shrieked, "dissemble no more! I admit the deed!—tear up the planks! here, here!—it is the beating of his hideous heart!" (p. 296).

In "The Imp of the Perverse" the same theme is repeated with singularly little variation. After several pages of speculation on the nature of *perversity,* the author speaks rather abruptly of having killed a man by causing him to inhale the fumes of a poisonous candle. "The next morning he was discovered dead in his bed, and the coroner's verdict was—'Death by the visitation of God!' "

Having inherited his estate, all went well with me for years. The idea of detection never once entered my brain. Of the remains of the fatal taper I had myself carefully disposed. I had left no shadow of a clew by which it would be possible to convict, or even suspect, me of the crime. It is inconceivable how rich a sentiment of satisfaction arose in my bosom as I reflected upon my absolute security. For a very long period of time I was accustomed to revel in this sentiment. It afforded me more real delight than all the mere worldly advantages accruing from my sin. But there arrived at length an epoch, from which the pleasurable feeling grew, by scarcely perceptible gradations, into a haunting and harassing thought. It harassed because it haunted. I could scarcely get rid of it for an instant. It is quite a common thing to be thus annoyed with the ringing in our ears, or rather in our memories, of the burthen of some ordinary song, or some unimpressive snatches from an opera. Nor will we be the less tormented if the song in itself be good, or the opera air meritorious. In this manner, at last, I would perpetually catch myself pondering upon my security, and repeating, in a low under-tone, the phrase, "I am safe."

One day, whilst sauntering along the streets, I arrested myself in the act of murmuring, half aloud, these customary syllables. In a fit of petulance, I re-modelled them thus: "I am safe—I am safe—yes—if I be not fool enough to make open confession!"

No sooner had I spoken these words, than I felt an icy chill creep to my heart. I had had some experience in these fits of perversity (whose nature I have been at some trouble to explain), and I remembered well that in no instance I had successfully resisted their attacks. And now my own casual self-suggestion that I might be fool enough to confess the murder of which I had been guilty, confronted me, as if the very ghost of him whom I had murdered—had beckoned me on to death.

At first, I made an effort to shake off this nightmare of the soul. I walked vigorously—faster—still faster—at length I ran. I felt a maddening desire to shriek aloud. Every succeeding wave of thought overwhelmed me with new terror, for, alas! I well, too well, understood that to *think,* in my situation, was to be lost. I bounded like a madman through the crowded thoroughfares. At length, the populace took alarm, and pursued me. I felt *then* the consummation of my fate. Could I have torn out my tongue, I would have done it—but a rough voice resounded in my ears—a rougher grasp seized me by the shoulder. I turned—I gasped for breath. For a moment I experienced all the pangs of suffocation; I became blind, and deaf, and giddy; and then some invisible fiend, I thought, struck me with his broad palm upon the back. The long-imprisoned secret burst forth from my soul.

They say that I spoke with a distinct enunciation, but with marked emphasis and passionate hurry, as if in dread of interruption before concluding the brief but pregnant sentences that consigned me to the hangman and to hell.

Having related all that was necessary for the fullest judicial conviction, I fell prostrate in a swoon.

But why shall I say more? To-day I wear these chains, and am *here!* To-morrow I shall be fetterless!—*but where?* (Cameo Edition, Vol. V, pp. 196–98).

"The Black Cat" is a longer story than either of those just alluded to, with more highly developed symbolism, but the theme is essentially the same.

The narrator begins this tale by again briefly debating the question of his sanity, but he says it is of little importance since he is to die on the morrow (for a crime which he gradually reveals). What he wishes to describe is a series of events which "have terrified—have tortured—have destroyed me."

To me, they have presented little but *Horror*—to many they will seem less terrible than *baroques.* Hereafter, perhaps, some intellect may be found which will reduce my phantasm to the commonplace—some intellect more calm, more logical, and far less excitable than my own, which will perceive, in the circumstances I detail with awe, nothing more than an ordinary succession of very natural causes and effects (p. 297).[16]

[16] We may surmise that Poe is here speaking half sarcastically, half seriously. Although he undoubtedly knew a great deal about anxiety and succeeded probably better than any other writer in conveying the experience to others, yet it is apparent that there were some things about it which he did *not* understand.

As a child, says the narrator, he was very fond of pets. His wife, knowing of this fondness for animals, added a number to their *menage,* including a beautiful *black cat.*

Pluto—this was the cat's name—was my favorite pet and playmate. I alone fed him, and he attended me wherever I went about the house. It was even with difficulty that I could prevent him from following me through the streets (p. 298).

For a number of years this association continued, but eventually the narrator succumbed to "the Fiend Intemperance . . . (I blush to confess it)," and he became irritable with and periodically mistreated both his wife and the pets—all save Pluto. But "at length even Pluto, who was now becoming old, and consequently somewhat peevish—even Pluto began to experience the effects of my ill temper."

One night, returning home, much intoxicated, from one of my haunts about town, I fancied that the cat avoided my presence. I seized him; when, in his fright at my violence, he inflicted a slight wound upon my hand with his teeth. The fury of a demon instantly possessed me. I knew myself no longer. My original soul seemed, at once, to take its flight from my body; and a more than fiendish malevolence, gin-nurtured, thrilled every fibre of my frame. I took from my waist-coat-pocket a pen-knife, opened it, grasped the poor beast by the throat, and deliberately cut one of its eyes from the socket! I blush, I burn, I shudder, while I pen the damnable atrocity (p. 299).[17]

---

[17] The eye is sometimes interpreted as a female sexual symbol; its enucleation might therefore be regarded here as a form of female castration. I believe the eye is here, as in "The Tell-Tale Heart," more correctly interpreted as a conscience-symbol, and the enucleation as an attempt to get rid of, repress, destroy it. Stern notes that both "The Black Cat" and "The Tell-Tale Heart" "have to do with an eye, the symbol of watchfulness, of censure, and the reminder of guilt. . . . The associative links that connect the Poe stories are numerous" (p. 289).

In rereading "The Fall of the House of Usher," I came upon the following lines, which singularly reinforce the surmise that Poe recognized, at least intuitively, the relationship between conscience and anxiety: "I looked upon the scene before me—upon the bleak walls—upon the vacant *eye-like windows*—upon a few rank sedges—and upon a few white trunks of decayed trees—with *an utter depression of soul*. . . . There was an iciness, a sinking, a sickening of the heart—an unredeemed dreariness of thought which no goading of the imagination could torture into aught of the sublime. *What was it*—I paused to think—*what was it* that so unnerved me in the contemplation of the House of Usher? It was a mystery all insoluble; nor could I grapple with the shadowy fancies that crowded upon me as I pondered. I was forced to fall back upon the unsatisfactory conclusion, that while, beyond doubt, there *are* combinations of very simple natural objects which have the power of thus affecting us, still the analysis of this power lies among considerations beyond our depth. . . . I reined my horse . . . and gazed down . . . upon the remodelled and inverted images of the gray sedge, and the ghastly tree-stems, and the vacant and *eye-like windows*" (p. 245, italics added). Note in the passages which are reproduced from "Ligeia" in Section VI the recurrence of the question, "What was it? What *was* it?" Poe was concerned with psychological "mysteries" long before he invented the "mystery" story.

The cat lived, and the narrator forgot his chagrin. Eventually even his old annoyance with the cat returned:

One morning, in cool blood, I slipped a noose about its neck and hung it to the limb of a tree;—hung it with the tears streaming down from my eyes, and with the bitterest remorse at my heart;—hung it *because* I knew that it had loved me, and *because* I felt it had given me no reason of offence. . . . (p. 300; see Poe's earlier comments on "perversity").

A number of events transpire, until the narrator finds himself wishing for another cat:

I went so far as to regret the loss of the animal, and to look about me, among the vile haunts which I now habitually frequented, for another pet of the same species, and of somewhat similar appearance, with which to supply its place (p. 302).

Another large black cat is found and incorporated into the household. But soon the old feelings of disgust and loathing reasserted themselves. "What added, no doubt, to my hatred of the beast, was the discovery, on the morning after I brought it home, that, like Pluto, it also had been deprived of one of its eyes": [18]

With my aversion to this cat, however, its partiality for myself seemed to increase. It followed my footsteps with a pertinacity which it would be difficult to make the reader comprehend. Whenever I sat, it would crouch beneath my chair, or spring upon my knees, covering me with its loathsome caresses. If I arose to walk it would get between my feet and thus nearly throw me down, or, fastening its long and sharp claws in my dress, clamber, in this manner, to my breast. At such times, although I longed to destroy it with a blow, I was yet withheld from so doing, partly by a memory of my former crime, but chiefly—let me confess it at once—by absolute dread of the beast.

The cat continues to haunt the narrator by day, and in his dreams at night, until:

One day she [my wife] accompanied me, upon some household errand, into the cellar of the old building which our poverty compelled us to inhabit. The cat followed me down the steep stairs, and, nearly throwing me headlong, exasperated me to madness. Uplifting an axe, and forgetting, in my wrath, the childish dread which had hitherto stayed my hand, I aimed a blow at the animal which, of course, would have proved instantly fatal had it

[18] The selection of the *cat* as a conscience symbol in this story can hardly be accidental, for the cat is proverbially *hard to kill* and, if taken away, will always *come back*. After the death of the "first" Pluto, an apparition of it appears the morning after the narrator's house has burned up; and the "second" Pluto, because of its singular likeness to the first, must be regarded as merely a reincarnation thereof.

descended as I wished. But this blow was arrested by the hand of my wife. Goaded, by the interference, into a rage more than demoniacal, I withdrew my arm from her grasp and buried the axe in her brain. She fell dead upon the spot, without a groan (p. 305).

With cool deliberation the murderer considers various ways of disposing of his wife's dead body. "Finally I hit upon what I considered a far better expedient than either of these. I determined to wall it up [repression?] in the cellar [the unconscious?]—as the monks of the middle ages are recorded to have walled up their victims" (p. 305).[19]

This design was carried through to the narrator's complete satisfaction:

The wall did not present the slightest appearance of having been disturbed. The rubbish on the floor was picked up with the minutest care. I looked around triumphantly, and said to myself—"Here at least, then, my labor has not been in vain."

My next step was to look for the beast which had been the cause of so much wretchedness; for I had, at length, firmly resolved to put it to death. Had I been able to meet with it, at the moment, there could have been no doubt of its fate; but it appeared that the crafty animal had been alarmed at the violence of my previous anger, and forebore to present itself in my present mood. It is impossible to describe, or to imagine, the deep, *the blissful sense of relief which the absence of the detested creature occasioned in my bosom"* (p. 306, italics added, by way of indicating the surcease of anxiety which occurs with repression).

Once again I breathed as a free-man. The monster, in terror, had fled the premises forever! I should behold it no more! My happiness was supreme! The guilt of my dark deed disturbed me but little. Some few inquiries had been made, but these had been readily answered. Even a search had been instituted—but of course nothing was to be discovered. I looked upon my future felicity as secured (p. 307).

On the fourth day after the murder a party of policemen came again to make inquiry and to search the premises; but the narrator was again completely calm and compliant with their every wish. Repeatedly they descended into the cellar but found no trace of evidence there.

"Gentlemen," I said at last, as the party ascended the steps, "I delight to have allayed your suspicions. I wish you all health, and a little more courtesy. By the bye, gentlemen, this—this is a very well constructed house." (In the rabid desire to say something easily, I scarcely knew what I uttered at all.) "I may say an *excellently* well constructed house. These

[19] Cf. "The Cask of Amontillado," also Poe's preoccupation with premature burial and related matters (Section VI).

walls—are you going, gentlemen?—these walls are solidly put together"; and here, through the mere phrenzy of bravado, I rapped heavily, with a cane which I held in my hand, upon that very portion of the brickwork behind which stood the corpse of the wife of my bosom.

But may God shield and deliver me from the fangs of the Arch-Fiend! No sooner had the reverberation of my blows sunk into silence, than I was answered by a voice from within the tomb!—by a cry, at first muffled and broken, like the sobbing of a child, and then quickly swelling into one long, loud, and continuous scream, utterly anomalous and inhuman—a howl—a wailing shriek, half of horror and half of triumph, such as might have arisen only out of hell, conjointly from the throats of the damned in their agony and of the demons that exulted in the damnation.

Of my own thoughts it is folly to speak. Swooning, I staggered to the opposite wall. For one instant the party upon the stairs remained motionless, through extremity of terror and of awe. In the next, a dozen stout arms were toiling at the wall. It fell bodily. The corpse, already greatly decayed and clotted with gore, stood erect before the eyes of the spectators. Upon its head, with red extended mouth and *solitary eye of fire,* sat the hideous beast whose craft had seduced me into murder, and whose *informing voice* had consigned me to the hangman. I had walled *the monster* up within the tomb! (pp. 307–8, italics added).

V. "The Raven"

If there be any doubt that this composition is but a poetic version of the central theme—of misconduct, repression of guilt (conscience), and threatened return of the repressed, with ensuing anxiety—which was previously developed, in prose form, in the works already reviewed, then let us note some parallels of detail which can hardly be dismissed as accidental.

Let us recall, first of all, that both the cat and the raven are *black.* Although the raven has no name, he is from "the Night's Plutonian shore." The cat's name *is* Pluto. Black is a conventional symbol for death, and Pluto is the keeper of the realm of the departed. Conscience is in a very real sense the voice of the dead—the wisdom and virtue of past generations—call it "the culture" or call it "God," speaking within us. Thus in Shakespeare's *Measure for Measure,* when Claudio says, "If I must die I will encounter darkness as a bride, and hug it in mine arms," his sister, Isabella, wishing to say that he is a man of courage and good principle, replies, "There spake my brother; there my father's grave did utter forth a voice" (Act III, Scene I). It can hardly be supposed otherwise than that the black, Plutonian figures of the cat and the raven are superego symbols, the living voices of the dead.

Moreover, both the cat and the raven make their appearance

through window-like apertures, and in the end both are *sitting on a human head*—surely an exquisite, if somewhat malignant, super-ego symbol—in the one case, on the head of the author's murdered wife and, in the other case, "On the pallid bust of Pallas just above my chamber door." [20]

In reviewing "William Wilson" and "The Black Cat," I have quoted at length, but "The Raven" is so well known and so readily available that in discussing it I shall reproduce only what seem to be the key lines or phrases in each stanza, reserving for full quotation only the last two.

The first noteworthy item of information in the poem is that the author was "weak and weary, . . . nearly napping." Freud (1935) repeatedly made the point that repression is most likely to be abrogated when there is an impairment of "ego strength," as in fatigue, illness, or the twilight period just before sleep.[21]

Under just such circumstances, "suddenly there came a tapping," a disturbance, which the author tried to interpret as someone "rapping at my chamber door."

In the second stanza, it is apparent that the author is depressed, uneasy: "Eagerly I wished the morrow. . . . " He is brooding on the "lost Lenore." Who "Lenore" was or what she signified is less easy to say. In "The Philosophy of Composition," where Poe attempts to show that he wrote "The Raven," not intuitively, but precisely by design, he says:

> My next thought concerned the choice of an impression, or effect, to be conveyed: and here I may as well observe that, throughout the construction, I kept steadily in view the design of rendering the work *universally* appreciable (p. 553).

---

[20] For another usage of essentially the same imagery, see the passage quoted below from "Shadow—A Parable." For an account of the house in which Poe was reputedly staying when he wrote "The Raven," see Harrison's (The Virginia) Edition of Poe's *Complete Works* (1902). Here the editor quotes an informant of Dr. H. H. Minor as saying "Above the door opening into the hallway, there stood the 'pallid bust of Pallas.' It [actually a bust of Minerva] was a little plaster cast and occupied a shelf nailed to the door casing, immediately behind the bust, and occupying the space between the top casing and the ceiling; a number of little panes of smoke glass took the place of the partition.

"This bust of Minerva was either removed or broken by one of the Brennan tenants after the family had moved to the city, and no trace of it can be found at the present time" (Vol. I, p. 226).

[21] Poe's brief essay, "Between Wakefulness and Sleep," comes appositely to mind here. In it he remarks that there is "an inappreciable *point* in time," just as sleep is approaching, when one has "fancies" of supreme "novelty." By practice he had learned to "startle myself from the point into wakefulness—*and thus transfer the point itself into Memory*—convey its impressions . . . to a situation where . . . I can survey them with the eye of analysis" (p. 659). Are we to infer that Poe thus tapped his own "unconscious" as a source of material for his writing? In passages to be cited shortly, he scornfully repudiates such a notion.

To this end Poe selected, he says, *beauty* and *sadness.* To enhance the beauty of the poem he decided to have a refrain, and to make this a melancholy one.

"Of all melancholy topics, what, according to the *universal* understanding of mankind, is the *most* melancholy?" Death—was the obvious reply. "And when," I said, "is this most melancholy of topics the most poetical?" From what I have already explained at some length, the answer, here also, is obvious—"When it most closely allies itself to *Beauty:* the death, then, of a beautiful woman is, unquestionably, the most poetical topic in the world—and equally is it beyond doubt that the lips best suited for such topic are those of a bereaved lover" (p. 557).

Bergler (1946) has advanced the interesting hypothesis that the transports of romantic love occur because the beloved takes on the function of conscience (the superego is "extrojected" upon the other person, somewhat as it is in "transference"), and since the beloved is in turn loving, much of the usual self-criticism and tension between ego and superego is eliminated, with resulting feelings of well-being and euphoria. When, therefore, love is suddenly lost, as in death, a reintrojection of the superego may be expected, perhaps with ensuing depression.

Here we cannot pursue further this intriguing topic,[22] but we have proceeded far enough to perceive that "Lenore" represents, in some rather vague way, "lost love"—whether the love of a sweetheart or of a mother seems not to matter materially, and the indications are that in Poe's mind they were singularly indistinct.[23]

The first two lines of the third stanza are particularly important and should be quoted in full:

And the silken, sad, uncertain rustling of each purple curtain
Thrilled me—filled me with fantastic terrors never felt before.

Curtains, tapestries, draperies—coverings in general—held a peculiar fascination for Poe: behind them lurked terrifying mysteries. For example, in "The Fall of the House of Usher," he remarks:

---

[22] Cf. Freud's "Mourning and Melancholia" (1917) and the work of Lindemann (1944) and of Liebman (1946).

[23] The first stanza of a poem entitled "Romance," which Poe wrote at the age of twenty, is much in point here. In real life Poe's marriage has been said to have been a double one: to Virginia Clemm's mother as much as to the girl herself. And in "Eleonora" he speaks of having married his "own cousin" and of dwelling, in the Valley of the Many-Colored Grass, with "my cousin, and her mother." All of which Poe knowingly prefaces by saying: "or, if doubt it ye cannot, then play unto its riddle the Oedipus."

Sleep came not near my couch—while the hours waned and waned away. I struggled to reason off the nervousness which had dominion over me. I endeavoured to believe that much, if not all of what I felt, was due to the bewildering influence of the gloomy furniture of the room—of the dark and tattered draperies, which, tortured into motion by the breath of a rising tempest, swayed fitfully to and fro upon the walls, and rustled uneasily about the decorations of the bed (p. 261; see similar imagery in "Ligeia," Section VI).

And again, in "Shadow—A Parable," Poe says:

And lo from among those sable draperies
Where the sounds of the song departed,
There came forth a dark and undefined shadow—
A shadow such as the moon, when low in heaven,
Might fashion from the figure of a man:
But it was the shadow neither of man,
Nor of God,
Nor of any familiar thing.

. . . .

And the shadow rested upon the brazen doorway,
And under the arch of the entablature of the door,
And moved not, nor spoke any word,
But there became stationary and remained (pp. 597–98).

The "fantastic terrors never felt before" in the lines quoted above from the third stanza of "The Raven" obviously represent an anxiety attack; and in order to try to gain control over it, the author repeats the reassurance that the noise he has heard is nothing more than "Some late visitor entreating entrance at my chamber door."

In the next stanza the author recovers somewhat from his anxiety ("Presently my soul grew stronger") and attempts to confirm his earlier interpretation of the reason for his fear. As he apologizes to the caller, he opens the door: "Darkness there and nothing more."

The fifth stanza reveals the author's renewed perplexity, and the indefinite fantasies that follow. He turns back into the room, "all my soul within me burning," and presently hears the noise again. He now attempts to master his anxiety by interpreting the noise as wind at the window. But his heart continues to pound; so that, in stanza seven, he flings wide the shutter; and the raven, "with mien of lord [father] or lady [mother]"—clearly a superego symbol—enters the room.

At this point let us digress for a moment in order to indicate how similar an analogy Freud used to represent the relationship between consciousness and the repressed or unconscious. In a passage previously (18) quoted, he says:

The unconscious is a large anteroom, in which the various mental excitations are crowding upon one another, like individual beings. Adjoining this is a second, smaller apartment, a sort of reception room, in which consciousness resides. But on the threshold between the two there stands a personage with the office of doorkeeper . . . (1935, p. 260).

For Freud the unconscious was populated with impulses of forbidden lust and hostility; here we are exploring the thesis that what falls under repression is far more likely to be man's "nobler" impulses, rather than those of the "id"; but for the time being this distinction is unimportant. According to *either* interpretation, it is when repression *breaks down* that anxiety is most likely to be experienced; and here Poe is giving an immortal example.

Whereas the "return of the repressed" has been preceded and accompanied by inexplicable terror, once the source of the "noise" (remember that we speak of *hearing* conscience, rather than sensing it in some other way, and that the raven *speaks*)—once the source of the "noise" had entered the room and been identified, the narrator felt better. The grotesque creature beguiles his "sad fancy into smiling." In fact, the author becomes rather mocking and contemptuous: "Tell me what thy lordly name is on the Night's Plutonian shore."

The whole atmosphere of this, the eighth stanza, is reminiscent of the way in which neurotic patients behave in therapy during the early stages of transference: with the intrapsychic conflict that has previously tortured them now converted into an interpersonal conflict, their anxiety and symptoms disappear, and all that remains, seemingly, is distrust of and hostility toward the therapist (see 18).

The ninth stanza is remarkable for only one new thought: Although the raven speaks "so plainly," the author really does not *understand* it, since "its answer little meaning—little relevancy bore." In this context it is appropriate to recall that although Poe and his foster father, John Allan, spoke the same language, literally, yet they did not understand each other, never really communicated.

The central idea in stanza ten is that parent figures are unreliable; you cannot depend on them: "On the morrow *he* will leave me, as my hopes have flown before." It should be observed that Poe had had singularly bad luck with *both* father and mother figures: His real father had deserted at Poe's birth; his mother had died when he was two years and eleven months old; Poe's foster mother, to whom he is said to have been deeply devoted, died when he was twenty; and his foster father seems to have *rejected* him more or less completely from the beginning of their association. The instability of *all* Poe's early affectional relationships appears to have been of fateful importance in determining his character and his whole outlook on life. (This thesis will be further developed in the concluding section.)

The third and fourth lines of the next stanza give as apt a characterization of the general tenor of Poe's own life as can well be imagined:

> Caught from some unhappy master whom unmerciful Disaster
> Followed fast and followed faster till his songs one burden bore—[24]

Attention has already been called to the fact that, in "The Philosophy of Composition," Poe was at pains to show that he had written "The Raven" "with the precision and rigid consequence of a mathematical problem." This claim is extended as follows:

> Most writers—poets in especial—prefer having it understood that they compose by a species of fine frenzy—ecstatic intuition—and would positively shudder at letting the public take a peep behind the scenes, at the elaborate and vacillating crudities of thought—at the true purposes seized only at the last moment . . . which in ninety-nine cases out of the hundred, constitute the properties of the literary *histrio* (p. 551).

For reasons that will be developed shortly, it appears that Poe was here concocting a fiction (which, as we know from other evidence, he was not, on occasion, above doing). It is the central purpose of the present paper to show that "The Raven" has precisely the same theme that many of Poe's other compositions had. Poe's youth was certainly an unhappy one; during his second and third decades he was severely neurotic; and at forty he had sunk into an alcoholic psychosis: ". . . followed fast and followed faster till his songs one burden bore. . . ."[25]

Stanza twelve contains two distinct and important elements. The first is the notion of *attack* upon the superego symbol:

> But the Raven still beguiling all my fancy into smiling,
> Straight I wheeled a cushioned seat in front of bird, and bust and door.

[24] Krutch (1926) quotes Rufus Griswold as having remarked that "*The Raven* was probably much more nearly than has been supposed, even by those who were very intimate with [Poe], a reflection and an echo of his own history. He was the bird's 'unhappy master, whom unmerciful disaster followed fast and followed faster. . . .'" (p. 12).

[25] At another time I hope to show that the distinction commonly drawn between Poe's poetry and fantasies, on the one hand, and his "tales of ratiocination" and pseudo-scientific writings, on the other, is only superficially justified and that in *all* his *creative* writings (he sometimes wrote as a poorly paid hack), he was constantly preoccupied with the attempt to *resolve mysteries,* an attempt which, in its most fundamental sense, was never successful.

In "William Wilson," "The Tell-Tale Heart," "The Black Cat," and elsewhere, Poe has engaged in would-be conscience-killing; nor is this strategy unique in the writings of Poe—remember that Pinocchio killed the Talking Cricket (though not its ghost). Or if it seems that "attack" and "killing" are too strong an interpretation for these lines, let us replace them with "defense." If in "wheeling" the cushion "in front of bird, and bust and door," the author did not actually *throw* it, then he must have held it in such a position as to blot out the sight of the bird. Poe's cushion throughout his adult life was alcohol; with it he constantly "fought" conscience (anxiety),[26] though with no more permanent success than he had in attempting to get rid of the raven.

The other thing to be noted about this stanza is the twice-repeated reference to the raven as "this ominous bird of yore"—the conscience, representing the transmitted essence of human experience, is the old, incalculably old, part of the personality.[27]

We are already familiar with Poe's preoccupation with *eyes,* and it is not surprising to find, in stanza thirteen, reference to "the fowl whose fiery eyes now burned into my bosom's core." Only by thinking about *her* ("the lost Lenore") does the author find it possible to tolerate the ordeal. Only by recalling such fleeting love as he has previously known can he abide this omnipresent conscience symbol. As will be indicated shortly, love is an indispensable precondition for the assimilation of discipline and authority and for the establishment of an harmonious relationship between the ego (the infantile) and the superego (the parental) parts of the personality. But the fantasy of the lost loved one proves insufficient to prevent another outbreak of anxiety: "the air grew denser, perfumed from an unseen censer," and the author again, in stanza fourteen, reviles the raven, this time more strongly, by calling him a "Wretch."

---

[26] I recall the case of a male patient who first drank to the point of drunkenness on the way back to school after a disagreement with his father during an Easter holiday at home. This act was clearly designed as a form of revenge, and subsequent reversions to alcohol followed much the same pattern. It seems that Poe's pathological drinking began while he was a student at Charlottesville, a period of great stress between him and his foster father. This period was followed by Poe's violent denunciation of Allan and enlistment in the Army.

[27] "Those who have a liking for generalizations and sharp distinctions may say that the external world, in which the individual finds himself exposed after being detached from his parents, represents the power of the present; that his id, with its inherited trends, represents the *organic past;* and that the superego, which comes to join them later, represents more than anything the *cultural past, an after-experience of which, as it were, the child has to pass through during the few years of his early life*" (Freud, 1949, p. 123, italics added).

The reviling continues in stanza fifteen, but then gives way to supplication: ". . . tell me truly, I implore—is there—*is* there balm in Gilead?" Here the author, defeated in his attempt to banish the raven by means of either attack or insult, asks desperately if there is *no* means whatever of dealing with his anxiety. Is there no hope at all? "Quoth the Raven 'Nevermore.' "

Stanza sixteen, in which the author calls the raven "Prophet! . . . thing of evil! . . . devil!" has been alluded to in a previous section. Here once more we see an attack upon the raven and an attempt to control anxiety by thinking again of "a rare and radiant maiden whom the angels name Lenore."

This attempt, like the others, fails, and the author, in a frenzy, tries to deal with the bird by means of expulsion (repression). Stanza seventeen, as a whole, is so significant that it should be reproduced:

> "Be that word our sign of parting, bird or fiend!" I shrieked, upstarting—
> "Get thee back into the tempest and the Night's Plutonian shore!
> Leave no black plume as a token of that lie thy soul hath spoken!
> Leave my loneliness unbroken!—quit the bust above my door!
> Take thy beak from out my heart, and take thy form from off my door!"

Obviously the author is saying to the bird, much as a peevish child might shout to a parent, "Go away; I hate you!"

But what does Poe himself have to say about the two concluding stanzas of this poem? His interpretation, when compared with the poem, seems frivolous and contrived. He says:

> Holding these opinions, I added the two concluding stanzas of the poem—their suggestiveness being thus made to pervade all the narrative which has preceded them. The under-current of meaning is rendered first apparent in the lines—
>
> "Take thy beak from out my heart, and take thy form from off my door!"
> Quoth the Raven "Nevermore!"
>
> It will be observed that the words, "from out my heart," involve the first metaphorical expression in the poem. They, with the answer, "Nevermore," dispose the mind to seek a moral in all that has been previously narrated. The reader begins now to regard the Raven as emblematical—but it is not until the very last line of the very last stanza that the intention of making him emblematical of *Mournful and Never-ending Remembrance* is permitted distinctly to be seen (p. 564).

Here Poe quotes stanza eighteen and, in so doing, ends "The Philosophy of Composition":

And the Raven, never flitting, still is sitting, still is sitting
On the pallid bust of Pallas, just above my chamber door;
And his eyes have all the seeming of a demon's that is dreaming,
And the lamplight o'er him streaming throws his shadow on the floor;
And my soul from out that shadow that lies floating on the floor
Shall be lifted—nevermore.

This stanza contributes little that is new, except the notion of melancholic resignation to an insoluble conflict. Poe, however, seemed to feel that it contained the "punch line" for the whole poem; but anyone who can, with a straight face, contend that there is nothing "metaphorical," nothing "emblematical" in the poem until the concluding lines of the next to last stanza commands little confidence as a commentator and interpreter, even though the production in question be his own. In "The Raven," Poe has given the world a never-to-be-forgotten poem, but his account of its psychological significance is either incredibly naïve or a premeditated farce. Viewed *clinically,* and more particularly against the background of other productions, it is an eminently personal document and one whose "universality" of appeal (which Poe correctly estimated) rests precisely upon the communality between the fundamental dilemma of Poe's life and that of every neurotic, in some measure that of every human being.

VI. Basler's Interpretation of "Ligeia"; Krutch on Poe's "Sexlessness"

In his recent book, *Sex, symbolism, and psychology in literature,* Basler (1948) makes a pertinent distinction between the *manifest* and the *latent* content of many literary productions: "There is the story which the narrator means to tell, and there is the story which he tells without meaning to, as he unconsciously reveals himself" (p. 194). Here, of course, this author is stating the principle of *projection,* which is well established in clinical psychology. But when he becomes more specifically analytical, there is room for a reasonable difference of opinion.

In his analysis of Poe as a personality, Basler gives major attention to "Ligeia." In essence, this story is very simple: it tells of a man, married to a very remarkable woman who, seized by an incurable illness, struggles valiantly, but vainly, against death. After the death of the wife—Ligeia by name—this man marries again, this time to one Rowena Trevanion. After a short time, the new wife becomes ill, dies; but as her husband keeps vigil the following night, he notices the corpse showing signs of reanimation. These become more and more pronounced, until at length the body rises from the bed; and it is evident that it has undergone transfiguration and is now—Ligeia!

The first remarkable detail in Poe's narration is this:

> I cannot, for my soul, remember how, when, or even precisely where, I first became acquainted with the Lady Ligeia. . . . Of her family—I have surely heard her speak. . . . And now, while I write, a recollection flashes upon me that I have *never known* the paternal name of her who was my friend and my betrothed, and who became the partner of my studies, and finally the wife of my bosom (Basler, 1948, pp. 160–61).

There is nothing singular in Poe's physical description of Ligeia until he comes to her *eyes*. Then he says:

> They were, I must believe, far larger than the ordinary eyes of our own race. . . . The expression of the eyes of Ligeia! How for long hours have I pondered upon it! How have I, through the whole of a midsummer night, struggled to fathom it. What was it—that something more profound than the well of Democritus—which lay far within the pupils of my beloved. What *was* it? (pp. 162–63).[28]

---

[28] This passage, with its emphasis upon *eyes,* will recall to the reader Footnote 17 on page 631. The *mystery* which is specifically associated with Ligeia's eyes is of a type which neurotic patients often express. Here is an excerpt from a therapeutic session with a middle-aged woman:

PATIENT: Now I, I don't think that there's much of anything else that I wanted to tell you unless you want me to play the record that I said goes around in my mind every night and all day. Oh *yeah,* not only at night but in the daytime too. Now that, that's a funny thing. It's just as if I was thinking all the time on two planes. Now after that thing [rejection by a man she expected to marry] happened and I knew I was kind of going to pieces, well, I, I tried to do all the mental hygiene things and the sensible things. I went about my daily work and my daily activities just as normally as I possibly could, and I kept myself busy and, and did everything I could think of to do to keep myself busy. And as I'd say, I'd read late at night so I wouldn't go to bed and just think. And I kept my—tried to take good care of my health and get a little exercise and do all the things I knew would be just normal about it and also to keep a good perspective. I mean, I just sat down and said to myself, "Well, now look! This is nothing unique. It's happened to thousands of other people, and it happens all the time and much *worse* things. And it's something that you can take in your stride and so, what about it." But all the time, while I was doing all these good, normal, sensible things, uh, there was this record playing, too, over and over and over and over. And it's as if there is something that I don't, uh, don't know. It always seems to me as if, if there's something that doesn't fit in, something that I can't understand, something that, uh— It's like—kind of like a key that's lost. And I keep thinking if I think about it *enough,* I'll surely find that thing that's lost. And uh, so I'll be working at the office and, uh, this—and I'll be doing my work, and as far as I know reasonably adequately, and at the same time on this other plane, this same process of thinking is going on—or whatever it is: it's not exactly thinking. And uh, *so many* a time I've just stopped and pushed my typewriter away and turned around and said, "Well, now look! This is getting you nowhere, and there's no sense to it. Now we'll just think this thing out right here and now." And I'd sit and look out the window and look at the branches on the trees and begin from the beginning and go over the *whole* thing, and I'd say, "Now that's settled, and we'll go back to work." But there'd still be this thing that I couldn't get hold of, this lost piece to the puzzle, or the lost

There is no point, among the many incomprehensible anomalies of the science of mind, more thrillingly exciting than the fact—never, I believe, noticed in the schools—that in our endeavors to recall to memory something long forgotten, we often find ourselves *upon the very verge* of remembrance, without being able, in the end, to remember. And thus how frequently, in my intense scrutiny of Ligeia's eyes, have I felt approaching the full knowledge of their expression—felt it approaching—yet not quite be mine—and so at length entirely depart! (p. 163).

Of all the women whom I have ever known, she, the outwardly calm, the ever-placid Ligeia, was the most violently a prey to the tumultuous vultures of stern passion. And of such passion I could form no estimate, save by the miraculous expansion of those eyes which at once so delighted and appalled me. . . . (p. 164).

Another striking characteristic of Ligeia was her *knowledge.*

I have spoken of the learning of Ligeia: it was immense—such as I have never known in woman. . . . I saw not then what I now clearly perceive, that the acquisitions of Ligeia were gigantic, were astounding; yet I was sufficiently aware of her infinite supremacy to resign myself, with a child-like confidence, to her guidance through the chaotic world of metaphysical investigation at which I was most busily occupied during the earlier years of our marriage. . . . Without Ligeia I was but a child groping benighted (p. 165).

Poe then takes up the plot proper:

I saw that she must die—and I struggled desperately in spirit with the grim Azrael. And the struggles of the passionate wife were, to my astonishment, even more energetic than my own. There has been much in her stern nature to impress me with the belief that, to her, death would have come without its terrors; but not so. Words were impotent to convey any just idea of the fierceness of resistance with which she wrestled with the Shadow. I groaned in anguish at the pitiable spectacle (p. 165).

At high noon of the night on which she departed, beckoning me, peremptorily, to her side, she bade me repeat certain verses composed by herself not many days before. I obeyed her (p. 166).

She died: and I, crushed into the very dust with sorrow, could no longer endure the lonely desolation of my dwelling in the dim and decaying city by the Rhine. I had no lack of what the world calls wealth; Ligeia had brought me far more, very far more, than ordinarily falls to the lot of mortals. After a few months, therefore, of weary and aimless wandering, I purchased and put in some repair, an abbey, which I shall not name, in one of the wildest and least frequented portions of fair England (p. 168).

---

key or whatever it was. And so I'd think, "Well, now maybe if we go over it carefully, item by item, once more we can get that." So then I would. And then, of course, I never did get it so then eventually I'd push it down into the other plane and go on working anyway. But that's the thing that always comes back to me, and I don't know what that is.

I had become a bounden slave in the trammels of opium, and my labors and my orders [concerning redecoration of the abbey] had taken a coloring from my dreams. But these absurdities I must not pause to detail. Let me speak only of that one chamber, ever accursed, whither, in a moment of mental alienation, I led from the altar as my bride—as the successor of the unforgotten Ligeia—the fair-haired and blue-eyed Lady Rowena Trevanion, of Tremaine.

There is no individual portion of the architecture and decoration of that bridal chamber which is not now visibly before me. Where were the souls of the haughty family of the bride, when, through thirst of gold, they permitted to pass the threshold of an apartment *so* bedecked, a maiden and a daughter so beloved? (p. 169).

The phantasmagoric effect was vastly heightened by the artificial introduction of a strong continual current of wind behind the draperies—giving a hideous and uneasy animation to the whole.

In halls such as these—in a bridal chamber such as this—I passed, with the Lady of Tremaine, the unhallowed hours of the first month of our marriage—passed them with but little disquietude. That my wife dreaded the fierce moodiness of my temper—that she shunned me, and loved me but little—I could not help perceiving; but it gave me rather pleasure than otherwise. I loathed her with a hatred belonging more to demon than to man. My memory flew back (oh, with what intensity of regret!) to Ligeia, the beloved, the august, the beautiful, the entombed (pp. 170–71).

About the commencement of the second month of the marriage, the Lady Rowena was attacked with sudden illness. . . .

One night, near the closing in of September, she pressed this distressing subject with more than usual emphasis upon my attention. She had just awakened from an unquiet slumber, and I had been watching, with feelings half of anxiety, half of vague terror, the workings of her emaciated countenance. . . . She partly arose, and spoke, in an earnest low whisper, of sounds which she *then* heard, but which I could not hear—of motions which she *then* saw, but which I could not perceive (pp. 171–72).

Having found the wine, I recrossed the chamber, and poured out a goblet, which I held to the lips of the fainting lady. She had now partially recovered, however, and took the vessel herself, while I sank upon an ottoman near me, with my eyes fastened upon her person. It was then that I became distinctly aware of a gentle foot-fall upon the carpet, and near the couch; and in a second thereafter, as Rowena was in the act of raising the wine to her lips, I saw, or may have dreamed that I saw, fall within the goblet, as if from some invisible spring in the atmosphere of the room, three or four large drops of a brilliant and ruby-colored fluid. If this I saw—not so Rowena. She swallowed the wine unhesitatingly, and I forbore to speak to her of a circumstance which must, after all, I considered, have been but the suggestion of a vivid imagination, rendered morbidly active by the terror of the lady, by the opium, and by the hour.

Yet I cannot conceal it from my own perception that, immediately subsequent to the fall of the ruby-drops, a rapid change for the worse took place in the disorder of my wife; so that, on the third subsequent night, the hands of her menials prepared her for the tomb, and on the fourth, I sat alone with her shrouded body, in that fantastic chamber which had received her as my bride. Wild visions, opium-engendered, flitted, shadow-like, before me. . . .

It might have been midnight, or perhaps earlier, or later, for I had taken no note of time, when a sob, low, gentle, but very distinct, startled me from my revery. I *felt* it came from the bed of ebony—the bed of death. I listened in an agony of superstitious terror—but there was no repetition of the sound. . . . I resolutely and perseveringly kept my attention riveted upon the body. Many minutes elapsed before any circumstance occurred tending to throw light upon the mystery. At length it became evident that a slight, a very feeble, and barely noticeable tinge of color had flushed up within the cheeks, and along the sunken small veins of the eyelids. Through a species of unutterable horror and awe, for which the language of mortality has no sufficiently energetic expression, I felt my heart cease to beat, my limbs grow rigid where I sat.

An hour thus elapsed, when (could it be possible?) I was a second time aware of some vague sound issuing from the region of the bed. I listened—in extremity of horror.

And again I sunk into visions of Ligeia—and again (what marvel that I shudder while I write?) *again* there reached my ears a low sob from the region of the ebony bed. But why shall I minutely detail the unspeakable horrors of that night? Why shall I pause to relate how, time after time, until near the period of the gray dawn, this hideous drama of revivification was repeated; how each terrific relapse was only into a sterner and apparently more irredeemable death; how each agony wore the aspect of a struggle with some invisible foe; and how each struggle was succeeded by I know not what of wild change in the personal appearance of the corpse? Let me hurry to a conclusion.

There was a mad disorder in my thoughts—a tumult unappeasable. Could it, indeed, be the *living* Rowena who confronted me? Could it, indeed, be Rowena *at all*—the fair-haired, the blue-eyed Lady Rowena Trevanion of Tremaine? Why, *why* should I doubt it? . . . What inexpressible madness seized me with that thought? One bound, and I had reached her feet! Shrinking from my touch, she let fall from her head, unloosened, the ghastly cerements which had confined it, and there streamed forth into the rushing atmosphere of the chamber huge masses of long and dishevelled hair; *it was blacker than the raven wings of the midnight!* And now slowly opened *the eyes* of the figure which stood before me. "Here then, at least," I shrieked aloud, "can I never—can I never be mistaken—these are the full, and the black, and the wild eyes—of my lost love—of the Lady—of the Lady Ligeia" (pp. 171–76).

It was James Russell Lowell who described Poe as "Three-fifths of him genius and two-fifths sheer fudge." In "Ligeia" there is certainly a fair portion of "fudge," of obvious melodramatics. But there is also much that deserves to be taken seriously. One thing stands out, clearly and substantially: this story, like so many of Poe's, deals with the experience of neurotic anxiety, and it shows a penetrating perception of the relationship between anxiety and the dynamism of repression.[29] On this much there can be general agreement; but when we attempt to go further, and identify *what* it is that is repressed, the matter of interpretation becomes more subtle.

The average man of letters, like the layman, knows enough about psychoanalysis to believe that if anything is repressed, it must be sex. This is the essence of Krutch's wisdom concerning the psychology of Poe, and the same assumption, more narrowly conceived, dominates Basler's interpretations. Recognizing the self-revealing nature of Poe's writings, Krutch (1926) remarks:

> The stories are too full of life and in detail too richly varied to be mechanical copies of one another, but they are in essence too similar not to be expressions of a mastering interest. Dreamlike in their power to make fantastic unrealities seem real, they are dreams in essence, experiences, that is to say, which satisfy in some way the desires of the dreamer. That these desires were abnormal and that they were ones not likely to be wholly realized in waking life, both the character of the dreams and the character of the dreamer would of themselves suggest; and to consider a little more closely certain aspects of the story is to connect them even more intimately with the character of their creator (pp. 77–78).

A few pages later, the same author continues:

> Perhaps the key to his morbidity may be found in a negative characteristic of his writings which has not yet been mentioned—namely their complete sexlessness. Of Poe it has often been said with entire truth that whatever objections might be made to the tone of some of his stories, it could not be denied that they are without a single exception "pure," and that though they may deal with every other horror and corruption known to man they are free from every taint of sexual indelicacy.[30] . . . The hero of *Berenice,* who described at some length how his love for the heroine turned gradually and

[29] Poe, like many another neurotic, in attempting to understand himself became a psychologist of sorts. It will be recalled that on an earlier page of "Ligeia" he remarks that: "There is no point, among the many incomprehensible anomalies of the science of mind, more thrillingly exciting than the fact—never, I believe, noticed in the schools—that in our endeavors to recall to memory something long forgotten, we often find ourselves upon the very verge of remembrance, without being able, in the end, to remember." In the story that follows, the death of Ligeia becomes the symbolic equivalent of repression, and her revivification portrays a *return of the repressed.* The anxiety which the hero of the story experiences in connection with Ligeia's return to life shows a remarkable intuitive discernment on the part of Poe of the relation between anxiety and threatened eruption into consciousness of repressed forces. (Cf. Basler's dubious later interpretation of this being "on the very verge" as Poe's inability to experience orgasm.)

[30] Cf. Section VIII.

without cause into such an irrational hate that he murdered her in a trance which came upon him, would be diagnosed by any psychiatrist, no matter to what school he might belong, as a sexual pervert of some kind. And yet, however full the tales may be of sex disguised and perverted, there is never from the first to the last any recognition of the existence of normal amorousness, which is indeed excluded in exactly the same way that all the other interests of normal life are excluded.

Poe was, it should be remembered, in his own character morbidly pure. For women he had all his life an intense regard which degenerated in his later days into a disgustingly weak dependence upon them, and he tended strongly toward that overevaluation of the opposite sex which is common among even those neurotics who are intensely jealous, as he himself was, of any distinction recognized in members of their own sex; but he was not, in the ordinary sense, a lover (pp. 82–83).

In an earlier chapter bearing a title which is a quotation from Poe, "My Passions Were Always of the Head," Krutch makes these remarks:

Doubtless he was aware in his own mind of nothing except the charm which feminine beauty divorced from any suggestion of conscious sex had for him and he would call his admiration for Virginia [his first cousin, whom he married when she was only a little over thirteen and he was twenty-seven] a worship of purity; but when we consider the distaste which his writings reveal for the whole idea of sexual passion and the unhappy history of his constantly frustrated flirtations with other women, we may guess that this abnormal absorption in purity was but one of the outward signs of a deep-lying inhibition, and we may guess also the function which Virginia was to perform in his life, though he himself did not clearly understand the fascination which she had for him. Her youth would serve as an excuse for leaving her untouched, and the fact that he was already married would furnish him with possible reason why all his affairs with other women must remain, if not exactly platonic, at least unconsummated. Events to be discussed later will make it clear that the effort to escape from a realization of his own condition was part of one of the essential processes in Poe's life, but no act reveals more clearly than this both his abnormality and the fact that he was desperately determined that it should not be admitted even to himself (pp. 53–54).

But one thing is fairly certain. Poe could not love in a normal fashion, and the reason lay, or at least seemed to him to lie, in the dream of some woman upon whom his desire had irrevocably fixated itself. If we knew who lay behind the doors of that tomb in the "ghoul-haunted woodland of Weir," we should know the answer to the greatest riddle of Poe's life (p. 62).

In the concluding paragraph of the chapter entitled, "The Misty Mid Region of Weir," Krutch shows an appreciation not only of the mechanism of repression but also of the tendency for the repressed to return, and in so doing to produce anxiety. He says:

> Nor does it seem to be too fanciful to suggest one other parallel. These charming maidens whom death takes away will not rest in their graves but struggle with an indomitable will against dissolution. Sometimes they break forth, like the Lady Madeline, from their tombs, or again, like Ligeia, they take possession of the body of another. Thus, like the erotic imagination which gave them birth, they never really die but rise to plague their victim even at the moment when he thinks that he is done with them forever (p. 87).

Basler takes much the same thesis as does Krutch. After noting that many of Poe's stories deal "deliberately with the psychological themes of obsession and madness," Basler says:

> Such a story is "Ligeia," the most important of a group of stories, generally but inadequately classified as "impressionistic," which includes the kindred pieces "Morella" and "Berenice." . . . Even a casual comparison of these stories will reveal not merely the similar theme of obsession but also the dominant concepts which provide the motivation in all three: the power of the psychical over the physical and the power of frustrate love to create an erotic symbolism and mythology in compensation for sexual disappointment. Although Poe grinds them differently in each story, they are the same grist to his mill (1948, p. 143).

Then follows a series of similar interpretations, selected and reproduced here somewhat randomly:

> [The hero's] imaginative desire has outrun his capabilities. . . . The key to his failure is hinted in the paragraph which reveals his symbolic deification of Ligeia as a sort of personal Venus Aphrodite who personifies the dynamic urge of life itself but who, because of the hero's psychic incapacity, cannot reveal to him the "forbidden knowledge" (p. 146).
>
> She becomes not merely a woman but a goddess, through the worship of whom he "feels" that he may "pass onward to the goal of wisdom too divinely precious not to be forbidden." There is for him, however, no possibility of fathoming the mystery which she symbolizes, though in the height of passionate adoration he feels himself to be "upon the very verge," which experience he likens to that of almost but not quite recalling something from the depths of his unconscious (p. 147).
>
> The analogy of the will's inability to dictate to the unconscious and its inability to dictate to love reveals something more than the hero's vague awareness of the source of the obsession which dominates in a compensatory process his struggle to achieve by power of mind what he cannot achieve through love (p. 148).
>
> But the hero's approach to power is thwarted by Ligeia's death. Just at the point when triumph seems imminent, when he feels "that delicious vista by slow degrees expanding before me, down whose long, gorgeous, and all

untrodden path, I might at length pass onward to the goal of a wisdom too divinely precious not to be forbidden"—just then Ligeia dies, because of the weakness of her own mortal will and in spite of the fervor with which the hero himself "struggles desperately in spirit with the grim Azrael" (p. 148).

Hence, the important elements in the hero's description of Ligeia are of primary significance as they reveal his feelings of psychic inadequacy, his voluptuous imagination, and his megalomania and fierce obsession with the idea that by power of will man may thwart death through spiritual love (p. 149).

Up to this point of her death the hero's obsession has taken the form of adoration and worship of her person in an erotomania primarily sexual (though frustrated by a psychic flaw which he is aware of but does not understand) and hence projected into a symbolic realm of deity and forbidden wisdom. Following her death, however, his obsession becomes an intense megalomania motivated by his will to restore her to life in another body through a process of metempsychosis (p. 150).

I. A. Richards once observed that the literary passages which seem to have survived best in the course of history are those with maximal ambiguity. Expressing the same thought a little differently, one might say that the possibility of multiple interpretation is the essence of art, a true work of art being one that allows each contemplator to have his own fantasies about it, dream his own dreams. As Krutch has already indicated, many of Poe's productions had a dreamlike quality; and Basler reproduces the following quotation from Poe:

The poem ["To Helen"—1848] which I sent you contained all the events of a *dream* which occurred to me soon after I knew you. Ligeia was also suggested by *a dream*—observe the *eyes* in both tale and poem (p. 157).

A work of art, like a dream, characteristically makes use of the principle of condensation, according to which a single element or statement is made to do double (or even triple) duty; it is made to carry two or more meanings and by its ambiguity achieves the level of "delicacy," i.e., disguise, noted in the quotation from Poe on an earlier page. It would not be surprising, therefore, if in "Ligeia" and other stories by Poe we have productions which can be legitimately interpreted in different ways. Thus, when the hero in "Ligeia" refers to his bride, Rowena, as "the successor of the unforgotten Ligeia," when we remember that Ligeia was older and wiser than Rowena, and when we note the reference to "the unhallowed hours of the first month of our marriage," we may legitimately infer that Poe is here describing heterosexual impotence arising from a "mother fixation." Hence I do not say that there is none of the sexual meaning which Krutch and Basler see in this story; I only say that there is something more, and that this "more" has a higher order of psychological importance than do the sexual elements. Put most simply, my thesis is that Poe's impotence with the maiden, Rowena, arises from the anxiety associated with the repressed ("dead") Lady Ligeia. Ligeia is a mother figure, a conscience symbol, "disloyalty" to whom deprives the hero of the possibility of normal sexual satisfaction. The impotence is thus derivative, the repression of conscience primary.

In earlier sections we have seen Poe's unmistakable preoccupation with the theme of conscience repression and the return of the repressed, symbolized by murder and ultimate confession of the guilty knowledge. In most of these stories the person (or animal) involved is masculine; but in another series a woman is the central figure. Some interpreters of Poe have concentrated upon the latter, stressing, as we have just seen, the theme of abnormal, repressed sexuality. This theme can be applied with some justification to these particular stories; but it seems much less apposite as regards the stories featuring male figures and having a paramount concern with conscience. However, it is relatively simple to see the stories with heroines as likewise involving the conscience-killing theme; and if the generality of application is any index of validity, the latter is superior to the thesis of inhibited sexuality. This is not to say that Poe was not sexually inhibited, or that this trait did not show in his literary works. It does, however, make his sexual "incapacity," or implied impotence, secondary and the moral issue basic.

That Ligeia was indeed a conscience symbol is indicated by many features of the story. As we have seen, Poe could not remember how or where he first met "Ligeia," and he knew nothing of her antecedents. How like conscience, with its origins trailing dimly off into the nothingness of early life and the infancy of mankind! Almost immediately we note the emphasis upon her *eyes,* a symbol which Poe has repeatedly, and unmistakably, used to represent conscience.[31] Then there was her *great learning, wisdom,* and the fact that in her presence he felt "childlike," "but a child groping benighted." He was *instructed* by her, and he *obeyed* her. Here we have unmistakable allusions to a *mother figure.*

[31] It should be noted that the eye is also commonly believed in analytic circles to symbolize the female sex organ. If it had any such significance for Poe, we must suppose that the eye, then, had for him a *double* meaning, combining both sexuality and conscience. Perhaps we here get an intimation of what might be called the *sexualization of conscience.* We shall return to this possibility in the concluding Section.

Through Ligeia he had received a heritage, ". . . far more, very far more, than ordinarily falls to the lot of mortals"; and (as Basler notes with a different intent) he *deifies* her, appropriately enough, since conscience by religious precept is "the voice of God speaking in man." And if, as Basler proposes, the revivification of Ligeia represents the author's successful attempt to recapture sexuality, why is he so terrified, rather than pleased, by his *success?*

It may at first seem strange that a writer should select a woman to portray conscience; but we must remember that one ordinarily has both a male and a female parent (teacher) and that a part of one's "learning" comes from each of them. One gets the impression that Ligeia was older than Rowena, thus more of a mother figure—surely no maiden, as was Rowena.

Having made the inference that Ligeia is a conscience figure, then the latter part of the story follows the familiar pattern: repression of conscience (death) and its mysterious, terrifying return to consciousness (life). But in this story we can, with some confidence, take a further step. Because of repressed conscience (the "dead" Ligeia), Poe is unable to enjoy his marriage to Rowena: "the unhallowed hours of the first month of our marriage . . . she shunned me, and loved me but little. . . . I loathed her with a hatred belonging more to demon than to man." In "The Black Cat" we have seen how conscience was the cause of the hero's losing his wife, but in "Ligeia" the sequence is more explicit. As we know clinically, Poe is not the first man who was impotent because of a "bad," i.e., repressed, conscience.[32] Other writers have stressed the notion of "mother fixation" as the basis for Poe's sexual difficulties; but this is a very partial and unsatisfactory concept. If we were to say "mother identification," we would be coming nearer the truth; for the man who feels he is womanly, unmanly, is sure to find his conscience troublesome and, on occasion, to wish it were out of his way (21).

This line of thought does not give us a complete or perfect understanding of Poe, but it is, I believe, more instructive than the single-minded emphasis upon sexuality. Perhaps our exploration in the two following sections will further illuminate the matter.

---

[32] Since writing the above, it has occurred to me that there is also a clear intimation of this sort of thing in "The Raven." In stanza sixteen, the author asks if, "within the distant Aidenn," his soul shall "clasp a rare and radiant maiden whom the angels name Lenore." Then "Quoth the Raven, 'Nevermore.'" If we are justified in identifying the Raven as conscience, then here again we see its inhibiting influence upon sexuality and the author's conscious reason for its repudiation; for the stanza immediately following begins, "Be that word our sign of parting. . . . Get thee back into the tempest and the Night's Plutonian shore!" How better to depict repression?

VII. Princess Bonaparte's Analysis of Poe, with Special Reference to "The Black Cat"

The two authors cited in the preceding section are literary men; perhaps it is too much to expect them to offer an entirely convincing interpretation of Poe's personality and writings along psychoanalytic lines. Let us turn, then, to the two-volume work *Edgar Poe* by Princess Marie Bonaparte (1933), a professional analyst.[32a]

In the introduction which he wrote for this work, Freud simply remarks:

> My friend and student, Marie Bonaparte, has, in this book, thrown the light of psychoanalysis on the life and work of a great writer with pathological tendencies.
>
> Thanks to her interpretations, one now sees how many features of Poe's work were conditioned by his personality, and one can also see that this personality was the product of powerful affective fixations and of unhappy events dating from earliest youth. Such researches do not purport to explain the genius of creative writers, but they do show what factors have given them inspiration and what sort of material has been imposed on them by destiny. . . .

But Bonaparte herself is less restrained; she holds back nothing as regards bold applications of all the intricate and bizarre features of analytic theory and produces a truly remarkable document. While the work is ingenious and scholarly throughout, one cannot escape the feeling that the author has followed Freudian theory rather slavishly and, in places, has been perhaps more zealous of preserving her status as *amie et élève* than in observing her obligation, as scholar and scientist, to keep close to the data.

Desirous of getting an impression of the work as a whole as quickly as possible, I first turned to the concluding section of Volume II, on "Poe and the Human Spirit." Here the author begins by elaborating Freud's familiar emphasis upon the similarity between dreams and artistic productions. Writers, she says, vary along an objectivity-subjectivity continuum; and she places Poe at the extreme of subjectivity.

Shortly we pick up the central theme of the author's analysis: she refers to "the most tragedic drama of the life of Edgar Poe, his sexual impotence" (p. 795). And it is this impairment of

---

32a [Since this chapter was written, a one-volume edition of this work has appeared. It is entitled, *The Life and Works of Edgar Allan Poe,* and was published in 1949 by the Imago Publishing Co, London. John Rodker is the translator.]

normal sexual functioning that leads to the manifold "displacements," i.e., disguised and perverse expressions of frustrated sexuality, which are to be found in his writings.

The author divides all of Poe's works into what she calls *Les Cycles du Mère* and *Les Cycles du Père.* By way of summary we then read the following:

> In the series of stories having to do with the "assassinated mother," the displacement of the affective forces is very clear. The murderous father, of the infantile sadistic conception of coition, appears there in the guise of the mysterious traits of an unknown one, with a profoundly criminal disposition, of whom the insane rave; this is particularly true as regards the orangutan of "La Rue Morgue." The penetrating phallus is symbolized now by a dagger, then by a razor. Thus, displacement—the closed room which, in the same "Rue Morgue," represents the mother, especially the behavior of the old Spanish woman—; displacement again in the case of the chimney, image of the maternal cloaca where the daughter is wedged. Always displacements, the gouged-out eye of the black cat, symbol of a castration wound, its rephallization in connection with hanging, and the cat itself, so general a symbol of woman and her organ.
>
> In the series of stories having to do with the father, the psychic accent on the phallus continues—in "The Tell-Tale Heart," which characteristic carries one back to the maternal entrails, in the "Cask of Amontillado," in the "Cave of Montresor." And all the representations, in "Hop-Frog" and "The Red Death," by courtiers, princes, or kings, of the parents of our infancy, are also displacements designed to render unrecognizable, in their true natures, the personages involved and to permit them, unsuspiciously, to play their "culpable" erotic role (p. 796).
>
> This is without doubt the reason that the displacement is made necessary in large part by moral censure, which dominates to such a degree our waking hours, and in the course of our sleep (p. 797).

Then follows a neat bit of circularity:

> And our readers, in following our analysis, have probably come to feel that we abuse these symbolisms which monotonously reduce all objects in the universe to human representations of the father, the mother, the infant, or to the various parts of the body, especially the genital organs. However, we cannot help it. We are not responsible for the monotony of the human unconscious, where our most archaic instincts and our most primitive memories rule as sole masters (p. 799).

The foregoing excerpts prepare one for the discovery that Bonaparte overlooks many of the continuities between "William Wilson," "The Black Cat," and "The Raven" which have been traced above.[32b] In fact, she puts the first of these in the "father series" of stories, the second in the "mother series," and makes no systematic analysis or classification of the latter at all.

Bonaparte's treatment of "William Wilson" is not greatly different from the one given in Section IV of the present study; but this is perhaps not surprising, since the symbolism is so transparent that there is hardly any latitude in the matter of interpretation. We find Bonaparte, for example, making such observations as the following:

> Mr. Allan, especially at the beginning, despite his austere manner, had in effect loved, in his way, the little Edgar. Now it is he who, in the double of William Wilson, is reincarnated partially in the representation of the moral conscience (p. 672).

After quoting the passage concerning the *whisper,* Bonaparte says:

> One knows not how to depict better the voice of conscience, which commands but speaks low (p. 673).
>
> The superego, in effect, is formed little by little in the course of infancy, and it is only gradually that the parental authority, or force, is introjected and takes on the same coloration as oneself (p. 674).
>
> Thus the self of Wilson, exasperated by the tyranny of his moral superego, dreamed of freeing itself, and we are to see the introjected conflict between the son and the father expose itself anew, as in the "Masque of the Red Death," "Hop-Frog," and the "Cask of Amontillado," against the background of a masked ball (pp. 280–81).

In the final scene of the story, says the author, Poe "has assassinated his superego, his moral conscience" (p. 682) and becomes the most depraved of men.

> It seems that Poe himself had partly known the symbolic meaning of this production, and this is without doubt why "William Wilson," despite its qualities of virtuosity and style, had a poorer reception than the majority of

---

[32b] [On rereading, in the translation previously mentioned, Bonaparte's discussion of "William Wilson," I discover a passage which I had previously overlooked: "Thus, the same confessional urge which forced the murderer in *The Black Cat* to knock on the wall behind which he had immured his victim; which in *The Tell-Tale Heart* drove the man with the lantern to reveal, to the police, the old man's heart beating beneath the floor; which, in *The Imp of the Perverse* caused the poisoner to cry his crime in the market-place; dictates the revelations of William Wilson's double, revelations no less compromising for being whispered. Here, conscience speaks, even to others, in its own true, *inner* voice and finds means to make others hear, though not by the way of the human voice nor by the symbolic scream of a cat" (p. 549). Bonaparte thus acknowledges certain continuities in these stories, but because of her theoretical presuppositions these continuities are given only secondary significance and do not influence either the organization of her two volumes or her principal conclusions.]

his other great stories. . . . Poe, this time, understood a little too well what he was writing—certainly more than he did as to why he wrote "The Raven" (p. 683).

After recalling the threefold division of the personality proposed by Freud—id, ego, and superego—Bonaparte makes a comment that is unusual in orthodox analytic writings. She says:

> Now the division of the personality from which the conception of the "double" originates can occur in one direction or the other: either the ego, allied with the moral superego, projects into the external world its worst tendencies in the form of a double which is immoral and tempting and in which is reincarnated the id—this, according to Rank, is the primitive form of the dynamism; or, what is a later variation, the self, confirmed accomplice of the id, proves itself to be very bad, and then it is the moral superego which inhabits the fatal double. "William Wilson" is perhaps the extreme case of the latter (pp. 685–86).

Although Bonaparte thus admits the possibility of the ego's being id-dominated and repressing—and then projecting—the conscience, and although she concedes that this is what happened in "William Wilson," she finds no other application of this theme in Poe's writings. While classifying "William Wilson" among the stories constituting *Les Cycles du Père,* it alone falls under the subheading of *Le Conflict avec la conscience.* How differently Bonaparte was inclined to perceive Poe's other stories is indicated by her treatment of "The Black Cat."

It is difficult to summarize in any orderly way the interpretation which Bonaparte makes of this story. The author herself remarks that: "The theme of castration of the mother, so strange to consciousness, to adult thought, but so familiar to the infantile mode of thought and to the unconsciousness of all ages, is found to be the tap-root of this great story by Edgar Poe" (p. 602). But the avenue by which she arrives at this conclusion involves some strange and unexpected turns of thought. One of the earliest and most surprising of these is her postulation that the cat in the story is a *female symbol,* this despite the fact that the cat has a masculine name and is referred to throughout the story in the male gender. More specifically, the cat is seen as a *mother symbol,* an interpretation that is bolstered by such observations as these: the second cat had a little patch of white fur on his chest—meaning milk in mother's breast; there are two cats in the story, and Poe had two mothers (his biological mother and his foster mother).

Observing that "perhaps our readers will find our identification of the mother with a male cat forced" (p. 579), Bonaparte makes the rejoinder that the cat is a "classic symbol for the female genital organ" and that witches (who portray "the bad mother") are always accompanied by cats. It is the mother who, oftener than not, discovers the little boy's masturbation, and the cat's mouth, full of sharp teeth, becomes an instrument of castration. Bonaparte notes that in the story the first Pluto *bites* the author's hand (the vehicle of masturbation), rather than scratching it, and that this fact so infuriates the hero that he cuts out the cat's eye, which Bonaparte interprets as an act of castration. The fact that *chat* (cat) and *chatrée* (castrated) have a punlike similarity is further pointed to as justification for this line of thought. In summary, then, Bonaparte remarks:

> Could it be, then, that the man is impotent? And impotent by the fear of castration, castration not only *of* women, but also *by* a woman, in virtue of the feminine vagina, with imaginary teeth? Now such seems to have been the case of Edgar Poe, and it is the hate, the hatred first of the castrated and castrating mother, of the mother, incarnation of castration both active and passive, which constitutes the profound inspiration for "The Black Cat" (p. 582).

Later on the same page the author states her thesis more specifically:

> Why is it on the occasion of a wound inflicted by the cat with its *teeth*—contrary to the habits of cats, who usually rely on their claws,—that the master of the animal finds himself seized by the first surge of cruelty, if there is not here an allusion to the betoothed cloaca, of which the world of Poe is filled? The mother has wounded the son on the hand, that frequent phallic symbol, that executive organ of masturbation: the son retaliates by taking his knife from his pocket, the bourgeois equivalent of the dagger of "The Man in the Crowd" or the razor of the "Rue Morgue." And he, himself, then inflicts on the totemic animal, which he has taken by the throat, the mutilation for which he hates the mother, castration; identifying himself with the all-powerful father to whom, as we have seen above *à propos* of the orang-utan, he attributed the crime, he *cuts* the mother,—in English it is the same word ("cut"); he cuts her, not at the throat, but around the eye, which he pops out. One knows, as elsewhere, from dreams and myths, from that of the Oedipus in particular, . . . what a universal symbol of castration the act of blinding is (p. 582).

Bonaparte does not overlook the fact that the hero in "The Black Cat" was alcoholic and that his enucleation of the cat's eye occurred when he was deeply intoxicated. She posits that alcohol serves to obliterate the moral ("inhibitory") part of the personality and to release the original, instinctive elements. In the enucleation incident we see, says Bonaparte, an expression of Poe's perverse sexual "sadism." On grounds of parsimony, if for no other reason, I prefer to interpret this act as being of a piece with the alcoholism: both can be reasonably interpreted as strategies of conscience-killing. And here we encounter an interesting question concerning the psychodynamics of alcohol. It is generally agreed that alcohol is a conscience depressant, but there are two quite different ways in which it might be supposed to achieve its distinctive psychic effects. The Freudian view is that alcoholics, i.e., neurotic drinkers, are persons whose sexuality and other "instincts" are deeply repressed and that they imbibe alcohol as a means of weakening the inhibitory forces of an "excessively severe superego" and thus allowing some expression and satisfaction of the imprisoned impulses. This, obviously, is the line of thought which Bonaparte follows.

My own impression is that the alcoholic (like neurotics in general) is a person in whom there is conscience repression and that the attempts of the conscience to escape from repression produce the characteristic neurotic experiences of anxiety, depression, and inferiority feeling. The alcoholic drinks, then, as a means of silencing conscience and lessening his neurotic (moral) suffering. Thus it would seem that alcohol serves to weaken, not the repressing forces (as Freudian theory holds), but the *repressed forces*. Thus inactivated, conscience ceases to struggle for readmission into consciousness, and the individual secures a transient relief from his anxieties.

This conception of the function of alcohol in the life of a neurotic has an important logical consequence. If psychotherapy has the objective of undoing repressions, then intoxication, according to the Freudian view, might be expected to be therapeutic too, for it neutralizes the repressing forces and allows the pent-up impulses to come forward into consciousness and demand gratification. Under these circumstances one might suppose that there would be an opportunity for "reality testing"; and if it was found that reality permitted satisfaction of the hitherto repressed impulses, then the fears connected therewith might be expected to undergo extinction and the repression, even in the sober state, to disappear. But this is not how the matter seems to work. I have never seen it argued that alcoholism is therapeutic; and the reason why we do *not* have alcohol therapy is that the effects of alcohol, far from opposing the dynamics of neurosis, actually parallel and reinforce them. Alcohol is an aid to and ally of repression, rather than a counteractant; it merely dulls perception of the remote consequences of action, i.e., quiets conscience, and permits the individual to continue to behave nonintegratively, just as repression is designed to do. That Poe was preoccupied with conscience-killing in his stories and with the same process in his addiction to alcohol is no coincidence.

Bonaparte's analysis of "The Black Cat" is long—extending to some thirty-three pages—and contains many ingenious ideas which we have not been able here to discuss. However, enough has been said to show how radically different it is from the treatment accorded this same story in Section IV of the present study. Perhaps the reader will be tempted to observe that enough has also been said to show how utterly indeterminate and noncrucial are *all* analyses of this kind. For example, in connection with her discussion of "The Black Cat," Bonaparte interprets "The Purloined Letter" as symbolizing a stolen penis. I would see it rather as a variation on the theme of the mystery which accompanies every repression; the "letter" being the intelligence, the wisdom, the "word" which is contained in conscience which, when lost (repressed), causes a sense of helplessness and anxiety. Let me grant that in the case of a writer, like Poe, the materials which one has at one's disposal are never complete or crucial, that alternative interpretations are always possible. But they serve to high-light general method and conceptual differences, which, in actual clinical practice, have real consequences and which will eventually be tried and tested by the common canons of evidence.

VIII. Summary: Dynamics and Diagnosis

Since Poe had no therapist, no one to interpret to him the unconscious meanings of his literary productions, he continued to be neurotic and to repeat endlessly, albeit with great skill and virtuosity, the same primal themes. Thus we lack in his productions the fresh material which is released by interpretations when we are working therapeutically with living persons. We do not know what he would have done and said in response to the ideas which have been expressed in the foregoing pages, and such information is indispensable for the final verification of clinical hypotheses. We have, in fact, in Poe's case only a portion of the total evidence which we obtain in the course of a regular analysis. But since the information which we glean from his writings and the known details of his life fit into a pattern which is clinically very familiar and well substantiated, we may venture to round out the picture somewhat more fully than the available data might alone justify.

With impressive frequency one finds in neurotic men a family history of the following kind. There have been frequent, often violent, conflicts between the father and mother. As a small boy, the patient has witnessed quarrels and arguments and has found his sympathies powerfully drawn to *the side of the mother,* with fateful consequences. It is from the father that a boy normally acquires the self-image that securely guides him into adult manliness. But in a situation of the kind just depicted, it is as if the boy is driven to a conclusion which can be expressed something like this: "If being a man means being like my father—who in my eyes stands for brutality and hatefulness—if being a man means being *like him,* I'd rather die!" The boy thus *will not* be like his father, and he obviously cannot, in a final sense, be like his mother; but he is likely to feel an affiliation with women that he does not share with men. Instead of developing a sense of "*We,* the men," and "*They,* the women," he is unable to identify himself fully with either sex, with resulting feelings of isolation, guilt, and alienation.[33]

In the nomal, harmonious family, alignment with the father brings the small boy the support and approval of both his father and his mother. By being a "chip off the old block" he wins the father's profound acceptance; and since the mother loves the father, she, too, will be glad to see his qualities being reproduced in her son. But where distrust and ill-will characterize the marital relationship, the boy is thrown into an acute identification dilemma: if he patterns himself after the father, he loses his mother's love; and if he tries to be like his mother, he risks alienation from his father, and men in general.

What happens to boys who, in such familial conflicts, choose the father and reject the mother we have no very satisfactory way of knowing, for such individuals seem not to appear very often in clinics. However, for the boy who, as noted earlier, attempts to resolve his dilemma by rejecting the father in favor of the mother, there is a high probability of neurosis which will ultimately cause him to seek professional help. The author now has complete psychotherapeutic recordings of a number of neurotic men in whom this pattern stands out with dramatic clarity (21).[34]

---

[33] A student recently reported that her small nephew, at the age of three, in starting off to Sunday school one morning with his father noted that their coats were made in much the same fashion and pridefully remarked: "We's men, isn't we, Daddy!" It is this kind of firm alignment with the father that is the boy's best assurance of healthy character and normal development.

[34] If the identification with the opposite-sexed parent is relatively complete, one may expect, not neurosis, but perversion. In order for one individual to regard

A similar constellation provides a no less serious impediment in the development of women. The normal, wholesome family situation is one in which a little girl finds that if she acts, thinks, and feels like her mother, she wins the affection and devotion of both her father and her mother. If, on the other hand, as a result of parental disharmony, she is forced to choose between her parents, and if her sympathies go with her father and against her mother, the result is likely to be pathological.

Let me take, for illustration, the case of a young woman who came for treatment during the terminal stages of her marriage to a man of about the same age. After the early resistances had been worked through, it was apparent that there were marked schizoid tendencies in her personality. At the age of twelve she had retreated into what she called "a dream world" and had fantasied quite continuously, for approximately two years, about a woman teacher who had been kind to her. During her marriage, as it became ever more apparent that she and her husband could not be happy together, she began to have fantasies about her elderly physician; and when these became so vivid that she was having difficulty in distinguishing them from reality, she became frightened and sought professional help.

It shortly emerged that this girl's mother had worked outside the home throughout her childhood and had delegated her care very largely to an aged grandmother (who eventually became psychotic) and to a very strict unmarried maternal aunt. The father appears to have been the only person (aside from the grandmother) from whom the child received much affection; and when he and the wife quarreled, or rather when the wife criticized and attacked him without much response on his part, the little girl's sympathies

another as an object of sexual interest, there must apparently be a feeling of difference, a polarization. Thus the man who feels *fully* aligned with women finds, not women, but men attractive. It is the person not completely identified with his own sex but likewise not fully identified with the opposite sex who is most predisposed to neurosis. Such a person suffers from an *identification dilemma,* whereas the normal person, on the one hand, and the full-fledged homesexual, on the other, do not. (It should be noted, incidentally, that this line of thought assumes that homosexuality in the male arises, not because of a "mother fixation" in the libidinal sense, but in the *characterological* sense. It is *mother identification,* rather than "fixation," that causes the difficulty. Sexual attraction to the mother may be taken as an early, and for that stage a healthy, sign of identification *with the father.*) In this context, the neurotic and the psychotic can be usefully differentiated by noting that for the former the dilemma is: To be a man or to be a woman? In the psychotic, or prepsychotic, the dilemma is more profound: To be a human being or not to be? Clinically this distinction is reflected by the neurotic's greater capacity and eagerness to reach out and utilize human contacts in a therapeutic relationship. This is the distinction which Freud apparently had in mind when he spoke of "transference neuroses" (neurosis proper, in contemporary usage) as opposed to the "narcissistic neuroses" (or psychoses) (cf. 18, Footnote 30).

went out to him and turned more and more away from her mother. In her desperation and despair, she sought consolation in masturbation; and the extremity of her dilemma is indicated by the fact that her masturbation often involved, not human, but *animal* fantasies. The following is a brief extract from the sixteenth interview:

PATIENT: There is another—and one thing I was—well, well, I wanted to tell you about: there was the relationship between my parents and me. I think that has probably something to do with why I married my husband. Because, uh, I don't, well, sometimes I think that I—I mean, my mother is very good to me. And she'll buy me anything I want and things like that, even now. And, uh, I mean, in that respect she's very good to me. But, uh, I mean, it's, it's always almost like as if she's trying to make up for something. . . . And I, I was wondering whether maybe she ever resented me actually. She had a—I don't know whether I told you this or not, but I just found out, found out very recently. She had told my boy friend about it. She had a—first she had a, a miscarriage, and then she had twins that died. And one of them—see, there were the doctors. Oh, she had a—well, she got hurt slightly, and she went to the hosptial for a check-up, and they could still feel the child in there; so they said to her it was all right. But actually one child was living, and one was dead. And, uh, she must have gone through an awful lot of pain and things like that. And then, well, and then this all happened successively and maybe a year in between, and then I came along. See, it was all within three years. I guess at that time they didn't know much about, um, birth prevention. And I was—and I was wondering sometimes whether she actually resented me or anything. Subcons—not consciously, I mean, but subconsciously.

And, well, I mean . . . well, she worked in a—we lived in one part of the city, and she worked in another part. And when I was, well, small, I used to—she used to just carry me around it—with her in the morning and in the evening. And there was a peculiar triangle with my grandmother. . . . Oh, when I got older, when I went to school, she, she had one of her sisters come up; and she was going to take care of me. And she wasn't—she was a young girl, and she thought that the less love she showed the more authority she'll get.

And I remember one time, my . . . My, my father was always treated as—as far as I can remember, my father always treated my mother with re—with respect and in a fairly loving way and— But my mother always—I mean, he'd never make a remark about, a derogatory remark about, about my mother, I don't think even to himself. But my mother would to my father. And I was attached to my father in a normal way; and whenever my mother said something like that, it—I was quite sensitive to that. And, uh . . . well, I don't know whether it was when I was around between five or ten or something like that—and my father used to play cards quite a lot. And, uh, my mother had to get him out of that habit. I mean, she, she didn't have a particularly easy time. But I just recall it was very disagreeable to me to find out that my father—I mean, he played cards during the day when he should have been working. My father was, uh, well, he seemed like a weakling or something like that. Bad habits. I remember once he came home drunk. That was only one time, and then I don't know why I should have been so sensitive to it. But my mother thought he was sick and started putting him to bed; and then my aunt said, "Well, can't you smell [P. laughs] it?" or something like that. I mean, my mother, my—mother wasn't particularly mad at him at the time. She just treated—I mean, he just did it once, and she just— He met somebody, and she treated it—oh, I don't know. As far as I was—I, I knew, she didn't—treated it fairly lightly since he, he didn't, didn't do it too often. But I was awfully sensitive to that, too. Maybe it was because I used to think highly of my father and those things sort of broke it up or something.

THERAPIST: Well, I would like to suggest a, a little different view of those facts. And I think they have a bearing upon your present life in a number of ways perhaps. You had—your, your father apparently was a more affectionate, a more responsive person with you than your mother was. There was more love between you and him than there was between you and your mother. Now—then, then there came these, uh, they weren't quarrels or fights because your father didn't, uh, didn't fight back. He was, as you say, very respectful and gentle with your mother and so on. But your mother behaved in a kind of quarrelsome, unwomanly, un—unladylike fashion. Now as a small child I think that presented a dilemma something like this for you. You said, "I'm a"—it's as if you said to yourself, "I'm a little girl, and little girls have a way of growing into women. But if being a woman means being like my mother and doing such heartbreaking things as she seems to do, I don't know. Maybe it would be better if I wasn't a woman." And I think it's out of that context that some of your confusion about femininity and masculinity arises. Back to the dream then: are you going to marry a girl or a boy? Are you a man, or are you a woman?

PATIENT: I dream of other things too that I dislike. Like I think when they're snooping around trying to find out what I did during the day from my aunt. I did something bad, and then she'd come out and say she dreamt I did something bad. And that was quite hateful for me. I mean, there was nothing I disliked more than, than—I mean, to her it was—as though she [laughs] probably thought she used psychology; but I, I hated that roundabout way of, of telling me things. I mean, if, if she would have spanked me once in a while, I wouldn't have—I would have felt that was all right maybe, I don't know. But that—it was just like somebody sneaking up; and I, I hated that.

And then most of the time I didn't—. And well then another thing, most of the time she always wanted me to kiss her, and I didn't want to. It's like with my husband, on a smaller scale, as it was with my mother. I didn't want to kiss her because I didn't, just didn't care for her. I mean, it was all right if she left me alone and I left her alone. That's the way I felt when I was around ten. And then if we left each other alone, everything was just fine. . . .

And, and then she, she would always tell me the things she did for me. That was another thing I couldn't stand. I didn't care—I mean, I'm still a little sensitive about it. I don't care if somebody doesn't do anything for me at all, but to do something and then tell me about it fifty times. I just—well, she just seemed to rub me the wrong way in all respects. And she once—and she, she even—well, I don't know, I was scratching myself between my legs or something like that once, and she told me not to do it, and little girls don't do it. I mean—just did it—I mean, in that respect she did everything you're not supposed to do. Because I was just—I, I didn't think anything of it at all. [Pause.]

Well, I, and then—and when—and then when she had this—I mean, I found out now that she even thought of divorcing my father because of, of, uh, of my grandmother. And she probably had a good reason there. She probably couldn't stand it. My, my, my grandmother was practically about nuts at the time. Probably at the beginning stage, I don't know. And my mother probably couldn't stand it. When she, she would—my, my mother tries to please everybody. But I guess there's just so much you can do. [Laughs.] And she actually thought of divorcing my father. And there was some way she was talking about, and I sort of could feel it. And she—when she said something against my grandmother, I, well, then I really got mad at her because I liked my grandmother. And, and the way my, my mother would kiss me all over the place, and my grandmother would kiss me on my forehead. And those—the things like that seemed to make all the difference in the world to me.

THERAPIST: Well, I have a thought I'm going to suggest here. It seems to me that what, uh, these facts seem to lead up to is this. You got confused about whether you were a—you wanted to be a man or you wanted to be a woman. And by that very fact you became confused about whom you could love. If you were a woman, and to the extent that you wanted to be a woman, you would expect to love a man; if you were a—tended to be, to have a masculine identification, however, then men would not be love objects, but women would be. So that you got thoroughly fouled up, thoroughly mixed up in terms of who you were yourself, in terms of your personal identifications and the kinds of love objects that you might have. Thus, you can't marry a wom—a girl, and you can't marry a man for whatever reason. This is your option, but you can't really—it's really not an option. You can't really—you can't marry—you don't want—you don't feel that you *can* marry either of them. And thus, if you can't marry either a woman or a man, the only thing that's left is for you to love yourself. And I think this dilemma is one of the things that has driven you back so powerfully on, on masturbation as a, as a recourse. Self-love, or masturbation, was the—seemed to be the way out. Instead of your being able to take the normal way out in terms of a good, strong, healthy, uh, feminine identification and a relation—and a love relationship with a man; or, on the other hand, a thoroughly perverse relationship in which you would say, "Well, yes, I, I, I like women; uh, they are of much more interest to me than a man," uh, you were not able to take the healthy or normal way, uh, out of the sexual dilemma: you were not able to take a thoroughly perverse way out and become an outright pervert. And you were just sort of stopped in between with masturbation being the only way in which you could find any—masturbation with fantasy being the only way in which you could find any, uh, really satisfying sexual, uh, gratification.

PATIENT: Well, that masturbation came out—it, it seemed just like—I don't know how I discovered it. And, all I seemed to remember is I was twelve; and I was sick; and, well, the Nazis had just overrun the place; and it was shortly after that; and I couldn't sleep much; and I, I must have read some kind of books—sex-stimulating books . . . because—but then it was—there it was. I just came to my vaginal, and I felt that I could sleep, and I felt that I had discovered something pretty wonderful—

THERAPIST: Yes.

PATIENT:—just—I had found a way to fall asleep.

THERAPIST: All right, I guess we'll have to stop here for tonight.

As in the case of the young woman whose words have just been quoted and many another seriously neurotic person, Poe's family experiences were anomalous and his socialization seriously disturbed. His own father disappeared shortly after his birth, and his contacts with his mother during the two years and eleven months which she subsequently lived must have been extremely unsatisfactory, since during this time she continued to work as a singer and actress in order to support her infant son and two older children. Shortly after his mother's death, Edgar was taken into the home of Mr. and Mrs. John Allan, of Richmond, Virginia. It appears that this action was prompted mainly by the desires of Mrs. Allan, who was childless; and we may reasonably conjecture that the Allans' marriage was an unhappy and unstable one, since Mr. Allan later had a number of illegitimate children by another woman. Mrs. Allan, we may thus suppose, was motivated in taking the young Edgar into her home more by the desire to hold the attention and assure the loyalty of her husband than by a special interest in a child as such. The indications are that she was as good a mother as she knew how to be, but the household was by no means a wholesome one for the rearing of a boy.

The fact that John Allan never legally adopted Edgar Poe indicates his reservations concerning him from the outset, and we have evidence that Allan was unsympathetic and critical of him throughout their association. In the altercations between husband and wife which we may infer Edgar witnessed or at least knew about, we may suppose that he aligned himself much more strongly with the foster mother than with the foster father.

Knowledge concerning the details of daily life in the Allan household while Edgar was a boy is meager, but when Edgar entered the university, at the age of seventeen, correspondence between him and his foster parents began which leaves little doubt as to the general nature of his relationship to them. Referring to the Allan-Poe letters which he reproduces in his volume on Poe, Stern (1945) says:

> The first two letters were written about three months after Allan had refused to let Poe return to the University of Virginia. They reflect the quarrel which must have taken place between them and show Poe's determination to leave his foster father's home. . . . The third letter was written after the death of Poe's beloved foster mother and after Allan had remarried. . . . On the back of [another] letter Allan wrote: "I do not think the boy has one good quality" (p. 1).

Elsewhere, in discussing Poe's addiction to the use of alcohol, Stern gives the following compact picture of Poe's adult personality and subjective world. He says:

> No man drinks without cause. In Poe's case the causes are not difficult to determine. He was a sensitive and neurotic child, orphaned at an early age, who was unable to find in the Allan home the feeling of security every young person needs. As a result, his dead mother came to represent the maternal protection he was so desperately seeking. All the women in his life were substitutes for her, and poor substitutes they must have been for an idealized creature who never existed and never could exist. The unstable element in Poe kept twisting him farther and farther from the norm, and every disaster in his ill-starred life contributed to the warping. To him the real world was intolerable, and he sought escape from it in his writing, in his sexless quest for the perfect woman, and in alcohol. The fact that he happened to be a poor drinker is immaterial. Alcohol gave him surcease from his troubles, and he took to it as a drug-addict takes to opium. Insanity lay close beneath the surface, and he knew how near it was. In fact he once complained that his "enemies referred the insanity to the drink rather than the drink to the insanity." Toward the end of his life he said: "I have absolutely no pleasure in the stimulants in which I sometimes so madly indulge. It has not been in pursuit of pleasure that I have periled life and reputation and reason. It has been in the desperate attempt to escape from torturing memories, from a sense of insupportable loneliness, and a dread of some strange impending doom."
>
> However, he was not all dreamer and escapist; underneath was a hard core of practicality that expressed itself in unceasing labor and that is best seen in his critical and analytical work. Because of it he was able to preserve his sanity for most of his life and accomplish so much. Toward the

end, when his wife died and his household seemed threatened, he went to pieces and sought refuge in alcohol, in narcotics, and finally in death (pp. xix–xx).

In Stern's quotations from Poe the phrase "insupportable loneliness" warrants special attention. It is through his father that a boy ordinarily finds his passport to the world of men and develops sympathy and enthusiasm for the human enterprise generally. As we have seen, Poe's experience was sadly defective in this respect. Throughout his life he "walked alone," yet he was never able to accept his isolation and loneliness. At one and the same time he despised other men and yet longed for their approbation with a passion rarely equaled.

Poe's heroes were often exceedingly apt projections of his own personality. He describes the recluse Legrand, in "The Gold-Bug," as "well educated, with unusual powers of mind, but infected with misanthropy, and subject to perverse moods of alternate enthusiasms and melancholy" (p. 463). In "The Murders in the Rue Morgue," C. Auguste Dupis is represented in a singularly similar fashion: "This young gentleman was of an excellent—indeed an illustrious family, but, by a variety of untoward events, had been reduced to such poverty that the energy of his character succumbed beneath it, and he ceased to bestir himself in the world, or to care for the retrieval of his fortunes" (p. 336). And in "Hop-Frog," the dwarf's (child's) abiding hatred for authoritative male figures (represented by the fat king and his seven ministers) is consummated as follows:

> Owing to the high combustibility of both the flax and the tar to which it adhered, the dwarf had scarcely made an end of his brief speech before the work of vengeance was complete. The eight corpses swung in their chains, a fetid, blackened, hideous, and indistinguishable mass. The cripple hurled his torch at them, clambered leisurely to the ceiling, and disappeared through the sky-light.
>
> It is supposed that Trippetta, stationed on the roof of the saloon, had been the accomplice of her friend in his fiery revenge, and that, together, they effected their escape to their own country: for neither was seen again (pp. 328–29).

This story of retaliation was published in 1849, the last year of Poe's life, and was therefore not a mere adolescent fantasy; it is rather the protest of a forty-year-old man who had never been able to regard himself, unconsciously, as anything more than a jester and a fool in a court of royal villains.

Krutch (1926) has perceived Poe's "misanthropy" with special clarity and has used some unforgettable phrases in describing it: "one whose hatred of the world, almost demoniacal in its intensity, constantly recoiled upon himself" (p. 123); "hardly to be trusted in polite society" (p. 137); "no love for the human race" (p. 157); "a spiritual outcast from his age" (p. 158); "he felt himself a superman forced to dwell among pygmies, and it was impossible for him to reveal anything except scorn for this race of men whose admiration he had to have at the same time that he despised them" (p. 160); "one who never for an instant regarded himself as the servant of the public" (p. 162); "not a large, brotherly, helpful man" (p. 194); "in a complete moral vacuum and cannot possibly teach any lesson, moral or immoral, since questions of morality never enter into them" (p. 199); deaf "to the still sad music of humanity" (p. 200).

In a manner typical of the neurotic, Poe was on such bad terms with himself that in order to keep down his own self-criticism and inferiority feeling, he had a perpetual need to belittle others. With his own conscience ever ready to seize upon external facts as an occasion for condemning him, Poe strove continually to interpret reality in such a way as to avert comparisons which might be in any way unfavorable. Somewhere he remarks that the very thought of there being anyone superior to him was intolerable.

Literary criticism provided, therefore, a natural vehicle for the expression of this need. At an early date Poe became known in connection with his critical appraisals for "a fearlessness bordering upon malicious severity" (Krutch, p. 216). "Men were to be slaughtered, but in women praiseworthy intentions were sufficient defense" (p. 220). And Lowell, a contemporary of Poe, remarked that he "sometimes seems to mistake his phial of prussic acid for his inkstand" (p. 222). By thus devaluating other men, both personally and intellectually, Poe strove to lessen his own chronic self-doubts and depression. Discrediting others, maximizing his own accomplishments, and, when the pain became too great, resorting to intoxication—these were Poe's principal strategies for managing his anxieties.

Poe introduces "The Murders in the Rue Morgue" with a quotation from Sir Thomas Browne which refers to the "name Achilles assumed when he hid himself among women." In an important sense, it was both Poe's salvation and his shame that he, too, *hid himself among women.* As a boy in Richmond, he formed strange attachments to the mothers of some of his schoolmates; later, for a number of years, his child-bride, Virginia, and her mother, Maria Clemm, provided a kind of sanctuary for Poe; and, after Virginia's death, Poe ran foolishly from one woman to another, unable to play either a fully masculine role with them or to reconcile himself to the childlike dependence which he so obviously sought.

Much has been made of Poe's "mother fixation," as if this were the primal cause of his personality difficulties. As emphasized elsewhere in this volume (18), neurosis is not so much the result of a learning excess as of a learning deficit. It was not that Poe loved his mother or some other mother figure *too much;* rather did the difficulty lie in *the lack of* strong and secure identification with a father figure. Poe's basic trouble was moral, not libidinal. If he had had the strength of character necessary to lead a fully manly existence in the ethical and social sense, there would have been no problem of unmanliness in the sexual sphere.

That Poe was, in fact, impotent with woman much of or perhaps all his life is a common conjecture among his biographers. And he has written at least one story in which the theme of impotence is but thinly veiled. In "Loss of Breath" there appear two early paragraphs which may be quoted without comment:

> "Thou wretch!—thou vixen!—thou shrew!" said I to my wife on the morning after our wedding, "thou witch!—thou hag!—thou whipper-snapper!—thou sink of iniquity!—thou fiery-faced quintessence of all that is abominable!—thou—thou" here standing upon tiptoe, seizing her by the throat, and placing my mouth close to her ear, I was preparing to launch forth a new and more decided epithet of opprobrium, which should not fail, if ejaculated, to convince her of her insignificance, when, to my extreme horror and astonishment, I discovered that *I had lost my breath.*
>
> The phrases "I am out of breath," "I have lost my breath," etc., are often enough repeated in common conversation; but it had never occurred to me that the terrible accident of which I speak could bona fide and actually happen! Imagine—that is if you have a fanciful turn—imagine, I say, my wonder—my consternation—my despair! (Cameo Edition, Vol 8, pp. 180–81).

Nor does it require great subtlety of interpretation to see the hidden meaning in the following passage:

> Long and earnestly did I continue the investigation [designed to lead to the recovery of his breath]; but the contemptible reward of my industry and perseverance proved to be only a set of false teeth, two pair of hips, an eye, and a number of billets-doux from Mr. Windenough to my wife. I might as well here observe that this confirmation of my lady's partiality for Mr. W. occasioned me little uneasiness. That Mrs. Lackobreath [the wife] should admire any thing so dissimilar to myself was a natural and necessary evil. I am, it is well known, of a robust and corpulent appearance, and at the same time somewhat diminutive in stature. What wonder, then, that the lath-like

tenuity of my acquaintance, and his altitude, which has grown into a proverb, should have met with all due estimation in the eyes of Mrs. Lackobreath (pp. 183–84).

After a succession of improbable adventures, which Poe evidently intended to be humorous, Mr. Lackobreath ends up *holding the nose* of Mr. Windenough.[35] Since it is through the nose that one ordinarily breathes and since we are exploring the possibility that "loss of breath" is the author's term for impotence, the symbolism of the nose-holding is clearly indicated.

If this line of thought seems debatable, let us turn to another story, "Lionizing," which was written in the same year (1835) as was "Out of Breath." Beginning with the second paragraph, the story reads:

> The first action of my life was the taking hold of my nose with both hands. My mother saw this and called me a genius—my father wept for joy and presented me with a treatise on Nosology. This I mastered before I was breeched.
>
> I now began to feel my way in the science, and soon came to understand that, provided a man had a nose sufficiently conspicuous, he might, by merely following it, arrive at a Lionship. But my attention was not confined to theories alone. Every morning I gave my proboscis a couple of pulls and swallowed a half dozen of drams.
>
> When I came of age my father asked me, one day, if I would step with him into his study (Cameo Edition, Vol. VIII, p. 162).

Here, then, in "Lionizing" and "Out of Breath," are but flimsily disguised references to masturbation and homosexuality. What role these practices played in Poe's own life we have no way of knowing; we can only say with confidence that his heterosexual adjustment was at best tenuous. But to stress Poe's psychosexual peculiarities is to confuse cause for effect. It was not that his normal libidinal impulses had fallen under some fateful repression, from which the resulting frustrations produced the observed character disorders; rather does it seem that the character disturbance, in the sense of poor masculine identification, was primary and the sexual peculiarities secondary. Because Poe did not have a father with whom he could identify, he did not have a conscience or superego which he could accept. And it was the continual battle between ego and superego which constituted the core of Poe's neurosis and kept him immature, socially and sexually.

---

[35] "Poe's frequent use of characters who pulled their enemies' noses is well known" (Quinn, 1941, p. 760).

CHAPTER 23

LANGUAGE AND LEARNING—AN EXPERIMENTAL PARADIGM

[The last two papers in this volume are concerned with the topic of language. More specifically, they are concerned with the question of how it is that human infants acquire the capacity to solve problems (both in the sense of *thought* and of *social control*) by the use of those particular noises and noise combinations which are conventionally designated as words and sentences. On the basis of trial and error alone, it is most unlikely that any child would acquire language, at least not in the short space of time in which most children do acquire it. The paper which immediately follows offers one explanation of this feat, an explanation which importantly involves the phenomenon of conditioning or associative shifting. However, the reader should note that this paper was published (jointly with Dr. Peter Viek, in the *Harvard Educational Review,* 1945) before a two-factor conception of learning had been fully developed, with the result that the terminology here employed will call for occasional revision (see Footnote 3).

In the concluding paper, a more elaborate mechanism is proposed to account for language learning, but one that again derives from familiar principles. The two mechanisms thus suggested, while different, are not mutually exclusive. Indeed they may both operate as indicated, importantly supplementing one another.

In some ways, it would have been more logical if these two papers had appeared earlier in this volume; certainly they will seem prosaic enough coming, as they do, immediately after the discussion of Poe. But the psychology of language is still, properly speaking, a thing of the future. Astonishingly little is known about it; perhaps it is not inappriate, therefore, if we let these two papers serve as a bridge to the future—and to a more definitive type of inquiry.]

I. Introduction

It is a commonplace that one can do almost anything more easily if told how than if one has to discover the solution independently, on the basis of one's own random (or even well-reasoned) exploratory efforts. On this assumption is predicated the widespread tendency of human beings to try to "profit from the experience of others," to "teach" and "study."

But this passing on of knowledge and skills presupposes, on the part of giver and receiver alike, a still more basic skill—*language*.

Learning to use and understand words is one of the monumentally important events in a child's life. It is the key which for him unlocks the storehouse of man's accumulated discoveries and wisdom, i.e., culture. Must the child find this key alone, or do his elders even here attempt to "tell him how"?

Throughout the formal school career of children, much attention is paid to the various language skills, to helping them develop more and more "effective communication." But even before they enter kindergarten, most children have the rudiments of language at their command, that is, they can use and understand not only words but also simple (sometimes relatively complex) sentences, and in some instances they can even read and write.

Educators have taken little interest in the teaching and learning of language which goes on in the home, before the child starts to school; yet these are crucial procedures upon which much of the success or failure of the child's subsequent career, in school and out, seems to hinge.

Observation indicates that parents are almost certain to spend a good deal of time with their small children telling them "what to say." "Mary, say 'mama,'" "Johnnie, say 'ball,'" and a thousand other variants of this familiar formula can be heard throughout the day in any well-ordered household where there is a baby who is in the early stages of language acquisition. The experimental paradigm with laboratory rats here reported suggests that this practice is indeed well founded, leading to much quicker establishment of the specific stimulus-response "connections" or habits involved in speech than could possibly occur without such tutelage.

If telling the child "what to say" continues too long, after he has already acquired the rudiments of speech, it can of course seriously retard his further development, especially along the lines of self-reliance, resourcefulness, and spontaneity. But in the beginning of language-learning this procedure is extremely useful—provided that the words which the parent commands the child to say prove genuinely functional *from the child's standpoint* and do not serve merely to gratify parental pride.

However, even more basic to language development than the

procedure of "telling" children how to solve their early problems of communication is the task of getting them to "catch on" to the utility of saying what they are told to say. Once they find what a wonderful new world words open up to them, they often begin to parrot the speech of parents with almost magical enchantment. But since there is no means of telling infants about the wonders of language before they themselves have language, this discovery must always be an outgrowth of their own experience. The question is: How can we contribute most effectively to their having this experience?

If learning to repeat upon command a particular word uttered by a parent or other older person must thus proceed without benefit of "explanation" or "instruction," it must of necessity come about on the basis of preverbal learning principles, namely, trial and error and conditioning. We still know only imperfectly how this important—and difficult—feat is accomplished, but certain conjectures made in the following pages may provide a basis for further inquiry and analysis.

II. Conditioning and Teaching

An eighteen-month-old child leaned forward, grunted, and groped for a dish of butter which sat on the table before her. The child's mother, seated nearby, said: "Mary, say 'butter.'" The little girl said something roughly approximating "butter" and was given a small amount of this substance in a spoon.

Anyone who has observed small children in a normal home environment knows how frequently parents and others are likely to use the procedure just described as a means of facilitating the acquisition of language, but the writers are unaware of this procedure having been previously analyzed in the light of modern learning theory. It is the purpose of this paper to offer such analysis and an experimental paradigm.

Conditioning or associative learning is generally recognized as a process whereby it becomes possible to elicit by a new, formerly indifferent stimulus a response which originally could be called forth only by means of another so-called unconditioned stimulus. Pavlov (1927), Hull (1929), and others have commented upon the biological utility of this form of learning as a means whereby living organisms are able to acquire anticipatory responses, of both an avoidant and an appetitive nature and thereby greatly increase their chances of survival. And Bertrand Russell (1927), Ogden and Richards (1938), Bloomfield (1914), Korzybski (1933), and other students of logic and language have pointed out the connection between the meaning or understanding of words and the conditioning process: a word (symbol) as heard or seen is the conditioned stimulus, the thing which the word symbolizes (the referent) is the unconditioned stimulus, and the meaning which the word has for the subject (its reference) is the conditioned response. What we wish to add is simply that conditioning plays an important role in teaching children those habits which are involved, not alone in the understanding, but also in the *use* of words.

Russell has clearly differentiated between words as understood and words as used and has suggested that the understanding of a word is a matter of conditioning, whereas skill in using a word, as a means of influencing the behavior of others, is acquired on the basis of trial-and-error learning. That the untutored exploratory babbling of infants sometimes leads to the production of sounds which are responded to as meaningful by parents is well known. As a matter of fact, if parents listen carefully and respond consistently to certain wordlike sounds which infants spontaneously make, the latter can learn to use a limited number of such sounds (*ma-ma, pa-pa, ba-ba,* etc.) amazingly early (at three to six months of age). This observation controverts the common assumption that a child must "understand" words before he can use them. We have repeatedly seen infants use words long before they began to respond meaningfully to these same sounds as made by others.[1] However, if language had to be acquired solely on such a trial-and-error basis, learning to speak in a really fluent manner would be an agonizingly slow and inefficient process. Normally the acquisition

[1] The same observation holds for infantile gesturing. The reason it is generally assumed that a child must "understand" the meaning of a word before he can use it is that most parents respond to the wordlike sounds made by their offspring only when these sounds are uttered with adult, dictionary connotations. Thus, "mama" is the symbol used by adults (and older children) to refer to a particular person in the household and normally serves as the subject of a sentence: "Mama is gone," "Mama will bring us a present," etc. It is not surprising that the ability to use the word "mama" in this relatively sophisticated manner usually does not develop until the second, sometimes the third or even the fourth year of life. But if the attendant adults will at first interpret "mama" as "I am uncomfortable," and will do something about this discomfort, the average child can learn to use this word and at least a few others within the first half-year of life. The same is true of the use of gestures. However, in saying that a child can thus learn to "use" words or gestures at such an early age, we should point out a certain ambiguity in this term. Words have two major types of use: the first we have just described; the second involves, not mere signaling of wants and desires, but the communication of "ideas" or "knowledge." In order to use words in this second sense, a child must indeed first "understand" these words. Whether there is any practical advantage in helping a child learn to "use" words in the first of these two ways, as an intermediate step to the second type of usage, is a problem for further research and analysis.

of speech proceeds relatively rapidly once it is begun, a circumstance which makes it sufficiently apparent that trial and error is superseded or at least importantly supplemented by some other mechanism.

The all-too-facile traditional explanation of language development is that it is "due to imitation." Miller and Dollard (1941) have shown how inexact, even mystical, are the ways in which this concept has often been employed, and these writers have succeeded in deriving from basic learning principles many of the behavioral phenomena often characterized as imitative. There is no doubt that, at later stages, children model their speech as well as other actions upon the behavior of others, both through self-conscious copying and unconscious identification (21). Important as "imitation" may thus be, it nevertheless fails, no less than does the trial-and-error hypothesis, to give us a completely satisfactory account of speech development: neither approach sufficiently acknowledges the active tuitional roles which parents and other adults continually play in this connection.

When the senior author began teaching courses in education, he was unable to decide how the word "teaching" ought to be defined. If one interprets it to mean the process whereby one individual influences the learning of another, the term becomes so broad as to be useless, or at least equivalent to "social interaction." But how can it be used in a narrower, more exact sense? Various writers have attempted to define teaching as the "guidance of learning," "helping others learn," etc., but it remained for a student (Mrs. Roger Lyndon) to suggest a more satisfying and precise definition, namely, that teaching is the process whereby one individual enables another to learn something (solve a problem) more quickly than he would on the basis of his own trial-and-error behavior.[2] With this definition in mind, we quickly see that Mary's mother was engaging in an unmistakable act of teaching when she commanded Mary to say "butter."

How likely a small child is to say "butter," or even "buh-buh," on a purely trial-and-error basis at a time when the child wants a

[2] Linton (1936), Ford (1939), and others have defined human culture as an accumulation of ready-made solutions to problems which are transmitted from generation to generation. (It is therefore not without significance that Mrs. Lyndon, before taking up psychology, had studied anthropology.) Language is the prime vehicle of culture transmission (teaching), but language as a social invention is itself a part of culture and has to be transmitted, as a prerequisite to the child's more formal "education." Teaching is likewise a social invention which, together with language, makes culture possible.

particular edible substance cannot be precisely estimated (cf. Thorndike, 1943), but the chances are obviously slight. On the other hand, if a child who has learned to say "butter" on command is given this command while wanting butter, and if the child obeys this command and gets some of the desired substance, only a few repetitions of this procedure will be required for the child to learn to utter this word whenever he wants butter. In this way the child is enabled to acquire the habit of using the word "butter" far more directly and quickly than he could ever do on the basis of unaided trial-and-error.

Schematically, we may say that once the response "butter" has become attached (conditioned) to the command, "Say 'butter,'" the latter can be used as a sort of ladle or handle for transferring the butter response to another stimulus (butter-want) to which it is initially very unlikely to occur. Once this "transplantation" has been carried out a few times, the butter response "takes root" and becomes firmly connected to the butter motive, because of the reinforcement which occurs when the butter is received and the butter want reduced.

This analysis leaves unanswered the important question as to how the child initially learns to say what he is commanded to; this problem must ultimately be considered. First, however, let us exemplify the process just described by a simple laboratory paradigm.

III. The Paradigm

How likely is an untutored laboratory rat to leap into the air when hungry? Without, for the moment, attempting to be very precise, we can be sure that such a response is relatively unlikely to occur. On the other hand, if a rat is placed on a metal grill and given an electric shock, the response of leaping into the air is almost certain to occur fairly promptly. Our problem, then, let us assume, is to get this jumping reaction "transplanted" from the latter situation, in which it is readily elicited by shock, to the former situation, so that it will also occur in response to hunger. How can this be done?

The foregoing discussion provides the clue. If we can get the jumping response conditioned to some neutral stimulus, such as the sound of a buzzer, we can use this stimulus as a means of eliciting the jumping response in a situation in which the rat is hungry and will receive food as a result of reacting in this manner. The jumping response should then become connected to the hunger motive and should occur whenever the rat is hungry, without external prompting of any kind.[3]

IV. The Experimental Group [4]

Using a standard procedure, 8 male rats (Lashley strain) about five months of age were trained, with electric shock as the unconditioned stimulus, until they all gave a conditioned jumping reaction 90 per cent of the time when a buzzer was sounded. The rats were then reduced to and held at 85 per cent of their normal body weight. On the first day of the experiment proper, each rat—now reduced in weight and hungry—was put back into the conditioning apparatus (described elsewhere, Mowrer and Miller, 1942) and treated as follows. If, at the end of 60 seconds, the rat had not jumped, it was caused to do so by means of the buzzer. Following this "forced" reaction, the rat received a small pellet of food.[5] This procedure was repeated until 10 trials had been given; but if, at any time during the 60-second interval between trials the rat jumped "spontaneously," it was likewise given food, and the buzzer was omitted for that trial. In other words, the rat was fed for jumping not only in response to the buzzer (and hunger) but also for jumping to hunger alone, the presumption being that this procedure would lead to an increase in "spontaneous" jumps to the point where their "forced" elicitation would become entirely unnecessary.[6]

---

[3] [This paragraph, if revised in the light of the two-factor conception of learning elaborated earlier in this book (9, 10), would go as follows: "The foregoing discussion provides the clue. If we can get the *emotion of fear* conditioned to some neutral stimulus, such as the sound of a buzzer, and if we can get our subject to learn to leap into the air as *a means of relieving this emotion,* we can then use the buzzer stimulus (and the ensuing fear) as a means of eliciting the jumping response in a situation in which the rat is hungry and will receive food (as well as fear reduction) for reacting in this manner. The jumping response should then become connected, through the law of effect, to the hunger motive, etc."]

[4] The writers are indebted to Mrs. John L. Bakke for assistance in carrying out the experimental procedures about to be described.

[5] If a rat failed to respond to the buzzer within 5 seconds, the electric shock was applied, just as in the preliminary training sessions. However, the shock was very rarely necessary, partly because of the high level to which the conditioning had previously been brought and partly because the giving of food for jumping in response to the buzzer seemed to reinforce this connection considerably, even though this connection was originally established by reinforcement provided by the termination of the shock. Our evidence on this point is not well controlled, but it is supported by Brogden's (1939) finding that a conditioned paw retraction in dogs which was set up with electric shock as the unconditioned stimulus could be kept alive indefinitely if food was substituted as a means of reinforcement. Cf. Allport's (1940) discussion of habits which are acquired on the basis of one motive being perpetuated by other motives; also the psychoanalytic concept of "overdetermination" (Freud, 1924).

[6] One of us has previously used the term "parasitic" reinforcement to refer to the way a response becomes connected to a conditioned stimulus as a result of the

How well this supposition was verified is indicated by the solid line in Figure 73. Here it will be seen that by the end of 10 days (100 trials), the 8 animals in the experimental group were making, on the average, 7 out of 10 of the required daily jumps on a "spontaneous" basis, i.e., were responding to their hunger alone, without

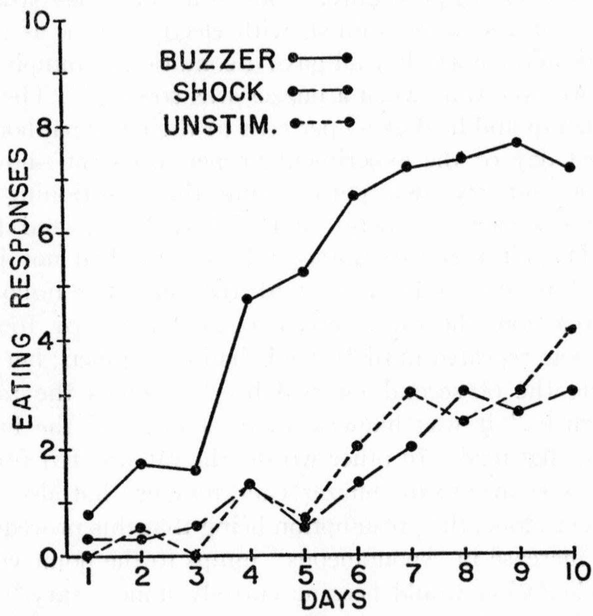

Fig. 73.—Incidence of spontaneous jumping responses followed by eating in the Experimental Group (buzzer), Control Group I (shock), and Control Group II (unstimulated).

external instigation. Unfortunately, this average curve gives a rather poor picture of what actually happened. By the end of the

---

reward provided by the termination or reduction of the unconditioned stimulus. In the present instance one may speak of a reversal of this process: a response, having become attached to the conditioned stimulus by means of parasitic reinforcement, becomes grafted onto a new "unconditioned" stimulus (the hunger) by means of the "intrinsic" reinforcement provided by a reduction in this stimulus (cf. Mowrer, 1941a; Mowrer and Lamoreaux, 4). Skinner (1935), following Konorski and Miller (1937), has made a distinction between two forms of conditioned responses: *respondant* conditioning and *operant* conditioning; and Hilgard and Marquis (1940) have drawn a somewhat parallel distinction between *classical* and *instrumental* conditioning. However, these dichotomies are hard to justify theoretically. Should we not rather speak of responses which occur to stimuli which do not provide their own source of reinforcement and to those which do? In our judgment, the latter type of response should not be referred to as "conditioned" at all, unless one wishes to make conditioning a mere synonym for learning. We prefer to keep the term "conditioning" for those responses which are acquired on the basis of "parasitic" reinforcement (which includes all sign learning), as distinct from responses which are acquired on the basis of "intrinsic" reinforcement (as in the case of trial-and-error learning and in the type of "guided learning" or teaching described above).

10 days, 6 of the 8 animals were responding almost entirely to hunger alone, whereas 2 animals had not yet "caught on" and were still having to be forced to jump by means of the buzzer. Thus, on the tenth day, the numbers of spontaneous leaps made by the 8 animals were 0, 10, 10, 9, 10, 0, 8, and 10. In other words, this type of learning had a certain all-or-none quality. If the experiment had been continued sufficiently long, animals Nos. 1 and 6 would presumably have also solved this problem, but at the end of 100 trials they had obviously not done so, whereas the other 6 animals had. Therefore, instead of saying that at the end of the experiment the 8 animals were, on the average, about 70 per cent proficient, it is more accurate to say that 6 of the 8, or 75 per cent, of the animals had solved the problem almost perfectly, while the remainder had made no evident progress toward its solution.

The behavior shown by the "successful" animals in this experiment, while no different in principle from a dog's "begging" for food by sitting up, or a horse's neighing, or little Mary's saying "buh-buh," was nevertheless very striking. To see a rat jumping into the air as a means of obtaining food (which was supplied from below the grill on which the animal stood) was an arresting experience, and since the genesis of this behavior was carefully controlled and observed, it serves satisfactorily to illustrate the hypothesis previously put forward.

V. Control Group I

It will probably have occurred to the reader to ask: Why condition the rats to jump to the buzzer as a means of "showing" them that this response will secure food? Why not simply force them to jump by means of the unconditioned stimulus, namely, the electric shock, without the intermediary action of the buzzer? It was by no means certain that this method would not prove to be as satisfactory as the more complicated method actually employed with the experimental group. However, one could anticipate that the more direct method would involve an important difficulty: namely, that the emotional upset produced by the shock would be so great that it would inhibit the animals from eating when the food was presented and that they would therefore fail to learn to jump in response to the hunger motive alone.[7]

In order to obtain empirical evidence on this score, we reduced

[7] Estes and Skinner (1941) have shown that fear retards the rate of eating in rats in a free-feeding situation.

the body weight of 8 naïve animals as already indicated and subjected them to the following procedure. Each animal was put into the experimental apparatus and, after an interval of 60 seconds, was shocked until it leaped into the air, after which it was offered a pellet of food. After a few presentations of the shock and food, the animals nearly always began to make "spontaneous" jumps, which were likewise followed by the presentation of food. These jumps were allowed to count as trials. However, it was evident that these animals were responding less to hunger than to another internal stimulus, namely, *fear*. This was indicated by the fact that they showed almost as much hesitation to eat following these "spontaneous" responses as they did following the shock-instigated jumps.

The broken line in Figure 73 shows the comparatively small number of times that the 8 animals in this group made so-called spontaneous jumps and then ate the food they thus obtained. As will be seen by comparing the curves for the experimental group and this control group, the use of a conditioned stimulus as a means of "telling" or "showing" the rats how to obtain the food was markedly superior to the use of a stimulus which had intense motivational value rather than primarily "sign-function." Although the buzzer undoubtedly aroused some fear (1), this emotion was manageable and did not interfere with the eating as much as did the fear produced by the traumatic shock stimulus.

In this group, as in the experimental group, the learning tended, in individual animals, to have an all-or-none quality. On the last day of the experiment, the 8 animals in this control group made the following scores: 0, 0, 0, 0, 6, 0, 8, 10. Thus, 3 out of the 8 animals may be said to have solved the problem, as contrasted with twice that number in the experimental group.

VI. Control Group II

A second control group seemed indicated, as a means of determining just how likely hungry rats are to learn to leap into the air for food without any "guidance" or "instruction" whatever. In other words, this group was designed to determine how quickly they could learn to leap into the air and thereby solve their hunger problem, on a purely trial-and-error basis, without the use of either a conditioned or an unconditioned stimulus to "point out" the solution.

With their body weights reduced in the manner already described, the 8 rats comprising this second control group were individually placed in the experimental apparatus and subjected to the following procedure. If a rat did not jump during 10 minutes (10 60-second periods), it was simply taken out of the apparatus, returned to its home cage, and fed. If a rat made 1 or more but fewer than 10 jumps during the 10 minutes, it was given a pellet of food following each jump but again left in the apparatus the full 10 minutes. On the other hand, if it made 10 jumps in less than 10 minutes, it was fed following each jump but was taken out of the apparatus after it had consumed the food received for its tenth jump. This procedure seemed to provide a fair control for our experimental group concerning the question as to how likely our experimental subjects were to solve the problem with which they were presented on an unaided, trial-and-error basis.

The results obtained with Control Group II were somewhat surprising in that the animals in this group showed a greater original tendency to jump in response to hunger alone than we had anticipated. As will be seen by the dotted line in Figure 73, the animals in this group learned, on the average, to obtain food by jumping as well as or better than did the animals in Control Group I, with final-day scores of 3, 0, 10, 10, 0, 10, 0, and 0. However, they still fell far below the experimental animals.

VII. Reliability of Group Differences

Inspection of Figure 73 suggests that the results obtained for the experimental group are significantly different from those for the two control groups. In order to test this impression statistically, it is necessary, first of all, to know how many successful responses ("spontaneous" jumps followed by eating) each animal in each group made throughout the 10 days of the experiment. The 8 animals in the experimental group made, respectively, the following scores: 1, 48, 70, 70, 2, 63, 95, 61; those in the first control group: 0, 0, 0, 0, 40, 0, 36, 45; and those in the second control group: 3, 0, 60, 54, 0, 20, 0, 0. Thus, the *average* number of successful responses made by the 8 animals in the experimental group was 51.250; by the 8 animals in the first control group, 15.125; and by the 8 animals in the second control group, 17.125. How reliable are the differences between these means? When subjected to "Student's" t-test, the differences between the mean for the experimental group and the means for the two control groups both turn out to be significant well beyond the .05 level, which is conventionally accepted as the standard of scientific trustworthiness. On the other hand, the difference between the means of the two control groups is completely nonsignificant, as inspection of the learning curves for these two groups would lead one to expect.

Unfortunately, the applicability of the *t*-test to our data is open to question. We need not go into the details of this difficulty except to say that it hinges upon the fact that in all three groups there appear to be *two* points of concentration of individual scores, rather than one, as in a normal distribution. The reason for this bimodality of individual scores is the tendency, already mentioned, for the animals to solve the problem in an all-or-none manner, i.e., to make a score either of 0 or somewhere around 40 to 70.

Although this fact renders the *t*-test suspect, it opens up the possibility of applying another statistical technique, namely, the method of chi square. Since 6 of the animals in the experimental group (those with scores of 48, 70, 70, 63, 95, and 61) solved the problem and 2 (those with scores of 1 and 2) did not, and since only 3 of the animals (those with scores of 40, 36, and 45) in the first control group solved it whereas 5 (with scores of 0, 0, 0, 0, 0) did not, we can ask how likely one would be to get such a difference in the behavior of the animals in 2 such groups if these 2 groups were treated in precisely the same manner, or, what is equivalent, if the 2 groups were treated differently but without this difference in treatment producing any real difference in the animal's behavior. The chi-square method tells us that the difference between the 2 groups—for 1 of which the ratio of successful to unsuccessful animals was 6/2 and for the other, 3/5—is reliable well beyond the .05 level. Since there were also only 3 animals (with scores of 60, 54, and 20) in the second control group which can be said to have solved the problem, the chi square test will naturally give the same value for the reliability of the difference between the experimental group and this second control group.[8]

VIII. The Relative Frequency of "Nervous" Responses

Thus far we have restricted the analysis of our data to a comparison of the number of times which the animals in our three groups "spontaneously" leaped into the air and then ate the food

[8] In theory, this test is designed to ascertain the reliability of the difference between a standard or known ratio of some kind (a *parameter*) and an empirically obtained ratio (known as a *statistic*). In our case, *both* of the ratios (6/2 and 3/5) are empirically derived (and therefore subject to error). However, it would seem justifiable to take either of these ratios as the best available estimate of a parameter with which the other ratio could be compared. Somewhat different results are obtained depending upon whether one takes 6/2 or 3/5 as the parameter, but in both cases the obtained *P*-value is beyond the .05 level of significance.

which was presented to them as a reward for this performance. The reader will certainly not be surprised to learn that some of our animals sometimes made the required response but then refused to eat the pellet which was offered to them. As can be seen in Figure 74, this type of behavior occurred very frequently in Control Group I (the shocked animals), very rarely in the Experimental Group

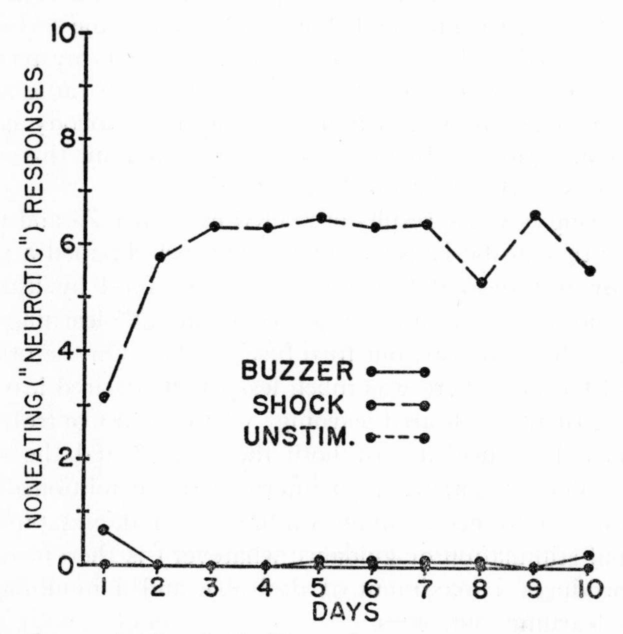

FIG. 74.—Curves showing the incidence of spontaneous jumping responses not followed by eating in the 3 groups.

(the conditioned animals), and not at all in Control Group II (the externally unstimulated animals). What do these results mean?

If an animal failed to eat the food offered following a jump, it was not because the animal was not hungry. It was rather because the animal, although hungry, was still more frightened and was more intent upon reducing fear than the hunger. Here we have a type of behavior comparable to the so-called "nervous" acts and mannerisms seen so commonly in human beings, children and adults alike, but so rarely (save in the experimental laboratory) in animals. There is, however, this important difference. In the case of our rats which leaped into the air but then refused to eat the food, we are not in the least mystified: we know that these animals were afraid of being shocked and were making anticipatory responses which, in all probability, somewhat reduced their fear. On the other hand, the "nervous" movements of human beings are often only a little less mysterious to the person manifesting them than they are to the casual, untrained observer.

In theory we know, of course, that so-called nervous actions or "symptoms" on the part of human beings are likewise instigated by anxiety (or "nervous tension"); we can also be fairly certain that they, too, are the unintended by-products of some sort of earlier training, or "education." They impress us as mysterious and meaningless only because the time interval between cause and effect in the human situation is often so great that nobody can easily "see the connection." In our laboratory paradigm, this complication and source of confusion does not arise.

Comparing now the results presented in Figure 73 and in Figure 74, we see that in the Experimental Group we obtained a good deal of the (by us) desired learning (to obtain food by leaping into the air) and very little undesired, "concomitant" learning (to leap into the air through fear, but to refuse food). On the other hand, in Control Group I there was much less of the desired learning and much more of the undesired learning; whereas, in Control Group II there was a low incidence of both the desired and the undesired learning. The advantage of an intermediary, conditioned stimulus (over an unconditioned stimulus, on the one hand, and, on the other, no external stimulation or guidance whatever) is therefore a double one: it produces a maximum of desirable and a minimum of undesirable learning outcomes.

Without wishing to overextend the application of our experimental paradigm, we are nevertheless tempted to observe that schools do not ordinarily care to undertake the education of children until they are skilled in the understanding and use of the exquisitely complex set of conditioned stimuli which we call language. Parents would probably also do well to delay many of the learning tasks they must impose upon their offspring until after speech is well established, concentrating their early tuitional efforts upon the development of this uniquely valuable vehicle for profiting from the experiences of others instead of prematurely creating for the infant learning dilemmas at a stage at which the only possibility of achieving solutions is through the painful, and precarious, process of trial and error (Mowrer, 1941a).[9]

---

[9] It can scarcely be supposed that the ability to "think independently" or "originally" will be much facilitated by confronting the infant with difficult problems before he has learned (through the medium of language) to think at all.

IX. Conditioning, Imitation, and Obedience

In the preceding pages we have seen how useful conditioned responses can be in teaching, i.e., in helping children as well as lower animals solve certain types of problems which would be extremely difficult for them on a purely trial-and-error basis. But there is one rather striking difference between little Mary's mother teaching her to say "butter" and our experimental paradigm in which rats were taught to jump as a means of showing that they were hungry.[10] In the latter case the conditioned stimulus for the jumping reaction was the sound of the buzzer, but in the case of the little girl, the conditioned stimulus (as presented by the mother) and the conditioned response (as made by the child) were much the same, namely, the sound "butter." How significant is this difference?

Cowles and Pennington (1943) have reported that they were able to condition rats to squeak in response to a pure tone of high pitch (which symbolized impending electric shock). Some years ago one of us attempted a similar experiment but failed to get the expected conditioning. After reading the report just cited, we again attempted to obtain this type of conditioning, but the results were still negative (see Mowrer, Palma, and Sanger, 1948). If we could have conditioned our subjects to respond to an artificial "squeak" by making a natural one, we might then have been able, by the technique already described, to teach them to squeak ("speak") for food, instead of jumping for it. In principle, there is, of course, no difference between the two procedures, but since we more readily think of the symbolic function of sounds than of other types of behavior, our paradigm would have seemed more like the "real thing" (see 24).

We now know how it was that our experimental subjects became conditioned to jump when we sounded the buzzer, and we

---

[10] It is easy to fall into the habit of assuming that the difference between instrumental and symbolic behavior (i.e., between "work" and "words") is definite and absolute. But this is not the case. If the jumping of our rats had operated an automatic food-delivery mechanism, as well it might, we could scarcely have referred to this behavior as expressive, communicative, or symbolic. It is only because this behavior produced the desired results *through the interpolated activity of another living organism* that we think of it as symbolic. The same is true of orally made noises. The sound "Rex" is ordinarily a symbol, but a clever advertising toy distributed some years ago by a drug company took advantage of the fact that this noise may also be directly instrumental, i.e., has a certain amount of inherent energy capable of performing work. The toy consisted of a little house containing a celluloid dog which jumped out when one loudly called "Rex!" Thus we see that identically the same act may be in the one case symbolic, in the other not. (For further discussion on the definition of a "symbol," see Yerkes, 1943.)

know, at least in principle, how it would be possible to make them squeak in response to a similar auditory stimulus. But we have not as yet accounted for the fact that little Mary responded to her mother's command, "Say 'butter,'" by saying "butter" or something roughly equivalent. This, as we have seen, is an essential preliminary to the mother's being able to teach her to use this word meaningfully, i.e., as a means of asking for some of this substance when she wanted it or, at a later stage, being able to make statements about it.[11]

We have already had reason to doubt the adequacy of the imitative theory of speech development as a comprehensive explanation. Let us, therefore, return to observation. When a mother is trying to train a child to say "Bye-bye," what is she likely to do? Not uncommonly one will observe her gently jostle or tickle him, all the while saying "Say 'Bye-bye.'" We can see that the jostling or tickling would motivate the child to do or say something, but how does he ever happen to say just what the mother is saying? This might occur on the basis of pure trial and error, but it would be very improbable, considering the large assortment of other sounds that the child might equally well make. It might also occur on the basis of so-called imitation; but as we have already indicated, it can no longer be taken for granted that imitation is something which children do instinctively or automatically. In all probability the child's saying what he is told to say is a subtle form of learned behavior, the circumstances of which are not ordinarily fully identified (see 21 and 24).

We are indebted to Dr. John Whiting, of Yale University, for what seems to us a crucial observation in this connection. Dr. Whiting has noticed the almost universal tendency for human parents, especially mothers (both primitive and civilized), to babble, jabber, coo, and otherwise *imitate their infants'* own early vocalizations. Thus, if an infant is spontaneously saying "ba, ba, ba, ba," the mother is likely to make the same sound simultaneously. This means that although the child starts the performance, the parent gets in at least a few similar sounds before the child stops. In this way the mother's "ba, ba," becomes a conditioned stimulus for the child to utter the same sound. After this learning has occurred, the child is said to "imitate" the mother, but this behavior originates, according to Dr. Whiting's interpretation, in the mother's, and sometimes even the father's, having first repeatedly imitated

[11] In a later paper we shall extend the present analysis to include that stage of language development in which children begin to "put words together." Cf. Footnote 1 (see 24).

the child.[12] When, subsequently, the mother holds the child in her arms, agitates him, and says, "Say 'bye-bye,' " the stage is set for this response (or the closest possible approximation) to occur. If the mother then rewards the child (as she is likely to do by smiles, caresses, and no more jiggling), the response is reinforced and is likely to occur, not only on command, but "spontaneously," i.e., when the child wishes attention or affection.

Soon the child is likely to discover that "doing what mama says" is, in general, rewarding and will develop an increasingly strong tendency, at least during the years of dependency, not only to do but also to say what "mother says." (This, we can assume, was true in little Mary's case.) On the other hand, if obedience, i.e., following parental commands and injunctions, is not thus rewarding, a sullen, indifferent, or anxious—and linguistically retarded—child is likely to result.

---

[12] For a somewhat similar analysis see Holt (1931); for a critique thereof, see Miller and Dollard (1941). [See also chapters 21 and 24.]

CHAPTER 24

ON THE PSYCHOLOGY OF "TALKING BIRDS"—A CONTRIBUTION TO LANGUAGE AND PERSONALITY THEORY

[This paper consists of three parts, the first and second of which were initially prepared as lectures. Of these, the first gives a general overview of the beginnings of what it is hoped will be an extended investigation of the psychology of talking birds and of its implications for language learning and other aspects of personality development—notably the phenomenon of identification—in human beings. The second, more technical and limited in scope, expands upon a crucial portion of the theoretical analysis which is adumbrated in the first part. Finally, in the third part, the author attempts to supplement what has been said earlier and to articulate it with the views and findings of other investigators.

This paper was presented, in substance, before a meeting of the Psychology Section of the New York Academy of Sciences, in May, 1948. Portions of it had been presented earlier: at the 1947 meeting of the American Psychological Association (Mowrer, 1947) and to the psychological colloquia of Johns Hopkins University and Harvard University. Many helpful suggestions and criticisms were received on these occasions. The author's special thanks go to Dr. Wallace Craig, good friend and neighbor, who has generously read and criticized the typescript of this chapter against the background of his long and scholarly study of bird behavior. The author also wishes to acknowledge the assistance, in several phases of this study, of Allyn Johnson.

The research here reported was made possible by a grant from the Laboratory of Social Relations, Harvard University.

After completion of this paper, the writer had an opportunity to read the concluding chapter, on language, of Dr. Charles E. Osgood's forthcoming book, *Method and theory in experimental psyhology* (1951). It is reassuring to discover that Dr. Osgood, working independently, has arrived at a view of the language-learning process very similar to the one here proposed (see Footnotes 5 and 26).]

I. The Speech of Birds and Babies

For a number of years I had felt that talking birds offered exciting scientific opportunities. We have used almost every conceivable type of "dumb" animal in psychological experiments; but no one, so far as I have been able to determine, has worked with those extraordinary creatures, the talking birds. Naturalists and fanciers have, of course, written highly illuminating accounts, and psychologists have sometimes reported casual observations.[1] But as subjects for exact research, these birds have gone begging.

This neglect seems all the more remarkable when one considers how incomplete is our knowledge of the process whereby human infants learn to talk; and it is entirely possible that a great deal may be learned from the study of birds that can be transferred to babies. A friend of mine is fond of saying that no one should undertake to bring up children until he has done an experiment with rats, or at least trained a puppy. Perhaps teaching a bird to talk would be an equally valuable experience!

The reader will therefore understand my delight when, early in 1947, I received a grant from the Laboratory of Social Relations at Harvard, with the understanding that a part of this money could be used to begin some research with talking birds. As speedily as some students and I could, we constructed quarters and purchased subjects: a Mexican double yellow-headed parrot, an Indian hill mynah, two magpies, and eight shell parakeets—two pairs for breeding and the rest as "prospective talkers."

But from that point on, things moved anything but swiftly. The mynah was very shy and quiet; the magpies were full grown, and the only one of them that showed signs of talking died; the

[1] Lashley, writing in 1913, makes the following comments: "The older literature of animal psychology abounds with anecdotes designed to display the intelligence of the parrots, but there has been no experimental study of the birds and nothing is known of the manner in which they learn to speak; whether by direct imitation, by the gradual imitative modification of instinctive notes, or by chance combinations of instinctive notes which, meeting the approval of the trainer, are rewarded and so 'set' in memory" (p. 362). Later in the same article Lashley remarks: "There is no experimental evidence bearing upon the motive which impels parrots to imitate sounds foreign to their species. The bird described in this note was in a constant state of rage during the experiments. . . . These facts suggest that reward is not an important factor in the parrot's reproduction of sounds. The whole attitude of the bird in reacting suggests the action of an instinct for competition. His movements during reaction frequently suggest the courting activities of other birds, and it seems not improbable that the principal motive for the parrot's reproduction of sounds is to be sought in a perverted form of sex rivalry. However, much more extensive experiments with observations upon the birds under natural conditions will be necessary to settle this question" (p. 365). (See Section III, particularly the references to the work of Craig, Lorenz, and Nice.)

breeding parakeets would not breed, and the "talkers" remained wild and untalkative. Only the parrot was in any way rewarding during the first two or three months. He learned to say a few words; but, having been badly treated before we got him, he continued to be suspicious and dangerous.

During the early summer I came across a young crow for sale in a local petshop. He was already somewhat tamed, and by the time I had had him for two or three weeks I was able to turn him loose in the yard of our summer home in New Hampshire. He became very playful and affectionate (except with strangers, to whom he was most impudent), and he was soon making a valiant attempt to say "Hello." Had it seemed feasible to bring him back to the city and keep him indoors, I think that he would have developed much further.[2]

In the fall I had the good fortune to obtain a young and highly gifted African gray parrot. Although he was wild and completely untrained, to my amazement he was trying to say "Hello" within two weeks, and from that point on his progress was most astonishing, in respect to both the fluency and clarity of his speech and his great friendliness.

Little by little in the beginning and then more and more rapidly, the mynah bird also made good progress, so that approximately one year after I obtained him, he was finger-tame, said a number of words, whistled beautifully, and was a great show-off and favorite with everyone around the laboratory. The Mexican parrot was undoubtedly talented enough, as indicated by the way he would "come out" with remarks which he had heard infrequently and a long time previously; but I was never able to overcome his hatred and distrust of human beings. After two students and I had each failed to teach parakeets to talk, we gave up the attempt until such time as we can raise our own birds and thus be able to start work with them at a much earlier age.

I have given our experiences in some detail in order that the reader will be able properly to evaluate the impressions we have gained and will not infer that we have as yet done anything that might be called an "experiment." As soon as we succeed in establishing a colony of breeding parakeets, I have no doubt that we shall have subjects available in sufficient numbers to make full-fledged experiments possible. Moreover, there are many very interesting questions which we look forward to investigating in this way.

---

[2] A report recently received indicates that this bird has come into the hands of an invalid lady who has devoted much time and attention to him and that he has responded by becoming, in the intervening two years, a fluent "talker."

But thus far we have just been getting "experience," highly unsystematic but suggestive.

TEACHING METHODS. Anyone who undertakes to teach birds to talk, and who has as little knowledge of this art as we did in the beginning, will be confronted by many questions concerning the procedure to be followed. What, precisely, does one do? Does one merely "repeat" over and over the word one wishes the bird to learn? Should one perhaps attempt to "imitate" the noises which the bird spontaneously makes? Should one try to get each word "associated" with something in the bird's experience? Should one use food and water in connection with the training? And if at last the bird says something, what should one then do?

After a good deal of speculation and trial-and-error, we hit upon the following procedure. We made a practice of feeding and watering a new bird entirely by hand, thus facilitating its taming, and as we did so we said the word or phrase we wished to teach. For example, we might say, "How are you?" and then present a bit of food; again, "How are you?" and more food; and so on. This method worked well, and one can conjecture that the way it works goes something like this. Since the word or phrase that is being taught is connected with eating (and/or drinking), the word will become a "good sound," one the bird likes to hear; and we may suppose that when the bird is later alone and hungry (or thirsty), if it happens to *make* a noise something like the word previously heard, the bird will be rewarded and will be prompted to "practice" and perfect it.

Elsewhere (see Section II) I have described this method and the theory behind it in considerable detail; but the gist of the procedure is that you try to make the bird *like* to hear the sounds you make so that it will also *like to hear itself make them.* This is sometimes known as the process of "identification" and is importantly involved in the psychological development of small children. I believe—though much more evidence will be required to prove—that this is the way in which one gets both birds and babies to say their first words (see 23).

Once a bird has learned to say a word, it may then be taught to say the word, not just because it likes to hear the noise involved, but as a means of begging for food. One may at this stage follow any one of three different procedures: (1) one may reward the bird for saying whatever word or phrase happens to come to it; (2) one may reward the bird only if it says a particular word, let us say, the name (previously taught in the manner described above) of the food which is being presented; or (3) one may reward the bird for saying a word only if that word has first been said by the trainer. In the third case, it will be noted that we are using a method of teaching the bird to "repeat" or "imitate" which is different from the method initially employed. In the beginning procedure, we say the word and then *give food,* as a means of making the word "sound good." In the procedure just described, we say the word and then *withhold food* until the birds says what we want it to say, namely the word we have just said. In the latter case, our word becomes a kind of "command," and is followed by reward only when the bird "obeys" by saying what we have said.

LATER DEVELOPMENT OF TALKING BIRDS. While one has been following the training procedures just described—which are all directed toward getting the bird to talk—one has also been doing something else: one has been training the bird to be tame, affectionate, and dependent. This latter part of the total procedure is no less important than the part which is more specifically directed toward getting the bird to say its first words; for it is only after a very close relationship has been established between bird and trainer that the bird's greatest possibilities as a talker will be realized.

In the early stages of training, I have found it useful to tie up the training procedure, as I have said, with the feeding and watering of the bird. But once a bird has learned a few words and has become gentle and attached to the trainer, a very different type of procedure may be followed. When this stage has been reached, one can feed and water the bird more or less routinely. Then the *presence* and *attention* of the trainer are important to the bird. When the bird is perfectly comfortable as far as its physical wants are concerned, it will now still make every effort to keep the trainer near at hand.[3] It soon finds that "talking" is one of the best ways

[3] It may be said that the bird thus tries to "hoard" the trainer. Just as a rat, after having been deprived of food, will when satiated accumulate large quantities in its nestbox—Wolfle (1939), Hunt (1939), Mowrer (1939), Miller and Postman (1946), Morgan (1947), Bindra (1948)—so will a bird try to keep its source of food (the trainer) near at hand—and presumably for much the same reason. Just as the rat presumably feels more comfortable (has less apprehension of a possible recurrence of a painfully intense hunger) when there is a visible quantity of food close by, so does the bird feel more relaxed and assured when the medium through which it obtains food is present (cf. 12). As is well known, talking birds are often extremely "jealous"—presumably because they feel threatened when a rival takes away from them the attentions of the beloved keeper; since they are dependent upon the keeper, losing him or having to share him with another means that he may not be able to respond so promptly as he otherwise would. "Sibling rivalry" in children probably has much the same basis; though it is on occasion troublesome to parents, such rivalry is probably unavoidable in any society which demands as intense identification with parents as is believed necessary in ours.

of doing this, and the stage is set for the bird's very best performance.

But one must still keep in mind the fact that a bird talks because and only because such behavior is, in one way or another, *rewarding.* Initially it is rewarding to the bird to make and hear sounds which it has heard the trainer make in pleasant contexts. At this first level of performance, words may be said by the bird without much reference to the outward effects they produce. In this respect they may be compared to the "babbling" or "vocal play" of human infants. Only at the next stage—when the bird finds that by means of saying words it can get food or water from the trainer—does talking become useful in the practical sense; but at both of the stages so far mentioned, we can see the operation of the principle of reward. And finally the bird becomes so attached to the trainer that it is rewarding just to *be with* him or her. This may be shown in any of several ways. The bird may scold when the trainer starts to leave or may beg to be taken with the trainer. If the bird is encouraged to talk on these occasions, it will often do so with special enthusiasm and clarity.[4]

Friends (Mr. and Mrs. A. T. Alper) have reported the following incident. Some years ago they were vacationing in Bermuda and were told to be sure to visit a certain park. They also learned that near one of the gates of the park was a parrot, famed for his remarkable fluency. But my friends were disappointed: they stood in front of this bird's cage for a long time and tried, all in vain, to get him to talk. However, the moment they started to *leave,* the bird opened up with the repertoire for which he was justly famous. In other words, as long as these persons were standing in front of this wise old fellow's cage, entertaining *him,* why should he exert himself? But as soon as they started to leave, then he went into action.

When I recently remarked to a visitor in my laboratory that it looked as if some of my birds talk to me as a means of getting me to talk to them, the visitor remarked: "In other words, there seems to be some question of who is training whom!"[5] Only by

---

[4] Here we seem to have an excellent example of what Allport (1937, 1940) has termed "functional autonomy." It is not, as this writer seemed at first to imply, that a given type of performance, once stably acquired, continues indefinitely, without benefit of motivation or reward. Instead, the "autonomy" is only apparent in that what looks like a case of performance without motivation turns out to involve simply a *shift* in motivation, in which the new, substitute motive is so subtle as to be difficult to identify. [See Section III.]

[5] "It is a question frequently as to who imitates whom—often fond parents hear the little one produce 'da-da' and vigorously imitate the child" (Osgood, not yet published). (See also 23.)

indeed letting the bird gain some control over the trainer by means of vocalization does it seem possible to bring the bird's powers as a talker to their fullest development.

This point of view throws light upon the old but rather mystifying practice of covering a bird's cage as a means of getting it to talk. The explanation seems to go as follows. The bird likes both to see and to hear its trainer. Naturally, if the bird can *see* the trainer, it is less important to *hear* him. By covering the cage, the trainer makes it impossible for the bird to be sure the trainer is "there" unless the trainer talks. It may therefore be supposed that the bird will be more highly motivated to talk, as a means of getting the trainer to talk and thus reassure the bird that he has not departed.

DO BIRDS "HAVE LANGUAGE"? Fellow psychologists and others have repeatedly asked if the words that birds reproduce have any "meaning" to them or if they simply repeat them "parrot-like." The first thing we can say with any certainty is that birds can be taught to indicate their wants by means of words, i.e., to say the name of whatever it is they want to eat or drink. It is also clear that birds can "associate" certain words or phrases with particular events. For example, last summer a number of children came into our yard to see the Mexican parrot, whose cage had been set out of doors. It was a cool day and the parrot was a bit on the grumpy side. As a result he would say not a word to the children, but as they started to walk away across the yard, he said very clearly, "Don't go." No attempt had ever been made to teach him this expression, and only once since has he been heard to utter it. What had apparently happened was this, that he had occasionally heard the writer's wife use the expression when guests were starting to depart. The least we can say is that this expression had become "associated" with people walking away. We can also surmise that the parrot, in the case cited, did not want the children to walk away. How much the expression, "Don't go," *really* meant to the parrot, I leave to the reader to decide.[6]

In a state of nature, birds and other creatures undoubtedly *communicate* with one another, but this is not the same as saying that they have *language*. Animal communication seems to consist

[6] A correspondent reports that in the summer her parrot, upon seeing the iceman approach the back porch, will regularly call out, "Fifty pounds today, please." Our own mynah bird, when saluted with a "Hello," will commonly ask, "How are you?" If the first speaker says, "Fine," the mynah is then likely to say, "What's up?" In both instances we are presumably dealing simply with common sequences of events which release "meaningful" responses on a purely associative basis.

simply of the use of *signals*—signals of danger, food, sex, etc. But one of the most distinctive things about "real" language, i.e., language as used by human beings, is that it involves putting *two* (or more) signals, or words, together into novel combinations so as to produce *sentences,* which can accomplish much more than can simple signaling. For example, if I take the words "John" and "steals," and put them together to form the sentence, "John steals," I can change others' attitudes and behavior toward John even though John himself be a thousand miles away. Birds seem wholly incapable of doing this sort of thing.[7] I do not, for example, expect my birds to tell me what has happened in the laboratory during my absence, although they can "tell" me well enough what they want when I am there. As a student recently remarked, birds can "communicate," but they cannot "converse." They cannot, in other words, use words with the same degree of *abstraction* as do human beings.

II. The Autistic Basis of Language Development

One of the chapters in a recent book on child development is aptly entitled "The Mystery of Language." "Despite the central role that language plays in the development of children," say the authors, "the first crucial steps in language learning remain a mystery to scientists" (Davis and Havighurst, 1947, p. 107). And Susanne Langer, in *Philosophy in a new key* (1948), begins her discussion of language as follows:

> Language is, without a doubt, the most momentous and at the same time the most mysterious product of the human mind. Between the clearest animal call of love or warning or anger, and a man's least, trivial *word,* there lies a whole day of Creation—or in modern phrase, a whole chapter of evolution (p. 83).

Despite a great deal of astute observation and ingenious speculation concerning language, there are still a number of problems to which we have no assured solutions. How language was originally invented will probably forever remain a matter of uncertain conjecture. Someone has said that it is too bad that behavior, unlike bones, does not fossilize. Writing is, of course, a kind of fossilized speech, but since spoken language had probably existed for some hundreds of thousands of years and had already reached a

[7] For a similar emphasis upon "predication" as the distinguishing feature of human language, see De Laguna (1927) and Stewart (1946).

state of high perfection and complexity when writing first made its appearance (a mere six thousand years ago), the origin of language is engulfed in the same obscurity that holds the secret of many of man's other great social and cultural discoveries.

But unlike the origin of language in the race, its appearance and development in the individual provide a drama which is constantly being re-enacted under our very eyes, and yet it is hardly less of a mystery, for all its ubiquity.

There seem to be two closely related reasons for this state of affairs. First and foremost is the fact that every society puts such great pressure upon parents to teach their children to talk, and parents are so intent that this shall be done in the manner which is most approved and is presumably best for the child, that we understandably do not venture into the systematic variation in method which is so useful in sharpening perceptions and in decisively confirming hypotheses. In short, language learning is regarded as so vital that we tend to be "culture-bound" with respect to our everyday treatment of it.

In the second place, it is to be noted that we psychologists have not yet approached language as a part of the more general, systematic study of *behavior*. Our great books on behavior theory have astonishingly little to say about language, and genetic studies of children are almost wholly normative in their treatment of language.[8] Philosophers and linguists seem, by and large, to have been more concerned with the psychology of language than the psychologists themselves; and it is from such writers as Ogden and Richards, Bloomfield, Sapir, Malinowski, De Laguna, Korzybski, Morris, Hayakawa, Jesperson, Langer, and Schaluch that we have had the most exciting treatments of the subject.[9] Psychologists are showing an awakening of interest in the language problem, as evidenced by Johnson's recent book (1946) and by the 1947 William James Lectures at Harvard by B. F. Skinner on "Verbal Behavior." Yet the assertion seems to stand that language has failed to receive as careful attention from psychologists as they have devoted to many other, seemingly less important problems.

Although there are those who would perhaps dispute the point, it seems that most of our *exact* knowledge of the dynamics of

---

[8] For a review of this work, prior to 1936, see *Infant speech* by M. M. Lewis.

[9] "Curiously enough it was not the psychologists who led the way in the analysis of the psychological processes relevant to the meaning of words. With some notable exceptions, they are still struggling with the self-imposed task of reducing word meaning to stimulus-response conditioning or association. Meanwhile neurologists and philosophers have been making the important contributions to this field" (Scheerer, 1949).

behavior, especially our knowledge of motivation and learning, has come, directly or indirectly, from the study of lower animals. But since the animals which have proved most valuable in this connection—apes, rats, dogs, etc.—seem incapable of learning to say so much as a single word,[10] our systematic behavior studies have not greatly advanced our understanding of human language; and since language plays so conspicuous a role in the lives of human beings, there has remained a kind of hiatus between the scientific studies of animal behavior and the study and understanding of human behavior.

For reasons which were not at all apparent to me, at first, no systematic attempt seems ever to have been made to bridge this gap by the use of those organisms which come nearest to human beings in their capacity to learn language and which we are at the same time free to utilize experimentally. The parrot family, which includes the macaws, cockatoos, parakeets, and other species, and the ravens, crows, mocking-birds, starlings, jays, and that fabulous talker and whistler, the mynah bird of India—these two groups offer a great variety of subjects which can reproduce human speech and which can also, at least in limited measure, meaningfully use and understand it. And yet, to the best of my knowledge, there is not a single behavior laboratory in the world in which these birds have been systematically studied. All we know about them is contained in the writings of naturalists and of persons who have kept and trained them as pets.[11]

It is from the latter type of literature, reinforced by actual experience with a few birds, that one learns why it is that these birds have not previously been employed as laboratory subjects. Liddell and his students (1944) found that they could not make pigs and certain other domestic animals "neurotic" unless they first made pets of them. And neither can one teach a bird to talk unless

[10] Recent unconfirmed newspaper reports suggest that dogs may learn to utter words, but the work of Kellogg and Kellogg (1933) and Yerkes and Learned (1925) gives no indication that chimpanzees possess this capacity. And a study by Mowrer, Palma, and Sanger (1948) indicates how severely limited is vocalization in rats. In a personal communication, K. J. Hayes, of the Yerkes Laboratories, remarks: "In regard to your statement that animals, including apes, 'seem incapable of learning to say so much as a single word,' are you familiar with the work of Furness [1916]? He taught an orangutan to use two words—cup and papa—appropriately. This is an isolated case, but it may merit mention in an unexplored field like this." Dr. Hayes is currently engaged in an attempt to get young chimpanzees to learn to utter words, on the basis of an hypothesis similar to the one set forth on a later page of this paper.

[11] This literature is large, running to scores of titles. Here only a few of the most useful and best known need be cited: Bechstein, 1871; Bronson, 1947; Feyeraband, 1943; Greene, 1884; Page, 1906; Russ, 1884.

a great deal of time and attention go into its taming. Although birds which are capable of talking can be caught in large numbers in a state of nature or purchased by the dozen from dealers,[12] yet in two respects we are almost as limited in working with them experimentally as we are with children. I am referring not only to the time required to produce a good talking bird but also to the necessity of keeping prospective talkers isolated from others of their own species. Ideally, a prospective talker should spend several hours of each day in the exclusive company of his trainer. This requirement obviously puts a severe limit on the number of birds of any one species which one individual can work with either simultaneously or successively.

I hope that eventually we can devise methods which will make possible full-fledged experiments (see Section III), with well-controlled laboratory conditions and subjects in statistically respectable numbers; but during the year that we had birds in our laboratory, I cannot say that we performed anything approximating an experiment. However, the scientific opportunities seem so numerous with the talking birds that further observations of an unsystematized, exploratory nature will probably be profitable, although we hope also to get some systematic experimentation under way.

A TENTATIVE HYPOTHESIS. Of the numerous problems which seem feasible of attack with talking birds, both at the observational and at the experimental level, the following may be cited as illustrative. Although the children in every well-ordered household learn language as a matter of course, it is little short of miraculous that they should do so; for language learning involves a remarkable feat, the feat of learning to reproduce, *as responses,* certain of the noises which impinge upon them *as stimuli.* Because language learning is such a commonplace, we are likely not to be properly impressed with the magnitude of the accomplishment which it represents. We say, of course, that this accomplishment is "due to imitation," but to name a process is not to explain it.

Darwin stressed the expressive function of the infant's early sounds and believed that from this emotionally toned behavior articulate speech somehow evolved. Others have sought to solve the problem—but have succeeded only in glossing it over—by positing an "instinct of imitation." E. B. Holt attacked the problem more squarely, but his reflex-circle principle falls far short of

[12] Subject to public health regulations concerning importation and interstate transportation.

providing a really satisfactory solution.[13] That language is learned on a strictly trial-and-error basis has been suggested, but this theory, too, has important weaknesses. Still other hypotheses have been put forward, but they are even less complete and give us no really integrative principle.

On the basis of many converging lines of evidence, it now appears that the most plausible explanation of the *first* stage of language learning lies along lines quite different from those usually suggested—lines which can be clearly traced only against the background of modern behavior theory and clinical theory. The essence of the hypothesis here proposed is that babies and birds alike first learn to reproduce the conventionalized noises which we call words, not because they can either understand or use those words in any ordinary sense, but because of what is, at first, a purely *autistic* function. Birds and babies, according to this hypothesis, both make their first efforts at reproducing words because these words *sound good to them.*

It is very generally agreed, in all human societies, that a good mother is one who is loving and attentive to the needs of her child, and it is also a common expectation that mothers will coo and make other gentle noises when caring for their young. These two practices—loving care combined with vocalization—presumably create in the infant a predisposition to react with emotional satisfaction, first to the vocalizations of others and later to his own vocalizations. Since the sound of the mother's voice has often been accompanied by comfort-giving measures, it is to be expected that when the child, alone and uncomfortable, hears his own voice, it will likewise have a consoling, comforting effect. In this way it may be supposed that the infant will be rewarded for his own first babbling and jabbering, without any necessary reference to the effects they produce on others.

Gradually, from what the infant probably perceives as an inarticulate murmuring or warbling on the part of the mother,[14] certain specific, recognizable words emerge which are especially welcome and reassuring, so that when, in the course of random vocalization, the child hits upon a sound that is recognizably like a sound which the mother (or possibly the father) makes, the child is motivated to reproduce that noise over and over and to try to perfect

[13] For a detailed critique of Holt's theory of language learning and for a synopsis of scientific and speculative views concerning imitation in general, see, respectively, Appendices 1 and 2 in *Social learning and imitation* by Miller and Dollard (1941).

[14] For a literary interpretation of what the speech of the mother may sound like to an infant, see Hudson's *Green Mansions* (pp. 64ff.).

it, since a perfect reproduction of it is more satisfying than is an imperfect one. If one wishes to call this a kind of self-contained trial-and-error learning, there can be no objection, provided we remember that it has been preceded by important emotional conditioning and that the success of the infant's efforts at vocalization is not necessarily dependent upon the reactions of others. *It is the child's own reactions to the sounds he makes which seem all-important at this stage.*

In suggesting that the utterance of word-like noises occurs first on a purely autistic basis, I mean, specifically, that when a child or a bird is lonely, frightened, hungry, cold, or merely bored, it can comfort and divert itself by making noises which have previously been associated with comfort and diversion. These sounds have become "sweet music"; and they are reproduced, not because of their social effectiveness, but because of the intrapsychic satisfaction they provide (see Section III). Later, once particular sounds have been learned on this autistic basis, the stage is set for them to function instrumentally, in connection with the child's (or bird's) interactions with the external world; but this appears to be a second stage in language learning, not the first one.

SUBSTANTIATING EVIDENCE. The evidence in support of this interpretation of language acquisition is varied and impressive. The five following sources of corroboration may be cited as most pertinent.

1. It is commonly agreed among bird fanciers that if you want to teach a bird to talk you must, in effect, behave toward it like a good mother. One writer remarks that "parakeets, like children, . . . are 100 per cent a reflection of the time and attention spent with them."[15] And another writer (Russ, 1884), summarizing his own and others' experiences, remarks that the one thing that a parrot needs above all else if he is to learn to talk is "to love and to be loved." That the appearance of the trainer shall be a rewarding event to the bird seems universally accepted as a condition of effective speech learning by the bird. And it is probably no accident that birds more readily learn to repeat their trainer's "Hello" than his "Good-bye."

2. While good care and affection for the prospective talking bird are emphasized in all writings on the subject, I am not aware that anyone has previously suggested the specific method which we believe is most effective. After trying other methods, we have

[15] S. O. Figland, personal communication.

found that the best way of inducing a bird to talk is to feed and water it exclusively by hand and, just as the food or water is presented, to utter the word which we wish the bird to learn. This procedure has two consequences: (*a*) it makes the sound of the word become a "good" sound, and (*b*) it specifically connects this sound with a particular kind of "goodness." Thus, as we offer water we say "water," and as we offer bread we say "bread." This procedure insures that these sounds will be ones which—once acquired on an autistic basis—can be later used for indicating, respectively, thirst and hunger.[16]

Actually, the proverbial "Polly want a cracker?" is probably taught in roughly this manner in most instances; but explicit description of the process seems not to have gotten into the literature. Most writers stress the importance of "repetition" but make little or no reference to the *context* in which it occurs.

Since the trainer is present when these primary drives of hunger and thirst get reduced, it is undoubtedly satisfying to the bird at the level of the secondary drives or emotions to have the trainer appear, and if "Hello" or any other word is characteristically associated with his appearance, it, too, will be readily learned [17] and may then be used as a means of calling to the trainer, as an expression of the bird's wish to see him.

Later, after a few words have been stably acquired on an autistic basis and then put to use communicatively, one can establish a more direct type of imitation. Thus, one may say "water" and withhold the water until the bird has said this word. Eventually, if this procedure is used in a variety of situations, the bird will learn that the trainer's utterances provide the solutions to his

[16] Whether they ever come to mean, respectively, water and bread, without reference to the bird's *wish* for them, is a question which requires further research. It seems unlikely, however, that any organism other than man ever achieves this degree of "abstraction." Cf. the discussion by Kellogg and Kellogg (1933) of the vocalizations of a baby chimpanzee. (See also the discussion in Section III of the theories of Langer.)

[17] In fact, this word may be learned *before* any of the words specifically associated with food or drink. It is as if the word which the trainer characteristically makes as he appears tends, for the bird, to become "his sound." When, subsequently, the bird has a need for the trainer to present himself, it finds that although it cannot make the trainer as a whole reappear, it can reproduce a part of him, namely, his characteristic noise. This noise presumably has secondary reward value for the bird, just as the actual arrival of the trainer himself (signaling food and drink) has. (A severely neurotic young woman has provided, in the course of psychotherapy, the following clinical illustration of this mechanism. About two years ago she developed an imaginary love affair with her physician, an elderly man who in reality had always behaved in a strictly professional manner in his associations with her. The young woman reported that she had a "nickname" for her fantasy-lover and that whenever she became anxious she would find it "enormously comforting" merely to repeat this term to herself.)

(the bird's) problems, and will attempt directly to reproduce them. This is the form of imitation which Miller and Dollard (1941) have so effectively analyzed; but it should be emphasized that this is apparently a later, not the initial, step in language learning (see 21 and 23).

3. Next we may mention the factor of age in language learning. It is well known that children who, through isolation, neglect, or other circumstances have not learned to speak by the time they are six or seven years old rarely develop normal language, even though the innate capacity is abundantly present. And bird trainers likewise stress the desirability of getting subjects when they are very young if they are to be trained as talkers. However, in the case of adult birds, it is possible to produce a kind of forced or artificial "regression." This is done by clipping their wings, caging them, and, in the present investigation, feeding and watering them exclusively by hand.[18] That children beyond the age of six or seven years do not learn to speak well, if at all, comes presumably in part from the fact that this kind of forced dependency is less easily possible with them than with birds and that no woman would ordinarily be able, even if the dependency could be established, to treat these older children as she would a real infant, lavishing on them the same love and "babying." She would intuitively expect them to "act their age," an expectation that would militate against its own fulfilment.[19]

4. Our hypothesis suggests why it is that infants as well as birds often seem to be "practicing" or "rehearsing" words all by themselves. One not infrequently hears a parrot or a crow "talking to himself," and mothers sometimes report that they can hear their infants making wordlike noises in their beds in the morning, noises which they commonly cannot be induced to make later in the day. Assuming that some degree of subvocal rehearsal (or vocal "imagining") is possible in small children, we can also explain why it is that children often "come out," as we say, with well-formed words which we have never before heard them attempt to utter. It is as if the practice has gone on covertly.[20] With birds it

[18] In the case of two birds, a magpie and a Mexican parrot, it has been observed that when they were exceptionally hungry they would move their wings up and down rhythmically in precisely the way young birds, while still in the nest, can be observed doing when they beg for food from their parents. This observation gives special point to the belief that food deprivation and caging serve to produce a very literal form of "regression."

[19] For a different analysis of this problem, see Langer (1948).

[20] For a more detailed discussion of the probable role of rehearsal in connection with learning, see Coppock and Mowrer (1948).

appears—although the evidence is not as yet definitive—that the practice must be overt. Even adult birds, as they are learning language, talk a kind of "baby talk," which gets corrected only with much overt repetition.[21]

5. Our theory also suggests why it is that a human being usually cannot compete as a vocal model for one bird when a second bird of the same species is present. At best a human being is probably a poor substitute as a love object for a bird and cannot therefore make noises that sound as good to the bird as do those of another bird. Since incubator hatching of the eggs of talking birds has apparently never been attempted, all such birds have presumably had at least a brief but important period during which they have seen, and heard the sounds of, their own species, a fact which may permanently predispose them to respond favorably to these sounds and to other sounds made by birds which are reminiscent of the parents. Thus when our mynah bird learned to caw like the laboratory crow, it was presumably not because this sound had been made by the mynah bird's parents but because the crow, of the various birds in the laboratory, looked most like the mynah bird's parents. By a kind of "transference" the crow presumably became a love object and his vocalizations attractive enough to be worth reproducing.

The question has sometimes been raised as to whether it would help in getting a bird to talk if the trainer *imitated the bird*—as mothers often imitate their babies. Assuming that a bird would be most likely to make, spontaneously, noises such as it had heard its parents make, if the trainer then made these noises the bird might be expected to "transfer" to him some of the emotional attitudes which it had previously acquired toward its parents. In other words, if the trainer thus made himself somewhat like the bird's parents, perhaps it would be easier for the bird then to identify with, or become like, him.

The work of Sanborn, Lorenz, and others with birds hatched by

[21] Continuing observations suggest that, at least in some types of birds and particularly after training has already progressed to a rather advanced stage, words may be almost perfect when first spoken. For example, on the first occasion when the author's gray parrot was heard to say, "Well, well," the words were said very clearly and precisely; and the same was true of the first occasion when this bird was heard to whistle the first bars of "Mary Had a Little Lamb." With subsequent repetitions both of these performances distinctly deteriorated—in part, it would appear, because this bird seems to enjoy burlesquing the sounds which it acquires. If more refined inquiry should show that birds can indeed reproduce words and other sounds perfectly, without overt practice, it would suggest a degree of covert activity or "thought" which the scientific investigator would otherwise be very cautious in attributing to them.

other species is very much in point here, as would be experiments involving the artificial deafening or perhaps direct devocalization of parent birds.

Finally, it is relevant to note that once a bird—the statement is often made of shell parakeets (Feyeraband, 1943)—has thoroughly identified with and learned to talk like a human being, it is useless for breeding purposes, being unable to care for its young and probably even incapacitated for mating. It is as if the human being has become so powerfully "cathected" that the bird is unable to direct either sexual or parental love toward members of the same species. It is also noteworthy that among parakeets only cocks learn to talk, although this is not necessarily the case with other species.[22] (For further discussion of these and related points, see Section III.)

Some Possible Objections. The autistic theory of language learning provides a plausible explanation of a wide range of known phenomena and posits a number of promising research problems. And the fact that it was observations made with birds which suggested this theory tends to confirm the supposition that they offer some generally overlooked scientific uses and opportunities. But it should be noted that this theory of language development, like other theories which have been proposed, is not entirely free of objections. Three of these are listed below.

1. It may be pointed out that some of the first words which children learn—such as "hot" and "ouch"—are not "good" words, at least not by adult standards. But such words apparently have a very different implication to the small child, since they seem first to be learned because they have been heard in association with reassurances on the part of the parent in frightening or painful situations. When a child is subsequently in pain or frightened, he may attempt to reassure himself by making the same noises. We probably err, therefore, in assuming that these words have the same implications for the infant that they have for adults, or even for the child at a somewhat later stage.

This interpretation can be illustrated as follows. When one of

[22] In the case of shell parakeets, it has been regularly found that women succeed better in teaching them to speak than do men. Since it is the male parakeet that learns most readily, it has been intimated that the opposition of sexes is in some way involved here. However, we need only recall that the woman's voice is an octave higher than the man's to realize that the parakeet, whose voice is naturally "small" and high-pitched, can reproduce the speech of women more easily than that of men, for purely mechanical reasons. In the language of learning theory, the generalization of secondary reinforcement from the trainer's voice to that of the bird occurs more readily where the trainer's voice is maximally similar to that of the bird.

the writer's little girls was about twelve months old, she would crawl under a kitchen stove to get the kitten, which liked to sleep there curled up in a paper bag. When the little girl got the kitten, she would try to stand up, bump her head, and cry. Since she seemed not to know how to get out from under the stove and would get frightened, the child's mother would go to her aid, laughingly saying, "Ouch, ouch," while extricating her. Later, in the same situation—sometimes after and sometimes before she had actually bumped her head—the little girl could be heard murmuring "Ouch, ouch." Since the appearance of aid and relief in that situation had been associated with these words, the child, in uttering them, probably reassured herself—and, secondarily, communicated with her mother.

2. Another objection that can be urged against our hypothesis is this. It may be supposed that the first occasions on which the young infant hears his own voice are not particularly pleasant ones. His first vocalizations are those of crying and may be assumed to accompany pain and other drive states. If, therefore, the self-satisfying quality of his own voice is important in the infant's learning of language, it might be supposed that the occurrence of crying would tend to militate against such learning.

This may, in fact, be the case; but it should also be noted that infant crying often precedes, and thus comes to "mean," drive reduction. Only under very exceptional circumstances is a baby already crying when something painful happens, thus resulting in "punishment" of the crying. The more common sequence is: drive, crying in response to the drive, and drive reduction. We may argue, therefore, that at least in the case of those infants whose crying is promptly responded to, even this sound takes on a slightly positive emotional tone. In this event, it would hardly be expected to function as a serious hazard to language learning. If, on the other hand, an infant's crying is rarely or never responded to, one might expect the sound of his voice to have largely negative connotations: since the sound of his own cries is usually followed by continued discomfort and mounting fatigue, the child cannot expect anything good to come of his crying. And the work of a number of investigators (Spitz, 1945; Teagarden, 1946, pp. 142 and 154) indicates that infants, in those institutions where care is highly impersonal and routine, do indeed tend to give up crying—and to show marked retardation in language learning.[23] A similar retarda-

[23] Brodbeck and Irwin (1946) state: "It is . . . a general observation that children who grow up in the ordinary orphanage home are somewhat retarded in their

tion might likewise be expected if the sounds which an infant hears others make are associated with pain rather than with pleasure. Perhaps it is partly in recognition of this principle that mothers do not usually start using their voices for disciplinary purposes, i.e., for "scolding," until after a period in which they have spoken only lovingly, and the child has progressed through at least the first critical stages of language acquisition.

3. The third objection which can be offered to an autistic theory of language acquisition is more serious than the two just described; but it is not necessarily fatal.

At about the same age that infants start to babble, they also commonly begin to show "social smiling," i.e., someone smiles at them and they smile back. Here, obviously, is a good example of "imitation," yet it would not seem that this behavior could be acquired on the autistic basis here proposed for language learning. When a child chances to make a sound which resembles a gratifying sound he has previously heard others make, he hears his own voice and will be rewarded by this sound. But when a child whose mother has smiled at him under pleasurable circumstances happens himself to smile, he cannot see it. It is not, in other words, the same stimulus for the infant that the mother's smile is. Therefore, his production of a smile does not have the same immediately self-satisfying consequences as does his production of a pleasant word. It is accordingly hard to see how the smiling of infants can be acquired on an autistic basis, and yet acquired it is, early and well. And if an imitative response such as smiling can be acquired without the autistic satisfaction which has been posited in the case of language, perhaps language likewise develops on some basis other than the one here proposed.

This is a serious problem and cannot be lightly dismissed. There is, nevertheless, one important difference to be noted between smiling and the utterance of words: there is a reflexive stimulus for smiling, namely, so-called "gas pains," whereas there is no known reflexive stimulus for words. Even the assumption that certain rudimentary sounds, such as "ma ma" and "da da," occur wholly as a consequence of the child's "maturation" is called into question by

---

speech development" (p. 146). "A recent study by William Goldfarb showed that this deficiency with regard to speech sounds, as well as to other uses of language, continues right up to the third year of life among institutional children, and even after a period of foster home replacement" (p. 153). See also the numerous references cited by Teagarden on the pages indicated above.

the purported fact that infants who are deaf from birth do not babble normally, if at all.[24]

Given a reflexive basis for the initial occurrence of smiling, it is by no means impossible for it to be transformed into a response which can be stimulated by others. If, for example, when the infant smiles reflexly, the mother smiles back at him, says a loving word, or rewards him in some other way, the kinesthetic stimuli associated with the infant's smiling will become at least faintly pleasurable to him, and he may be expected to learn in this manner to smile autistically. From this stage he can then progress to genuinely imitative, or social, smiling. But in the case of words, there in no reflexive mechanism which can be relied upon for their original production, and it is at this point that the autistic interpretation seems uniquely useful. (See Tompson, 1941.)

III. Language, Learning Theory, and Psychoanalysis

The present section is essentially a series of "texual footnotes" which serve to elaborate and further document what has already been said. The two preceding sections are based largely upon the writer's own observations and upon inferences drawn therefrom. Here we shall re-examine these observations and inferences from a more technical standpoint and in the light of evidence reported by others.

Autism and Secondary Reinforcement. It has been suggested in Sections I and II that, in both human infants and talking birds, the *first* stage of word learning is autistic; and by this is meant that a word, having been associated with satisfactions (drive reductions) provided by the parent or "foster parent," becomes satisfying in its own right, i.e., satisfying not only when uttered by another but also when uttered by the bird or baby itself. And from this it is but a short step to the conclusion that the capacity to

[24] In the communication previously referred to, Dr. Keith J. Hayes has asked if I could "cite some references for 'the purported fact that infants who are deaf from birth do not babble normally, if at all.' Ewing and Ewing [1938] contend that the early babbling of congenitally deaf children is normal." I have consulted Mrs. Leo Zittzus, head of the department for the teaching of the deaf-blind at the Perkins Institute and Massachusetts School for the Blind (Watertown, Massachusetts), and she reports that the congenitally deaf "do not babble because babbling is associated with the pleasure of hearing the sounds uttered, which, of course, the deaf infant cannot do. All the congenitally deaf child does is to make weird sounds, which he perceives only through the vibrations produced in his larynx." Asked to evaluate the report of Ewing and Ewing, Mrs. Zittzus stated that "many American educators do not agree with Ewing and Ewing; they do not confirm their findings."

utter the conventional noises called words develops because the organism is automatically, or "autistically," rewarded whenever it makes a noise somewhat like a word which has thus become satisfying. The organism is thus prompted to perfect this noise, with or without tutelage.

In the words of Langer (1948), we may say that a word becomes a *symbol* well before it becomes a *sign,* in the sense of having an objective *denotation.* As symbol it has, at this very beginning stage, an emotional *connotation* for the infant or the bird, but it is not yet looked upon or used as an item of behavior whose primary function is that of communication with others.

Anyone who is familiar with modern learning theory will at once tend to translate what has just been said into a somewhat different, and in some respects more precise, language. He will call the word a *conditioned stimulus,* and he will call the satisfaction which it becomes capable of eliciting a *secondary reinforcement.* When Pavlov's dogs which had been subjected to a few paired presentations of a bell and a bit of meat powder began to salivate to the bell alone, Pavlov (1927) called this a conditioned reaction; but he completely overlooked the fact that the sounding of the bell did something besides make the animal salivate: Pavlov had no interest in the fact that the bell, having been associated with hunger reduction, itself became capable of producing a kind of satisfaction, *emotional* satisfaction. Hearing the bell would not, to be sure, make the animal any the less hungry; but what the bell could do was to *reassure* the animal. When an animal is hungry, there is often added to this primary drive the apprehension or fear that the hunger may persist or perhaps even grow worse (12, 17). When Pavlov's dogs heard the bell, which had previously been followed by food, we may be sure that they were "glad," i.e., experienced a reduction in the fear or apprehension which had accompanied their hunger but which was now dispelled by the "promise" which the bell gave of food to come.

There is rapidly growing literature on this phenomenon of "secondary reinforcement," and the basic concepts involved have already shown themselves applicable in a number of areas which have long defied systematic scientific analysis (Miller, 1950; Postman, 1947; 5, 8). The theory which has been advanced in earlier portions of this paper to account for the first stage in language learning is a case in point. All that this theory says, in essence, is simply that words, as a result of being combined with "loving care," take on alike for the bird and baby secondary reinforcing value and that they have this value when uttered, not only by others, but also by the bird or baby. This, it is believed, lays the basis for the "self-contained" or "autistic" trial-and-error learning which, in the favorable instance, eventuates in the bird's or baby's reproducing the word—but, in the beginning, more as a *self-signal* than as a signal to others.[25]

Miller and Dollard, in their book *Social learning and imitation* (1941), were among the first to see the great and varied significance of secondary reinforcement and rightly turned their attention to the problem of language learning. In the following words they set forth an hypothesis concerning the development of babbling in babies which is very similar to the one previously developed in this paper. They say:

> Since the mother talks to the child while administering primary rewards such as food, the sound of the human voice should acquire secondary reward value. Because the child's voice produces sounds similar to that of his mother's, some of this acquired reward value generalizes to it. . . . From this hypothesis it may be deduced that children talked to while being fed and otherwise cared for should exhibit more iterative and imitative babbling than children not talked to while being rewarded (p. 277).[26]

Somewhat surprisingly, Miller and Dollard do not, however, extend this hypothesis to account for the acquisition of true word sounds or "vocables." For this purpose they posit a different theory (p. 207); but, as can be seen, their explanation of babbling

---

[25] From what has just been said it follows that if a laboratory animal, such as a dog, cat, or rat, were taught to expect food to follow a given signal, let us say a bell or a tone, and if conditions were then arranged so that, by pressing a bar or pulling a cord, the animal could make the signal sound at will, the animal ought to "learn to make" this noise much more readily than if no such prior conditioning had occurred. An experiment by Mowrer and Kunberger (11) indicates that this inference is well founded, and it gives an objective paradigm for thinking somewhat more concretely about the particular theory advanced above to account for the way in which birds and human infants "learn to make" those noises which we call words. The fact that in the one case the noise is "made" by the organism's own vocal apparatus and in the other case by a mechanical device which is actuated by some response such as pressing a bar should not obscure the basic similarities in the two situations. In both cases it is the effect which the noise has upon the *maker* that is important, not its function as a means of "communicating" to others.

[26] In the work previously cited, Osgood (1951) puts forward a similar hypothesis: "The infant pattern gradually becomes more like that of the speech he hears about him, elements foreign to the culture into which he is born dropping out and those indigenous to it becoming more prominent. Since a large part of this 'acculturation' occurs before the child can actually be said to speak, it appears that the infant in its babbling is differentially reinforced for making parent-like sounds—and much of this reinforcement is probably self-administered, i.e., the child obtains greater pleasure from produced sounds that facsimilate those heard about him." Here Osgood is referring to events that transpire at the age of about five months, before "true language" has appeared.

is precisely the same as the one previously advanced in the present paper.[27]

Another writer who has come excitingly close to the autistic theory of language acquisition as herein developed, but who has just missed it, is Langer. In her brilliant and engaging book, *Philosophy in a new key* (1942), she takes as a point of departure the following excerpts from Sapir:

It is probable that the origin of language is not a problem that can be solved out of the resources of linguistics alone but that it is essentially a particular case of a much wider problem of the genesis of symbolic behavior and of the specialization of such behavior in the laryngeal region which may be presumed to have had only an expressive function to begin with. . . .

The primary function of language is generally said to be communication. . . . The autistic speech of children seems to show that the purely communicative aspect of language has been exaggerated. It is best to admit that language is primarily a vocal actualization of the tendency to see reality symbolically, that it is precisely this quality which renders it a fit instrument for communication and that it is in the actual give and take of social intercourse that it has been complicated and refined into the form in which it is known today (Sapir, 1938, p. 159).

To this Langer then adds:

If it is true that "the tendency to see reality symbolically" is the real keynote of language, then most research into the roots of the speech-function have been misdirected. Communication by sound is what we have looked for among the apes; . . . What we should look for is *the first indication of symbolic behavior,* which is not likely to be anything as specialized, conscious, or rational as the *use* of semantic (p. 89).[28]

But after this auspicious beginning, Langer makes a series of assumptions of doubtful validity. First of all, she assumes that

[27] Since the above was written, it has been discovered that on p. 81 of their book Miller and Dollard make a statement very similar to the one quoted above from p. 277, after which they have a footnote which reads as follows: "It would be interesting to compare the babbling behavior of different children after an attempt had been made to give different phonemes a special acquired reward value. One child would be talked to with a certain phoneme while being fed and with a different but equally pronounceable phoneme while being dressed or having some other routine performed which seems to annoy him. A second child would be talked to with the first phoneme while being dressed and the second while being fed. Each child would be talked to with both phonemes for an equal length of time. The prediction would be that the child would learn to babble with the phoneme which had been given an acquired reward value more than with the other." From this it is apparent that Miller and Dollard came even closer to the autistic theory of language development than the passage concerning babbling would alone suggest.

[28] For a discussion of what may be "the first indication of symbolic behavior" in chimpanzees and rats, see Mowrer and Ullman (16), with particular reference to the phenomenon of VTE (vicarious trial-and-error).

there is a babbling or "lalling" instinct in human infants. She says:

> The ape has no instinctive desire to babble in babyhood. He does not play with his mouth and his breath as human infants do; there is no crowing and cooing, no "goo-goo" and "ba-ba" and "do-de-da" in his otherwise uproarious nursery. Consequently there are no sounds and syllables *that please or frighten him by their sheer aesthetic character,* as he is pleased, frightened, or comforted by purely phenomenal sights (p. 94, italics added).

Because this author does not see the way in which the human voice, without reference to the particular words uttered, at an early stage acquires secondary reinforcement value; and because she is apparently also unaware of the way in which infant babbling is diminished by failure to hear the human voice in association with rewarding experiences (for example, because of deafness, isolation, or neglect—see Section II), she is forced to posit in man "an instinctive tendency to produce sounds, to play with the vocal apparatus" (p. 95); and from this she then proceeds to make the added assumption that these instinctively made sounds, "by their sheer aesthetic character," please or frighten him!

In support of this thesis Langer alludes to seemingly unaccountable fears in young chimpanzees and to what she regards as equally mysterious attachments which these animals sometimes develop. As an instance of the latter she reports the following:

> Not only fear, but also delight or comfort may be inspired in these animals by objects that have no biological significance [!] for them; thus Gua [studied by Kellogg and Kellogg, 1933], who was so attached to Mr. Kellogg that she went into tantrums of terror and grief whenever he left the house, could be comforted by being given his pair of coveralls. "This she would drag around with her," the account reads, "as a fetish of protection until his return. . . . Occasionally, if it was necessary for him to go away, the leave-taking could be accomplished without emotional display on the part of Gua if the coveralls were given to her before the time of departure" (p. 92).

Langer astutely observes that "Gua was using the coveralls even in his [the 'foster-father's'] presence as a help to her imagination which kept him near whether he went out or not" (p. 92). On an earlier page we have posited that talking birds use their trainer's "noises" in precisely the same way: long before a word is used as a name for or means of calling the trainer,[29] it appears to func-

---

[29] The word "call" has an instructive double meaning. It may be used in the sense of "calling *for*" someone, or it may be used in the sense of *naming,* as when we say, "What do you call him?" That there is an inherently close relationship between the summoning and the denotative features of a word is indicated by the fact that in some languages one says, not "What do you call him?" but "*How* do

tion precisely like a fetish, a little part of the beloved one which the bird can "have near" even though the real person is far away.[30] It is therefore all the more astonishing that Langer should take the position that these rudimentary symbols inspire "delight or comfort" by their sheer aesthetic quality and have "no biological significance."

Nothing could be clearer than the "biological significance" of the coveralls in the example quoted from Kellogg and Kellogg: they were a part of the individual most significant biologically in Gua's life! However, some of the other examples cited by Langer are less easily accounted for. For example:

> Kohler describes how the chimpanzees will hoard perfectly useless [?] objects and carry them between the lower abdomen and the upper thigh, a sort of natural trouser pocket, for days on end. Thus Tschego, an adult female, treasured a stone that the sea had rounded and polished (p. 92).

Tschego's stone can be said to be "useless" only in the sense of playing no observable external role in her life; but we may suppose that emotionally it was very far from being useless. Precisely how the stone acquired its emotional utility as a fetish or comforter we cannot in this case say; but the careful experimental studies of Wolfe (1936) with chimpanzees show that if poker chips, initially reacted to with indifference, are made to have "token" value, i.e., serviceable as a means of obtaining food, they quickly acquire much the same sort of fascination which Tschego's stone had for her. In other words, although, in some cases, we may not happen to know the circumstances which have caused a particular object to acquire "token" or "symbolic" value for an organism, yet we un-

---

you call him?" From the primitive function of calling for other persons we may conjecture that there evolved the more refined use of "call," or names, as means of merely pointing or referring.

[30] A letter from Mrs. W. L. Wetmore of Corning, New York, interestingly confirms this interpretation. Mrs. Wetmore says: "Three parrots I have known enjoyed talking, and when they are alone—all three—they will entertain themselves with the whole repetition of their learning. Once when I was ill, my neighbor's parrot hung on the back porch all by himself. Pretty soon he started whistling, then he sang 'East Side, West Side'—he dances to this—and thereafter he continued for 40 minutes with one thing after another, without repeating himself. He called 'There Kitty, Kitty, Kitty,' and invariably his last act will be whatever he learned last; in this case it was 'Vote for Al!'" Apropos of the denotative use of words by parrots, Mrs. Wetmore adds: "He used to call both his master and mistress by name. At morning he yelled for his 'coffee,' and he most certainly knew many other foods and seemed to know what he wanted when he asked for them." Finally, this correspondent reports an observation of a type which I have had from others: "Just lately a parrot almost made me have hysterics from laughing. I went to deliver eggs and when I came in I was under the impression that there were several people in the next room; but it was only Polly—all alone—giving a *perfect* imitation of a whole gang of chattering, giggling females!" Was this the parrot's way of creating his own "company"?

derstand very accurately how to make this sort of interest and attachment come about. It is done by the conditioning process already discussed, and we do not at all need to accept Langer's asseveration that "An ape that can transfer the sense of her master's presence to a memento of him, and that reacts with specific emotions to the sheer quality of a perception, certainly is nervously organized above the level of purely realistic conditioned response" (p. 92).[31]

As for Langer's assumption that "instinctive babbling" is a prerequisite for word learning, we need only note that birds do not instinctively make the sounds which a normal infant does during the "babbling stages," and yet certain of their species can be taught to say human words with great distinctness. Shell parakeets often engage in what fanciers call "little bird talk"—a kind of garbled chattering—but it is considerably removed from infantile babbling, as are the sounds which the larger talking birds make "spontaneously."

In the chapter from which the above quotations have been taken, Langer moves on from the problem of initial utterance of words, as self-symbols, to the question of how these then get converted over into the elements of social communication (or a "second kind" of symbol), how and why words are then given a syntax, what the role of metaphor is, and a number of other considerations which are central in language theory. Because this author has made a number of initial assumptions of dubious worth, much of her later analysis suffers accordingly. But what should here again be emphasized is the essentially correct nature of her most basic proposition, which she summarizes as follows:

> The notion that the essence of language is the formulation and expression of conceptions rather than the communication of natural wants (the essence of pantomime) opens a new vista upon the mysterious problem of origins. For its beginnings are not natural adjustments, ways to means [in any practical, realistic sense]; they are purposeless lalling-instincts, primitive aesthetic reactions, and dreamlike associations of ideas that fasten on such material. . . .
>
> Moreover, this originally impractical, or better *conceptual* use of speech is borne out by the fact that all attempts to teach apes or the speechless "wild children" to talk, by the method of making them ask for something, have failed; whereas all cases where the use of language has dawned on an in-

[31] Here again it is evident that Langer's whole analysis suffers from lack of conversance with the concept of secondary reinforcements and with the concept of problem solving, not only in the sense of reducing primary drives but equally in the sense of alleviating emotional tensions.

dividual, simian or human, under such difficult circumstances, have been independent of the practical use of the word at the moment (p. 96).[32]

Young children learn to speak, after the fashion of Victor [the "Wild Boy of Aveyron"], by constantly using words to bring things *into their minds,* not *into their hands* (p. 98).

Any attempt to trace [language] back entirely to the need of communication, neglecting the formulative, abstractive experience at the root of it, must land us in the sort of enigma that the problem of linguistic origins has long presented (p. 103).

. . . the utilitarian view of language is a mistake . . . (p. 97).

IMITATION, IDENTIFICATION, AND THE "OEDIPUS COMPLEX." When the author began the research reported in the preceding pages of this paper, he thought of it only as a means of learning something more about the psychology of language and language learning. But almost immediately it was apparent that in order to understand even the rudimentary phenomena observed in the talking birds, we perforce encounter one of the most basic problems of personality theory: the problem of *identification.*[33]

After this research had recently been reported to a professional audience, one member of the group made a remark that went something like this: "We used to use the word 'imitation' a good deal in psychology, and we thought we knew what we meant by it. But since psychoanalysis has introduced the term 'identification,' it has largely taken the place of 'imitation,' and I am not at all sure that we know what *it* means."

Perhaps a superficial distinction that is worth drawing between these two terms is this: When one individual serves as a model for the behavior of the other, with both individuals present, we may speak of imitation; but when one individual acts like, or copies, another individual in the latter's absence, we may speak of *identification.* A student recently reported that a friend of hers had related the following observation (possibly unreliable, but one that will serve to illustrate a point). The friend's brother-in-law has a dog which is much attached to him, and when the brother-in-law walks around in the back yard, he has to stoop as he passes under the clothesline to avoid hitting his head on it. The dog, in walking under the clothesline, likewise stoops, although the line hangs well above his head. If the dog does this only as he follows his master

---

[32] Cf. the distinction made in Section I of this paper between the repetition of a word as a *command* and its repetition as a signal that something *good* is to follow.

[33] For an extended analysis of the role of identification in formal education and a review of the literature, see Courtney (1949) and Lair (1949). This discussion should also be compared with Chapter 21.

around, we might speak of imitation, but if he does it even in the master's absence, one might call it identification.

It would appear that some such distinction as this was in the minds of Miller and Dollard when they wrote: "It is possible that a more detailed analysis would show that the mechanisms involved in copying ['imitating'] are also involved in that aspect of character, or superego, formation which the Freudians have described as 'identification' " (p. 164). For whether one does what one is supposed to do only when others are "looking" or does it in private as well as in public is surely a sound pragmatic test of conscience and good character.

All of which suggests the possibility that identification is a *more dynamic* conception than is imitation. Certainly the psychoanalytic account of identification is a very complex affair, far more so than most accounts of imitation, and one that involves not only the question of copied means but also of copied motives.[34] In other words, identification carries the implication that the identifier not only acts like but also likes (and fears) the individual identified with. That both liking and fearing a parent is one of the primal conditions for *becoming like* the parent in the fundamental sense of identification was early recognized by Freud, as was the connection between identification and the *oral* gratifications in particular. In a paper written in 1917, Freud remarks:

> We have elsewhere described how object-choice develops from a preliminary stage of identification, the way in which the ego first adopts an object and the ambivalence in which this is expressed. The ego wishes to incorporate this object into itself, and the method by which it would do so, in this oral or cannibalistic stage, is by devouring it. Abraham is undoubtedly right in referring in this connection to the refusal of nourishment met with in severe forms of melancholia (p. 160).

And in a different context Freud (1933) has this to say:

> . . . it will suffice if you will grant that the establishment of the superego can be described as a successful instance of identification with the parental

[34] This statement may be illustrated by the following quotation from Lorenz: "On seeing one animal beginning to perform some action and thereby inciting a fellow-member of the flock or herd to do likewise, the human observer is prone to assume an 'instinct of imitation' on the part of the second individual to explain its behavior. The process, however, on which this seeming imitation is really based very closely resembles that very direct transmitting of moods from one individual to another which we can so often observe in ourselves. The 'contagious' reactions of laughing, yawning, and the like at first sight seem very different from the complicated serial actions transmitted in a similar way in animals, yet, being also inherited possessions of the species, they are directly comparable to them" (1937, p. 256). For a discussion of motivation in connection with the instinct problem generally, see Craig (1918).

function. The fact that is decisively in favor of this point of view is that this new creation of a superior function within the ego is extremely closely bound up with the fate of the Oedipus complex, so that the superego appears as the heir of that emotional tie, which is of such importance for childhood. When the Oedipus complex passes away the child must give up the intense object-cathexes which it has formed toward its parents, and to compensate for this loss of object, its identifications with its parents, which have probably long been present, become greatly intensified (16, p. 91).[35]

Now it is not here maintained that what is said in the foregoing quotations is either fully clear or fully correct, but it can hardly escape notice that there is a connection between what Freud is here discussing and the conditions posited in the present paper as requisite for the development of that form of identification with, or being like, a human being which is involved in a bird's learning to talk.

Let us begin by referring to the well-known experiments of Craig (1914) with blond ringdoves. From the date of their weaning, they were kept in isolation as far as other members of their species were concerned and were fed and attended exclusively by human beings. The behavior of "Jack" as described below is typical of the results obtained with other subjects:

Each time I put food in his cage he became greatly excited, charging up and down the cage, kahing and bowing-and-cooing to me, and pecking my hand whenever it came within the cage. From that day [about six months after weaning] until the time of his death, Jack continued to react in this social manner to human beings. . . . Growing up in isolation from all companions of his own species, he gave himself completely to the companionship of human beings (p. 122).

When this male dove was placed with a female of the species, he was distractible and inept as a sex partner. Even more striking results were obtained with another male ("Frank"), which actually became so attached to the experimenter's hands that he would attempt to copulate with them. Of him Craig writes:

After these experiences with another [female] dove, Frank readily and persistently bowed-and-cooed to my face and to my hand, as he had not done before. He continued for a long time, even after he was mated, *to jump on the hand that fed him,* so persistently that he was a nuisance. But though he

[35] For a more extended account of identification, see Freud (1922). One of the commonest, albeit subtle, indications of the relationship between identification and oral gratification is in Christian communion; here the "wafer and wine" are consumed in "remembrance" of the flesh and blood of the Savior. Cannibalism in even its frankest forms is believed always to have symbolic overtones. (See 21.)

jumped on the hand he did not show sexual behavior toward it, not after his first contact with the feathers of another dove. . . [italics added, p. 130].

And elsewhere Craig (1908) summarizes these observations by saying:

. . . we must believe that young doves have no inherited tendency to mate with birds of a particular kind; they learn to associate with a particular kind during the period when they are being fed, when the characteristics of their nursing-parents are vividly impressed upon their young minds (p. 90).

Observations of this general type are by no means unique in the literature on bird behavior. In a personal letter from the Austrian investigator, Konrad Z. Lorenz, to Craig, under date of August 26, 1937, we read the following:

Your suspicion that I started rather early in studying birds is quite correct. My first bird was a one-day-old domestic Mallard whom [sic] I got as an Easter present. I remember perfectly well how I found out that this duckling would run in pursuit of me and how I realized that it took me for its mother. For the following weeks it seems that I did not do anything else but foster it and play mother duck to it. I actually reared that bird, which is a wonder for I was but six years old at the time. (Quoted with the permission of Dr. Craig.)

In one of his scientific papers, Lorenz (1937) extends this line of thought further, as follows:

It is a fact most surprising to the layman as well as to the zoologist that most birds do not recognize their own species "instinctively," but that by far the greater part of their reactions, whose normal object is represented by a fellow-member of the species, must be conditioned to this object during the individual life of every bird. If we raise a young bird in strict isolation from its kind, we find very often that some or all of its social reactions can be released by other than their normal object. Young birds of most species, when reared in isolation, react to their human keeper in exactly the same way in which, under natural conditions, they would respond to fellow-members of their species (pp. 262–63).

Heinroth failed to breed hand-reared Great Horned Owls, Ravens and other birds, for no other reason than that these tame individuals responded sexually to their keepers instead of to each other. In a very few cases known, the bird whose sexual reactions were thus directed toward man, finally accepted a fellow-member of the species which, however, was always regarded as a rather poor substitute for the beloved human and was instantly abandoned whenever the latter appeared (p. 263).

The principle which emerges from these observations, that both species identification and sexual choice are determined by the nature of the parent or foster parent, is particularly well confirmed by the following passage, again from Lorenz:

> I once had a pair of Greylag Geese hatch a Muscovy Duck's eggs. The parent-child relations in this artificial family dissolved sooner than is normal. . . . From the seventh week of their life, . . . the young Muscovies had nothing more to do with the former foster parents nor with any Greylag Geese, but behaved socially toward one another, as well as toward other members of their species, as a perfectly normal Muscovy Duck should do. Ten months later the one male bird among these young Muscovies began to display sexual reactions and, to our surprise, pursued Greylag Geese instead of Muscovy Ducks, striving to copulate with them, but he made no distinction between male and female geese (p. 264).

To this process of becoming affectionally and sexually attached to the early source of nourishment, Lorenz gives the name of "imprinting," concerning which he says:

> . . . it is a purely conceptual dispute whether imprinting is to be regarded as a special sort of learning, or as something different. The decision of this question depends entirely upon the content we see fit to assign to the conception of "learning." Imprinting is a process with a very limited scope, representing an acquiring process occurring only in birds and determining but one object of certain social relations (p. 266).

In his assumption that "imprinting" (cf. Craig's word "impressed") occurs "only in birds" Lorenz is apparently mistaken. The author, as a boy, once captured a litter of very young skunks which he succeeded in rearing "by hand." When these little creatures were large enough to walk efficiently, they would line up in single file and follow their "foster mother" wherever he went. However the human being here involved regarded himself, it was perfectly evident that the young skunks were reacting to him precisely as they would have to their natural mother.

Despite his contention that imprinting occurs only in birds, Lorenz makes an implicit admission to the contrary when he says:

> While being completely indifferent to any fellow-member of the species and most intensely and affectionately attached to its keeper as long as it stays on the ground or on the water, it [a man-reared greylag goose] will suddenly and surprisingly cease to respond to the human in any way whatever at the moment it takes to wing in pursuit of another Greylag. My Greylags used to follow me on my swimming tours in the Danube *as a dog would* . . . (italics added p. 271).

That dogs, no less than birds and skunks, are capable of forming very close attachments to human beings—sometimes to the virtual exclusion of any interest, sexual or otherwise, in other members of their species [36]—is dramatically indicated by the following report, for which I am indebted to Hector Chevigny:

> I was also deeply interested in your remarks about the apparent disorientation in the sexual cycle of your birds [see Section II]. This, I think you'll find, is common experience with creatures showing a tropic inclination to proximity with man. My own ["Seeing Eye"] dog is all but altogether indifferent to females, even under conditions which would cause most males considerable anguish. My gag about it is that he has taken holy orders. Occasionally he has shown what seems to be clearly homosexual interest in younger male dogs, but this does not seem to be his constant drive in this realm.[37]

Anent Lorenz's assumption that imprinting occurs only in birds is the remark by Chevigny that "it may interest you to know that at Seeing Eye [Morristown, New Jersey] the belief is rather fixed that this proximity tropism [in dogs], if I may call it that, is unique in its field of work with animals."

Although I am not aware of its having been pointed out previously, it would seem that in the foregoing accounts we have rather striking confirmation of the psychoanalytic tenet that early oral (and other?) gratifications in human beings exercise a powerful

---

[36] It is likewise a common observation of the staff at the Yerkes Laboratories of Primate Biology that chimpanzees which have been exclusively cared for by human foster parents show extreme social and sexual aberrations when introduced to ordinary life in the laboratory colony. For an account of a "neurosis" in such an animal and of its possible clinical meaning, see Hebb (1947) and Mowrer (1947).

[I am indebted to Mrs. F. J. Corsairt for the following observations: "We have two pure-bred Togenberg milk goats which we have had for four years. They were bred twice but their kids did not do well because it was obvious that the mothers resented them, fighting with them over our favors. With one of the goats, there was rejection of the kid whenever my husband or I went out to pet the goats. Now, for two years neither goat will breed. They just avoid the buck, play tricks on him, etc. They are still heavy milkers, but give milk only if *we* milk them." And Miller (not yet published) describes a similar phenomenon in sheep: "Scott (1945) has observed that adult sheep generally seem to follow their mothers in the flock. When he fed two orphan lambs from bottles, he found that afterwards they did not show nearly as much gregariousness as was characteristic of the other sheep. The flock would be grazing in a tightly knit group while the sheep that had been bottle-fed would graze by itself. Furthermore the bottle-fed sheep seemed to show much more tendency than others to follow people around. It seems likely that this suggestive observation will open up a fruitful line of experimental analysis."]

[37] The following comments by Mrs. Nice (1943) are interesting in this connection: "It is well known that under conditions of captivity homosexual unions are formed by many birds. . . . Homosexual pairs often occur in captivity among pigeons, anatidae, and parrots; they have been reported in Emus, Griffon Vultures, other birds in zoos. . . . Homesexual pairs seem to be very rare in the wild" (pp. 194–95).

influence in determining both personal and sexual orientation in later life. But the observations just reported raise an interesting question: Why is it that of the wide variety of species in which "imprinting" can evidently occur, it is only in the human infant and certain species of birds that it can result in the reproduction of human speech?

In the work previously referred to, Langer has attempted to answer this question as follows:

> [The ape] is conceptually not very far from the supreme human achievement, yet never crosses the line. What has placed this absolute barrier between his race and ours?
>
> Chiefly, I think, one difference of natural proclivities. The ape has no instinctive desire to babble in babyhood. . . . Man, though undoubtedly a simian, must trace his descent from a vocalizing race—a genus of ape, perhaps, in which the rudiments of symbolic conception, that apparently are dawning in the chimpanzee, were coupled with an instinctive tendency to produce sounds [and] play with the vocal apparatus (1948, pp. 94-95).

Furness (1916) is probably nearer the truth when he attempts to explain this difference, not on the basis of an "instinctive tendency to produce sounds," but on the basis of differences in specialized brain capacities. "It seems well-nigh incredible," he remarks, "that in animals otherwise so close to us physically there should not be a rudimentary speech-center in the brain which only needed developing" (p. 281). Why certain species of birds, far less closely related to man than are the other anthropoids and indeed even mammals in general, should be "almost human" in their ability to reproduce speech is a puzzling question. It is common lore among bird-fancies that parrots and parakeets have larger brains in relation to body weight than does any other avian species. Whether this is an accurate statement I have been as yet unable to determine; but even if it is, the problem is not necessarily solved, for birds such as the hill mynah, which appear to have relatively small brains, also learn to talk fluently. A careful neurological study of the brains of talking and nontalking birds, in relation to those of mammals (including man), might disclose some illuminating facts.

Although the review made in the foregoing pages clearly indicates that "imprinting" is a relatively widespread phenomenon in the animal kingdom, there are some striking negative instances. Indeed, a moment's reflection will show that in birds which nest parasitically, imprinting must necessarily *not* occur if the species is to be perpetuated. On this score Mrs. Nice makes these comments:

> As pointed out by Cushing (1941), with some birds the recognition of mates must be an inherited matter—witness Cowbirds and parasitic Cookoos. With others, however, the mating preference is acquired apparently at a very early age—Pigeons, Ducks, Raven, Shell Parakeet, etc. Social birds, when hand-raised, are very apt to transfer their reactions to man. Some of Lorenz's Jackdaws treated him as their wife, others as their husband (p. 192).

And to these remarks Lorenz himself adds:

> With very many species it is practically impossible to direct experimentally social reactions of the young to any but the normal object, because their innate perceptory patterns are so highly differentiated as to prevent the successful "faking" of the corresponding sets of stimuli. This is the case with most birds of the Limicolae. Especially Curlews (*Numenius arcuatus*), even when hatched artificially and never having seen any living creature but their keeper, cannot be brought to respond to him with any reactions but those of escape (p. 267).

Mockingbirds offer the "mirror image" of this problem: although reared by members of their own species, they still show a tendency to identify with other species at least to the extent of reproducing their songs. It is commonly believed that parrots and other birds that learn, under domestication, to repeat human speech never do so in a state of nature, that is to say, when reared by their natural parents and never subsequently fed by human beings. Nor am I aware of it if they are given in the wild to "mocking" other birds. Just why this remarkable tendency has evolved, just what its survival value might have been in mockingbirds is a problem which, on the authority of Dr. Craig, has not received much scientific attention. (See, however, his discussion of the evolution of bird song in general, Craig, 1943.)

The question as to whether bird's songs, in a state of nature, are characteristically inherited or learned has been subjected to much investigation but with ambiguous results. These findings have recently been reviewed by Mrs. Nice (1943, pp. 139–50) and by Craig (1943, pp. 141–43; cf. also his remarks on "responsive singing," pp. 140–41); and although the findings indicate that learning often plays a role in the perfection or variation of a song, yet the basic pattern seems to be genetically fixed. A priori it could hardly be otherwise, for to suppose that bird songs were entirely learned would be to credit birds with "culture." In her monograph, Mrs. Nice has a section entitled, "Primitive Culture in

Birds and Animals," but she does not venture to conclude that songs are in any very important way "cultural." [38]

Metfessel (1940) has shown that canaries do at least to some extent acquire their songs by learning, and Craig (in a personal communication) has called attention to the practice of German canary-breeders of "teaching" their young singers by means of *eine Kanarienorgel.* This instrument, operated automatically by means of compressed air, ordinarily has five pipes, each of which can be made to produce a distinctive "song" which the young canary is supposed to learn to reproduce. It is also noteworthy that an American concern is now producing phonograph records which are designed to facilitate the speech of talking birds. However, these records are recommended merely as a supplement to the regular, personalized training. "Once your Budgie can talk he'll pick up new words that you want him to know much faster," say the makers of these records; but they do not claim that the records alone will suffice. The author has in mind a number of experiments in which systematic comparison will be made of the ease with which birds learn recorded speech as opposed to direct human speech.

The age at which birds can be taught to talk, and at which "imprinting" in general may occur, is another large problem which can be touched on but briefly here. Most parakeet trainers insist that the young "Budgie" must be brought into exclusive contact with human beings at a very early age (as soon as it spontaneously leaves the nest) if it is readily to be taught to talk; and our own experiences bear this out. However, it is evident that the age factor, while probably still important, is not so crucial in some of the larger talking birds, notably the parrots. As indicated earlier (Sec-

---

[38] Although all birds (save a few mute forms) have their native cries and songs, it is interesting how, in talking birds, these get replaced by the acquired human sounds. I am indebted to Bernard F. Riess for the report that a crow which has lived for many years at the Bronx Zoo has long since given up his natural cawing in favor of a more urbane "Hello" and "Oh, Boy!" Lorenz (p. 72) reports a comparable instance of a learned utterance taking the place of an instinctive one. And the writer has noted with both his mynah bird and gray parrot how the "wild" noises which they originally made have gradually given way to words and learned whistles. Closely related to this phenomenon is the whole question of the *function* of birds' songs and cries in nature. Mrs. Nice summarizes present knowledge of the function of bird song as follows: "Song is one of the most important signals between members of the species. In most 'song birds' the male's role is primarily defense of his family; he sings tirelessly to assure himself of territory and a mate and to defend both. Song has been highly developed here as a weapon, as a symbol of ownership to warn other males and attract females. It may also function in courtship and in sustaining the bond between the mated pair" (p. 149). It is perhaps not surprising that under the highly abnormal conditions of human socialization, vocalization, now serving very different functions, may also take on new forms. One may also conjecture that the natural functions of bird song, whatever they are, must be highly important if they are to offset the hazards to which frequent vocalization might be expected to lead [cf. Mowrer, Palma, and Sanger, 1948].

tion II), one reason, though perhaps not the only reason, why young birds learn more quickly from human beings is that they are still somewhat helpless and therefore more readily become dependent than do older birds. If, however, by the measures earlier referred to one can produce, at a later stage, an "artificial regression," it is possible to reproduce, in a degree at least, the same psychological condition existing in the younger bird.

The following passage from Craig's (1908) account of his experiments with the ringdoves indicates how this can be done:

> Since the bird was uncomfortably shy and afraid of human beings, I began about the last of April to starve him mildly and compel him to feed from the hand. He quickly learned to take his seed in this way, and he always jumped on the hand—but not in a friendly manner, often with a few sharp pecks or a blow of the wing. But on May 11th, after jumping on the hand as usual, he gave the sexual reaction of the male (p. 129). [This bird was hatched the preceding July.]

It would thus appear that the following passage from Lorenz is open to reinterpretation:

> These few observational examples are sufficient to illustrate in a general way the peculiarities of the acquiring process in question, but I wish to call the reader's attention more especially to the points in which this process differs from what we call associative learning. (1) The process is confined to a very definite period of individual life, a period which in many cases is of extremely short duration; the period during which the young partridge gets its reactions of following the parent birds conditioned to their object lasts literally but a few hours, beginning when the chick is drying off and ending before it is able to stand. (2) The process, once accomplished, is totally irreversible, so that from then on, the reaction behaves exactly like an "unconditioned" or purely instinctive response. This absolute rigidity is something we never find in behavior acquired by associative learning, which can be unlearned or changed, at least to a certain extent (1937, p. 264).

The following extended passage is reproduced from the communciation from Chevigny already mentioned. He says:

> Several of the points you made in connection with your remarks about your work with the birds . . . have a remarkable correspondence with experience in training dogs for blind-guiding work. In particular I was interested in your notion that the birds seem to pass from the food-reward level to another, namely, the inducement of proximity to the master itself, during their training. For many reasons I believe you have made an entirely accurate observation here, . . .
>
> Your New Haven guide-dog user is mistaken when he says the training of the dog does not begin on the food-conditioning level. The school at

Morristown does not try to teach much dog-training theory to the students, so this is not surprising [that I had been told that food rewards did not enter into the training procedure]. The dogs receive about three months' training, after which they are paired off with a class of students to spend another month of training. The same trainer who had been working with the dogs during the three months' period also takes on the students, and an important element in the students' experience is *the job of winning the dog he has been assigned away from the trainer.* The student must feed the dog himself or the thing is a failure from the beginning. The school's injunction is strict to keep on feeding the dog in person for some time after taking him from the school [italics added].

Varying, I suppose, with the personality of the dog, the time comes when the question of who feeds him is no longer of the slightest consideration with the animal. His entire motivation seems to be to be with the master at all times. I have a male boxer, aged six. I've had him four years. During the past three years I have not fed him fifty times; my wife or children do that chore, and also often take him out for night or morning curbing. Indeed, apparently all the rules usually considered to be necessary to keeping an animal's regard may be broken in his case, but one: he cannot be abandoned for any length of time. There is little doubt about his preferences. He would rather be with me, lying under conference tables in cramped positions, at offices, under bar stools, so long as he does not have to remain behind at home. His resentment at being left is unmistakable. He lets me know about it when I come home, by showing his anger. There is little doubt that he interprets being left behind as a punishment for nonperformance of some duty. After an evening when, for various reasons, I've had to leave him at home he throws himself into his job with much display of ability.

Occasionally students at Seeing Eye and the dogs assigned to them fail to bring a union off, in which case the student fails, doesn't go home with an animal. In every case of this, I've been told, it has been due to a personal disinclination on the part of the would-be master to show the animal that he will give him the proximity he craves.

First through the food-conditioning, and then through the rewards of proximity—exactly as you've noted with your birds—the animal is induced to do what the master wants." [39]

The reader may sense an ambiguity in the foregoing: How is it that one *ever* succeeds in getting a dog to transfer his affection and loyalty if, after a preliminary period, the matter of feeding becomes unimportant? In other words, Chevigny says that the dog still prefers him even though other members of the family now do the feeding; yet he was able to win the dog away from the original trainer by means of feeding. The answer to this apparent riddle is contained in Chevigny's own remarks when he says that the only

---

[39] The reader will also find most interesting the two works by Chevigny which are listed in the bibliography (1946, 1947).

thing he must not now do, if he wishes to keep his dog's affection, is to "abandon" him. Presumably this is what the trainers at the "Seeing Eye do, at least partially, when they want to effect a "transference" to the new master. One may also conjecture that if a dog were "mildly starved," to use Craig's term, the question of feeding might take on more importance than it appears to have in a well-fed animal.

After reporting some highly suggestive observations concerning the methods of training the guide dogs for the blind and lead dogs for dog teams, Chevigny offers these speculations concerning the precise nature of the gratification which a dog derives from close association with a human master:

> For a time I thought that the smell of man was the answer. The dog's sense of smell is keen beyond human comprehension, and is part of his sexual equipment. The cat, too, it seemed to me, was attracted by the smell of men. But what you had to say about your birds throws this idea for me. I wonder now if stroking may not be the source of special pleasure. It would seem a fair assumption that, whatever it is, it would have to be something the creature would not find in Nature. . . . Do you stroke your birds as part of your attempts to train them?

This is a very discerning inquiry, for it is well known among the keepers of parrots and parakeets that they love nothing better than to have their "necks scratched." I have not been able to achieve sufficient intimacy with my Mexican parrot for him to submit to this treatment, but the African gray parrot actively courts it, in fact, would almost any time rather be played with in this manner than eat. And Craig reports a similar proclivity in the ringdove: "The hand could *stroke him, preen his neck,* even pull the feathers sharply; Jack had absolutely no fear, but ran to the hand to be stroked or teased, showing the joy that all doves show in *the attentions of their companions*" (1914, p. 122, italics added). Thus it would appear that the force that holds beast to man in relations of this kind is something which one indeed finds "in Nature," but which the isolated, "domesticated" animal is able to find only in his human relationships.

From the foregoing and other sources which have been cited, one can only conclude that when a parrot, a dog, or any other animal becomes a "pet," it becomes, to its own way of thinking, a human being. It is, in other words, *identified* with this foster species rather than with its own, and human rejection has all the threat that is involved when a normally socialized individual is "banished." A bird's learning to talk, therefore, is merely a part of a much larger process of becoming like human beings and is unique to birds because they alone possess the special neurological equipment needed for the requisite articulation of sounds.

Finally, in concluding this report I wish to quote a few sentences from a letter from Percival M. Symonds. He says:

> There is no doubt that your dynamic theory of the origin of spoken language has considerable merit. It fits in well with dynamic theory in general. However, I wonder if you shouldn't push it back a step or two. As I understand your theory, it is that the infant's first language sounds come at a period of frustration and are the infant's attempts to recapture, in this somewhat symbolic fashion at least, satisfactions or reactions that were coincident with previous satisfactions. The sounds are in the nature of a conditioned reaction in the frustrating situation. Isn't it necessary, however, to introduce the further factor that in the frustrating state the infant is afraid of loss or separation and the sounds are an attempt to recapture, at lease symbolically, the presence of the mother who is the source of the satisfaction? [40] This sort of dynamic explanation as an attempt to avoid anxiety has been used to explain other similar phenomena.

This communication from Professor Symonds was based upon the material contained in Section II of this paper. It is hoped that when this material is viewed in conjunction with Sections I and III it will be evident that the writer is in full accord with Dr. Symonds' suggestions. We may appropriately recall—and thus summarize the central argument of the present paper—Langer's trenchant remark that human infants (and birds?) first use words to bring something *into their minds* rather than into their hands. And we may surmise, again with Mrs. Langer, that this way of thinking about the beginnings of the symbolic process holds a number of unexplored possibilities for illuminating the many "mysteries of language."

---

[40] Perhaps the most exact way of formulating this notion is as follows. The bird (baby) discovers that when it is alone it may get hungry, thirsty, cold, hurt. On the other hand, when the trainer is present, these discomforts vanish. Therefore the presence of the trainer is an important stimulus element in the total situation, serving to convert it from situation-in-which-I-may-be-uncomfortable (helpless) to situation-in-which-everything-will-be-all-right. In this way the bird will be rewarded by the appearance of the trainer and disturbed by his departure, even though none of the primary drives mentioned is actually operative at the moment. It is fully understandable that, when alone, the bird should try to reduce its apprehensions by reproducing the trainer symbolically, i.e., by making his noises (in somewhat the same manner, perhaps, as human beings are said to "whistle in the dark"). As we have seen, creatures which are less talented vocally must use something more tangible for this purpose, e.g., the coveralls on which little Gua became so dependent. Cf. Lair's (1949) remarks concerning the "hallucination wish mechanism used by the child in the first half of the first year to bring back or recall the nurse who had sole charge of her and was a substitute mother" (p. 255). (See 21.)

BIBLIOGRAPHY

ACKERSON, L. 1931. *Children's behavior problems.* Chicago: University of Chicago Press.

ADAMS, D. K. 1931. A restatement of the problem of learning. *Brit. J. Psychol.,* 22, 150–78.

ADDIS, R. S. 1935. A statistical study of nocturnal enuresis. *Arch. of Disease in Children,* **10**, 169–78.

ADRIAN, E. D., and MATTHEWS, B. H. C. 1934. The Berger rhythm: potential changes from the occipital lobes of man. *Brain,* **57**, 355–84.

AICHHORN, A. 1935. *Wayward youth.* New York: The Viking Press, Inc.

ALEXANDER, F., and FRENCH, T. M. 1946. *Psychoanalytic therapy: principles and application.* New York. The Ronald Press Co.

ALLPORT, F. H. 1924. *Social psychology.* Boston: Houghton Mifflin Co.

ALLPORT, G. W. 1937. *Personality: a psychological interpretation.* New York: Henry Holt & Co., Inc.

———. 1940. Motivation in personality: reply to Mr. Bertocci. *Psychol. Rev.,* **47**, 533–54.

———. 1943. The ego in contemporary psychology. *Psychol. Rev.,* **50**, 451–78.

———. 1946. Effect: a secondary principle of learning. *Psychol. Rev.,* **53**, 335–47.

———. 1947. Animal models and human morals. *Psychol. Rev.,* **54**, 182–92.

ANDERSON, A. C. 1932. Time discrimination in the white rat. *J. comp. Psychol.,* **13**, 27–55.

ANDERSON, F. N. 1930. The psychiatric aspects of enuresis. *Amer. J. Pediatrics,* **40**, 591–618 and 818–50.

ANDERSON, CAMILLA M. 1949. Unpublished MS.

ANDERSON, O. D., and LIDDELL, H. S. 1935. Observations on experimental neurosis in sheep. *Arch. Neurol. Psychiat.,* Chicago, **34**, 330–54.

ANDERSON, O. D., and PARMENTER, R. 1941. A long-term study of the experimental neurosis in the sheep and dog, with nine case histories. *Psychosom. Med. Monogr.,* **2**: 3 and 4.

ANGEL, A. 1935. From the analysis of a bedwetter. *Psychoanal. Quart.,* **4**: 1, 120–34.

ANGYAL, A. 1941. *Foundations for a science of personality.* New York: The Commonwealth Fund, Division of Publications.

BACH, G. R. 1946. Father-fantasies and father-typing in father-separated children. *Child Development,* **17**, 63–80.

BAGCHI, B. K. 1937. The adaptation and variability of response of the human brain rhythm. *J. Psychol.,* **3**, 463–85.

BAKES, F. P. 1939. Effect of response to auditory stimulation on the latent time of blocking of the Berger rhythm. *J. exp. Psychol.,* **24**, 406–18.

BARETZ, L. H. 1936. A new treatment for enuresis in the male. *Urologic and cutaneous Rev.,* **40**: 321–22.

BARKER, R., DEMBO, T., and LEWIN, K. 1937. Experiments on frustration and regression in children. *Psychol. Bull.,* **34**, 754–55.

BASLER, R. P. 1948. *Sex, symbolism, and psychology in literature.* New Brunswick, N. J.: Rutgers University Press.

BATESON, G. 1942. Social planning and the concept of "deutero-learning." In T. M. Newcomb and E. L. Hartley (eds.), *Readings in social psychology.* New York: Henry Holt & Co., Inc., 1947.

BECHSTEIN, J. M. 1871. *Cage and chamber birds.* Revised and partly rewritten by George B. Barnesby. London: Robert Hardwicke.

BENTHAM, J. 1780. *Principles of morals and legislation.* Oxford: Clarendon Press.

———. 1934. *Deontology* (Part I, *Theory of virtue*), ed. John Bowreng. London: Longmans, Green & Co., Ltd.

BERGLER, E. 1946. *Unhappy marriage and divorce.* New York: Intern. Universities Press.

BERNARD, L. L. 1926. *Introduction to social psychology.* New York: Henry Holt & Co., Inc.

BEVERLY, B. I. 1933. Incontinence in children. *J. Pediatrics,* St. Louis, **2:** 6, 718.

BIBRING, E. 1937. Therapeutic results of psychoanalysis. *Intl. J. of Psychoa.,* **18,** 170–90.

BIRCH, H. G., and BITTERMAN, M. E. 1949. Reinforcement and learning: the process of sensory integration. *Psychol. Rev.,* **56,** 292–308.

BLANCO, I. M. 1941. On introjection and the process of psychic metabolism. *Int. J. Psycho-Anal.,* **22,** 17–36.

BLOODFIELD, L. 1914. *An introduction to the study of language.* New York: Henry Holt & Co., Inc.

BODER, D. P. 1949. *I did not interview the dead.* Urbana, Ill.: University of Illinois Press.

BONAPARTE, M. 1933. *Edgar Poe.* 2 vols. Paris: Denoël et Steele.

BONJOUR, J. 1931. Un moyen pour quérir l'incontinence d'urine nocturne. *Rev. med. de la Suisse Rom,* **51,** 82–83.

BORING, E. G. 1933. *The physical dimensions of consciousness.* New York: Appleton-Century-Crofts, Inc.

———. 1941. Statistical frequencies as dynamic equilibria. *Psychol. Rev.,* **48,** 279–301.

BOTT, E. A., BLATZ, W. E., CHANT, N., and BOTT, H. 1928. Observation and training of fundamental habits in young children. *Genet. Psychol. Monogr.,* **4:** 1, 1–161.

BREITWIESER, J. V. 1911. Attention and movement in reaction time. *Arch. Psychol., N. Y.,* **2,** 1–49.

BRODBECH, A. J., and IRWIN, O. C. 1946. The speech behavior of infants. *Child Devel.,* **17,** 145–56.

BROGDEN, W. J. 1939a. The effect of frequency of reinforcement upon the level of conditioning. *J. exp. Psychol.,* **24,** 419–31.

———. 1939b. Unconditioned stimulus-substitution in the conditioning process. *Amer. J. Psychol.,* **52,** 46–55.

———. 1940a. Conditioned flexion responses in dogs re-established and maintained with change of locus in the application of the unconditioned stimulus. *J. exp. Psychol.,* **27,** 583–600.

———. 1940b. Retention of conditioned responses tested by experimental extinction. *Amer. J. Psychol.,* **53,** 285–88.

BROGDEN, W. J., and CULLER, E. 1936. Device for the motor conditioning of small animals. *Science,* **83,** 269–70.

BROGDEN, W. J., LIPMAN, E. A., and CULLER, E. 1938. The role of incentive in conditioning and learning. *Amer. J. Psychol.,* **51,** 109–17.

BRONSON, J. L., 1947. Talking hill mynahs. *All-Pets Magazine,* **18,** 17 ff.

BROWN, C. H. 1937. The relation of magnitude of galvanic skin responses and resistance levels to the rate of learning. *J. exp. Psychol.,* **20,** 262–78.

BROWN, J. F. 1940. *Psychodynamics of abnormal behavior.* New York: McGraw-Hill Book Co., Inc.

BROWN, J. F., and FEDER, D. D. 1934. Thorndike's theory of learning as Gestalt psychology. *Psychol. Bull.,* **31,** 426–37.

BROWN, J. S. 1939. A note on a temporal gradient of reinforcement. *J. exp. Psychol.,* **25,** 221–27.

Brunswik, E. 1939. Probability as a determiner of rat behavior. *J. exp. Psychol.*, **25**, 175–97.

Bugelski, R. 1938. Extinction with and without sub-goal reinforcement. *J. comp. Psychol.*, **26**, 121–34.

Burton, W. H. 1944. *The guidance of learning activities.* New York: Appleton-Century-Crofts, Inc.

Calvin, J. S. 1939. Decremental factors in conditioned response learning. Ph.D. dissertation, Yale University.

———. 1948. Learning of probable occurrences. *Amer. Psychol.*, **3**, 236. Abstract.

Cameron, H. C., *et al.* 1924. Discussion on enuresis. *Proc. Roy. Soc. Med.*, **17**, 27–40.

Cameron, N. 1938. Reasoning, regression and communication in schizophrenics. *Psychol. Monogr.*, **50**: 1.

Campbell, C. N. 1918. A case of childhood conflicts with prominent reference to the urinary system; with some general considerations on urinary symptoms in the psychoneuroses and psychoses. *Psychoanal. Rev.*, **5**, 269–90.

Campbell, K. 1933. *The mind of Poe and other studies.* Cambridge, Mass.: Harvard University Press.

Cannon, W. B. 1927. The James-Lange theory of emotions: a critical examination and an alternative theory. *Amer. J. Psychol.*, **39**, 106–24.

———. 1932. *The wisdom of the body.* New York: W. W. Norton & Co., Inc.

Chein, I. 1944. The awareness of self and the structure of the ego. *Psychol. Rev.*, **51**, 204–14.

Chevigny, H. 1946. *My eyes have a cold nose.* New Haven, Conn.: Yale University Press.

———. 1947. Personality problems in the guide dog relation. *Outlook for the Blind*, **41**, 91–96.

Cole, L. E. 1939. A comparison of the factors of practice and knowledge of experimental procedure in conditioning the eyelid response of human subjects. *J. gen. Psychol.*, **20**, 349–73.

Collins, T. F. 1922. *Arboreal life and the evolution of the human eye.* Philadelphia: Lea & Febiger.

Commins, W. D., McNemar, Q., and Stone, C. P. 1932. Intercorrelations of measures of ability in the rat. *J. comp. Psychol.*, **14**, 225–35.

Cook, S. W., and Harris, R. E. 1937. The verbal conditioning of the galvanic skin reflex. *J. exp. Psychol.*, **21**, 202–10.

Coppock, H. W., and Mowrer, O. H. 1947. Inter-trial responses as "rehearsal": a study of "overt thinking" in animals. *Amer. J. Psychol.*, **60**, 608–16.

Courtin, W. 1923. Relations between enuresis and sleep. *Arch. Kinderheilk.*, **74**, 40–50.

Courtney, P. D. 1949. Identification and learning: a theoretical analysis. Ph.D. dissertation, Harvard University.

Cowgill, D. O. 1948. Variant meanings of the terms conditioning and conditioned response. *J. soc. Psychol.*, **28**, 247–55.

Cowles, J. T., and Nissen, H. W. 1947. Reward-expectancy in delayed responses of chimpanzees. *J. comp. Psychol.*, **24**, 345–58.

Cowles, J. T., and Pennington, L. A. 1943. An improved conditioning technique for determining auditory acuity in the rat. *J. Psychol.*, **15**, 41–49.

Craig, W. 1908. The voices of pigeons regarded as a means of social control. *Amer. J. Sociol.*, **14**, 86–100.

———. 1914. Male doves reared in isolation. *J. Animal Behavior*, **4**, 121–33.

———. 1918. Appetites and aversions as constituents of instincts. *Biol. Bull.*, **34**, 91–107.

———. 1943. *The song of the wood peewee.* N. Y. St. Museum Bull. No. 334, 186.

CRUIKSHANK, R. M. 1937. Human occipital brain potentials as affected by intensity-duration variables of visual stimulation. *J. exp. Psychol.,* **21,** 625–41.

CRUTCHFIELD, R. S. 1939. The determiners of energy expenditure in string-pulling by the rat. *J. Psychol.,* **7,** 163–78.

CULLER, E. A. 1938. Recent advances in some concepts of conditioning. *Psychol. Rev.,* **45,** 134–53.

CULLER, E., FINCH, G., and GIRDEN, E. 1934. Apparatus for motor conditioning in cats. *Science,* **79,** 525–26.

CULLER, E., FINCH, G., GIRDEN, E., and BROGDEN, W. 1935. Measurements of acuity by the conditioned-response technique. *J. gen. Psychol.,* **12,** 223–27.

CUTSFORTH, M. G. 1930. A study of successive discriminations of brightness in chicks. Unpublished Ph.D. dissertation, University of Kansas.

DABROWSKI, C. 1937. Psychological basis of self-mutilation. *Genet. Psychol. Monogr.,* **19,** 1–104.

DARROW, C. W. 1935. Emotion as relative functional decortication: the role of conflict. *Psychol. Rev.,* **42,** 566–78.

———. 1938. The equation of the galvanic skin reflex curve. I. The dynamics of reaction in relation to excitation background. *J. gen. Psychol.,* **16,** 285–309.

DAVIDSON, J. R., and DOUGLASS, E. 1950. Nocturnal enuresis: a special approach to treatment. *British Medical Journal,* **1,** 1345–46.

DAVIDSON, W. C. 1924. Enuresis. *Abt's Pediatrics, Philadelphia,* **4,** 867–78.

DAVIS, A. 1941. American status systems and the socialization of the child. *Amer. sociol. Rev.,* **6,** 345–56.

DAVIS, A. W., and HAVIGHURST, R. J. 1947. *Father of the man.* Boston: Houghton Mifflin Co.

DAVIS, G. G. 1908. Gersuny's operation for the cure of enuresis. *Ann. Surg. Phila.,* **48,** 792–93.

DE LAGUNA, GRACE. 1927. *Speech: its function and development.* New Haven, Conn.: Yale University Press.

DENNIS, W. 1939. Spontaneous alternation in rats as indicator of persistence of stimulus effects. *J. comp. Psychol.,* **28,** 305–12.

DENNY, M. R. 1946. The role of secondary reinforcement in a partial reinforcement learning situation. *J. exp. Psychol.,* **36,** 363–89.

DEWEY, J. 1938. *Experience and education.* New York: The Macmillan Co.

DODGE, R. 1931. *Conditions and consequences of human variability.* New Haven, Conn.: Yale University Press.

DOLLARD, J. 1935a. *Criteria for the life history.* New Haven, Conn.: Yale University Press.

———. 1935b. Mental hygiene and a "scientific culture." *Int. J. Ethics,* **45,** 4.

———. 1943. *Fear in battle.* New Haven, Conn.: Institute of Human Relations.

DOLLARD, J. DOOB, L. W., MILLER, N. E., MOWRER, O. H., and SEARS, R. 1939. *Integrational possibilities of the frustration-aggression hypothesis for the social sciences.* New Haven: Yale Univ. Press.

DUNBAR, H. F. 1938. *Emotions and bodily changes: a survey of literature on psychosomatic interrelationships, 1910–1933.* New York: Columbia University Press.

DUNLAP, K. 1932. *Habits: their making and unmaking.* New York: Liveright Publishing Corp.

DUNLAP, K., GENTRY, E., and ZEIGLER, T. W. 1931. The behavior of white rats under food and electric shock stimulation. *J. comp. Psychol.,* **12,** 371:78.

DURUP, G., and FESSARD, A. 1936. L'électrencéphalogramme de l'homme. Donnees quantitatives sur l'arret provoqué par des stimuli visuels et auditifs. *C. R. Soc. Biol. Paris,* **122,** 756–58.

ELIOT, T. S. 1948. *From Poe to Valéry.* New York: Harcourt, Brace & Co., Inc.

ELLIOTT, M. H. 1934. The effect of hunger on variability of performance. *Amer. J. Psychol.,* **46,** 107–12.

ELLSON, D. G. 1939. A quantitative study of spontaneous recovery as a function of the interval following extinction. Ph.D. dissertation, Yale University.

ENGLISH, O. S., and PEARSON, G. H. J. 1937. *Common neuroses of children and adults.* New York: W. W. Norton & Co., Inc.

ERICKSON, E. H. 1940. Problems of infancy and early childhood. In G. M. Pierson (ed.), *Cyclopedia of medicine, surgery, and specialties.* Philadelphia: F. A. Davis Co.

———. 1943. Clinical studies in childhood play. Chapter 24. In *Child Behavior and Development,* Barker, Kounin, and Wright, eds. New York: McGraw-Hill Book Co.

ESTES, W. K. 1949. Generalization of secondary reinforcement from the primary drive. *J. comp. physiol. Psychol.,* **42,** 286–95.

ESTES, W. K., and SKINNER, B. F. 1941. Some quantitative properties of anxiety. *J. exp. Psychol.,* **29,** 390–400.

EVERALL, E. E. 1935. Perseveration in the rat. *J. comp. Psychol.,* **19,** 343–69.

EWING, I. R., and EWING, A. W. G. 1938. *The handicap of deafness.* London: Longmans, Green & Co., Ltd.

FARBER, I. E. 1948. Response fixation under anxiety and non-anxiety conditions. *J. exp. Psychol.,* **38:** 2, 111–31.

FENICHEL, O. 1934. *Outline of clinical psychoanalysis.* Albany: Psychoanalytic Quarterly Press.

———. 1945. *The psychoanalytic theory of neurosis.* New York: W. W. Norton & Co., Inc.

FERGUSON, L. W. 1941. The cultural genesis of masculinity-femininity. *Psychol. Bull.,* **38,** 584–85. Abstract.

FEYERABEND, C. 1943. The budgerigar or small parakeet as a talker. Fond du Lac, Wis.: *All-Pets Magazine* Publishing Co.

FINCH, G., and CULLER, E. 1935. Relation of forgetting to experimental extinction. *Amer. J. Psychol.,* **47,** 656–62.

FINGER, F. W. 1942a. The effect of varying conditions of reinforcement upon a simple running response. *J. exp. Psychol.,* **30,** 53–68.

———. 1942b. Retention and subsequent extinction of a simple running response following varying conditions of reinforcement. *J. exp. Psychol.,* **31,** 120–34.

FINNER, P. F. 1935. *An introduction to experimental psychology.* New York: Prentice-Hall, Inc.

FISHER, R. A. 1937. *The design of experiments.* London: Oliver & Boyd, Ltd.

———. 1938. *Statistical methods for research workers.* London: Oliver & Boyd, Ltd.

FITTS, P. M. 1940. Perseveration of non-rewarded behavior in relation to food-deprivation and work-requirement. *J. genet. Psychol.,* **57,** 167–91.

FLETCHER, F. M. 1939. Effects of quantitative variation of food-incentive on the performance of physical work of chimpanzees. Ph.D. dissertation, Yale University.

FORD, C. S. 1938. Unpublished notes on the Fiji Islanders.

———. 1939. Society, culture, and the human organism. *J. gen. Psychol.,* **20,** 135–79.

FORDYCE, A. D., *et al.* 1924. Discussion on enuresis. *Proc. Roy. Soc. Med.,* **17,** 37–40.

FRANK, L. K. 1939. Time perspectives. *J. soc. Philos.,* **4,** 293–312.

———. 1944. The adolescent and the family. *Yearb. nat. Soc. Stud. Educ.,* **43,** 240–54.

FREEMAN, G. L. 1939. Postural tensions and the conflict situation. *Psychol. Rev.,* **46,** 226–40.

FREEMAN, W., and WATTS, J. S. 1942. *Psychosurgery.* Springfield, Ill.: Charles C Thomas, Publisher.

FRENCH, T. M. 1933. Interrelations between psychoanalysis and the experimental work of Pavlov. *Amer. J. Psychiat.,* **89,** 1165–1203.

French, T. M. 1937. Reality testing in dreams. *Psychoanal. Quart.,* **6**, 62–77.

Freud, A. 1928. *The technique of child analysis.* New York: Nervous and Mental Disease Publishing Co.

———. 1931. Psychoanalysis of the child. In C. Murchison (ed.), *Handbook of child psychology.* Worcester, Mass.: Clark University Press.

———. 1935. *Psychoanalysis for teachers and parents.* Trans. B. Low. New York: Emerson Books, Inc.

———. 1937. *The ego and the mechanisms of defence.* London: The Hogarth Press, Ltd.

Freud, Anna, and Burlingham, Dorothy. 1944. *Infants without families.* New York: Medical War Books, International Universities Press, Inc.

Freud, S. 1894. The defence neuro-psychoses. In *Collected papers,* Vol. I, pp. 59–75. London: Hogarth Press, Ltd., 1924.

———. 1908a. Character and anal erotism. In *Collected papers,* Vol. II, pp. 45–50. London: Hogarth Press, Ltd., 1924.

———. 1908b. "Civilized" sexual morality and modern nervousness. In *Collected papers,* Vol. II, pp. 76–99. London: Hogarth Press, Ltd., 1924.

———. 1911. Formulations regarding the two principles in mental functioning. In *Collected papers,* Vol. IV, pp. 13–21. London: Hogarth Press, Ltd., 1925.

———. 1912. Types of neurotic nosogenesis. In *Collected papers,* Vol. II, pp. 113–21. London: Hogarth Press, Ltd., 1924.

———. 1915a. Some character-types met with in psycho-analytic work. In *Collected papers,* Vol. IV, pp. 318–46. London: Hogarth Press, Ltd., 1925.

———. 1915b. The unconscious. In *Collected papers,* Vol. IV, pp. 98–136. London: Hogarth Press, Ltd., 1925.

———. 1916a. Metapsychological supplement to the theory of dreams. In *Collected papers,* Vol. IV, pp. 137–51. London: Hogarth Press, Ltd., 1925.

———. 1916b. *Three contributions to the theory of sex.* New York: Nervous and Mental Disease Publishing Co.

———. 1917. Mourning and melancholia. In *Collected papers,* Vol. IV, pp. 152–70. London: Hogarth Press, Ltd., 1925.

———. 1918. *Totem and taboo.* New York: Moffat, Yard & Co.

———. 1920a. *A general introduction to psychoanalysis.* New York: Liveright Publishing Corp.

———. 1920b. *The interpretation of dreams.* New York: The Macmillan Co.

———. 1922a. *Beyond the pleasure principle.* New York: Boni & Liveright.

———. 1922b. *Group psychology and the analysis of the ego.* New York: Boni & Liveright.

———. 1923. A neurosis of demoniacal possession in the seventeenth century. In *Collected papers,* Vol. IV, pp. 436–72. London: Hogarth Press, Ltd., 1925.

———. 1924a. A reply to criticisms on the anxiety neurosis. In *Collected papers,* Vol. I, pp. 107–27. London: Hogarth Press, Ltd., 1924.

———. 1924b. The passing of the oedipus complex. In *Collected papers,* Vol. II, pp. 269–76. London: Hogarth Press, Ltd., 1924.

———. 1924c. The economic problem in masochism. In *Collected papers,* Vol. II, pp. 255–68. London: Hogarth Press, Ltd., 1924.

———. 1925. Mourning and melancholia. In *Collected papers,* Vol. IV, pp. 152–70. London: Hogarth Press, Ltd.

———. 1930. *Civilization and its discontents.* London: Hogarth Press, Ltd.

———. 1933. *New introductory lectures on psycho-analysis.* New York: W. W. Norton & Co., Inc.

———. 1935. *The ego and the id.* London: Hogarth Press, Ltd.

———. 1936. *The problem of anxiety.* New York: W. W. Norton & Co., Inc.

———. 1949. *An outline of psychoanalysis.* New York: W. W. Norton & Co., Inc.

Fromm-Reichmann, F. 1939. Transference problems in schizophrenics. *Psychoanal. Quart.,* **8**, 412–26.

Fuchs, A., and Gross, S. 1916. Incontinentia vesicae und Enuresis nocturna bei Soldaten. *Wiener klinische Wochenschrift,* **29,** 1483–86.

Fulton, J. F. 1943. *Physiology of the nervous system,* 2d ed. New York: Oxford University Press.

Furness, W. H. 1916. Observations on the mentality of chimpanzees and orang-utans. *Proc. Amer. phil. Soc.,* **55,** 281–90.

Gantt, W. H. 1944. Experimental basis for neurotic behavior. *Psychosom. Med. Monogr.,* **3,** 203.

Garrett, H. E. 1939. *Statistics in psychology and education.* New York: Longmans, Green & Co., Inc.

Gates, A. I. 1942. Connectionism: present concepts and interpretations. *Yearb. nat. Soc. Stud. Educ.,* **41,** (II), 141–164. Bloomington, Ill.: Public School Publishing Co.

Gengerelli, J. A. 1930. The principle of maxima and minima in animal learning. *J. comp. Psychol.,* **11,** 193–236.

Genouville. 1908. Incontinence d'urine. *L'association Française d'urologie.* Paris, **12,** 97–107.

Girden, E. 1938. Conditioning and problem-solving behavior. *Amer. J. Psychol.,* **51,** 677–86.

———. 1943. Role of the response mechanism in learning and in "excited emotion." *Amer. J. Psychol.,* **56,** 1–21.

Girden, E., and Culler, E. 1937. Conditioned responses in curarized striate muscle in dogs. *J. comp. Psychol.,* **23,** 261–74.

Glaser, J., and Landau, D. B. 1936. A simple mechanical method for the treatment of enuresis in male children. *J. Pediatrics,* **8,** 197–99.

Goldman, M. R. 1934–35. Treatment of enuresis: past and present. *Penn. Med. J.,* **38,** 247–51.

Goldstein, K. 1939. *The organism.* New York: American Book Co.

Grant, D. A. 1939. The influence of attitude on the conditioned eyelid response. *J. exp. Psychol.,* **25,** 333–46.

Grant, D. A., Riopelle, A. J., and Hake, H. W. 1950. Resistance to extinction and the pattern of reinforcement. I. Alternation of reinforcement and the conditioned eyelid response. *J. exp. Psychol.,* **40,** 53–60.

Greene, W. T. 1884. *Parrots in captivity.* London: George Bell & Sons, Ltd.

Grether, W. F. 1938. Pseudo-conditioning without paired stimulation encountered in attempted backward conditioning. *J. comp. Psychol.,* **25,** 91–96.

Guthrie, E. R. 1935. *The psychology of learning.* New York: Harper & Bros.

———. 1940. Association and the law of effect. *Psychol. Rev.,* **47,** 127–48.

———. 1946. Recency or effect: a reply to Captain O'Connor. *Harv. educ. Rev.,* **16:** 4, 286–89.

Guthrie, E. R., and Horton, G. P. 1937. A study of the cat in the puzzle-box. *Psychol. Bull.,* **34,** 774.

Gwinn, G. T. 1949. The effects of punishment on acts motivated by fear. *J. exp. Psychol.,* **39,** 260–69.

Haire, M. 1939. A note concerning McCulloch's discussion of discrimination habits. *Psychol. Rev.,* **46,** 298–303.

Hale, G. C. 1914. A case of peresistent enuresis: *Canadian med. Ass. J. Toronto,* **4,** 413–17.

Hall, C. S. 1936. Emotional behavior in the rat. IV. The relationship between emotionality and stereotyping of behavior. *J. comp. Psychol.,* **24,** 369–75.

Hamel, I. A. 1919. A study and analysis of the conditioned reflex. *Psychol. Monogr.,* **27:** 118.

Hamill, R. C. 1929. Enuresis. *J. Amer. med. Ass.,* **93** (I), 254–57.

Hamilton, D. M. 1939. Some aspects of homosexuality in relation to total personality development. *Psychiat. Quart.,* **13,** 229–44.

HAMILTON, G. V. 1916. A study of perseverance reactions in primates and rodents. *Behav. Monogr.*, **3**: 2.

HAMILTON, J., and ELLIS, W. D. 1933. Behavior constancy in rats. *J. genet. Psychol.*, **42**, 120–39.

HAMILTON, J. A., and KRECHEVSKY, I. 1933. Studies in the effect of shock upon behavior plasticity in the rat. *J. comp. Psychol.*, **16**, 237–53.

HANNAY, J. 1853. *Edgar Allan Poe.* London: Addey and Co.

HARLOW, H. F. 1949. The formation of learning sets. *Psychol. Rev.*, **56**, 51–65.

HARRIS, J. D. 1941. An analysis of certain nonassociative factors inherent in avoidance conditioning in the rat. *Psychol. Bull.*, **38**, 572.

———. 1944. *Recent developments in conditioning.* New London, Conn.: Medical Research Dept., U. S. Submarine Base.

HARRISON, J. A. (ed.). 1902. *The complete works of Edgar Allan Poe..* **2** vols. New York: The Thomas Y. Crowell Co.

HARTMANN, G. W. 1935. *Gestalt psychology.* New York: The Ronald Press Co.

———. 1941. *Educational psychology.* New York: American Book Co.

HATHAWAY, S. R. 1935. An action-potential study of neuromuscular relations. *J. exp. Psychol.*, **18**, 285–98.

HEATHERS, G. L. 1940. The avoidance of repetition of a maze reaction in the rat as a function of the time interval between trials. *J. Psychol.*, **10**, 359–80.

HEBB, D. O. 1947. Spontaneous neurosis in chimpanzees. *Psychosom. Med.*, **9**, 3–16.

HEIDBREDER, E. 1945. Toward a dynamic psychology of cognition. *Psychol. Rev.*, **52**, 1–22.

HELSON, H. 1942. Multiple-variable analysis of factors affecting lightness and saturation. *Amer. J. Psychol.*, **55**, 46–57.

HENDRICK, I. 1939. *Facts and theories of psychoanalysis.* New York: Alfred A. Knopf., Inc.

HENRY, G. W. 1934. Psychogenic and constitutional factors in homosexuality. *Psychiat. Quart.*, **8**, 243–64.

HERNAMAN-JOHNSON, F. 1921. The treatment of urinary incontinence by electrical methods. *The Lancet,* **200**, 1295–96.

HERON, W. T. 1942. Complex learning process. In F. A. Moss (ed.), *Comparative psychology.* New York: Prentice-Hall, Inc.

HEWER, E. E. 1927. The development of muscle in the human foetus. *J. Anat.*, **62**, 72–78.

HEYER, A. W., JR. 1950. Need establishment and reduction in learning and retention. Ph.D. dissertation, University of Illinois.

HILGARD, E. R. 1937. The relationship between the conditioned response and conventional learning experiments. *Psychol. Bull.*, **34**, 61–102

———. 1948. *Theories of learning.* New York: Appleton-Century-Crofts, Inc.

HILGARD, E. R., and BIEL, W. C. 1937. Reflex sensitization and conditioning of eyelid responses at intervals near simultaneity. *J. gen. Psychol.*, **16**, 223–34.

HILGARD, E. R., and MARQUIS, D. G. 1940. *Conditioning and learning.* New York: Appleton-Century-Crofts, Inc.

HOFFER, W. 1945. Psychoanalytic education. *Psychoanal. Stud. the Child,* **1**, 293–307.

HOFFMAN, R. L. 1919. Bladder stutterers. *Military Surgeon,* **45**, 107–9.

HOLLINGWORTH, H. L. 1928. General laws of redintegration. *J. gen. Psychol.*, **1**, 79–90.

———. 1949. *Psychology and ethics,* New York: The Ronald Press Co.

HOLT, E. B. 1931. *Animal drive and the learning process.* New York: Henry Holt & Co., Inc.

HOPKINS, L. T. 1937. *Integration—its meaning and application.* New York: Appleton-Century-Crofts, Inc.

HORNEY, K. 1937. *The neurotic personality of our time.* New York: W. W Norton & Co., Inc.

HOVLAND, C. I. 1936. "Inhibition of reinforcement" and phenomena of experimental extinction. *Proc. nat. Acad. Sci., Wash.,* **22,** 430–33.

HOVLAND, C. I., and SEARS, R. R. 1938. Experiments on motor conflict. I Types of conflict and their modes of resolution. *J. Exp. Psychol.,* **23,** 477–93.

HOWARD, H. 1935. Action potentials from the intact human brain in visual and auditory stimulation. Unpublished master's thesis, Brown University

HOWELLS, T. H. 1940. *Hunger for wholiness.* Denver: World Press, Inc.

HUDSON, W. H. 1931. *Green mansions.* New York: Three Sirens Press.

HULL, C. L. 1929. A functional interpretation of the conditioned reflex. *Psychol. Rev.,* **36,** 498–511.

———. 1930. Knowledge and purpose as habit mechanisms. *Psychol. Rev.,* **37,** 511–25.

———. 1931. Goal attraction and directing ideas conceived as habit phenomena. *Psychol. Rev.,* **38,** 487–506.

———. 1932. The goal gradient hypothesis and maze learning. *Psychol. Rev.,* **39,** 25–43.

———. 1934a. Learning. II. The factor of the conditioned reflex. In C. Murchison (ed.), *Handbook of general experimental psychology.* Worcester: Clark University Press.

———. 1934b. The concept of the habit-family hierarchy and maze learning. *Psychol. Rev.,* **41,** 33–54, 134–52.

———. 1937. Mind, mechanism, and adaptive behavior. *Psychol. Rev.,* **44,** 1–32.

———. 1938. The excitatory-potential hypothesis and behavior theory. Unpublished MS. on file at Yale University, Institute of Human Relations.

———. 1941. Psychology seminar memoranda. Bound mimeographed copies on file in the University of Iowa, University of North Carolina, and Yale University libraries.

———. 1942. Conditioning: outline of a systematic theory of learning. *Yearb. nat. Soc. Stud. Educ.,* **41** (II), 61–95. Bloomington, Ill.: Public School Publishing Co.

———. 1943. *Principles of behavior.* New York: Appleton-Century-Crofts, Inc.

———. Oct., Nov., 1949. Memorandum on behavior theory. Mimeographed. New Haven, Conn.

HUMPHREYS, L. G. 1939a. Acquisition and extinction of verbal expectations in a situation analogous to conditioning. *J. exp. Psychol.,* **25,** 294–301

———. 1939b. The effect of random alternation of reinforcement on the acquisition and extinction of conditioned eyelid responses. *J. exp. Psychol.,* **25,** 141–58.

———. 1940a. Extinction of conditioned psychogalvanic responses following two conditions of reinforcement. *J. exp. Psychol.,* **27,** 71–76.

———. 1940b. The strength of a Thorndikian response as a function of the number of practice trials. *Psychol. Bull.,* **37,** 571.

———. 1943. The strength of a Thorndikian response as a function of the number of practice trials. *J. comp. Psychol.,* **35,** 101–10.

———. 1948. The generalization of verbal expectations following two conditions of reinforcement. *Amer. Psychol.,* **3,** 347. Abstract.

HUMPHREYS, L. G., MILLER, J., and ELLSON, D. G. 1940. The effect of the intertrial interval on the acquistion, extinction, and recovery of verbal expectations. *J. exp. Psychol.,* **27,** 195–202.

HUNT, J. McV. 1941. The effects of infant feed-frustration upon adult hoarding behavior. *J. abnorm. soc. Psychol.,* **36,** 338–60.

HUNT, J. McV. (ed.). 1944. *Personality and the behavior disorders.* 2 vols. New York: The Ronald Press Co.

HUNTER, W. S. 1912. The delayed reaction in animals and children. *Behavior Monogr.,* **2:** 1.

HUNTER, W. S. 1935a. Conditioning and extinction in the rat. *Brit. J. Psychol.,* **26** (II), 135–48.

———. 1935b. Conditioning and maze learning in the rat. *J. comp. Psychol.,* **19,** 417–24.

HUNTER, W. S., and PENNINGTON, L. A. 1939. A new apparatus and method for training the rat in auditory discrimination problems. *Science,* **89,** 87–88.

ISRAELI, N. 1936. *Abnormal personality and time.* Lancaster, Pa.: Science Press.

———. 1941. The psychology of planning. *Psychol. Rec.,* **4,** 253–56.

JAMES, W. 1890. *The principles of psychology.* 2 vols. New York: Henry Holt & Co., Inc.

JAMES, W. T. 1941. Experimental observations indicating the significance of work on conditioned motor reactions. *J. comp. Psychol.,* **32,** 353–66

JANET, P. 1890. *Les troubles psychopathiques de la miction.* Essai de psychophysiologie normale et pathologique (thèse). Angiers: imprim. Burdin et Cie.; Paris: Librairie Lefrançois.

JASPER, H. H. 1937. Electrical signs of cortical activity. *Psychol. Bull.,* **34,** 411–81.

JASPER, H. H., CRUIKSHANK, R. M., and HOWARD, H. 1935. Action currents from the occipital region of the brain in man as affected by variables of attention and external stimulation. *Psychol. Bull.,* **32,** 565.

JENKINS, W. O., and STANLEY, J. C., JR. 1950. Partial reinforcement: a review and critique. *Psychol. Bull.,* **47,** 193–234.

JOHNSON, W. 1946. *People in quandries.* New York: Harper & Bros.

KANNER, L. 1935. *Child psychiatry.* Springfield, Ill.: Charles C Thomas, Publisher.

KAPPAUF, W. E., and SCHLOSBERG, H. 1937. Conditioned responses in the white rat. III. Conditioning as a function of the length of the period of delay. *J. genet. Psychol.,* **50,** 27–45.

KARN, H. W., and PORTER, J. M., JR. 1946. The effects of certain pre-training procedures upon maze performance and their significance for the concept of latent learning. *J. exp. Psychol.,* **36,** 461–69.

KATONA, G. 1940. *Organizing and memorizing.* New York: Columbia University Press.

KELLER, F. C. 1941. Light-aversion in the white rat. *Psychol. Rec.,* **4,** 235–50.

KELLOGG, W. H., and KELLOGG, L. A. 1933. *The ape and the child.* New York: Whittlesey House.

KELLOGG, W. N., SCOTT, V. B., *et al.* 1940. Is movement necessary for learning? An experimental test of the motor theory of conditioning. *J. comp. Psychol.,* **29,** 43–73.

KEMPF, E. J. 1918. *The autonomic functions and the personality.* Nerv. ment. Dis. Monogr. No. 28, 156.

KENDLER, H. H., and UNDERWOOD, B. J. 1948. The role of reward in conditioning theory. *Psychol. Rev.,* **55,** 209–15.

KENSHALO, D. R., and KRYTER, K. D. 1949. Middle ear infection and sound-induced seizures in rats. *J. comp. physiol. Psychol.,* **42,** 328–31.

KIDD, D. 1906. *Savage childhood: a study of Kafir children.* London: A. & C. Black, Ltd.

KILPATRICK, W. H. 1925. *Foundations of method.* New York: The Macmillan Co.

KIMBLE, G. A. 1949. An experimental test of a two-factor theory of inhibition. *J. exp. Psychol.,* **39,** 15–23.

KINGSLEY, H. L. 1946. *The nature and conditions of learning.* New York: Prentice-Hall, Inc.

KLEIN, D. B. 1944. *Mental hygiene.* New York: Henry Holt & Co.

KLUCKHOHN, C., and KELLY, W. H. 1945. The concept of culture. In R. Linton (ed.), *The science of man in world crisis.* New York: Columbia University Press.

KNOTT, J. R. 1939. Some effects of "mental set" on the electrophysiological processes of the human cerebral cortex. *J. exp. Psychol.,* **24,** 384–405.

KOFFKA, K. 1928. *The growth of the mind.* New York: Harcourt, Brace & Co., Inc.

———. 1935. *Principles of Gestalt psychology.* New York: Harcourt, Brace & Co., Inc.

KÖHLER, W. 1927. *The mentality of apes.* New York: Harcourt, Brace & Co., Inc.

KONORSKI, J., and MILLER, S. 1937. On two types of conditioned reflex. *J. gen. Psychol.,* **16,** 264–72.

KORZYBSKI, A. 1933. *Science and sanity.* Lancaster, Pa.: Science Press.

KRECHEVSKY, I. 1932a. Antagonistic verbal discrimination habits in the white rat. *J. comp. Psychol.,* **14,** 263–77.

———. 1932b. "Hypotheses" in rats. *Psychol. Rev.,* **39,** 516–32.

———. 1935. Brain mechanisms and "hypotheses." *J. comp. Psychol.,* **19,** 425–62.

———. 1937. Brain mechanisms and variability. I. Variability within a means-end readiness. *J. comp. Psychol.,* **23,** 121–38.

———. 1938. A study of the continuity of the problem-solving process. *Psychol. Rev.,* **45,** 107–33.

KRECHEVSKY, I., and HONZIK, C. H. 1932. Fixation in the rat. *Univ. Calif. Publ. Psychol.,* **6,** 13–26.

KRUTCH, J. W. 1926. *Edgar Allan Poe.* New York: Alfred A. Knopf, Inc.

KUBIE, L. S. 1939. A critical analysis of the concept of a repetition compulsion. *Int. J. Psycho-Anal.,* **20,** 390–407.

———. 1941. The repetitive core of neurosis. *Psychoanal. Quart.,* **10,** 23–43.

LAIR, W. S. 1949. Psychoanalytic theory of identification. Ph.D. dissertation, Harvard University.

LAMOREAUX, R. R. The place of secondary motivation in conditioning. Unpublished MS.

LAMOREAUX, R. R., and MOWRER, O. H. Conditioning as discrimination—A study of "spontaneous" (interval) responses and their significance. Unpublished MS.

LANDIS, C., and HUNT, W. A. 1939. *The startle pattern.* New York: Rinehart & Co., Inc.

LANGE, N. 1888. Beiträge zur Theorie der sinnlichen Aufmerksamkeit und der activen Apperception. *Philos. Studien,* **4,** 390–422.

LANGER, S. K. 1948. *Philosophy in a new key.* New York: Penguin Books, Inc. (First issued by Harvard University Press, 1942.)

LASHLEY, K. S. 1913. Reproduction of inarticulate sounds in the parrot. *J. Anim. Behav.,* **3,** 361–66.

———. 1916. The human salivary reflex and its use in psychology. *Psychol. Rev.,* **23,** 446–64.

———. 1929. *Brain mechanisms and intelligence.* Chicago: University of Chicago Press.

———. 1942. The problem of cerebral organization in vision. *Biol. Symposia,* **7,** 301–22.

———. Personal communication. (See HILGARD, E. R., and MARQUIS, D. G., 1940, p. 12.)

LASHLEY, K. S., and WADE, M. 1946. The Pavlovian theory of generalization. *Psychol. Rev.,* **53,** 72–87.

LEEPER, R. W. 1948. A motivational theory of emotion to replace "emotion as disorganized response." *Psychol. Rev.,* **55,** 5–21.

LEWIN, K. 1935a. *A dynamic theory of personality.* New York: McGraw-Hill Book Co., Inc.

LEWIN, K. 1935b. *Principles of topological psychology.* New York: McGraw-Hill Book Co., Inc.

———. 1937. Psychoanalytic and topological psychology. *Bull. Menninger Clin.,* No. I, 202–11.

———. 1942a. Field theory of learning. *Yearb. nat. Soc. Stud. Educ.,* **41** (II), 215–42.

———. 1942b. Time perspective and morale. In G. Watson (ed.), *Civilian morale.* Boston: Houghton Mifflin Co.

LEWIS, M. M. 1936. *Infant speech.* London: Kegan Paul, Trench, Trubner & Co., Ltd.

LICHTENSTEIN, P. E. 1950. Studies of anxiety. I. The production of a feeding inhibition in dogs. *J. comp. physiol. Psychol.,* **43,** 16–29.

LIDDELL, H. S. 1944. Conditioned reflex method and experimental neurosis. In J. McV. Hunt (ed.), *Personality and the behavior disorders.* New York: The Ronald Press Co.

LIDDELL, H. S., JAMES, W. T., and ANDERSON, O. D. 1935. The comparative physiology of the conditioned motor reflex based on experiments with the pig, dog, sheep, goat, and rabbit. *Comp. Psychol. Monogr.,* **2:** 51.

LIEBMAN, J. L. 1946. *Peace of mind.* New York: Simon & Schuster.

LINDEMANN, E. 1944. Symptomology and management of acute grief. *Amer. J. Psychiatry,* **101** (ii), 141–48.

LINDNER, R. M. 1938. An experimental study of anticipation. *Amer. J. Psychol.,* **51,** 253–61.

LINDQUIST, E. F. 1940. *Statistical analysis in educational research.* Boston: Houghton Mifflin Co.

LINTON, R. 1936. *The study of man.* New York: Appleton-Century-Crofts, Inc

LIPMAN, E. A., and CULLER, E. 1938. The role of incentive in conditioning. *Amer. J. Psychol.,* **51,** 109–17.

LOOMIS, A. L., HARVEY, E. N., and HOBART, G. 1936. Electrical potentials of the human brain. *J. exp. Psychol.,* **19,** 249–79.

LORENZ, K. 1932. Betrachtungen über das Erkennen der arteigenen Triebhandlungen der Vogel. *Journal für Ornithologie,* **80,** 50–98.

———. 1937. The companion in the bird's world. *Auk,* **54,** 245–73.

LUMLEY, F. H. 1931. An investigation of the responses made in learning a multiple choice maze. *Psychol. Monogr.,* **42:** 189.

———. 1932. Anticipation as a factor in serial and maze learning. *J. exp. Psychol.,* **15,** 331–42.

LUND, F. H. 1939. *Emotions: their psychological, physiological, and educative implications.* New York: The Ronald Press Co.

LURIA, A. R. 1932. *The nature of human conflicts.* New York: Liveright Publishing Corp.

LYND, R. S. 1940. *Knowledge for what?* Princeton, N. J.: Princeton University Press.

MACDONALD, A. 1946. The effect of adaptation to the unconditioned stimulus upon the formation of conditioned avoidance responses. *J. exp. Psychol.,* **36,** 1–12.

MACKINNON, D. W. Unpublished MS.

MAGOUN, F. A. 1943. *Balanced personality.* New York: Harper & Bros.

MCCULLOCH, T. L. 1939a. Comment on the formation of discrimination habits. *Psychol. Rev.,* **46,** 75–85.

———. 1939b. Reply to a note on discrimination habits. *Psychol. Rev.,* **46,** 304–7.

MCCULLOCH, T. L., and PRATT, J. G. 1934. A study of the pre-solution period in weight discrimination by white rats. *J. comp. Psychol.,* **18,** 271–90.

MCGEOCH, J. A. 1942. *The psychology of human learning.* New York: Longmans, Green and Co., Inc.

MCGILL, V. J. 1938. An answer to Kurt Lewin. *Science and Society,* **2,** 527–31.

McGuinness, A. C. 1935. The treatment of enuresis in childhood. *Med. Clinics of N. Amer.*, **19**, 287–94.

Maier, N. R. F. 1929. Reasoning in white rats. *Comp. Psychol. Monogr.*, **6**, 1–93.

———. 1931. Reasoning and learning. *Psychol. Rev.*, **38**, 332–46.

———. 1949. *Frustration: the study of behavior without a goal.* New York: McGraw-Hill Book Co., Inc.

Maier, N. R. F., and Schneirla, T. C. 1942. Mechanisms in conditioning. *Psychol. Rev.*, **49**, 117–34.

Marcuse, M. 1924–25. Das Bettnässen (Enuresis nocturna) als sexualneurotischen Symptom. *Z. Sexualwissensch.*, **2**, 229–37.

Markey, O. B. 1932. Psychiatric implications in enuresis. *Arch. Pediat.*, **49**, 269–78.

Martin, R. F. 1937. An attempt at the experimental demonstration of regression in hypotheses in rats. Unpublished master's thesis, University of Oregon.

———. 1940. "Native" traits and regression in the rat. *J. comp. Psychol.*, **30**, 1–16.

Maslow, A. H. 1948. "Higher" and "lower" needs. *J. Psychol.*, **25**, 433–36.

Maslow, A. H., and Mittleman, B. 1941. *Principles of abnormal psychology.* New York: Harper & Bros.

May, M. A. 1945. Illustrations of stimulus-response principles in educational psychology. Unpublished MS.

———. 1948. Experimentally acquired drives. *J. exp. Psychol.*, **38**, 66–77.

May, M. A., *et al.* Personal communication.

May, R. 1950. *The Meaning of Anxiety.* New York: The Ronald Press Co.

Mead, M. 1930. *Growing up in New Guinea.* New York: Blue Ribbon Books, Inc.

———. 1935. *Sex and temperament in three primitive societies.* New York: William Morrow & Co., Inc.

———. 1942. *And keep your powder dry.* New York: William Morrow & Co., Inc.

Metfessel, M. 1940. Relationships of heredity and environment. *J. Psychol.*, **10**, 177–98.

Meyer, M. F. 1922. *Psychology of the other-one.* Columbia, Mo.: Missouri Book Co.

Michaels, J. J. 1939. Enuresis: a method for its study and treatment, by O. H. Mowrer and W. M. Mowrer: a critique. *Amer. J. Orthopsychiat.*, **9**, 629–34.

Miller, G. A., and Postman, L. 1946. Individual and group hoarding in rats. *Amer. J. Psychol.*, **59**, 652–68.

Miller, J. 1939. The effect of facilitatory and inhibitory attitudes on eyelid conditioning. Ph.D. dissertation, Yale University.

Miller, N. E. 1935. A reply to "Sign-Gestalt or conditioned reflex?" *Psychol. Rev.*, **42**, 280–92.

———. 1937. Reaction formation in rats: an experimental analog for a Freudian phenomenon. (Film presented before the A.P.A. at Minneapolis.)

———. 1941. An experimental investigation of acquired drives. *Psychol. Bull.*, **38**, 5–34.

———. 1948. Studies of fear as an acquirable drive. I. Fear as motivation and fear-reduction as reinforcement in the learning of new responses. *J. exp. Psychol.*, **38**, 89–101.

Miller, N. E., and Dollard, J. 1941. *Social learning and imitation.* New Haven, Conn.: Yale University Press.

———. 1944. Experimental studies of conflict. In J. McV. Hunt (ed.), *Personality and the behavior disorders.* New York: The Ronald Press Co.

Miller, N. E., and Miles, W. R. 1935. Effect of caffeine on the running speed of hungry, satiated, and frustrated rats. *J. comp. Psychol.*, **20**, 397–412.

———. 1936. Alcohol and removal of reward: an analytical study of rodent maze behavior. *J. comp. Psychol.*, **21**, 179–204.

MILLER, N. E., and STEVENSON, S. S. 1936. Agitated behavior of rats during experimental extinction and a curve of spontaneous recovery. *J. comp. Psychol.*, **21**, 205–31.

MORGAN, C. T. 1947. The hoarding instinct. *Psychol. Rev.*, **54**, 335–41.

MORGAN, J. J. B., and WITMER, F. J. 1939. The treatment of enuresis by the conditioned reaction technique. *J. genet. Psychol.*, **55**, 59–65.

MORGAN, J. J. B., and LANNERT, V. Z. 1941. The element of habit in persistence. *J. educ. Psychol.*, **32**, 465–70.

MORRIS, C. 1946. *Signs, language, and behavior.* New York: Prentice-Hall, Inc.

MOWRER, O. H. 1934. The modification of vestibular nystagmus by means of repeated elicitation. *Comp. Psychol. Monogr.*, **9**: 45.

———. 1937. Reaction to conflict as a function of past experience. *Psychol. Bull.*, **34**, 720–21.

———. 1938a. Apparatus for the study and treatment of enuresis. *Amer. J. Psychol.*, **51**, 163–66.

———. 1938b. Enuresis: a method for its study and treatment. *Amer. J. Orthopsychiat.*, **8**, 436–59.

———. 1938c. Preparatory set (expectancy): a determinant in motivation and learning. *Psychol. Rev.*, **45**, 62–91.

———. 1938d. Some research implications of the frustration concept as related to social and educational problems. *Character & Pers.*, **7**, 129–35.

———. 1939a. Animal studies in the genesis of personality. *Trans. N. Y. Acad. Sci.*, 3, 4 pp.

———. 1939b. A stimulus-response analysis of anxiety and its role as a reinforcing agent. *Psychol. Rev.*, **46**, 553–65.

———. 1940a. An experimental analogue of "regression," with incidental observations on "reaction-formation." *J. abnorm. soc. Psychol.*, **35**, 56–87.

———. 1940b. Preparatory set (expectancy): some methods of measurement. *Psychol. Monogr.*, **52**, No. 2, 43.

———. 1940c. Anxiety reduction and learning. *J. exp. Psychol.*, **27**, 497–516.

———. 1941a. Motivation and learning in relation to the national emergency. *Psychol. Bull.*, **38**, 421–31.

———. 1941b. Preparatory set (expectancy): further evidence of its "central" locus. *J. exp. Psychol.*, **28**, 116–33.

———. 1943. A cumulative graphic work-recorder. *J. exp. Psychol.*, **33**, 159–63.

———. 1946. The law of effect and ego psychology. *Psychol. Rev.*, **53**, 321–34.

———. 1947a. Discipline and mental health. *Harv. educ. Rev.*, **17**, 284–96.

———. 1947b. On the dual nature of learning: a re-interpretation of "conditioning" and "problem-solving." *Harv. educ. Rev.*, **17**, 102–48.

———. 1947c. Discussion of Dr. Hebb's paper: spontaneous neurosis in chimpanzees. *Psychosom. Med.*, **9**, 16–19.

———. 1947d. On the utility of parrots and other birds in the study of language development: a preliminary report. *Amer. Psychol.*, **2**, 279–80. Abstract.

———. 1948a. Learning theory and the neurotic paradox. *Amer. J. Orthopsychiat.*, **18**, 571–610.

———. 1948b. What is normal behavior? In L. A. Pennington and I. A. Berg (eds.), *An introduction to clinical psychology.* New York: The Ronald Press Co.

———. 1949. Biological vs. moral "frustration" in personality disturbances. *Progressive Educ.*, **26**, 65–69.

———. 1950. Review of N. R. F. Maier, *Frustration—the study of behavior without a goal. Science,* III, 434.

MOWRER, O. H., and JONES, H. 1943. Extinction and behavior variability as functions of effortfulness of task. *J. exp. Psychol.*, **33**, 369–86.

———. 1945. Habit strength as a function of the pattern of reinforcement. *J. exp. Psychol.*, **35**, 293–311.

MOWRER, O. H., and KLUCKHOHN, C. 1944. Dynamic theory of personality. In J. McV. Hunt (ed.), *Personality and the behavior disorders.* New York: The Ronald Press Co.

MOWRER, O. H., and LAMOREAUX, R. R. 1942. Avoidance conditioning and signal duration: a study of secondary motivation and reward. *Psychol. Monogr.,* **54**: 5.

MOWRER, O. H., and MILLER, N. E. 1942. A multi-purpose learning-demonstration apparatus. *J. exp. Psychol.,* **31**, 163–70.

MOWRER, O. H., and ORBISON, W. D. 1939. Signal intensity and rate of presentation as factors influencing conditioning. Unpublished MS.

MOWRER, O. H., PALMA, F., and SANGER, M. D. 1948. Individual learning and "racial experience" in the rat, with special reference to vocalization. *J. genet. Psychol.,* **73**, 29–43.

MOWRER, O. H., RAYMAN, N. N., and BLISS, E. L. 1940. Preparatory set (expectancy)—an experimental demonstration of its "central" locus. *J. exp. Psychol.,* **26**, 357–72.

MOWRER, O. H., and ULLMAN, A. D. 1945. Time as a determinant in integrative learning. *Psychol. Rev.,* **52**, 61–90.

MOWRER, O. H., and VIEK, P. 1945. Language and learning: an experimental paradigm. *Harv. educ. Rev.,* **15**, 35–48.

———. 1948. An experimental analogue of fear from a sense of helplessness. *J. abnorm. soc. Psychol.,* **43**, 193–200.

———. 1950. Some problems in the empirical derivation of gradients of reinforcement. Unpublished MS.

MUENZINGER, K. F. 1934a. Motivation in learning. I. Electric shock for correct response in the visual discrimination habit. *J. comp. Psychol.,* **17**, 267–77.

———. 1934b. Motivation in learning. II. The function of electric shock for right and wrong responses in human subjects. *J. exp. Psychol.,* **17**, 439–48.

———. 1938. Vicarious trial and error at a point of choice. I. A general survey of its relation to learning efficiency. *J. genet. Psychol.,* **53**, 75–86.

———. 1948. Concerning the effect of shock for right responses in visual discrimination learning. *J. exp. Psychol.,* **38**, 201–3.

MUENZINGER, K. F., BERNSTONE, A. H., and RICHARDS, L. 1938. Motivation in learning. VIII. Equivalent amounts of electric shock for right and wrong responses in a visual discrimination habit. *J. comp. Psychol.,* **26**, 177–85.

MUENZINGER, K. F., and Fletcher, F. M. 1936. Motivation in learning. VI. Escape from electric shock compared with hunger-food tension in the visual discrimination habit. *J. comp. Psychol.,* **22**, 79–91.

———. 1937. Motivation in learning. VII. The effect of an enforced delay at the point of choice in the visual discrimination habit. *J. comp. Psychol.,* **23**, 383–92.

MUENZINGER, K. F., and GENTRY, E. 1931. Tone discrimination in the white rat. *J. comp. Psychol.,* **12**, 195–206.

MUENZINGER, K. F., and NEWCOMB, H. 1935. Motivation in learning. III. A bell signal compared with electric shock for right and wrong responses in the visual discrimination habit. *J. comp. Psychol.,* **20**, 85–93.

———. 1936. Motivation in learning. V. The relative effectiveness of jumping a gap and crossing an electric grid in a visual discrimination habit. *J. comp. Psychol.,* **21**, 95–104.

MUENZINGER, K. F., and WALZ, F. C. 1934. An examination of electrical current stabilizing devices for psychological experiments. *J. gen. Psychol.,* **10**, 477–82.

MUENZINGER, K. F., and WOOD, A. 1935. Motivation in learning. IV. The function of punishment as determined by its temporal relation to the act of choice in the visual discrimination habit. *J. comp. Psychol.,* **20**, 95–106.

MULLER, G. E., and SCHUMANN, F. 1889. Ueber die psychologischen Grundlagen der Vergleichung gehobener Gewichte. *Pflug. Arch. ges. Physiol.,* **45**, 37–112.

MURRAY, H. A. 1938. *Explorations in personality.* New York: Oxford University Press.

MURRAY, J. M. 1947. Normal personality development. Chapter 4. In *Teaching psycho therapeutic medicine* (Helen L. Witmer, ed.). New York: Commonwealth Fund.

NICE, M. M. 1943. Studies in the life history of the song sparrow. II. The behavior of the song sparrow and other Passerines. *Transactions of the Linnaean Society,* **6,** 329.

NUNBERG, H. 1926. The sense of guilt and the need for punishment. *Intl. J. Psycho-Anal.,* **7,** 420–34.

OCHSENIUS, K. 1923. Auf Behandlung der Enuresis. *Munch. med. Wschr.,* **70** (i), 432.

———. 1925. Zur Behandlung der Enuresis. *Munch. med. Wschr.,* **72** (ii), 1342.

O'CONNOR, V. J. 1946. Recency or effect?: A critical analysis of Guthrie's theory of learning. *Harv. educ. Rev.,* **14,** 194–206.

OGDEN, C. K., and RICHARDS, I. A. 1938. *The meaning of meaning.* New York: Harcourt, Brace & Co., Inc.

O'KELLY, L. I. 1940a. An experimental study of regression. I. Behavioral characteristics of the regressive response. *J. comp. Psychol.,* **30,** 41–53.

———. 1940b. An experimental study of regression. II. Some motivational determinants of regression and perseveration. *J. comp. Psychol.,* **30,** 55–95.

O'KELLY, L. I., and HEYER, A. W., JR. 1948. Studies in motivation and retention. *J. comp. physiol. Psychol.,* **41,** 466–78.

OLTMAN, J. E., and FRIEDMAN, S. 1938. Acute heterosexual inadequacy. I. In the male. *Psychiat. Quart.,* **12,** 609–78.

———. 1940. The correction of homosexuality. II. In the female. *Psychiat. Quart.,* **14,** 194–204.

PAGE, C. N. 1906. *Parrots and other talking birds.* Privately printed. Des Moines, Ia.

PARMENTER, R. 1940. Avoidance of nervous strain in experimental extinction of the conditioned motor reflex. *J. gen. Psychol.,* **23,** 55–63.

PASSEY, G. E. 1948. The influence of intensity of unconditioned stimulus upon acquisition of a conditioned response. *J. exp. Psychol.,* **38,** 420–28.

PATTON, R. A. 1947. The incidence of middle-ear infection in albino rats susceptible to sound-induced seizures. *Amer. Psychol.,* **2,** 320.

PAVLOV, I. P. 1927. *Conditioned reflexes.* Trans. G. V. Anrep. London: Oxford University Press.

———. 1928. *Lectures on conditioned reflexes.* New York: International Publishers Co., Inc.

———. 1941. *Conditioned reflexes and psychiatry.* Trans. W. H. Gantt. New York: International Publishers Co., Inc.

PFAUNDLER, M. 1904. Demonstration eines Apparates zu Selbsttätigen Signalisierung Stattgehabter Bettnässung. *Verhandlungen der Gesellschaft für Kinderheilkunde, Wiesbaden,* **21,** 219–20.

PHILIP, R. 1928. The measurement of attention. *Stud. Psychol. Psychiat. Cathol. Univ. Amer.,* **2,** 1–81.

POE, E. A. Cameo Edition, 1904. *The works of Edgar Allan Poe.* 9 vols. New York: Funk & Wagnalls Co.

PORTER, E. H., and BIEL, W. C. 1943. Alleged regressive behaviour in a two-unit maze. *J. comp. Psychol.,* **35,** 187–95.

POSTMAN, L. 1947. The history and present status of the law of effect. *Psychol. Bull.,* **44,** 489–563.

PRENTICE, W. C. H. 1946. Operationism and psychological theory: a note. *Psychol. Rev.,* **53,** 247–49.

———. 1949. Continuity in human learning. *J. exp. Psychol.,* **39,** 187–94.

PRESTON, G. H. 1940. *Psychiatry for the curious.* New York: Rinehart & Co., Inc.

QUINN, A. H. 1941. *Edgar Allan Poe: a critical biography.* New York: Appleton-Century-Crofts, Inc.

RATTRAY, R. S. 1929. *Ashanti law and constitution.* Oxford: Clarendon Press.
RAZRAN, G. H. S. 1936. Attitudinal control of human conditioning. *J. Psychol.,* **2,** 327–37.
REDFIELD, R. 1942. *Levels of integration in biological and social systems.* (*Biological Symposia,* ed. J. Cattell, Vol. VIII.) New York: The Ronald Press Co.
RÉMY-ROUX. 1908–11. Nouvel appareil électrique contre l'incontinence nocturne d'urine. *Bulletin et Mémoires de la Société de Médecine de Vaucluse, Avignon,* **2,** 337–40.
RHEINBERGER, M. B., and JASPER, H. H. 1937. The electrical activity of the cerebral cortex in the unanesthetized cat. *Amer. J. Physiol.,* **119,** 186–96.
RICE, P. B. 1946. The ego and the law of effect. *Psychol. Rev.,* **53,** 307–420.
RICHARDS, I. A. 1938. *Interpretation in teaching.* New York: Harcourt, Brace & Co., Inc.
———. 1942. *How to read a page.* New York: W. W. Norton & Co., Inc.
RIESS, A. 1943. An analysis of children's number responses. *Harv. educ. Rev.,* **13,** 149–62.
ROBERTS, W. H. 1930. The effect of delayed feeding on white rats in a problem cage. *J. genet. Psychol.,* **37,** 35–58.
ROBINSON, E. E. 1940. An experimental investigation of two factors which produce stereotyped behavior in problem situations. *J. exp. Psychol.,* **27,** 294–310.
ROCK, R. T., JR. 1940. Thorndike's contributions to the psychology of learning. *Teach. Coll. Rec.,* **41,** 751–61.
ROHRER, J. H. 1947. Experimental extinction as a function of the distribution of extinction trials and response strength. *J. Exp. Psychol.,* **37,** 473–93.
RUSS, K. 1884. *The speaking parrots—a scientific manual.* London: L. Gill.
RUSSELL, B. 1927. *Philosophy.* New York: W. W. Norton & Co., Inc.
SACHS, H. 1944. *Freud: master and friend.* Cambridge, Mass.: Harvard University Press.
SADGER, J. 1910. Ueber Urethralerotik. *Jahrb. f. psychoan. u. psychopath. Forsch.,* **2,** 409–50.
SANDERS, M. J. 1937. An experimental demonstration of regression in the rat. *J. exp. Psychol.,* **21,** 493–510.
SAPIR, E. 1921. *Language: an introduction to the study of speech.* New York: Harcourt, Brace & Co., Inc.
———. 1938. Language. In E. R. A. Seligman (ed.), *Encyclopedia of the social sciences,* Vol. IX, pp. 155–69.
SCHACTER, M. 1932. Considérations générales sur l'enuresis nocturne infantile. *J. de Med. de Paris,* **52,** 619–21.
SCHILDER, P. 1929. Conditioned reflexes. *Arch. Neurol. Psychiat., Chicago,* **22,** 425–43.
SCHLOSBERG, H. 1934. Conditioned responses in the white rat. *J. genet. Psychol.,* **45,** 303–35.
———. 1936. Conditioned responses in the white rat. II. Conditioned responses based upon shock to the foreleg. *J. genet. Psychol.,* **49,** 107–38.
———. 1937. The relationship between success and the laws of conditioning. *Psychol. Rev.,* **44,** 379–94.
SCHWARZ, O. 1915. Versuch einer Analyse der Miktionsanomalien nach Erkältungen. *Wien klin. Wschr.,* **28,** 1057.
SCOTT, J. P. 1947. "Emotional" behavior in fighting mice. *J. comp. Psychol.,* **40,** 275–82.
SEARS, R. R. 1943. *Survey of objective studies of psychoanalytic concepts.* New York: Social Science Research Council.
SEARS, R. R., PENTLER, MARGARET H., and SEARS, PAULINE S. The effect of father-separation on preschool-children's dollplay aggression. *Child Development,* **17,** 219–243.
SEIGER, H. W. 1946. A practical urine or wet diaper signal. *J. Pediatrics, St. Louis,* **28**:6, 733–36.

SEWARD, G. H. 1946. *Sex and the social order.* New York: McGraw-Hill Book Co., Inc.

SEWARD, J. P. 1949. An experimental analysis of latent learning. *J. exp. Psychol.*, **39**, 177–86.

SHAFFER, L. F. 1930. *The psychology of adjustment.* Boston: Hougton Mifflin Co.

———. 1947. The problem of psychotherapy. *Amer. Psychol.*, **2**, 459–67.

SHEEN, MSGR. F. J. 1948. *The modern soul in search of God.* Washington: National Council of Catholic Men.

———. 1949. *Peace of soul.* New York: McGraw-Hill Book Co., Inc.

SHEFFIELD, F. D. 1941. A simple conditioning explanation of an avoidable vs. unavoidable shock training study. *Psychol. Bull.*, **38**, 569. Abstract.

———. 1948. Avoidance training and the contiguity principle. *J. comp. physiol. Psychol.*, **41**, 165–77.

———. 1949. Hilgard's critique of Guthrie. *Psychol. Rev.*, **56**, 284–91.

SHEFFIELD, V. F. 1949. Extinction as a function of partial reinforcement and distribution of practice. *J. exp. Psychol.*, **39**, 511–26.

SHERRINGTON, C. S. 1906. *The integrative action of the nervous system.* New Haven, Conn.: Yale University Press.

SHOBEN, E. J., JR. 1949. Psychotherapy as a problem in learning theory. *Psychol. Bull.*, **46**, 366–92.

SIIPOLA, E. M. 1938. The measurement of reversion and its relation to similarity in habit-structure. Unpublished Ph.D. dissertation, Yale University.

SKINNER, B. F. 1935. Two types of conditioned reflex and a pseudo type. *J. gen. Psychol.*, **12**, 66–77.

———. 1937. Two types of conditioned reflex: a reply to Konorski and Miller. *J. gen. Psychol.*, **16**, 272–79.

———. 1938. *The behavior of organisms.* New York: Appleton-Century-Crofts, Inc.

———. 1948. "Superstition" in the pigeon. *J. exp. Psychol.*, **38**, 168–72.

SMITH, G. E. 1928. The new vision: Bowman lecture. *Trans. Ophth. Soc. Utd. Kgdm.*, **48**, 64–85.

SMUTS, J. C. 1926. *Holism and evolution.* New York: The Macmillan Co.

SNEDECOR, G. W. 1938. *Statistical methods.* Ames, Ia.: Collegiate Press, Inc.

SOLOMON, R. L. 1948a. The influence of work on behavior. *Psychol. Bull.*, **45**, 1–40.

———. 1948b. Effort and extinction: a confirmation. *J. comp. physiol. Psychol.*, **41**, 93–101.

SOLOMON, R. R., and WYNNE, L. C. 1950. Avoidance conditioning in normal dogs and in dogs deprived of segments of autonomic functioning. *Amer. Psychol.*, **5**, 264.

SPENCE, K. W. 1936. The nature of discrimination learning in animals. *Psychol. Rev.*, **43**, 427–49.

———. 1940. Continuous versus non-continuous interpretations of discrimination learning. *Psychol. Rev.*, **47**, 271–88.

———. 1945. An experimental test of the continuity and non-continuity theories of discrimination learning. *J. exp. Psychol.*, **35**, 253–366.

SPITZ, R. 1945. *The psychoanalytic study of the child.* Vol. I. New York: International Universities Press, Inc.

SPRAGG, S. D. S. 1933. Anticipation as a factor in maze errors. *J. comp. Psychol.*, **15**, 313–29.

———. 1934. Anticipatory responses in the maze. *J. comp. Psychol.*, **18**, 51–73.

———. 1936. Anticipatory responses in serial learning by chimpanzee. *Comp. Psychol. Monogr.*, **13**:62.

STECKLE, D. C., and O'KELLY, L. I. 1940. The effect of electrical shock upon later learning and regression in the rat. *J. Psychol.*, **9**, 365–70.

STERN, P. V. D. 1945. *Edgar Allan Poe.* New York: The Viking Press, Inc.

STEVENS, J. M. 1942. Expectancy vs. effect—substitution as a general principle of reinforcement. *Psychol. Rev.,* **49**, 102–16.

STEWART, G. R. 1946. *Man, an autobiography.* New York: Random House, Inc.

STOKE, S. M. 1940. An inquiry into the concept of identification. *J. gen. Psychol.,* **76**, 163–89.

SULLIVAN, H. S. 1931. The modified psychoanalytic treatment of schizophrenia. *Amer. J. Psychiat.,* **11**, 519–40.

———. 1945. *Conceptions of modern psychiatry.* Washington: William Alanson White Psychiatric Foundation. (Reprinted from *Psychiatry,* **3**:1 and **8**:2.)

SWIFT, S. K. 1949. *The cardinal's story.* New York: The Macmillan Co.

SYMONDS, P. M. 1927. Laws of learning. *J. educ. Psychol.,* **18**, 405–13.

SYNGG, D., and COMBS, A. W. 1949. *Individual behavior: a new frame of reference.* New York: Harper & Bros.

TAYLOR, W. S. 1926. *Readings in abnormal psychology and mental hygiene.* New York: Appleton-Century-Crofts, Inc.

TEAGARDEN, F. M. 1946. *Child psychology for professional workers.* New York: Prentice-Hall, Inc.

THOMPSON, J. 1941. Development of facial expression of emotion in blind and seeing children. *Archives of Psychol.,* No. 264.

THORNDIKE, E. L. 1898. The association process in animals. In *Biological Lectures from the Marine Biological Laboratory of Woods Hole.*

———. 1900. *The associative processes in animals.* Boston: Ginn & Co.

———. 1931. *Human learning.* New York: Appleton-Century-Crofts, Inc.

———. 1932. *The fundamentals of learning.* New York: Teachers College, Columbia University.

———. 1935. *The psychology of wants, interests, and attitudes.* New York: Appleton-Century-Crofts, Inc.

———. 1938. The law of effect. *Psychol. Rev.,* **45**, 204–5.

———. 1943. *Man and his work.* Cambridge, Mass.: Harvard University Press.

———. 1946. Expectation. *Psychol. Rev.,* **53**, 277–81.

TOLMAN, E. C. 1932. *Purposive behavior in animals and men.* New York: Appleton-Century-Crofts, Inc.

———. 1935. Sign-gestalt or conditioned reflex? *Psychol. Rev.,* **40**, 246–55.

———. 1938. The determiners of behavior at a choice point. *Psychol. Rev.,* **45**, 1–41.

———. 1949. There is more than one kind of learning. *Psychol. Rev.,* **56**, 144–55.

TOLMAN, E. C., HALL, C. S., and BRETNALL, E. P. 1932. A disproof of the law of effect and a substitution of the laws of emphasis, motivation and disruption. *J. exp. Psychol.,* **15**, 601–14.

TOMKINS, S. S. 1943. *Contemporary psychopathology.* Cambridge, Mass.: Harvard University Press.

TRAVIS, L. E., and EGAN, J. P. 1938. Conditioning of the electrical response of the cortex. *J. exp. Psychol.,* **22**, 524–31.

TSAI, L. S. 1932. The laws of minimum effort and maximum satisfaction in animal behavior. *Monogr. nat. Inst. Psychol.* No. 1.

TUTTLE, H. S. 1946. Two kinds of learning. *J. Psychol.,* **22**, 267–77.

TUTTLE, W. W. 1924. The effect of attention or mental activity on the patellar tendon reflex. *J. exp. Psychol.,* **7**, 401–19.

ULRICH, R. 1945. *The history of educational thought.* New York: American Book Co.

UPTON, M. 1929. The auditory sensitivity of guinea pigs. *Amer. J. Psychol.,* **41**, 412–21.

UTEAU, and RICHARDOT, I. 1916. Appareil pour dépister la simulation dans l'incontinence nocturne d'urine. *Paris Medical,* **6** (ii), 233–35.

VALENTINE, W. L. 1938. *Experimental foundations of general psychology.* New York: Rinehart & Co., Inc.

Warden, C. J., and Haas, E. L. 1927. The effect of short intervals of delay in feeding upon speed of maze learning. *J. comp. Psychol.*, **7**, 107–16.

Warner, L. H. 1932a. An experimental search for the "conditioned response." *J. genet. Psychol.*, **41**, 91–115.

———. 1932b. The association span of the white rat. *J. genet. Psychol.*, **14**, 57–90.

Washburne, C. 1926. *New schools in the old world.* New York: John Day Co., Inc.

Waters, R. H. 1937. The principle of least effort in learning. *J. gen. Psychol.*, **16**, 3–20.

Watson, J. B. 1914. *Behavior: an introduction to comparative psychology.* New York: Henry Holt & Co., Inc.

———. 1916. The place of the conditioned reflex in psychology. *Psychol. Rev.*, **23**, 89–116.

———. 1924. *Behaviorism.* New York: W. W. Norton & Co., Inc.

———. 1926. Experimental studies on the growth of the emotions. In *Psychologies of 1925.* Worcester, Mass.: Clark University Press.

Weaver, E. G. 1930. The upper limit of hearing in the cat. *J. comp. Psychol.*, **10**, 212–33.

Weissenberg, S. 1925–26. Über das Bettnässen und die Rolle der Träume in seinem Bilde. *Z. Kinderheilk.*, **40**, 343–52.

Wells, F. L. 1916. Mental regression: its conception and types. *Psychiat. Bull.*, **9**, 445–92.

———. 1935. Social maladjustments: adaptive regression. In C. Murchison (ed.), *A handbook of social psychology.* Worcester, Mass.: Clark University Press.

Wendt, G. R. 1936. An interpretation of inhibition of conditioned reflexes as competition between reaction systems. *Psychol. Rev.*, **43**, 258–81.

Werner, H. 1940. *Comparative psychology of mental development.* New York: Harper & Bros.

Whatmore, G. B., and Kleitman, N. 1946. The role of sensory and motor cortical projections in escape and avoidance conditioning in dogs. *Amer. J. Physiol.*, **146**, 282–92.

Whatmore, G. B., Morgan, E. A., and Kleitman, N. 1945–46. The influence of avoidance conditioning on the course of nonavoidance conditioning in dogs. *Amer. J. Physiol.*, **145**, 432–35.

Weeler, R. H. 1940. *The science of psychology.* New York: The Thomas Y. Crowell Co.

Whipple, G. M. 1924. *Manual of mental and physical tests.* Baltimore: Warwick and York.

Whiting, J. W. M. 1938. Unpublished notes on the Waskuk peoples of New Guinea.

———. 1941. *Becoming a Kwoma.* New Haven, Conn.: Yale University Press.

Whiting, J. W. M., and Mowrer, O. H. 1943. Habit progression and regression—a laboratory study of some factors relevant to human socialization. *J. comp. Psychol.*, **36**, 229–53.

Wickens, D. D. 1938. The transference of conditioned excitation and conditioned inhibition from one muscle group to the antagonistic muscle group. *J. exp. Psychol.*, **22**, 101–23.

Wickens, D. D., and Platt, C. E. 1949. The effect of response termination of the conditioned stimulus on learning rate in classical and instrumental conditioning. *Amer. Psychol.*, **4**, 226.

Willoughby, R. R. 1935. Magic and cognate phenomena: an hypothesis. In C. Murchison (ed.), *A handbook of social psychology.* Worcester, Mass.: Clark University Press.

Wischner, G. J. 1947. The effect of punishment on discrimination learning in a non-correction situation. *J. exp. Psychol.*, **37**, 271–84.

effect of punishment on
xp. Psychol., **38,** 203–4.
f response in a non-
medicine. New York:
esis of peptic ulcer in
chimpanzees. *Comp.*
ntal tests of reasoning
chol. Monogr., **17**:76.
York: Henry Holt &
logie, 2d ed. Vol. II.
nt but functionally re-
41, 111–23.
nparative study of in-
Psychol., **16,** 235–57.
erval upon the rate of
New Haven, Conn.:
elligence and its vocal
on-Century-Crofts, Inc.
nd dietary habit. VIII.
comp. physiol. Psychol.,
to Professor Leeper.
pontaneous recovery in
n response in the rat.
onse following the ex-
der, Berlin, **18,** 109–88.

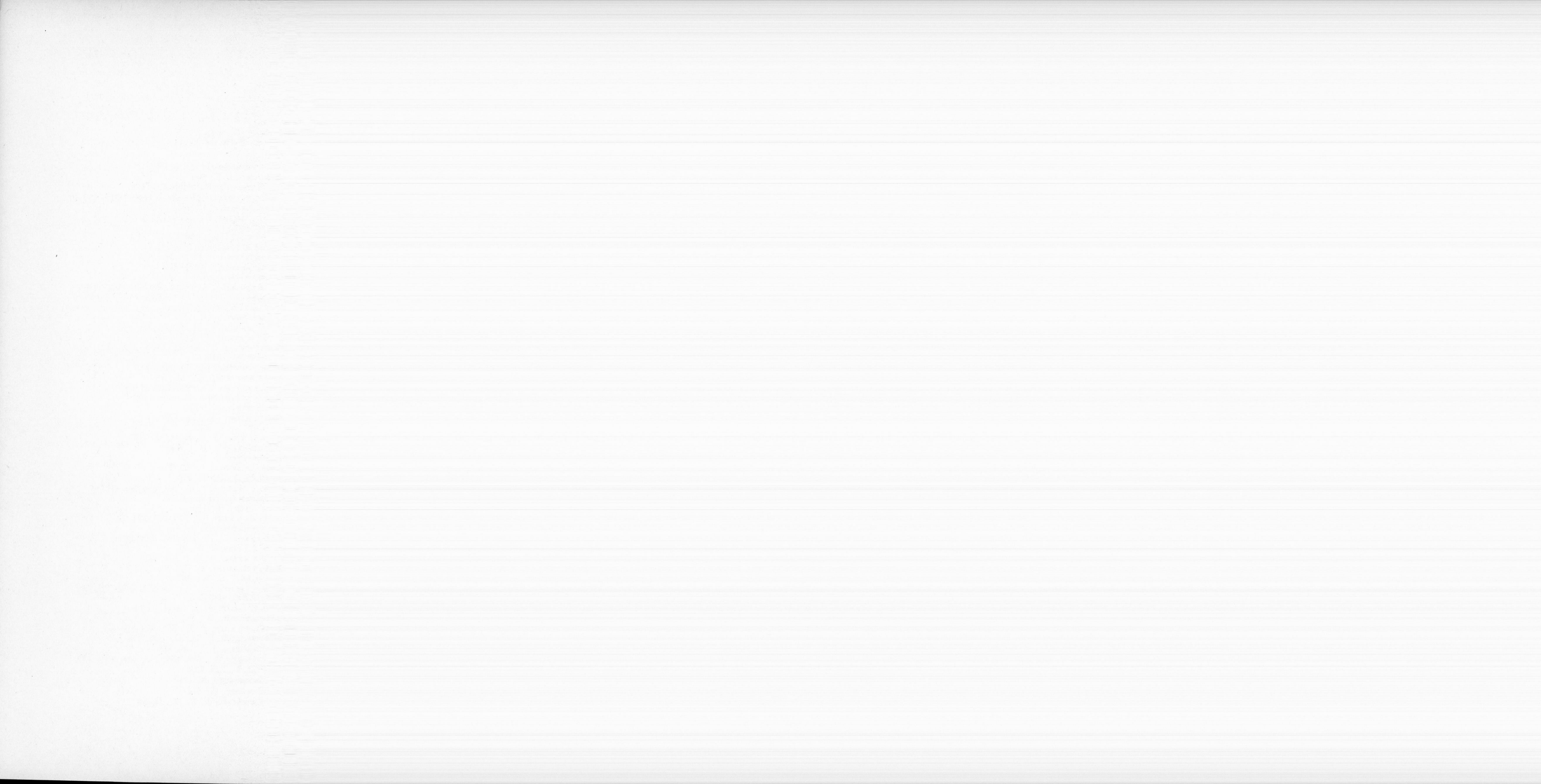

INDEX OF NAMES

INDEX OF SUBJECTS